CRITICAL COMPANION TO

J. K. Rowling

A Literary Reference to Her Life and Work

KARLEY ADNEY AND HOLLY HASSEL

An imprint of Infobase Publishing

Critical Companion to J. K. Rowling

Copyright 2011 by Karley Adney and Holly Hassel

Facts On File, Inc.
An imprint of Infobase Publishing
132 West 31st Street
New York NY 10001

Library of Congress Cataloging-in-Publication Data
Adney, Karley.
Critical companion to J. K. Rowling / Karley Adney and Holly Hassel.
p. cm.
Includes bibliographical references and index.
ISBN 978-0-8160-7574-4 (alk. paper)
1. Rowling, J. K. I. Hassel, Holly. II. Title.
PR6068.O93Z5226 2010
823'.914—dc22
[B]
2009054326

Facts On File books are available at special discounts when purchased in bulk quantities for businesses, associations, institutions, or sales promotions. Please call our Special Sales Department in New York at
(212) 967-8800 or (800) 322-8755.

You can find Facts On File on the World Wide Web at
http://www.factsonfile.com

Text design by Erika K. Arroyo
Composition by Mary Susan Ryan-Flynn
Cover printed by Sheridan Books, Ann Arbor, Mich.
Book printed and bound by Sheridan Books, Ann Arbor, Mich.
Date printed: December 2010

Printed in the United States of America

10 9 8 7 6 5 4 3 2 1

This book is printed on acid-free paper.

CONTENTS

ACKNOWLEDGMENTS

This book has been a labor of love, but labor indeed. I want to acknowledge first here my coauthor, Karley, for her insights, perspective, and knowledge, all of which strengthened this book immeasurably and made for a productive partnership during the years of writing, researching, and revising. I also want to thank sincerely and heartily our wonderful editor at Facts On File, Jeff Soloway. His constructive suggestions were invaluable in shaping the book. Special thanks goes to the University of Wisconsin–Marathon County for supporting work on the manuscript through summer research grants, giving us the time to read, write, and research. Finally, a sincere thank you to my husband, Jason, and daughter, Trixie, who gave the gifts of time, understanding, support, and love so that I could pursue this project.

—Holly

First and foremost, I thank my good friend and coauthor Holly for her passion and dedication to this project; collaborating with Holly always feels less like work and more like fun. Thank you to the University of Wisconsin–Marathon County and the University of Wisconsin Colleges English Department for their support. I also extend many thanks to Jeff Soloway, our editor, whose feedback was always helpful and encouraging. I thank my students for the discussions we have had and the insights I have gained from them. I also send a heartfelt thank you to my parents, Karen and Dave, and my sisters, Gina and Chelsea, who have always supported and encouraged my writing (and who even share my passion for Harry). And I offer my deepest thanks to my best friend and husband, Christoph, for his support, interest, and love.

—Karley

INTRODUCTION

A simple train delay in 1990 can be held partly responsible for the creation of one of the most successful book series of all time, J. K. Rowling's Harry Potter books. Of course, the groundwork was laid long before. Without Rowling's passion for stories and writing, cultivated since her youth, as well as her extensive education (as a student at Exeter, a teacher in Europe, and an employee at AMNESTY INTERNATIONAL, among other jobs), the stories never would have come together in the same way. Still, Rowling claims that it was during that fateful train delay that the entire Harry Potter universe entered her mind. She quickly made it a personal goal to finish the first novel, *Harry Potter and the Philosopher's Stone*, and see it published. She never anticipated the commercial and critical success she and Harry would experience over the coming years.

Rowling's works have aroused endless public and critical debate. Millions of fans sported wizard robes and waited hours for the release of each of the Harry Potter books or films. Over the decade from the initial publication of *Harry Potter and the Philosopher's Stone* in 1998 to the ultimate release of the final Harry Potter film, *Harry Potter and the Deathly Hallows*, in 2011, "POTTERMANIA" exploded. Indeed, the cultural and commercial frenzy over the texts, films, merchandise, and products associated with the "Boy Who Lived" has become as important to understanding these literary works as the works themselves.

As Harry Potter fans were eagerly anticipating each new book or movie, detractors gathered just as passionately to shred and even burn copies of Rowl-ing's novels. Some have claimed that the books glorify dark magic; others have accused Rowling herself of being a practicing witch, of even of using her novels to recruit followers of Satan. Related objections have been voiced by concerned parents and teachers who disagree with the series's tacit endorsement of subversive and antisocial behavior, arguing that the books undermine figures of authority by approving of the frequent occasions when Harry, Ron, and Hermione break rules or the less frequent ones when they physically attack teachers. By contrast, others have argued that the books reinforce valuable lessons about personal journeys and the importance of selflessness, as well as about friendship, courage, self-sacrifice, loyalty, and many other virtues.

Other critics claim that Rowling's depictions of race, class, and gender roles are highly traditional—even retrograde. They say that she incorporates only token minorities into her Harry Potter universe and that the series reinforces patriarchal social norms. However, many readers have defended Rowling's choice of racial representations, arguing that they reflect the demographics of a typical boarding school, and still others believe that Rowling challenges rather than reinforces patriarchal values.

The literary merit of the series also serves as fodder for debate. Regardless of her book sales, some critics charge Rowling with writing formulaic detective novels that, although popular at the present, are ultimately fated to prop up wobbly table legs or remain buried away in back corners of moldy basements. Conversely, other critics suggest that, like J. R. R. Tolkien, Rowling has mastered the genre of high fantasy and presents her readers with a secondary world to which they may escape and enjoy themselves while thinking critically about weighty philosophical and intellectual questions and improving both their reading and their analytic skills.

It is hard to deny that Rowling and her work have caused people to read more and have generated important critical conversations. Literally hundreds of critical collections, scholarly articles, guides to the series aimed at the general reader, encyclopedias, and other critical works have appeared since Rowling first published *Harry Potter and the Philosopher's Stone* in Britain in 1998. One of the many purposes of this book is to educate readers about these debates and to encourage them to consider Rowling's novels thoughtfully while understanding the vivid contexts in which they were written.

About This Book

Rowling's story and those she has written have quickly grown to mythic proportions. This book presents important biographical, critical, literary, and cultural contexts. It contains four parts. Part I, Rowling's biography, traces her early life, her personal development as a writer, her authorship of each of her novels, and her recent activity.

Part II examines Rowling's works. It contains extensive entries on each of the Harry Potter novels, each entry providing a synopsis and critical commentary, as well as subsections covering the novel's reviews, scholarship, film adaptation, and major characters. The subentries on characters not only highlight the characters' development over the course of the specific novel, but also discuss the characters' contributions to the book's plot and central thematic concerns. Following the entries on the novels are two broader entries on secondary sources. The first is an entry entitled "Scholarship on the Harry Potter Series," providing an overview of the critical articles published by academics and literary scholars on the series. The second is an entry entitled "Additional Resources on the Harry Potter Series," which discusses resources written by nonscholars, such as Harry Potter enthusiasts. Together, these entries provide an understanding of how lay readers, critics, scholars, and reviewers have received the books and and have attempted to explicate their themes and meanings. Finally, a section called "Minor Works" provides brief entries on Rowling's nonfiction pieces and each of her short books that complement the Harry Potter series.

Part III, "Related People, Places, and Topics," presents relevant information about Rowling's life and work, including writers past and present who have influenced her work, towns where she has lived, contextual subjects such as "British boarding schools" and "Celtic mythology," and more.

Part IV contains the appendices, including a bibliography of Rowling's works, a secondary source bibliography, a chronology, and cast information on the Harry Potter movies.

References to terms that are themselves subjects of entries in Part III are given in CAPITAL AND SMALL CAPITAL LETTERS the first time they appear in an entry.

PART I

Biography

J. K. Rowling

(1965–   )

On June 5, 2008, J. K. Rowling gave the commencement speech at Harvard University's graduation. Harvard's president, Drew Gilpin Faust, praised Rowling's selection by alumni, noting that "no one in our time has done more to inspire young people to . . . read" (T. Smith). Some students crowed over Rowling's selection; one college senior, Kevin Ferguson, for example, claimed, "She's a rock star!" Others, however, were less impressed with Rowling, such as the disappointed computer science major Kevin Bombino, who critiqued Rowling's lack of gravitas: "I think we could have done better" (T. Smith). The range of reactions captured in news coverage of Rowling's speech encapsulates the larger critical conversation that has taken place over the last decade about the value, significance, and credibility of Rowling's work. Though Rowling admitted experiencing "fear and nausea" in anticipation of her addressing the Harvard class of 2008, her speech, "The Fringe Benefits of Failure, and the Importance of Imagination," offers insights drawn from Rowling's own life story. It was, she argued, her failures that allowed her to pursue her one true passion—writing; equally important, she noted, are the power of imagination and a sense of empathy, both of which inform Rowling's own passion for social justice, a theme in both her literary world and her professional activities.

EARLY LIFE

Sources differ about the details of the meeting of Anne Volant and Peter Rowling, though most agree that a train was involved. Rowling herself writes on her official Web site that her parents "met on a train travelling from King's Cross station to Arborath in Scotland when they were both eighteen" ("Biography"). Peter Rowling was in the Royal Navy and Anne Volant in the Women's Royal Navy Service, which provided primarily clerical support to the navy (Kirk 10); another source asserts both were 18 and being sent to Scotland for service (Compson 12). Her parents married on March 14, 1965 (already expecting their baby girl, Jo), after their

return to civilian life, in BRISTOL, ENGLAND, where her father worked as an apprentice production engineer at Siddeley, an aircraft engine company (Sexton 12), and her mother, as a lab technician (Lovett 3).

Joanne (Jo) Rowling was born to Peter and Ann Rowling on July 31, 1965, at the General Hospital, in CHIPPING SODBURY, SOUTH GLOUCESTERSHIRE, ENGLAND ("J. K. Rowling"). Her own July 31 birth date would later be immortalized for readers everywhere as Harry Potter's. Rowling has said that her first memory is of the birth of her sister, Diana (known affectionately as "Di"), on June 28, 1967, but that she remembers eating the play dough her father gave her to entertain herself while her mother labored in the adjacent bedroom more than she remembers her sister's birth (Fraser 1).

Rowling has fond memories of her childhood; her parents were avid readers, and her grandparents similarly fond of telling tales. Her grandfathers, Ernie and Stanley (the driver and conductor of the wizarding Knight Bus introduced in *Prisoner of Azkaban* were named after them), were both an influence on her life. As the owner of a supermarket, Ernie would let Jo and Di play "store" after hours, with "real tins and packets and money," an exercise in imagination that Rowling recalls fondly (Fraser 2). Stanley, a dreamer, remembers Rowling "had trouble telling fact from fiction" (Fraser 2), and it was the influence of her immediate and extended family that cultivated the love of reading and language that led her to a career as a writer. Both parents read to their eldest daughter frequently, and Rowling in turn would tell stories to her younger sister. Rowling's biography on her Web site claims that though the girls were best friends as children, they also fought "like a pair of wildcats imprisoned together in a very small cage" ("Biography").

The Rowlings yearned for a country life, and while the girls were still young (Rowling was four), they moved to WINTERBOURNE, SOUTH GLOUCESTERSHIRE, ENGLAND. The *Toronto Star* reports that it was here that Rowling played with the children of a local family, THE POTTERS, a story confirmed in *Readings on J. K. Rowling,* whose editor, Gary Wiener, explains that the two children, Ian and Vicki, "witches and wizards" with Rowling 4 the Rowling family moved to a coun- ocated a half-hour's drive from Bristol in Ր ...... , ENGLAND, occupying Church Cottage, named for its proximity to a church and its grave- yard. Rowling recalls in an interview with Lindsey Fraser, "All our friends thought it was spooky liv- ing next to a graveyard but we liked it. I still love graveyards—they are a great source of names. We lived near Offa's Dyke on the River Wye—a wonderful place" (4). Rowling's father commuted to nearby Bristol and continued his work as an engineer, though the company had now merged with Rolls-Royce (Sexton 13). The girls were so close in age that they were often compared, with the lively, brown-haired Di often thought of as the "pretty" one and bookish Jo, with her freckles and reddish hair, the "smart" one; Rowling has said of their youthful pigeonholing that she always felt she "had to achieve . . . always had to be right" (Sexton 21). The bucolic environment provided a safe and quiet childhood for both girls, though around this time Rowling's favorite grandmother, Kathleen, passed away from a heart attack at the age of 52 (S. Smith 39).

Rowling's literary proclivities were obvious from a young age. She wrote her first story, about a rab- bit named Rabbit who has a bout of measles and is visited by a spider named Miss Bee, at age six (Lovett 3) and later wrote a mystery called "The Seven Cursed Diamonds" (Gaines 10). Rowling notes in an interview early in her career, "My life's ambition has been to write full time. . . . This is all I have wanted from the age of six. I cannot overstate how much I wanted that. But I didn't talk about it at all. I just never really spoke about it, because I was embarrassed" (Feldman 139). Rowling refers frequently in interviews to this secret desire to make her living as a professional writer, but she feared telling people largely because she "was afraid they'd tell me I didn't have a hope" (Lovett 3). Her literary ambitions were fueled by her own passion for reading. Rowling's childhood tastes for books were varied and many. She reports reading books with both her parents—*The Wind in the Willows* with her father, and one of her mother's favorites by her side, *Noddy* (by Enid Blyton). Rich-

ard Scarry books were a favorite, and as were Anna Sewell's *Black Beauty,* Louisa May Alcott's *Little Women,* and most especially *The Little White Horse* by ELIZABETH GOUDGE. Rowling calls Goudge's book "very well-constructed and clever" and has claimed that "perhaps more than any other book, it has a direct influence on the Harry Potter books" (Fraser 11). As a teenager, Rowling received a copy of *HONS AND REBELS* (known as *Daughters and Rebels* in America) by JESSICA MITFORD from her aunt, and Rowling has called the writer the "most influential on her career" (Compson 20). Mitford was so influential on Rowling professionally and personally that she named her first daughter after the writer. The works of another woman, JANE AUSTEN, including *Emma, Sense and Sensibility,* and *Pride and Prejudice,* were also especially influ- ential on Rowling.

SCHOOLING

Rowling started school in Bristol; as might be expected, bookish young Jo loved school. But, her positive views of school would be changed by the family's 1974 move to Tutshill. Multiple sources document Rowling's experience at the village school, which Rowling calls "Dickensian," particularly the class of Mrs. Morgan, who seated children according to her perception of their intel- ligence. After Rowling scored a 0 out of 10 on the pop math quiz (she had never done fractions before), Mrs. Morgan placed her "in the stupid row" (Lovett 3; "J. K. Rowling"). Rowling has said that Mrs. Morgan, unsurprisingly, was the inspiration for the character of Severus Snape (Compson 15). As a new student in school, she had difficulty making friends, but by the end of the academic year she had redeemed herself in the eyes of Mrs. Morgan; when she was finally "promoted" to the left side of the room (where the "smart" kids were seated), though, she took her best friend's seat (Shapiro 34).

Rowling has said in an interview with *Salon* magazine that she was "obsessed with achieving academically, but that masked a huge insecurity. I think it is very common for plain young girls to feel this way" (Shapiro 33). She later told Margaret Weir in an interview with Salon.com that Herm- ione "was very easy to create because she is based almost entirely on myself at age 11. She is really a caricature of me." She further explains her basing Hermione's character on her own adolescent personality: "I think I was always very insecure, a real worrier, but I would put on a show of confidence to mask it. I might just have been a tiny bit Hermione-ish" (Wiener 17–18).

Rowling next attended WYEDEAN SCHOOL, a comprehensive school, roughly equivalent to American high school, located in Sedbury, a town two miles away from her home in Tutshill. She developed a greater sense of confidence as she moved out of her early teen years and away from feeling awkward and insecurities exacerbated by the fact that, in Rowling's own words, she was "quiet, freckly, short-sighted, and rubbish at sports" (Shapiro 35). Other sources have noted that while she was not much good at some of the popular team sports such as hockey, she enjoyed more individual activities, including swimming and dancing (Fraser 9). Around this time Rowling acknowledges reading more sophisticated novels, such as C. S. LEWIS's Narnia series, as well as novels geared toward adults in the romance and spy genres, including Austen's celebrated work *Pride and Prejudice* (Kirk 33) and Ian Fleming's James Bond novels.

Once she conquered the initial anxiety of going through puberty and starting at a school with older students, Rowling's confidence grew. She found a group of girls who shared similar qualities and continued to cultivate the storytelling and writing she had always enjoyed, sometimes sharing it with her new friends. She also developed a friendship with Sean Harris, a boy who entered her school in upper sixth (equivalent of 12th grade at U.S. high schools). Many sources (and Rowling herself) enjoy the relationship between the real-life Harris and his literary counterpart, Ron Weasley. Though Rowling has said that "Ron Weasley isn't a living portrait of Sean" (Fraser 7), she notes that he is inspired by Harris, partly because Harris was the owner of a turquoise Ford Anglia that "spelled freedom" for Rowling as a teenager. Living in a rural village, Sean and his unique car used to "rescue her from [her] boredom" living in the isolated area (Fraser 8). Rowling has said, "Some of the happiest memories of my teenage years involve zooming off into the

darkness in Sean's car," reminiscent of Harry's feeling of liberation when Ron and his twin brothers rescue him from his Privet Drive prison in *Chamber of Secrets* (Sexton 26). As a teen, Rowling began to favor the fringe elements of popular culture and adopted a semigothic look with heavy black eyeliner and clothing to match (along with a smoking habit), an image that complemented her growing affinity for such punk music groups as the Clash and the Smiths (S. Smith 61).

In 1980 the Rowlings felt concerned when Anne Rowling began to have difficulty with motor control and grasping objects along with tingling in her right arm. Rowling was 15 years old when she learned that her mother was diagnosed with multiple sclerosis, a disease of the nervous system that is degenerative and incurable, sometimes punctuated with periods of recovery that, however, Anne did not experience. Instead, Anne's health began a general decline that continued through the next decade (Sexton 24–25). Rowling admits that home life became difficult, as her father nursed her mother, whose physical abilities deteriorated in ways that prevented her from maintaining her previously active involvement in the lives of her daughters (Kirk 40).

Though she often regaled her friends with stories of adventure and action at their lunch table, Jo still kept her more intimate and serious creative work to herself. Rowling was generally reluctant to share her creative work with her instructors, but one of her secondary school English teachers, Miss Shepherd, did make an impact. Rowling's love for the English language and literature was cemented by Miss Shepherd, whom Rowling describes as "a feminist, and clever" (Fraser 7). Rowling has called Miss Shepherd "the only teacher I ever confided in. She inspired trust" (Fraser 7), and it was the teacher's rigorous standards of accuracy and clarity of language and her rigor, passion, and high expectations that helped shape the young Rowling's affinity for reading and writing as an area of academic study.

Rowling's academic excellence and obedient nature rewarded her with the position of "head girl" at Wyedean. Though the title suggested great authority, in reality, the position had "very little responsibility," reports Shapiro, and usually involved escorting important visitors around the campus and giving a speech to the student body (39). Prior to 1988, students in English and Welsh schools took two sets of exams, O levels, or Ordinary levels, at age 16, and A levels (Advanced levels) after their last two years of school, which were devoted to studying a more focused curriculum. Rowling, because of her love of language, focused on English, French, and German (Compson 19). Rowling graduated from Wyedean with honors and appeared to have a bright future. She had hoped to attend the highly regarded Oxford University and was encouraged by her teachers to take the examinations that would qualify her to do so. Rowling's wish would not be granted, however; she was rejected by Oxford and settled instead on Exeter University, within a few hours from her home.

Rowling entered Exeter in 1983, attracted partly by her belief that the school was a bastion of progressive ideas; she admits she expected to be among other students "thinking radical thoughts" (Fraser 17) but discovered, in fact, that the university was quite traditional. Rowling had not discussed her writing aspirations with her parents, both of whom found it hard to understand their daughter's lack of direction. They encouraged her to study French and the classics, presuming that she would find a productive career as a bilingual secretary. Rowling later said, "I was—am—totally unsuited to that kind of work. Me as a secretary? I'd be your worst nightmare" (Fraser 18). Her study of the French language also included a year studying abroad and working as a teacher in PARIS, FRANCE, in order to earn college credit. It was the first time she had been out of the country without her family, and the year there helped her mature. She returned to England a more confident young woman.

Rowling has said that she was "influenced by [her parents'] belief that languages would be better [than literature or creative writing] for finding a job" (Fraser 18). As Kirk notes, Rowling was a much less impressive student in college—skipping classes, handing in work late, or simply not at all. As one professor in the languages department recalled, Rowling was an "average student" (45). It was advised she drop Greek and Roman studies from

her program of study after she failed to register for a final exam (45). Rowling graduated in 1987 with a GPA of 2.2 (Kirk 47). Wiener's biography confirms that "surprisingly for a student of her abilities, her grades were only average" (18).

After graduation Rowling went to London to begin her course on bilingual secretarial work. She worked a series of office jobs including one with the Manchester Chamber of Commerce and two years with AMNESTY INTERNATIONAL, the international agency focused on human rights violations (T. Smith). Her employment at Amnesty International was significant to Rowling's future development both as an adult and as a writer.

ADULTHOOD

Rowling's stint in clerical work influenced her later life in two ways: She developed her passion for writing in cafés, and she cultivated the sense of empathy that would become central to her literary themes and to the charity work she began to engage in after the success of the Harry Potter series.

During Rowling's postgraduate period of office work she maintained her quiet passion for writing, writing stories on the office computer and ducking out during lunch to write stories in cafés. More important, her job at Amnesty International, though fairly dreary and monotonous clerical work, had an impact on her in significant ways. Rowling's work at the agency involved using her training in French to research human rights abuses in francophone Africa (Kirk 50). Her favorite writer, Mitford, was a strong advocate for social justice and proponent of activism for human rights; Rowling's shared passion for social justice was fostered by her work at the agency.

Rowling later memorialized how her work at Amnesty International informed her worldview and her writing in the 2008 commencement address at Harvard University. Calling her work at Amnesty International one of the "greatest formative experiences of [her] life," Rowling described the horrors she was privy to through her employment in the African research department. This work exposed her to stories of rape, kidnapping, disappearances, torture, murder, and exile; many coworkers were former political prisoners who had experienced such atrocities in their own lives because of their willingness to speak out against injustice in their own countries. In her speech Rowling looked back upon that time in her life as highly instructive and used it to illustrate the importance of empathy and imagination.

Rowling suffered her own woes in the early 1990s as well as some moments of inspiration. In 1990 Rowling was 26. After being released from some of her office jobs, she rekindled a relationship with an old boyfriend and moved to MANCHESTER, ENGLAND, where she obtained employment at the Manchester Chamber of Commerce. It was on a train from Manchester to London on a trip looking for an apartment when the train broke down and Harry Potter was born.

THE BIRTH OF HARRY POTTER

Rowling claims that her entire vision of Harry and his world formed during that four-hour train delay. Her daydreaming and writing on her off-hours and at times during her working hours paid off, as her imagination seemed ripe to become home to the character whose life would be one of the best-selling stories of all time. Rowling recalls that "the idea that we could have a child who escapes from the confines of the adult world and goes somewhere where he has power, both literally and metaphorically, really appealed to me" (Lovett 4), and perhaps her own sense of lacking a direction drove her vision of Harry as developing a self-knowledge that is both literal and figurative: "I suddenly had this basic idea of a boy who didn't know who he was," Rowling states (Shapiro 49). Though Rowling usually carried a pen and paper with her, as many writers make a habit of doing, the day of the train delay was the exception, and she later reflected that she was able to linger over and detail Harry's world precisely because she did not stop her imagination to write down details (Kirk 67).

By the time she arrived at her destination, Rowling had begun fleshing out the plotline and already had some ideas for characters, such as Ron, Nearly Headless Nick, Hagrid, and Peeves. She also says that she concentrated first on Hogwarts, imagining "a place of great order, but immense danger, with children who had skills with which they could overwhelm their teachers" (Fraser 20). She spent the next few months of her life adding detail to the story line of the first novel and developing the supporting characters, including inventing the sport of Quidditch after a "huge row" with her boyfriend, after which she stormed off to the pub (Fraser 23) and later spent the night at a hotel (Kirk 54).

Her mother had been diagnosed with multiple sclerosis a decade earlier, and on December 30, 1990, at the young age of 45, Anne Rowling died. Jo was heartbroken, and the grief she felt over her mother's death surely informed the plot and characterization of the books, especially Harry's own sense of loss and longing as an orphan. One of Rowling's biographers, William Compson, notes that the loss of Rowling's mother led to the inclusion in *Philosopher's Stone,* of the Mirror of Erised, the magical mirror that allows its user to see his or her heart's desire. Harry's temptation is to return to the mirror each night to see his parents in the only way he can, but Dumbledore's wise intervention removes the temptation, as Dumbledore knows that the mirror lures its users into fixing on "what could be" rather than "what is."

Rowling's troubles continued when her apartment was robbed and the things her mother had left her were stolen. After losing her position at the Manchester Chamber of Commerce, Rowling went to work briefly at the local university but, as with her other clerical positions, found the job mostly unsatisfying. As Shapiro reports, Rowling was deeply saddened, her greatest regret that she had not let her mother read any of the Harry Potter novel she was working on, the one thing in life that gave her joy as she struggled through her grief and boredom at work. In a 2006 interview Rowling described how the loss of her mother affected her daily: "Barely a day goes by when I do not think of her. There would be so much to tell her, impossibly much" ("J. K. Rowling Says").

By early 1991, as Rowling recovered from her mother's death, she knew she needed a change in her life. Deeply dissatisfied with the clerical work she had been doing since her college graduation, Rowling started looking in a new direction. She stumbled upon a newspaper advertisement looking for English teachers in Portugal. Rowling describes her thought process about her eventual move to the Continent this way: "I knew that I'd enjoy teaching English as a foreign language in Paris and I thought to myself, how would it be if I went abroad, did some teaching, took my manuscript, had some sun . . . ?" (Fraser 23). Rowling was eventually hired for a position teaching English as a second language in the port town of Oporto, Portugal, teaching students, as Rowling explains, from "age eight to eighty-two" (Fraser 23); most of the students were teenagers preparing for exams and adult community members as well. She taught night school from 5:00 P.M. to 10:00 P.M. on weeknights and also taught on Saturday mornings (Kirk 55). Rowling occupied a roomy four-bedroom apartment reserved for the school's teachers and formed fast friendships with her new roommates, an Irishwoman named Aine Kiely and a fellow Briton, Jill Prewett (Sexton 51). During her first week in Portugal she wrote one of her favorite chapters in *Philosopher's Stone*, "The Mirror of Erised."

About five months after her arrival, in March 1992 at a local jazz bar, Meia Cava, Rowling met a man who caught her attention (Sexton 52). His name was Jorge Arantes, referred to variably in sources as a Portuguese journalism student, a journalist, and "a journalist for one of the leading television stations in Portugal" (Shapiro 58). They had a whirlwind courtship, becoming engaged on August 28, 1992, and married on October 16 of that same year, even though their relationship had become increasingly strained by bickering that grew into larger arguments.

After a miscarriage before they married, Rowling quickly became pregnant again after their fall marriage and gave birth to her daughter, Jessica (named for her favorite author, the feminist and humanitarian Jessica Mitford), on July 27, 1993. The demands of Arantes's work kept him away from home frequently, and Rowling's relationship with him became even more strained. The addition of a newborn only increased the tension, and Rowling

recalls that she "was very depressed. . . . Having a newborn child made it doubly difficult. I simply felt like a nonperson. I was very low and I felt I had to achieve something" (Shapiro 60). Further, Arantes had just completed eight months of mandatory military service with the Portuguese army and had not found gainful employment, adding further pressure on Rowling as their family's sole financial supporter on a teacher's salary (Sexton 52). In November 1993 Arantes threw Rowling out of the house they shared after she told him she no longer loved him. It was only with the help of a local friend and the police that she was able to return and collect their daughter, then four months old (Sexton 54). Arantes later sold his story to Dennis Rice at the *Daily Express* (United Kingdom) after Rowling had rocketed to fame.

With a deteriorating marriage, few employment prospects (she was not paid during the holiday breaks from her teaching job), and a new baby, Rowling was desperate for a supportive environment where she could continue writing Harry's story. She had the first three chapters completed and many, many more ideas, but Portugal was not the place to fulfill her dreams. A phone call from her sister changed Rowling's future.

RETURN TO ENGLAND

Her sister Di, now also grown, was living with her husband in Edinburgh, Scotland. Rowling had always been close to her sister, so when Di suggested she relocate to Edinburgh with her baby so Rowling could have family support while she decided what to do next, she agreed. A Christmas stay with her sister turned into a permanent residence. This is the period most often referred to in media reports of Rowling's life, her stint as a divorced and unemployed single parent. In an interview in *School Library Journal* Rowling recalls this time: "It was more difficult to write because at the time I was a single parent and I had no money for child care at all. It is absolutely true that I used to go to cafes. I had to basically find out which cafes would allow me to sit in for a bit of coffee and let me just write for a couple of hours while my daughter napped" (Feldman 138). Because few cafés approved of the would-be novelist's sitting for hours on end, having bought a single cup of coffee, it was lucky that her brother-in-law, Roger Moore, had just opened a café called Nicolson's; she spent many hours there finishing the draft of the manuscript that would eventually be titled *Harry Potter and the Philosopher's Stone*. Later she would sneak into the open computer labs on a local college campus on weekends in order to type the manuscript so she could submit it to a publisher, hoping no one would discover she was not working on college coursework (Fraser 26). Rowling later rejected some of the claims circulated in the media that she wrote in cafés because her apartment did not have heat. Though times were desperate for her, she admits that her house was less cold than it was dirty because of the amount of time she spent on the book rather than doing housework.

Rowling later recalled "how collecting her welfare checks from the post office felt terribly humiliating" (Compson 45). Though the story of Rowling's writing of the Harry Potter story as a "penniless mother" has reached a height bordering on nearly mythological, Rowling herself felt "mildly indignant" (Feldman 138) about the inaccuracies that were circulated about her "rags-to-riches" story. She asserts, "When I had the idea for Harry and when I started writing the [first] book, I was working full time, as I was for my entire adult life, and I was *not* a single parent. I finished the book under those conditions" (Feldman 138). As a college graduate she had nearly always been productively employed, but as a new mother with child care responsibilities, Rowling was in fact struggling to scrape by financially and availing herself of public assistance (£69, or $103.50, per week) as she worked diligently to complete her first Harry Potter novel.

Though Harry gave her a sense of hope about her future, Rowling struggled with depression, and Compson notes that she spent nine months visiting a counselor, an experience that would eventually help her create the Dementors, creatures that serve as a "way of showing depression through characters" (47). In a 2008 interview Rowling described her mental state at the time as having "suicidal thoughts" and admitted that "the thing that made me go for help was probably

my daughter. . . . She was something that earthed me, grounded me, and I thought, this isn't right, this can't be right, she cannot grow up with me in this state" ("*Harry Potter* Author Reveals"). In the same interview Rowling reaffirmed that depression is not a condition to be ashamed of and that she had never remotely felt uncomfortable admitting her struggles with it or addressing difficult personal issues, including her past with Arantes. In March 1994 Rowling filed the British equivalent of a restraining order against Arantes, who had gone to England in search of his wife and daughter. By that fall she had filed for divorce, which was finalized in June 1995 (Sexton 61).

Rowling had decided to pursue postgraduate certification in education so she might return to teaching; after an interview at Heriot-Watt University (now part of the University of Edinburgh), she began the course of study in August 1995, about the same time she was finishing the manuscript of *Philosopher's Stone*. The child care center on the campus had closed, and for a brief time, Rowling was unsure of how she would afford day care expenses while she went to school; luckily friends and family lent her money or otherwise supported her, and between support from her friends and family and public assistance, Rowling was able to continue writing through the period, when, she confesses, "my self-respect was on the floor. I didn't want Jessica to grow up this way, so she became my inspiration and writing about Harry became my safe haven" (Shapiro 67). When Rowling completed the manuscript, she had been working on the novel in varying stages for five years. In 1994 she had received a grant from the Scottish Office of Education and Industry to help support her as a full-time student and to find good-quality child care for her daughter. She also eventually obtained a job as a French teacher at a local school and was by this point significantly past her worst low points as an unemployed single mother; she was self-sufficient and feeling a great sense of accomplishment.

Despite the financial challenges, she soldiered on, inspired by her daughter and by her sister Di's good cheer and support. When Di read the first three chapters of *Philosopher's Stone* and laughed out loud, the approval was enough to keep Rowling writing (Sexton 60). The next step, she knew, was to find a literary agent, though she expected it to be difficult because most handbooks in publishing recommend children's novels be about 40,000 words and the manuscript she had completed was near 90,000. Because she could not afford to have it photocopied, she retyped the manuscript completely twice (Kirk 73). Her first submission to a literary agent was rejected, but in an inspiring burst of luck, her second submission to CHRISTOPHER LITTLE LITERARY AGENCY was accepted. Rowling has said that

> all I ever wanted to do is to see the book published. That was the truth. I was very, very, very realistic. . . . I knew that most children's writers don't make any money. They will never ever, ever be very well known. I was totally OK with that. I just wanted someone to publish Harry so I could go to bookshops and see it. [I wanted] to be able, somehow, to support myself writing so I didn't have to give it up (Feldman 139).

Her agent, Christopher Little, had cautioned her that she would "never be rich or famous as the author of children's books" (T. Smith), but even knowing that she would probably never make a living as a writer, Rowling was overjoyed that she had secured a literary agent. After Little received 12 rejections from the major local publishers, a small local publisher named BLOOMSBURY agreed to buy the book in 1996 for the equivalent in U.S. dollars of approximately $3,000; Rowling was thrilled (Compson 51). Barry Cunningham, the editor who accepted the manuscript, was interviewed and asked about the 12 other publishers who had rejected Rowling's manuscript. Cunningham said, "It's a little like turning down the Beatles."

A 2005 interview with Nigel Newton, chairman of Bloomsbury Publishing, revealed the poignant story of how he decided to publish the novel. John Lawless reports in the *Sun-Herald* that when Rowling's agent handed a sample of the book to Newton to read, he took it home. Instead of reading it himself, he handed it to his eight-year-old daughter,

Alice, to read. Newton confessed that "she came down from her room an hour later, glowing . . . saying, 'Dad, this is so much better than anything else'" (Lawless). His daughter's nagging to find out what happened next led him eventually to agree to publish the novel. The editor asked Rowling to develop Neville Longbottom as a more substantial character and to make Quidditch a larger part of the story, and Rowling was happy to do so (Kirk 74). Even the small printing of 500 copies could not dim Rowling's enthusiasm at the mere fact that she was going to achieve her dream of seeing her novel in bookstore windows.

As the book was being edited by the publisher, she began a part-time teaching job at Leith Academy after earning her teaching certificate in July 1996, and she also received a writer's grant from the Scottish Arts Council in the amount of £8,000 ($12,400) to support her writing of the sequel *Chamber of Secrets*. The funds allowed her to purchase a personal computer (Sexton 71–72).

But, a surprising future awaited Rowling. The next year she was shocked to discover via a phone call from her literary agent that the New York publisher SCHOLASTIC was bidding on her novel for the American rights; Little told her that a number of publishing houses were competing for the right to publish the manuscript. Arthur Levine, representing Scholastic, took a huge risk in offering the nearly unheard-of amount of $105,000 for the rights (Compson 53; Shapiro 76). Unprepared for the high expectations for her book's success, Rowling was at once excited at the prospect of her book's success and terrified of the growing pressure on the book to succeed.

On June 26, 1997, *Harry Potter and the Philosopher's Stone* was published in the United Kingdom. Prior to its publication the publisher, Bloomsbury, initially requested she use two initials on the front cover instead of her first name, stating that it would be more noticeable. Suspicious, Rowling asked for more information, and the publishers expressed concerns about an explicitly female name on the cover since, as Compson notes, "boys supposedly don't like books written by women" (52). Similarly, Christopher Little had "researched the effect of authors' names on book sales" and recommended she adopt more gender-neutral initials so as not to "alienate the young males whom he believed were the most likely readers of the novel" (Wiener 24). Rowling saw no reason to disagree and honored the request, though since she did not have a middle name at birth, she adopted the use of her grandmother's first name, *Kathleen*, to arrive at *J. K. Rowling*, contrary to documented claims (Fraser 2).

SMASHING SUCCESSES

The publication of *Philosopher's Stone* was met with widespread success, primarily through word of mouth, and both adults and children bought and read the book in droves. Shapiro calls Rowling's first novel an "immediate smash, selling more than 150,000 copies in a matter of months" (82–83). But, it was more than commercially successful. The books received critical acclaim by reviewers and accumulated a number of book awards: the Nestlé Smarties Book Prize, the Federation of Children's Books Group Award, and the British Book Awards Children's Book of the Year (Shapiro 83). The new fame and fortune allowed Rowling to rent a new home in Edinburgh and put her fears about money to rest. The book was published as *Harry Potter and the Sorcerer's Stone* in the United States in August 1998 to similar acclaim. A few changes were made to "Americanize" both *Sorcerer's Stone* and *Chamber of Secrets* such as changing English words to prevent confusion, but most changes were very minor (Fraser 31). By the end of the year Scholastic had produced 190,000 copies in seven printings (Sexton 79).

Rowling decided to devote herself to writing full time, even though she harbored worries that "this was all just a flash in the pan" and knew that if she gave up her teaching career she would also be losing the experience that would make it possible for her to return to teaching if needed (Fraser 27). Rowling had already been hard at work on the second book in the series but experienced much anxiety: "I was worried that it wouldn't live up to readers' expectations," she confessed in an interview with Lindsey Fraser (28). Though she

submitted the complete manuscript for *Chamber of Secrets* to her publisher on time, she felt dissatisfied with the quality; she asked Bloomsbury to return it to her for further editing and kept it for an additional six weeks until it met her exacting standards (Sexton 77).

Chamber of Secrets was published in the United Kingdom in July 1998 to positive reviews and stunning sales, almost immediately taking the top spot on best-seller lists. Rowling outsold such popular adult novelists as Tom Clancy and John Grisham (T. Smith), and as each book met with inevitable success, Rowling's U.K. and U.S. publishers agreed that the series's popularity was likely to continue and began to draw up contracts for the seven novels Rowling had initially planned to constitute the series. Thrilled but fearful about the enormous pressure of writing five more novels, and concerned about her ability to sustain the same level of quality and enthusiasm for the books, Rowling outlined the plots of the next five novels so she could sign the contract with confidence in her story line and themes (Shapiro 87).

She later recalled in a 2003 interview that she "never dreamed this would happen," speaking of her breathtaking commercial and critical success. She added, "My realistic side had allowed myself to think that I might get one good review. That was my idea of a peak. So everything else really has been like stepping into Wonderland for me" (Treneman). After the publication of *Chamber of Secrets* Rowling was having enough financial success between advances on the next book and royalties from the first to become a full-time writer. As part of a reward for her success, she bought a home on Hazelbank Terrace in Edinburgh (Sexton 80).

Prisoner of Azkaban was published in Britain in July 1999 to similarly enthusiastic critical and reader praise. By 1999 the first three books in the series held the top three spots on the *New York Times* fiction best-seller list, raising questions about whether children's books should be included on the list; ultimately a second list was created for children's fiction largely because of the Harry Potter phenomenon. In Britain the book sold 60,000 copies on the first day of its release, and by summer

1999 the worldwide book sales neared 30 million copies. They had been translated into 27 languages; Rowling received her first million-dollar royalty check that summer (Sexton 81).

Initially Rowling resisted adapting the books into films. She told the interviewer Lindsey Fraser that she declined all the offers she was inundated with after the success of the books, including one by WARNER BROTHERS. Eventually Rowling agreed to make films based on the novels. Filmmakers assured her that the plot would remain faithful to the book, Rowling would have input on certain aspects of the creative process, the films would be live action (not animated), and British actors would play the characters. It was also agreed that Rowling would be granted final approval over the finished script. In 2000 she shared her perspective on the film adaptation, telling *Newsweek*'s Malcolm Jones that while she did not "have any right to jackboot in there and say this or that," she "sold it to people she trusted, and so far my trust has not been misplaced."

In March 2000 complications interrupted Rowling's otherwise rapidly rising star. In addition to a "tell-all" interview that her ex-husband, Arantes, had given to a tabloid TV show, a U.S. writer named Nancy Stouffer filed a lawsuit against Rowling, accusing her of plagiarism. Stouffer claimed that the Harry Potter books drew substantially from her 1984 novel *The Legend of Rah and the Muggles*. Stouffer said, "I have been accused of stealing; some children believe I am the one that followed J. K. Rowling" ("Author to Face"). Stouffer accused Rowling of taking the term *Muggle*, character names including *Lily* and *James Potter*, themes, plotlines, and scenes from her book. Judge Allen G. Schwartz of the New York District Court not only threw out Stouffer's case, ruling that "publication, distribution, and exploitation of the Harry Potter books does not violate any of Stouffer's intellectual property right" (Steger), but also fined Stouffer $50,000, claiming that Stouffer had "perpetuated a fraud on the court through her submission of fraudulent documents that were willfully altered" (Wapshott). Stouffer's counsel adamantly denied claims that she had falsified records, but Judge Schwartz ordered Stouffer to discontinue "making false representa-

tion to third parties" (Steger). After the dismissal of the lawsuit, Rowling was widely quoted as saying, "The clouds have lifted and I no longer have to worry" (Schlink).

With the rapidly increasing popularity of the books, the release of the fourth novel in the series, *Goblet of Fire*, reached frenzied proportions. Rowling missed her deadline for the first time with the fourth novel. Compson reports that Rowling rewrote chapter 9, "The Dark Mark," 13 times and had to begin rewriting the book itself halfway through because of a plot hole (63). Rowling herself recalls that time with a mix of anxiety and regret: "Writing Book Four was an absolute nightmare," she told Ann Treneman. She explained that she had to rethink the plot halfway through writing it and immediately regretted having agreed to move so quickly into the writing of the next book after finishing *Prisoner of Azkaban*. In the same interview she said, "The first thing that I did when I finished *Prisoner of Azkaban* was to discuss repaying the advance for the next book. . . . People were a bit shaken, I think. I said: I want to give the money back and then I will be free to finish it in my own time rather than have to produce it for next year" (Treneman). She described the process of writing *Goblet of Fire* to interviewer Margot Adler of National Public Radio in 2000: "My muse went wrong. She led me up a blind alleyway, and I had to scrap out of the book, and I went back and I rewrote and I still love the writing of it, but it was very pressured at one point." Though she had to "write like fury to make the deadline" (Treneman), she was able to produce the final version for a July 2000 publication date.

The book's publication on July 8, 2000 (simultaneously in both the United States and United Kingdom) set numerous records, including the largest first printing ever for a hardcover book: 300,000 copies (T. Smith). It became the fastest-selling book in history at the time of its publication ("J. K. Rowling Biography"). With the fourth episode in the Harry Potter series, it could be said that "Pottermania" was fully in effect. In a 2000 *Newsweek* interview Malcolm Jones asked Rowling whether she thought the mania had reached a peak. Rowling answered, "At some point things have got to calm down." Bookstores throughout the world stayed open past midnight for special midnight sales of the book, and online bookshops such as Amazon.com arranged for and guaranteed special Saturday deliveries of the book to its customers. By the time *Goblet of Fire* was published, Rowling's books had sold 192 million copies worldwide and had been published in 55 languages, and Rowling's net worth was estimated at $444 million (Cawley 50). Despite her prodigious wealth, Rowling told the interviewer Malcolm Jones that "the main difference between where I was five years ago and now is the absence of worry." Rowling dismissed the conspicuous consumption favored by some of her wealthy coevals, noting that the major victory for her was not her ability to purchase new luxuries but to provide for herself without worry. This same year Rowling's alma mater, Exeter University, conferred upon her an honorary doctorate and invited her to speak at the ceremony. Rowling's speech focused on the themes of making mistakes, taking risks, and luck, three elements that had all shaped her own experience in life (Kirk 114).

By this time objections to the series began to emerge on the basis of religious critiques of the "witchcraft" featured in the books. For example, in September 2000 Christian parents in North Carolina charged that the books promoted Satanism and demanded that the novels be banned from classrooms; the school board rejected their request (S. Smith). Rowling used the protest as an opportunity to speak out forcefully against censorship, noting "the idea of censorship deeply offends me. They [objectors] have the absolute right to decide what their children read. I think they're misguided, but they have that right. But to prevent other people's children from reading something, at that point, I would be very happy to face them and argue that one out" (Jones). In fact, Rowling has been quoted as saying, "I believe in God, not magic" and asserting that she is a member of the CHURCH OF SCOTLAND, making the accusations of Satanism even more puzzling for Harry Potter fans (Nelson). Rowling told the *Times* (UK) that some fanatics believed that she was a witch. Rowling remembers finding "death threats" on the Internet: "And then about

halfway through this message board," she remembers, I found well, people being advised to shoot me, basically" (Treneman). Nonetheless, critics of the series organized large-scale protests including book burnings: At least one high-profile book burning took place in December 2001 in Alamogordo, New Mexico, and involved throwing copies of the novel into burning piles (Kirk 104). On the other hand, Rowling expressed a great deal of joy in her devoted fans and child readers. The benefit to her fame was the interaction with her readers. Rowling described these interactions with her fans as "hugely enjoyable" and declared in her interview with NPR, "There's absolutely no negative in meeting the readers, none. . . . I've never met a child who was anything less than delightful" (Adler).

Rowling at this time in her life was reflective about where she was both personally and professionally. With such amazing success Rowling admitted that though quite content with her school-age daughter, Jessica, and her success, she had "always wanted to have more children" but "did not expect to meet anyone," because of the "baggage" of her previous marriage, her child, and her fame (Treneman). She acknowledged in her interview with Anne Treneman that "you do meet people [when you are famous] but it tends to be those who are very keen to approach you and maybe not those you would really want to meet" (Treneman).

In 2000 a mutual friend introduced Rowling to Dr. Neil Murray, an anesthetist who worked at St. John's Hospital and Edinburgh Hospital. Though he admitted he had read 10 pages or so of her book on a late-night shift at the hospital, Rowling was thrilled that he "didn't really have a clear idea of who I was. It means that we could get to know each other in quite the normal way" (Sexton 91–92). They married on Boxing Day (December 26), 2001. Bridesmaids included her daughter, Jessica; her sister, Di; and Murray's sister, Lorna. An earlier plan to marry at the Galápagos Islands was thwarted by news leaks, and, instead, the couple settled on the library of their home, the estate KILLIECHASSIE HOUSE, in Perthshire, Scotland.

After the rushed writing of *Goblet of Fire*, Rowling asked her publishers for a delayed release for the

In keeping with the tradition of secrecy surrounding the plots of the last four novels in the series, publishers were prohibited from releasing advance copies of *Harry Potter and the Deathly Hallows. (Photo by Gabriel Pollard/Used under a Creative Commons license)*

next volume, taking a break of nearly a year before getting to work on *Order of the Phoenix*. Rowling told Treneman that she needed "to try to come terms with what had happened to [her]," that is, her rocketing from obscurity to wealth and fame. The gap between *Goblet of Fire* and *Order of the Phoenix* was the longest of her books, nearly three years.

As she moved forward with the drafting of the fifth book, *Order of the Phoenix*, several life circumstances interfered. The Stouffer plagiarism case had "hindered her work on the eagerly awaited fifth episode," according to the *Australian,* as well as the publication of *Goblet of Fire*. During this same period, fall 2002, Rowling also announced that she and her husband were expecting their first child together, due in spring 2003 ("JK, Harry"). Their son, David, was born on March 30. Her 2003 interview with the *Times* (U.K.) noted that her net worth had crept from £15 million three years previous to £280 million in 2003, with book sales of 200 million copies (Treneman). Before *Order of the Phoenix* was released, Rowling told an interviewer that the book was "a departure" and that "there is a nasty death in it as well. Nasty because it is someone I care about as a character" (Treneman). Scholastic printed 8.5 million copies of the fifth

book, which was scheduled for release on June 21, 2003; this was the largest first printing of any book in history (Sexton 97). Rowling announced her third pregnancy on her Web site, assuring readers that it would not interfere with the 2005 publication of *Half-Blood Prince.*

Mackenzie Jean's birth on January 23, 2005, was more than good cause for Rowling to take a break before writing the final novel in the series. By the time Rowling began writing *Deathly Hallows,* the commercial and critical excitement surrounding her creation was still in full force, sustained for a full decade. Fans shared their fears that Rowling might kill Harry, and Rowling admitted that she could "completely understand . . . the mentality of an author who thinks: 'Well, I'm gonna kill them off because that means there can be no non-author-written sequels. So it will end with me and after I'm dead and gone they won't be able to bring back the character'" ("Harry Might"). Rowling said in an interview for a British television show, "The final chapter is hidden away, although it's now changed very slightly. One character got a reprieve," noting that she had written it almost 17 years previously when she had first conceived the series.

A news story published the month before the release of *Deathly Hallows* reported on Rowling's interview with the BBC in which she "walked into the kitchen crying" because she had killed off a major character. Rowling admitted that her husband responded, "Don't do it then," to which she responded, "It just doesn't work like that. You are writing children's books, you need to be a ruthless killer" ("*Harry Potter* Author Says"). It is this willingness to confront head-on what some critics find to be matters too dark for children's literature that has garnered such praise for Rowling's books; she has not shied away from what could even be called a preoccupation with death, immortality, the human soul, good and evil, and many other weighty philosophical issues that the series explores.

In her interview with the *Times* (U.K.), Rowling responded to Treneman's observation that she is frequently asked why the Harry Potter series is so successful. Rowling mused, "I cannot answer that question. I can't. It sounds coy. It sounds disingenuous. I never think of it like that. I think it would be dangerous for me to think about it like that, to sit down and analyse it, to decide why. It would be an exercise in navel gazing. It would possibly lead me to deduce that I was doing certain things right and maybe certain things I should drop and if you start writing like that . . ." Though Rowling herself cannot explain (or chooses not to hypothesize) how Harry has captured the hearts of so many readers, many readers are eager to see what future literary works will emerge from Rowling's imagination.

ROWLING RECENTLY

Five years after she settled the lawsuit against Nancy Stouffer for plagiarism, Rowling found herself on the other end of a legal tussle, instigating a lawsuit to prevent RDR BOOKS from publishing STEVE VANDER ARK's 160,000-word encyclopedia, *The Harry Potter Lexicon,* based on his Web site, in existence since 2000. Filed by Rowling and Warner Brothers in October 2007, the lawsuit was widely regarded as important because of the potential impact it could have in setting precedent for the publishing industry on the kinds of works that could be published commenting on a writer's work, more narrowly defining what constitutes infringement on an author's reserved rights. Vander Ark, a devoted Rowling fan, was "devastated" by the lawsuit. In Rowling's witness-stand testimony, she said, "I never ever once wanted to stop Mr. Vander Ark from doing his own guide, never ever. Do your book, but, please, change it so it does not take as much of my work" (Reardon).

The court found that Vander Ark's proposed book did offer something beyond the primary work, or could be considered a "transformative" secondary work that would add to readers' understandings of the original series; however, it also concluded that the *Lexicon* "appropriated far too much of Rowling's masterpieces" to constitute the legal definition of "fair use" (Siskind 303) and exceeded reasonable copying to fulfill the purpose of the reference work. The court also found that the Vander Ark lexicon would cause some market harm to the encyclopedia planned by Rowling herself because the purpose of the lexicon was commercial gain (Siskind 304).

In the end, ruling judge Patterson, "found that the defense of fair use failed in this specific case" but did not rule out future reference works that would support a finding of fair use (Siskind 305). Implicit in the case was the assumption that Rowling would be issuing her own encyclopedic companion or companions to her popular series.

Rowling continues to support philanthropic causes she has actively involved herself in for over a decade. In fall 2000 Rowling made a major donation of $785,000 to the charitable organization National Council for One-Parent Families (now known as Gingerbread) (Compson 40; S. Smith). This was the beginning of what would become a long record of philanthropic work and large charitable donations. Rowling's 2001 donation funded the creation of a research center on multiple sclerosis (MS) in Edinburgh, Scotland, partly because Scotland has the highest rate of MS in the world (Reid). Her April 2001 gift of $375,000 funded research, pain-relief drugs, and accessible therapies for sufferers of the disease (Kirk 94). Also in 2001 Rowling wrote the two books *Quidditch through the Ages* and *Fantastic Beasts and Where to Find Them* with all proceeds to be donated to Comic Relief, supporting "some of the poorest and most vulnerable people in the poorest countries of the world" (Compson 42). They were both published in 2001, with $3 of each copy sold going to the charity, raising nearly $30 million as of 2009 for Comic Relief. *The Tales of Beedle the Bard* hit bookshelves in November 2008, and Rowling donated the proceeds from the collection of fables to the charity she cofounded, the CHILDREN'S HIGH LEVEL GROUP. In 2006 Rowling was estimated to have a net worth of more than $1 billion by *Forbes* magazine ("Harry Might"). By mid-2007 her books had sold nearly 325 million copies ("J. K. Rowling").

What readers are probably most interested in is whether we will see more about Harry or some new and enchanting character from Rowling. In an interview with the BBC, when asked whether she would write more stories about Harry Potter in the future, Rowling cryptically responded, "Never say never" (Romano), though she had said previously that there would be only seven novels in the series. She hinted in a 2007 interview with *Time* magazine at an eighth book, saying, "There have been times since finishing, weak moments, when I've said, 'Yeah, all right' to the eighth novel," but that "if—and it's a big if—I ever write an eighth book, I doubt that Harry would be the central character" ("J. K. Rowling Ponders"). An interview on BBC had Rowling discuss her plans to write another children's book series, probably under a pseudonym and aimed at a younger reading audience than the Potter books ("Rowling Moves On").

At the time of this printing Rowling is not publicly discussing her current writing projects. However, in October 2010, in an interview with Oprah Winfrey at Edinburgh's elegant Balmoral Hotel, Rowling said that "characters are still all in my head," and "I could easily write an eight or ninth." Reports have suggested she is working on an encyclopedic companion to the Harry Potter series.

WORKS CITED

Adler, Margot. "Interview: J. K. Rowling on her 'Harry Potter' Series of Books and Protecting Herself from the Celebrity Caused by the Books' Success." *Morning Edition* (NPR), 27 October 2000. Newspaper Source Plus. Available online by subscription. Accessed August 25, 2009.

"Author to Face Plagiarism Writ." *Courier Mail* (Brisbane), 16 March 2001. Newspaper Source Plus. Available online by subscription. August 25, 2009.

Cawley, Janet. "15 Extraordinary Women: Joanne Kathleen (J. K.) Rowling." *Biography* 7, no. 7 (July 2003): 50. MasterFILE Premier. Available online by subscription. Accessed August 25, 2009.

Compson, William. *J. K. Rowling.* New York: Rosen Central, 2003.

Feldman, Roxanne. "The Truth about Harry." *School Library Journal* 45, no. 9 (September 1999): 136–139.

Fraser, Lindsey. *An Interview with J. K. Rowling.* London: Mammoth Books, 2000.

Gaines, Ann Graham. *J. K. Rowling: A Blue Banner Biography.* Hockessin, Del.: Mitchell Lane, 2005.

"Harry Might Not Survive Potter Finale, Rowling Hints." *Winnipeg Free Press,* 28 June 2006. Newspa-

per Source Plus. Available online by subscription. Accessed August 25, 2009.

"*Harry Potter* Author Reveals Suicidal Thoughts." Zap2It.com, 24 March 2008. Newspaper Source Plus. Available online by subscription. Accessed August 25 2009.

"*Harry Potter* Author Says She Cried after Writing Death Scene." *Canadian Press,* 18 June 2003. Newspaper Source. Available online by subscription. Accessed August 25, 2009.

"JK, Harry to Rise from Ashes of Court Case." *Australian,* 21 September 2009. Newspaper Source Plus. Available online by subscription. Accessed August 25, 2009.

"J. K. Rowling." *Contemporary Authors.* Updated 24 March 2009. Gale Literary Databases. Available online by subscription. Accessed May 11, 2009.

"J. K. Rowling Biography." Biography.com. Available online. URL: http://www.biography.com/articles/ J.K.-Rowling-40998. Accessed May 11, 2009.

"J. K. Rowling Has Gone from Welfare to Riches." *Toronto Star,* 21 October 2000.

J.K. Rowling Official Site. "Biography." Available online. URL: http://www.jkrowling.com/en/. Accessed July 5, 2010.

"J. K. Rowling Ponders No. 8." *Daily Telegraph* (Sydney), 31 December 2007. Newspaper Source Plus. Available online by subscription. Accessed August 25, 2009.

"J. K. Rowling Says Her Mother's Death Influenced Harry Potter Books." *Canadian Press,* 10 January 2006. Newspaper Source Plus. Available online by subscription. Accessed August 25, 2009.

Jones, Malcolm. "The Woman Who Invented Harry." *Newsweek,* 17 July 2000. MasterFILE Premier. Available online by subscription. Accessed August 25, 2009.

Kirk, Connie Ann. *J. K. Rowling: A Biography.* Westport, Conn.: Greenwood Press, 2003.

Lawless, John. "How This Man's Daughter Saved a Legend." *Sun-Herald* (Sydney), 10 July 2005.

Lovett, Charles. *J. K. Rowling: Her Life and Works.* New York: SparkNotes, 2003.

Nelson, Michael. "Fantasia: The Gospel According to C. S. Lewis." *American Prospect,* 25 February 2002. Available online URL: http://www.prospect.org/

cs/articles?article=fantasia the gospel_according_to_cs_lewis. Accessed September 1, 2009.

Reardon, Patrick. "Harry Potter and the Battle of the Lexicon." *Chicago Tribune,* 4 May 2008.

Romano, Carlin. "Classic 'Harry': With Six Novels Down, at Least One to Come, J. K. Rowling Has Elevated Herself to among the Masters of Children's Literature." *Philadelphia Inquirer,* 16 July 2007.

Rowling, J. K. "The Fringe Benefits of Failure and the Importance of Imagination." *Harvard University Gazette,* 5 June 2008.

"Rowling Moves On." *Sunday Telegraph* (Sydney), 4 December 2005. Newspaper Source Plus. Available online by subscription. Accessed August 25, 2009.

Schlink, Leo. "Christmas with Harry Potter." *Advertiser* (Adelaide), 21 September 2009. Newspaper Source Plus. Available online by subscription. Accessed August 25 2009.

Sexton, Colleen. *J. K. Rowling.* Minneapolis, Minn.: Twenty-First Century Books, 2008.

Shapiro, Marc. *J. K. Rowling: The Wizard behind Harry Potter.* New York: Macmillan, 2000.

Siskind, Shira. "Crossing the Fair Use Line: The Demise and Revival of the *Harry Potter Lexicon* and Its Implications for the Fair Use Doctrine in the Real World and on the Internet." *Cardozo Arts and Entertainment Law Journal* 27, no. 1 (2009): 291–311. Wilson OmniFile. Available online by subscription. Accessed August 25, 2009.

Smith, Sean. *J. K. Rowling: A Biography.* London: Michael O'Mara Books, 2003.

Smith, Tovia. "Rowling's Harvard Speech Doesn't Entrance All." NPR. 6 June 2008. Available online. URL: http://www.npr.org/templates/story/story.php?storyId=91232541&ft=1&f=1001. Accessed August 11, 2009.

Steger, Jason. "Harry Potter Works His Magic in Case of the Muggles." *Age* (Melbourne), 20 September 2002.

Stritof, Sheri, and Stritof, Bob. "J. K. Rowling and Neil Murray Marriage Profile." About.com. Available online. URL: http://marriage.about.com/od/thearts/p/jkrowling.htm Accessed September 1, 2009.

Treneman, Ann. "I'm Not Writing for the Money; It's for Me and Out of Loyalty to Fans." *Times* (London), 20 June 2003.

Wapshott, Nicholas. "Harry Potter Plagiarism Case Rejected by Judge." *Times* (London), 19 September 2009. Newspaper Source Plus. Available online by subscription. Accessed August 25, 2009.

Warner Brothers Entertainment, Inc. and J. K. Rowling v. RDR Books. 84E3WAR1. United States District Court of the Southern District of New York. 2008. Center for Internet and Society. Stanford University Law School. Accessed September 1, 2009.

Weir, Margaret. "Of Magic and Single Motherhood." Salon.com. 31 March 1999. Available online. URL: http://www.cesnur.org/recens/potter_022.htm. Accessed September 3, 2009.

Wiener, Gary, ed. *The Greenhaven Press Literary Companion to Contemporary Authors: Readings on J. K. Rowling.* San Diego, Calif.: Thomson/Gale, 2003.

PART II

Works A–Z

HARRY POTTER NOVELS

Harry Potter and the Sorcerer's Stone
(*Harry Potter and the Philosopher's Stone*)
(1997)

SYNOPSIS

Chapter 1: "The Boy Who Lived"

Vernon and Petunia Dursley live at Number Four, Privet Drive, with their son, Dudley. They consider themselves very normal people and refuse to associate with anything unusual or mysterious. For this reason the Dursleys never mention Petunia's sister (or that sister's husband and son) because they are "abnormal."

The story begins on a usual day. Vernon leaves for work and is unsettled by a cat he sees on the street corner reading a map. He convinces himself he could not have seen such a spectacle and continues his drive to work, during which he is further unnerved by seeing many funnily dressed people wearing cloaks. During a break at work Vernon walks to a nearby shop and overhears people happily whispering about "The Potters" and their son, Harry. Vernon is sure the muffled gossip concerns his wife's sister; he considers asking Petunia about what he has heard when he gets home but, knowing it will upset her, decides against it. After hearing reports about flying stars (coupled with an unusual number of owls in the sky) Vernon feels compelled to say something to Petunia. When she confirms that her sister's son is named Harry, Vernon realizes the events of the day most definitely somehow concern his relatives.

That very night Albus Dumbledore appears on Privet Drive. He is met by Professor Minerva McGonagall, who asks whether the rumors she heard that day are true. Dumbledore confirms that You-Know-Who (Voldemort) appeared at the Potters' home. While there Voldemort killed Lily (Petunia's sister) and her husband, James Potter; he also attempted to kill their son, Harry, but for some reason was unable to do so and was forced to flee. Within minutes the roar of a flying motorcycle disturbs the night's silence. Hagrid, Dumbledore's trusted friend and staff member at Hogwarts, lands the bike and presents Dumbledore with Harry, whom Hagrid rescued from the rubble of the Potters' house in Godric's Hollow. McGonagall is uneasy with Dumbledore's decision to leave Harry with the Dursleys since they are some of the worst Muggles (people with no magical ability) she has ever seen. Dumbledore assures her that he made his decision with Harry's best interest in mind and that it will be beneficial for Harry to grow up without knowing his past. He lays Harry, swaddled in blankets, on the steps to Number Four, Privet Drive. Then he, Hagrid, and McGonagall leave while throughout the wizarding world overjoyed people toast Harry, saying, "To Harry Potter—the boy who lived!"

Chapter 2: "The Vanishing Glass"

Chapter 2 begins almost 10 years later. It is Dudley's birthday, and Aunt Petunia rudely awakens Harry in his cupboard under the stairs; she immediately puts Harry to work in the kitchen. Harry is a small boy with dark unruly hair and green eyes. His clothes are always too big (they are hand-me-downs from the overweight Dudley), but the distinguishing aspect of his appearance is the lightning-shaped scar on his forehead. When he asked years ago where the scar came from, his aunt hurriedly explained he got it in the car crash in which his parents died, then reprimanded him with "Don't ask questions," a phrase Harry heard often from the Dursleys.

Dudley pitches a fit since he received only 36 presents (two fewer than last year), and Petunia can only calm him by assuring him he will get more gifts when they go out. The Dursleys will take Piers Polkiss, Dudley's friend, to the zoo while Harry stays with a neighbor, Mrs. Figg. Plans change since Mrs. Figg has broken her leg; the Dursleys are forced to take Harry with them to the zoo, much to Dudley's consternation. During the car ride Harry reminisces about a dream he had in which there was a flying motorcycle. Vernon screams at Harry for mentioning something so silly. In the reptile house Harry is intrigued by a boa constrictor. The snake winks at Harry and then engages him in conversation. Piers screams for Vernon and Dudley to see the snake now that it is moving around its cage; they rush over, and Dudley shoves Harry out of the way. Suddenly, the glass at the front of the snake's cage disappears, and the snake escapes while Dudley, his friend, and the zoo staff remain dumbfounded by the event. After calming down, Piers asks Harry whether he was talking to the snake. The very suggestion infuriates Vernon, who orders Harry to his cupboard, where he is to remain without meals. Harry reflects on his unfortunate state: He has no friends, and Dudley's gang makes him their favorite target. Harry wishes he had somewhere else to go, as he has wished many times before in his life.

Chapter 3: "The Letters from No One"
For the upcoming school year Dudley will attend private school while Harry will go to public school. Although Harry will continue to be bullied by Dudley and his gang, he cannot help but laugh at Dudley in his private school uniform.

One morning at breakfast Harry is told to get the mail. He is completely shocked to find a letter addressed to him. The Dursleys seize the letter and appear violently unsettled by its arrival. They destroy the letter, but to no use. Another letter arrives for Harry, and then another. Soon multiple copies of the letter arrive each day. Harry, determined to find out what the letter contains, attempts to outsmart his uncle by waking up early to get to the mail before anyone else. His determination pales in comparison to that of his uncle, however, who sleeps on the doorstep to prevent Harry from obtaining a copy of the letter.

Completely unraveled by the constant barrage of letters, Vernon gathers everyone into the car in an attempt to escape their relentless delivery. Their stay at a dumpy, faraway hotel cannot even stop the letters from finding them. Angry and mentally unstable, Vernon hauls the family out to a rickety shack built on a rock in the middle of the sea. A rainstorm causes waves to crash against the cliffs while Harry remembers his 11th birthday is only minutes away. Harry counts down the final seconds, and with the arrival of midnight and his birthday there is a ferocious knock at the shack door.

Chapter 4: "The Keeper of the Keys"
Rubeus Hagrid, keeper of keys and grounds at Hogwarts, breaks down the door. His abrupt entrance shocks Harry and angers the Dursleys. When Hagrid learns that Harry knows nothing about the magical school Hogwarts, he becomes infuriated with the Dursleys; his disgust only mounts when he discovers the Dursleys told Harry his parents died in a car crash. Instead, Hagrid explains, Harry's parents (James and Lily Potter) were murdered by the evil wizard Voldemort, whom most of the wizarding community refers to as "You-Know-Who" out of fear. Harry learns that he has been famous among wizards since the night of his parents' murder because, although Voldemort wanted to murder Harry as well, for some reason Harry was left unharmed when Voldemort attempted to kill him. Hagrid explains that many of the powerful good witches and wizards who fought against Voldemort died, but Harry, even at the infant age of one, was able to withstand Voldemort, who disappeared the night he murdered Harry's parents and tried to kill Harry.

In the midst of learning all this information, Harry also finally gains access to a copy of the letter addressed to him that Vernon had worked so tirelessly to keep from him. Inside the envelope are several important pieces of information including a letter from Professor McGonagall welcoming him to Hogwarts and a list of supplies he must take with him to school. Vernon furiously informs Hagrid that Harry will not be allowed to attend the wizarding school, but Hagrid assures him that Harry will indeed be attending Hogwarts at the start of term. He reassures Harry of this fact as well and then— after letting slip that he himself was expelled from Hogwarts—Hagrid stays in the shack with Harry since they will go shopping for his school supplies together the next morning.

Chapter 5: "Diagon Alley"
Hagrid and Harry set off for Diagon Alley, a street in London hidden from Muggles, which witches and wizards travel to in order to buy special supplies ranging from potion ingredients to magical schoolbooks. Harry expresses his concern to Hagrid about purchasing the necessary supplies for school

This steam locomotive, no. 5972 "Olton Hall," pulls the Hogwarts Express in the film adaptations of the novels and is shown here on display at Doncaster Railway Works in England. *(Photo by Phil Scott/Used under a Creative Commons license)*

because he does not have any money. Hagrid quells Harry's fears by assuring him that his parents left him a large inheritance, a portion of which they can attain from Gringotts, the wizarding bank, so Harry can complete his necessary shopping.

Diagon Alley can only be accessed by traveling through the Leaky Cauldron, a dodgy pub frequented by witches and wizards. When Harry enters the pub, he is swarmed by members of the wizarding community, who recognize him by his lightning-shaped scar and feel extremely honored to meet him. One such person is Professor Quirrell, who will be one of Harry's teachers at Hogwarts. He is a nervous man with a stutter. He tells Harry he has his own errand to run in Diagon Alley, and then Harry is once again barraged by excited people glad finally to make his acquaintance.

Hagrid finally gets Harry through the mass of people in the pub and takes him to Diagon Alley. Harry withdraws money from Gringotts, which is staffed by goblins, protected by many enchantments, and even guarded by dragons in some parts. Hagrid tells Harry one would have to be mad to try to rob Gringotts. While at the bank Hagrid also accesses a vault with special permission from Dumbledore, retrieving a package for the headmaster.

While waiting to be fitted for his school robes, Harry meets a young boy who reminds him of Dudley. The boy is rude, makes fun of Hagrid, and makes offensive comments that only people who have wizard parents should be allowed to attend Hogwarts. After this encounter Hagrid helps Harry acquire the rest of his school supplies, last of all, a wand. In the wand shop Ollivander's, Harry meets

Mr. Ollivander, who helps suit him with a proper wand. Mr. Ollivander remembers every wand he has ever sold and expresses obvious curiosity when Harry is finally fitted with a proper wand, since, as Mr. Ollivander puts it, "The wand chooses the wizard," and the wand that chooses Harry is the brother wand of Voldemort's. After this eventful day Harry feels self-conscious about his lack of knowledge of the wizarding world, but Hagrid assures him he will learn quickly enough and then escorts Harry to the train station and says his farewell.

Chapter 6: "The Journey from Platform Nine and Three-Quarters"

The Dursleys agree to take Harry to catch his train to Hogwarts. When Harry informs his uncle Vernon that his train will leave from platform nine and three-quarters, his uncle seizes the opportunity to comment on the wizarding world and asserts that catching a train at platform nine and three-quarters demonstrates that they are "barking mad."

Once at the train station Harry asks for help in locating his train and its platform, but a guard assures Harry no train leaves at 11 o'clock and then, irritated, leaves Harry standing alone. Just when Harry begins to get really nervous, he hears someone talking about how the train station is "packed with Muggles." Harry takes this as a clue that whoever is speaking must be a member of the wizarding community, and he is right. Molly Weasley, along with her children, Percy, Fred, George, Ron, and Ginny, helps Harry get to the magical platform by walking through a pillar between platforms nine and ten. Once the Hogwarts Express, a scarlet steam engine, departs the station, Harry's excitement grows. Harry sits in a compartment by himself, but not for long: Ron Weasley joins him, and the two become fast friends. When they buy some candy, Harry becomes particularly interested in the chocolate frogs, which include a picture of a famous witch or wizard. Harry is surprised to learn that the people in pictures in the wizarding world have the ability to move. Harry gets an Albus Dumbledore card, from which he learns Dumbledore defeated Grindelwald, discovered 12 uses for dragon's blood, and made important alchemical advancements with his friend, Nicolas Flamel.

A worried boy enters their compartment looking for his lost toad. Ron attempts to perform some magic for Harry but feels unsettled when a nosy, bossy bushy-brown-haired girl barges in. Her name is Hermione Granger, and she already knows who Harry is (she has been reading about Hogwarts since she received her acceptance letter). She reminds the boys they should put on their school robes since they will arrive at Hogwarts shortly and leaves brusquely, taking Neville (the toadless boy) with her.

Harry learns from Ron that someone tried to break into Gringotts; the discussion turns quickly to Quidditch. A pale snarky boy interrupts their conversation: He is the same snooty boy Harry met in Diagon Alley while being fitted for his school robes. His name is Draco Malfoy, and he teases Ron about his family's poor economic situation. A fight ensues but quickly ends when Ron's pet rat bites one of Draco's friends. The train arrives at Hogwarts, where Hagrid meets the first-year students. They board boats, and Hagrid finds Neville's toad, Trevor. The boats sail across a huge black lake. The students disembark and follow Hagrid to the Hogwarts castle front door.

Chapter 7: "The Sorting Hat"

Professor McGonagall greets the students and explains that they will be sorted into one of four houses: Slytherin, Gryffindor, Ravenclaw, and Hufflepuff. Students work together in their houses to earn house points (these points can also be deducted); the house with the most points at the end of the year will win the House Cup, an important honor. Professor McGonagall escorts the students into Hogwarts' Great Hall, which has a bewitched ceiling that mimics the real sky.

At the front of the great hall is a stool upon which an old hat rests. Suddenly, the hat starts singing: It introduces itself as the Sorting Hat, and its ensuing song reveals important qualities associated with each of the four houses at Hogwarts. Gryffindors are brave, daring, and chivalrous; Hufflepuffs are loyal, patient, and hardworking; Ravenclaws are witty and learned; and last, Slytherins are known for their ambition and cunning. One by one the students are called forward to be sorted. The hat assigns Draco to Slytherin, while Ron, Hermione, and Neville all are sorted into Gryffindor. Harry is also sorted into Gryffindor, but not without some difficulty; Harry possesses qualities important to each house. Harry thinks about how he does not want to be in Slytherin, so the talking hat sorts him into Gryffindor.

The students are treated to a magical feast, during which Harry peruses the teachers sitting at the head table. He notices a hook-nosed teacher sitting next to Professor Quirrell, whom he met earlier in the Leaky Cauldron. Harry's eye shifts from Professor Quirrell's turban to the hook-nosed professor, and when their eyes lock, a searing pain occurs at Harry's scar on his forehead. Percy informs Harry the professor at whom he has been staring is Professor Snape, the Potions teacher, who has always longed to be the Defense Against the Dark Arts teacher.

After dinner Dumbledore makes some announcements, after which the students head to their dormitories. Harry, exhausted, falls into a deep sleep interrupted by a strange dream in which Harry wears Quirrell's turban and is told he must transfer houses to Slytherin. Draco appears and laughs at Harry, then Draco transforms into Snape. Harry has no recollection of the dream the next day.

Chapter 8: "The Potions Master"

Harry cannot walk down a corridor of the castle without people staring at him. Harry is unsettled by Peeves the Poltergeist, but worse yet are the caretaker, Argus Filch, and his cat, Mrs. Norris. They spy relentlessly on the students, seizing any opportunity to report someone for punishment.

The students attend their first classes: History of Magic is boring; Charms seems more interesting because of the small and squeaky-voiced Professor Flitwick; McGonagall's Transfiguration class is impressive because of her trick of turning her desk into a pig and back again. Quirrell's class turns out to be more boring than everyone expected. Harry finds a sense of relief in learning that he is not very far behind most of his classmates, who all have a lot to learn. In Potions Harry learns just how much Snape hates him. Snape repeatedly puts Harry on the spot, asking him difficult questions, the answers to which, of course, Hermione knows. Harry is puzzled why Snape dislikes him so much.

After lessons Harry and Ron go to visit Hagrid. At his house Harry sees an article from the wizarding newspaper, the *Daily Prophet;* the story covers a recent break-in at Gringotts on July 31, the same day (the paper reports) that the vault was emptied. Harry realizes that this was on his birthday, the very day they were in Gringotts. He remains suspicious as to how and why Hagrid emptied the vault just in time.

Chapter 9: "The Midnight Duel"

The first years learn they will be having their first flying lesson. Harry feels concerned that he will make a fool of himself in front of Draco, who seems to have a lot of experience on a broomstick. Neville has no experience flying since his grandmother would never let him try; Hermione is just as nervous about flying as Neville since one cannot learn to fly just from reading a book. At breakfast Neville receives a Remembrall from his grandmother. Draco and his cronies, Crabbe and Goyle, steal the object from Neville; McGonagall senses trouble and makes them give it back to Neville.

At their flying lesson Neville nervously pushes off the ground and goes flying. He lands, breaking his wrist. Madam Hooch escorts him to the hospital, telling all the students they are forbidden to fly. Draco sees Neville's Remembrall and snatches it up. Harry commands that Draco return it. Draco flies off and tells Harry if he wants it for his friend, he will have to come get it. Harry's first time flying is exhilarating. Draco throws the Remembrall, and Harry maneuvers expertly to catch it. McGonagall suddenly yells Harry's name; he knows he has been caught, and Draco and his cronies are delighted.

Harry worries what fate awaits him. Curiously McGonagall takes Harry to a classroom and retrieves a student, Oliver Wood, who Harry learns plays Quidditch for Gryffindor. Professor McGonagall tells Wood that she has found him a seeker, a position on a Quidditch team. McGonagall tells Harry that his dad would be proud of him, since he was an excellent Quidditch player himself.

Later that day Draco challenges Harry to a wizard's duel. They agree to meet in the trophy room at midnight. Hermione overhears their plans and tells the boys they must not go wandering at night about the castle, to which Harry responds that what they decide to do is none of her business. When Ron and Harry leave for the duel, Hermione follows them, asking them whether they care at all about their fellow Gryffindors. They tell her they are going anyway. When Hermione turns to get back in the dormitory, the Fat Lady (the woman in the portrait who guards the Gryffindors common room) has disappeared, and she is locked out. She insists that she accompany them since she does not want to be caught just standing outside the common room door. Neville is also stuck outside after forgetting the password. He, too, must accompany Ron and Harry to the duel. Upon arriving at the trophy room, they hear Filch snooping around. They are able to escape without being caught and realize that Draco tricked them in hopes they would get caught.

On their way back to the Gryffindor dormitory they end up on the third floor, the forbidden corridor. They find themselves face to face with a huge three-headed dog. They decide to run, at the risk of running into Filch. When they finally arrive back at the common room, Hermione informs Harry and Ron that the dog was standing on a trapdoor, indicating that it is guarding something. Harry thinks he knows where the package Hagrid retrieved from Gringotts has ended up.

Chapter 10: "Halloween"

Upset by their antics Hermione refuses to talk to Harry and Ron, but they appreciate this since she is bossy and nosy. One morning at breakfast Harry receives a package with a note instructing him not to open it at the table since it contains his broom, a *Nimbus Two Thousand*. The note also instructs him to meet Oliver Wood for his first training session that night. Harry learns many details about Quidditch from Wood. Each team has seven players: three Chasers, two Beaters, one Keeper, and one Seeker. The Chasers use the Quaffle to score 10 points at a time. The Beaters use bats with balls called Bludgers to distract the Chasers. The Keepers defend the goals, and the Seeker (Harry's role on the team) is to capture the Golden Snitch. Capturing the Snitch is worth 150 points and automatically ends the game.

In Charms class the students learn how to make things fly. They spend the hour learning about the Wingardium Leviosa spell. Harry hears Hermione telling Ron that he is performing the spell wrong. Hermione executes the spell beautifully. After class Ron characterizes Hermione as a "nightmare"; a few moments later she bumps into them, walking quickly past and crying. She spends the rest of the day in the bathroom in tears.

That evening the Halloween feast is disrupted by Quirrell's cries that a troll has entered the Hogwarts dungeons. While the students make their way back to the dormitories, Harry realizes Hermione does not know about the troll. On their way to finding her they discover the troll and triumphantly lock him in a room; they then realize they have locked him in the girls' bathroom, with Hermione. Hermione is terrified, and the boys have to battle the troll themselves. They end up knocking out the troll with his own club, courtesy of the Wingardium Leviosa spell performed by Ron.

When the professors find the three students, Hermione takes the blame, saying that since she had read all about trolls, she thought she could handle one by herself. After the encounter with the troll and taking responsibility for the situation and saving them from trouble, Hermione becomes very good friends with Ron and Harry.

Chapter 11: "Quidditch"

Harry learns more about the history of the exciting sport of Quidditch thanks to a book from the library, *Quidditch through the Ages*. He takes the book with him one day into the courtyard, and Snape confiscates it since no library books are supposed to be taken outside the school. Harry also notices Snape limping and becomes curious about what may have caused his injury. Harry decides that he would like his library book back. He interrupts Snape and Filch, who seem to be tending to Snape's injured leg. Snape screams at Harry to leave. Of course, this incident causes Harry to become suspicious of Snape, but Hermione still defends the professor.

The Quidditch match proves exciting, and dangerous even, when Harry's broom appears to be possessed. Hermione and Ron notice Snape staring at Harry and muttering something. Hermione disrupts Snape by setting his cloak on fire. Harry regains control of his broom, catches the Snitch, and wins the match for Gryffindor. After the match Harry, Ron, and Hermione visit Hagrid and share their theories that Snape was trying to curse Harry. Hagrid assures them that Snape would never do anything to harm Harry, sabotage Hogwarts, or try to get whatever is hidden in the castle. Hagrid, as is his habit, tends to reveal more information than he should in conversations with the three students; he discloses that whatever seems to be hidden in the castle involves a man by the name of Nicolas Flamel.

Chapter 12: "The Mirror of Erised"

The Christmas holidays approach rapidly, and in the meantime, Harry, Ron, and Hermione spend a lot of their time in the library trying to uncover some information about Nicolas Flamel. When Christmas arrives, Harry and Ron have the entire dormitory to themselves. Harry feels overwhelmed at actually receiving thoughtful Christmas gifts (compared to what the Dursleys had given him in the past). Harry's most puzzling present arrives anonymously. It is an Invisibility Cloak (a garment that, when worn, prevents the wearer from being seen). The note accompanying the gift instructs Harry to "use it well" (202).

Harry does make good use of the cloak by wearing it to sneak into the restricted section of the library in his pursuit to learn more about Nicolas Flamel. One night while he goes exploring he runs into Filch; to escape him, he runs into an empty classroom. Inside it stands a huge mirror. Harry approaches the mirror and is taken aback by what he sees: himself, standing surrounded by his family, with his mother and father right beside him. Harry makes Ron go with him to see the mirror, explaining that Ron will see Harry's parents when he looks in it; instead, however, Ron sees himself as Quidditch captain, holding the Quidditch Cup and the House Cup and wearing the head boy badge. Harry returns to gaze in the mirror for several nights. One night Dumbledore arrives in the room and tells Harry that men have wasted away in front of this very

mirror before and that the mirror will be moved to a new location.

Chapter 13: "Nicolas Flamel"

Harry starts having nightmares about his parents' disappearing, surrounded by a flash of green light. He is also unsettled when he learns that Snape will be refereeing the next Quidditch match. On a brighter note Neville gives Harry a chocolate frog card since he knows he collects them; although it is of Dumbledore and Harry already has a copy of the card, he turns it over and reads that one of Dumbledore's accomplishments is work in alchemy with Nicolas Flamel. With some research Harry, Ron, and Hermione discover that Flamel made the Sorcerer's Stone, used to turn metal into gold and make the Elixir of Life, granting immortality to the drinker.

At the next Quidditch match Harry catches the Snitch in record time. After the match Harry sees Snape going into the Forbidden Forest. Harry uses his broom to spy on Snape and overhears him talking to Quirrell. Snape asks Quirrell whether he knows how to get past Hagrid's three-headed dog, Fluffy; mentions that the Sorcerer's Stone is indeed in the castle; and threatens Quirrell that he does not want Snape as his enemy. Harry tells Ron and Hermione what he overheard, and they realize the stone is only safe as long as Quirrell stands up to Snape, which, they assume, probably will not last very long.

Chapter 14: "Norbert the Norwegian Ridgeback"

With exams approaching Hermione takes it upon herself to make study schedules for herself, Ron, and Harry. They spend a lot of time in the library and one day run into Hagrid there. They tell him what they know about the stone, and Hagrid tells them to visit him later. After Hagrid leaves, they look at what section of books he was interested in: dragons, which are illegal in Britain.

Once Harry, Ron, and Hermione mention the stone, Hagrid again divulges more information than he should, telling them that Professors Sprout, Flitwick, McGonagall, Quirrell, Snape, and Dumbledore help guard the stone. They are shocked at Snape's involvement. Their attention is drawn toward the fire, in which a dragon egg sits. Astounded, Ron asks where Hagrid obtained the egg; Hagrid explains that the previous night he visited a pub, had a few drinks, and won the dragon egg in a bet. The person from whom he won the egg seemed very glad to be rid of it.

A few days later the egg begins to hatch. They go to Hagrid's and see the baby dragon. Hagrid suddenly looks startled: Someone had been spying on them through the window. It was Draco. Since it is illegal to keep a dragon as a pet, they try to help Hagrid find a place for Norbert (as Hagrid has named him); Ron suggests that they ask his brother, Charlie, for help since he works with dragons in Romania, and Charlie agrees to help. One day Ron goes to assist Hagrid in feeding Norbert, and the dragon bites his hand. He tries to keep the injury a secret, but it eventually swells so badly he must go to the hospital wing. Harry and Hermione take Norbert to the top of a tower at midnight to meet Charlie. They see Draco being reprimanded by McGonagall for being out of bed at night: He claims that Harry will be arriving with a dragon, but McGonagall dismisses this as nonsense. They successfully deliver the dragon by means of the Invisibility Cloak. They make their way back inside but forget the cloak. They enter the castle, and Filch catches them.

Chapter 15: "The Forbidden Forest"
Filch takes Harry and Hermione to McGonagall, who happens to be accompanying and reprimanding Neville (he had been trying to find Harry and Hermione to warn them about Draco, who was out to get them both in trouble). For being out of bed and roaming the castle, they are punished, including Draco. They all receive detention and lose 50 house points each.

Soon after, Harry, walking past a classroom, hears Quirrell's voice saying, "No, not again please" and then "All right." He assumes Snape is bullying Quirrell. They all serve their detention in the Forbidden Forest with Hagrid. He explains they will be looking for an injured unicorn. Harry, Hermione, and Hagrid go one way, and Draco, Neville, and the boarhound Fang go another. Harry's group runs into some centaurs (creatures

that are half-horse and half-man). Draco and Neville signal for help, so Hagrid goes to them, telling Harry and Hermione to wait where they are. When Hagrid takes the other group back, they redivide, and then Harry, Fang, and Draco go off together. They follow a trail of unicorn blood leading, unfortunately, to a dead unicorn.

Suddenly, a cloaked figure appears out of the forest, makes its way to the unicorn, and starts to drink blood from its side. Draco screams, and Harry is overcome with pain radiating from his scar. A centaur named Firenze comes to their rescue. He explains that killing a unicorn is a terrible crime and that drinking unicorn blood will keep one alive, no matter how close to death he or she may be. The penalty for drinking the blood is that the drinker's life becomes cursed for killing something so innocent and beautiful. Firenze then also helps Harry to understand that the Sorcerer's Stone resides in the castle and that Voldemort will do what he must to obtain it. Harry feels apprehensive since he thinks Voldemort will kill him. When he returns to his dormitory, he finds his Invisibility Cloak underneath his sheets with another anonymous note: It reads, "Just in case" (261).

Chapter 16: "Through the Trapdoor"
Harry's scar continues to bother him, and he assumes the pain is a warning of danger; he also suddenly becomes very suspicious of how Hagrid obtained the dragon egg. He thinks it is odd that when Hagrid wanted nothing more than a dragon, someone arrived with one for him. When Harry, Ron, and Hermione go to ask Hagrid about it, he tells them that he did not see what the person looked like because of his cloak, but that the stranger was very interested in Fluffy. Hagrid let slip to the cloaked person that to calm Fluffy down, one only needed to play music for the gigantic dog. The threesome decides to talk to Dumbledore about what they have learned, but he is, for the time being, gone from the castle. When they tell McGonagall they know about the stone and that someone is after it, she is flabbergasted that they know any of the information but tells them to stay out of trouble. She becomes very agitated when she finds the three of them standing outside the door to

the room housing Fluffy. Back in the common room they decide to use the Invisibility Cloak to go after the stone themselves that night.

As they plan to leave, Neville stops Harry, Ron, and Hermione and tells them not to go since all of Gryffindor will suffer from their bad behavior. He means well, but this does not stop Hermione from performing the Body-Bind spell on him, knocking him to the ground, immobile. She apologizes, and the three of them duck out of the common room and head toward the door to the third floor corridor that hides Fluffy.

When they arrive, a harp is playing, and Harry reports that Snape must have already gotten past Fluffy. All of them go through the trapdoor and land in a patch of Devil's Snare, which is the protection for the stone created by Professor Sprout. After that, they encounter Professor Flitwick's obstacle, hundreds of flying keys, only one of which will open the door that will take them to the next room. Harry's talents as Seeker are especially helpful here. In the next room they find a giant chessboard, which they must cross to get to the next room. This is Professor McGonagall's obstacle, and the only way to get to the next stage is to win the game of chess against giant, transfigured living chess pieces. Ron, as a brilliant chess player, leads them to victory, becoming injured in the process. Harry then pushes Hermione along into the next room, in which a troll lies, unconscious; Snape has already taken care of Quirrell's obstacle so that Hermione and Harry do not have to. The next room involves a complex riddle using potions created by Snape; Hermione solves the riddle quickly, and since, according to the riddle, only one of them can proceed to the next room, Harry goes on alone. He enters the last room and finds someone whom he least expected.

Chapter 17: "The Man with Two Faces"
Quirrell stands in the last chamber. Harry is completely shocked, explaining he thought Snape would be here. Quirrell says Harry is mistaken about Snape. When Harry mentions that Snape tried to kill him at a Quidditch match earlier in the year, Quirrell explains that he was actually trying to kill Harry by jinxing his broom while Snape was mut-

tering spells to try to save him from falling to his death. Harry asks Quirrell whom he was talking to a few days ago in a classroom, whom Quirrell was begging to leave him alone. Quirrell responds by saying that he was speaking to his master, a master who is always with him.

They stand in front of the mirror Harry saw his parents in. Quirrell says that he sees himself presenting the stone to his master. Harry sees himself reaching into his pocket and pulling out the Sorcerer's Stone; then, he feels something drop into his pocket. He actually possesses the stone. Harry becomes overwhelmed, trying to make sense of what Quirrell is saying. Then Quirrell removes his turban. Underneath it is Voldemort's face; he has been using Quirrell as a host the entire year. That is why Harry's scar hurt.

Voldemort explains to Harry that since his near-destruction, he has had to live off others and has been able to stay alive by drinking unicorn's blood. He wants the Sorcerer's Stone so he can take the Elixir of Life. Voldemort senses Harry has the stone, and when he refuses to give the stone up, Voldemort commands Quirrell to seize Harry. When he attempts to do so, Quirrell starts screaming in pain, explaining that his hands are burning after touching Harry. When Quirrell attempts to touch Harry again, Harry realizes that he must keep touching Quirrell to prevent him from doing anything worse. Harry hears Voldemort screaming for Quirrell to find a way to kill Harry, and then everything goes dark for Harry.

Harry wakes up in the hospital wing to see Dumbledore smiling down at him. Dumbledore tells Harry that the stone has been destroyed, but Harry knows this does not mean that Voldemort is gone and will not try to return to power. Harry asks Dumbledore why Voldemort wanted to kill him 11 years ago, but Dumbledore tells Harry he cannot answer that question for him now. A question he can answer for Harry, though, is why Quirrell was unable to touch him. Dumbledore explains that Harry's mother died out of love to save her son's life, and for that reason Quirrell—a man possessed by hatred and greed and connected so closely to Voldemort—could not stand to touch him.

Harry has a few other questions answered by Dumbledore. When he asks whether Snape and his father, James, hated each other, Dumbledore acknowledges they did not like each other and that Snape could not forgive Harry's father for saving his life since that put him in James Potter's debt forever. Dumbledore also explains to Harry that he was able to find the stone because he did not want to use it for himself but to save it from being used by Voldemort. The year ends positively for Harry, whose house wins the House Cup and who receives an album from Hagrid filled with pictures of his parents. He arrives back in London and says good-bye to his friends. He knows he will have a nice summer because even if he knows he is not allowed to do magic outside school, the Dursleys do not.

CRITICAL COMMENTARY

Published in June 1997 in Britain as *Harry Potter and the Philosopher's Stone* and in September 1998 in the United States as *Harry Potter and the Sorcerer's Stone,* the first novel in the Harry Potter series launched what would become one of the largest cross-media merchandising industries in history, making Rowling one of the richest people on the planet and globally igniting a passion for reading unprecedented among children, adolescents, and adults. Rowling's personal tale of hardships inspired almost as much public interest as Harry's story did and became woven into the fabric of both the character and his creator's success stories. In the first book Rowling introduces important themes such as identity, self-discovery, and good versus evil, themes that are more fully explored in the later novels. The strongest appeal of *Sorcerer's Stone* seems to be not simply the fantasy world of witchcraft and wizardry but the character of Harry himself. As have most successful children's book writers, Rowling has an aptitude for identifying the fears, insecurities, desires, and dreams of young readers and bringing them vividly to life through her young protagonist and his friends. The invention of the sport of Quidditch, the scatological humor, and the realities of children's lives (bad dreams, spats with family members and friends, academic difficulties, sibling rivalry) all serve as appealing aspects to Rowling's intended audience.

Rowling has said that "all [she] ever wanted to do is to see the book published. . . . I knew that most children's writers don't make any money. They will never ever, ever be very well known. I was totally OK with that. I just wanted someone to publish Harry so I could go to bookshops and see it" (Feldman 139). In the same 1999 interview in the *School Library Journal* she rejected the idea that she became famous "overnight or it came out of nowhere"; rather she worked diligently over a long period since she first conceived of the character of Harry Potter and Hogwarts School of Witchcraft and Wizardry in 1990. Though Rowling's interview emphasizes her passion for her stories and her view of writing as a form of avocation rather than a moneymaking venture, her books have nonetheless become some of the best-selling and most beloved books in the world. Many critics have focused attention on what makes these books so widely admired by readers, and well-known literary critics and creative writers have tangled over their literary merit.

Identity and Self-Discovery

One of the most important themes developed throughout the series and introduced in this first novel is the dramatization of the human journey of self-discovery and identity that Harry experiences, which young readers find especially compelling because of their own developing sense of self. When we are introduced to Harry, he lives with his contemptible relatives, who treat him with little respect and even less compassion. When Rowling reveals Harry as a wizard whose magical lineage has earned him a spot at the Hogwarts School of Witchcraft and Wizardry, Harry's previously held assumptions about his family, his place in the world, and himself are all destabilized. When Hagrid appears to relay the message of Harry's admission to Hogwarts, Harry is stymied: "Instead of feeling pleased and proud, [Harry] felt quite sure there had been a horrible mistake. A wizard? Him? How could he possibly be? He'd spent his life being clouted by Dudley and bullied by Aunt Petunia and Uncle Vernon" (57). As he considers some of the odd occurrences of his childhood, he begins the transformation that the novel documents, from slightly odd, abused boy to the "right famous" wizard Hagrid believes him to be.

Previously something of a loner both among classmates and in his family, Harry is quickly introduced to his new environment by Hagrid, the Hogwarts gamekeeper, though his new friend cannot create a social circle for Harry. Harry sets about this task almost immediately upon boarding the Hogwarts Express. Harry and Ron quickly share more than a train compartment in chapter 6: Besides sharing the candy from the mobile treat cart, Harry confides his anxieties to Ron. "I bet I'm the worst in class," he worries, after he makes the mistake of saying Voldemort's name out loud (100). Ron quickly reassures him, "There are loads of people who come from Muggle families and they learn quick enough" (100). This theme of anxiety over social relationships resonates strongly with young readers, who themselves have to navigate the shifting landscape of schools and other communities of peers, a navigation often tricky, unstable, and fraught with peril. Coupled with the sort of culture shock Harry experiences as he moves from the Muggle to the wizarding world, Harry's identity development is at the core of the first novel's plotline.

One of the most satisfying elements of the first book is the gradual sense of community that Harry begins to build as he forges a friendship with Ron Weasley and Hermione Granger, who will be his boon companions throughout the series. In his Muggle life Harry is the victim of bullying and exclusion by his cousin, Dudley, and Dudley's friends. Despite his embryonic magical abilities, Harry is the victim of his dependence on the goodwill of his relatives. Outcast and relegated to a small closet under the stairs, Harry has virtually no friends and little in the way of real family. Upon discovering his magical heritage, however, Harry is thrust into a world of not simply fellowship but admiration, as he discovers that beyond his magical powers, he is well known in the wizarding community for his historical role in vanquishing Voldemort. When he first arrives at platform nine and three-quarters in chapter 6, children from wizarding families stare curiously at him, whisper about him, or ask him directly, as Ron does, "Are you really Harry Potter?" (98). Even Hermione, raised in a Muggle family, reports, "I know all about you, of course—I got a few extra books for background reading, and you're in *Modern Magical History* and *The Rise and Fall of the Dark Arts* and *Great Wizarding Events of the Twentieth Century*" (106). Though his sudden fame disorients Harry, it also serves as a natural social lubricant, and Harry is soon catapulted from lonesome obscurity to social celebrity.

Social Development

Helping him navigate this transition, as well as the conflict underpinning all the books—his battle with Voldemort—are the sort of loyal friends most readers will envy: the bookish Hermione Granger and the affable Ron Weasley. Though Hermione is a bit of a latecomer to the trio because of her overeager "know-it-all" attitude, the confrontation with the troll in the girls' bathroom solidifies the three friends' relationship, as the narrator concludes in the chapter "Halloween": "But from that moment on, Hermione Granger became their friend. There are some things you can't share without ending up liking each other, and knocking out a twelve-foot mountain troll is one of them" (179). After a lonely childhood filled with alienation and rejection, Harry's fast friendships, forged intensely, remain all the more important to his life and to his growth as a character.

Though competition is emphasized through the sorting into the four houses and through the house Quidditch teams, Rowling also emphasizes intrahouse unity in the books; the Sorting serves as one mechanism through which characters, especially Harry, develop a sense of themselves. In chapter 7 the Sorting Hat delineates the qualities of each house, from the "daring, nerve, and chivalry" of Gryffindor to the "patient Hufflepuffs," the "wit and learning" of Ravenclaw, and the "cunning folk" of Slytherin (118). It seems that the Weasleys, for example, are foreordained to belong to the Gryffindor house, with its characteristics of loyalty and bravery, and that Draco and his friends are born for Slytherin, having inherited their parents' elitist attitudes and smug demeanor.

Harry, in contrast, appeals as a hero because Rowling gives him wider latitude to make his own decisions about the sort of characteristics he wants to develop and the kinds of people with whom he wants to identify. When the Sorting Hat drops onto Harry's head, he seems to exert a level of choice over his placement that his classmates do not. The Sorting Hat muses, "Difficult. Very difficult. Plenty of courage, I see. Not a bad mind either. There's talent, oh my goodness yes—and a nice thirst to prove yourself" (121), seeming to imply that Harry shares qualities of all houses. However, Harry's pleading "*Not Slytherin, not Slytherin*" becomes central to the series as his identity develops and his crisis over his status as "chosen one" becomes increasingly agonizing; he wonders frequently whether he has been placed in the right house. Harry's quest for identity and his continual self-questioning are two of the qualities his readers find most likable and reinforce an ideology of self-determination that is attractive to readers young and old.

Death and Mortality

Though some critics and reviewers have cited *Goblet of Fire* as the point when the series becomes dark, perhaps even overly focused on death, others have suggested that this theme is central even to the first book. The audience for *Sorcerer's Stone* is clearly a youth readership, but one feature of Rowling's work that distinguishes it from other FANTASY FICTION series for children is its tragicomic approach to difficult questions, including facing mortality and the loss of loved ones. For example, Harry begins the story as an orphan, a long tradition in British and other national literatures (*see* ORPHANS IN LITERATURE). As a result, Harry struggles with their death and subsequent absence from his life; chapter 2 has Harry thinking mournfully about this absence: "He couldn't remember his parents at all. His aunt and uncle never spoke about them, and of course he was forbidden to ask questions. There were no photographs of them in the house" (30). Harry's situation is certainly made all the more bleak by his loss.

Paradoxically Rowling also incorporates a lighthearted approach to death in the form of the house ghosts such as Nearly Headless Nick and the Bloody Baron (a tension that Harry grapples with throughout the series, including events in *Order of the Phoenix* that cause Harry to question Nearly Headless Nick about those who return to the earthly plane).

In *Sorcerer's Stone* Harry gasps when "twenty ghosts . . . streamed through the back wall. Pearly-white and slightly transparent, they glided across the room talking to one another and hardly glancing at the first years" (115). The Friar, Bloody Baron, Grey Lady, and Nearly Headless Nick, though dead, are employed with highly humorous effect throughout the series, complicating its tone.

Flawed Characters, Flawed Institutions

Human character flaws are also the subject of Rowling's exploration in *Sorcerer's Stone*. Though Harry demonstrates many human virtues, the book is populated by characters who are less temperamentally gifted, exhibiting greed, cowardice, and prejudice. Voldemort's quest for ultimate power and immortality is the catalyst for the entire series, while Professor Quirrell's perceived cowardice in the face of Snape's pressure to give up the Sorcerer's Stone is subverted by the story's plot. Overhearing a strained conversation between Snape and Quirrell, Harry concludes that "Snape's trying to force Quirrell to help him get [the stone]" (227). Unfortunately, Harry's rush to judgment is another of those human flaws Rowling seems to target, as he discovers in the book's closing chapters that Snape's distasteful appearance and attitude do not reflect his allegiance or moral character; instead, it is Quirrell who seeks the stone as a way of resurrecting Voldemort.

Sorcerer's Stone thus nicely sets up one of the central themes of the series: questions about justice and corrupt authority. When the series moves to a mixed readership of adults and youth, Rowling questions institutional authority more vigorously, mainly in her presentation of the Minister of Magic (from Fudge to Scrimgeour), who typically either fails to act or acts inappropriately in the face of the threats of Dark Magic to the social order. However, in the early books in the series Rowling seems to confine her questions about the implications of corrupt authorities to those in Harry's immediate sphere of influence—not necessarily those imbued with the power to influence institutions. For example, the Dursleys wield a great deal of power over Harry and demonstrate moral and character weaknesses that make them easy targets for readers' contempt.

Similarly, Snape and Quirrell, both teachers who are supposed to be authority figures and role models for Harry and his friends, have very real human frailties that call into question the admonition that children listen to their elders.

Literary Conventions

Rowling also uses a tragicomic tone in her handling of Harry's pre-Hogwarts life. From the beginning she draws upon the fairy tale and literary tradition of the "Cinderella" figure, who has been abused and/or cast aside and treated with an undeserved contempt. His surrogate family makes no effort to conceal their hatred for him, as an exchange very early in the novel reveals: "Don't be silly, Vernon, she hates the boy," says his aunt Petunia when her husband suggests leaving Harry with a relative during Dudley's birthday trip to the zoo. The narrator continues, "The Dursleys often spoke about Harry like this, as though he wasn't there—or rather, as though he was something very nasty that couldn't understand them, like a slug" (22).

Clearly, Harry's story begins in a lowly place, and though this common literary trope can feel formulaic, readers nonetheless empathize with the squalid conditions in which Harry lives. As do other literary protagonists such as the young Arthur, or "Wart," in T. H. WHITE's *The Sword in the Stone*, Harry suffers mistreatment by his cousin, Dudley ("Dudley's favorite punching bag was Harry, but he couldn't often catch him" [20], the narrator tells us), and from his aunt and uncle: "He'd lived with the Dursleys almost ten years, ten miserable years, as long as he could remember" (29). Though Harry has suffered an abused childhood with little warmth or love, he has nonetheless avoided bitterness, and it seems that his relatively cheerful disposition despite his upbringing ultimately earns him rewards.

Formally and stylistically, one of the most frequent refrains of praise for Rowling is her incorporation of folklore, mythology, and literary traditions in the Harry Potter books in fresh and innovative ways. Of course, the staples of fairy tales populate the books—witches, wizards, dragons, and trolls—but Rowling also draws in more substantive ways upon the connotations of particular mythological creatures in a way that adds depth to her novel.

A good deal of formal and literary criticism has focused on Rowling's introduction of and use of mythical elements and narrative features of some of the most beloved of stories in the British school story and fantasy fiction traditions. As Joan Acocella has written, "Part of the secret of Rowling's success is her utter traditionalism. The Potter story is a fairy tale, plus a Bildungsroman, plus a murder mystery, plus a cosmic war of good and evil."

Acocella and others have also drawn attention to the way in which Rowling's first book in the series adheres to Vladimir Propp's *Morphology of the Folk Tale* (1928), with its outlining of the common structure of such tales. Propp defines "morphology" as "the study of forms" (xxv), and his study outlines 31 features or categories of events typical in folktales and myths. Though the Harry Potter series does not incorporate all 31 features, Harry's story contains many of them, ranging from number 8, "The villain causes harm or injury to a member of a family" (30), as Harry is orphaned because of Voldemort's murder of his parents; to 11, "The Hero Leaves Home" (39), when Harry leaves the Dursleys to begin his magical education at Hogwarts; to 14, "The Hero Acquires the Use of a Magical Agent" (43): Though Harry performs magic himself, his trip to Diagon Alley equips him with his magic wand. Other typical features include the hero and villain's joining in combat (as at the conclusion of most of the books in the Harry Potter series except *Prisoner of Azkaban*) and the hero's being branded (such as when Harry receives the scar on his forehead when Voldemort attacks him when he is a baby).

Aside from the structural traditions Rowling uses, creatures from GREEK AND ROMAN MYTHOLOGY are also fruitfully employed in the books. The centaurs Ronan, Bane, and Firenze, the latter of whom whisks Harry from the horrific scene of Voldemort's feeding on the dead unicorn, are makeshift ambassadors between humans and the creatures of the forest, at least through their grudging respect for Hagrid and their awareness that the wizards of Hogwarts are their allies against the dark creatures who support Voldemort. Rowling draws upon the mythologies of ancient Greece in crafting her modern-day centaurs; as *Bulfinch's Mythology* explains, "The ancients were too fond of a horse to consider the union of his nature with man's as forming a very degraded compound, and accordingly the Centaur is the only one of the fancied monsters of antiquity to which any good traits are assigned" (105). As creatures who were "admitted to the companionship of man," these mythical beings who are human from the head to the loins and the other half horse are, in mythology, also possessed of many human talents and virtues including skills in arts such as music, hunting, medicine, and prophecy, according to *Bulfinch*.

Rowling's centaurs also use the gift of prophecy, demonstrated in *Sorcerer's Stone*. Hagrid and Harry encounter them in the Forbidden Forest, and the two centaurs respond with observations about astronomy ("Mars is bright tonight") rather than direct answers about who killed the unicorn, prompting Hagrid to call them "ruddy stargazers" (254), a modern epithet for their historical connections. Rowling capitalizes on this association between centaurs and prophesying later in the series as a way of challenging assumptions about what constitutes teaching, learning, and knowledge.

Further, the unicorn, whose blood Voldemort drinks after killing the gentle creature in chapter 15, has origins in Indian, Chinese, and biblical mythology as well as Greek natural history. Its traditional associations with benevolence and gentleness are reinforced in Rowling's novel by the centaur Firenze, who tells Harry, ". . . it is a monstrous thing, to slay a unicorn. . . . Only one who has nothing to lose, and everything to gain, would commit such a crime" (258). Rowling makes use of the unicorn's affiliations with medicinal properties, as Firenze further explains: "The blood of a unicorn will keep you alive, even if you are an inch from death, but at a terrible price. You have slain something pure and defenseless to save yourself, and you will have but a half-life, a cursed life, from the moment the blood touches your lips" (258). Firenze's impassioned explanation of the unicorn's symbolism sets the narrative stage in establishing Voldemort's brutal nature and callous disregard for life.

The three-headed dog that guards the Sorcerer's Stone is, in the book, named "Fluffy" but is in reality a descendant of Cerberus, the mythical canine guardian of Hades, the underworld of Greek mythology. Edith Hamilton's classic guide, *Mythology*, describes him as a "three-headed, dragon-tailed dog, who permits all spirits to enter but none to return" (43). The last of the mythical demigod Hercules' 12 labors was to bring Cerberus up from the underworld, which he accomplished through brute strength, though in the *Aeneid*, the tales of the warrior hero Aeneas, Cerberus is "easily mollified by a bit of cake" (Hamilton 330). Rowling's use of this mythical creature, retooled with a modern twist, as the guardian of the set of obstacles leading to the Sorcerer's Stone is the sort of inventive updating that critics and readers of the series have enjoyed. Though Fluffy is soothed by music rather than cake (as in the ancient myth), his appearances add a layer of mythological allusion that deepens and enriches the first novel.

Sorcerer's Stone also introduces a mythical creature that will make recurring appearances in the novel, playing central roles in *Goblet of Fire* and the *Deathly Hallows*: the dragon. As Karl Shuker's book *Dragons: A Natural History* documents, dragons or dragonlike creatures appear in the myths, histories, and folktales of cultures across the globe—from Quetzalcoatl of Mexico to the Icelandic basilisk to the wyvern of Great Britain to dragon deities of China. In almost all cultures, snakes, serpents, and lizards have evolved from "simple, serpentine forms to much more complex, specialized beasts" (Shuker 9). Rowling draws upon this rich tradition to infuse her books with the traditional dragon of literary fantasy but places an inventive new spin by attaching names and nationalities to the dragons of the wizarding world. *Sorcerer's Stone* uses Hagrid's fascination with dangerous magical creatures to draw Norbert the Norwegian Ridgeback into the plotline, a precursor to Rowling's use of dragons in *Goblet of Fire* and *Deathly Hallows*. According to Shuker, dragons have been associated with "malevolence or beneficence, paganism or purity, death and devastation, life and fertility, good or evil," a contradictory tangle of symbolisms that Rowling invokes throughout Harry's story.

Names in Rowling's books are also critically remarked upon because of her innovative use of her educational training and wide reading in the French language, which manifests itself in character names. Rowling has revealed, for example, that the roots of Voldemort's name are French: The verb *voler* (to fly) and the noun *morte* (death) combine to suggest the Dark Lord's quest for immortality. The last name *Malfoy* also has French etymology suggesting the phrase "bad faith" (based on *mal,* which translates to "bad," and *foi,* which means "faith"). Remus Lupin's last name originates in the French word *lupine,* meaning "wolf." Certainly, Rowling also makes use of puns and plays on words in sometimes barely noticeable ways such as her play on the word *diagonally* in the name *Diagon Alley.*

Rowling's target audience for *Sorcerer's Stone* may have been young readers, but this first entry in the series is notable because it initiated the phenomenon that is POTTERMANIA and hooked millions of children and teens on reading. Rowling's imaginative use of myth, folklore, linguistically complex character names and place-names, and appropriation of multiple literary traditions sparked the interest of both readers and critics and launched Rowling into the limelight, a public journey that would only intensify as the rest of the series was published. Her compelling personal story and Harry's own triumph over his humble origins engaged the reading public at an unprecedented level and, coupled with the critical success the books enjoyed, became part of literary history.

INITIAL REVIEWS

Because the first three books of the Harry Potter series did not achieve widespread popularity or reach adult readers on a broad scale until several years after their publication, reviews of the books are found primarily in trade journals for librarians and teachers and some mainstream magazines and newspapers. Early reviews from these texts appear somewhat mixed, with some reviewers musing over the series's potential appeal to young American readers who might be unfamiliar with the British slang and style of wry humor. A majority of the positive reviews praise the book's style, character development, and engaging plot. A few reviews critique the novel for a lack of character development and insubstantial themes.

A few early reviews find fault with Rowling's debut novel. Deborah Stevenson in *Bulletin of the Center for Children's Books* wondered whether the "the stakes are anything to get excited about" in the novel's plot and whether some elements such as the sport of Quidditch seemed "inserted largely because the author laboriously created them" and would "interfere with the plot rather than advancing it" (110). The same reviewer compared *Sorcerer's Stone* unfavorably with Phillip Pullman's *The Golden Compass,* claiming the latter offers thrills that the former simply does not. From a readerly perspective Daniel Beach's review in *Book Report* expressed concern over the difficult words and the novel's length, suspecting both would dissuade young readers when coupled with complicated "fantastical" elements. Gail Gawkwell further observes: "Harry Potter as a character, and the plot itself, seemed to me to lack the depth of development that I have learnt to read and expect in literature. The plot seemed to consist of a series of bite-sized sequences that together created a series of constantly moving events" in her review featured in *the Journal of Adolescent and Adult Literacy* (669). However, these critical observations are at odds with what are largely positive responses to the first novel in the series.

It is difficult to read reviews from *New York* magazine and *Book Report* that wonder whether the Harry Potter series will "gain a following on this side of the Atlantic" or judge the book "an enhancing purchase, not a necessary one" without a sense of irony, given the series' record-breaking success in the last 10 years. A handful of these reviews simply do not recognize the book's potential to become the blockbuster success it did. Gawkwell, for example, sees the novel as fractured and the narrative disconnected, surmising that perhaps this style is the product of "the intertextual world of multimedia computer game narratives" and Beach states tepidly, "It is an interesting story" (669), but emphasizes that aspects of the novel's language and story will be alienating for young readers.

By contrast, in reviewing the American edition of *Sorcerer's Stone*, numerous reviewers heralded Rowling's inventive use of narrative convention and classic literary genres to create an entirely new and imaginative fantasy world. As Eva Mitnick notes in *School Library Journal*, "The delight of this book lies in the juxtaposition of the world of Muggles (ordinary humans) with the world of magic." This mixing of the "mundane and the marvelous" is also commended by June Cummins in the *Michigan Quarterly Review*, but more frequent are reviewers' applause of her formulation of a work of fantasy that fits into multiple classic literary genres such as the orphan story, boarding school tale, quest narrative, and fairy tale. Like Cummins, reviewers in *Booklist* and *Fantasy and Science Fiction* appreciated Rowling's fresh entry into these literary traditions.

Similarly, reviews in *Publishers Weekly, Horn Book Magazine,* and the *New York Times Book Review* all comment favorably on Rowling's literary resemblance to ROALD DAHL, though not one finds Rowling derivative; instead, they see Rowling "dancing in the footsteps of," "traveling through territory owned by," or simply as "like" the late Dahl. These comparisons are always complimentary, usually to comment on the two authors' similarities in creating a "delightful romp" or "light-hearted caper." At least one review compares Rowling's style to that of P. L. Travers, the pen name of Helen Lyndon Goff, who created the Mary Poppins series.

The engaging plot, sympathetic hero, accessible style, and character development are also mentioned in the initial reviews of the novel. Michael Winerip calls the characters "impressively three-dimensional" in the *New York Times Book Review* (26), while Kathleen Dolgos in *Childhood Education* calls it "riveting" and "suspenseful." Mitnick praises Harry as a "perfect confused and unassuming hero" while Deborah Stevenson in *Bulletin of the Center for Children's Book,* calls Harry an "unappreciated young hero" whose triumph will keep readers turning pages (311).

SCHOLARSHIP

Little scholarship exists that treats *Harry Potter and the Sorcerer's Stone* in isolation. Please see the "Scholarship on the Harry Potter Series" section for critical work that analyzes this novel as part of the larger series.

Because the target audience for *Sorcerer's Stone* was primarily young readers, the bulk of the critical work published in scholarly journals focuses on the pedagogical value or use of the book. Andrew Frank and Matthew McBee in "The Use of *Harry Potter and the Sorcerer's Stone* to Discuss Identity Development in Gifted Adolescents," in the *Journal of Secondary Gifted Education,* use the psychologist Erik Erikson's theory of identity development in adolescents as a framework for advocating the value of "bibliotherapy," or using reading to foster "social, emotional, or psychological growth" (35). The authors recommend the first book in the series as a mechanism for facilitating discussion with adolescents about navigating identity crises and the formation of self. Donna Gibson, in "Empathizing with Harry Potter: The Use of Popular Literature in Counselor Education," also advocates the pedagogical usefulness of the *Sorcerer's Stone,* specifically in the education of counselors. Gibson's article promotes the book and a specific classroom application designed to help students develop empathy. Susan Nelson Wood and Kim Quackenbush similarly offer specific classroom practices in "*The Sorcerer's Stone:* A Touchstone for Readers of All Ages," suggesting that classroom study of the book can help students understand the fantasy genre, promote understanding of other genres such as poetry, and cultivate an understanding of literary studies.

Several scholarly articles address the literary value and heritage of the first book. Peter Gottesman in his review of *Harry Potter and the Sorcerer's Stone* in *Teachers College Record* speculates on what psychological and emotional needs the book fulfills in young readers. Gottesman believes that, as a work of fantasy fiction, the book appeals to children's imagination. He also argues that the book is both relevant to youngsters' contemporary stresses and subversive in its advocacy of Harry's rejection of particular, corrupt authority systems. Finally, Gottesman argues that the book addresses children's need to see justice in cosmic battles of good and evil and that the story line appeals to children's sense of sympathy for Harry's plight and the value of community it promotes. Evelyn

Perry's essay, "Metaphor and MetaFantasy: Questing for Literary Inheritance in J. K. Rowling's *Harry Potter and the Sorcerer's Stone*," by contrast, focuses on the literary lineage of the book, taking a historical rather than reader-response perspective. Perry traces the many literary influences that are demonstrated in the first book in the series, ranging from the King Arthur stories in White's *The Once and Future King* tetralogy to works by LEWIS CARROLL, J. R. R. TOLKIEN, C. S. LEWIS, E. NESBIT (Edith Nesbit), and SUSAN COOPER. "Children's Literature or Adult Classic? The Harry Potter Series and the British Novel Tradition" by Paige Byam similarly locates the series within the British novel tradition, arguing that they are not simply children's literature but part of the great tradition of British novels.

Extratextual concerns are the subject of Jodi H. Levine and Nancy Shapiro's as well as Gillian Lathey's articles. Published in *About Campus,* a periodical whose target audience is university administrators and faculty, Levine and Shapiro's essay, "Hogwarts," draws analogies between Hogwarts school and the experience of first-year students moving into college life. The writers focus on diversity, the challenges of the first-year experience, learning communities, practices in teaching and learning, and civic responsibility in their discussion of parallels between the books and college life in the United States. Lathey's essay, "The Travels of Harry: International Marketing and the Translation of J. K. Rowling's Harry Potter Books," takes a materialist approach, discussing the growth of the series as a literary and cultural phenomenon but focusing primarily on the cultural specificity of the first book—its inherent "Britishness"—and its impact on the global consumerism of the Harry Potter phenomenon, specifically as it relates to translation. Lathey recounts a small summer seminar group that studied specific translations of the first book and the impact of translation—the ability of translation to convey tone, humor, names, idioms, and language of the book.

CHARACTERS

Albus Dumbledore   Hogwarts School of Witchcraft and Wizardry headmaster and mentor to Harry. Dumbledore's character exemplifies thoughtfulness, intelligence, and the importance of trusting and believing in others. From the outset of the series, Dumbledore's dedication to Harry and to Harry's best interest is obvious. While readers may question Dumbledore's initial decision to leave baby Harry with the Dursley family, readers learn quickly that the headmaster does so in the interest of conferring the maximal magical protection on the infant Harry. Though he knows Harry will have a difficult life, by placing him in a Muggle home, Dumbledore guarantees Harry will develop into a young boy appreciative of even the smallest gifts in life; this life path provides a stark contrast to the life Harry would have lived in the wizarding world, known already as the "Boy Who Lived," a savior to the wizarding community.

Dumbledore also serves in the archetypal role of the wise old man. Perhaps it is his age (more than 100 years old) or his long white beard, but Dumbledore radiates intelligence to his students, his colleagues, and the novel's readers. More important, he consistently demonstrates his wisdom, the careful and apt application of the knowledge he has accumulated over his long life. Although he often offers cryptic advice or words that seem nothing other than nonsense (consider his "Nitwit! Oddment! Blubber! Tweak!" remark at the Welcoming Feast [123]), nearly all students respect him and take him seriously, as Percy Weasley confirms to Harry in chapter 7 at the Sorting: "Is he—a bit mad?" he asks Percy, who responds "Mad? . . . He's a genius! Best wizard in the world! But he is a bit mad, yes. Potatoes, Harry?" (123). Percy, like many of Dumbledore's students and his colleagues, embraces both Dumbledore's quirky ways and his dazzling intellect and sterling moral character. His other admirers know Dumbledore cares deeply that they be educated properly and make the most of their potential while at Hogwarts.

Other themes Rowling emphasizes through Dumbledore's character early in the series are the importance of trusting in others and the power of friendship and solidarity, points she develops throughout the series even more fully. Dumbledore seems aware that Harry eventually will have to confront Voldemort (in some capacity), and the headmaster not only trusts that Harry will carry out this mission but believes that Harry will ultimately be successful. This is illustrated in the novel's conclusion, when Harry relates to his friends Ron and Hermione his experience confronting Voldemort. "I think he sort of wanted to give me a chance," muses Harry in chapter 17. "I don't think it was an accident he let me find out how the mirror worked. It's almost like he thought I had the right to face Voldemort if I could" (302). Ron announces that this is evidence that Dumbledore is "off his rocker" (302), though it is clear throughout the books that Dumbledore is in control of the events—even when it appears on the surface to the characters and to readers that he is not.

It may appear strange that such a wizened old man wholeheartedly believes in the adolescent Harry's abilities to defeat the Dark Lord and his servants, but Dumbledore's belief in Harry reminds readers that the youngest or smallest people are capable of great feats.

Dursley family   Harry's adoptive family. Uncle Vernon, Aunt Petunia, and Cousin Dudley form the Muggle family in which Harry is raised. They live on Privet Drive, symbolically, since they desire to keep the fate of Harry's parents and Harry's background of being born a wizard "private." Rowling's having the Dursleys reside on Privet Drive is also ironic since one of Petunia's favorite pastimes is gossiping. The Dursleys treat Harry as a second-class citizen, and it is obvious to critics, readers, and reviewers that the way they treat Harry (forcing him to wear clothes so large that he trips, only providing him with broken glasses, making him sleep in a cupboard under the stairs full of spiders, or requiring that he make them meals or clean up after them) can be considered child abuse or, at the very least, neglect.

The Dursleys fear change, and even more they fear what others might think of them, so they try by all means possible to hinder Harry from attending Hogwarts because of its association with something they find "abnormal." When Hagrid arrives at the ramshackle cabin where they have hidden in

chapter 4, Petunia admits bitterly that the Dursleys knew of Harry's magical lineage. Of her sister, Lily, she gripes, "I was the only one who saw her for what she was—a freak!" and later "I knew you'd be just the same, just as strange, just as *abnormal!*" (53). The Dursleys and their hateful attitude are a major obstacle in Harry's life and continue to be throughout the series. Simultaneously, they provide the protective function that Dumbledore refers to throughout the books; Lily Potter's gift of the sacrifice of her life out of love for her son retains its power because Harry resides with his blood relatives. Even though they treat him with contempt, they nonetheless are necessary.

Hermione Granger   Best friend of Harry and Ron, fellow Gryffindor, and a Muggle-born witch. Hermione's most important characteristics include the virtues of reason and loyalty. When Rowling introduces her to readers, some may be put off by her attitude. She acts in an overbearing and bossy manner. Immediately upon entering Harry and Ron's train compartment on the Hogwarts Express in chapter 6, Hermione launches into her signature know-it-all tone: "Are you sure that's a real spell?" she asks Ron, who is trying to turn a rat yellow. "Well, it's not very good is it?" she offers (105). She peppers their conversation with references to having read all the assigned course books prior to the start of the term—in addition to "a few extra books for background reading" (106).

She clearly values rules and book knowledge above all else, and her main unwavering priority remains not only to succeed in school but also to be the top in her class. In one of her most famous lines, Hermione reflects how important school is to her; after a trip to the third-floor corridor, she admonishes Harry and Ron, telling them their behavior could have resulted in their being "killed, or worse, expelled" (162). She studies more than any other student and seems to know more about the history of the wizarding world than even those born into it. Rowling has revealed that Hermione's birthday is September 19; since a student receives the acceptance letter to Hogwarts on his or her 11th birthday and term begins on September 1, it is worth noting that Hermione had almost a year more to prepare herself for entering Hogwarts than Harry and probably the majority of other students as well. Regardless of this advantage Hermione is a dedicated student who values reason and logic over all else. Without her, Harry never would have reached Quirrell and the Sorcerer's Stone because he found himself stumped by the logic puzzle.

Hermione is also fiercely loyal. Even though Harry and Ron find her annoying when they meet her, they begin to appreciate and value her friendship. In honor of her friendship with the two boys, Hermione starts to break some rules. Near the end of the novel she sneaks out with Harry and Ron to find the Sorcerer's Stone and in doing so openly flouts curfew. More important, however, Hermione lies to protect Harry and Ron. When the boys rescue her from the troll on Halloween, Hermione takes responsibility for the incident, claiming she went searching for the troll. After this incident Harry, Ron, and Hermione become the best of friends. Throughout the rest of the book and the rest of the series Hermione serves as a sort of friendship glue for the trio, often negotiating conflicts between Harry and Ron, as in *Goblet of Fire*, when Ron resents Harry for his unplanned entry into the Triwizard Tournament. She helps her friends in their times of need (and often compensates for their shortcomings), and that is one of the strongest aspects of her character.

Rubeus Hagrid Hogwarts groundskeeper and close friend of Harry. Hagrid, a bumbling but lovable character, ushers Harry into the wizarding world. By giving Hagrid such an honored role, Rowling emphasizes his trustworthiness and his genuineness. Hagrid consistently reveals information that should be kept confidential, such as his letting slip how to get past Fluffy, the three-headed dog who is guarding the Sorcerer's Stone, to a hooded stranger while he is drunk. Nonetheless, since Dumbledore trusts Hagrid without reservation, Rowling suggests that readers should as well.

In the character of Hagrid Rowling confronts and debunks several stereotypes. To begin, readers may view a man of Hagrid's stature—big and hulk-

ing—as physically threatening. Contrarily, Hagrid remains one of the gentlest characters in the series. He might rebuke Vernon for insulting Dumbledore and give Dudley a pig's tail, but Hagrid does not regularly resort to violence. One would not typically assume a man like Hagrid's favorite hobby would be caring for animals, but this activity gives him great reward and happiness. Even in a poker game at the local pub Hagrid is most interested in winning a dragon egg so that he might have a baby dragon to call his own, as chapter 16 reveals, with Harry noting, "Hagrid told that stranger how to get past Fluffy, and it was either Snape or Voldemort under that cloak—it must've been easy, once he got Hagrid drunk" (266). Hagrid's reverence for nature and its creatures emphasizes his sensitivity to the needs of others—both animals and people—but in this case, as well as subsequent novels, his soft spot for creatures from spiders to dragons sometimes leads to the unintentional endangerment of others.

Neville Longbottom Close friend of Harry, Ron, and Hermione; a fellow Gryffindor. Rowling imparts to readers via the character of Neville Longbottom that all people have potential, and when they put their mind to the task of fully realizing that potential, they will succeed. Rowling first emphasizes the importance of potential when Neville tells the story that his family worried that he was only a Squib (someone born into a wizarding family who has no magical powers, like Argus Filch and Mrs. Figg), a status that would have been disastrous since the Longbottoms are a pureblood family. When several of Neville's relatives had already given up on him, he suddenly demonstrated his magical powers. Something of a late bloomer, Neville reminds readers that people grow and mature at different rates but that this developing will eventually happen.

Neville lives with his "Gran," as he affectionately calls her. Gran seems to doubt Neville's abilities and puts a great deal of pressure on her grandson to succeed, as his account of his childhood at the Sorting reveals to his fellow Gryffindors: "My gran brought me up and she's a witch . . . but the family thought I was all-Muggle for ages" (125). She routinely sends him Remembralls and Howlers, mechanisms of shame in the wizarding world.

Under the weight of this pressure, combined with the way his grandmother doubts his abilities, Neville often fumbles—notoriously so in Potions. But when Neville finally starts to believe in himself, Rowling shows readers that self-confidence is key to realizing one's potential. The most convincing example that stresses the importance of believing in one's self occurs when Neville asserts himself to Harry, Ron, and Hermione when they plan to sneak out of the Gryffindor Tower in an attempt to recover the Sorcerer's Stone, challenging them outside the dormitory for breaking the rules. Even though Hermione puts a spell on Neville and she, Harry, and Ron seek the stone as they had planned, it is the 10 points Dumbledore awards Neville for having the courage to stand up to his friends that results in Gryffindor's winning the House Cup.

A final theme Rowling stresses through Neville's character is the importance of memory. Obviously Neville is quite forgetful: His grandmother sends him a Remembrall to help him remember something important, but Neville even forgets what the object was intended to remind him of. Rowling only hints at the importance of remembering and memories in *Sorcerer's Stone*, but she continues to stress and develop the theme throughout the rest of her novels.

Draco Malfoy One of Harry's nemeses, and member of Slytherin House. Draco is the epitome of class snobbishness. When Harry meets Draco, Draco discusses blood status and how Hogwarts should be a more exclusive institution, complaining, "I really don't think they should let the other sort in, do you? They're just not the same, they've never been brought up to know our ways. Some of them have never even heard of Hogwarts until they get the letter, imagine. I think they should keep it in the old wizarding families" (78). His views on blood status (which become much more evident and unsettling in the second novel of the series), coupled with his appearance—a boy with white blond hair and blue eyes—appear to be stereotypically Aryan. Rowling's describing Draco in such

terms does not seem coincidental since the Malfoys support the Dark Lord, whom critics have likened to Adolf Hitler.

Malfoy also serves as the characteristic bully. His cronies, Crabbe and Goyle, follow Draco wherever he goes; his two minions even seem to follow Draco out of fear rather than really valuing his companionship. In this first novel Draco suggests he and Harry participate in the wizard's duel, "Tonight, if you want. . . . Wands only—no contact. What's the matter? Never heard of a wizard's duel before, I suppose?" taunts Draco in chapter 9. Harry is horrified to discover that Ron's agreement to be his "second" means that he is "there to take over if you die" (154). Draco lacks character and integrity, evident not only in his willingness to hurt others physically and emotionally but in his underhanded and manipulative actions. Draco's proposing to engage in a wizard's duel also emphasizes his violent nature; he would rather resort to physical violence than address the conflict in another manner. In the end this event also suggests Draco's amorality and manipulation, as it turns out this invitation to Harry to duel at midnight is in fact treacherous, as he never intends to show up and instead sends Argus Filch, who could punish Harry and his friends if he discovers them out of their dorms after curfew.

As does Harry, Draco openly flouts the rules, such as when he steals Neville's Remembrall and flies off on his broom even though Madam Hooch has explicitly forbidden anyone to fly. An important distinction between Harry and Draco, however, is that Harry often rejects unfair rules and breaks them in the service of a greater good or in an effort to help someone else; Draco's rule breaking is usually self-serving or intended to torment a classmate. As do many typical bullies, Draco targets some of the weakest characters, such as Neville, who lack confidence and will not retaliate. Another similarity Draco shares with bullies in general is that, in all reality, bullies are more cowardly than those they tease. When Draco is sentenced to visit the Forbidden Forest with Harry, Hermione, Neville, and Hagrid, he is the most scared of them all, shrieking and bolting from the scene of the unicorn's murder without so much as a backward glance (256).

Like many children's authors, Rowling suggests that bullies such as Draco will get their comeuppance. Even though Slytherin officially holds the title of House Cup winner and all the members of that house bask in the victory, their happiness is cut short when Dumbledore revises the final point totals in order to reward Harry, Hermione, Ron, and Neville for their courage in the face of danger in navigating the obstacles guarding the Sorcerer's Stone. Draco, the typical Slytherin, suffers great disappointment when the honor of House Cup champion is stripped from his house and awarded instead to the Gryffindors.

Minerva McGonagall Transfiguration professor and head of Gryffindor House. Readers meet McGonagall in her Animagus form of a cat; Rowling's symbolism here is well chosen, considering that cats sometimes represent intuition, the ability to comfort, and independence. All of these are characteristics McGonagall possesses. One of her main functions in the novel is to act as a mother figure for Harry (though this duty is also fulfilled by Mrs. Weasley). Even though she trusts Dumbledore, she questions his judgment when he decides to leave Harry with the Dursleys. When McGonagall explains that she feels the Dursleys are a poor choice to care for Harry, readers know immediately that she, as do many other characters, has Harry's best interest at heart.

Rowling first describes McGonagall as "a tall, black-haired witch in emerald-green robes . . . She had a very stern face and Harry's first thought was that this was not someone to cross" (113), and the use of the descriptor *stern* recurs throughout the first book. Readers discover through that book that she is known for her strictness and fondness for the rules. To a degree she represents fairness: Even when students of her own house are caught disobeying the rules, she punishes them (as when Harry and his friends are given detention in the Forbidden Forest for wandering the castle grounds after curfew). However, McGonagall makes allowances for Harry that she probably would not grant other students because

of her affection for him and her awareness of his importance within the coming cosmic battle.

In *Sorcerer's Stone* a prime example of this favoritism occurs when McGonagall catches Harry flying his broom on the Quidditch pitch after Madam Hooch had forbidden any of the students to do so. Instead of punishing Harry, McGonagall rewards him by making him the Gryffindor Seeker and then sees that he gets his own broom, crowing, "The boy's a natural. I've never seen anything like it. . . . He caught that thing in his hand after a fifty-foot dive," to Oliver Wood, the Gryffindor Quidditch captain (151). She ignores several rules with this decision. Perhaps Rowling's point in having McGonagall disregard the rules she usually honors so strictly so Harry can play Quidditch is twofold. First, McGonagall—as head of Gryffindor House—would really enjoy seeing Gryffindor win the Quidditch cup; this motivation is a selfish one, and it humanizes her as a character. But, Rowling's more significant point in McGonagall's making an exception for Harry might be that even the strictest people can occasionally disregard rules to offer someone like Harry (whose life until he arrived at Hogwarts was quite miserable) a special opportunity out of compassion and love.

Harry Potter Protagonist and member of Gryffindor House; the hero of the series. Harry exhibits many of the traits noted by OTTO RANK in his seminal work *The Myth of the Birth of the Hero*, including being born to distinguished parents, being raised by lowly people, and avenging his father's death. Readers learn that Harry exhibits more of Rank's typical hero traits, including the achieving of honors and being the subject of a prophecy made about the hero's birth, in later novels.

In this first novel Harry begins the archetypal hero journey also discussed at length by JOSEPH CAMPBELL. He faces many of the experiences noted by Campbell, including the call to adventure (receiving his letter from Hogwarts), the road of trials (adjusting to Hogwarts and battling Voldemort to protect the Sorcerer's Stone), and mastery of the two worlds (the Muggle world and the wizarding world). Similarly, Harry meets many of figures who serve in archetypal roles: Hagrid is the herald who announces Harry's adventure, Dumbledore serves as one of Harry's mentors, and Snape fulfills the role of shape-shifter, since the Potions professor misleads Harry about his allegiance, time and again.

This first novel introduces us to the modest and appealing young boy who will become the center of the cosmic conflict that is the centerpiece of the seven-book series. Mistreated by his family and bullied by his cousin, Harry nonetheless has preserved a kind of humble self-confidence; though he is occasionally wracked with moments of self-doubt, Harry's visit from Hagrid and his invitation to attend Hogwarts confirm a suspicion he has had his entire childhood, that he is not deficient or inadequate, but simply different. The journey he experiences in *Sorcerer's Stone* is spiritual, emotional, and cultural, as he begins to navigate the unfamiliar territory that his friends seem so comfortable in and to discover his role within a historic and epic battle, the contours of which he is only beginning to understand. However, it is the internal evolution of Harry the character that serves as a touchstone for the novel's plot, though certainly readers find the external conflicts with Voldemort and his followers as engaging as Harry's own journey to self-understanding. Readers learn, along with Harry, about the imaginative parallel wizarding world of J. K. Rowling's magical invention so vividly drawn in *Sorcerer's Stone* just as we take Harry's internal journey with him. Harry only begins his quest in *Sorcerer's Stone,* and Rowling continues to develop his heroic traits with each new installment in the series.

James and Lily Potter   Harry's parents. Even though they have both been murdered within hours of the opening of *Sorcerer's Stone,* they still serve as important characters, through whom Rowling highlights important themes of her work. The most significant themes James and Lily emphasize are those of love and sacrifice. Their strong and unwavering love for their son leads them both to sacrifice themselves to protect him; it is their love—specifically Lily's—that allows Harry to survive Voldemort's attack and send the Dark Lord's curse rebounding on him. Rowling reveals more reasons that Harry

was able to survive Voldemort's killing curse in later novels, but she imparts to her readers that unconditional love is the greatest form of protection and support a parent can give his or her child.

Quirinus Quirrell   Defense Against the Dark Arts professor and servant of Lord Voldemort. Rowling starts one of the great traditions in her series with Quirrell: The post of Defense Against the Dark Arts professor is cursed and will be the position that serves as a way to introduce some of her most memorable characters. In *Sorcerer's Stone* Quirrell, the professor responsible for teaching students how to protect themselves, ironically appears quite cowardly. Quirrell's fearfulness is a clue to readers to be suspicious of his abilities. For example, late in the novel, Harry spies Quirrell after a confrontation with an unidentified voice, noting that "he was pale and looked as though he was about to cry" (246), hardly the appearance of the defender against the Dark Arts.

As readers discover, he is literally nothing more than a host on which Voldemort lives, whom the Dark Lord lets perish without remorse; by placing Quirrell in such a position, Rowling suggests that those who let others use them will fail and will not be provided for or protected by those whom they serve. She continues to emphasize this commentary on human relationships throughout the series, primarily through Voldemort's Machiavellian intimidation and exploitation of his followers.

Severus Snape   Potions professor and head of Slytherin House. Snape is the epitome of ambiguity and often serves as a red herring in *Sorcerer's Stone.* Rowling lays the foundations for the evolution of most of her major characters in this novel, and one of the most important characteristics she reveals about Snape is his ethical ambiguity. Even until almost the end of the last novel, readers will question where Snape's allegiance lies.

He obviously holds grudges, and by the way he treats Harry, Rowling encourages readers to question the value of holding a grudge (if any), especially after one considers the consequences of doing so, as Snape does. In "The Potions Master," Snape humiliates Harry during the first Potions class, deducting points from Gryffindor after Harry is unable to answer Snape's questions and accusing him of sabotaging Neville: "You—Potter—why didn't you tell him not to add the quills? Thought he'd make you look good if he got it wrong, did you? That's another point you've lost for Gryffindor" (139). Harry feels stymied by this unfairness and disturbed by Snape's vindictiveness.

Though readers do not discover the source of the grudge to which Snape clings until later novels, Rowling reveals that Snape's hurt stems from many years ago and concerns James Potter; since James is dead, Snape takes his anger out on Harry, causing Harry to suffer for an act he neither was involved with nor had any knowledge of. Dumbledore later clarifies that Snape and James Potter "did rather detest each other," because James saved Snape's life. "Professor Snape couldn't bear being in your father's debt. . . . I do believe he worked so hard to protect you this year because he felt that would make him and your father even" (300). Consequently, Rowling emphasizes the foolishness of feuds and how they can damage those who have no responsibility for what occurred years earlier.

Snape also fulfills the role of the archetypal "mean teacher" figure popular in children's novels (notably those by ROALD DAHL). He has a dungeon for a classroom, he has an abrasive personality, and he frequently taunts and mocks his students. He does not provide a classroom environment in which students can prosper and succeed but rather fuels competition and resentment. He quite obviously favors his Slytherins and leaves students in other houses feeling hopeless since they feel they cannot effectively combat Snape's (a teacher's) attacks.

Voldemort Harry's archnemesis and enemy of the wizarding community. Voldemort's motives for killing the Potters and attempting to murder Harry remain unclear in the first novel. In turn, Rowling dramatizes one of the great mysteries of her series. Voldemort evokes fear, evidenced clearly by members of the wizarding community, who refer to him only as "He-Who-Must-Not-Be-Named." Voldemort's name—

when translated from French—literally means to "fly from death."

According to Rowling, Voldemort also epitomizes greed. It is not material greed that Voldemort demonstrates but a kind of sinful greed to become immortal. He viciously sacrifices animals (he murders unicorns for their enchanted blood) and has no regard for human life (he is an unrepentant killer, of Harry's parents and even occasionally his followers, and in *Sorcerer's Stone*, of Quirrell) to obtain his goal of immortality.

In the figure of Voldemort Rowling suggests that those who are as self-serving and self-absorbed as Voldemort will never obtain what they desire. In *Sorcerer's Stone* and the next two volumes of the series, he cannot exist in corporeal form but must rely on the assistance of others; those who make great sacrifices to resurrect him, including Quirrell (and in later novels, Peter Pettigrew and Lucius Malfoy) are discarded when their purpose has been served or severely punished because they do not complete the task set to them. Voldemort's using his followers in this way seems to be Rowling's method of reinforcing that people obsessed with gaining power and status for themselves—such as Voldemort—will use and abuse those loyal to them in order to achieve their ends with no regard for others. They have no care except for themselves, but paradoxically, they could not survive without the aid of others. It is this lack of awareness that is ultimately Voldemort's undoing.

Ron Weasley Best friend of Harry and Hermione and fellow Gryffindor. Ron and Harry share a genuine friendship. Ron does not seek out Harry to gain fame or status by being his companion; conversely, he feels quite surprised to find that the lonely and anxious boy he shares a train compartment with on the way to Hogwarts is the legendary Harry Potter. Ron serves as a cultural guide to Harry since Harry is new to the wizarding community and Ron was raised as a wizard. Harry feels comfortable asking Ron about the norms of the new environment, whether it is the different sorts of wizarding candy or the complex rules, history, and teams for the sport of Quidditch. Ron and the Weasley family in general serve as invaluable resources to Harry.

The exterior of the St. Pancras Midland Hotel, the most visible portion of the St. Pancras Railway Station. In the film adaptations, exterior shots of King's Cross Station—where Harry and his friends board the Hogwarts Express—are of this building. *(Photo by Andrew Dunn/Used under a Creative Commons license)*

Ron has a large family. He is the second youngest child and the youngest boy. In turn, Ron faces expectations established by the successes of his older brothers. These expectations place pressure on him at a very young age, and these pressures are sometimes difficult for him to bear. When Ron sees himself in the Mirror of Erised, he sees an image of himself as head boy and Quidditch captain; he is only able to "tear his eyes away from this splendid sight to look excitedly" at his friend, who sees something entirely different (211). Both are demanding positions, and Ron quite often lacks focus and determination. In turn, readers might question whether what Ron sees reflected in the mirror is actually what he truly desires to be happy, or whether the reflection shows what he desires to please his parents and siblings.

The Weasley family also represents the lower socioeconomic class. They have little money and many family members, and the children rarely receive new clothing or belongings, a consistently sensitive subject for Ron, who frequently compares his financial situation with that of Harry. With the Weasleys Rowling emphasizes that love and support are the elements necessary for a happy family and that money is less important. Regardless, the Weasleys (and Ron in particular) are often targets of ridicule by elitist and class-conscious members of the upper class, such as Draco Malfoy.

FILM ADAPTATION

The film version of *Sorcerer's Stone* was highly anticipated, both by members of the movie-making community and, even more so, by Rowling's fans.

Critics wondered whether the success of Rowling's first book would indicate a winning formula translated to screen.

The film, like the first novel, was released under two different titles. In the United Kingdom (and most of the rest of the world), the original title for Rowling's first novel, *Philosopher's Stone,* was used; the movie premiered on November 4, 2001. In the United States WARNER BROTHERS released *Sorcerer's Stone* 10 days later. The movie was released for general viewing in both countries on November 16 (hence one of the film's taglines: "The magic begins November 16"). The film experienced an astonishing opening weekend, grossing more than $90 million during its opening in the United States and £20 million in the United Kingdom.

With taglines like "Let the magic begin" and "Journey beyond your imagination," expectations for the 152-minute film were high. Critics debated which sections of the film the screenwriter Steve Kloves would emphasize or sacrifice to enhance the film-viewing experience. Initial reviews of the director Chris Columbus's first Harry Potter movie installment were mixed, but points many critics could agree on were the film's faithfulness to Rowling's text and the way in which this faithfulness left little room for invention by Columbus. David Ansen of *Newsweek* claimed, "Team Harry has bent over backward to cram everything everybody loves about the book into its two-and-a-half-hour movie, being careful to invent as little as possible." Ansen further pressed his concern with his readers in posing the question "Has there ever been a big-budget movie adaptation as faithful to its source as *Harry Potter and the Sorcerer's Stone?*"

Kenneth Turan in the *Los Angeles Times* complained that the filmmakers treated Rowling's text "like holy writ." The problem, Turan concluded, was that the film merely copies the book, and "copies don't leave much to object to or get excited about." Joe Morgenstern of the *Wall Street Journal* also complained of the "cautious approach" the filmmakers took by remaining so faithful to the novel but also noted that "the most magical part of the movie is what kids will bring to it."

One aspect of the film that critics and viewers alike agreed upon was the incredible cast: an ensemble of award-winning, lovable, and respected British actors. Richard Harris performed expertly as Hogwarts headmaster Albus Dumbledore. Dame Maggie Smith complemented Harris as Hogwarts deputy headmistress Minerva McGonagall. Robbie Coltrane was cast as Rubeus Hagrid (an event to which Coltrane's children responded by cheering). The performer who garnered the most glowing reviews, however, was Alan Rickman in the role of the Potions professor, Severus Snape.

Perhaps *Newsweek*'s Ansen captured Rickman's performance best in saying, "Who could imagine a more perfect fit for the sinister Snape than Alan Rickman, who brings a mesmerizing mixture of menace and drollery to his scenes." Other noteworthy actors in adult roles include Warwick Davis as Professor Flitwick and a bank teller at Gringotts, Ian Hart as Professor Quirrell and Voldemort, Verne Troyer as Griphook, and John Hurt as Mr. Ollivander, who Ansen says, "lights up his one, fine scene."

Actor Rupert Grint, who plays Harry Potter's affable pal Ron Weasley, is known for his comic talent. *(Photo by John Griffiths/Used under a Creative Commons license)*

But, the most-anticipated casting choices concerned the roles of Harry, Ron, and Hermione. Daniel Radcliffe, Rupert Grint, and Emma Watson play the starring students. None of the three main characters was exceptionally easy to cast, and no child had been cast to play Harry even at the time production began. The casting of the character of Harry Potter has already been transformed into legend. As the producer David Heyman reminisces, one night he and Kloves (the film's screenwriter) saw a production of *Stones in His Pockets*. Heyman and Kloves happened to run into a friend, Alan Radcliffe, who had his son, Daniel, with him. Heyman says, "It was like lightning" when he saw Daniel; the rest is movie history.

Rupert Grint as Ron Weasley is known for his mastery of facial expressions, which capture and portray his emotions so well. Whether it be his look of disgust after first meeting Hermione or the anxiety his face expresses during the Sorting Hat ceremony, Grint's use of expression has earned him praise since his first appearance as Ron Weasley.

Emma Watson was cast as the bookish Hermione Granger. While reviews on her acting ability remained inconsistent, many viewers agreed that Watson's did not accurately reflect Hermione's physical appearance; Watson, many fans felt, was too "pretty" or "cute" to play Rowling's Hermione. The disparity in physical appearance was not the only aspect of Hermione that troubled film critics. For instance, Catherine Wallace of the *Christian Century* objected to Columbus and Kloves's depiction of Hermione: "She is portrayed as far more overbearing than she is in the novel. . . . The film seems guilty of the classic antipathy to smart, capable women—exaggerating her clumsy self-confidence and willingness to help others into an insufferable arrogance."

For the most part the critical reception of the first Harry Potter film remains overwhelmingly negative. Columbus and Klove's choice to stray very little from Rowling's novel serves as the main point of contention. Jami Bernard of the *New York Daily News* refers to her complaint of the movie's being "powered solely by the book" as "surely quibbling," but other critics would disagree, arguing that viewers have done a disservice to the filmmakers, causing their lack of experimentation. Rita Kempley of the *Washington Post* offers that "*Potter*-philes are sure to get what they want—if what they want is, in fact, an exacting version of J. K. Rowling's charming children's fantasy. If it's enchantment they are after, that's quite another matter." The *New York Times*'s critic Elvis Mitchell asserts that "the most highly awaited movie of the year has a dreary, literal-minded competence, following the letter of the law as laid down by the author." Mitchell's review reaches its most scathing when he writes, "Someone has cast a sleepwalker's spell over the proceedings, and at nearly two and a half hours, you may go under, too." The *Toronto Star*'s Peter Howell describes the film as "a case where giving the people what they want outweighs any grander artistic pretensions"; similarly Rob White of *Sight and Sound* states: "The motto seems to have been: keep it bland." Wallace of the *Christian Century* encourages readers not to substitute seeing the movie for reading the book and senses that young viewers will be disappointed: "If the director had taken youngsters as seriously as Rowling does, we might have had less of chocolate frogs jumping out of windows and more of engaging kids laying sturdy claim to their own emergent identities despite the timeless array of adolescent hazards: mean teachers, bullying classmates, too much homework, personal insecurities and clueless authorities." Richard Corliss in *Time* writes that "the film lacks moviemaking buoyancy" but adds that "the picture isn't inept, just inert." The *Boston Globe*'s Jay Carr seems to capture general critical reception best, stating that the film "remains a thing of calculation rather than inspiration." Even the film's music did not escape critique; though John Williams's music has become beloved by fans (serving, even, as some of their cell phone ringtones), critics widely found fault with his music, claiming it mirrored his other work too closely.

The reviews were not without praise, however. Critics for *People Weekly* summarized their reaction with "Bottom line: Kids will fall under Harry's spell." Ansen of *Newsweek* credits Columbus for his "valiant first effort." Roger Ebert of the *Chicago Sun-Times* describes the first film in the series as "an enchanting classic that does full justice to a story that was a daunting challenge. . . . It isn't just a movie, but a world with its own magical rules."

Although critics consistently criticized the film for its faithfulness and hence lack of creativity, Columbus and Kloves did make some important changes by sacrificing some components of Rowling's novel when translating the work from page to screen. For instance, almost an entire chapter of the book focusing on Norbert (Hagrid's illegal pet dragon) was cut from the film. While the scene would have obviously lengthened the movie and its absence does not drastically affect one's understanding of the plot, viewers miss important details about characters, such as Ron, because of the deletion. Harry, Ron, and Hermione have grown close to Hagrid and will do anything to protect him; in the book they devise the plan to remove Norbert from the Hogwarts grounds. Without the help of Charlie, Ron's older brother who works at a dragon colony in Romania, deporting Norbert safely would not have been possible. Deleting the scene not only means a shorter film and one less character for viewers to acquaint themselves with (Charlie) but also deprives readers of better understanding the emotional dynamics of some of Rowling's characters. Harry, Ron, and Hermione's devotion to Hagrid is more obvious in the novel, and the strong familial bond between the Weasleys becomes less apparent because viewers do not see Charlie go to the aid of his younger brother.

Another significant revision of Rowling's text concerns Neville Longbottom. Numerous instances in the novel present Neville with Harry, Ron, and Hermione, including, most notably, the detention served in the Forbidden Forest. Deleting Neville from such scenes in the film weakens the bond he shares with the three main characters and shifts Neville to a more minor role. Some critics have questioned the emphasis, especially considering the more significant role Neville plays in ensuing books.

Even though the film was roundly criticized for its lack of "magic," it was nominated for a plethora of awards, including a Grammy (for Williams's heavily and negatively reviewed score) and three Oscars. Probably the greatest reward the film received, however, was Rowling's own reaction to the film.

The producer David Heyman recounts how nervous he felt during the screening of the film for Rowling, waiting anxiously for her reaction. When the screening finished, Rowling rose from her seat, walked over to Heyman, and hugged him. Heyman says, "To say the least, I was greatly relieved." Critics may not have had such a warm reception, but the film became a blockbuster nonetheless and created a strong and successful foundation for the Harry Potter film franchise.

WORKS CITED AND FURTHER READING

Acocella, Joan. "Under the Spell: Harry Potter Explained." *New Yorker,* 31 July 2000, 74–78.

Ansen, David. "The Trouble with Harry: The Ingredients Are Right, but Where's the Alchemy?" *Newsweek,* 19 November 2001.

Beach, Daniel. "Review of *Harry Potter and the Sorcerer's Stone.*" *Book Report* 17, no. 5 (March/April 1999): 63–64. Academic Search Premier. Available online by subscription. Accessed September 22, 2009.

Bernard, Jami. "A Great Start to the Wonder Years *Harry Potter* Remains True to Its Sorcery." *New York Daily News,* 16 November 2001.

Black, Sharon. "Harry Potter: A Magical Prescription for Just about Anyone." *Journal of Adolescent and Adult Literacy* 46, no. 7 (April 2003): 540–544.

Brown, Stephen. "Harry Potter and the Marketing Mystery: A Review and Critical Assessment of the Harry Potter Books." *Journal of Marketing* 66, no. 1 (2002): 126–130.

Bulfinch, Thomas. *Bulfinch's Mythology: The Age of Fable, the Age of Chivalry, Legends of Charlemagne.* New York: Modern Library, 1934.

Byam, Paige. "Children's Literature or Adult Classic? The Harry Potter Series and the British Novel Tradition." *Topic: The Washington and Jefferson College Review* 54 (Fall 2004): 7–13.

Carr, Jay. "On the Screen, *Harry Potter* Has Its Charms but Lacks Magic of the Books." *Boston Globe,* 16 November 2001.

Cart, Michael. "Review of *Harry Potter and the Sorcerer's Stone.*" *Booklist.* 15 September 1998. Academic Search Premier. Available online by subscription. Accessed September 22, 2009.

Corliss, Richard. "Wizardry without Magic." *Time,* 19 November 2001.

Cullinan, Bernice. "Timeless Books Expand the Boundaries of Time." *Reading Teacher* 57, no. 1 (September 2003): 101–102.

Cummins, June. "The Secret World of Harry Potter." *Michigan Quarterly Review* 39, no. 3 (2000): 661–666.

De Lint, Charles. "Books to Look For." *Fantasy and Science Fiction* 98, no. 1 (2000): 35–39.

Diffendal, Lee Ann. "Questioning Witchcraft and Wizardry as Obscenity: *Harry Potter's* Potion for Regulation." *Topic: The Washington and Jefferson College Review* 54 (2004): 55–62.

Dolgos, Kathleen. "Review of *Harry Potter and the Sorcerer's Stone.*" *Childhood Education* 75, no. 5 (Fall 2009): 311. Academic Search Premier. Available online by subscription. Accessed September 22, 2009.

Ebert, Roger. "*Harry Potter and the Sorcerer's Stone.*" *Chicago Sun-Times,* 16 November 2001.

Ensor, Barbara. "Spellbinding." Review of *Harry Potter and the Sorcerer's Stone. New York,* 31 August 1998. Available online by subscription. Academic Search Premier. Accessed September 22, 2009.

Feldman, Roxanne. "The Truth about Harry." *School Library Journal* (September 1999): 136–139.

Flowers, Ann. "Review of *Harry Potter and the Sorcerer's Stone.*" *Horn Book Magazine* 75, no. 1 (January/February 1999): 71. Academic Search Premier. Available online by subscription. Accessed September 22, 2009.

"Forecasts: Review of *Harry Potter and the Sorcerer's Stone.*" *Publishers Weekly,* 20 July 1998. Academic Search Premier. Available online by subscription. Accessed September 22, 2009.

Frank, Andrew, and Matthew McBee. "The Use of *Harry Potter and the Sorcerer's Stone* to Discuss Identity Development with Gifted Adolescents." *Journal of Secondary Gifted Education* 15, no. 1 (2003): 33–39.

Gawkwell, Gail. "Not Spellbound by Harry." Review of *Harry Potter and the Sorcerer's Stone. Journal of Adolescent and Adult Literacy* 44, no. 7 (April 2001): 669.

Gibb, Alexandra, Martha McGovern, and Suzanne Nelson. "Magic in the Classroom: Using *Harry Potter.*" *Reading Today* 25, no. 1 (2007): 46.

Gibson, Donna. "Empathizing with Harry Potter: The Use of Popular Literature in Counselor Education." *Journal of Humanistic Counseling, Education, and Development* 46, no. 2 (2007): 197–210.

Glieck, Elizabeth. "The Wizard of Hogwarts." Review of *Harry Potter and the Sorcerer's Stone. Time,* 12 April 1999, 86.

Gottesman, Peter. Review of *Harry Potter and the Sorcerer's Stone. Teachers College Record* 106, no. 2 (2004): 267–270.

Hallett, Cynthia Whitney. *Scholarly Studies in Harry Potter: Applying Academic Methods to a Popular Text.* Studies in British Literature. Lewiston, N.Y.: Edwin Mellen Press, 2005.

Hamilton, Edith. *Mythology.* Boston: Little, Brown, 1949.

Harrell, Pamela Esprivalo, and Andrea Morton. "Muggles, Wizards, and Witches: Using Harry Potter Characters to Teach Human Pedigrees." *Science Activities* 39, no. 2 (Summer 2002): 24–28.

Howell, Peter. "*Harry Potter and the Sorcerer's Stone.*" *Toronto Star,* 16 November 2001.

Hurst, Carol Otis. "Crowd Pleasers." *Teaching Pre-K–8* 30, no. 2 (October 1999): 86–87.

Jacobs, Alan. Review of *Harry Potter and the Sorcerer's Stone. First Things* 99 (January 2000): 35–38.

Kempley, Rita. "Harry Flies off the Page: The Wizard Loses a Little of His Charm." *Washington Post,* 16 November 2001.

Lathey, Gillian. "The Travels of Harry: International Marketing and the Translation of J. K. Rowling's Harry Potter Books." *Lion and the Unicorn* 29 (2005): 141–151.

Levine, Jodi, and Nancy Shapiro. "Hogwarts." *About Campus* 5, no. 4 (September 2000): 8–13.

Lurie, Alison. "Not for Muggles." *New York Review of Books* 46, no. 20 (December 16, 1999): 6–7.

Mitchell, Elvis. "*Harry Potter and the Sorcerer's Stone.*" *New York Times,* 16 November 2001.

Mitnick, Eva. "Review of *Harry Potter and the Sorcerer's Stone.*" *School Library Journal* 44, no. 10 (October 1998): 145–146. Academic Search Premier. Available online by subscription. Accessed September 22, 2009.

Morgenstern, Joe. "Hyped Harry Potter Is a Pleasant Ride, Hogwarts and All." *Wall Street Journal,* 16 November 2001.

Mullen, Alexandra. "Harry Potter's Schooldays." *Hudson Review* 53, no. 1 (2000): 127–135.

Neithardt, Leigh A. "The Problem of Identity in *Harry Potter and the Sorcerer's Stone*." In *Scholarly Studies in Harry Potter: Applying Academic Methods to a Popular Text*. Lewiston, N.Y.: Edwin Mellen Press, 2005.

Nel, Phillip. "Bewitched, Bothered, and Bored: Harry Potter, the Movie." *Journal of Adolescent and Adult Literacy* 46, no. 2 (2002): 172–175.

Nye, Lesley. "Editor's Review." *Harvard Educational Review* 71, no. 1 (2001): 136–145.

Pashak, Barrett. "Magic-Lite for the Pre-Teen Set." *Report/Newsmagazine* (Albert Edition) 26, no. 44 (1999): 53.

Perry, Evelyn M. "Metaphor and MetaFantasy: Questing for Literary Inheritance in J. K. Rowling's *Harry Potter and the Sorcerer's Stone*." In *Scholarly Studies in Harry Potter: Applying Academic Methods to a Popular Text*. Lewiston, N.Y.: Edwin Mellen Press, 2005.

Power, Carla. "A Literary Sorceress." Review of *Harry Potter and the Sorcerer's Stone*. *Newsweek*, 7 December 1998, D7.

Propp, Vladimir. *Morphology of the Folktale*. Rev. 2d ed. Translated by Laurence Scott. Austin: University of Texas Press, 1968.

Puig, Claudia. "The Lore of 'Harry Potter': A Treasure Trove of Myths and Legends is Delighting Kids and Scholars Alike." *USA Today*, 16 November 2001, E1.

Rollin, Lucy. "Among School Children: The *Harry Potter* Books and the School Story Tradition. *South Carolina Review* 34, no. 1 (2001): 198–208.

Shuker, Karl. *Dragons: A Natural History*. New York: Simon & Schuster, 1995.

Siegel, Lee. "Fear of Not Flying." Reviews of *Harry Potter and the Sorcerer's Stone, Harry Potter and the Chamber of Secrets, Harry Potter and the Prisoner of Azkaban*. *New Republic* 221, no. 21 (1999): 40–44.

Stevenson, Deborah. Review of *Harry Potter and the Sorcerer's Stone*. *Bulletin of the Center for Children's Books* 52, no. 3 (1998): 110.

Stuttaford, Andrew. "It's Witchcraft." *National Review* 51, no. 19 (1999): 60–62.

Treneman, Ann. "I'm Not Writing for the Money: It's for Me and Out of Loyalty to Fans." *Times* (London), 20 June 2003.

Turan, Kenneth. "*Harry Potter and the Sorcerer's Stone*." *Los Angeles Times*, 16 November 2001.

Wallace, Catherine M. "Missing Harry." *Christian Century* 118, no. 35 (December 2001): 31.

White, Rob. Review of *Harry Potter and the Philosopher's Stone* (movie). *Sight and Sound* 129 (January 2002): 43–44.

Winerip, Michael. Review of *Harry Potter and the Sorcerer's Stone*. *New York Times Book Review*, 14 February 1999, 26.

Wood, Susan Nelson, and Kim Quackenbush. "*The Sorcerer's Stone*: A Touchstone for Readers of All Ages." *English Journal* 93, no. 3 (2001): 97–103.

Harry Potter and the Chamber of Secrets (1998)

SYNOPSIS

Chapter 1: "The Worst Birthday Ever"

The second book opens on Harry's 12th birthday. Harry is breakfasting with the Dursleys at their home at Number Four, Privet Drive, in Little Whinging, England. Harry is home from school for the summer, and his uncle Vernon has locked away all magical items because he fears Harry's magical abilities. The narration recaps Harry's past as the survivor of Voldemort's deadly attack and his initiation into the magical world on his 11th birthday. The Dursleys prepare for a dinner party that evening and shut Harry in his room because they are ashamed of having a wizard in the family. While avoiding his aunt Petunia, Harry spends time in the yard, where he sees a mysterious creature lurking in the hedge. Dudley appears and taunts Harry about not having received any gifts or cards for his birthday, something Harry feels acutely aware of, as he has received no letters from his friends Ron and Hermione all summer. Rising to Dudley's bait, Harry pretends to utter a spell, which leads his aunt to assign him numerous cleaning duties in preparation for the evening's cocktail party. That evening, banished to his room, Harry finds something waiting for him.

Chapter 2: "Dobby's Warning"

Harry is introduced to Dobby the house-elf, who appears awestruck at their meeting. Though Harry tries to deter him from making noise (as the Dursleys' dinner party has begun), Dobby feels overwhelmed with gratitude at being treated with kindness and being asked to "sit down" by a wizard and in turn makes a great deal of noise. Dobby serves an unnamed family and will need to punish himself with self-inflicted physical violence for betraying them; simply by visiting Harry to warn him that he must not return to Hogwarts, Dobby has disrespected and disregarded his masters (whose identity the house-elf refuses to reveal). Harry rejects this admonition as he has already reached his tolerance for the Dursleys. Dobby reveals that he has been intercepting Harry's letters from Ron and Hermione. Dobby next tries to extort Harry to stay in Little Whinging by threatening to keep the letters from Hermione and Ron. Dobby eventually uses magic to drop Aunt Petunia's finely crafted violet pudding on the floor in front of their important guests (who are associated with Uncle Vernon's business). An owl arrives to tell Harry that he should not use magic outside school, something he neglected to tell the Dursleys; of course, it was Dobby who actually used magic, and not Harry. Uncle Vernon promptly locks Harry in his room, putting bars on the windows and a cat flap in the bedroom door. After three days, Harry's low spirits improve when Ron Weasley arrives at his window.

Chapter 3: "The Burrow"

Harry quickly realizes that Ron and his brothers, the twins Fred and George, hover outside his window in an enchanted Ford Anglia. They pull the bars out of his bedroom window and grab his trunk and myriad possessions (including Hedwig, Harry's owl). The ruckus wakes Uncle Vernon, who tries to pull Harry back in the window before he can escape with the Weasley brothers. Harry, Ron, Fred, and George make a spectacular escape. During their enchanted car ride to the Weasley home, the boys speculate on who could have sent Dobby to deter Harry from returning to Hogwarts and wonder whether the Malfoys could be the culprits. Harry learns more about Ron's family, including about Percy's obsession with his new role as prefect and Arthur's work for the Misuse of Magical Artifacts Office. After the boys arrive at the Weasley home (the Burrow), Mrs. Weasley berates them for their rash actions but welcomes Harry to their home. Mrs. Weasley consults *Gilderoy Lockhart's Guide to Household Pests* before sending the boys out to degnome the garden. Arthur Weasley returns from investigating some magicked Muggle artifacts, and Molly informs her husband that Ron, Fred, and George used the enchanted car to save Harry. Instead of punishing the boys, though, Arthur asks eagerly about the car's performance. Harry learns a lot about the Weasley family while staying in their home, including such details as Ron's favorite Quidditch team is the Chudley Cannons (posters for which splash the walls of his bedroom).

Chapter 4: "At Flourish and Blotts"

Harry marvels about life at the Burrow, where everyone treats him with care and respect, so different from his life at the Dursleys'. Letters from Hogwarts reveal that Harry and Ron need seven books by Gilderoy Lockhart. Hermione sends a letter to the Burrow by owl post to confirm a meeting in Diagon Alley. Readers learn that Ron's brothers Charlie and Bill have already left Hogwarts; the former works in Romania studying dragons and the latter works in Egypt for the wizard's bank, Gringotts. To travel to Diagon Alley, the Weasleys introduce Harry to Floo network travel, in which wizards sprinkle powder into a fireplace, announce their destination, and are quickly transported to the place they name. In his first attempt Harry mistakenly transports himself to a dimly lit shop, where he quickly hides in a cabinet to avoid encountering Draco Malfoy and his father, who enter as Harry arrives. Draco complains loudly about Harry's fame and place on the Gryffindor Quidditch team. Harry overhears the conversation of the owner, Mr. Borgin, and Lucius Malfoy, who announces he is selling certain items that might incriminate him in wrongdoing if the Ministry were to learn of them.

After their departure Harry rushes from the store and sees he is in Knockturn Alley, which appears to be the location of a number of stores selling Dark Arts items. Luckily he runs into Hagrid, who escorts him to Gringotts, where they meet Hermione, her parents, and the Weasleys. The kids tour Diagon Alley and observe Percy reading the book *Prefects Who Gained Power*, confirming his ambitious nature. At Flourish and Blotts, Gilderoy Lockhart holds a book signing and immediately embraces Harry for a photo opportunity. The Malfoys taunt Harry, Ron, Ginny (Ron's sister), and Arthur (Ron's father), who starts a fistfight with Lucius. The group leaves the store in a grimmer mood than that in which they arrived.

Chapter 5: "The Whomping Willow"

Reluctant to leave the Burrow after his enjoyable summer month, Harry (and the Weasley children) must leave for Hogwarts. The Weasleys drive their Ford Anglia (enchanted with a special backseat-expanding spell by the Muggle-artifact-loving Arthur Weasley) in Muggle fashion (driving), even though they are running late and could use some magical assistance to ensure they do not miss the Hogwarts Express. They arrive at platform nine and three-quarters, invisible to Muggles, with only five minutes to spare. Last to go, Harry and Ron attempt to pass through the wall that leads to the Hogwarts Express, but it mysteriously will not allow them to do so. They decide to fly the Ford Anglia to school, presuming themselves in an emergency situation. They use the invisibility function to ensure they will not be seen and follow the train on their journey. As they near the school, the car's engine groans and dies. Near enough to school, they attempt a crash landing but instead smash the enchanted Anglia into the Whomping Willow, an aggressive tree that attacks them. The car ejects their luggage and its passengers and disappears into the Forbidden Forest, seemingly disgusted by Ron and Harry. In the melee Ron's wand breaks. They scramble to the castle, but Snape interrupts their observation of the Sorting Ceremony and punishes them for having flown the car, which the evening edition of the *Daily Prophet* reveals was seen by several Muggles. Snape fetches Mc-

A sign has been placed at King's Cross railway station, along with a luggage trolley appearing to pass through the brick wall, as a tribute to the Harry Potter series. *(Photo by Oxyman/Used under a Creative Commons license)*

Gonagall and Dumbledore, and the boys explain their story, fearful they will be expelled as Snape has suggested; instead, McGonagall gives them detention and some sandwiches. They return to their common room to an admiring welcome at their derring-do.

Chapter 6: "Gilderoy Lockhart"

At breakfast the next morning Ron receives a red envelope by owl post, a Howler from his mother, reprimanding him and Harry for stealing the car. During Herbology that day Lockhart stops by to speak to Professor Sprout and pulls Harry aside, conspiratorially suggesting that Harry flew the Ford Anglia to school as a ploy to gain publicity. Returning to class, Harry, Ron, and Hermione work with mandrakes, plants that work as a restorative but are also dangerous. Transfiguration reveals that Ron's wand is dysfunctional.

Later in the day Harry has another confrontation with Draco over a first-year student, Colin, who asks Harry to take a picture with him and sign it. Their first Defense Against the Dark Arts class begins with a quiz on Gilderoy Lockhart's likes and dislikes, much to Harry's chagrin and amusement. After some self-congratulatory remarks Lockhart releases a cageful of Cornish pixies and sets the students to recapturing them.

Chapter 7: "Mudbloods and Murmurs"
Saturday Harry is awakened early (and regrettably) by the Gryffindor team captain, Oliver Wood, for a surprise Quidditch practice. On his way to the pitch he again encounters the admiring Colin Creevey, to whom he explains the rules of the game. After a long-winded strategy speech by Wood they practice while Colin takes photos. Unfortunately, the Slytherin team shows up with a special note to practice on the pitch in order to train Draco Malfoy as their new Seeker; the entire Slytherin Quidditch team all possess new *Nimbus Two Thousand and One* brooms, gifts from Draco's father. When Ron and Hermione arrive at the field, Draco refers to Hermione as a "Mudblood," a term unfamiliar to Harry. Ron attempts to stun Draco, but the spell backfires since Ron's wand is broken; the misfired spell causes Ron to throw up slugs. Harry and Hermione take Ron to Hagrid, who is unperturbed by Ron's condition. He tells Harry that *Mudblood* is a "foul name for some-one who is Muggle-born" (115), then he describes the elitist views held by some pureblood wizards such as the Malfoys. He also shows them his magically enhanced garden and implies, as others have, that Ginny has a crush on Harry. When they return to the castle, McGonagall assigns Ron to polish silver in the trophy room and Harry to help Lockhart with his fan mail, a task Harry does not relish. At the end of detention Harry hears a strange, chilling voice and realizes Lockhart does not.

Chapter 8: "The Deathday Party"
October presents cold weather, sickness, and uncomfortable Quidditch practices. On his way back from a particularly muddy practice Harry happens upon an unhappy-looking Nearly Head-less Nick, the Gryffindor Tower ghost. Nick feels despondent over being rejected from the Headless Hunt. The caretaker Argus Filch finds Harry drip-ping mud on the floor and calls him into his office to write him up. Distracted by a large bang made by Peeves the poltergeist, Filch storms out and leaves Harry to observe a purple envelope for a magic cor-respondence course, revealing that Filch is a Squib, a pureblood wizard who has no magical abilities. He escapes Filch's office without detention, and Nick invites him to attend his 500th Deathday party on Halloween. At the party Hermione, Ron, and Harry avoid Moaning Myrtle, who Hermione explains is an adolescent ghost who haunts the girls' first-floor bathroom. A pack of headless, horse-riding ghosts interrupt the deathday party and taunt Sir Nicholas about having only a mostly severed head. On his way out of the party Harry hears the chilling voice again; after following the sound of the voice, Harry, Hermione, and Ron find a painted message on the wall of a deserted corridor announcing that the Chamber of Secrets has been opened again. Near the message they also find Filch's cat, petrified (frozen). The other students, returning from the Halloween feast, happen upon the scene.

Chapter 9: "The Writing on the Wall"
Filch arrives, horrified. Dumbledore takes Harry, Ron, and Hermione along with several professors to Lockhart's nearby office. In examining Mrs. Norris, the cat, Dumbledore asserts that she has been petrified, not killed, as Lockhart claims. Filch blames Harry, but Dumbledore notes that the dark magic required would be too advanced for a second-year student. Snape tries to discover why Harry, Hermione, and Ron did not go to the feast after the Deathday party, implying he knows about Harry's ability to hear the strange voice. Hermione and Ginny are both emotionally affected by the cat's fate, and Hermione spends many hours seeking out information in the library about the Chamber of Secrets, eventually asking History of Magic profes-sor Binns about the subject.

Binns reluctantly presents his students with the legend, noting its origin in Hogwarts' history. A rift between two of the school's founders—Salazar Slytherin and Godric Gryffindor—arose over whether to limit Hogwarts' enrollment only to pureblood wizards. Binns tells them that according to legend, Slytherin built a secret chamber in the castle and sealed it so that no one but his true heir could open it when she or he arrived at the school. The heir could use its magic, and the creature it harbored, to purge the school of all non-purebloods. On the way back from class they find leaking water and multiple spiders at the site of the attack and enter Moaning Myrtle's bathroom to ask her whether she saw anything on the night of the attack. On the way out Percy spies them and deducts five points from Gryffindor for boys being in the girls' bathroom. The kids speculate that Draco Malfoy is the heir of Slytherin, and Hermione suggests that they brew a batch of Polyjuice Potion, which allows the drinker to take on the appearance of another person. They plan to transform themselves into Slytherins and trick Draco into revealing information. However, they can only access the potion recipe book with the permission of a teacher.

Chapter 10: "The Rogue Bludger"

In Defense Against the Dark Arts class Lockhart requires Harry to play the role of various creatures so the professor can reenact the exploits documented in his books. Ron, Harry, and Hermione flatter Lockhart into giving them permission to sign out the much-needed potion book from the Restricted Section of the library to make the Polyjuice Potion. The three of them meet in Moaning Myrtle's bathroom to plan their potion making.

The first Quidditch match of the season arrives. The hotly contested match features Slytherin pitted against Gryffindor. A bewitched Bludger sets its sights on Harry, who manages to catch the Snitch before the Bludger beans him and sends him careening to the ground with a broken arm, which Lockhart tries to mend; Lockhart actually ends up removing the bones rather than mending them, and Harry is sent to the hospital wing. Harry spends the night there while his arm heals. Dobby wakes him suddenly and confesses he blocked the barrier at the train station and bewitched the Bludger in order to keep Harry

safe from whatever wicked force has opened the Chamber of Secrets, confirming indeed that the chamber has been unlocked and the beast within unleashed. Harry also learns that house-elves can only be freed if their master gives them an item of clothing. Later in the evening Dumbledore and McGonagall enter carrying a statue. Harry learns the statue is Colin Creevey, petrified and holding his most beloved possession, his camera.

Chapter 11: "The Dueling Club"

Madam Pomfrey discharges Harry, and he immediately meets Ron and Hermione in the girls' bathroom. They speculate that Lucius Malfoy opened the chamber when he was in school and Draco did this time. Along with Draco, Crabbe, and Goyle, Ron, Hermione, and Harry all plan to stay at Hogwarts over the Christmas break. Hermione, Harry, and Ron realize they need two ingredients from Snape's office for the Polyjuice Potion and figure they will need to create a distraction, and Hermione volunteers to do the stealing since she has gotten into much less trouble than Ron and Harry while at Hogwarts.

Lockhart starts a Dueling Club for students, which he debuts by practicing spells with a reluctant and displeased Snape. Maliciously Snape partners Harry and Draco and asks them to model a duel for the class. When Malfoy produces a large snake that Lockhart inadvertently makes larger in his attempt to keep it at bay, Harry unknowingly uses Parseltongue—the language of snakes—to keep it from biting Justin Finch-Fletchley. His classmates are horrified; Harry learns from Ron and Hermione that being a Parselmouth, an individual able to talk to snakes, is a rare gift—and even more troubling, Salazar Slytherin, one of the Hogwarts' founders who was fanatical about purebloodedness, was also a Parselmouth. The next day Harry goes to the library to explain himself to Justin but overhears a group of scared Hufflepuffs speculating that he is the heir of Slytherin. Wandering the halls in dismay later, Harry runs into Hagrid carrying a dead rooster while musing over what creature is killing animals like roosters on the grounds; shortly thereafter, Harry stumbles across Justin Finch-Fletchley and Nearly Headless Nick, both petrified and lying in a corridor. Peeves the poltergeist calls attention to the scene, and McGonagall escorts Harry to see Dumbledore.

Chapter 12: "Polyjuice Potion"

Harry visits Dumbledore in his office for the first time. While he is waiting, he cannot resist trying on the Sorting Hat in hopes that it will assuage his anxieties about having been placed in Gryffindor, but the hat is no help and reiterates that Harry would have done well in Slytherin. Fawkes, Dumbledore's phoenix (an elegant bird), looks decrepit and bursts into flames. Harry is apologetic when Dumbledore enters, until the headmaster explains that phoenixes burst into flame when they are ready to die and are then reborn from their own ashes. Hagrid bursts in to defend Harry from the suspicion that he opened the Chamber of Secrets, but Dumbledore reassures them both he does not suspect Harry is the culprit.

Everyone leaves for Christmas break, but Harry, Ron, and Hermione stay, as do Crabbe, Goyle, and Draco, giving the three Gryffindors an opportunity to use the Polyjuice Potion on the Slytherins. They each take a hair from the person they intend to transform into and drink the potion in Moaning Myrtle's bathroom. Ron turns into Crabbe, Harry into Goyle, and Hermione will not come out of her stall but encourages them both to go on. They run into Percy in a hallway while searching for the Slytherin common room. Percy is evasive about his whereabouts. Draco shows up and leads them to the Slytherin common room to show them something "really funny." It turns out to be an article from the *Daily Prophet* reporting Arthur Weasley's fine for bewitching the Ford Anglia (that Ron and Harry crashed earlier in the book), much to Ron's consternation, since he has to pretend to be amused in the guise of Crabbe. They learn that Draco wants to know as much as they do who the heir of Slytherin is and also that he does not know who opened the Chamber of Secrets the last time. He also refers for the first time to Azkaban, the wizard prison. After Draco makes a number of hateful comments about "Mudbloods" and a confession that his father has a lot of "Dark Arts stuff" concealed at the Malfoy estate, the Polyjuice Potion wears off and Ron

and Harry have to abruptly exit and race back to the bathroom. There they learn that Hermione accidentally used Millicent Bustrode's cat's hair instead of one of Millicent's hairs; Hermione has a fur-covered face and a tail, so Ron and Harry take her to the hospital wing.

Chapter 13: "The Very Secret Diary"

Hermione spends the next several weeks in the hospital. Ron and Harry stumble upon Filch mopping Moaning Myrtle's bathroom; they find her sobbing because someone threw a book at her. Ron warns Harry about the dangers of strange books, but Harry looks at it anyway, discovering it is T. M. Riddle's personal diary. Ron recognizes the name from his detention polishing school plaques; Riddle won an award for special service to the school 50 years ago. The diary has no writing in it, but they figure Riddle was Muggle-born because it was purchased on Vauxhall Road in London, and they speculate it might be a clue because Riddle was at school when the chamber was last opened. Further investigation reveals that Riddle also received a medal for magical merit and served as Head Boy at Hogwarts.

Lockhart attributes the lulls in attacks from the chamber beast's fear of him. On Valentine's Day Lockhart decorates the Great Hall in the holiday spirit and brings in a phalanx of dwarves to deliver singing valentines; Harry tries to avoid having one delivered, spilling the contents of his bag—including the diary—in his effort to run away, while Ginny looks on terrified. Harry notes the diary remains pristine even though the rest of his books are covered in ink. He tries writing on it and discovers it writes back in the voice of Tom Riddle. The diary explains that the Chamber of Secrets was opened and the monster attacked several students, killing one. Riddle reports he caught the guilty party who was expelled, but the monster was not imprisoned. The page for June 13 turns into a miniature television and sucks Harry into Riddle's memory. Harry finds himself in the office of Armando Dippet, the headmaster at Hogwarts 40 years earlier, and sees Riddle asking to stay at Hogwarts over the summer rather than return to the orphanage. Dippet refuses because of the attacks. Harry follows Riddle to a dark corridor where they come across Hagrid talking to an unseen creature that slinks away as Hagrid blocks Riddle's attempts to stun it.

Chapter 14: "Cornelius Fudge"

Harry tells Ron and Hermione about the opening of the Chamber of Secrets he witnessed in Riddle's diary. It has been four months since the last attack. One day, Harry returns to his dorm to find his belongings strewn about and the diary missing. He concludes it had to have been a Gryffindor since no one else knows the password to their dormitory. On the way to the next Quidditch match Harry hears the sinister voice he heard several times earlier in the novel; he tells Hermione, who suddenly runs to the library because of an epiphany she has had. McGonagall calls off the Quidditch match before it starts and sends everyone back to their houses. She takes Ron and Harry to the hospital wing where they learn Hermione and Ravenclaw Penelope Clearwater have been petrified. A small mirror was found next to them. McGonagall announces new curfews and greater limitations on student movement in the hallways. Harry and Ron decide to talk to Hagrid about their new knowledge and circumvent the new security by using the Invisibility Cloak. Shortly after they arrive at Hagrid's cabin, someone knocks on the door—the Minister of Magic, Cornelius Fudge, followed by Draco Malfoy's father, Lucius. Fudge announces he has to take some action because of the rash of events involving the supposed Chamber of Secrets and so he takes Hagrid to Azkaban. Dumbledore enters to defend Hagrid, at which point Lucius Malfoy, one of the 12 school governors, presents an Order of Suspension to Dumbledore, who enigmatically comments that he will "only *truly* have left this school when none here are loyal to me. You will also find that help will always be given at Hogwarts to those who ask for it" (264). Hagrid, for the benefit of Harry and Ron who still hide under the Invisibility Cloak, comments that those who want to know what is going on should follow the spiders.

Chapter 15: "Aragog"

Dumbledore's forced absence from Hogwarts causes Harry to reflect on his mentor's assertion that he will only have left the school when none there is loyal to him. All the spiders seem to have disappeared, making Hagrid's suggestion difficult to follow, and the school staff implements even stricter security measures, including teacher escorts in the hallway. Malfoy gloats about Dumbledore's absence and unctuously urges Snape to apply for the post of headmaster. Lockhart appears cheerful and confident that the problem concerning the chamber is solved.

During Herbology one day Ron and Harry see spiders heading for the Forbidden Forest. They decide to use Harry's Invisibility Cloak to collect Hagrid's pet wolfhound Fang from Hagrid's cabin and venture into the forest, following the path of the spiders diligently. They encounter both the bewitched Ford Anglia, which has "turned wild," and a group of spiders the size of cart horses who scoop the boys up and take them to a clearing where they meet Aragog, an aged, blind, elephant-sized spider who orders them killed until Harry says they are friends of Hagrid. From Aragog they learn that he was the creature Riddle suspected as the beast from the Chamber of Secrets, but Aragog assures Harry and Ron that he was not the creature who killed the girl in the bathroom. Aragog refuses to speak the name of the actual creature but says it is "an ancient creature we spiders fear above all others" (278). He refuses to allow Harry and Ron to leave, and the tribe of spiders turns on them. Harry and Ron avoid being eaten by the other spiders when the rogue Ford Anglia bursts into the clearing and carries them back to the safety of Hagrid's cabin. Frustrated and traumatized, they head to bed until Harry realizes that the girl killed by the creature 50 years ago must be Moaning Myrtle.

Chapter 16: "The Chamber of Secrets"

Students feel dismayed to find exams will be held as planned but cheered by the reinstatement of Quidditch. Ron and Harry have not been able to escape teacher escorts to visit Moaning Myrtle's bathroom, but since the Mandrakes have almost reached maturity, they will soon be able to make the potion that will reverse the petrifications. At breakfast Ginny approaches Ron and Harry, seemingly about to confess something about the Chamber of Secrets, but Percy shoos her away.

Later that day Ron and Harry, about to go to Moaning Myrtle's bathroom, run into McGonagall; to explain their whereabouts and why they are unescorted, they lie and say they are visiting Hermione in the hospital wing and detour there. They find Hermione, clutching a page from a library book that describes the basilisk, the King of the Serpents, whose gaze freezes its victims; it has venomous fangs, spiders flee it, and the crow of the rooster is fatal to it. The creature in the chamber is a basilisk, and all those petrified did not look directly at it. Hermione's note on the page, "pipes," explains how the basilisk has been moving around Hogwarts. They realize the entrance to the Chamber of Secrets must be in Moaning Myrtle's bathroom; they make their way to the staff room to wait for McGonagall to inform her of this discovery when another announcement orders them back to the dorms. They hide in the staff room wardrobe, and, when a group of teachers enter, they overhear that Ginny has been kidnapped. The teachers insincerely encourage Lockhart to confront the creature since he is Defense Against the Dark Arts teacher, and he nervously returns to his office to "get ready" for the ensuing confrontation.

Harry and Ron go to Lockhart's office to tell him what they have discovered about the Chamber of Secrets and find him packing his belongings, indicating that he intends to leave Hogwarts. Lockhart admits that in his books he takes credit for the accomplishments of others. Outraged over his lack of regard for Ginny, Harry and Ron disarm him of his wand as he begins to utter a memory charm, and then they march Lockhart to Moaning Myrtle's bathroom to ask her how she died. As she recalls the story of her death, Harry and Ron realize the entrance to the chamber must be behind the sink, which magically opens when Harry speaks Parseltongue. They slide down a chute into a cavelike tunnel littered with small animal bones. Encountering a 20-foot snake skin, Lockhart takes advantage of their surprise to snatch Ron's damaged wand and attempts to utter a memory erasing charm but the wand explodes, causing a small rockslide—trapping Ron and Lockhart away from the chamber and muddling Lockhart's mind. Harry realizes he must proceed alone. Reaching a wall

decorated with carvings of snakes, Harry commands, in Parseltongue, a door in the wall to open; it does, and he enters the chamber.

Chapter 17: "The Heir of Slytherin"
In the stone-pillared and dimly lit chamber Harry finds Ginny lying on the floor at the base of a statue of Salazar Slytherin. Tom Riddle appears, and Harry realizes he is not a ghost, as he first assumes, but instead, as Riddle explains, a memory preserved in the diary Harry had been reading earlier. Harry mistakes Riddle for an ally until Riddle explains he used the diary to win Ginny's confidence and to take over her soul to control her actions. He takes Harry's wand and explains that he used Ginny to commit some of the incidents at the school without her being aware of it—until she grew suspicious and tried to get rid of the diary; that was when Harry found it. Riddle admits that Harry has been his target since the chamber was reopened and recalls some of his own schooldays when he felt Dumbledore suspected that Riddle, not Hagrid, was the real culprit behind the opening of the chamber.

Riddle wants to know how Harry survived Voldemort's attack on him as a baby and then confesses that he is the young Lord Voldemort, claiming to be the greatest sorcerer in the world. Harry asserts that Dumbledore is in fact the greatest sorcerer, and Fawkes the phoenix arrives with the Sorting Hat in its beak. Riddle mocks the "songbird and an old hat" (316) that the "greatest sorcerer" has given his young protégé as a weapon. Harry affirms the importance of his mother's sacrifice for him as the explanation for his surviving the attack by Voldemort. Riddle challenges the weapons Dumbledore has given Harry to use against the powers of Lord Voldemort and calls forth the basilisk, which emerges from the statue of Salazar Slytherin's mouth. Fawkes blinds the basilisk, giving Harry a new advantage, though he still lacks a weapon and mutters desperately for help to some unseen force. The Sorting Hat drops into his hands, and as if in response to his request, the sword of Gryffindor appears out of the hat. Harry manages to plunge the sword into the roof of the serpent's mouth, his arm subsequently impaled by one of the fangs, which splinters as the creature falls dead to the floor.

Fawkes goes to Harry's side while Riddle mocks Harry about his sure death, and the phoenix sheds its healing tears on Harry's arm. Realizing the phoenix's healing powers, Riddle starts to utter a spell, but Harry plunges the splintered basilisk fang into the diary that Fawkes drops at his feet, causing Riddle to disappear. Ginny wakens and appears horrified by what has happened and fears being expelled. They follow Fawkes back to the tunnel, where they call to Ron, who has been digging a hole through the rock collapse. Lockhart has lost his sense of identity and memory. Fawkes again goes to their rescue by pulling them back up the pipe by its tail feathers, the ability to bear heavy loads another of the phoenix's many gifts.

Chapter 18: "Dobby's Reward"

Arriving at McGonagall's office, Harry, Ron, and Ginny find the Weasleys waiting for them along with Dumbledore. Harry tells the eager listeners what transpired but stops before explaining who opened the chamber since he hopes to avoid incriminating Ginny. Dumbledore rescues him by wondering how Voldemort managed to enchant Ginny when he is rumored to be in Albania. She explains being bewitched by the diary and Dumbledore assures her no punishment will be issued. The Weasleys leave with Ginny to go to the hospital wing, and Dumbledore dispatches McGonagall so he can address Ron and Harry privately. He grants them Special Awards for Services to the School and 200 points apiece for Gryffindor. Ron takes Lockhart to the infirmary, and Dumbledore talks to Harry alone.

Harry confesses his fears about being like Riddle to Dumbledore, who reassures him that even though Voldemort might have transferred some of his powers to Harry when he attacked Harry so many years ago, the difference between them is that Harry asked to be in Gryffindor. Dumbledore remarks that this choice "makes [Harry] very different from Tom Riddle. It is our choices, Harry, that show what we truly are, far more than our abilities" (333). As Dumbledore sits down to write a letter to Azkaban requesting Hagrid's release and a posting

for a new Defense Against the Dark Arts teacher, an outraged Lucius Malfoy arrives with Dobby. Dumbledore suggests that Lucius planted Voldemort's diary on Ginny as a way of spreading resentment of Muggle-borns throughout the wizarding community. Infuriated, Lucius turns to leave, and Harry has an idea. Harry takes the diary, stuffs it into his sock, and hands it to Lucius, who promptly casts the sock aside and tells Harry he will meet a bitter end as his parents did. Dobby catches the sock and is delighted to be free since he has been presented with a piece of clothing from his master, the only way a house-elf can be freed of its service. The final year feast is filled with excitement including Hagrid's return and the canceling of exams.

CRITICAL COMMENTARY

After the steadily increasing popularity of *Sorcerer's Stone*, hopes were high for a repeat of the popular appeal that the first novel had so readily garnered. This second novel cemented the world and work of Rowling as commercially and critically successful and launched the global phenomenon—including merchandising and film deals—"POTTERMANIA." The book is more predictable and less rich narratively than some of the others in the series, or at least was assessed as such before the publication of all seven novels; however, once Rowling released *Half-Blood Prince* and *Deathly Hallows*, her longterm view toward plot became more obvious, and aspects of *Chamber of Secrets* took on new resonance within the larger picture of the entire series.

Chamber of Secrets is distinguished by its role in introducing some of the most important themes explored in the rest of the series that are not present in the first novel. Whereas culture shock and questions about identity are introduced in *Sorcerer's Stone*, others—including the interspecies conflict exploited by Voldemort, campaigns for social justice initiated on behalf of house-elves, and Rowling's specific critique of institutional corruptions and bureaucracy—do not emerge until the second novel. Similarly *Chamber of Secrets* introduces readers to a humanized Voldemort—Tom Marvolo Riddle—and while readers do not learn as much in the second book about him as in *Half-Blood Prince*, they begin to understand the charismatic young wizard who went on to become the powerful and destructive force that sparked a war.

Identity

One of the central concerns of the series is identity, which critics hypothesize at least partly explains the books' broad appeal to child, adolescent, and young adult readers, who intimately relate to Harry's struggle to understand himself and his place in the world. In the first novel Harry's experience depicts him as a "child of destiny." This literary strategy has been the basis for many successful works for both adults and children, especially in fantasy, from the pig Wilbur in *Charlotte's Web* to "Wart," or the young King Arthur, in *The Sword and the Stone* to the comparatively recent *Eragon* series by Christopher Paolini. This "child of destiny" construct forms the center of Rowling's plot: Harry discovers that he is not, as has long believed, a penniless and average orphan but a wizard, one who does not simply possess the ability to execute magic but also is the linchpin in a historical drama of good and evil and has the admiration of the population of an entire parallel world. For example, though any wizarding family would be familiar with house-elves as a species, Harry has the troubling experience of coming face to face with one in the chapter "Dobby's Warning," when the admiring house-elf who later becomes central to the series both fawns over and sabotages Harry as part of a larger plan to protect him from the Malfoys' evil machinations and Voldemort's clutches. Harry learns quickly that Dobby reflects the views of a number of magical species who see him as the symbol of Voldemort's defeat—and the end of an oppressive and dark era in wizarding history. Coming to grips with this knowledge—and continuing to live up to unstated expectations from classmates, teachers, and perfect strangers—is Harry's struggle, and it continues into the second book.

In addition to discovering that he is indeed something and someone far greater than the humble and unloved orphan he has lived as for 11 years, Harry explores other questions about who he is and what his values are. These questions dramatize the same sort of struggles that his young readers also experience. Though Harry's experience is in a far different context—as a kind of "destined child" with magical powers—one of the primary appeals of the series is the protagonist's feeling of "not belonging." From the first chapter of the series Harry experiences conflicts and a feeling of alienation from his adoptive family, the Dursleys. When he discovers his true heritage and transitions to Hogwarts, he still struggles to find a place to belong. Even though he finds a niche in Gryffindor and in his good friends, Hermione and Ron, one of the series's central tensions is Harry's quest to find a place that he can call home. In *Chamber of Secrets* the social landscape becomes an especially important part of the narrative. Though child and adolescent readers will not relate to the exact conflict—Harry's fear of being the "heir of Slytherin" and his social ostracism because of it—most or all readers will identify with the fear of being different from peers and the seemingly all-encompassing problem of conforming to the social expectations of peer culture.

Though Harry does not encounter the teenage Voldemort, Tom Riddle, until late in the novel, he begins much earlier than that to explore the increasingly troubling similarities between himself and Voldemort. In *Sorcerer's Stone* Harry learns that his holly and phoenix-feather wand shared a twin core with Voldemort's—a feather from Dumbledore's phoenix Fawkes. By the end of the second novel Harry is even more troubled by the other common traits he shares with Riddle: Both were orphaned as small children and raised in the Muggle world; both have the suspicion–arousing trait of speaking Parseltongue, the language of snakes; both Tom Riddle and Harry Potter have, as Dumbledore notes, a "certain disregard for rules" (333), though it is clear that Harry's inclination is to disregard rules in the service of others while Tom acts only in his own interest. The Sorting Hat reinforces its earlier assertion that Harry "*would* have done well in Slytherin" (206) when he dons it again in Dumbledore's office, making Harry more uneasy about the qualities he shares with Voldemort.

Because the entire series is concerned with Harry's evolving identity, *Chamber of Secrets* only begins to explore its protagonist's emotional and psychological journey of personal development. However, readers see Harry begin to cultivate some of the important moral qualities that will serve him later in the series, including his trademark courage in the face of danger, adherence to an ethical framework, and humility. Harry intervenes when the snake attacks Justin Finch-Fletchley during Lockhart's Dueling Club practice, he rescues Ginny from the basilisk at the book's conclusion and takes on the treacherous teen Voldemort, and he defends Hermione from Malfoy's elitist attack. He and Ron confront the cowardly Gilderoy Lockhart as he is about to abandon Hogwarts rather than face the basilisk. Harry continually proves himself a hero even as he experiences fear, insecurities, and anxiety about who he is.

Social Pressures
His mysterious affiliation with Voldemort and the dark powers he represents also introduce some complex social dynamics that foreshadow the conflicts that emerge in *Goblet of Fire* and *Order of the Phoenix*, including the stigma and disbelief that Harry experience in the fifth book over his assertions that Voldemort has returned. *Chamber of Secrets* gives Harry a taste of this social stigma when he bids a snake that appears during their Dueling Club to leave one of his classmates alone, when he ". . . shouted stupidly at the snake, 'Leave him alone!' And miraculously—inexplicably—the snake slumped to the floor, docile as a thick, black garden hose" (194). Harry is more than shocked to find his classmates angry and frightened rather than grateful, and the incident leads to ostracism from fellow students who have previously been friendly, even admiring.

Even though his Parseltongue skills are handy at the end of the novel, they are viewed with suspicion and sometimes horror by other students because of their association with the Dark Arts. After the Dueling Club incident Harry overhears a group of Hufflepuffs in the library in chapter 12 speculating that he is the heir of Slytherin; Ernie McMillan even proposes that "The Boy Who Lived" is not the hero of the wizarding world but rather someone to be viewed with skepticism: "Only a really powerful Dark wizard could have survived a curse like that" (199). This social ostracism foreshadows the alienation he will experience throughout his years at Hogwarts because of his status as the "chosen one" as well as

his unpopular habit of predicting Voldemort's return, as Rowling emphasizes in *Order of the Phoenix*.

Culture Shock
As does the first novel, *Chamber of Secrets* further develops Harry's experience of "culture shock" as he continues to learn about the new world to which he is so central—and starts to realize that human personal and social flaws are as prominent in the wizarding community as they are in Little Whinging. The Dursleys' shallow elitism and contempt for difference are matched if not exceeded by the Malfoys' hatred of nonmagical and nonpureblood people. Part of Harry's heroic quest in *Chamber of Secrets* is to become acculturated to a world that is simultaneously strangely familiar and vastly foreign and that even natives sometimes have difficulty navigating. For example, Ginny is scolded by her parents at the end of the novel for trusting a magical item: "What have I always told you?" says Mr. Weasley. "Never trust anything that can think for itself *if you can't see where it keeps its brain?*" [emphasis in original] (329). If even cultural natives occasionally falter in significant ways in keeping to the "rules" of the community, it is predictable that Harry has plenty of learning—and of course characteristic of a BILDUNGSROMAN, or "coming of age" novel, as the Harry Potter series has been categorized.

Harry demonstrates a growing comfort with his role in the wizarding world, though Ron Weasley often has to serve as a cultural ambassador for him in translating some of the cultural norms that he takes for granted. When Draco calls Hermione a "Mudblood" on the Quidditch pitch, only Ron's angry reaction communicates the offensiveness of the word to Harry. This extends the kind of guidance that Ron has provided throughout the first book, whether explaining what Quidditch is or how wizarding photos work. Hagrid, as well, serves as a respite and a comrade at arms as a fellow nonpureblood in guiding Harry through the complexities of wizarding society.

The mentoring and support of Hogwarts headmaster Albus Dumbledore, which was essential in *Sorcerer's Stone* in orienting Harry to the expectations of his new environment, continues to be important for Harry in *Chamber of Secrets*. The headmaster's tolerance of—if not encouragement of—the subversive methods of Harry and his friends is illustrated in chapter 14, "Cornelius Fudge," when Dumbledore seems aware of the presence of Harry and Ron under the Invisibility Cloak in Hagrid's cottage. When, "speaking very slowly and clearly so that none of them could miss a word," he advises, "I will only truly have left this school when none here are loyal to me. You will also find that help will always be given at Hogwarts to those who ask for it" (264–265). Dumbledore is sometimes cryptic in his advice and evasive in sharing real details about his own background, but, as readers learn later in the series, this is partly a function of his desire to protect Harry from some of the more disturbing details of Harry's childhood—and his seemingly fated confrontation with Voldemort.

Free Will and Destiny

The sorts of choices that Harry will face in *Deathly Hallows* are foreshadowed in this novel: Harry's stories as well as the stories of Tom Riddle (teenage Voldemort) and Ginny Weasley invite readers to consider the philosophical debate over free will versus determinism, choice versus fate. This is a central question in the series: How much control do we have over our fate? By the sixth book in the series Tom Riddle's birth in an orphanage and subsequent institutional childhood clearly invite readers to consider the degree to which he experienced freedom of choice in the kind of character and values he developed, questions that are introduced in this second novel and developed more fully in *Half-Blood Prince*. In *Chamber of Secrets* we see only young Voldemort's thirst for power and his manipulative nature as a young Hogwarts student. It seems that he makes clear choices about his actions, especially since he deliberately frames Rubeus Hagrid for opening the titular Chamber of Secrets.

Harry, as well, struggles with understanding how much of his "destiny" is foreordained and how much is within his control. In *Sorcerer's Stone* Harry begs the Sorting Hat not to put him in Slytherin because even his brief introduction to the wizarding culture has shown him that most of the dark wizards in wizarding history have been from that house, and Harry's impulse for good is strong. However, he is

distraught over the Sorting Hat's initial offer to put him in Slytherin in the first novel. He is equally disturbed while waiting in Dumbledore's office when the Sorting Hat once tells him, "I stand by what I said before . . . you *would* have done well in Slytherin" (206). As he becomes increasingly confused by his knowledge of Parseltongue and his ability to hear the eerie voices others cannot, Harry has to wonder whether he has some inborn predisposition toward dark magic that his will cannot overcome. In the end Rowling seems to speak through the voice of Dumbledore when he advises Harry, "It is our choices, Harry, that show what we truly are, far more than our abilities" (333). The fact that Harry chose Gryffindor over Slytherin seems significant to Dumbledore, and Rowling's message of personal empowerment seems to resonate with most readers.

Celebrity and Fame

A parallel theme in this novel—and one that perhaps became increasingly more important to the author as the series's popularity grew—is that of celebrity, especially the corruptive power of fame. *Chamber of Secrets* is a trenchant indictment of the power of fame to distort those of weak moral character in the figure of Gilderoy Lockhart. Rowling introduces Lockhart when Harry escapes to the Burrow for the remainder of summer holiday; Mrs. Weasley peruses a set of Lockhart's "household manuals" for advice on how to rid the garden of gnomes, her children mocking her addlepated admiration of his winking countenance on the cover: "Oh, he is marvelous," muses Mrs. Weasley, to which Fred remarks, "Mum *fancies* him" (36). Her embarrassment is warranted, as the next chapter introduces readers to the blustering, arrogant, shallow Lockhart, whose book signing at Flourish and Blotts functions as a precursor to the larger role he plays in the book.

An attention monger, Lockhart feels immediately drawn to Harry because of the latter's notoriety, and Lockhart capitalizes on it at every opportunity. As the new Defense Against the Dark Arts teacher he is his own best marketing department, his classroom instruction more an opportunity to showcase his interests and products than education, as evidenced by their first test on

Lockhart's "favorite color," "secret ambition," and "greatest achievement to date" (100). His inflated self-opinion is certainly unequal to his abilities as he demonstrates an inability to execute even the most basic of Defense Against the Dark Arts skills, such as when he sets loose Cornish pixies that he is then unable to recapture, abandoning his young students to the task. Even more irritating to Harry than Lockhart's self-promotion is his condescending attitude. In the chapter "Gilderoy Lockhart," when one of Harry's admirers, Colin Creevey, asks for a photo, Lockhart interrupts and then admonishes Harry, "Let me just say that handing out signed pictures at this stage of your career isn't sensible—looks a tad bigheaded, Harry, to be frank" (98). Rowling's exaggerated portrayal of Lockhart as a smug pretender may possibly critique pretentious celebrities or his fans—such as the swooning females throughout the novel, including Mrs. Weasley and Hermione—who find his braggadocio quite appealing.

The ultimate insult occurs at the end of the novel when Ron and Harry find their Defense Against the Dark Arts teacher packing to leave rather than embarking to rescue the kidnapped Ginny Weasley. Lockhart is not only vapid; he is a fraud and admits as much to Harry and Ron in chapter 16 when he says, "Books can be misleading" and deflects Harry's accusation that he's "just been taking credit for what a load of other people have done" by claiming "it's not nearly as simple as that. There was work involved" (297–298). Boasting of casting memory charms on those who actually accomplished the feats described in his many books, Lockhart evinces outrage and anger at his cowardice from Harry and Ron. As two who have risked their own young lives already for the greater good, they find Lockhart's selfish motives all the more distasteful when he attempts a Memory Charm on Harry and Ron in the Chamber of Secrets and is rendered an amnesiac.

Corrupt Institutions

Chamber of Secrets also introduces Rowling's critique of corrupt institutions and inefficient—and sometimes malicious—bureaucracies. Rowling's most evident critique occurs in Hagrid's cabin in the chapter "Cornelius Fudge" when Minister of Magic Cornelius

Fudge and Lucius Malfoy, Draco's father, manage in a span of several minutes to arrest the gameskeeper Hagrid and unseat Dumbledore as headmaster of Hogwarts. In this chapter Rowling introduces readers to the Minister of Magic of the chapter title. Fudge's actions in response to the crisis over the Chamber of Secrets set the stage for his subsequent cowardly and morally suspect approach to future crises in *Goblet of Fire* and *Order of the Phoenix*. Unpersuaded by Dumbledore's assertion that "Hagrid has my full confidence," Fudge claims that the "Ministry's got to act" and "Hagrid's record's against him. Ministry's got to do something" (261). Motivated by external pressures from powers that be rather than the moral imperative to solve the problem, Fudge considers it more important to be seen as taking action than to take the right action: "I'm under a lot of pressure. Got to be seen to be doing something. If it turns out it wasn't Hagrid, he'll be back and no more said" (261), overlooking, of course, that Hagrid will be spending the interim at Azkaban and exposed to the soul-sucking prison guards. Fudge's failure to show real leadership and his quick acquiescence to the will of Lucius Malfoy's political and social influence foreshadow the minister's future weak-willed nature when Voldemort eventually gains power in later novels. Though both of these mistakes—Hagrid's arrest and Dumbledore's suspension—are rectified quickly, they call attention to the efficient exertion of power that is possible when it is concentrated in few—or the wrong—hands.

Moral Ambiguity

One of the major critiques of the series besides the objections from some religious groups over the novel's use of "witchcraft" has been what could be called its moral ambiguity or perhaps even moral hypocrisy: Seemingly objective moral rules that disapprove of lying and stealing and approve of obeying authority figures and laws are directly contradicted by the actions of the main characters. This moral relativism is sometimes viewed with concern by parents who believe the series promotes inappropriate values and behavior. However, using moral frameworks can be useful in placing the characters' moral development in a context for understanding how and why they make choices that in fact demonstrate a sophisticated rather than inappropriate approach to moral conduct and decision making.

Critics of the series's moral ambiguity typically cite Rowling's characters' subversive actions that are counter to established norms about good conduct and yet are rewarded. For example, Arthur Weasley, a civil servant ministry employee, regularly magically enchants Muggle objects such as the Ford Anglia, even though doing so is against magical law. Similarly Arthur's bewitching of the car enables Harry and Ron to steal it to return to Hogwarts after the platform shuts them out. Other examples of Rowling's alleged promotion of subversive morality include Harry, Ron, and Hermione's stealing ingredients from Snape's office to make the Polyjuice Potion, taking on Crabbe and Goyle's identities to trick Malfoy (including feeding the two Slytherins a sleeping potion and hiding them in a broom closet), and stunning and disarming Lockhart in order to prevent him from fleeing the castle instead of rescuing Ginny.

One way to understand Rowling's portrayal of the rightness of her characters' actions is through the psychologist William Perry's theory of intellectual and moral development that categorizes moral decision making, outlined in his *Forms of Intellectual and Ethical Development in the College Years: A Scheme.* Though the scheme is applied to college students, its general framework can be useful for considering stages of moral development across the human life span. The earliest stage, dualism, defines the knower's attitude toward knowledge as either "right" or "wrong," with little consideration of context. In the more advanced position, "multiplicity" or "subjective knowledge," the thinker either relies entirely on a personal value system because of the sense that "no one" really knows the right answer or presumes that every position or opinion is equally valid. The final stage of Perry's scheme is "contextual relativism" or "procedural knowledge," in which solutions and their appropriateness differ with context and involve making choices dependent upon the situation.

Perry's scheme (and a useful follow-up, *Women's Ways of Knowing: The Development of Self, Voice, and Mind,* by Mary Belenky et al.) can educate readers about the claims of moral ambiguity often directed at the main characters in the Potter series and the books' lack of a definitive moral framework in which lying and stealing are always wrong. Though some readers might be tempted to adopt an "end justifies the means" attitude à la Machiavelli's *Prince,* a more appropriate reading might recognize, as Hermione increasingly does throughout the series, that moral decision making always occurs in a context. Rowling's "message" here seems to be not necessarily to promote disobedience or nonconformity but rather to support a critical evaluation of circumstances—the stakes involved and the risks of inaction—rather than a blind adherence to universal rules that may not account for every context, exigency, or intention.

Blood Status and Prejudice

Other important themes that begin to emerge in this second novel include recurring conflicts over racism, chauvinism, and social hierarchies. Readers have been introduced to the elitism over pureblood status in the first novel by Draco Malfoy, whose early encounters with Harry reveal his preoccupation with the "right sort" of people, which Harry quickly decodes as chauvinism. He rejects Draco because of it, but it is not until *Chamber of Secrets* that readers fully begin to see the extent of the wizarding community's internal strife over divisions based on species and blood status.

The first major conflict over blood status—used for humorous effect but powerful nonetheless—occurs in chapter 7, "Mudbloods and Murmurs," when Malfoy and the Slytherin Quidditch team not only take over the Quidditch pitch but also hurl epithets at Hermione Granger, calling her a "filthy little Mudblood," sparking a duel between Draco and Ron. These are the first but certainly not the last magical exchanges over blood status that will propel the series's narrative.

It is not just, however, blood status and hierarchies within the wizarding community that produce conflict; this second novel also sets the stage for the series's exploration of the oppression and, in the case of house-elves, virtual enslavement, of other species by wizards. For example, *Chamber of Secrets* in chapter 2 introduces Dobby the house-elf, who is essentially a member of a slave class and cannot be freed except by the gift of clothing from his masters. This slave-master relationship is normalized by pureblood wizards, who argue that house-elves enjoy and prefer this relationship to the responsibility that autonomy entails. The oppression of "inferior" classes based on species or blood status becomes a central belief distinguishing the Death Eaters from the Order of the Phoenix and their supporters, and this distinction is complicated by the fact that many of the good characters in the books—including Harry and Ron—are not entirely disturbed by the slavery of house-elves. This tension is illustrated later in the series by the relationship between wizards and other species including goblins, giants, and centaurs.

Though this second novel was slightly less well received than its predecessor and is considered by some critics to be one of the weakest in the series, it plays an important role in introducing and advancing some of the key themes, questions, and character developments of the series. Harry's developing questions about his identity and his role in wizard society and the growing epic battle of good and evil, his relationship with his friends and mentors, thematic questions about racial and interspecies power struggles, and the critical assessment of bloated, corrupt, and inefficient institutions are all key components of this second novel.

INITIAL REVIEWS

Because the Harry Potter series did not gain its enormous popularity and cultural traction until after the third book of the series was published, the first three novels rated fewer and lower-visibility initial reviews than the last four books, which were reviewed in prominent and well-respected newspapers and periodicals. Reviews of the first three books can be found largely in trade periodicals for teachers, newspapers, and popular magazines, while the last four novels merited hotly awaited reviews in prominent publications, such as Michiko Kakutani's *New York Times* review. *Harry Potter and the Chamber of Secrets*, released on July 2, 1998, garnered almost entirely positive reviews praising the novel's inventiveness, imagination, and pacing,

although reviewers offered minor criticisms about the plot's predictability.

Initial reviews of *Chamber of Secrets* highlighted its brisk pacing and successful use of suspense. For example, Janice Del Negro, in the *Bulletin of the Center for Children's Books*, whose target audience is school and public librarians, comments on the dramatic and suspenseful pace, plot twists, and pithy characterization, an assessment that concurs with Martha Parravano's claim in *Horn Book Magazine* that "the atmosphere Rowling creates is unique; the story whizzes along; Harry is an unassuming and completely sympathetic hero". Elizabeth Bukowski in the *Wall Street Journal* calls *Chamber of Secrets* a "refreshing break from the all-too-familiar settings of many of today's novels" (W9) Most reviews comment positively on the novel's ability to hook readers and keep them engaged.

Reviewers also remark on Rowling's brilliant execution of an inventive and fresh entry in the fantasy adventure tradition and Rowling's portrayal of a hero to whom kids can relate. June Cummins in the *Michigan Quarterly Review* writes that the novel's minor weaknesses are balanced by the way the "parallel world at Hogwarts is so well-maintained". Yvonne Zipp in the *Christian Science Monitor* calls it a "charming tale" with all the "staples of a fantasy adventure—secret passageways, swords, monsters, and of course, a hero" (19). The richness of Rowling's literary imagination and her ability to make classic features of the fantasy novel fresh rather than derivative also garnered praise from reviewers. Susan Rogers in the *School Library Journal,* the most influential print journal reviewing children's and young adult media, praised the novel's humor and "inventive, new, matter-of-fact uses of magic that will once again have readers longing to emulate Harry and his wizard friends." *Publishers Weekly* confirms Rogers's assessment, remarking jauntily, "Rowling might be a Hogwarts graduate herself, for her ability to create such an engaging, imaginative, funny, and above all, heartpoundingly suspenseful yarn is nothing short of magical." Deborah Loudon in the *Times Literary Supplement* not only notes that "Hogwarts is a creation of genius" but also remarks upon Rowling's fresh use of traditional narrative elements: "The ingredients of Rowling's success are traditional—strong plots, engaging characters, excellent jokes, and a moral message which flows naturally from the story." Also commended by many periodicals geared toward parents, librarians, and teachers is the family-friendly nature of Rowling's novel. Christine Loomis in *Family Life* calls the novel the "perfect read-aloud for the entire family" (91).

Only a handful of reviews acknowledged weaknesses of the novel. For example, Del Negro claims the book has minor plot inconsistencies and laments the small role of Hermione in this sequel. Other critics, including Cummins and Parravano, believe the book is predictable and formulaic. Cummins calls it "a slightly inferior book" to the first novel because it is "too predictable," while Parravano commends and condemns Rowling's second novel in the same sentence, remarking, "Rowling clearly hit on a winning formula with the first Harry Potter book; the second book—though still great fun—feels a tad, well, formulaic." Even though Andrew Stuttaford in the conservative publication *National Review* found much to praise in the book, from a political perspective he argued that Rowling "reveals typical leftish social prejudices all too typical of the British intelligentsia," citing specifically her portrayal of the villainous Malfoy as rich and aristocratic, the tacky and dreadful bourgeois Dursleys, and the poor but honorable bureaucrat Arthur Weasley.

In the end, however, many reviewers specifically affirm the book's appeal to devotees, and this affirmation suggests the significant role of *Chamber of Secrets* in the series because of its importance in continuing to build not only the larger series narrative but to fulfill the expectations of devoted readers who waited anxiously to determine whether the appeal of the first book could be repeated in the second—and beyond. Many reviewers frame their assessment of *Chamber of Secrets* as comparative—how well it measured up to the first in the series. Charles De Lint in *Fantasy and Science Fiction* articulates this dilemma in his review, noting that the book "proves to be just as enchanting and entertaining as the first book—a rarity in itself, when it comes to books in a series." Rogers

in *School Library Journal* believes that Rowling had succeeded, writing that "fans . . . won't be disappointed," an evaluation echoed by Tena Natale in *Book Report.* A *Publishers Weekly* reviewer confirms that "fans who have been anxiously awaiting the return of young British wizard Harry Potter . . . will be amazed afresh." Loudon comments in the *Times Literary Supplement* that "unlike many sequels, it is as good as its predecessor," and Geraldine Brennan's review in the *Times Educational Supplement* also measures the second book against the first, specifically in the context of its appeal to adult versus child readers: "*Chamber of Secrets* is a tighter, more complex read than *Sorcerer's Stone,* with fewer of the stray story lines that irritated some adult readers (but not children, who seem to appreciate the books for being the kind of sprawling stories they like to write themselves, with unwieldy plots, cliffhangers, sharp asides, and in-jokes)." Overwhelmingly, reviewers agreed that *Chamber of Secrets* satisfies both new and devoted readers.

SCHOLARSHIP

Little current scholarship treats *Chamber of Secrets* in isolation; please see the "Scholarship on the Harry Potter Series" section for works that analyze this novel as part of the larger series.

Two articles address the second book in the series specifically, and each does so in limited ways. The literary theorist Mary Eagleton, in "The Danger of Intellectual Masters," takes a Freudian approach to *Chamber of Secrets,* discussing it in conjunction with the novelist A. S. Byatt's novel *Possession.* Eagleton applies the Freudian notion of "erotic-theoretical transference," or a confusion of the erotic and the instructional, examining the two novels in light of the cultivation of romantic relationships between teacher and student, or the conflation of intellectual admiration with romantic interest. This framework is then applied to the relationship between the celebrity Defense Against the Dark Arts teacher Gilderoy Lockhart and Hermione Granger, who throughout the book is mocked by Ron and Harry for her obvious romantic interest in Lockhart. Eagleton also suggests the climactic scene in which Lockhart botched his attempt to modify Ron's and Harry's memories reflects a transfer of phallic power, with the loss of Lockhart's wand a stand-in for loss of the phallus.

A second brief critical piece, Bill McCarron's "Literary Parallels in *Harry Potter and the Chamber of Secrets*," delves into the etymological significance of multiple character names in *Chamber of Secrets*, tracing the linguistic and literary heritage of characters such as Madam Pince, Gilderoy Lockhart, Marcus Flint, Severus Snape, the mandrake, and Moaning Myrtle. He cites the English poets John Milton and John Donne and the American novelist Thomas Pynchon as sources for Rowling's inspiration in her naming selections.

CHARACTERS

Dobby The Malfoys' house-elf. Dobby first appears as an anguished but mischievous presence at Number Four, Privet Drive, by dropping a cake when the Dursleys have dinner guests. It is later revealed that Dobby's errands are intended to protect Harry from Lucius Malfoy, a suspected supporter of Lord Voldemort, and of Voldemort's plan to kill Harry and restore the Dark Lord to power. As a character, Dobby reflects the allegiance of the many magical species who suffered under the Dark Lord's reign of terror and who feel gratitude for Harry because he vanquished Voldemort. Throughout the novel Dobby intercedes by using the house-elves' own powerful brand of magic. He is to blame for diverting Harry's letters from friends all summer, blocking Ron and Harry's access to platform nine and three-quarters, bewitching the Bludger to target Harry during the match against Slytherin, all at personal risk to himself, as house-elves must punish themselves if they betray their owners. Ultimately Harry's developing sense of social justice manifests itself at the end of the novel when he tricks Lucius Malfoy into freeing Dobby.

Albus Dumbledore Hogwarts headmaster and mentor to Harry. In *Chamber of Secrets* Dumbledore plays a background role. Rowling continues to emphasize his character as wise, patient, and almost omniscient. In *Chamber of Secrets* readers see Dumbledore in his administrative role, issu-

ing or forgiving infractions, such as his rejection of Snape's suggestion early in the novel that Ron and Harry be expelled for arriving at school in the stolen bewitched Ford Anglia and crashing into the Whomping Willow.

Rowling shows Dumbledore as both merciful and judicious throughout—whether siding with those unjustly accused (Hagrid's sentencing to Azkaban) or absolving the innocent (pointing out Ginny as an unwilling participant in Riddle's scheme). Dumbledore always uses his keen insight to relieve Harry's anxieties. Dumbledore's authority is paradoxically reinforced in this novel when Lucius Malfoy, as a member of the school's Board of Governors, orchestrates Dumbledore's suspension by manipulating the other members into signing an order to remove Dumbledore from his position as headmaster. Harry's allegiance to his mentor, even in Dumbledore's absence, is in part the means through which he is able to defeat teenage Voldemort, Tom Riddle, Jr., with the help of Dumbledore's phoenix, Fawkes—whose loyalty, ability to carry heavy loads, and healing tears are all central to Harry's victory over Riddle in the chamber.

Finally, Dumbledore's sagacity appears in his reassurance to Harry in the book's final chapter when he notes, "It is our choices, Harry, that show what we truly are, far more than our abilities" (333), a comment that reflects the series's thematic consideration of the age-old debate of free will versus determinism. In this book Dumbledore continues to assuage Harry's fears that the similarities between Harry and Tom—both determined, both flouters of rules, both Parselmouths—do not predetermine either their character or their course in life. Rowling reinforces Dumbledore's ability to judge character well: Readers learn that Dumbledore was Riddle's Transfiguration teacher and always suspected Riddle's earnest, high-achieving persona was a facade.

Hermione Granger Muggle-born friend of Harry and Ron. Hermione continues to demonstrate her academic skill in this book and is widely regarded as the top student in her year, though quite inflexible about rules and regulations. This novel introduces movement away from this rigid, black-and-white view of human behavior toward a more complex sense of moral responsibility that balances a passion for justice with respect for authority. This is a trajectory the entire series follows concerning the character of Hermione, since her earliest characterization in *Sorcerer's Stone* centers on her inflexibility and shrewish scolding of her classmates—qualities that alienate her from her peers. Beginning with the battle with the troll in the girls' bathroom in *Sorcerer's Stone*, when Hermione lies to save Harry and Ron from punishment, she earns the respect and friendship of the two boys, but it is important that her breaking away from rigid rule following precipitates this change. Hermione earns social credibility the more she challenges authority.

Chamber of Secrets continues this trend. For example, Hermione suggests and spearheads Harry, Ron's, and her brewing of the Polyjuice Potion: She capitalizes on Lockhart's enormous ego as a way of persuading him to sign their permission sheet to check out the Potions book with the recipe. She also suggests they create a distraction in Potions so she can steal the ingredients they need from Snape's office. This evolving sense of morality moves away from her dichotomous view of right and wrong (lying and stealing are always wrong) toward a nuanced and context-specific (though not relativistic) framework that accounts for motives, ends, and the greater good. We continue to see this evolution in Hermione's character throughout the series. Although Hermione learns the identity of the monster through an insight that takes her back to the library, in *Chamber of Secrets* she spends the last part of the novel petrified after an encounter with the basilisk and plays almost no role in the novel's denouement.

Rubeus Hagrid   Hogwarts gamekeeper. Readers learn in this second book in the series that Rubeus Hagrid, the beloved gamekeeper at Hogwarts, was expelled from Hogwarts 50 years ago after being framed by Tom Riddle as the student responsible for opening the Chamber of Secrets. While his role in the second novel is limited, he nonetheless plays an important part in advancing one of the series's overarching themes—justice and injustice, as the Minister of Magic himself appears at Hagrid's cabin midway through the book to sentence him to Azkaban. This is largely because the ministry's own attempts to determine the perpetrator of the attacks on the students have been ineffective, and they need to appear as if they are making progress toward capturing whoever or whatever is attacking Hogwarts.

Readers also learn, through Riddle's memories and Aragog's words, that Hagrid's boundless love for all creatures, regardless of their appearance, penchants, or eating habits, has been lifelong, as we meet the giant spider whom Hagrid lovingly tended from an egg, took to the Forbidden Forest, and helped to create a home.

Gilderoy Lockhart   Defense Against the Dark Arts teacher, wizarding celebrity, and winner of *Witch Weekly*'s Most Charming Smile Award five times in a row. Rowling first refers to Lockhart when Mrs. Weasley consults his book *Gilderoy Lockhart's Guide to Household Pests* to determine the best way to degnome the Weasley family garden. Widely published, Lockhart's book details his exploits—fabricated and plagiarized, readers later learn—vanquishing various magical creatures around the globe. His narcissism is rivaled only by his incompetence as a teacher, as Harry learns at Flourish and Blotts, when he, Hermione, and the Weasleys are purchasing their schoolbooks. Lockhart has required them to purchase his entire oeuvre. During a bookstore press conference he capitalizes on Harry's widespread public visibility for a photo opportunity. As the school year begins, Lockhart's first Defense Against the Dark Arts lesson sets loose pixies, to a disastrous end, and the rest of the year's lessons consist of dramatic reenactments of his alleged victories over malevolent creatures, much to the chagrin of most of his students. Hermione is strangely mesmerized and forgiving of Lockhart's shortcomings, as are most of the witches, who are dazzled by his smooth talking and luxuriant locks.

Determining the target of Rowling's scathing critique in the figure of Gilderoy Lockhart remains difficult. Does she attack the easily duped females of the book who overlook his obvious personality flaws because of his charms, or a culture that showers shallow hams like Lockhart with book contracts and magazine covers? Lockhart plays a significant role in the novel's climax as his true persona is revealed. His cowardice in attempting to slink away from responsibility rather than take on the basilisk shocks and disgusts Harry and Ron, as do his egocentrism and his moral laxity when he attempts to erase both of their memories to camouflage that cowardice. Ultimately, Lockhart is revealed to be ineffective as a teacher as well as a Defense Against the Dark Arts practitioner. At the end of the novel his backfired memory charm is a suitable punishment as his erased memory leaves all of his charming personality with none of the inflated ego.

Neville Longbottom   Friend of Harry's and a fellow Gryffindor. Neville appears sporadically in the second book and as such plays a very small role in the plot of *Chamber of Secrets,* appearing primarily in scenes in the Gryffindor common room, at meals, or in classroom scenes. His role is diminished from the first book, when Neville's courageous challenge of his friends' rule breaking earned Gryffindor the winning 10 points they needed to earn the House Cup, and his role increases steadily throughout the series when he becomes one of the core group of Hogwarts students who stand against Voldemort beside Harry, Ron, and Hermione, among others.

Draco Malfoy   Harry's rival and a member of the House of Slytherin. Draco Malfoy emerges as a villainous figure in the series and a prototypical Slytherin whose unctuous demeanor wins him the approval of professors like Snape even as his insincerities are obvious to others, including Harry, Ron, and Hermione. Later in the series readers will learn more about Draco as a complex figure, but by *Chamber of Secrets* Draco has a malicious sheen with few redeeming qualities. New developments in the second novel for Draco include his bribing his way onto the Slytherin Quidditch team as Seeker when his father provides the entire team with new state-of-the-art *Nimbus Two Thousand and Ones.* Readers also learn the extent to which Draco has

inherited his father's mania for pureblood status and his zeal for tormenting Muggle-borns and half-bloods. Readers are introduced to Malfoy's father, Lucius, whose single-minded pursuit of the eradication of nonpureblood wizards from Hogwarts manifests itself in his attempts to unseat Dumbledore as headmaster, a crusade that continues throughout the series.

Minerva McGonagall   Transfiguration professor and head of Gryffindor House. Like Dumbledore, McGonagall serves administrative functions throughout the second book but tends to be simultaneously nurturing and protective. It is McGonagall who bears the troubling news that Hermione has been petrified to Ron and Harry; this is not coincidental since McGonagall, in many ways, functions as a mother figure for students at Hogwarts. McGonagall assigns detentions for Harry and Ron when they arrive at school so infelicitously via flying car; she announces new security measures and cancels Quidditch practice; McGonagall often assists Dumbledore with tasks, escorts students, and grants reprieves, but she is on the whole a static and minor character who develops little over the course of *Chamber of Secrets.*

Harry Potter   The novel's protagonist and a member of Gryffindor. As does the first novel in the series, *Chamber of Secrets* documents not only Harry's epic battle between the brewing forces of good and evil but also his internal struggle to learn more about himself—his history, his family, and the world he has been ushered into so abruptly. The series focuses primarily on Harry's struggle to define his identity. Like the average teen, Harry is struggling to determine his values, goals, and priorities, but he is also learning more about the wizarding world, which is relatively new to him, as well as his own already notorious place in it. *Chamber of Secrets* continues exploring that struggle.

Further, the book introduces readers to Tom Marvolo Riddle, the teenage version of Lord Voldemort; Rowling also examines the many similarities he and Harry share. Harry mulls over, often with great anguish, how he defines himself and whether he knows himself, especially as he learns about the multiple parallels between them: Both orphans and Parselmouths, raised in the Muggle world, with natural magical talents and an irreverent spirit, Riddle and Harry share backgrounds and characteristics that are only beginning to be revealed in *Chamber of Secrets*. Further Rowling cultivates Riddle and Harry as sort of doppelgangers, two sides of the same coin, who advance one of the series's major themes about the power of individual moral agency—everyday choices over predestination.

Harry's relationships with his new friends and mentors continue to evolve over the course of *Chamber of Secrets*, as well. Only in his second year at Hogwarts and still becoming oriented to the culture and history of the wizarding world, Harry continues to learn about the stories, myths, and practices that those raised within it take for granted. Harry and readers become oriented to some of the tensions of wizard England, an opportunity for Rowling to enrich some of the important themes of the series. Harry learns about the term *Mudblood*, an offensive epithet for wizards from nonmagical families. Harry begins to understand that some of the elitist hierarchies, prejudices, and forms of discrimination that trouble the Muggle world are equally present in his new environment. He also must acknowledge the injustices, corruption, and hypocrisies such as Hagrid's unjust imprisonment in Azkaban and Lucius Malfoy's contemptible treatment of his house-elf Dobby, as well as his strong-arming of the school Board of Governors, which enables him to suspend Dumbledore as headmaster.

His friendships with Hermione and Ron continue to grow. Upset and feeling betrayed at the novel's opening because he has not received any letters from his two supposed friends (Rowling later reveals Dobby has been intercepting the letters), Harry deepens his friendship with Ron as he spends time at the Burrow, the Weasleys' home, before the school year begins. He gains an appreciation for the warm and welcoming Weasley family, especially Molly, who takes on an adoptive mother role. Harry's respect and admiration for the brainy Hermione are also confirmed when she not only discovers the identity of the mysterious creature, the basilisk, but

is petrified. Harry and Ron are motivated to find the truth as much to save Ginny as to save their friend from this fate.

Harry also begins to learn more about Albus Dumbledore, and even though he is still reluctant to confide entirely in the headmaster, he learns to trust in the vision and wisdom of Dumbledore, especially when that trust and loyalty are key in helping him defeat both Tom Riddle, Jr., and the basilisk in the climactic battle in the Chamber of Secrets. It is this growing self-confidence that also shapes Harry's growth as a character in this early book in the series. Harry is beginning to define himself as a wizard, a friend, and a leader in addition to understanding his important role as a central figure in wizarding history.

Tom Riddle, Jr./Voldemort   Harry's nemesis; a powerful dark wizard and former member of Slytherin House. *Chamber of Secrets* introduces readers to the teenage version of Voldemort, the dark wizard whose epic story in some ways makes up the plot trajectory of the entire series. Having apparently been banished but not destroyed at the end of *Sorcerer's Stone*, Voldemort reappears in the form of a bewitched diary that has been finagled into Ginny Weasley's possession via Lucius Malfoy, though details are not revealed about where Lucius obtained it. Teenage Tom Riddle, Jr., proves an important narrative innovation by Rowling in that he allows the book to position Harry and Tom as foils or doppelgangers, two sides of the same coin, who, beyond being protagonist and antagonist in this series, also serve as a literary meditation on the nature of free will and determinism.

Chamber of Secrets remains an important book in the series because of the role it plays in setting up the last two books, *Half-Blood Prince* and *Deathly Hallows*. Beyond learning Voldemort's given name—*Tom Marvolo Riddle*—readers also see a little about Riddle's tenure at Hogwarts and how his charisma and determination manifested themselves even in his youngest years, explaining partially how he grew to such power and with such a devoted legion of followers after leaving Hogwarts. A master manipulator from the beginning, Tom Riddle, Jr., tells his story to Ginny and then to Harry, and readers can start to understand Riddle's compelling nature. A favorite of the then-headmaster, Armando Dippet, Riddle confesses to Harry in the Chamber of Secrets confrontation that the one person he could not charm was Transfiguration professor Albus Dumbledore, another example of the paradoxes and dichotomies that define the Riddle-Potter relationship: Even as they could not be more opposite in their appeal to the patriarchs of the novels, they bear disturbing similarities to each other—both orphans, both raised in the Muggle world, both Parselmouths. *Chamber of Secrets* begins to introduce readers to the complexities of Voldemort's and Harry's relationship.

Further, the teenage Tom Riddle, Jr., holds important clues to the adult Voldemort readers will encounter in later books. Along with *Half-Blood Prince, Chamber of Secrets* serves as one of the two books in the series that begin to document Riddle's evolution into the nefarious Voldemort and that try to explain the origins of the evil mastermind—in some ways the book seeks to humanize Voldemort even as it seems Tom Riddle, Jr., had very few choices in his life (though they may have been the important ones).

Severus Snape The Potions professor and head of Slytherin House. As is the case of many of the teachers in *Chamber of Secrets,* Snape evolves little as a character. Readers continue to see the strained and hostile relationship that persists between Snape and Harry, though this relationship will grow more complex over the next five books. The initial and growing interpersonal hostility is first illustrated in the chapter "The Whomping Willow," when Ron and Harry arrive at Hogwarts via a flying car. Snape immediately commandeers them from the Sorting Ceremony and argues that they deserve punishment not just for their flagrant disrespect for Hogwarts rules, but also for their disregard for wizarding protocol, since the flying car's invisibility function failed and several Muggles saw them on their trip. Snape goes so far as to recommend expulsion, which Dumbledore and McGonagall, their head of house, wisely reject. Nonetheless, Snape's

venom toward Harry is demonstrated through his contemptuous treatment of Harry in class and in the dueling club, where Snape deliberately partners Draco and Harry, knowing their animosity for each other.

Ginny Weasley Sister of Ron Weasley and new Hogwarts student; member of Gryffindor. Readers see little of Ginny in the first book, except a minor appearance at the train station. Even though she is central to the plotline of *Chamber of Secrets,* we also see little of her in this book, when compared with the other, more central characters of the novel. Rowling introduces Ginny in the third chapter when Harry, Ron, and the Weasley twins arrive at the Burrow. Rowling implies throughout the novel through the words of various Weasleys and even Hagrid that Ginny has a schoolgirl crush on Harry. However, Rowling does not reveal Ginny's most important role in the novel until the last two chapters: Ginny has been used as a vehicle by Tom Riddle for returning to corporeal form via a secret diary that made its way into her possession.

Throughout the book Ginny struggles to assert herself and has difficulty adjusting to the new world of boarding school in her first year; Rowling suggests that Ginny feels lonely and has a hard time creating a social circle. She appears intermittently in scenes with Harry, Ron, and Hermione and often behaves shyly. At this point in the series she has not entered the inner circle of friends including Harry, Ron, Hermione, and Neville, among others.

Nonetheless, Ginny is essential to *Chamber of Secrets* because she has been confiding in Tom Riddle's magical diary and through her growing emotional intimacy with the memory of Tom Riddle, Jr., has empowered him to reenter the wizarding world in at least this limited form. She has also been enchanted to open the titular Chamber of Secrets and perform other troubling acts, such as murdering the roosters (basilisks flee from their cry as it is fatal to them) and painting the disturbing messages on the castle walls that appear throughout the novel. It is Ginny's abduction that inspires Harry and Ron to take action, as her kidnapping propels them to disarm Lockhart, use their knowledge to locate the

Chamber of Secrets, and puzzle out access to it in order to rescue her.

Ginny is unconscious for most of the book's climax—Harry's battle with the memory of Tom Riddle and the basilisk—but in the final chapter, she figures heavily in the way Rowling begins to develop thematic questions of free will, choice, and identity. Ginny is horrified that she has participated in Riddle's evil project, and Dumbledore's assurance that she is not to be held responsible for her actions in this case may foreshadow (and call on the past) curses employed by both Voldemort and his supporters in their relentless quest for power and control. This is a theme explored through Harry's character as well.

Ron Weasley   Harry and Hermione's best friend and a fellow Gryffindor. At first, Ron seems to have abandoned his best friend because Harry has not received any letters from him over the summer, but eventually we learn that Dobby has been intercepting the letters, and in fact Ron remains a true and dedicated friend. This is confirmed when he, Fred, and George go to great—illegal, even—lengths to free Harry from the prison that the Dursleys' house has literally become, including its bars on the windows. Harry's and Ron's friendship deepens in this novel as their relationship takes on brotherly contours because Harry stays with the Weasleys at their home, the Burrow, for a period before the school year starts. Harry is immediately taken with the Weasley family because of the warm, loving, and jovial environment of their home and the gracious welcome and genuine love they show for him even from the beginning of their acquaintance.

Ron often serves as a cultural ambassador for Harry, as he is the only one of their trio who has grown up in the wizarding world (Hermione's parents are Muggle dentists). Pureblood but poor, Arthur and Molly Weasley have instilled in their children an inherent sense of appreciation for diverse cultures and creatures as well as a sense of justice and egalitarianism, such that Ron does not demonstrate the chauvinism and elitism of some of his fellow purebloods, such as Draco Malfoy

(although he does scoff at one of his family members, who lives in the Muggle world). Instead, he often takes on the defense not only of his friends but of a larger sense of justice and equality that Voldemort and his followers do not possess (though this does not translate into his attitude toward house-elves, unfortunately). This is illustrated during the fight that erupts before a Quidditch practice when Draco insults Hermione with the term *Mudblood,* a racial epithet that Harry only learns to understand through his association with cultural guides like Ron and Hagrid.

The adventures of *Chamber of Secrets* often involve Ron and Harry, most notably their trip into the Forbidden Forest to "follow the spiders" as Hagrid directs them and their foray into the Chamber of Secrets with Lockhart. While the series as a whole charts the relationship of the friendship of Ron, Harry, and Hermione, *Chamber of Secrets* accounts for the growing bond between Harry and Ron, who not only survives confrontation of one of his greatest fears—spiders—but also feels gratitude toward Harry for saving his sister.

FILM ADAPTATION

"Hogwarts is back in session," one of the taglines for the second Harry Potter film, enticed new and dedicated fans alike. WARNER BROTHERS released the film in November 2002; it first premiered in the United Kingdom on November 3, premiered in the United States on November 14, and was released for the general public on November 15 (hence the tagline "The second year begins November 15"), almost exactly one year after the release of the first Harry Potter film, *Philosopher's/Sorcerer's Stone.* Five days before the release of *Chamber of Secrets* Rowling announced that she had completed the fifth novel in the series, *Order of the Phoenix.* With this announcement frenzy built around all things Harry Potter, accounting for its $88 million opening weekend. The box office figures were slightly lower than the sales the first Harry Potter film had generated, but *Chamber of Secrets* was in strict competition with one of Britain's other most famous and beloved heroes, James Bond. *Chamber of Secrets* proved to be serious competition for the Bond film

Ron Weasley and his twin brothers use a bewitched turquoise Ford Anglia to rescue Harry from Number Four, Privet Drive, in *Harry Potter and the Chamber of Secrets;* this car used in the film adaptation is on display at Warner Brothers Studios. *(Photo by Jan Klaver/Used under a Creative Commons license)*

Die Another Day, which just slightly edged ahead of *Chamber of Secrets.*

At 161 minutes the second Harry Potter film is longer than the first and, in fact, remains the longest of the first six films, despite the second novel's comparatively short length. David Ansen of *Newsweek* refers to the running time of the film as "bloated," a descriptor that captures some fans' reactions about the sluggish pace of selections of the movie wedged between moments of intense action. Even while the credits roll to their close, the filmmakers continue to tell the story of *Chamber of Secrets* and provide entertainment for the audience with the often-missed scene involving Gilderoy Lockhart; the camera pans down to Flourish and Blotts and a humorous adver-

tisement of Lockhart in a straitjacket, speaking as one whose mind had been obliviated.

Chris Columbus and Steve Kloves returned as director and screenwriter for the second Harry Potter film. They used many of the same techniques they had with *Philosopher's/Sorcerer's Stone,* such as remaining very faithful to Rowling's text and using a palette of vibrant colors to maintain the Disneyesque atmosphere they had created for Rowling's world with the first film. The filmmakers accurately portrayed Rowling's text, but, as Dominic Mohan of the *London Sun* observes, they do "a much better job than the first of unlocking the magic from her wizard prose." And as Brian Bethune of *Maclean's* suggests, "Columbus can hardly be faulted for refusing to argue with success" (73). Bright colors cannot mask the darker elements of the film, however, including prevalent racism and creatures scarier than what children encountered in the first film. Taglines like "Dobby has come to warn you sir," "The Chamber of Secrets has been opened. Enemies of the heir . . . beware!" and "Something evil has returned to Hogwarts!" testify to the more mature aspects of the film, which earned the movie its PG rating. The director cautioned parents about the rating and darker content, stating, "If you have a seven-year-old or under and you are thinking about taking them to the movie then talk to them about it. Parents tend to ignore the PG rating, which is a mistake."

The cast for *Chamber of Secrets* was built upon the exceptional cast already assembled for the first Harry Potter film, with some very notable and successful additions. The most praised actor to join the ensemble was Kenneth Branagh, who won British Supporting Actor of the Year for his performance as Lockhart by the London Critics Circle Film Awards. Lisa Schwarzbaum of *Entertainment Weekly* offers that Branagh's role is one "for which the preternaturally seasoned fellow has apparently waited all his life." Eleanor Gillespie of the *Atlanta Journal-Constitution* referred to Branagh's performance as "shamelessly funny" and described the actor as a "welcome addition" to the Harry Potter cast. Jason Isaacs also received glowing reviews for his performance as Draco Malfoy's father, Lucius. Bethune writes that "Jason Isaacs as Lucius Malfoy and Kenneth Branagh as the narcissistic fop Gilderoy Lockhart, turn in note-perfect performances" (73). Ansen of *Newsweek* writes that Isaacs's performance resonates with viewers because he seems to "[ooze] freeze-dried evil." Schwarzbaum calls Isaacs a "worthy adversary" for Branagh, ultimately toasting them both.

Other actors who either joined the cast or played larger roles in *Chamber of Secrets* include Robert Hardy as Cornelius Fudge, Julie Walters as Molly Weasley, Mark Williams as Arthur Weasley, and Toby Jones (who supplied the voice of Dobby the house-elf).

The largest roles, naturally, belonged to the students, about whom critics from *Sight and Sound* also claimed, "Some of [their] performances might have been better rendered by pixels". Conversely, Ansen of *Newsweek* argued that the three kids "radiate a newfound confidence." James Parker of the *American Prospect* provides a sarcastic view on how the children, specifically Hermione, have aged since the last film: "Hermione (Emma Watson)—now she's a great girl, every young boy's dream, a literal spellbinder. Dark hair, dark eyebrows; she rubs together a couple of Latin-sounding syllables and the sparks of magic fly. Wand in hand, she could light your cigarette for you." Bethune's review of the children is tamer, offering that "Hermione is very good [. . . but] Radcliffe has grown the most" (73). Rupert Grint remains a master of the art of facial expression. The scene in which he attempts to curse Malfoy but instead curses himself because of his faulty wand serves as a particularly striking example of his talent. The slugs that he vomits up were flavored like different types of fruit, so holding them in his mouth and then releasing them, he says, were not painful experiences at all. His faces of utter disgust during the scene, however, were so convincing that they actually had adverse effects on some of his viewers. In at least one theater in Norway, a movie complex manager reported children vomiting at least once a showing during the aforementioned scene because of the way Grint reacted to the "slugs."

Other actors joined the ranks of Hogwarts students in *Chamber of Secrets*, including Bonnie Wright as Ginny Weasley, Christian Coulson as Tom Riddle, Jr., and, most notably, Shirley Henderson as Moaning Myrtle. Henderson is the oldest actor to play a Hogwarts students (in her 30s) and is remembered for her shrill voice and constant sobbing; Schwarzbaum of *Entertainment Weekly* writes that Henderson "squeaks eloquently."

Reviews on the film in general tackled issues similar to those critics had with the first film: Critics from *Sight and Sound* claim that the movie "[follows] slavishly close to its J. K. Rowling source novel," a criticism also offered by the screenplay writer Steve Kloves. The London *Times*'s Barbara Ellen offers that "like its predecessor, *The Chamber of Secrets* lacks the kind of delicacy and intensity that will ensure its ultimate memorability." Similarly, Ansen claims that "the Harry Potter movies aren't half as wonderful as they ought to be" and that "they feel created from the outside in. Magic isn't made by committee."

Ansen also describes the film as "a kiddie monster movie"; Harry's final battle with the basilisk would surely have earned it such a title. Some critics praised the special effects used for creatures like the basilisk and Dobby the house-elf, but others argued the creatures were poor excuses for computer animation.

On the whole critics seem to agree that the second *Harry Potter* film is better than the first. The *Atlanta Journal-Constitution*'s Eleanor Ringel Gillespie writes that "[Harry's] back, and he's better. Much better." Similarly Schwarzbaum of *Entertainment Weekly* claims that the film is "an improvement" over *Philosopher's/Sorcerer's Stone.* Joe Morgenstern of the *Wall Street Journal* writes, "This new *Harry Potter* has its flaws, but it's better, as well as darker, than the first." And Steven Rea of the *Philadelphia Inquirer* summarizes the movie as "darker, scarier and somewhat better than *Sorcerer's Stone.*" Roger Ebert describes the film as "a glorious movie," and Parker of the *American Prospect* calls the film "sumptuous."

Like the first Harry Potter film, *Chamber of Secrets* received nominations for many awards and was actually awarded the Empire Award for Special Contribution to British Cinema and a BMI Film Music Award for John Williams, as well as the Critics Choice Award from the Broadcast Film Critics Association (for his combined work on *Harry Potter, Minority Report,* and *Catch Me If You Can*). The director, Chris Columbus, started a talent-rich and successful tradition with the first two Harry Potter films. New directors would learn from his choices, build upon the foundation he created, and find success of their own while indebted to the founder.

WORKS CITED AND FURTHER READING

Albertazzi, Paola. "Academic Medicine: Time for Reinvention." *BMJ: British Medical Journal* 328, no. 7,430 (2004): 46–47.

Ansen, David. "Mild about Harry." *Newsweek,* 18 November 2002. Available online. URL: http://

www.newsweek.com/id/66444. Accessed November 22, 2009.

Belenky, Mary, Blythe McVicker Clinchy, Nancy Rule Goldberger, and Jill Mattuck Tarule. *Women's Ways of Knowing: The Development of Self, Voice, and Mind.* New York: Basic, 1986.

Bethune, Brian. "Chamber of Marvels: Harry Potter, Take Two, Is as Stylish as the Original." *Maclean's,* 25 November 2002, 73.

Binnendyk, Lauren, and Kimberly Schonert-Reichl. "Harry Potter and Moral Development in Pre-Adolescent Children." *Journal of Moral Education* 31, no. 2 (2002): 195–201.

Brennan, Geraldine. "Absolutely Wizard." *Times Educational Supplement,* 25 December 1998, 22–24.

Brown, Jennifer, and Roback, Diana. "Forecasts: Children's Books." *Publishers Weekly,* 31 May 1999, 94–98.

Brown, Stephen. "Harry Potter and the Marketing Mystery: A Review and Critical Assessment of the Harry Potter Books." *Journal of Marketing* 66, no. 1 (2002): 126–130.

Bukowski, Elizabeth. "Mad about Harry." *Wall Street Journal: Eastern Edition,* 25 June 1999, p. W9.

Carey, Brycchan. "Hermione and the House-Elves: The Literary and Historical Contexts of J. K. Rowling's Antislavery Campaign." In *Reading Harry Potter: Critical Essays.* Westport, Conn.: Praeger, 2003.

Cummins, June. Review of *Harry Potter and the Sorcerer's Stone* and *Harry Potter and the Chamber of Secrets. Michigan Quarterly Review* 39, no. 3 (2000): 661–666.

De Lint, Charles. "Books to Look For." *Fantasy and Science Fiction* 98, no. 1 (2000): 35–39.

Del Negro, Janice. Review of *Harry Potter and the Chamber of Secrets. Bulletin of the Center for Children's Books* 53, no. 1 (1999): 28.

Eagleton, Mary. "The Danger of Intellectual Masters: Lessons from Harry Potter and Antonia Byatt." *Revista Canaria de Estudios Ingleses* 48 (2004): 61–75.

Ebert, Roger. "Review: *Harry Potter and the Chamber of Secrets.*" *Chicago Sun-Times,* 15 November 2002. Available online. URL: http://rogerebert.suntimes.com/apps/pbcs.dll/article?AID=/20021115/

REVIEWS/211150304/1023. Accessed November 22, 2009.

Eccleshare, Julia. "Letter from London." *Publishers Weekly*, 31 August 1998, 21.

Ellen, Barbara. "Review: *Harry Potter and the Chamber of Secrets.*" *Times*, 14 November 2002. Available online. URL: http://entertainment.timesonline.co.uk/tol/arts_and_entertainment/film/article828645.ece. Accessed November 22, 2009.

"Fiction Reprints." *Publishers Weekly*, July 24, 20005, 95.

Gillespie, Eleanor. "Review: *Harry Potter and the Chamber of Secrets.*" *Atlanta Journal-Constitution*, 15 November 2002. Available online. URL: http://www.imdb.com/name/nm0000110/news?year=2002. Accessed November 22, 2009.

Hurst, Carol Otis. "Crowd Pleasers." *Teaching Pre-K–8* 30, no. 2 (October 1999): 86–87.

Lipson, Eden Ross. "Books' Hero Wins Young Minds." *New York Times*, 12 July 1999, p. E1.

Loomis, Christine. Review of *Harry Potter and the Chamber of Secrets*. *Family Life* (September 1999), 91.

Loudon, Deborah. "At Hogwarts." Review of *Harry Potter and the Chamber of Secrets*. *Times Literary Supplement*, 19 September 1998, 28–33.

Lurie, Alison. "Not for Muggles." *New York Review of Books*, 16 December 1999, 6–7.

Margolis, Rick, and Amanda Ferguson. "There's Something about Harry." *School Library Journal* 45, no. 4 (April 1999): 18–20.

McCarron, Bill. "Basilisk Puns in *Harry Potter and the Chamber of Secrets.*" *Notes on Contemporary Literature* 36, no. 1 (2006): 2.

———. "Literary Parallels in Harry Potter and the Chamber of Secrets." *Notes on Contemporary Literature* 33 (2003): 7–8.

Mohan, Dominic. "New Potter Film Is Magic." 8 November 2002. Available online. URL: http://www.thesun.co.uk/sol/homepage/features/life/article182798.ece. Accessed November 22, 2009.

Morgenstern, Joe. "Chamber of Secrets Is More Sure in Its Magic." *Wall Street Journal*, 15 November 2002. Available online. URL: http://online.wsj.com/article/SB1037313235288318468.html. Accessed November 22, 2009.

Natale, Tena. "Reviews: Fiction." *Book Report* 18, no. 2 (September/October 1999): 62–63.

Nye, Lesley. "Editor's Review." *Harvard Educational Review* 71, no. 1 (2001): 136–145.

Oxoby, Marc. Reviews of *Harry Potter and the Chamber of Secrets* (2002) and *The Lord of the Rings: The Two Towers*. (movies). *Film and History* 33, no. 1 (2003): 67–69.

Parker, James. "Hero Worship: James Bond, Harry Potter, and the Big-Movie Machine." *American Prospect*, 30 December 2002. Available online. URL: http://www.prospect.org/cs/articles?article=hero_worship_123002. Accessed November 22, 2009.

Parravano, Martha. Review of *Harry Potter and the Chamber of Secrets*. *Horn Book Magazine* 75, no. 4 (July/August 1999): 472–473.

Pashak, Barrett. "Magic-Lite for the Pre-Teen Set." *Report/Newsmagazine* (Albert Edition) 26, no. 44 (1999): 53.

Perry, William. *Forms of Intellectual and Ethical Development in the College Years: A Scheme*. New York: Holt, Rinehart & Winston, 1968.

Rea, Steven. "Review: *Harry Potter and the Chamber of Secrets.*" *Philadelphia Inquirer*, 15 November 2002. Available online. URL: http://www.philly.com/philly/entertainment/movies/A_darker_creepier_funnier_Harry_Potter.html. Accessed November 22, 2009.

"Review: *Harry Potter and the Chamber of Secrets.*" *Sight and Sound* 13, no. 1 (January 2003): 47–49.

Rogers, Susan. "Grades 5 and Up: Fiction: Review of *Harry Potter and the Chamber of Secrets.*" *School Library Journal* 45, no. 7 (July 1999): 99–100.

Rollin, Lucy. "Among School Children: The Harry Potter Books and the School Story Tradition." *South Carolina Review* 34, no. 1 (2001): 198–208.

Schwarzbaum, Lisa. "Review: *Harry Potter and the Chamber of Secrets.*" *Entertainment Weekly*, 13 November 2002. Available online. URL: http://www.ew.com/ew/article/0,,389817~1~0~harrypotterandchamber,00.html. Accessed November 22, 2009.

Siegel, Lee. "Fear of Not Flying." *New Republic* 221, no. 21 (1999): 40–44.

Stuttaford, Andrew. "It's Witchcraft." *National Review* 51, no. 19 (1999): 60–62.

Tucker, Nicholas. "The Rise and Rise of Harry Potter." *Children's Literature in Education* 30, no. 4 (1999): 221–234.

Witschonke, Christopher. "Harry Potter Casts His Spell in the Classroom. *Middle School Journal* 37, no. 3 (2006): 4–11.

Yeo, Michelle. "*Harry Potter and the Chamber of Secrets:* Feminist Interpretations/Jungian Dreams." *Simile: Studies in Media and Information Literacy Education* 4, no. 1 (2004): 1.

Zipp, Yvonne. "Swooping to Stardom." *Christian Science Monitor* 91, no. 141 (June 17, 1999): 19.

Harry Potter and the Prisoner of Azkaban (1999)

SYNOPSIS

Chapter 1: "Owl Post"

The third installment of Harry's adventure begins with Harry studying secretly in his room, since the Dursleys have hidden away all of his school supplies in order to keep Harry's life as a wizard as secret as possible. The Dursleys are no more accepting of Harry's status as a wizard than when they first learned about it; Uncle Vernon, in fact, has lately become even more irritated with the wizarding community. When Harry's friend Ron attempted to contact him via telephone (unfamiliar with the way in which it works), he screamed into the receiver, asking for Harry. This angered Uncle Vernon and got Harry into a lot of trouble.

An hour into Harry's 13th birthday he notices something flying outside. The creature flies toward him, and he realizes it is Hedwig, Errol (one of the Weasleys' owls), and another owl. They are bearing birthday gifts for Harry from Ron, Hermione, and Hagrid. Ron sends Harry a clipping from a wizarding newspaper showing their family in Egypt; Arthur Weasley won a drawing and spent the winnings on taking his family to see his son Bill, who works on breaking curses for Gringotts in Egypt. Harry smiles at the picture, seeing the happy family

enjoying themselves; the picture even shows Ron's hand-me-down pet rat Scabbers on his shoulder. Ron also gives Harry a Sneakoscope, a kind of top that spins when someone untrustworthy is in its presence. Hermione gives Harry a broom-servicing kit, and Hagrid gives him the *Monster Book of Monsters,* a book that tries to attack him when he opens it.

Harry also receives a letter from Professor Mc-Gonagall with his usual supplies list, but accompanying it is a permission form for Harry to visit Hogsmeade, the only all-wizarding settlement in Britain. Harry doubts that his aunt or uncle will sign the form but feels better than usual because his thoughtful friends remembered his birthday.

Chapter 2: "Aunt Marge's Big Mistake"

When Harry awakes and goes downstairs the next morning, Uncle Vernon is watching a news broadcast about an escaped prisoner named Sirius Black, who is armed and dangerous. Vernon comments that the only way to deal with people like Black is to hang them. Harry learns that Vernon's sister Marge is going to stay with them for a week. She is a cruel woman who spoils Dudley and abuses Harry. The Dursleys concoct a story that Harry attends a school called St. Brutus's Secure Center for Incurably Criminal Boys. While the idea offends Harry, he finds a way to use it to his advantage. Since the Dursleys are desperate to keep Harry's wizarding world a secret from Aunt Marge, Harry makes an arrangement with his uncle Vernon: If he keeps up the facade about his attendance at St. Brutus's, Uncle Vernon agrees to sign Harry's permission slip for Hogsmeade.

Aunt Marge is a dog breeder and has one of her dogs, Ripper, with her. Aunt Petunia is disgusted by the way Aunt Marge spoils the dog, allowing him even to drink from Petunia's fine china. Aunt Marge shares some of her feelings about the practice of dog breeding, which seem to be passive-aggressive comments about Harry's parents, offering, "If there is something wrong with the bitch, there'll be something wrong with the pup." Harry's temper threatens to get the best of him, but he instead concentrates on the trips to Hogsmeade that a signed permission slip will get him and manages to control his anger.

On her last night with the Dursleys Aunt Marge asks about Harry's parents; Vernon says James Potter was unemployed, angering Harry. Aunt Marge then says they got themselves killed in a car crash, probably while drunk; this statement enrages Harry, who in his anger unintentionally works magic on Aunt Marge, who begins to inflate at an alarming rate. Harry runs to gather his things, followed by Uncle Vernon, who screams that Harry must fix the situation. Harry retorts that she got what she deserved, and with his trunk and Hedwig in her cage, Harry runs off into the night.

Chapter 3: "The Knight Bus"
The anger surging through Harry's veins is soon replaced with distress. Harry realizes he has just done magic outside Hogwarts, and that is grounds for expulsion (Harry is all too familiar with this situation since his similar trouble last year with Dobby and the pudding cake). Harry tries to formulate a plan and, while digging through his trunk, senses something behind him. After performing the lumos spell, Harry shines the light in the direction in which he senses the presence: The small ray of light from his wand outlines a large shaggy shape with two gleaming eyes. Frightened, Harry backs up and into his trunk. He trips and lands in the gutter when there is a loud bang, and a triple-decker purple bus pulls up in front of him: the Knight Bus.

The conductor welcomes Harry to the bus, explaining it is a form of emergency transportation for witches and wizards that will take them wherever they desire to go. Longing to remain unrecognized, Harry tells the conductor that he is Neville Longbottom and that he wants to be taken to the Leaky Cauldron. The bus ride is unsettling, jarred with abrupt stops and quick turns. Harry comments on the newspaper the conductor reads since it has a picture of the criminal who had been on the news earlier at the Dursley home: Sirius Black. Harry learns the nature of Black's crime: He was a staunch follower of Voldemort and killed 13 people with one curse. When officials arrived at the crime scene, they found Black standing alone, laughing eerily. Sirius Black was taken to Azkaban, the wizarding prison, from which no one had ever escaped before;

his ability to escape the prison makes him even more dangerous.

Soon the bus arrives in Diagon Alley, and when Harry disembarks, Minister of Magic Cornelius Fudge is there to greet him. Harry, sure that he will be punished severely for using magic outside school, feels stunned when the minister says Harry will not suffer consequences for what he did to his aunt. Confused, Harry follows Tom, the barkeep of the Leaky Cauldron, to his room, where he is to remain for the next two weeks until the start of the term at Hogwarts.

Chapter 4: "The Leaky Cauldron"
Harry spends most of his days wandering Diagon Alley. One day he notices quite a crowd amassing outside the Quality Quidditch Supplies store, so he stops to see what the fuss is about. A new broom model is on display in the window: the *Firebolt*. Harry sets to acquiring the rest of his school supplies. When he enters the bookstore (Flourish and Blotts), Harry sees copies of the book Hagrid sent him for his birthday; then he understands that Hagrid sent him the book because he would need it that year in school. While gathering the rest of his books, Harry becomes distracted by a book called *Death Omens: What to Do When You Know the Worst Is Coming*. On the cover of the book is a beast resembling the one that Harry thought he saw before boarding the Knight Bus. Disturbed, Harry finishes his shopping and returns to his room at the Leaky Cauldron.

On the last day of holiday Harry meets Ron and Hermione. They explore Diagon Alley together. Since Ron's rat Scabbers seems ill, they go to the Magical Menagerie, the wizarding pet store, in search of some medicine. A witch working at the shop tells Ron that Scabbers has outlived the normal rat life expectancy but still offers Ron some rat tonic that may help. Hermione purchases a large orange cat that she names Crookshanks and that subsequently attempts to attack Scabbers in the pet store.

Harry, Hermione, and the Weasleys enjoy a nice dinner together at the Leaky Cauldron. Afterward Harry hears Arthur and Molly talking about him and Sirius Black. From their hushed conversation

Harry gathers that Sirius Black is after him. Arthur mentions that while being trapped in Azkaban for 12 years, Black was heard mumbling, "He's at Hogwarts, he's at Hogwarts." Harry returns to his room, thinking that with the protection of Hogwarts and his record of escaping Voldemort, he will be safe from the threat of Black.

Chapter 5: "The Dementor"

The time has come to return to Hogwarts. The group boards Ministry of Magic cars, which take them to King's Cross Station. Mr. Weasley and Harry enter the station together; Arthur begins to explain to Harry about Black, but Harry interrupts to tell him he already knows that Black is after him. Arthur makes Harry promise that he will be more cautious than usual and that he will stay out of trouble. When the students board the Hogwarts Express, all the compartments are full except one, occupied by a shabbily dressed man. They deduce he is Professor R. J. Lupin, the new Defense Against the Dark Arts teacher. Harry informs Hermione and Ron about Black, and shortly thereafter, Harry's Sneakoscope goes off in his trunk. The conversation turns to Hogsmeade, which the students look forward to visiting, but Harry fears being left behind since he has not yet had his permission slip signed.

Rain falls steadily when the Hogwarts Express suddenly and much earlier than usual comes to a stop. The students hear strange noises and then the lights go out. Some people enter the compartment, including Neville and Ginny, but in the darkness they stumble over each other. Professor Lupin awakens and tells the students to remain quiet. The door to their compartment opens once again, and a cloaked figure with a scabbed-over mouth and what appear to be decayed hands enters. The air turns violently cold, and Harry, hearing screaming, faints. When he regains consciousness, Harry learns no one else fainted or heard the screaming. Professor Lupin gives Harry some chocolate, telling him that eating it will make him feel better. He explains to the students that the creature who had entered their compartment was a Dementor, one of the guards for the wizarding prison Azkaban.

After they arrive at Hogwarts, Professor McGonagall takes Harry and Hermione aside. She sends Harry to tell Madam Pomfrey of his encounter with the Dementor, and Hermione goes with Professor McGonagall to her office. When Hermione emerges, she seems quite happy. They go to the great hall in time for Dumbledore's start of term announcements, one of which informs the students that Dementors are posted around the school grounds; this is a precautionary measure against the escaped Sirius Black. Regardless, Dumbledore is unhappy about their presence and association with the Ministry of Magic. Dumbledore then introduces the new teachers, including Professor Lupin and, surprisingly, Hagrid, who will be the new Care of Magical Creatures professor. After the feast the students go to their assigned dormitories, and once there, Harry feels at home at last.

Chapter 6: "Talons and Tea Leaves"

The students receive their schedules at breakfast; Hermione, oddly, has too many subjects listed on hers. The students begin a new subject—Divination—the room for which is hard to find and located in the North Tower. Harry runs into Sir Cadogan, a knight in one of the castle's pictures, who agrees to show them the way to the classroom.

The Divination teacher is Professor Trelawney, a flighty woman who wears large glasses and a lot of jewelry. Her classroom is dark and cluttered. Professor Trelawney explains that Divination is a delicate art and that those who can "see" the future have the "inner eye." Though some of the students are skeptical of her abilities, she impresses them when she predicts that Neville will break his tea cup and will need another one. Indeed, her prophecy comes true. She also tells Lavender that something she dreads will happen on October 16. The students use their tea cups to tell each other's futures with the tea leaves. When Professor Trelawney sees what is in Harry's cup, she announces to the class that he has "the Grim," a shape of a large dog that is an omen of death. Most of the class becomes excited with her prediction that Harry will die; Hermione, however, considers the whole business of Divination "wooly."

In Transfiguration Professor McGonagall notes that the students are distracted and explains that Professor Trelawney predicts someone's death every year. McGonagall is frustrated that Trelawney's commotion has taken away from her lesson on animagi, people who are able to transform into animals at will. McGonagall is an animagus herself (she can take the form of a cat).

In Care of Magical Creatures class the students have two new experiences: a class taught by Hagrid and an introduction to hippogriffs. Hippogriffs are creatures that are part eagle and part horse. They must be approached carefully, and one can only get close to a hippogriff after it acknowledges your presence and welcomes you with a bow. Harry approaches one of the creatures and is allowed to ride him. Draco wants to show that Harry's feat is easier than it seems, and, completely disrespecting a hippogriff, approaches it without waiting for it to bow. The hippogriff, Buckbeak, attacks Draco by clawing his arm. Draco reacts dramatically and is rushed to the hospital wing. Hagrid becomes upset when the Malfoys file a suit with the Board of Governors; Buckbeak faces a trial and possible execution.

Chapter 7: "The Boggart in the Wardrobe"
In Potions class the students work to produce a Shrinking Solution. Snape instructs Ron to assist Draco in preparing his ingredients since Draco is wearing a sling because of his encounter with Buckbeak. While working on their potions, Draco makes snide remarks about Sirius and how if Malfoy were Harry, he would want revenge for what Black did. Harry becomes frustrated because he has no idea what Draco is talking about.

Between classes Harry and Ron notice that Hermione keeps suddenly disappearing and reappearing; her bag remains constantly overloaded with books. Ron and Harry discuss her odd behavior and how she manages to take so many classes at once. Ron remarks that Hermione must not be telling them everything going on with her.

The students have their first Defense Against the Dark Arts lesson with Professor Lupin. It is a practical lesson in which they must defeat a boggart, a type of shape-shifter that assumes the shape that most terrifies the person fighting it. Many of the students have a chance to battle the boggart, which takes the form of a severed hand, a banshee, and a

giant spider, among others. As Harry approaches for his turn, Lupin jumps between him and the boggart; for Lupin the boggart turns into a silvery white orb. Some of the students discuss why Lupin would be afraid of crystal balls, but they all agree he seems to be a very good teacher.

Chapter 8: "Flight of the Fat Lady"
Defense Against the Dark Arts quickly becomes everyone's favorite class. Conversely, hardly anyone likes Divination, and everyone dreads Care of Magical Creatures with Hagrid, who, after the incident with Buckbeak, has the students caring for uninteresting creatures called Flobberworms.

At the start of October Quidditch season arrives. Oliver Wood, in his seventh year, is especially eager to win the Quidditch Cup. On October 16 Lavender learns that her pet rabbit has died; some of the students think that this is one of Professor Trelawney's predictions coming true, but Hermione remains skeptical. The month continues to be exciting with the arrival of the first Hogsmeade weekend and the traditional Halloween feast. Harry asks McGonagall whether she will sign his permission form, but she tells him she cannot since the permission must be from a family member or guardian. Unable to go to Hogsmeade, Harry remains at the castle and runs into Lupin. While they visit in Lupin's office, Snape enters with a potion for Lupin then leaves. Terrified at what exactly the potion may do, Harry tells Lupin that Snape has always wanted Lupin's job in an effort to suggest Snape may have put something into the potion to harm Lupin.

Everyone enjoys the Halloween feast, sharing stories of their adventures in Hogsmeade. When the students return to their common rooms, there is a commotion at the Gryffindor entrance: The Fat Lady has gone missing. Her portrait seems to have been shredded. Dumbledore arrives and talks to Peeves, who witnessed the Fat Lady's attack. He says that the perpetrator was Sirius Black.

Chapter 9: "Grim Defeat"
The staff searches the castle thoroughly, but no trace of Sirius remains. Harry, Ron, and Hermione overhear Snape talking to Dumbledore about theories concerning how Sirius may have entered the castle. The Gryffindors are scheduled to play Sly-

therin in Quidditch, but because of Draco's injured arm, they play Hufflepuff. The day before the match Lupin does not show up for Defense Against the Dark Arts; instead, Snape substitutes for him. He disregards Lupin's lesson plans and tells the students they will spend their time studying werewolves.

The morning of the match Harry wakes up to find Crookshanks sniffing around the boys' dormitory. He ushers the cat out quickly. By the time of the match, a horrible storm has erupted. Harry competes directly with Cedric Diggory, the Hufflepuff Seeker. While chasing the Snitch, Harry thinks he sees the Grim sitting in the Quidditch stands. He is then overcome when Dementors guarding the castle grounds get too close to him. Harry hears Voldemort threatening Harry's mother and her futile pleas that he not harm Harry. Harry passes out and wakes up in the hospital wing to find out that not only did Gryffindor lose the match against Hufflepuff, but his *Nimbus Two Thousand* was completely destroyed by the Whomping Willow.

Chapter 10: "The Marauder's Map"
Lupin arrives back in class and, after hearing about the destruction of Harry's broom, tells him that the Whomping Willow was planted the year he arrived at Hogwarts. Harry tells Lupin that when the Dementors attack, he can hear Voldemort murdering his mother. He asks Lupin to teach him how to defend himself against the creatures.

Yet another Hogsmeade weekend arrives and Harry feels left out again. The Weasley twins seek Harry out and present him with a special gift: the Marauder's Map. They explain that the map shows all of the secret passageways around Hogwarts, one of which leads to Hogsmeade. All Harry has to do is utter, "I solemnly swear I am up to no good," and the map (which at first only looks like a blank piece of parchment) reveals a detailed map that also shows where and who everyone is.

Harry sneaks off to Hogsmeade and visits the Three Broomsticks with Ron and Hermione. While in the pub they overhear some of the professors talking about Sirius Black, James Potter, Remus Lupin, and Peter Pettigrew. These boys were very close, but Pettigrew was a bit of an outsider, who followed the others around and worshiped them. Sirius was

chosen to be the Potters' secret keeper, which meant that only he would know the location of James and Lily, who had gone into hiding because of Voldemort. When Sirius turned on the Potters by betraying them to Voldemort, he murdered Pettigrew as well. All that remained of Pettigrew was his finger. Fudge comments that Sirius is truly mad; one day when he visited the wizarding prison Azkaban, Fudge was confronted by Sirius, who asked Fudge for his newspaper to do the crossword. The minister and teachers then reveal that Sirius is, in fact, Harry's godfather.

Chapter 11: "The Firebolt"
Harry is completely shocked that no one ever told him what happened. He looks in the book of pictures Hagrid presented him at the end of his first year and sees Sirius standing with his parents. Draco's comments in Potions class about wanting to get revenge for what Sirius had done suddenly make sense to Harry. Hermione, Ron, and Harry go to visit Hagrid, who has learned that an official trial will be held to determine Buckbeak's fate; they agree to help build a defense for the hippogriff.

Christmas arrives with a special gift for Harry: a *Firebolt*, the broom he had admired in Diagon Alley. There is no card to inform Harry who sent him the gift, and in turn, Hermione becomes suspicious. She reports the incident to McGonagall, who takes Harry's broom away since she, as does Hermione, fears it may have been jinxed and sent by none other than Sirius Black.

Chapter 12: "The Patronus"
Ron and Harry are furious with Hermione for telling McGonagall about the *Firebolt*'s mysterious arrival. Harry is also still bothered about the effect the Dementors have on him, so he asks Lupin to give him lessons to defend himself against them. Lupin agrees to teach Harry about the Patronus spell, which produces a type of guardian that shields the wizard from the Dementor. To produce a Patronus, Lupin says, one must concentrate on his or her happiest memory. Harry makes his first attempt at the dementor but fails and hears his mother screaming and his father telling her to run. Lupin seems especially interested that Harry heard his father's

voice; he learns that Lupin knew his father well and consequently was once close to Sirius as well.

Ron and Harry both remain puzzled at how Hermione manages to get to all her classes since several of them meet at the same time and she has not yet missed a class. After testing for every possible jinx, Harry finally gets his *Firebolt* back. The chapter ends with yet another fiery encounter between Ron and Hermione: Scabbers has gone missing, and all that remains of him are a few drops of blood, mingled with some ginger cat hairs.

Chapter 13: "Gryffindor versus Ravenclaw"
With the disappearance of Scabbers Hermione and Ron's friendship seems doomed. Ron seems depressed but feels much better after Harry lets him ride the *Firebolt* after Quidditch practice. Harry sees a pair of eyes and worries that the Grim has appeared; the eyes belong to Crookshanks, and Ron yells at the animal.

During the Quidditch match between Gryffindor and Ravenclaw, Harry's attention is drawn to the ground at what seem to be Dementors crossing the field. Harry conjures a Patronus and then, magnificently, catches the Snitch. When he arrives on the ground, Harry learns what he saw was not a group of real Dementors but Draco and his cronies merely dressed as Dementors. With this Quidditch win, Gryffindor is one step closer to winning the Quidditch Cup. A huge celebration occurs in the common room and only ends when McGonagall arrives at one o'clock in the morning to end the festivities. Tired from all the excitement, Harry falls asleep but wakes with a start to Ron's screams. Ron tells everyone that Sirius was looming over his bed. McGonagall arrives to investigate, wary of Ron's claims. She asks Sir Cadogan (who has taken over the Fat Lady's duties since she was attacked by Sirius) whether he let someone into the Gryffindor dormitory. He answers in the affirmative, explaining that Sirius had the correct password to enter. McGonagall then severely reprimands Neville, who had written down multiple passwords on a scrap of paper and somehow lost them.

Chapter 14: "Snape's Grudge"
The Hogwarts atmosphere is charged with excitement and bound with tighter security after Sirius's break-in. Ron becomes an instant celebrity, but Harry remains puzzled as to why Sirius ran away without hurting anyone. Hagrid asks Harry and Ron to visit him. During the visit Hagrid urges them to be nicer to Hermione.

The next Hogsmeade weekend arrives, and Harry wants to go, but Hermione threatens to tell McGonagall if he plans to sneak out again. Harry decides he will fool her and everyone else (but Ron) by using the Marauder's Map and the Invisibility Cloak. He follows Ron to the Shrieking Shack, where Draco repeatedly insults the Weasley family. Harry throws mud at him, and in the ensuing fray his Invisibility Cloak slips off his head and Draco sees him. Harry races back to Hogwarts and is met by Snape, who immediately takes him to his office, saying that Draco saw him in Hogsmeade. Snape makes Harry empty his pockets and he sees the blank parchment that is the map. When Snape attempts to find out what the parchment really is, words begin to appear on the paper that insult Snape. Highly irritated, Snape insults Harry by saying he is arrogant and disobeys rules just as his father did. Harry responds that Snape is mad because his father saved his life when they were at school together. Snape assures Harry that Harry's father and friends were playing a trick on Snape and that James Potter was just too cowardly to go through with it.

Snape calls for Lupin since Snape thinks the map may involve some dark magic, which, as the Defense Against the Dark Arts professor, Lupin should know a great deal about. Lupin manages to get Harry and the parchment out of Snape's office but scolds Harry for taking the sacrifice his parents made for his life so lightly. Lupin also tells Harry he knows who made the map but does not reveal the information. When Harry arrives back at the common room, he and Ron find Hermione in tears: Hagrid lost his case, and Buckbeak has been sentenced to death.

Chapter 15: "The Quidditch Final"
Hermione tells Harry and Ron that they have a chance to appeal the ruling on Buckbeak's case. Ron says that this time he will help Hermione; Hermione then breaks down on his shoulder, and the two mend the rift between them. They overhear

Draco making remarks about how pathetic Hagrid is. Without hesitation Hermione slaps Draco and tells Harry that Gryffindor had better beat Slytherin in the Quidditch final because she could not stand to see Slytherin win.

That same day after lunch Hermione goes missing. They find her asleep in the common room, surrounded by books and parchment. She arrives in Divination already irritated by missing classes by falling asleep. Professor Trelawney instructs the students that they will be learning to use crystal balls, at which Hermione scoffs. In Harry's crystal ball Trelawney claims to see the Grim; at this Hermione begins to laugh. An argument ensues between Hermione and the professor, ending only with Hermione's storming out of the classroom.

The match between Gryffindor and Slytherin is one of the most highly anticipated matches in Hogwarts history. Harry wakes up in the middle of the night before the match and, looking outside, sees Crookshanks, accompanied by a huge black dog. He tries to get some more sleep before the match.

At the match the Slytherins play unfairly, so much so, in fact, that even Madam Hooch and McGonagall lose their composure. The game is an exciting one, ending with a Gryffindor victory. This victory gains Gryffindor the Quidditch Cup.

Chapter 16: "Professor Trelawney's Prediction"
The time for final exams arrives. Ron sees that Hermione has several finals at one time and remains baffled about how she can manage such a schedule. Harry, Hermione, and Ron see a team of people from the Ministry of Magic who have arrived ready to execute Buckbeak, even though the appeal has not yet been held. For Divination class Professor Trelawney sees each student separately: The task is to explain what he or she sees in a crystal ball. After Harry completes his exam, Professor Trelawney suddenly seems possessed and begins speaking in a harsh voice. She prophesies that before midnight one of Voldemort's faithful servants will return to him. Voldemort, with this servant's help, will rise again, more powerful than ever. When she seems to have returned to her senses, Harry asks her whether she remembers what just happened, and Professor Trelawney says it sounds like nonsense.

A note arrives from Hagrid saying that Buckbeak lost the appeal. Harry, Ron, and Hermione go to his cabin to comfort him. Hermione makes some tea to help Hagrid calm down. In the process she finds an empty jug, inhabited by Scabbers. Thrilled to see his lost pet, Ron holds Scabbers, who struggles madly to escape from his grip. Dumbledore, Fudge, and the executioner Macnair arrive at Hagrid's so Harry, Ron, and Hermione sneak out. While heading back to the castle, Scabbers continues to squeal wildly, but his noises cannot hide the swishing and thud of an ax.

Chapter 17: "Cat, Rat, and Dog"
Harry, Ron, and Hermione are stunned. Suddenly, they see a pair of eyes in the darkness. They belong to Crookshanks. Scabbers squeals wildly and looses himself from Ron's grip; Ron chases after him. As Ron pursues the rat, a huge black dog materializes out of nowhere. The dog pounces on Ron and drags him down into the passage guarded by the Whomping Willow, breaking Ron's leg in the process.

Hermione and Ron are desperate to make their way to the passageway but are impeded by the willow's branches, which are swinging violently. Crookshanks prods the willow tree with its paw and the branches remain still. Harry and Hermione chase the dog and Ron, ending up in the Shrieking Shack. They find Ron lying on a huge bed. He yells, "It's a trap!" and tells Harry and Hermione that the dog is actually not a dog at all but Sirius Black, who is an animagus. Sirius appears, and when Harry attempts to attack him, Crookshanks joins in the fight and wounds Harry's arm. The cat then curls up on Sirius's chest. Harry, flooded with rage, accuses Sirius of all the crimes he committed, including, most heinously, the murder of his parents. Sirius asks Harry to let him explain himself and says that Harry will regret it if he does not. Professor Lupin arrives and takes Harry's wand. He addresses Sirius as an old friend and asks him, "Where is he?" Sirius points at Ron. Completely dumbfounded, Ron says that Sirius must be crazy.

Lupin confuses the students by saying, "Why hasn't he shown himself before now? Unless you switched without telling me?" Sirius answers in the affirmative while Ron continues to look at them as if they are both crazy. Lupin hugs Sirius. Hermione is outraged, and says she cannot believe that she has been covering up for Lupin all year. She reveals he is a werewolf, and she learned this when Snape set the essay when he substituted for Lupin in his class. She also accuses Lupin of helping Sirius break in. Lupin says that he is indeed a werewolf but says he has not been helping Sirius. To show Harry, Ron, and Hermione that they can trust him, he gives them back their wands and then puts his own away. Lupin explains that the Marauder's Map revealed the real criminal was among them, and that he knows what the map is because he helped to write it.

Lupin was watching the map and saw Harry, Ron, and Hermione disappear through the willow, but they were accompanied by someone else. The students say it was only the three of them, and then Lupin tells them he saw Sirius pull two of them into the Whomping Willow. The three students say this is impossible. Lupin asks to see Ron's rat and Ron becomes scared, asking what his rat has to do with anything. Sirius tells him it is not a rat. When Ron begins to argue, Lupin jumps in and says it is no rat, but an animagus by the name of Peter Pettigrew.

Chapter 18: "Moony, Wormtail, Padfoot, and Prongs"

Ron still believes that Lupin and Sirius are crazy. Harry says that Pettigrew is dead and that Sirius killed him 12 years ago. Sirius tries to get Scabbers and Lupin tells him that the story must be explained to Harry, Ron, and Hermione so they understand the truth. Sirius tells Lupin to explain quickly because he wants to commit the murder he was imprisoned for. Lupin explains that everyone just thought Sirius killed Pettigrew but that really, Pettigrew committed the crime and then turned into a rat, his animagus form. Hermione tells Lupin there is no way this could be because when they learned about animagi in the beginning of the year with McGonagall, she looked up all the registered animagi and Pettigrew was not listed.

Lupin then explains the existence of the animagi that never would have officially registered with the ministry. Lupin was bitten by a werewolf when he was a child. Dumbledore, understanding, as always, agreed to let Lupin attend Hogwarts. They derived a plan so Lupin would not harm any fellow students

when he transformed into a werewolf once a month. Dumbledore had the Whomping Willow planted; the tree protected a passageway to the Shrieking Shack in Hogsmeade. Lupin would spend his time as a werewolf in the shack. His closest friends—Sirius, Pettigrew, and James Potter—knew he was a werewolf and wanted to keep him company. So finally in their fifth year of school they mastered the animagus spell and would transform themselves to keep Lupin company when he was in werewolf form. These young men—who went by names that reflected their animagus forms (*Moony, Wormtail, Padfoot,* and *Prongs*)—created the Marauder's Map.

Lupin explains that he has felt guilty all year for not telling Dumbledore that Sirius was an animagus and that may have been how he was getting into Hogwarts. If he told Dumbledore the truth, it would have meant revealing that he had taken advantage of Dumbledore's kindness as a child. Lupin admits that in a way, Snape is correct: He has been helping Sirius all year by not revealing this information.

Sirius asks what Snape has to do with anything, and Lupin explains he teaches at Hogwarts. Lupin recalls their animosity, and Sirius gets angry at the mention of him. Lupin explains that Snape was very interested in where Lupin went every month. Sirius took advantage of the situation and told Snape that all he had to do was prod the knot on the Whomping Willow and he could follow Lupin. If that had happened, he would have arrived at the Shrieking Shack and been met by a werewolf and probably killed. When James heard about the plan, he went after Snape and pulled him back, risking his own life in doing so. Snape then knew the truth about Lupin, and Dumbledore swore him to secrecy.

Harry asks Lupin whether that is why Snape does not like him, because he thought Lupin was in on the joke. From the hallway a voice says: "That's right." Snape stands in the doorway, with his wand pointed directly at Lupin.

Chapter 19: "The Servant of Lord Voldemort"

Snape explains he had visited Lupin's office because Lupin had forgotten to take his potion. On the desk he saw the Marauder's Map, and he used it to follow them all. Snape assumes that Lupin has been helping Sirius and that the Shrieking Shack has been their home base. Lupin says it is a mistake, but Snape will not listen; Snape conjures a spell to bind Lupin's wrists and ankles and cover his mouth. He then points his wand between Sirius's eyes. Hermione also tries to make Snape listen, but he is unyielding. He tells Sirius he enjoys this vengeance since Sirius now faces the Dementors' kiss. Harry tells Snape he is pathetic because he cannot get over how Sirius, Lupin, and his father made a fool of him in school. Snape makes a move to react, Harry, Ron, and Hermione all perform the *Expelliarmus* spell at once, knocking Snape unconscious. Black still wants Scabbers, but Ron will not hand him over. He asks how Sirius could know, out of the million of rats, how this one is definitely Scabbers. Sirius explains that when Fudge once visited Azkaban, Sirius asked him for his copy of the paper; in that issue was the same picture of the Weasley family in Egypt that Ron sent to Harry with his birthday gift. In the picture Scabbers is on Ron's shoulder, with a toe missing on his front paw. Sirius and Lupin remind Harry that all anyone found of Pettigrew was his finger. Sirius goes on to explain that Crookshanks stole the passwords for Sirius so he could break into the Gryffindor dormitory to kill Pettigrew/Scabbers.

Returning to the subject of the night of Harry's parents' death, Sirius reveals that at the last minute, the Potters made Pettigrew their secret keeper. Sirius arrived at the scene of the murders and realized what must have happened: Pettigrew betrayed the Potters to Voldemort. Lupin and Sirius take the rat and perform a spell that makes him turn back into a man. Pettigrew tries to blame Sirius and turns for help to Lupin, who ignores him. He appeals to Ron and Hermione as well, but they reject his pleas. Pettigrew continues to protest his innocence, and Lupin asks why an innocent man would spend 12 years as a rat; Sirius offers an answer to that question, based on his time in Azkaban. Pettigrew would stay a rat until he was sure Voldemort was back in power; otherwise, he was too frightened to reveal his identity.

Many of Voldemort's followers still caught in Azkaban were furious with Pettigrew since it was at the Potters' that Voldemort met his downfall.

Then the question arises as to how Sirius even escaped Azkaban. He says he was able to stay sane simply because he was innocent. Since Dementors feed off emotions and are blind, he one day transformed into a dog and snuck out when they opened his cell door.

Pettigrew appeals to Harry when Sirius and Lupin say they will kill him on the spot; Harry says to take him to the castle so the Dementors can settle his fate since he knows his father would not have wanted his best friends to become murderers. Pettigrew turns to Sirius and asks what good might have resulted if he had not joined Voldemort, who has powers even Sirius cannot fathom. Sirius, disgusted with such a question, says innocent lives would have been spared. Then they go as a group, with Pettigrew chained between Ron and Lupin, to the castle.

Chapter 20: "The Dementor's Kiss"

On the way back to the castle Sirius asks Harry whether he knows he is his godfather and tells him that he can live with him if he likes. Harry is overwhelmingly happy. The group emerges from the Whomping Willow. A cloud moves, revealing the Moon. Lupin, who has not taken his wolfsbane potion, turns into a werewolf. Sirius tells the kids to run, transforms into the shaggy black dog, and takes on Lupin himself. They fight intensely.

In the meantime, Pettigrew picks up Lupin's wand, casts a spell, transforms back into a rat, and escapes into the forest. Harry hears a dog yelping in pain and runs toward the lake, where the noises comes from. Sirius has turned back into a man and is moaning, "No." Hundreds of Dementors circle closely above him. Harry tells Hermione to think of something happy and attempts to conjure a Patronus several times, but there are too many Dementors for him to do so. Harry and Hermione become overwhelmed by Dementors themselves. Harry sees what they actually look like under the hood: scabbed skin over eye sockets and a gaping hole for a mouth. The sound of his mother's screaming overtakes him. Suddenly the screaming stops, and the coldness begins to disappear. Harry's eyes will not focus, but a bright shape like that of a unicorn has driven all the Dementors away. Then Harry faints.

Chapter 21: "Hermione's Secret"
Harry wakes up in the hospital to Fudge's congratulating Snape for his good work in rounding up Sirius and saving Harry, Ron, and Hermione. Madam Pomfrey sees Harry awake and tells him to relax since Sirius has been captured and will receive the Dementor's kiss at any moment. When Harry attempts to tell Fudge of Pettigrew's crime, Fudge only dismisses him. Fudge and Snape leave; Snape reminds Dumbledore that even if Sirius claims he is innocent, Sirius was capable of murder at 16. Dumbledore says he remembers, and with that Snape storms out of the hospital. Dumbledore assures Harry and Hermione that he believes their story and that Sirius is being held in Flitwick's office. Dumbledore also says that something might be done about the situation if only they had more time. Hermione understands what Dumbledore means by this, and Dumbledore leaves the hospital saying, "You must not be seen" and "Three turns should do it." Harry is very confused.

Hermione takes a chain from around her neck and places it around Harry's as well. A small hourglass hangs from it. She turns it three times. Harry feels as if he is flying very fast, and suddenly he is standing with Hermione in the entrance hall. He starts to talk and Hermione tells him to be quiet, and they go into a cupboard since she can hear someone approaching. She thinks the people they hear might be them as they were heading to Hagrid's.

Hermione then explains that the device she has is a Time-Turner. She has been using it all year to get to her classes. McGonagall gave it to her after the ministry approved. Hermione is puzzled why Dumbledore sent them back three hours when all the events with Sirius occurred only recently. Harry realizes Dumbledore also wants them to save Buckbeak. They know where Sirius is trapped: They can save them both, and the two accused can escape together.

Stealthily they make their way to Hagrid's hut. They wait outside and hear themselves chatting with Hagrid. Hagrid tells them to go because the executioner, Fudge, and Dumbledore have arrived. Harry, Ron, and Hermione leave Hagrid's, and as

soon as they are out of sight, the future Hermione and Harry take Buckbeak from where he is and run into the forest. The men walk out of Hagrid's hut, completely surprised that the hippogriff has disappeared.

From the forest Hermione and Harry see Ron scrambling off after Scabbers, who has just escaped from Ron's hands and run out from under the Invisibility Cloak. They see everyone enter the passage blocked by the Whomping Willow. Harry wants to intervene and stop Snape from getting to the shack, but Hermione reminds him they cannot take any chances of being seen. They must wait for the events to unfold as they did. In the meantime, Harry discusses the Patronus that drove the Dementors away. Hermione asks him who he thinks produced the Patronus, and Harry tells her he thinks it was his father.

Soon the group emerges from the Whomping Willow. Harry wants to do something to stop Pettigrew, and again Hermione reminds him they cannot interfere because they could be seen. They seek shelter in Hagrid's cabin (Hagrid has gone walking in a happy stupor because of Buckbeak's escape). Harry decides to go outside to see what exactly is happening at the lakeshore. He sees the Dementors surrounding Sirius and then Hermione and himself. He becomes anxious for his father to appear and save them all, but no one seems to be coming. Instead, Harry jumps forward and casts a Patronus spell. He saves Sirius, Hermione, and himself from the Dementors. Harry realizes the shape of his Patronus is a stag; he makes the connection that his Patronus is Prongs, his father's animagus form.

He tells Hermione what just occurred, explaining that the reason he could cast such a powerful Patronus was that he had already done it. Within moments they climb on Buckbeak and make their way to Flitwick's office. Without wasting any time, Hermione and Harry (Ron is still unconscious in the hospital wing) convince Sirius to mount the hippogriff. Before flying off into the night, Sirius tells Harry that he is truly his father's son.

Chapter 22: "Owl Post Again"
Hermione grabs Harry so they can get back to the hospital wing before Dumbledore leaves and locks it

from the outside. They make it back just in time. Ron is the only one left in the hospital wing. Madam Pomfrey attends to them, and they follow her directions intently. Suddenly a roar fills the castle. It is Snape, outraged that Black has disappeared. He is sure Harry is responsible. He bursts into the hospital wing, where he accuses Harry and Hermione of helping Sirius. Dumbledore tells Snape to remain calm while Madam Pomfrey assures everyone that the students have not left their beds but have been under her expert care. Fudge is embarrassed by Sirius's escape; Dumbledore asks him to remove the Dementors from the school grounds. Ron wakes up and asks what has happened, and Harry tells Hermione to explain while he helps himself to another piece of chocolate.

The students learn that Professor Lupin has decided to leave Hogwarts. His choice to resign rests on the possibility of transforming into a werewolf again and possibly attacking a student. Harry tries to convince Lupin to stay, but Lupin says he must go, in the best interest of the school and the children. Lupin tells Harry how proud he is of the Patronus he conjured. Before he leaves, Lupin returns the Marauder's Map to Harry.

Harry has a conversation with Dumbledore in which he expresses his feelings of disappointment that since Pettigrew escaped, nothing they did made any difference. Dumbledore corrects him: Because of what happened, an innocent man regained his freedom. Harry tells Dumbledore about Trelawney's prediction, and Dumbledore believes that her prediction was accurate. Harry expresses anger at not being able to prevent Pettigrew from rejoining Voldemort, but Dumbledore assures him that he did a noble thing in letting Pettigrew live since now Pettigrew would forever be in Harry's debt and, in fact, owed Harry his life. Harry tells Dumbledore he feels foolish for thinking his father had conjured the Patronus that saved his life. Dumbledore reassures him that that feeling is not foolish at all, as the dead never really leave us and through the form of his Patronus Harry found his father inside himself.

Harry, Ron, and Hermione pass all of their exams, a feat that shocks Harry since he was sure he would not have passed Potions because of Snape's intense dislike for him. They enjoy a pleasant ride back to King's Cross Station, discussing the ensuing Quidditch World Cup. Then something appears at Harry's window. It is a very small owl, with a letter for Harry from Sirius. He reads the letter aloud. In the letter Sirius reveals that he and Buckbeak have gone into hiding and that Sirius did send Harry the *Firebolt* (which causes Hermione to remind everyone that was what she suspected all along). Crookshanks placed the order for the *Firebolt* for Sirius. He also tells Harry that it was he whose eyes watched Harry when he first left the Dursleys', before he boarded the Knight Bus. As a special surprise Sirius has also enclosed a signed permission slip (as Harry's godfather), stating that he may visit Hogsmeade next year. Sirius adds a P.S. to the letter, stating that Ron should keep the small owl that delivered his letter since it is Sirius's fault that Ron no longer has a pet rat.

After disembarking from the Hogwarts Express, Harry is met coldly by Uncle Vernon, who sees Sirius's letter in Harry's hand. Harry tells him it is not another form for him to sign, but a letter from his godfather, his parents' best friend, a convicted murderer and escaped convict; this godfather, he tells Uncle Vernon, will be checking in periodically with Harry to make sure he is happy. This news horrifies Uncle Vernon but leaves Harry feeling happy and ready for his summer vacation.

CRITICAL COMMENTARY

Realizing that Harry's story entertained and touched readers of all ages, Rowling incorporated themes into *Prisoner of Azkaban* that adults were more likely to appreciate. *Prisoner of Azkaban* is the first novel in the Harry Potter series that, when examined critically, obviously includes content geared toward a more mature audience. The novel lends itself to a critical examination of a range of themes and issues including the importance of family, secrecy and security, betrayal, revenge, the representation of women, time, justice, and personal transformation.

Subtext

Though the novel appeals to readers of all ages, Rowling writes for her more mature readers specifically with small but clever remarks that younger readers may understand generally but will not necessarily appreciate fully. Rowling playfully addresses those who attack and brand her series as dangerous for young readers, she incorporates comments that carry multiple (and critical) meanings, and she subversively remarks on capital punishment.

The novel opens with Harry at Number Four, Privet Drive, studying in his bedroom. This is a familiar scene to fans, since Harry must study privately so as not to enrage his aunt and uncle, who wholeheartedly disapprove of his studying magic at Hogwarts. Harry is working on an assignment that asks him to discuss why "Witch Burning in the Fourteenth Century Was Completely Pointless." Harry's research leads him to discover that "on the rare occasion that they did catch a real witch or wizard, burning had no effect whatsoever. The witch or wizard would perform a basic Flame Freezing Charm and then pretend to shriek with pain while enjoying a gentle, tickling sensation" (2). All readers can appreciate this statement's humorous suggestion that, as usual, Muggles truly do not understand witches, wizards, and their abilities. This statement also provides an example of Rowling's responding playfully to the objections from conservative religious critics, typically Christian, who conflate witchcraft with Wicca and charge Rowling with promoting a brand of witchcraft associated with the supernatural, occult, and Satanism. Rowling answers these critics by hinting that witches have thrived and will continue to thrive, no matter the measures taken to prevent them from doing so.

Another incident in the novel geared specifically to mature readers involves Aunt Marge's comments about dog breeding. Marge informs the Dursleys of her cruel practices concerning the puppies she raises, and how she feels no sympathy for underbred dogs. During this conversation Marge also remarks, "If there's something wrong with the bitch, there'll be something wrong with the pup" (25). Some young readers might understand that *bitch* is a scientific term for a female dog; hence, they understand the sentence to mean that if something is wrong with a puppy's mother or father, something could also be wrong with the puppy. Mature readers, however, can also appreciate the intricacy in Marge's statement. Marge appears to be speaking about the dogs she breeds, but this comment simultaneously reflects her feelings about Harry and his parents. She feels the Potters were lazy, incompetent, and troublesome, and so Harry must be also. Young readers will understand the comment relating to dog breeding, but mature readers will also observe how the comment is a particularly pointed and cruel remark targeting Harry.

Also early in the novel Vernon Dursley comments on the death penalty in a way that speaks, in particular, to mature readers. When Vernon sees Sirius on the Muggle news, Vernon says, "When will they *learn* . . . that hanging's the only way to deal with these people?" (17). Young readers might assume that Vernon's comment means that the world would be safer if criminals, such as Sirius, no longer existed. Mature readers, however, will note Rowling's implied critique of capital punishment. Associating support of the death penalty with Uncle Vernon, who is a generally abusive, mean-spirited, and shallow man, suggests Rowling questions the value of capital punishment as a mechanism for achieving justice, a point that is likely to be unappreciated by young readers.

Importance of Family

Whether young or old a theme all readers of the Harry Potter series can identify with is family in varying configurations. Rowling, since *Sorcerer's Stone*, has presented various images of what makes a family, ranging from the nuclear families of the Weasleys (loving and functional) and the Dursleys (hateful and dysfunctional) to the close-knit best friends Harry, Ron, and Hermione, who, although not blood-related, form a makeshift family. In *Prisoner of Azkaban* the Weasley family in particular emphasizes the importance of making family a priority, while Harry's Patronus symbolizes that although loved ones may die, they remain with those they love.

Early in the novel readers learn that Arthur Weasley has won the *Daily Prophet* Grand Prize Galleon Draw. Ron informs Harry of this news in a letter: "I couldn't believe it when Dad won the *Daily Prophet* Draw. Seven hundred galleons! Most of it's gone on this trip, but they're going to buy me a new wand for next year" (9). Seven hundred galleons translates to approximately $5,860 (Rowling claims that a galleon is roughly worth five pounds sterling, which equated to approximately $8.30, as of September 2009). The Weasleys (who in *Chamber of Secrets* open their Gringotts vault to find one galleon and "a very small pile of silver Sickles" [57]) rarely, if ever, have discretionary money. This stroke of luck provides the family with possible funding for school or household supplies, but instead the Weasleys spend the bulk of their winnings on visiting their son Bill, who works in the pyramids as a curse breaker for Gringotts bank, in Egypt. The decision to spend almost all of their winnings on this trip to Egypt demonstrates that for the Weasleys, nothing is more important than family, even material comforts. The members of the Weasley family make one another their top priority, and in turn the family remains happy and supportive of one another, regardless of their financial situation.

Rowling also reinforces the importance of family through an important symbol in the novel—Harry's Patronus, which takes the shape of his father's animagus form, Prongs the stag. Harry feels foolish when he tells Hermione that he thinks he saw his father perform the Patronus spell that saved them from the Dementor attack after their return from the Shrieking Shack near the end of the novel. Harry reveals his feelings of confusion to Dumbledore, who provides Harry with some comfort. He says, "You think the dead we loved ever truly leave us? You think that we don't recall them more clearly than ever in times of great trouble?" (427). More specifically Dumbledore speaks to Harry's desperate yearning to know his murdered father: "Your father is alive in you, Harry, and shows himself most plainly when you have need of him. How else could you produce that *particular* Patronus? Prongs rode again last night" (428). Dumbledore's advice emphasizes that even death cannot sever the ties

between family members, a theme that resonates throughout the series. The headmaster's statements are also particularly moving considering the death of Rowling's mother of multiple sclerosis in 1990, a loss Rowling grieved deeply. She admits that the Harry Potter series explores death and the feelings experienced by those who lose a loved one. She insists that even though loved ones pass away, they never "truly leave us."

Secrecy

Flitwick explains an important charm in *Prisoner of Azkaban*: the Fidelius Charm, which involves a selected person's being sworn to guard a secret. This novel repeatedly addresses the theme of secrecy, focusing on why people keep secrets and the ramifications of doing so. Scores of characters keep secrets, including the Weasleys, Lupin, and Pettigrew, and the consequences of keeping those secrets are often disastrous. Ultimately Rowling emphasizes that being honest is always the best course of action.

Secrets propel the plot of the third novel as knowledge withheld from Harry becomes central to the story line. Harry does not suspect that Sirius hunts him specifically; he only suspects that he should be wary of the escaped convict because of Sirius's supposed connection to Voldemort. The Leaky Cauldron provides both the setting for a happy reunion of Harry, the Weasleys, and Hermione and, more important, the backdrop for some important and private conversations between Molly and Arthur Weasley. Harry assumes the Weasleys are discussing him and hears Molly tell Arthur that Harry is "*happy not knowing*" (65). The knowledge to which Molly refers is that Sirius is indeed tracking Harry. Before boarding the Hogwarts Express for the start of term, Arthur speaks to Harry privately, informing him of Sirius's intentions and dangerous nature. By revealing a secret about Sirius to Harry, Arthur reinforces that being honest, even with someone as young as Harry about as difficult a subject as Sirius, is the best choice.

Many members of the wizarding community, including McGonagall, Flitwick, Hagrid, Fudge, Dumbledore, and even Madam Rosmerta (the hostess at the Three Broomsticks pub), know the alleged truth about Sirius: He betrayed his best friends, the

Potters, and caused their deaths. They do not share this knowledge with Harry, however, and allow him to go through life in ignorance, though even some of his classmates have more information about Harry's parents' deaths than he does. Readers may sympathize with the decision to keep this information secret from Harry, a child, but others may rightfully question what gives them—whom Harry trusts—the right to conceal the truth from him. Granted, revealing the truth of the Potters' downfall to Harry would obviously cause him great sadness and anger, but the manner in which Harry actually learns the truth—through glimpses incited by Dementor attacks and by accidentally overhearing a conversation in the Three Broomsticks—causes Harry more pain and angst than learning the truth from someone close to him would. Even though people who knew the truth of the Potters' demise kept the information secret in an effort to protect Harry, Harry suffers upon learning the truth. It may be extremely difficult to find the appropriate time to tell the truth about a sensitive subject, but Rowling suggests that it is important the truth is revealed, and in the most sensitive manner possible.

The entire plot of the novel, of course, revolves around one secret kept for over a decade: Peter Pettigrew, not Sirius, betrayed the Potters to Voldemort. Pettigrew keeps the secret for no other reason but to protect himself. A man hungry for power, Pettigrew takes any action necessary to protect himself and gain status. The consequences of his secret are many, each one more devastating than the other. Pettigrew's secret leads to the imprisonment of an innocent man; the entire wizarding community's perception of Sirius is transformed; Harry loses his godfather, with whom he may have been able to live, saving him from the abusive childhood of Number Four, Privet Drive. Pettigrew's secret emphasizes just how much damage keeping a secret can cause.

Perhaps the greatest secret in the novel concerns Lupin and his hidden identity as a werewolf. As a student at Hogwarts Lupin was fortunate that he did not have to bear his secret alone: His confidantes James, Sirius, and Peter provided him with some comfort and company, helping him through difficult times. Now Defense Against the Dark Arts professor, Lupin must keep his lycanthropy secret from his students. He keeps this secret to protect himself and his students. Refusing to reveal publicly that he is a werewolf allows Lupin to keep his job because, as he tells Harry, the parents of Hogwarts students "will not want a werewolf teaching their children" (423).

Lupin also keeps his secret for the benefit of his students. People typically view werewolves as dangerous hunters always tracking their prey; surely if students knew that Lupin was a werewolf, they would have a very difficult time trusting him and, consequently, learning Defense Against the Dark Arts information from him. When Hermione realizes that Lupin is a werewolf, she is very quick to distrust him and forced to question his allegiance in the Shrieking Shack: She assumes Lupin has betrayed Harry and the rest of the wizarding community by being in league with Sirius, the supposed criminal.

Regardless of Lupin's motives for keeping his lycanthropy a secret, Rowling suggests that Lupin is the only one who should be allowed to disclose his secret to others. Lupin's situation mirrors that of a gay man or woman who has the right to decide at which time he or she will "out" his or her sexual identity, and to whom. In most scenes in *Prisoner of Azkaban* Rowling suggests that secrets lead to pain and trouble, but she clearly implies that Snape's deliberately outing Lupin by providing clues to their students is wrong. Rowling demonstrates that in most cases secrets only inflict pain, but she also reminds readers that they must use personal judgment to decide when and how to reveal the truth.

Of course, the background readers gain from the confrontation in the Shrieking Shack only reinforces the centrality of secrecy and honesty as themes within the novel, if only because Harry's story ultimately begins owing to Pettigrew's role as "Secret-Keeper," his failure to fulfill that responsibility, and the subsequent impact of that betrayal on Harry's future.

Betrayal and Revenge

A novel such as *Prisoner of Azkaban,* in which one of the central characters is wrongfully imprisoned for murder, must treat the themes of betrayal and revenge, and, indeed, these topics remain central to Rowling's third book in the series.

Rowling first stresses the theme of betrayal when Harry receives his birthday present from Ron, who sends him a Sneakoscope from Egypt. This gadget alerts its owner when someone untrustworthy is near. The object may seem unreliable but proves its worth on the train ride to Hogwarts for the start of the school year. Harry, Ron, Hermione, and a few others take their places in a compartment with the mysterious R. J. Lupin. The Sneakoscope goes off, but Harry dismisses it, knowing that he can trust his best friends (though his experience with the Defense Against the Dark Arts teacher in the first book, Professor Quirrell, might have excited his suspicions about the sleeping Lupin). Scabbers, however, is also in the train car, and by the end of the novel, readers learn that he (Peter Pettigrew) has betrayed many witches and wizards and, most important, Harry and his parents.

Pettigrew provides the most significant example of betrayal in *Prisoner of Azkaban*. Once the trusted companion of Sirius, Lupin, and James, Pettigrew transforms—literally—into a rat. McGonagall mentions how Pettigrew followed his friends loyally around the Hogwarts campus, and readers later learn that James and Lily Potter trusted Pettigrew so implicitly that they agreed to make him their secret keeper. The course of the entire Harry Potter saga hinges on Pettigrew's betrayal, as, without him, Voldemort might never have known where to find the Potters.

Another important example of betrayal in the novel concerns Ron and Hermione, whose pets—Scabbers and Crookshanks, respectively—battle with each other often, and intensely. Convinced that Hermione's cat ate his rat, Ron feels betrayed by her since she neither apologizes for Scabbers's disappearance nor offers to help him find his pet, if Scabbers is still even alive. The rift that develops in Hermione and Ron's friendship is the first serious argument that occurs between the friends. The anger, hurt feelings, and distrust quickly evaporate when Sirius and Lupin reveal the truth of the past in the Shrieking Shack, but until then, their bitter

conflict mirrors the situation between Sirius and Pettigrew, the catalyst for revenge, and foreshadows even more intense conflict between the two friends in future books.

The two characters most obsessed with revenge are Sirius and Snape. The only motivation Sirius seems to have to carry on after his escape from Azkaban is exacting revenge on Pettigrew for the heinous crimes he committed against Sirius and his best friends, the Potters. Seeing Pettigrew/Scabbers smiling at him from a picture with the Weasleys in the *Daily Prophet*, Sirius musters the energy and ingenuity finally to escape Azkaban and make his way to Hogwarts, where he knows he will find Pettigrew. Sirius's rage fuels his actions, and simultaneously, he does not kill the innocent, maintaining his focus on the object of his vengeful obsession. For example, when Sirius breaks into the Gryffindor dormitory, attempting to capture Pettigrew, he easily could have injured Ron but instead only scared him. Sirius's instinct is to contain his rage in an effort to protect the innocent, but his inability to abandon his obsession for revenge destroys him internally. His stay in Azkaban ravaged his body, but his thirst for revenge, to which he clings desperately, wreaks havoc on his spirit.

Snape allows himself to be possessed by a similar obsession with revenge. Deeply wounded and embarrassed by the way Sirius and James treated him during their time as students at Hogwarts, he refuses to forgive them and instead desires revenge. He exacts some of this revenge by treating Harry cruelly throughout the series, but in *Prisoner of Azkaban* Snape reveals to Harry explicitly why he hates James Potter (and his friends) so passionately. Snape was obviously jealous of James: He tells Harry that James was "exceedingly arrogant. A small amount of talent on the Quidditch field made him think he was a cut above the rest of us too. Strutting around the place with his friends and admirers" (284). Snape explains that Sirius told him to go to the Whomping Willow, knowing full well that if Snape did so, he would die. Even though James saves Snape from approaching the tree, Snape holds a dangerous grudge against him (which suggests Snape despises James for additional reasons as well). Because Snape is known for his petty and bitter nature, one cannot help but question that if he were less obsessed with revenge, perhaps he would be a kinder, happier soul. Ultimately, with the examples of Sirius and Snape, Rowling argues that one consumed by revenge will live a miserable existence, focused only on plotting to destroy enemies instead of issuing forgiveness and finding peace.

Gender Roles

Though Rowling does not seem to tackle the question of gender roles directly, the issue remains prominent in criticism about the series, primarily explorations of Rowling's depictions of female characters and whether the books participate in reproducing traditional scripts for masculine and feminine behavior. The most well-known women in *Sorcerer's Stone* and *Chamber of Secrets* include Hermione Granger, Minerva McGonagall, and Ginny Weasley; all three of these women are independent, strong, and rational, though they play comparatively minor roles in the story lines compared to their male counterparts—Harry, Ron, the Weasley brothers, Professor Dumbledore, for example. *Prisoner of Azkaban* introduces a new type of female character: the Divination professor, Sybill Trelawney. The inclusion of a woman so different from the others in the series raises questions about her and why so many of Rowling's other girls and women find Trelawney irritating and, at times, infuriating (especially when contrasted with Dumbledore's inexplicable tolerance for her).

Rowling's choice to cast a woman as Divination professor deserves attention. Students know that success in this subject requires an aura and a so-called inner eye. In contrast to a subject like Potions—a true science mirroring the Muggle academic discipline of chemistry—which requires one to locate ingredients and follow directions listed thoroughly in a textbook, Divination seems quite imprecise. Those who practice Divination rely more on their intuition than on acquired skills. Women are traditionally considered more intuitive and emotional than men, and Rowling's placing Trelawney in this role emphasizes that stereotype. Readers—girls and women in particular—may question Rowling's choice and consider this deci-

sion insulting, since few take Trelawney or her field of study seriously. Rowling, however, asks readers to feel sympathy for Trelawney. Dismissed by most (if not all) of her colleagues, Trelawney secludes herself high in the castle's North Tower and rarely descends to join the rest of the Hogwarts community. As with Bertha Mason in *Jane Eyre*, one cannot help but wonder whether Trelawney has been relegated to her tower, stored away and kept secret.

Rowling may encourage readers to view Trelawney sympathetically because of her marginalization and lack of intellectual credibility, but few characters within the Harry Potter series have compassion for the Divination teacher. Lavender Brown and Parvati Patil remain in awe of Trelawney after the professor accurately predicts the passing of Lavender's beloved pet rabbit (with some manipulating of facts, the prediction is accurate), but students who admire Trelawney as Lavender does are rare (and Lavender herself lacks credibility throughout the books, and Parvati is similarly dismissed by fellow characters and readers as flighty and unimportant).

Hermione and McGonagall, central female characters within the book, express contempt for Trelawney. Hermione objects to Trelawney and her subject of specialization for two reasons in particular: First, Hermione performs poorly in the course, and second, she considers Trelawney a poor teacher. Hermione early in her Divination coursework scoffs at Trelawney, who responds to Hermione, "You'll forgive me for saying so, my dear, but I perceive very little aura around you. Very little receptivity to the resonances of the future" (107). This remark infuriates Hermione, who has great difficulty understanding that one cannot gain expertise in a subject simply by reading about it. Hermione also abhors Trelawney because she considers her a poor teacher. Trelawney does not provide her students with any concrete suggestions on how to improve their understanding or performance, indeed seemingly rejecting the idea that the field of study can be understood through study or practice. It is this lack of precision that leads Hermione to leave the class.

Perhaps some of Hermione's dislike for Trelawney is modeled on McGonagall's attitude toward the Divination professor; Hermione obviously considers the rational and fair McGonagall as a role model and possibly imitates her attitude toward Divination, even unconsciously. Always respectful and kind (and strict), McGonagall is rarely witnessed behaving unprofessionally. Handling Trelawney's eccentricities causes McGonagall to react in a manner less professional than her custom. Christmastime at Hogwarts calls for all those remaining in the castle to gather for dinner. Trelawney, behaving even more dramatically than usual, creates a spectacle by suggesting the number of people dining together is unlucky and could result in the death of one of the dinner guests. Dumbledore convinces Trelawney to dine with the group, and when Trelawney takes her seat, McGonagall, quite pointedly, offers her some tripe (229). When her students arrive at their first Transfiguration lesson completely distracted by Trelawney's predictions of Harry's ensuing death, McGonagall says, "Divination is one of the most imprecise branches of magic. I shall not conceal from you that I have very little patience with it. True Seers are very rare, and Professor Trelawney—" (109). McGonagall catches herself before openly insulting Trelawney in front of their students, but this episode demonstrates how McGonagall, typically composed and controlled, becomes quickly rattled at even the mention of Trelawney.

Perhaps McGonagall and Hermione feel uncomfortable with Trelawney because the Divination professor behaves emotionally, a characteristic they both display very rarely. Do they feel disgusted by Trelawney, who perpetuates the idea that women are emotional, flighty, and dramatic, or are they possibly threatened by a woman so in tune with her emotions? These questions remain unresolved by the series.

Time

A central concern in *Prisoner of Azkaban* is time. Rowling's creation of the Time-Turner implies that time is nonlinear and can be manipulated. Strict rules govern those who are granted the power to manipulate time; Time-Turners cannot be purchased by simply anyone, and those allowed to use them must receive clearance from ministry officials. Hermione, allowed to use a Time-Turner to attend

more Hogwarts classes than an average day would allow, explains the dangers of manipulating time by such an instrument to Harry: "Professor McGonagall told me what awful things have happened when wizards have meddled with time. . . . Loads of them ended up killing their past or future selves by mistake!" (399). McGonagall advocates that Hermione have a Time-Turner, assuming she will use it responsibly. Hermione (with some friendly encouragement from Dumbledore) breaks the agreement under which the Time-Turner was assigned to her; Hermione's breaking the rules showcases how rules concerning Muggle time do not always apply in the wizarding world and takes up a recurring question within science fiction and fantasy works about the nature of and manipulatability of time.

A common misconception of readers about Time-Turners is that they allow the user simply to go back in time and alter the course of the future, as Marty McFly does in the popular 1985 Hollywood film *Back to the Future*. This is inaccurate. Within Rowling's wizarding world, Time-Turners grant their users the power to visit an appointed moment in time, coexisting with the self that has not used the device to arrive at that moment. For instance, when Harry and Hermione use the turner to rescue Sirius and Buckbeak, they hide in a closet in the Great Hall and hear themselves and Ron sneak by under the Invisibility Cloak on their way to Hagrid's (before they find Scabbers and go to the Shrieking Shack). They exist concurrently. This representation of time challenges readers to view time as malleable and nonlinear.

Though members of the wizarding community may be able to influence time in ways that Muggles cannot, Dumbledore reinforces that altering time does not present such manipulators with the opportunity to excuse past actions or decisions. Choices made, no matter the moment in time, resound into the future. Discussing Trelawney's prophecy with Dumbledore causes Harry to wonder about the future and attempt to decipher what events concerning Voldemort would now ensue. In response Dumbledore asks him, "Hasn't your experience with the Time-Turner taught you anything, Harry? The consequences of our actions are always so complicated, so diverse, that predicting the future is a very difficult business indeed. . . . Professor Trelawney, bless her, is living proof of that" (426). Dumbledore reminds Harry (and consequently readers) that those who think they can alter, master, or predict the course of time are gravely mistaken. Dumbledore's comments reflect the major premise of chaos theory, which in basic terms argues that a seemingly minor event (a butterfly's flapping its wings) can start a chain reaction that will result in a much more significant event (a tidal wave). As do the novels preceding it, *Prisoner of Azkaban* encourages readers to think about the significance of their actions, no matter how minor, and how those actions can alter the course of a story—the course of history—dramatically.

Justice

One of the most important themes in *Prisoner of Azkaban* is justice. Sirius's wrongful imprisonment, coupled with the impending execution of Buckbeak, reminds readers that justice may be swift but is not always fair.

Draco Malfoy taunts Buckbeak the hippogriff; he disregards all Hagrid's instructions for interacting with the animal and is blatantly disrespectful to it. When Buckbeak consequently attacks Malfoy, the latter tries to displace all blame onto others, insisting that Hagrid and Buckbeak are completely at fault for the incident. Malfoy flaunts the clout his family—his father, in particular—has with the board of Hogwarts and Cornelius Fudge, the Minister of Magic: He tells his fellow students that Lucius Malfoy "complained to the school governors. *And* to the Ministry of Magic. Father's got a lot of influence, you know" (125). He also adds that, because of the altercation, Hagrid will not "be a teacher much longer. . . . Father's not very happy about my injury" (125). Regardless of Draco and Lucius's threats, Hagrid retains his teaching position and ministry officials are not able to carry out Buckbeak's execution. Harry and Hermione help Buckbeak flee, and the beast must assume a new identity. Rowling allows the hippogriff to survive and in turn suggests that the creature does not deserve to be punished for its interaction with Mal-

foy and that Buckbeak's escape is justified because he is a victim rather than a perpetrator.

Dumbledore makes the most insightful observations about the concept of justice in *Prisoner of Azkaban*. Harry and Hermione rush to inform Dumbledore of Sirius's innocence, explaining to their headmaster that, in fact, Peter Pettigrew should be held responsible for the betrayal of the Potters and the murders of 12 other innocent wizards. Dumbledore quickly realizes that without Pettigrew in custody, few people—if any—will believe Harry and Hermione's story. He tells Harry, "There is not a shred of proof to support Black's story, except your word—and the word of two thirteen-year-old wizards will not convince anybody" (392). These words are harsh but accurate. Dumbledore reassures Harry and Hermione that he believes their story but reminds them that justice and truth can be clouded simply by a source's age, social status (as with Malfoy), or background. That Dumbledore, the symbol of authority in the series, endorses Harry and Hermione's use of the Time-Turner to save Buckbeak and Sirius from their fates under the laws of the land is a fairly subversive subtext; it is also one of the reasons that some parents, teachers, and librarians challenge the overall moral framework of Rowling's wizarding world, one, they argue, that promotes a lack of respect for the formal structures of power and encourages lawlessness.

Despite the positive outcomes (Sirius and Buckbeak's freedom), Harry feels extremely disappointed at the novel's end; though Sirius is innocent, he is still forced to flee and live as a fugitive. When Dumbledore asks Harry why he seems so discouraged, Harry explains that he thinks all he and Hermione accomplished—particularly in freeing Buckbeak and Sirius—"didn't make any difference" (425). Dumbledore, in response, says, "It made all the difference in the world, Harry. You helped uncover the truth. You saved an innocent man from a terrible fate" (425). These words provide Harry with comfort and remind him (and readers) that justice is not always the same as fairness. Sometimes people are unfairly and wrongly considered guilty, but what matters most is that someone—even one person—knows the accused is truly innocent.

Transformation and Identity

Prisoner of Azkaban presents readers with important questions about transformation and identity. Characters who are animagi, Lupin's secret life as a werewolf, and the introduction of the Patronus spell encourage readers to examine how all characters undergo changes, how all have the ability to change who they are, and that one's identity shifts and grows during these personal transformations.

Rowling hints that animagi will be an important part of the novel since they are mentioned early in the work, during McGonagall's first Transfiguration class with her third-year students. The students seem unimpressed that McGonagall is an animagus since they are preoccupied with Sybill Trelawney's prediction that Harry will die. Rowling usually mentions, in passing, magical spells or abilities early in each novel that eventually play a crucial role in the plot; her inclusion of animagi is no exception. Drawing attention to animagi, however, is also significant since *Prisoner of Azkaban* emphasizes the theme of transformation in the forms of Harry's father and his friends. Animagi symbolize the opportunities people have to change; people can decide to change or transform, just as Sirius, James, and Peter did. If one is not born an animagus (like McGonagall), however, becoming an animagus is a long, taxing, and painful process. As such, Rowling suggests that those who elect to make significant changes should prepare themselves for a challenge. Conversely, Rowling reinforces that change—even if difficult to bear—is rewarding, just as it was for Lupin's friends when they finally learned to become animagi and could join him during his time spent as a werewolf.

Characters who are animagi undergo very literal transformations: Their appearances change significantly. Characters also experience significant emotional transformations as well. Sirius, once a carefree rogue, shifts into a desperate, angry man obsessed with vengeance. Peter was a boy who followed his friends devoutly but becomes a man concerned more with acquiring status and power and less with allegiance to those he considers his friends, eventually leading him to a life of cowardice and betrayal. Even Hermione experiences a significant emotional transformation: She grows into a courageous young woman, confident enough in her own judgment to insult a professor and physically assault Malfoy. These characters, among others, deliberately choose to alter their identities; in some cases, however, characters are forced to change whether they actually desire to do so.

One such character, Remus Lupin, does not elect to change but is forced to change; since he suffers from lycanthropy. Lupin's situation emphasizes the importance of being willing to adjust to changes thrust upon one; surely Lupin would rather live as a healthy human, but Lupin manages his condition and consequently has transformed into a compassionate, caring, patient man. Similarly, Harry is confronted with details of his past (and consequently his parents' past). Like Lupin, he must adjust to the knowledge thrust upon him. Their resilience demonstrates that growth arises from change, especially change that is forced.

The introduction of the *Expecto Patronum* spell and the resulting Patronus also encourages readers to explore theories about identity. Lupin explains that to conjure a Patronus, one must find a happy memory from which to gain energy and strength; remembering a joyful moment is necessary to combating a Dementor's negative effects. Harry's remembering happy moments from his past requires him to examine his identity and recall with whom he has shared great joy: The people present in those memories, such as parents and closest friends, have helped shape Harry's identity. More significant, the shape of one's Patronus clearly reflects one's identity (a concept that Rowling explores in more depth during Dumbledore's army meetings in *Order of the Phoenix*). For instance, Harry's Patronus, a stag, mimics his father's animagus form. This mimicking illustrates that James Potter constitutes a significant part of Harry's identity. Harry's Patronus provides a connection between him and his father and encourages readers to understand that even though people pass away, their influence and importance remain strong.

Rowling conceptualized the third novel in the series as engaging a dual readership and began to take up increasingly complex and abstract themes in it. Her willingness to tackle weighty themes in this third novel is a prelude to the increasingly dark tone of the rest of the books.

INITIAL REVIEWS

Unlike reviews of the first two novels in the series, which often found faults in character, plotting, or style, initial reviews of *Prisoner of Azkaban* are almost universally and uniformly laudatory, even as they continue to make comparisons between Rowling and other writers of the children's fantasy genre, both contemporary and historical. Reviewers praised the book's humor, increasingly polished style, imagination, and interesting characters.

Rowling's ability to address classic themes of love and death in fresh ways was praised by reviewers of the third novel. *Commonweal* called *Azkaban* "a pleasure: superbly constructed, amazingly inventive, deliciously hyperbolic, psychologically insightful, successful in both humor and terror." This appreciation for both the reassuring and frightening aspects of the story was echoed by Nicholas Tucker in the *Michigan Quarterly Review*, who admired the way the book "provides moments of great imaginative fulfillment arising from episodes of suspense and occasional terror." Geraldine Brennan, as well, in the *Times Educational Supplement* believed the novel was more complex and more interesting than the previous two entries in the series in its handling of complicated themes. Yvonne Zipp's *Christian Science Monitor* review shared this evaluation, calling the third book an improvement on the first two because of its added layers of symbolism and adventure.

Deborah Loudon's review in the *Times Literary Supplement* mirrors this approval of the increasingly complex and multilayered narrative, noting that the book adds to the "mythopaeic power without losing narrative drive or wit." Loudon's additional observation that Rowling achieves this subtle and complex thematic exploration without didacticism or condescension confirms Verlyn Klinkenborg's *New York Times* review: "It is not a moralistic world, however, which is one reason boys and girls and even adults like it so much. Neither the good nor the evil at Hogwarts is metaphysical." By contrast, Tucker's review in the *Michigan Quarterly Review* disagrees

with this assessment, asserting that the book has nothing to say about concrete contemporary social issues and that the moral world Rowling creates is "black and white," citing Harry's hero worship of his parents as an example and the cruelty and malice of the one-dimensional school bullies, Malfoy, Crabbe, and Goyle. Tucker, unlike Loudon or Klinkenborg, does not recognize an increased thematic complexity related to moral questions, stating instead that "there is no room for any such subtlety in the Potter books."

Reviewers on the whole believed the plotting of the novel, along with what is referred to as a "thrilling" climax by Diane Roback of *Publishers Weekly*, to be a strength of the book. *Publishers Weekly* claims that Rowling's plotting is "genius"; Martha Parravano, in *Horn Book Magazine*, calls the climax "exciting," and Eva Mitnick in *School Library Journal* also singles out the nonstop pacing and stunning climax as strengths of the novel. Tena Natale Litherland in *Book Report* calls the novel "action packed" and "fantasy at its finest" (65). Even though Gregory Maguire concedes that "in terms of plot, the books do nothing very new," he asserts that "they do it brilliantly."

Parravano of *Horn Book Magazine* is one of the few reviewers who specifically identify characters—both development of continuing characters and the introduction of new ones—as a strength of the third installment. Calling Professor Lupin a "man with a howling secret" and a "particularly interesting" new teacher, Parravano also reserves praise for the evolution of the protagonist, noting that Harry is developing as a more complex character. Amanda Craig in the *New Statesman*, a British political magazine, praises Rowling's protagonist and explains that "Harry wins our hearts by displaying courage, modesty, intelligence, and humour."

Stylistically many reviewers found much to admire. Reviews in *Publishers Weekly*, the *Times Educational Supplement*, the *Michigan Quarterly Review*, and the *Times Literary Supplement* were all enthusiastic about Rowling's wit and use of humor. *Time* magazine's review commended the book as "consistently funny, adept at both broad slapstick and allusive puns and wordplay" (Corliss). Humor is not the only element of tone and style to garner positive response from reviewers: Lee Siegel's *New Republic* review calls Rowling's literary style "artful."

As with reviews of previous novels, the reviews for *Prisoner of Azkaban* frequently compare Rowling's work either favorably or unfavorably with other series or writers from the children's fantasy genre. Sally Estes in *Booklist* praises the story generally as well told and calls it "a cut above most fantasies for the age group." However, Craig in her *New Statesman* review, as do many reviewers, critics, and readers, compares Rowling to C. S. LEWIS, author of the *Chronicles of Narnia*, and J. R. R. TOLKIEN, author of the *Lord of the Rings*, because of their creation of secondary magical worlds, but where Craig sees the two men as "doomy academics," Rowling's "books sparkle with satire" and are "brilliant at the vivid pleasures and pains of childhood, from eating sweets to being bullied." However, Rowling falls short, according to Craig, in comparison with the work of Philip Pullman, writer of the His Dark Materials series, which Craig finds superior, preferring to rank Rowling along with E. NESBIT (Edith Nesbit) and ROALD DAHL.

SCHOLARSHIP

Little scholarship treats *Prisoner of Azkaban* in isolation; please see "Scholarship on the Harry Potter Series" section for additional reviews that analyze this novel as a contributing work to the larger series.

Ron Cooley's article, "Harry Potter and the Temporal Prime Directive: Time Travel, Rule-Breaking, and Misapprehension in *Harry Potter and the Prisoner of Azkaban*," addresses what he argues to be the common theme of subversion in children's literature. Cooley argues that the novel(s) does not encourage child readers to be disobedient but offers that stories like *Prisoner of Azkaban*, with its episodes of rule breaking, serve as social or ideological correctives to conformist social impulses. Rowling's third novel directly addresses the issue of how figures of power such as Dumbledore and Fudge or powerful institutions such as the Ministry of Magic apply rules inconsistently. Cooley argues that this inconsistent application of the rules is necessary to build the sense that the wizarding authority structures are in fact flawed and thus justify the civil

disobedience Harry engages in later in the book and the series as a whole.

Cooley claims that the ultimate rule breaking occurs with the use of time travel, which is a key plot element in the novel; he argues that Harry's transgressions are rarely punished, but his time-travel transgression is a required part of the plot that ultimately poses the ethical question "When is it right to break the time travel rule, and when, by analogy is it right to break any rule?" (35). Further, Cooley suggests that the book itself offers many opportunities to understand events from new perspectives, such as Peter Pettigrew's identity, Sirius Black's true intentions, and so forth; Cooley denotes these situations as part of a pattern of "error, revisitation, and correction" (38). The moral movement of the book is ultimately Harry's, and the final confrontation with Pettigrew, Lupin, Sirius, and Snape confirms this theory.

The other significant criticism reflecting on *Prisoner of Azkaban* in isolation is Maureen Katz's "Prisoners of Azkaban: Understanding Intergenerational Transmission of Trauma Due to War and State Terror (with Help from Harry Potter)." In *JPCS: Journal for the Psychoanalysis of Culture and Society*, Katz's analysis draws on her experiences as a psychiatrist, descendant of Holocaust survivors, and mother. Her work addresses the ways in which children of victims of terror (including children of Bosnian refugees, children of those accused under McCarthyism, and other descendants of Holocaust survivors) cope and how they try to find their own identities. She explains that the children of those who were terrorized usually have a sense of hopelessness inherited from the views of their parents. She compares these experiences to those Harry endures when attacked by Dementors. Katz reflects on how Harry is able to beat the Dementors, by picturing himself somewhere else altogether, and how victims of trauma such as Harry need to discuss their issues, paying special attention to the complicated and multilayered societal influences that shape the perceptions they have of themselves.

CHARACTERS

Sirius Black/Padfoot Wrongly accused of murder; the Potters' best friend; Harry Potter's godfather; an animagus. Referred to as "possibly the most infamous prisoner ever to be held in Azkaban fortress" (37), Sirius Black is an honest man who is unfairly considered guilty until proven innocent. In a classic case of being in the wrong place at the wrong time, Sirius Black is framed by Peter Pettigrew for murdering 13 people and for betraying the Potters to the Dark Lord. Completely consumed by revenge for his wrongful imprisonment, Sirius often acts rashly (a trait that will continue to cause him trouble in succeeding Harry Potter novels). Although unable to quench his thirst for revenge, Sirius finds some comfort in knowing his godson, Harry Potter, finally knows the truth about Sirius's relationship with the Potters.

Rowling makes a clever choice for Sirius's animagus form: an "enormous, pale-eyed, jet-black dog" (334). To begin, *Sirius* is the name of an incredibly bright star; astronomers also refer to this star as the "Dog Star." Rowling's choices of name and animagus form complement each other well and hint at Sirius's true identity and abilities. More important, however, is what Sirius's animagus form symbolizes. Dogs are considered loyal and friendly; people who truly know Sirius would define him as having both traits. Perhaps the worst feeling Sirius had to bear while wrongfully imprisoned was that the wizarding community believed he had betrayed his best friends, the Potters. Sirius explains, "I think the only reason I never lost my mind was that I knew I was innocent" (371). Only an innocent man trapped in Azkaban—much like Hagrid in *Chamber of Secrets*—could survive a sentence in the prison.

Sirius does not have the opportunity to exact revenge on Pettigrew because the traitor escapes to rejoin Voldemort at the end of the novel. With Sirius Rowling suggests that justice is not always served: Because of the use of the Time-Turner, the nearly unbelievable appearance of Peter Pettigrew, and other various factors, Sirius's reputation cannot be restored publicly. Instead, just a few people know of Sirius's innocence. At the very least, Harry knows that truth, and that knowledge provides Sirius with some comfort. With the character of Sirius Rowling emphasizes that even

if only a few people know the truth of a matter, those few people are enough, simply because the truth is known.

Although Harry and Sirius will hardly see or be able to contact each other, Sirius finds that he can take pride in and enjoy being Harry's godfather. With the signing and sending of Hogsmeade visit permission slips, Sirius fulfills a role in Harry's life he has not known since the death of his parents: Someone in his extended family truly cares for him and wants to see him happy. As in many other cases Rowling reminds readers that one's choices influence one's happiness, and Sirius's choice to ignore his desire for revenge leaves him with more energy and time to focus on getting to know and being able to help his best friends' son, his godson, Harry.

Albus Dumbledore Headmaster of Hogwarts. In *Prisoner of Azkaban* Dumbledore continues to cultivate the trust of his young charge Harry. While the Hogwarts headmaster has always allowed Rowling to explore the concept of trust, his specific interactions with Hagrid, Lupin, Harry, and Hermione demonstrate that Dumbledore's relationships with Harry, Ron, and Hermione illustrate the importance of trusting in others as a key part of human relationships.

Dumbledore demonstrates this importance of faith in human potential when he gives Hagrid the position of Care of Magical Creatures professor. Because Dumbledore is a man who values learning highly, Rowling makes an important statement about him when the headmaster gives Hagrid a teaching position. Dumbledore would never jeopardize his students' education, so he places a great deal of trust in Hagrid to teach the students well.

Likewise, Dumbledore exhibits trust in his interactions with Lupin, both when Lupin was a student at Hogwarts and when Lupin serves on the Hogwarts staff in this third book. When Lupin wants to attend Hogwarts as a boy, Dumbledore welcomes him openly over what were sure to be predictable protests about Lupin's threats to the safety of other students: Lupin explains that "Dumbledore . . . was sympathetic. He said that as long as we took certain precautions, there was no reason I shouldn't come to school" (353). With the planting of the Whomping Willow, Hogwarts becomes Lupin's home. Dumbledore also shows great trust in Lupin when he hires him as a teacher. First, Lupin could pose a threat to students, but Dumbledore trusts that Lupin will follow the careful potion regimen prescribed to him, which will keep his symptoms under control. Second, Dumbledore welcomes Lupin into Hogwarts knowing full well the werewolf was best friends at school with Sirius who is now considered a dangerous escaped convict. Dumbledore respects all people and creatures, and one of the ways he offers respect is to offer his trust, balanced with his judgment.

Perhaps the most important comments Dumbledore makes about trust involve Hermione, Sirius, and Harry. After Hermione and Harry save Buckbeak and Sirius, Dumbledore gives them a very truthful answer: "There is not a shred of proof to support Black's story, except your word—and the word of two thirteen-year-old wizards will not convince anybody" (392). Dumbledore adds that he has "no power to make other men see the truth" (393) but reassures Harry and Hermione that he believes their story and believes that Sirius is innocent. Dumbledore further instills the value of trust in others when he entrusts Harry and Hermione to use the Time-Turner to save Buckbeak's life and Sirius's soul. But, Rowling makes her most vital statement about truth with Dumbledore when he tells Harry that saving Sirius and Buckbeak "made all the difference in the world" because Harry "helped uncover the truth [. . . and] saved an innocent man from a terrible fate" (425). Dumbledore not only embodies truth in *Prisoner of Azkaban* but also reminds Harry (and Rowling's readers) that uncovering the truth is always worth one's time and energy.

Cornelius Fudge   Minister of Magic. As usual, Fudge seeks complacency and preservation of the image of his authority, even if with this attitude justice is not always served. He tries to uphold the image that he is both capable and fair, whereas he is actually bumbling, easily swayed, and willing to bend the rules to appear competent. The first instance of Fudge's ignoring rules set forth by

the ministry in order to preserve his image occurs when he allows Harry to enjoy his stay in Diagon Alley rather than being punished for blowing up his Aunt Marge. Fudge assuages Harry's very reasonable anxiety about expulsion from Hogwarts for his actions by remarking, "Oh, my dear boy, we're not going to punish you for a little thing like that! . . . It was an accident! We don't send people to Azkaban just for blowing up their aunts" (45). This erratic treatment of rule breaking reinforces the overall skepticism with which authority figures are treated in the books.

Fudge seems genuinely to care about Harry's welfare and safety. When he confronts Harry at the Leaky Cauldron, he reprimands him for disappearing and then adds, "But you're safe, and that's what matters" (43). On the other hand, Fudge's concern customarily appears to be less for other people and more for himself. When Sirius escapes at the end of the novel, Fudge worries that "The *Daily Prophet's* going to have a field day! We had Black cornered and he slipped through our fingers yet again! All it needs now is for the story of the hippogriff's escape to get out, and I'll be a laughingstock" (420). Even with a so-called murderer on the loose and, in turn, the threat that the convict poses to his community, Fudge remains most concerned with himself and with appearing capable in his leadership role.

Hermione Granger   Best friend of Harry Potter and Ron Weasley; fellow Gryffindor. In the first two Harry Potter novels Hermione plays the role of the successful student; other than occasionally breaking a few school rules, Hermione takes few chances. But, in *Prisoner of Azkaban* Hermione demonstrates significant character development and begins taking risks with her education, her friends, and her reputation.

Characters view Hermione as the highly intelligent young woman who helps Harry and Ron with their homework and their adventures. Lupin calls her "the cleverest witch of [her] age" (346). Hermione's age may explain her new risk-taking behavior. She has now spent two years at Hogwarts and, as a Muggle, has not only adjusted to but flourished in the wizarding world. She takes her education seriously and, in typical Hermione fashion, enrolls in extra classes and overworks. The first major risk Hermione takes concerns her Divination class. After appearing "startled at the news that books wouldn't be much help in this subject" (103), Hermione takes the subject less seriously since books represent knowledge to her. In fact, Hermione calls Divination "woolly" and based on "a lot of guesswork, if you ask me!" (111). When Ron tells Hermione he thinks she does not like Divination simply because she is not talented at the subject, Hermione becomes very defensive: "If being good at Divination means I have to pretend to see death omens in a lump of tea leaves, I'm not sure I'll be studying it much longer! That lesson was absolute rubbish compared with my Arithmancy class!" (111). Truth resounds in Ron's claim, though; Hermione does not like subjects for which she cannot read a book and be immediately knowledgeable, just as in *Sorcerer's Stone* when she dislikes flying because one cannot learn to fly simply by reading about it.

Hermione not only dislikes Divination; she dislikes the subject's teacher, Professor Trelawney, as well. The imprecise nature of Divination unnerves Hermione, but Hermione dislikes her professor for another more significant reason: Trelawney and her "woolly guesswork" represent neglect of her students' education, an act Hermione would consider nothing less than a crime. Tired of sitting through lessons in which she learns nothing, Hermione takes a significant risk in walking out of a class, never to return. Her dismissal of Trelawney also hints at Hermione's evolving sense of intolerance for women ruled by emotions rather than reason. Trelawney's very nature offends Hermione, who thrives on reason and logic, even though later in the series Hermione lets her actions be governed by emotion rather than reason.

Hermione also takes risks in her relationships with Harry and Ron. The risk she takes concerning Harry is for his benefit, but the risk she takes with Ron rises partly from her stubborn nature. When Hermione reports the *Firebolt* Harry receives from an anonymous sender to McGonagall, both boys—Harry especially—are furious with her. As Hermione points out, though, she reports the gift only because she is worried about Harry's safety.

Hermione cares for Harry and wants him to be safe, as evidenced by the broom servicing kit she gives him for his birthday: If his broom is kept in pristine condition, it will be safer for Harry to fly; more important, her gift giving reflects her attention to Harry's most cherished interest—Quidditch.

The fight Hermione has with Ron is based solely on the stubbornness of both characters. The fight between Hermione and Ron is the first serious argument to occur since the three become friends after rescuing Hermione from the troll in *Sorcerer's Stone*, though it is not the last. After Scabbers disappears, Hermione tells Ron only that cats naturally hunt rodents and in her defensive state does not apologize to Ron for Crookshanks's potential involvement in the rat's disappearance, nor does she offer to help her friend find his pet. Both characters and their stubbornness perpetuate their argument. Rowling suggests that lack of communication and the refusal to air the grievances frankly, especially between close friends, have no place in relationships and lead only to frustration and hurt feelings.

Hermione seems even more easily frustrated and impatient with ignorance than in the preceding Harry Potter novels (probably partly because of her use of Time-Turner, which results in overwork and lack of sleep). Her frustration reaches its climax with Malfoy, who spends most of the novel making snide comments about Hagrid and how Buckbeak will be executed. In a fit of aggravation Hermione slaps Malfoy. This action is also a serious risk since being physically violent with a fellow student could result in harsh punishment. This risk, completely out of character for Hermione, alters her reputation. After she slaps Malfoy and later storms out of Trelawney's classroom, Ron says, "Hermione, I don't know what's gotten into you lately!" After this statement, Rowling describes Hermione as "look[ing] rather flattered" (326).

Hermione took some risks in the earlier novels, including sneaking out after hours, venturing to the third-floor corridor, and even stealing ingredients to make the Polyjuice Potion painstakingly, but the risks Rowling has her take in *Prisoner of Azkaban* prove her character's growth into a spirited, principled, and passionate young woman.

Rubeus Hagrid Care of Magical Creatures professor at Hogwarts; school groundskeeper. In this novel Rowling continues to emphasize Dumbledore's trust in Hagrid, as well as Hagrid's dedication to and care for Hogwarts and all those who call it home.

When Dumbledore announces that Hagrid will fulfill a new position—that of teacher of Care of Magical Creatures—the students are "stunned" by the headmaster's choice (93). The Hogwarts community views Hagrid as a friendly but bumbling character who does well with animals but always somehow finds himself duped by people. Dumbledore's granting Hagrid a teaching post showcases the trust the headmaster has in his loyal staff member; Dumbledore signals that Hagrid will flourish in the role of teaching students in a formal capacity.

In his new role as professor Hagrid attempts to increase student engagement by requiring a somewhat dangerous textbook and an opening lesson on hippogriffs. Hagrid gives Harry a copy of the textbook for his birthday because he cares about Harry and wants him to do well in class. Hagrid's best intentions are thwarted, however, when both of these choices backfire. Even though Hagrid thinks that the book and how to use it are common sense, students are miserable with their textbook *Monster Book of Monsters*, a book that snaps and bites at its owner. Hagrid's choice of textbook demonstrates this fascination (and obsession) with strange creatures.

As the *Monster Book of Monsters* is Hagrid's first misstep in his attempt to help students cultivate the same love of dangerous creatures that he has, his first Care of Magical Creatures lesson is equally ill fated. He introduces students to the hippogriff, a dangerous creature that demands respect and patience. Hagrid shares his thorough knowledge of the magical creature with his students, demonstrating he is qualified—to some degree—for his teaching position: "Yeh always wait fer the hippogriff ter make the firs' move . . . It's polite, see? Yeh walk toward him, and yeh bow, an' yeh wait. If he bows back, yeh're allowed ter touch him. If he doesn' bow, then get away from him sharpish, 'cause those talons hurt" (115). Rowling emphasizes here another of Hagrid's important traits: respect for all creatures, a trait he encourages students to develop as well.

After Draco Malfoy disregards Hagrid's rules and is disrespectful of the hippogriff, the creature attacks Draco and Hagrid loses all composure. Even though Hagrid knows that responsibility lies with Malfoy for the incident, his passion and courage for teaching leave him, especially when Lucius Malfoy informs the ministry of the accident. Hagrid does not focus on student growth and learning and instead is overtaken with grief, nearly losing his ability to continue to educate and instead retreating into safe and unchallenging activities. Harry, Ron, and Hermione visit Hagrid shortly after the accident in class, and they find him in a compromising state: "Hagrid was sitting in his shirtsleeves at his scrubbed wooden table; his boarhound, Fang, had his head in Hagrid's lap. One look told them that Hagrid had been drinking a lot; there was a pewter tankard almost as big as a bucket in front of him, and he seemed to be having difficulty getting them into focus" (120). Rowling's description here is important for two reasons. First, it stresses Hagrid's sadness at how his lesson went poorly, a student was injured, and the hippogriff would now face trial at the ministry. But, even more important, the description emphasizes Hagrid's inappropriate behavior of drinking, and drinking until he is drunk, at that. Rowling suggests that Hagrid's drinking is a problem, especially since he jeopardizes the students' safety when he is drunk: He does not realize he should reprimand Harry, Ron, and Hermione for being out of the castle after dark (with Dementors ready to attack) because he is intoxicated. Though Hagrid's dependence on alcohol is rarely commented on within the books, some critics have called attention to the narrative's tacit permission for alcohol abuse and underage drinking, partly in the figure of Hagrid and partly because of the consumption of Butterbeer by Hogwarts students.

Hagrid also serves as a liaison for Hermione and Ron during their fight about Crookshanks and Scabbers. When Ron and Harry visit Hagrid, he tells the boys he is surprised they have not been kinder to Hermione and even adds "Ah, well, people can be a bit stupid abou' their pets" (274). This statement, from Hagrid, resounds with Harry and Ron since no one at Hogwarts cares more about pets than Hagrid.

Neville Longbottom   Harry Potter's friend and fellow Gryffindor. In this novel Neville remains the forgetful, bumbling classmate readers met in *Sorcerer's Stone* and *Chamber of Secrets* but also further develops as a character. While Neville must still endure Snape's torture and ridicule in Potions, Neville—in a way—sees that Snape gets his comeuppance. When called upon to battle the boggart first, Neville appears quite frightened, but with some encouragement from Lupin, Neville not only successfully defends himself against the shape-shifter but also humiliates Snape in the process: Neville's boggart reveals itself as Professor Snape dressed in Neville's grandmother's clothing. After the lesson students reminisce about how Snape looked in the old woman's clothes for days, delighting in even the memory of the scene. Rowling has Neville confront two of his worst fears simultaneously and publicly. In doing so, he becomes more comfortable with his own anxieties, with the support of some of his classmates and Lupin. This character growth prefaces the development of Neville experiences throughout the rest of the series.

Even though Neville does undergo some character development in confronting his fears publicly, his forgetfulness preserves him as a target for jokes and discipline. Because he frequently forgets the passwords to the Gryffindor common room, he writes them down but then loses them. His failure to protect this list leads to one of his most shameful moments: Black finds the list, gains access to Gryffindor Tower, and nearly attacks Ron (while actually trying to kill Scabbers). Enraged, McGonagall punishes Neville severely: "Professor McGonagall was so furious with him she had banned him from all future Hogsmeade visits, given him a detention, and forbidden anyone to give him the password to the tower. Poor Neville was forced to wait outside the common room every night for somebody to let him in" (271). Neville's shame is compounded with the arrival of a Howler from his grandmother.

Rowling's constant emphasis on Neville's forgetfulness establishes an important similarity between him and his parents, a similarity readers learn more about in *Order of the Phoenix*.

Remus Lupin   Professor of Defense Against the Dark Arts at Hogwarts; a werewolf. Readers learn in *Prisoner of Azkaban* that Lupin was a member of James Potter's circle of best friends, along with Sirius Black and Peter Pettigrew. Lupin is an understanding, encouraging teacher. Dumbledore allowed Lupin to attend Hogwarts even though other headmasters would not have, prioritizing concern for the safety of the other students over Lupin's desire for an education. Grateful to Dumbledore, Lupin returns to Hogwarts and takes pride in his job; he is very knowledgeable in his subject, is a hands-on teacher, and remains focused on student growth. As a werewolf, however, Lupin bears a secret that shrouds him in mystery and establishes him as an outsider.

Rowling's first description of Lupin depicts a worn, tired man: "The stranger was wearing an extremely shabby set of wizard's robes that had been darned in several places. He looked ill and exhausted. Though quite young, his light brown hair was flecked with gray" (74). As a young man who has become old before his time, Lupin is introduced as somewhat worn by the hardships he has endured, marking him as a sympathetic character who takes on the role of a caretaker and protector and whose concern for others overshadows his own needs and desires.

This initial description also provides a useful hint about Lupin's true identity, which readers encounter near the end of the novel. When Lupin finds himself in the presence of a full moon, he experiences a violent transformation: "There was a terrible snarling noise. Lupin's head was lengthening. So was his body. His shoulders were hunching. Hair was sprouting visibly on his face and hands, which were curling into clawed paws" (381). After this disastrous incident Lupin decides to resign from his teaching post at Hogwarts: His resignation symbolizes that he cares deeply about his students since, as he explains to Harry, he could never risk transforming again and possibly attacking a student.

From his introduction in the novel Rowling establishes Lupin as a competent, friendly, caring teacher. After the Dementor attack on the train ride to Hogwarts, Lupin gives Harry some chocolate. When Harry reports to the hospital wing, still shaken from the encounter, he tells Poppy Pomfrey that Lupin gave him chocolate afterward and she responds, "So we've finally got a Defense Against the Dark Arts teacher who knows his remedies!" (90). Similarly, after her first Defense Against the Dark Arts lesson with Lupin Hermione reflects that he "seems like a very good teacher" (140). Considering Hermione's high expectations, her comment is high praise for Lupin.

What appeals to students like Hermione, Ron, and Harry is Lupin's hands-on nature. He engages his students in every lesson, rather than lecturing to them throughout the class period as Professor Binns, or later in the books, Dolores Umbridge, does. Lupin gains student interest and holds it by making his lessons practical and relatable for his students. In addition to teaching his students about magic that is useful to them, Lupin is very supportive and encouraging, traits lacking in colleagues such as Professor Snape. When Lupin takes his class to battle the Boggart, they find Snape sitting in the room where the wardrobe with the Boggart trapped inside is. Snape makes some cruel remarks about Neville's being a poor student and humiliates him in front of the entire class: "Possibly no one's warned you, Lupin, but this class contains Neville Longbottom. I would advise you not to entrust him with anything difficult" (132). After Snape leaves, Lupin asks Neville to battle the Boggart first; this choice by Lupin demonstrates he believes in Neville. With some encouragement Neville succeeds and simultaneously pokes fun at Snape and his grandmother (the two people who cause him the most stress and worry).

Lupin also invests extra time and energy to teach Harry the *Expecto Patronum* spell. He spends time with Harry teaching him the spell not only so he can defend himself from Dementors, but so Harry can feel more confident in himself. Just as with Neville, Lupin assures and encourages Harry and supplies him with the confidence to feel proud of himself, rather than being obsessed with his troubles. When

Harry worries that he seems to be too affected by the presence of Dementors, Lupin explains that Harry has a more difficult past than others, and that even Muggles are affected by Dementors. Above all, Lupin wants his students to feel comfortable and confident in themselves, because only then are they prepared to learn and grow.

Because of his relationship with Harry's parents Lupin provides Harry with a deeper understanding of his past and appeals so much to Harry because of the information he can share about his parents, especially James, as a student at Hogwarts. Lupin clearly cares for and respects Harry's parents and makes these feelings obvious to Harry when he reprimands him for sneaking to Hogsmeade with Sirius Black, who has escaped from Azkaban. After he discovers that Harry has used the Invisibility Cloak to sneak back into Hogwarts, Lupin takes Harry to task: "Your parents gave their lives to keep you alive, Harry. A poor way to repay them—gambling their sacrifice for a bag of magic tricks" (290). Lupin wants Harry to understand his past, and a crucial part of Harry's past is how much his parents loved him and were willing to sacrifice for him—and, therefore, Harry's current choices must be sensible and honor that sacrifice. Lupin also stresses the importance of understanding the past when he and Sirius confront Pettigrew in the Shrieking Shack. Bent on revenge, Sirius wants to kill Pettigrew immediately, but Lupin stops him, explaining that before Sirius takes any action, Harry, Ron, and Hermione "need to understand" why Sirius wants to murder Pettigrew (349). Always focused on student understanding, Lupin requires that his students understand the situation; in doing so, Harry learns more valuable details about his past, and his respect for Lupin grows.

Draco Malfoy Harry's nemesis; member of Slytherin House. In *Prisoner of Azkaban* Rowling emphasizes Malfoy's sense of entitlement based on his social class. Rowling also stresses Malfoy's role as the school bully and his insensitivity to those who have suffered past trauma, namely, Harry.

Malfoy respects precious few of the staff members at Hogwarts, and Professor Remus Lupin is not one of them. When Malfoy sees Lupin, he says, "Look at the state of his robes. . . . He dresses like our old house-elf" (141). His disrespect for Lupin reflects Malfoy's superficial emphasis on appearances, and Lupin's outward appearance suggests an obvious lower social station than Draco's. Even worse is Malfoy's encounter with Hagrid during his first Care of Magical Creatures class. Malfoy completely disregards the rules Hagrid explains must be observed when interacting with a hippogriff, but because he feels he is above regulations, Malfoy viciously taunts Buckbeak: "'This is very easy,' Malfoy drawled, loud enough for Harry to hear him. 'I knew it must have been, if Potter could do it. . . . I bet you're not dangerous at all, are you?' he said to the hippogriff. 'Are you, you great ugly brute?'" (118). As exhibited in his encounter with the hippogriff, Malfoy has disrespect for animals and all creatures he perceives as being beneath him, an attitude that is consistent with the "Magic Is Might" philosophy embraced by his Death Eater family later in the series. Malfoy's behavior during this particular lesson also further emphasizes the difference between Harry and Malfoy since Harry approaches the creature cautiously, offering it his respect and patience.

Draco's mean-spiritedness is obvious when he discusses how Buckbeak will be executed in front of Hagrid, Harry, Hermione, and Ron. He poses as though he is severely injured: Harry describes him as acting "as though he were the heroic survivor of some dreadful battle" (123). Draco's injury is hardly serious, but he feigns its severity in an attempt to gain sympathy even as he demonstrates cruelty by taunting Hagrid over Buckbeak's impending death. He tries desperately to gain some attention with this injury since, sadly, Draco lacks any talent or reason for others to pay him a great deal of attention.

Draco's role as bully is stressed in *Prisoner of Azkaban* since he not only makes snide remarks about those he dislikes, causing them pain and embarrassment, but goes as far as to capitalize on his victim's worst fears, as with Harry and his feelings about the Dementors. Malfoy mocks Harry for being more susceptible to Dementor attacks than others and even poses as a Dementor during the Gryffindor/Ravenclaw Quidditch match. When Harry sees the so-called Dementor on the Quidditch pitch, he performs the Expecto Patronum spell, causing Malfoy and his goons to collapse in a pitiful heap (263), illustrating Malfoy's desire to humiliate Harry, whereas, as usual, Harry defeats Malfoy's attempts.

Minerva McGonagall   Transfiguration professor at Hogwarts; head of Gryffindor House. As with the preceding Harry Potter novels, in *Prisoner of Azkaban* McGonagall takes on a role as stern housemother, by turns nurturing and demanding depending on her students' needs. When students prepare for the first trip to Hogsmeade, Harry asks her whether she will sign his permission slip so he can join in the fun, but McGonagall refuses to do so. Harry's safety remains a priority to her, and even though a trip to Hogsmeade might pose little risk to Harry, she refuses to grant him permission to go. Her refusal to make an exception for Harry—even though she is fully aware of his situation with the stubborn, uncaring Dursleys—reinforces her fairness (especially when contrasted with the special dispensation granted to Harry by Cornelius Fudge after Harry's magical assault on his aunt Marge). McGonagall strives to treat all students equally (perhaps with the exception of securing a broom for Harry as a first-year student on her house Quidditch team) and by denying Harry permission, gains students' respect for holding him to the same rules as everyone else.

McGonagall is also stern and authoritative, providing a stark contrast to her colleague Sybill Trelawney. McGonagall as professor of Transfiguration views her subject as more of a science than she regards Divination, in which results are yielded by reading tea dregs in cups or peering into a crystal ball. McGonagall assumes her students will be highly impressed by her first Transfiguration lesson, in which she, as an animagus, transforms into a cat; instead, she is frustrated by their distractedness. Aware that her students just arrived from Trelawney's Divination course, she asks dismissively, "Tell me, which of you will be dying this year?" (109). This question quickly eases the tension in her classroom and simultaneously trivializes Trelawney's claims. Concerned that her students feel their safety may be at risk, McGonagall eases their fears, proving that their well-being is her priority and simultaneously calling into question the legitimacy of Divination as an area of academic study.

Peter Pettigrew/Scabbers/Wormtail   Villain and servant to Lord Voldemort. Pettigrew worshipped Sirius Black and James Potter while they were at Hogwarts together. Instead of remaining a loyal friend, however, he betrays the Potters (and Sirius) to Voldemort. Though readers do not learn yet why the Potters changed their Secret Keeper from Sirius to Pettigrew, Peter's weak character is apparent in the series, and it is only later that his friends see that his unctuousness and idol worship have a dark side that ultimately leads to their betrayal and deaths. Pettigrew proudly fakes his own death and is posthumously awarded the Order of Merlin, First Class (308). Some of Rowling's keenest symbolism occurs in the form of Pettigrew's living many years as a rat since he is no better than a scavenging rodent. Rowling's description of his appearance emphasizes his ratlike qualities: "He had the shrunken appearance of a plump man who has lost a lot of weight in a short time. His skin looked grubby, almost like Scabbers' fur, and something of the rat lingered around his pointed nose and his very small, watery eyes" (366).

Rowling also depicts Pettigrew as fairly strategic, manipulative, and exploitative. To begin, when he decides to live as a rat for more than a decade, he is smart enough to take up residence with the Weasley family. The Weasleys hardly ever own new clothes, books, or pets, so few (if any) would question an aged rat who had lived for so many years. Even the woman in the pet shop in Diagon Alley makes some remarks about the rat's age and condition, but no one is fazed by the seeming abnormality, since objects have to last in the Weasley home.

Rowling also hints at Pettigrew's strategic abilities since he only becomes a major character in a novel during which Voldemort's second rise to power seems inevitable. Sirius, when given the opportunity to confront Pettigrew in the Shrieking Shack, tells the betrayer, "You never did anything for anyone unless you could see what was in it for you" (370). Rowling paints Pettigrew as the epitome of selfishness but also places him in an odd position. After Harry saves Pettigrew's life, Dumbledore explains that Pettigrew will now remain in Harry's debt and that he and Harry are inextricably bound. Pettigrew, a man accustomed to serving and saving himself, now faces the future of serving someone else—Harry—a debt that is paid later in the series.

Readers and critics often compare Pettigrew to Neville for several reasons. As McGonagall mentions, Pettigrew worshipped James and Sirius, just as Neville looks up to Harry and Ron. The two characters share another similarity: Both Pettigrew and Neville are extremely shy. Rowling's decision to make such obvious connections between these two characters may be a way for her to remind readers that, as Dumbledore explains in *Chamber of Secrets*, choices are more important than abilities; Pettigrew's choices benefit only himself, while Neville's choices benefit those important to him.

Harry Potter   The protagonist; member of Gryffindor House. In *Prisoner of Azkaban* Harry finally begins to understand his complicated past and learns more about the way his parents died. The exploration of these details gives the book a darker tone, but Harry's trusted friends and new characters he meets, including Remus Lupin and Sirius Black, are able to help him through this painful growth process.

Harry knows little about his parents, but when Aunt Marge insults them in the early chapters of the book, he loses all control, magically inflating her body into an enormous bubble. Harry's anger reflects his love for and loyalty to his parents and, likewise, his strong dislike for classist, snobbish people like Marge (whose comments about drowning weak dogs eerily echo comments made by pureblood fanatics whose elitist attitudes toward other species, Muggles, and nonpureblooded wizards sometimes border on the fanatical).

New opportunities for independence and the development of moral judgment present themselves in this book as well. During his days in Diagon Alley Harry indulges in eating ice cream, purchases his school supplies, and looks longingly at the newest broom, which he finds completely fascinating: the *Firebolt*. Although Harry has mounds of gold in Gringotts, he practices discipline and does not purchase the new broom, deciding that since he has never lost a match on his *Nimbus Two Thousand*, no reason exists for him to purchase a new broom. Obviously tempted and deserving of a reward now and then, Harry, in deciding not to buy the broom, demonstrates his growing maturity and rationality, traits he will need to draw upon as he makes his way through life as an orphan and prepares for future battles with Voldemort.

Encounters with Dementors leave Harry shaken and feeling as though he is weaker than his friends and classmates since their reactions are not as strong those he experiences. He feels relieved when Lupin agrees to teach him the Expecto Patronum spell to defend himself against the creatures and takes great comfort in knowing that his past—more terrible than those of his friends—is the reason for his stronger reactions. Both the Dementor attacks and his private lessons with Lupin provide Harry with important details about his past. The Dementors evoke details about the death of the Potters. During Harry's first encounter with a Dementor on the train Harry hears "screaming, terrible, terrified, pleading screams. He wanted to help whoever it was" (84). Later, during a Quidditch match when Dementors swarm too close to the pitch, Harry hears a woman scream, "Not Harry, not Harry, please not Harry!" followed by "Stand aside, you silly girl . . . stand aside, now" (179). Harry realizes the voices he hears are those of his mother and Voldemort, and even though the exchanges haunt his dreams, Harry values the small details he can gather, no matter how awful, to understand finally the manner of his parents' deaths.

Eventually Harry learns the entire story of how his parents were betrayed by Peter Pettigrew to Voldemort, and he learns this story from people who care about him and who cared about the Potters. Much as Hagrid first welcomed Harry into the wizarding world, Lupin and Sirius reveal the truth of the Potters' deaths yet also function as sources of happy and pleasant memories of the Potters. These characters provide a direct link for Harry to his parents since they grew up with them, celebrated with them, and joined forces with them in the first war against Voldemort. Harry feels a definite connection to his father when Sirius tells him, "You are—truly your father's son, Harry" (415). Such a compliment from Sirius carries a great deal of weight since Sirius knew James so well. Rowling further emphasizes the connection between father and son by making Harry's Patronus a stag, an exact replica of Prongs, his father's animagus form.

Harry spends most of the novel enraged over Black's alleged betrayal of the Potters. Readers have not seen Harry as angry as he feels when he initially think about Sirius Black: "A hatred such as he had never known before was coursing through Harry like poison" (213). Similarly, when Harry and Hermione find Sirius and Ron in the Shrieking Shack, Rowling describes Harry's emotional state as follows: "He had forgotten about magic—he had forgotten that he was short and skinny and thirteen, whereas Black was a tall, full-grown man—all Harry knew was that he wanted to hurt Black as badly as he could and that he didn't care how much he got hurt in return" (340). Rowling captures Harry's grief and anger brilliantly. The pain he feels for the loss of his parents fully realizes itself now that Harry finally knows the details of his parents' deaths.

By the novel's conclusion, Harry is finally aware that Pettigrew holds all responsibility for the murder of his parents. He nevertheless rises above the anger that has arrested him for so much of the novel. Harry stops Sirius from killing Pettigrew, for which the traitor thanks Harry. Harry replies: "I'm not doing this for you. I'm doing it because—I don't reckon my dad would've wanted [Sirius and Lupin] to become killers—just for you" (376). Sirius lost his best friends the day that Pettigrew murdered the Potters; Harry lost his parents. Surely Harry would desire revenge even more than Sirius, but the 13-year-old wizard seeks justice through established channels, convinced that Pettigrew will meet a fate he deserves at the scabbed hands of the Dementors. Harry's choice to let the Dementors punish Pettigrew sets Harry apart from his godfather,

Sirius. Refusing to murder Pettigrew when given the chance emphasizes Harry's ability to behave rationally, a characteristic Sirius often lacks. This is also another pivotal moment in Harry's moral development in the series, when he chooses the delayed gratification of justice over the immediate reward of revenge and violence.

Sirius and Harry, bonded by the loss of the Potters, look forward to the possibility of living together as a family, the first real opportunity Harry has for that kind of relationship up until this point in the series. The prospect of never again having to live at Number Four, Privet Drive, overwhelms Harry, but within mere minutes the possibility disappears because Sirius must live on the run if he is to remain free. Harry does not feel discouraged, though, since returning to the Dursleys' for the summer months is a small sacrifice to make to secure his godfather's freedom. Just as Harry lost his parents, he loses a chance to establish an immediate connection with Sirius. Rowling makes Harry return to the Dursleys', but not without frightening them into being nice to Harry since his godfather, as he informs them, is an escaped convict. Though Harry will be without his friends for a few months, the valuable connections he makes—with Sirius and Lupin in particular—during his third year at Hogwarts sustain him during his time with the Dursleys.

Severus Snape Potions professor at Hogwarts; head of Slytherin House. In the third installment of the Harry Potter series, Rowling reveals important details about Snape's past that help readers understand Snape's animosity toward Harry. Snape's behavior in this novel is shaped by a grudge based on events that occurred when he was a student at Hogwarts with James Potter, Remus Lupin, Peter Pettigrew, and Sirius Black. Even though most of his actions are driven by this old grudge, Snape still protects Harry and his friends from danger, proving he is mature enough to ignore his anger when student safety is jeopardized.

As Snape reveals to Harry, when Harry's father and his friends were at school decades earlier, Sirius goaded Snape to follow him to the Whomping Willow to learn why Lupin needed to hide him-

self away each month. At the last moment James stopped Snape from approaching the tree, knowing that Snape could easily be killed by the willow's thrashing limbs: "Your saintly father and his friends played a highly amusing joke on me that would have resulted in my death if your father hadn't gotten cold feet at the last moment. There was nothing brave about what he did. He was saving his own skin as much as mine" (285). Even though much of the responsibility for the prank lay with Sirius, Snape's continued resentment is targeted at all four of the friends. Snape's jealousy of Lupin's securing the Defense Against the Dark Arts teaching job fuels his existing resentment of Lupin, and though he helps Lupin with his lycanthropy by making him a potion (at Dumbledore's request), he cannot resist subversively revealing Lupin's condition. When he substitutes for Lupin, he asks the students to write an essay about werewolves, alerting perceptive students such as Hermione to Lupin's secret. Rowling depicts Snape as clinging to an immature anger stemming from ill will nurtured over many years. The negative effects of holding staunchly to this grudge present themselves at the end of the novel when the usually collected, unfeeling Snape loses control of himself in the hospital wing. When Snape learns of Sirius's escape from Hogwarts, his screams draw the attention of many staff members, and even the pleasant Madam Pomfrey rebukes Snape and demands he take control of himself. This rare sign of emotion signifies how deeply hurt Snape was as a student by Sirius and James in particular. Although his behavior is adolescent, Rowling demands some sympathy for Snape and any other person who, bullied in school, may wrestle with the emotional pain for years afterward.

Readers may not think Snape cares for his students, but his actions near the end of *Prisoner of Azkaban* prove otherwise. When a group of Dementors swarm Harry and Hermione, Snape rescues them. Their safety is his priority, and even if he dislikes his students, he cares for their well-being, just as McGonagall and Lupin do. Although he is consumed by anger and ruled by a schoolboy grudge against James Potter in particular, Snape is, Rowling demonstrates, one of Harry's greatest allies.

Sybill Trelawney   Divination professor at Hogwarts. Her first name hearkens back to the sibyls of ancient Greece, who foretold the future. Many members of the Hogwarts staff (and larger magical community) target Trelawney, ridiculing her for a power she claims to possess ("seeing" the future). Few believe she, or her gift, is genuine. That some of the events she predicts transpire may indicate Rowling's reminder that even Trelawney deserves sympathy and, possibly, respect.

The way Rowling describes Trelawney warrants attention, since Harry's first thought upon seeing Trelawney is of a "large, glittering insect. Professor [Trelawney's . . .] large glasses magnified her eyes to several times their natural size, and she was draped in a gauzy spangled shawl. Innumerable chains and beads hung around her spindly neck, and her arms and hands were encrusted with bangles and rings" (102). Her appearance provides a striking contrast to that of the other female professors in the novels, most notably McGonagall, who dresses in dark, neat tartan robes. In comparison, Trelawney's wardrobe portrays her as highly feminized, expressive, and at odds with the expected decorum of the traditional professorial attire. Her gaudy, ornate appearance shrouds her in mystery and simultaneously suggests she attempts to draw attention to herself through her nonconformity to expectations.

Trelawney's self-promotion concerns the many predictions she makes, and the one that arrests her students' attention most significantly focuses on the forthcoming death of a student. She repeatedly discusses Harry's impending death with no concern for his feelings or the feelings of those students who care about him. After she predicts Harry's death, she revels in the attention; this behavior suggests that she cares little about her students' emotional well-being and more about her self-importance. It is no wonder she is eager to be taken seriously by her students, however, since so many of her colleagues (and some students) dismiss Divination as an imprecise branch of magic. She desperately tries to validate her profession for her students by suggesting those who do not believe in Divination simply are not gifted enough themselves to be Seers: "Many witches and wizards, talented though they are in the area of loud bangs and smells and sudden disappearing, are yet unable to penetrate the veiled mysteries of the future" (103).

Even though most of her colleagues, students, and members of the wizarding community consider Trelawney a fraud, Rowling suggests that she deserves some sympathy and respect because of the way she is viewed by her colleagues. Most readers (and characters in the novels) do not take Trelawney seriously, and some may even go so far as to consider her mentally unstable. Trelawney's office and classroom are in the North Tower, one of the highest points in the castle, far away from everyone else. In this way Rowling places Trelawney in the tradition of madwomen confined to attics, like those in *Jane Eyre* and *Wide Sargasso Sea*. Trelawney hardly ever descends from her tower to join others, a pattern that also alienates her from the rest of the Hogwarts community. Although Trelawney explains that her decision not to mingle is her own, one must question whether she has decided to avoid the company of others because of the way they ridicule her, a narrative convention that warrants at least some sympathy for Trelawney.

Rowling also suggests that Trelawney deserves respect because some of the predictions she makes—both minor and major—are indeed valid. For instance, she predicts that Neville will break a teacup and appears to predict the death of Lavender's pet rabbit. More significant, however, is the prediction she voices to Harry during his final Divination exam: "The Dark Lord will rise again with his servant's aid, greater and more terrible than ever he was" (324). This prophecy (and another from many years earlier further explored in *Order of the Phoenix*) prove that Trelawney is a true Seer, even if most consider her flighty and unreliable.

Lord Voldemort   Harry's nemesis; the antagonist of the series. Voldemort does not appear in *Prisoner of Azkaban*, but Rowling mentions him often through conversations between or revelation by other characters. Rowling stresses Voldemort's power in this novel: When Lupin and Sirius accuse Pettigrew of serving Voldemort because in doing so the traitor might acquire some power by association, the Dark Lord's status is once again confirmed for readers.

Readers also finally learn some very specific details about Voldemort's crime against the Potters. In the presence of the Dementors Harry hears his parents pleading with Voldemort and the dark wizard's unfeeling commands. These flashbacks supply readers with concrete details that portray Voldemort's callousness in his pursuit of ultimate power. Even though he is never directly present and appears only in whispered conversations (the Hogwarts professors' conversation at the Three Broomsticks) or nearly private prophecies (when Trelawney prophesies his return during Harry's Divination final), Voldemort remains a constant, looming threat to readers, which mirrors the wizarding community's barely repressed anxiety and panic over the possibility of his return.

Ron Weasley Harry Potter's and Hermione Granger's best friend; fellow member of Gryffindor House. In *Prisoner of Azkaban* Ron remains one of Harry's closest friends, concerned for his friend's safety but simultaneously envious of Harry's fame. Readers also see an aspect of Ron's character they have not yet seen: his ability to hold a grudge.

Ron sends Harry a Pocket Sneakoscope for Harry's 13th birthday. Ron's choice of gift is important because it alerts its owner when someone or something untrustworthy is present. Well aware of the dark wizards who threaten his friend, Ron through the gift evidences his concern for his friend's safety.

Ron obviously cares for Harry, but this feeling does not prevent Ron from also feeling jealous of him: He wants his friend to be safe, but he also wants some of Harry's fame. As the youngest of the six Weasley boys, Ron feels as though he does not always receive enough attention. He also feels immense pressure to reach the level of success of his older brothers, as when he looks into the Mirror of Erised in *Sorcerer's Stone* and sees himself as a successful leader at Hogwarts. When Sirius Black enters the castle and nearly attacks Ron, Ron finally has his taste of fame, which he finds refreshing after watching the attention lavished on Harry the past few years. Rowling explains Ron's behavior

after Sirius's intrusion as follows: "Ron had become an instant celebrity. For the first time in his life, people were paying more attention to him than to Harry, and it was clear that Ron was rather enjoying the experience . . . he was happy to tell anyone who asked what had happened, with a wealth of detail" (270). As Harry's trustworthy sidekick, Ron very rarely receives special attention, so Sirius's attempted attack, even if potentially very dangerous, gives him a small share of notoriety.

Also in *Prisoner of Azkaban* readers begin to learn more about the evolving feelings between Ron and Hermione, who engage in a fierce battle over their respective pets, Scabbers and Crookshanks. Ron behaves very defensively about his pet rat, partly because Ron is stubborn, but mostly because he treasures the aged rat that has been passed to him from his older brothers. The Weasleys could not afford to give Ron his own new pet, so he takes pride in the pet that his family is able to give him. His argument with Hermione over Crookshanks's allegedly killing Scabbers drags on seemingly without end. Ron refuses to acknowledge any possibilities other than death by Crookshanks for his missing rat, and his inflexibility angers Hermione and saddens Hagrid, who reminds Ron that people sometimes behave irrationally when their pets are concerned. This fight between Ron and Hermione is the first major incident in which the friends are pitted against each other since becoming best friends after saving Hermione from the troll in *Sorcerer's Stone*. Rowling suggests that friends one considers as trustworthy should not be punished rashly and unfairly.

FILM ADAPTATION

After two monumentally successful film, change occurred in the Harry Potter film franchise. Chris Columbus, exhausted after directing the first two films (which succeeded each other within a year), was followed by Alfonso Cuarón, best known for his well-received film *Y Tu Mamá También*. The third film installment, *Harry Potter and the Prisoner of Azkaban*, was released on May 31, 2004, in the United Kingdom and on June 4, 2004, in the United States. The film grossed more than $92 million on opening weekend in the United States and had the biggest box-office opening ever in Britain. With the tagline "Something wicked this way comes," filmmakers piqued viewer interest and suggested that if they had seen the first two films, they should expect a much darker and heavier film.

Cuarón and his team also worked to portray the complex layering of Rowling's novel with other taglines like "Everything will change," "Mysteries will unfold," "Secrets will be revealed," "Character will be tested," and "Darkness will descend." Each of these sayings could be seen splashed across the bottom of a poster on which three characters' faces appeared. For instance, Snape's, Hermione's, and Malfoy's faces filled most of a promotional poster at the bottom of which the statement "Character will be tested" was printed, asking readers to question to what lengths each of these characters would go to meet his or her goals. In other words, even promotional materials associated with Cuarón's film had viewers thinking critically about the film before they even saw it, a feat that had not been attempted nor accomplished with the first two films. The complexity and beauty of Rowling's literary works moved to the forefront, even if Cuarón took much more liberty with *Prisoner of Azkaban* than Columbus had with the first two films. As David Gritten of the *Daily Telegraph* suggests, "The third in the Potter series, released on Monday, has a new director, the Mexican Alfonso Cuarón, and it marks a huge stride forward. *The Prisoner of Azkaban* . . . is a film that does justice to Rowling's soaring imagination."

Cuarón received high praise from many critics. In Henry Haun's "Passing the Wand: *Y Tu Mamá*'s Alfonso Cuarón Conjures a Darker Potter" from *Film Journal International*, Cuarón explains that "you don't mess with a winning formula. I wanted to keep the series going without any telltale sign that there had been a change in command. After I did that, I looked around to see if there was something I could bring to the series that would be mine and mine alone". Viewers may experience shock from the drastic changes made between the first two films and the third, but those changes serve as Cuarón's signature, distinguishing the film from the first two. The London *Times*'s James Christopher reflects on how assigning Cuarón as director was a major gamble (since he had not directed any projects similar in scale and popularity to *Harry Potter*) but ends his review by stating that "any misgivings about his ability to bring home the lucrative bacon evaporate frame by lavish frame." Cuarón's painstaking efforts made the film aesthetically different from the previous two installments. He worked for more than six months just to master the appearance of the Dementors. The *Chicago Tribune*'s Mark Caro describes Cuarón as "[shaking] the candy coating off of the franchise without violating its spirit."

One event that did have an impact on the spirit of the films was the death of Richard Harris, the actor performing the role of Albus Dumbledore, headmaster of Hogwarts. Harris was so fond of his role that even when he was seriously ailing, he told filmmakers not to recast him. After his passing rumors circulated that Harris would be re-created via computer graphics. Instead, the highly coveted role of Dumbledore was recast. The filmmaking team considered actors such as Ian McKellen and Christopher Lee but ultimately the role of headmaster went to Michael Gambon. According to the critics Carla Power and Devin Gordon of *Newsweek* in their article "Caution: Wizard at Work," the director Cuarón "reimagined the role of Professor Dumbledore after Richard Harris's death. British actor Michael Gambon now plays the Hogwarts headmaster as an elegant old hippie." The loss of Harris was difficult for fans, and filmmakers knew casting someone to play Dumbledore just as Harris had played him would not necessarily work and might suggest that Harris was "replaceable." So, reinventing the role, as Cuarón and Gambon did, made the transition a smoother one; Dumbledore was a new character, played by a new actor. In Haun's "Passing of the Wand," Cuarón states that Michael Gambon is "wicked, always pulling pranks during the filming, making us laugh. Michael's not at all like the stern figure he's playing."

Other casting additions include a score of celebrated British actors, including Julie Christie as the Three Broomsticks hostess Madame Rosmerta, Timothy Spall as the traitor Peter Pettigrew/Scabbers/Wormtail, David Thewlis as Defense Against the Dark Arts professor Remus Lupin, Gary Oldman as escaped Azkaban prisoner and Harry's godfather Sirius Black, and, of course, Emma Thompson as flighty Divination professor Sybill Trelawney. And, as Haun notes, Cuarón shared some thoughts on his cast in general and specifically on Alan Rickman, who plays the sinister Potions professor Severus Snape: "[Rickman] knows more about the character than I do. He's actually talked to Rowling about the role, so I pretty much left him to his own resources, which are considerable. Indeed, our cast is the crème de la crème of English acting and they didn't need any help from me, so I mostly concentrated on the three kids."

Much has been written about Cuarón's talents in working with child actors. Richard Corliss of *Time* in his article "When Harry Met Sirius" reflects on the director's ability not only to work with but also to inspire young actors. Corliss reflects that Daniel Radcliffe (Harry), Rupert Grint (Ron), and Emma Watson (Hermione) seemed "uncertain in their first films [. . . but] are comfortable with the camera now, and have grown into their roles as into their maturing bodies." Similarly, Power and Gordon of *Newsweek* quote the producer, David Heyman, in their article "Caution: Wizard at Work" as saying that Cuarón "has a keen understanding of the nuances of teenage life." Cuarón's sensitivity to the needs and feelings of his central teenage characters, some critics argue, has made characters such as Harry, Ron, and Hermione more real and relatable.

Cuarón used some unique strategies both to learn about his child actors and to prepare them for their roles in this much darker film. For instance, he encouraged Radcliffe to prepare for his role by listening to music that would focus his energy and mood; Radcliffe took to listening to bands like the Sex Pistols, the Strokes, and the Dandy Warhols. Cuarón also asked each of the three teens to write reflections about the character he or she would play so they would better understand the roles. Radcliffe, as Harry, turned in a one-page paper. Watson, as Hermione, gave Cuarón a 17-page document. And, true to Ron's fashion, Grint did not turn in any reflection at all.

In several instances the depiction of Hermione in *Prisoner of Azkaban* serves as a point of con-

sternation for viewers, especially girls and women. While all the students appear in regular clothes (in comparison to the Hogwarts robes fans had become accustomed to seeing them in throughout the first two films), Hermione's clothes are stylish and trendy (so much so, in fact, that some of her shirts, belts, and other accessories were copied and sold for young girls to buy for their own wardrobes). Rowling's Hermione would, fans assume, care little about whether or not her clothing was stylish. She would take pride in her appearance but not concern herself with being a trendsetter.

A similar but more troubling depiction of Hermione occurs during her journey with Harry to save Buckbeak from his sentencing at Hagrid's hut. When she and Harry wait in the woods, they see themselves hiding in Hagrid's pumpkin patch. The Hermione waiting in the woods with Harry suddenly looks distressed and turns to Harry, asking, "Is that really what my hair looks like from behind?" Rowling's Hermione would never let herself be concerned with such a question; she cared about the appearance of her hair for the Yule Ball, a special occasion, but in the middle of a quest to save the lives of Buckbeak and Sirius, Rowling's Hermione would not worry about the appearance of her hair, which suggests her to be shallow, vain, and self-involved, even while the lives of others are at stake. Perhaps these changes were made to stress Hermione's femininity and the typical concerns of adolescent females. However, fans agree these additions were unnecessary; the maturing talents of the actors serve as enough of a reminder that they are growing and dealing with new teenage pressures.

Although critics seem to agree that the performance of the child actors has improved by volumes, they do not all agree as to whether the film, as a whole, is better than those before it. Only one critic completely panned the film: Ann Hornday of the *Washington Post* claims that the film is too long, "made all the more so by a turgid story, a dour visual palette and uninspiring action." Hornday's claim concerning the palette is worth noting; *Prisoner of Azkaban* is visually (as well as thematically) much darker. While Cuarón's film lacks the vibrant colors employed by Columbus's filmmaking team, many critics agree the darker palette is not only appropriate for the mood of the film but also a welcome change.

The *Chicago Sun-Times*'s Roger Ebert feels *Prisoner of Azkaban* does not equal the standard and quality of the first two Harry Potter films. Power and Gordon of *Newsweek* call *Azkaban* "the puberty movie in the Potter franchise." They also claim that "Rowling's sequels have a knack for getting better." But, other critics disagree, arguing that the third film is the best of the trio. A. O. Scott of the *New York Times* calls *Prisoner of Azkaban* "the most interesting" and says that the film is "the first one that actually looks and feels like a movie, rather than a staged reading with special effects." The *London Daily Mirror*'s Kevin O'Sullivan argues that "*The Prisoner of Azkaban* delivers the goods in spectacular fashion." The Associated Press's Christy LeMire calls *Prisoner of Azkaban* "the meatiest, most magical film in the series," and Richard Corliss of *Time* tells readers to "enjoy the savory witches' brew that Cuarón has cooked up in his Harry pot."

As were the other Harry Potter films, *Prisoner of Azkaban* was nominated for many awards, including two Oscars (for Best Achievement in Music Written for Motion Pictures and Best Achievement in Visual Effects); the film was nominated for a host of Saturn awards; it won the BAFTA Children's Award for Best Feature Film; *Prisoner of Azkaban* won two Visual Society Awards; the film was nominated for both a Grammy and a Hugo Award; and the movie won a World Soundtrack Award. Roundly a success with both critics and fans, it provided viewers with a fresh and intuitive presentation of Harry Potter.

WORKS CITED AND FURTHER READING

Brennan, Geraldine. "Another Wizard Adventure." Review of *Harry Potter and the Prisoner of Azkaban*. *Times Educational Supplement*, 16 July 1999. Academic Search Premier. Available online by subscription. Accessed October 5, 2009.

Caro, Mark. "Review: *Harry Potter and the Prisoner of Azkaban*." *Chicago Tribune*, Available online. URL: http://www.showbizdata.com/review/232465/HARRY-POTTER-AND-THE-PRISONER-OF-AZKABAN. Accessed November 22, 2009.

Christopher, James. "Review: *Harry Potter and the Prisoner of Azkaban*." *Times* (London), 3 June 2004. Available online. URL: http://uk.imdb.com/title/tt0241527/news?year=2004. Accessed November 22, 2009.

Cooley, Ron. "Harry Potter and the Temporal Prime Directive: Time Travel, Rule-Breaking, and Misapprehension in *Harry Potter and the Prisoner of Azkaban*." In *Scholarly Studies in Harry Potter: Applying Academic Methods to a Popular Text*, edited by Cynthia Hallett, 29–42. Studies in British Literature, vol. 99. Lewiston, N.Y.: Edwin Mellen Press, 2005.

Corliss, Richard. "When Harry Met Sirius." *Time*, 30 May 2004. Available online. URL: http://www.time.com/time/magazine/article/0,9171,1101040607-644206,00.html. Accessed November 22, 2009.

Craig, Amanda. "Wit and Wizardry." *New Statesman*, 12 July 1999. Business Source Premier. Available online by subscription. Accessed October 5, 2009.

Ebert, Roger. "Review: *Harry Potter and the Prisoner of Azkaban*." *Chicago Sun-Times*, 3 June 2004. Available online. URL: http://rogerebert.suntimes.com/apps/pbcs.dll/article?AID=/20040603/REVIEWS/406030301. Accessed November 22, 2009.

Estes, Sally. Review of *Harry Potter and the Prisoner of Azkaban*. *Booklist*, 1 September 1999. Academic Search Premier. Available online by subscription. Accessed October 5, 2009.

Gilbert, Sandra, and Susan Gubar. *The Madwoman in the Attic: The Woman Writer and the Nineteenth-Century Literary Imagination*. New Haven, Conn., and London: Yale University Press, 2000.

Gray, Paul, et al. "Wild about Harry." *Time Canada*, 20 September 1999. Business Source Premier. Available online by subscription. Accessed October 5, 2009.

Gritten, David. "Review: *Harry Potter and the Prisoner of Azkaban*." *Daily Telegraph*, 3 June 2004. Available online. URL: http://www.imdb.com/name/nm0190859/news?year=2004. Accessed November 22, 2009.

Haun, Harry. "Passing the Wand: *Y Tu Mamá*'s Alfonso Cuarón Conjures a Darker Potter." *Film Journal International* 107, no. 7 (July 2004): 16–18.

Heilman, Elizabeth H. "Blue Wizards and Pink Witches: Representations of Gender Identity and Power." In *Harry Potter's World: Multidisciplinary Critical Perspectives*, edited by Elizabeth H. Heilman, 221–240. New York: RoutledgeFalmer, 2003.

Hornday, Ann. "Harry-Raising Adventure: Only Fans Will Love 'Potter 3,' Hogwarts and All." *Washington Post*, 4 June 2004. Available online. URL: http://www.washingtonpost.com/wp-dyn/articles/A14361-2004Jun3.html. Accessed November 22, 2009.

Huey, Peggy. "A Basilisk, a Phoenix, and a Philosopher's Stone: Harry Potter's Myths and Legends." In *Scholarly Studies in Harry Potter: Applying Academic Methods to a Popular Text*, edited by Cynthia Hallett, 65–83. Studies in British Literature, vol. 99. Lewiston, N.Y.: Edwin Mellen Press, 2005.

Katz, Maureen. "Prisoners of Azkaban: Understanding Intergenerational Transmission of Trauma Due to War and State Terror (with Help from Harry Potter)." *JPCS: Journal for the Psychoanalysis of Culture and Society* 8, no. 2 (2003): 200–207.

Klinkenborg, Verlyn. "Editorial Notebook: Harry Potter and the Marveling Muggles." *New York Times*, 11 September 1999. Newspaper Source Plus. Available online by subscription. Accessed October 5, 2009.

LeMire, Christy. "Review: *Harry Potter and the Prisoner of Azkaban*." 4 June 2004. Available online. URL: http://www.showbizdata.com/review/232465/HARRY-POTTER-AND-THE-PRISONER-OF-AZKABAN. Accessed November 22, 2009.

Lewis, Jonathan P. "If Yeh Know Where to Go: Vision and Mapping in the Wizarding World." In *Scholarly Studies in Harry Potter: Applying Academic Methods to a Popular Text*, edited by Cynthia Hallett, 43–64. Studies in British Literature, vol. 99. Lewiston, N.Y.: Edwin Mellen Press, 2005.

Litherland, Tena Natale. Review of *Harry Potter and the Prisoner of Azkaban*. *Book Report* 18, no. 3 (Nov/Dec 1999): 65. Academic Search Premier. Available online by subscription. Accessed October 5, 2009.

Loudon, Deborah. Review of *Harry Potter and the Prisoner of Azkaban*. *TLS: Times Literary Supplement*, 10 December 1999. Academic Search Premier.

Available online by subscription. Accessed October 5, 2009.

Maguire, Gregory. "Lord of the Golden Snitch." *New York Times Book Review*, 5 September 1999. Academic Search Premier. Available online by subscription. Accessed October 5, 1999.

Mitnick, Eva. Review of *Harry Potter and the Prisoner of Azkaban*. *School Library Journal* 45, no. 10 (October 1999): 158. Academic Search Premier. Available online by subscription. Accessed October 5, 2009.

O'Sullivan, Kevin. "Review: *Harry Potter and the Prisoner of Azkaban*." *London Daily Mirror*, 4 June 2004. Available online. URL: http://www.cinema.com/news/item/7023/record-box-office-in-uk-for-azkaban.phtml. Accessed November 22, 2009.

Parravano, Martha. Review of *Harry Potter and the Prisoner of Azkaban*. *Horn Book Magazine* 75, no. 6 (November/December 1999): 744–745. Academic Search Premier. Available online by subscription. Accessed October 5, 2009.

Power, Carla, and Devin Gordon. "Caution: Wizard at Work." *Newsweek*, 4 August 2003. Available online. URL: http://www.newsweek.com/id/152656. Accessed November 22, 2009.

Roback, Diane. Review of *Harry Potter and the Prisoner of Azkaban*. *Publishers Weekly*. 15 October 2001. Academic Search Premier. Available online by subscription. Accessed October 5, 2009.

Scott, A. O. "Review: *Harry Potter and the Prisoner of Azkaban*." *New York Times*, 3 June 2004. Available online. URL: http://movies.nytimes.com/movie/review?res=980DE2D81431F930A35755C0A9629C8B63. Accessed November 22, 2009.

Siegel, Lee. "Fear of Not Flying." *New Republic*, 22 November 2009. Business Source Premier. Available online by subscription. Accessed October 5, 2009.

Tucker, Nicholas. "A Little Touch of Harry: Review of *Harry Potter and the Prisoner of Azkaban*." *Michigan Quarterly Review* 39, no. 3 (2000): 667–673. Humanities International Complete. Available online by subscription. Accessed October 5, 2009.

Zipp, Yvonne. Review of *Harry Potter and the Prisoner of Azkaban*. *Christian Science Monitor*. 23 September 2009. Academic Search Premier. Available online by subscription. Accessed October 5, 2009.

Harry Potter and the Goblet of Fire (2001)

SYNOPSIS

Chapter One: "The Riddle House"

In the town of Little Hangleton the Riddle House (where Lord Voldemort's father grew up) has been unoccupied for years. It has become run down and dilapidated, and stories circulate in the village of Little Hangleton that 50 years earlier the Riddles (son and parents) were found dead by their maid with no discernible cause. Their deaths were lamented by very few (if any) because Mr. and Mrs. Riddle and their son, Tom, were considered rich and snobbish. Frank Bryce, the caretaker for the estate, was arrested for the crime, though he maintained he had seen a pale, dark-haired teen loitering in the area. Because no cause of death could be determined, Bryce was released and continued to care for their place. He is 77 years old at the book's opening, during which he spies intruders in the unoccupied Riddle House and assumes hooligans are about. He comes upon Peter Pettigrew (also known as Wormtail and Ron's former pet rat, Scabbers), who escaped capture at the end of the third novel, *Prisoner of Azkaban*. Bryce hears a mysterious noise. Pettigrew, speaking with someone unseen, volunteers to procure another wizard to accomplish some important but ambiguous task. He speaks with Voldemort (who resides in the form similar to the stature of an infant), who insists no other wizard will do; readers are not made privy to whom, exactly, Voldemort and Pettigrew are referring. There is reference to the murder of someone named Bertha Jorkins, whose death will figure prominently throughout the book. A snake named Nagini arrives and announces the presence of Bryce, whom Voldemort promptly kills. At the end of the chapter Harry Potter awakens from a nightmare, his scar throbbing.

Chapter Two: "The Scar"

Now 14, Harry awakens from a vivid dream: He remembers the dark, a snake, Wormtail, an old man, and a murder being committed along with a plan to kill Harry himself. He ponders why his scar hurts, because the last time his scar troubled him was when Voldemort was near him. He wonders whether to tell anyone about this dream and finally decides to tell his godfather, Sirius Black. The narrative reviews Harry's troubles so far in the series and, specifically, what occurred at the end of the previous novel.

Chapter Three: "The Invitation"

At breakfast the narrator reveals new developments for the Dursleys: The school nurse says Dudley is too heavy and unhealthy and as such has been placed on a very strict diet (which does nothing to improve his poor attitude). The mail arrives, and it includes an invitation from the Weasleys for Harry to attend the Quidditch World Cup. Even though Uncle Vernon goes out of his way to deprive Harry of things that make him happy, he also has the competing impulse to be rid of him for two weeks of the summer. When Harry threatens to tell his godfather, Sirius, that Vernon is refusing him permission to visit Ron and attend the World Cup, Uncle Vernon agrees, as Sirius has an (inaccurate) reputation as a mass murderer and Vernon fears what Harry's godfather might do to him and his family if he discovers that Harry is unhappy. Harry sends an owl to Ron accepting the invitation.

Chapter Four: "Back to the Burrow"

The Dursleys tensely await the Weasleys' arrival on Sunday at 5:00 P.M. At 5:15 a clamor emerges from the fireplace, which Uncle Vernon has boarded up in order to use an electric fire; not knowing this, Arthur has arranged to pick up Harry via the Floo Network—travel by fireplace. The Weasleys blast out the blocked-up fireplace, and Arthur, Fred, George, and Ron arrive in the living room. It is obvious the Dursleys think the Weasleys are crazy. The twins collect Harry's trunk, and Arthur attempts to make small talk with the Dursleys, who are nervous. Fred and George spill some candies, which they later reveal they did on purpose, knowing Dudley's dietary restrictions. The candies are part of their efforts to taunt him as revenge for his relentless mistreatment of Harry. Harry says good-bye to the Dursleys, and when they ignore him, Arthur chastises them, much to Vernon and Petunia's annoyance. Right before Arthur and Harry are about to depart, Dudley's tongue swells up, and he begins to choke—the twins have given him Ton-Tongue Toffee, a magical substance they created themselves that causes the chewer's tongue to swell to giant proportions. Arthur tries to sort it out but to no avail, and Harry departs via Floo powder.

Chapter Five: "Weasleys' Wizard Wheezes"
Harry arrives at the Burrow and finds Ron's older brothers Bill and Charlie already there. Bill works with dragons in Romania while Charlie works for Gringotts, the goblin-run bank. Arthur arrives and berates Fred and George for dropping the candy. Hermione and Ginny enter and the younger teens go upstairs while the twins get a tongue lashing over Weasleys Wizard Wheezes, their joke stuff business. Harry learns that Mrs. Weasley is unhappy over the twins' low academic aspirations. Percy is at the Burrow as well and is now working for the Ministry of Magic. Ron's new owl, Pigwidgeon, annoys the kids. Percy is obsessed with his work for Barty Crouch, Sr. (referred to hereafter as Crouch), Percy's supervisor at the Ministry of Magic. At an outdoor dinner in the Weasleys' backyard, conversation about Ludo Bagman, head of the Department of Magical Games and Sports, turns to Percy's critique that Bagman has not done enough about the absence of Bertha Jorkins, who went on holiday in Albania (referenced in the introductory chapters) and has gone missing. A spirited discussion of the World Cup follows, and Percy alludes to a "top secret event" that his Department of International Magical Cooperation will be organizing. Harry reports to Ron and Hermione that he has heard from Sirius twice.

Chapter Six: "The Portkey"
Everyone at the Burrow arises at the crack of dawn. Bill and Charlie and Percy can Apparate, or disappear from one place and reappear almost instantly in another, because they are of age and have taken their apparition test, but everyone else has to use a Portkey, a magically bewitched object that will transport them to the Quidditch World Cup. Arthur

notes the logistical difficulty of organizing large wizarding events without attracting Muggle attention. Arthur, Hermione, Ginny, Ron, and Harry head to Stoatshead Hill and find Amos Diggory and his son, Cedric, waiting there to travel with the Portkey. Cedric is a Hufflepuff as well as Seeker and captain of the Hufflepuff Quidditch team. Amos brags that Cedric's Quidditch abilities are superior to Harry's. Regardless, they all take the Portkey to the match.

Chapter Seven: "Bagman and Crouch"
The group arrives at a deserted moor where two wizards process new arrivals. A Muggle employed by the campsite has to have his memory modified frequently. Bagman seems lax about anti-Muggle precautions. Harry and the Weasleys set up their tent, which is magically bewitched to appear as a two-person tent on the outside but inside is lavish and spacious. Harry and Hermione fetch water, and Harry marvels at the diverse witches and wizards from around the globe. They meet Seamus Finnegan and Dean Thomas, their Gryffindor classmates, in a patch of tents decked out in green gear supporting Ireland's Quidditch team.

Percy, Bill, and Charlie arrive, as does Ludo Bagman, who takes bets on the match from Fred and George over Arthur's objections. He reports there has been no new information on the disappearance of Bertha Jorkins, his Ministry of Magic coworker. Crouch appears, impeccably dressed, Muggle-style, and refers to Percy frequently as "Weatherby," challenging Percy's self-styled image as Crouch's right-hand man. Arthur and Crouch allude again to some forthcoming event at Hogwarts that remains an enormous secret. By evening the excitement grows and attempts by the ministry to quell the use of illegal (but good-hearted) magic are futile. Harry buys three pairs of Omnioculars (binoculars that allow the user to rewind and pause events or even to learn more information about that which the viewer sees—in this case, Quidditch positions and moves), for himself, Ron, and Hermione, in order to watch the game.

Chapter Eight: "The Quidditch World Cup"
Harry and the Weasleys head to their seats, with tickets in a prime location because of Arthur's connection with the ministry. The stadium is

enormous, seating 100,000 fans. Harry spots a female house-elf and strikes up a conversation, learning her name is Winky and she is Crouch's house-elf. She tells him Dobby, since being freed, now hopes to be paid for his work (to her horror), and she affirms the elfish value of strict obedience. She indicates she is saving a seat for her master at the top of the box seats despite her fear of heights. Crouch arrives at the box seats, as do the Malfoys, and a tense exchange between Lucius and Arthur ensues. Bagman serves as announcer. Team mascots precede the match—Veela for the Bulgarians and Leprechauns for the Irish. The Veela are seductive she-creatures who entrance the male players and the referee; the Leprechauns toss gold into the audience. A lively Quidditch match then begins; although the Bulgarian Seeker, Viktor Krum, gets the Snitch, Ireland wins, just as Fred and George bet Bagman.

Chapter 9: "The Dark Mark"
Harry and the Weasleys return to their tent for some cocoa and are about to head to bed when Arthur rouses them. Outside a group of hooded wizards is levitating the Muggle campsite manager and his family, tormenting them. Arthur rushes to help the Ministry of Magic official contain the chaos. He sends the kids to the woods to hide. Harry realizes he has misplaced his wand. They see Winky moving strangely through the forest as though being held back by some invisible force. Suddenly, the Dark Mark (a skull made of stars with a protruding snake as its tongue) is conjured in the sky. Harry, Ron, and Hermione try to run, but suddenly a large group of ministry wizards Apparates and begins firing Stunning Spells wildly, including Crouch, who accuses the children of conjuring the Mark. Others assert that the youngsters are unlikely to have done it, since conjuring the mark requires powerful and dark magic.

Farther on into the woods the ministry wizards find Winky, magically stunned. She denies having conjured the Dark Mark, though she is in possession of Harry's wand and is accused by Amos Diggory of performing the deed. Crouch, humiliated, threatens to set her free. Harry and his friends return to their

tents and converse, with Arthur explaining that the Dark Mark is Voldemort's symbol and has not been seen in 13 years. Readers also learn that the term *Death Eaters* refers to Voldemort's supporters and that during his reign of terror the Dark Mark was conjured above the location where a Death Eater murdered someone. They speculate that the Death Eaters scattered when the symbol appeared because those who are not already captured and in Azkaban probably betrayed Voldemort and would face his wrath if he were to return.

Chapter 10: "Mayhem at the Ministry"
Harry, the Weasleys, and Hermione pack and return quickly via Portkey to the Burrow, where Mrs. Weasley is panicked over a news story in the *Daily Prophet* by Rita Skeeter, a sensationalist journalist who targets the Ministry of Magic in her stories. Arthur and Percy go to work, and Harry explains to Hermione and Ron that he is awaiting a response to an owl he sent to Sirius about his scar's hurting. He recounts his dream and remembers that Trelawney predicted last year that Voldemort would rise again.

The public is whipped into a frenzy over Rita Skeeter's story. Hermione and Ron argue over house-elf rights; Ron claims that the elves are happy with their status, a notion with which Hermione disagrees completely (as illustrated by her adamant defense of Winky at the World Cup after the Dark Mark had been conjured). They rifle through the school supplies Molly bought at Diagon Alley for their return to Hogwarts. Ron complains about the shabby dress robes his mother bought for him since they are required for him as a fourth-year and the Weasleys cannot afford to buy him new robes; he laments being poor.

Chapter 11: "Aboard the Hogwarts Express"
Everyone at the Burrow is down in spirits about the end of summer vacation. Mr. Weasley sets off for an emergency that figures importantly in the novel's denouement; Mad-Eye Moody, a retired and paranoid ex-Auror (dark wizard hunter), is in trouble with the Improper Use of Magic Office.

They all take taxis to King's Cross Station, and Charlie suggests mysteriously to the kids that he may be seeing them soon. On the train they hear Draco alluding to Durmstrang, another wizarding school that only admits purebloods and favors the subject of the Dark Arts. Hermione reveals from her perpetual reading of *Hogwarts: A History* that Durmstrang, among many other wizarding schools, is in a secret location that is unplottable (impossible to locate on a map). Draco taunts Harry, Ron, and Hermione about not knowing about the Triwizard Tournament (the secret event many characters have alluded to thus far in the novel), bragging that his father has known about it for ages and that Arthur Weasley must be "too junior" to be involved with the planning. Because of this insult Ron remains angry for the rest of the trip to Hogwarts.

Chapter 12: "The Triwizard Tournament"
The trio discuss who the new Defense Against the Dark Arts teacher will be, since s/he has not arrived yet. This year the Sorting Hat's song provides historical background on the qualities of the four houses, specifically that Salazar Slytherin disagreed with his cofounders about the admission of non-pureblood students. Nearly Headless Nick reveals that Hogwarts has house-elves, and Hermione is horrified and refuses to eat the dinner she claims is prepared by slave labor. Dumbledore begins his start-of-term announcements, but the arrival of Mad-Eye Moody, the new Defense Against the Dark Arts teacher, interrupts the headmaster's announcement about the Triwizard Tournament, a competition among the three largest European schools of wizardry, each of which selects a champion to compete in three magical tasks. Established 700 years ago, the tournament was discontinued because of its death toll. Ministry of Magic officials put an age restriction on this year's competitors; students wishing to participate must be of age in the wizarding world, meaning they must be 17 or older. Dumbledore says the other school delegations will arrive in October. Everyone heads off to bed, the Weasley twins dreaming of hoodwinking the judge into selecting them as champions even though they do not meet the age requirement.

Chapter 13: "Mad-Eye Moody"
The next morning Fred, George, and their friend Lee Jordan try to think of magical aging methods in order to trick the tournament judge. Harry awaits word from Sirius via owl post but does not hear anything. The students go through their class day—Herbology and Care of Magical Creatures, where Hagrid has them raising thoroughly disgusting creatures named Blast-Ended Skrewts. After lunch Hermione takes off for a mysterious trip to the library. In Divination Trelawney predicts terrible things for Harry, just as she had the year before. At dinner Malfoy calls their attention to the *Daily Prophet* story about Arthur's visit to rescue Mad-Eye Moody the night before they departed for school. Draco and Ron insult each other's mothers, and just as Draco is about to stun Harry with his back turned, Mad-Eye Moody transfigures Draco into a ferret, even though he admits to McGonagall that Dumbledore warned him not to use transfiguration as a punishment for misbehaving students. Fred and George award high praise to Mad-Eye Moody's Defense Against the Dark Arts lessons, leaving Ron and Harry especially excited about that class.

Chapter 14: "The Unforgivable Curses"
Snape would like the Defense Against the Dark Arts job and is in a foul mood because he has not been appointed to it. The Gryffindors go to Moody's Defense Against the Dark Arts class. Moody tells them that they do not need their books but that they are behind on learning curses, and since he will only be there a year, they have to catch up on a lot. Moody illustrates the effects of the three Unforgivable Curses on three different spiders—the Imperius Curse, which forces the victim to do one's will; the Cruciatus Curse, which inflicts torturous pain on the victim; and *Avada Kedavra*, the Killing Curse, which has no countercurse. Harry is the only known survivor of the Killing Curse. When Moody kills the spider with the Killing Curse, Harry wonders whether his parents died similarly. Use of the three curses on a human sentences one to a life term in Azkaban. Moody utters his trademark phrase, "Constant Vigilance," cautioning the students always to be on their guard.

After class Neville is upset, and Moody invites him for tea after dinner. While Harry and Ron work on Divination homework, Neville arrives in the Gryffindor common room with the book *Magical*

Water Plants of the Mediterranean, a gift from Moody to lift the boy's spirits. Fred and George work on a document and behave suspiciously. Hermione's new purposeful use of the library becomes apparent when she introduces her S.P.E.W. (Society for the Promotion of Elfish Welfare) campaign, which Harry and Ron mock and the house-elves reject. She tries to recruit the two boys to her campaign but is interrupted by Hedwig with a message from Sirius announcing his return to England from his secret location elsewhere. Harry blames himself for Sirius's return, which will undoubtedly endanger his godfather.

Chapter 15: "Beauxbatons and Durmstrang"

Harry sends a message to Sirius recanting his story about his scar's hurting in an effort to prevent him from returning to the dangers he faces at home. Defense Against the Dark Arts becomes more difficult as Moody puts the Imperius Curse on the students. Hermione objects to this practice, since, even as an educational tool, performing the curse is illegal; Moody responds to this with the claim "Dumbledore wants you taught what it feels like" (230). They all notice increases in their homework this year at Hogwarts, due precisely to the fact that O.W.L. (Ordinary Wizarding Level) exams occur the following year. Cedric Diggory expresses interest in entering the Triwizard Tournament. Fred and George still conspire about a mysterious issue. Meanwhile, students learn the three tasks in the Triwizard Tournament are assigned points by judges, usually the heads of the participating schools. Hermione's continued campaign for the rights of the house-elves is met with widespread lack of interest.

Sirius writes back to Harry, explaining that Harry should keep him informed of what transpires at Hogwarts. The Beauxbatons delegation arrives via a house-sized carriage pulled by winged horses. Madame Olympe Maxime, a giantess, exits the carriage, accompanied by a dozen boys and girls. The Durmstrang delegation arrives by means of a ship emerging from underneath the Black Lake. Igor Karkaroff, their headmaster, leads a number of students, most notably the Quidditch superstar from the Bulgarian team, Viktor Krum.

Chapter 16: "The Goblet of Fire"

The Hogwarts students, including Ron, fawn over Krum because of his celebrity status as a professional Quidditch player, to Hermione's disgust. Bagman and Crouch arrive to have dinner with the Hogwarts students and the newly arrived delegations. Dumbledore announces that the two ministry officials will be joining Karkaroff and Maxime as judges for the tournament. Filch upon Dumbledore's command takes out a wooden chest encrusted with jewels. Dumbledore explains the tournament will consist of three tasks throughout the school year, tasks requiring magical prowess, cleverness, and bravery. The representatives—so-called champions—of each institution will be selected by the Goblet of Fire. Out of the bejeweled casket Dumbledore pulls a wooden cup erupting blue flames. He explains that aspiring champions should place their names on a slip of paper in the goblet during the next 24 hours. An age line will be drawn to prevent underage entrants from attempting to put their names in the goblet. Dumbledore notes that once a champion has been selected by the Goblet of Fire, a binding magical contract forms and the selected individual cannot withdraw from the tournament. Karkaroff crosses paths with Harry and seems wary; Moody also has a tense encounter with the Durmstrang headmaster over some unnamed past tension.

The next morning Fred, George, and Lee Jordan take an aging potion in an attempt to outwit the goblet but are promptly ejected from inside the magical age line, growing long white beards. A number of students from all three schools put their names in, hoping to be chosen as their school's champion. Harry, Ron, and Hermione visit Hagrid, who is excited about the tournament and refuses to join S.P.E.W. because he is of the mind that house-elves enjoy their station and do not desire freedom or a change in their status. They go to dinner, noting Hagrid has made some improvements to his appearance seemingly motivated by his romantic interest in Madame Maxime. The champions are announced: for Durmstrang, Viktor Krum; for Beauxbatons, an attractive blond young woman named Fleur Delacour; for Hogwarts, Cedric Diggory. Dumbledore is about to conclude the ceremony when the goblet ejects one more name: *Harry Potter.*

Chapter 17: "The Four Champions"

Dumbledore ushers Harry to the side room, where the champions have gathered over Harry's protestations that he did not enter his own name into the Goblet of Fire. Karkaroff and Madame Maxime strenuously object and cry foul over Hogwarts's second champion; however, rules state that whoever has his or her name issued from the goblet must compete in the tournament. Moody enters the room and argues that Harry's competing is dangerous and perhaps the result of dark magic, as tricking the goblet into both allowing and selecting Harry's name would require some very powerful and advanced magic. Crouch, also in attendance, concludes with Dumbledore that no choice exists but to have both Harry and Cedric compete on behalf of Hogwarts. Everyone leaves, with Harry contemplating how and why his name was entered into the Goblet of Fire. When he returns to Gryffindor's common room, everyone hails him as a hero, the students celebrating but disbelieving his claim that he did not enter his own name. Ron feels hurt and angry, believing Harry lied to him about entering the tournament.

Chapter 18: "The Weighing of the Wands"

The next morning Harry dreads breakfast but meets Hermione as he is leaving the Gryffindor dorm; she invites him for a walk. Hermione believes he did not enter his name in the tournament but shares his concern over who did and insists he write Sirius about the matter. She also explains why Ron is jealous of the attention Harry continually receives. All students, including Hufflepuffs, are cold to Gryffindor, especially to Harry, because they believe he stole their champion, Cedric's, glory. Hagrid, as does Hermione, believes that Harry did not enter his name. The next few days are miserable for Harry, mostly because Ron ignores him but also because all the students are wearing buttons that say "Support Cedric Diggory: The Real Hogwarts Champion" and that also flash "Potter Stinks!" Draco and Harry have a magical skirmish in the hall, and Hermione

gets hit by a spell that causes her teeth to enlarge, about which Snape makes a snide comment, sending Hermione in tears to Madame Pomfrey. Harry and Ron shout at Snape and get detention.

Harry is fetched for tournament business and finds Krum, Cedric, and Fleur sitting in a classroom with Bagman and a *Daily Prophet* photographer for a wand-weighing ceremony. Rita Skeeter is also there to do a story on the champions; she corners Harry in a broom closet and uses her "Quik Quotes Quill," which translates her utterances into flowery and inaccurate language, all the while trying to induce Harry to admit he entered himself in the tournament. The headmasters and headmistress enter to observe, along with ministry officials and the wandmaker Ollivander, who performs the wand assessment. The core of Fleur's wand (a Veela hair) reveals that she herself is part Veela (the hair was one of her grandmother's). Ollivander examines the wands and reminds Harry that his and Voldemort's wands share a phoenix feather core from Fawkes, Dumbledore's phoenix, which was so helpful to Harry in *Chamber of Secrets.* At dinner Harry is reminded that he needs to work on his Summoning Charm. He receives an owl from Sirius asking him to meet him at 1 A.M. in the Gryffindor common room, where he will appear in the fireplace. Meanwhile, Ron continues to be surly and cold to Harry.

Chapter 19: "The Hungarian Horntail"

Harry looks forward to the conversation with Sirius; he is starting to feel anxious about the first task of the Triwizard Tournament. Rita Skeeter's story on the tournament focuses entirely on Harry and includes lies and misrepresentations about his life and his family. Harry tries to reconcile with Ron to no avail. Hermione complains about Viktor Krum's spending a lot of time in the library because of the gaggle of female admirers who follow him everywhere. The Saturday before the first task Hermione and Harry (wearing the Invisibility Cloak) go to Hogsmeade. Harry observes the other students, carefree, and wishes he were one of them.

They see Hagrid and Moody talking, and as Moody approaches them, it becomes apparent that Moody's magical eye can see Harry even though he wears the Invisibility Cloak. Hagrid tells Harry he should meet him at his cabin at midnight. When he meets Hagrid, Harry learns that the first task of the tournament involves dragons. Madame Maxime learns this as well. On his way back to meet Sirius in the common room fireplace, Harry (wearing his Invisibility Cloak) bumps into Karkaroff, confirming that every champion will know about the dragons except Cedric. When Harry meets Sirius, they talk about Harry's worries. Sirius confides that Karkaroff used to be a Death Eater, that Bertha Jorkins is still missing, and that Jorkins is somewhat mentally dull but gossipy so could be a liability if lured into a trap. Ron approaches Harry, and Sirius disappears. The boys do not end the night on friendly terms.

Chapter 20: "The First Task"

Harry and Hermione review many books at the library trying to figure out how to get Harry past the dragons but struggle to figure out what sort of spell will help him. On the way to class one day Harry decides to tell Cedric about the dragons so he will not be the only champion who does not know what he will be up against during the first task. Cedric remains somewhat suspicious of Harry's goodwill but eventually thanks him for making him privy to the information. Moody calls Harry to his office and advises him to do two things in the first part of the tournament: play to his strengths and use a simple spell to get what he needs. Harry quickly realizes he needs to do a Summoning Spell so he can get his broom in order to fly when encountering the dragon. He and Hermione practice the spell until he feels comfortable with using it.

At the start of the tournament McGonagall, Bagman, and the champions gather in a tent. Each champion is instructed that he will battle a dragon (as they all already know), but their final goal is to retrieve a golden egg from each dragon's nest. Harry summons his *Firebolt* from the castle and successfully evades the Hungarian Horntail to capture the golden egg. Hermione and Ron approach Harry, while being patched up in the medical tent, and he and Ron resolve their conflict. Harry and Krum tie for first place on the basis of their scores. The next task will take place February 24 and will involve a message hidden inside the egg each champion has just secured from his dragon's custody.

Chapter 21: "The House-elf Liberation Front"

There is a celebration in the Gryffindor common room, where Harry opens his egg, which emits a shrill howl. Hermione realizes that Fred and George have stolen food from the kitchens and learns how to gain access; she wants to see the conditions in which the house-elves live. Her S.P.E.W. campaign remains widely mocked. In December Rita Skeeter arrives at a Care of Magical Creatures class to observe a lesson on the increasingly larger Blast-Ended Skrewts. Hagrid agrees to an interview with her, troubling Harry and Ron. Later Hermione rushes Ron and Harry to the kitchen, where they find Dobby and learn that both he and Winky work there (Dobby is the only elf to receive pay for his work, and he has come to take some pride in the fact). Winky feels miserable over being freed and works at Hogwarts as a last resort. We learn that part of house-elves' enslavement is keeping their masters' secrets, and Winky will not say bad things about her former master, Crouch. Winky suggests that Bagman is a "bad wizard."

Chapter 22: "The Unexpected Task"

McGonagall announces the Yule Ball, a traditional part of the Triwizard Tournament, will be held as part of the celebration for the tournament. Students in their fourth year or older may attend (and may invite someone younger), and champions and their partners are expected to open the ball with a special partner dance. As a champion, Harry realizes he needs to ask someone to accompany him, but he and Ron are both intimidated about asking girls on a date. Harry works up the courage to ask Cho, the Ravenclaw Seeker he seemed interested in the previous year, but learns she has already agreed to go with Cedric. He and Ron try to persuade Ginny and Hermione to go with them as their dates but learn they are committed—Ginny to Neville and Hermione to a boy whose name she will not reveal. Harry finally asks Parvati Patil, who accepts and offers to ask her twin sister, Padma, to accompany Ron.

Chapter 23: "The Yule Ball"

Winter falls, and Harry procrastinates puzzling the egg. Ron notices Hermione's teeth look less prominent and she reveals that when they were magically enlarged last fall, she let Madame Pomfrey shrink them more than necessary. Pigwidgeon arrives with a note from Sirius, who congratulates Harry on his success with the first task. The day of the Yule Ball Harry and Ron get ready and meet the Patil twins. To the astonishment of everyone Hermione enters the ball with her mystery date, Viktor Krum, and has had something of a makeover with a sleek hairstyle and fancy periwinkle dress. Percy announces to Harry that he has been promoted to the status of Crouch's personal assistant.

During a conversation with Krum and Karkaroff Dumbledore refers to an area of the castle known as the Room of Requirement. After dinner the dance begins, though Harry abandons the dancefloor as quickly as he can, much to the annoyance of his date. Hermione joins him and Ron at a table, and Ron, out of jealousy, implies that Krum only asked her to the dance to acquire inside information on Harry. Crouch's absence from the office is the subject of a conversation between Percy and Harry. On a walk through the grounds Harry and Ron overhear an ambiguous conversation between Snape and Karkaroff about something happening that is worrisome. They also overhear Madame Maxime and Hagrid, who are having an intimate conversation, during which Hagrid's suggestion that the Beauxbaton's headmistress appears part giant outrages and offends her. Ron later explains her outrage probably stems from the view that giants are widely regarded by wizards as vicious and brutal creatures.

Cedric approaches Harry and suggests enigmatically that he should visit the prefect's bathroom and take a bath with the egg he acquired from fighting the dragon in the first task. Ron and Hermione argue in the common room when Hermione correctly interprets Ron's snarky behavior as jealousy over her attending the ball with Krum instead of Ron. She informs Ron that if he wanted to go to the dance with her so badly, he should have asked her earlier, instead of waiting until the last minute.

Chapter 24: "Rita Skeeter's Scoop"
The next day the students rise late, and Hermione and Ron do not address the previous night's argument. As February approaches, Harry does not make much progress on the egg. In Care of Magical Creatures they have a new teacher, Professor Grubbly-

Plank, whose appearance is quickly explained when Malfoy produces the latest edition of the *Daily Prophet* with a story called "Dumbledore's Giant Mistake." It portrays Hagrid as a ferocious and ruthless giant who routinely subjects his students to dangerous creatures.

Over the weekend the students visit Hogsmeade and see Bagman conspiring with some goblins in a corner of the Three Broomsticks. Bagman reports to Harry that Crouch has stopped going to work, attempting to divert attention from his tête-à-tête with the goblins. He also inappropriately offers help to Harry with his second task. Skeeter enters, and Harry and Hermione confront her about the Hagrid story. Ron warns against getting on Rita's bad side. They visit Hagrid's cabin and find Dumbledore trying to refuse Hagrid's resignation. They encourage him to stay on as a teacher. Hagrid instead talks about wanting Harry to win the tournament so he can prove one does not need status as a pureblood to be great. Harry feels guilty that he has not made progress on the second task.

Chapter 25: "The Egg and the Eye"
Harry decides to take Cedric's suggestion and examine the egg in the prefects' bathroom, so he takes it there in the middle of the night with his Invisibility Cloak and the Marauder's Map in hand to keep track of Filch. Moaning Myrtle, camping out in the prefects' lavatory, tells him to open the egg in the water. He hears a song that is a riddle and determines that he will have an hour to conquer the depths of the lake and retrieve one of his valuable possessions from the merpeople.

On his way back to the dorm he sees Barty Crouch on the Marauder's Map. Momentarily distracted, he trips and loses the egg, which cracks open and creates a disturbance. Filch comes along and assumes the object belongs to Peeves, as does Snape, who claims someone has been searching his office. Moody goes to the rescue of Harry, who hides beneath his Invisibility Cloak. Moody rescues the egg and the map from Snape and Filch and asks Harry whether he saw who broke into Snape's office. Harry confesses it was Crouch, and they have an intense conversation about Death Eaters. Moody implies that Crouch could be searching for signs of dark wizardry or implements of it. He borrows the map and suggests Harry consider a career as an Auror.

Chapter 26: "The Second Task"

Harry sends Sirius an owl about Crouch's breaking into Snape's office. The trio of friends work tirelessly on a solution to the second task, but even the night before, they have no ideas. McGonagall summons Ron and Hermione to her office for unclear reasons, and Harry falls asleep in the library reading. Dobby wakes him the next morning, 10 minutes before the second task begins, and gives him part of a plant called Gillyweed. Dobby says he overheard Moody and McGonagall talking about the plant in the staffroom. Harry takes it and dashes to the lake's edge, where Bagman calls a start to the task. He hurriedly swallows the Gillyweed, which gives him gills and fins, so he dives in but is immediately attacked by Grindylows, underwater creatures, which he fends off. Meanwhile, Fleur suffers attacks from creatures in the lake and is unable to complete the task. Harry comes upon a merpeople village, where Cho, Hermione, Ron, and Fleur's little sister, Gabrielle, are tied to a giant statue. He frees Ron but feels torn about whether to leave the others behind. The merpeople tell him he can only take his own hostage, but Krum eventually arrives for Hermione and Cedric takes Cho. Desperate when Fleur does not arrive for her sister, Harry threatens the merpeople and takes Gabrielle and Ron to the surface. Afterward he feels foolish for thinking that the hostages were actually in danger, but after consultation with the Chief Merperson and Dumbledore, the judges award him second place for showing moral fiber in his determination to save all the hostages.

Chapter 27: "Padfoot Returns"

Sirius arranges a meeting in Hogsmeade. In Potions class the Slytherins circulate a *Witch Weekly* article entitled "Harry Potter's Secret Heartache" portraying Hermione as a scheming vixen who toys with both Harry's and Viktor's affections. Hermione wonders how Rita overheard a private conversation between her and Viktor, which happened to be quoted in the article. Snape confiscates the magazine and publicly

mocks them. He later threatens Harry with Veritaserum (a serum that forces the drinker to tell the truth) to induce him to admit that he has been stealing ingredients from his office. Karkaroff enters and shows Snape something on his arm that Harry cannot see.

The next day the trio of friends head to Hogsmeade. They meet Padfoot, Sirius's black dog animagus form, in a remote area and follow him to a nearby cave. They discuss Crouch's absence from his work at the Ministry of Magic and wonder whether it is even possible that Winky stole Harry's wand at the World Cup and used it to conjure the Dark Mark. Sirius also harbors resentment against Crouch because as the head of the Department of Magical Law Enforcement, Crouch sent Sirius to Azkaban without a trial. Sirius tells them that Crouch was an up-and-comer in the ministry until his son, Barty Crouch, Jr., was revealed to be a Death Eater. His father followed the law strictly and, even though it was his own son, Crouch unhesitatingly sent his son to Azkaban; Sirius recalls the Crouches' deathbed visit to their son in prison. Crouch lost some public sympathy because his careerism was seen to have driven his son toward the dark side. They discuss why Crouch would have been investigating Snape; they cannot understand why Dumbledore trusts the former Death Eater and Potions master. Sirius asserts that Snape has always been fascinated by the Dark Arts but was never proved a Death Eater. He asks Ron whether Percy can get any inside information from the ministry.

Chapter 28: "The Madness of Mr. Crouch"

Ron sends an owl to Percy asking about Crouch. On their next visit to the kitchen they give socks to Dobby; Winky appears drunk, depressed, and filthy. Hermione tries to cheer her up and asks about her former master, Crouch, but Winky asserts that she keeps her master's secrets. Hermione and Ron's romantic tensions continue to develop. The next morning Hermione starts receiving hate mail over Rita's story. In Care of Magical Creatures they work with nifflers, creatures who like to find shiny objects, and Hagrid designs a lesson around using the creatures to find buried Leprechaun gold, which he explains disappears eventually. Ron feels frustrated that Harry never told him that the gold Ron paid him at the World Cup for his Omniocu-lars disappeared, and Harry says he never noticed. Ron again suffers jealously and bitterness over being poor. Hermione continues her vendetta against Rita, determined to find out how she gains access to private information. Percy responds to their let-ter questioning Crouch's status defensively, saying that Crouch is taking a well-deserved break, that he sends regular owls with instructions, and that Percy has matters under careful control. The champions learn at the end of May about the tournament's third task, which will be completing a maze with many obstacles.

Krum corners Harry in a stretch of trees near Hagrid's cabin, asking whether his relationship with Hermione is romantic, and Harry truthfully denies that it is. In the midst of their conversation a bat-tered Crouch, seemingly delirious, emerges from the woods asking for Dumbledore. Harry leaves Viktor to watch him while he runs to the castle, but Snape interrupts him. When Harry finally returns with Dumbledore, Krum is unconscious and Crouch is gone. Once revived, Krum reveals that Crouch attacked him, and Karkaroff, also present, accuses Dumbledore of some conspiracy to prevent the Durmstrang champion from winning.

Chapter 29: "The Dream"
Harry, Ron, and Hermione try to figure out what happened with Viktor and Crouch, and they send an owl to Sirius about the incident. They overhear Fred and George Weasley approaching the Owlery talking about blackmail, but the twins say they are joking. The trio visit Moody, asking what he thinks happened to Crouch. Moody's response is to reas-sert his motto, "Constant Vigilance." Sirius writes back and berates Harry for going somewhere alone with Krum, admonishing him to prepare himself for the third task. Hermione and Ron help Harry practice curses, spells, and hexes. Harry falls asleep during Divination and dreams Voldemort punishes Wormtail for some undetermined blunder. Harry awakens and heads to Dumbledore's office to report the vision and finds the Minister of Magic, Cor-nelius Fudge, talking to Dumbledore and Moody about Crouch.

Chapter 30: "The Pensieve"
Leaving Harry to wait, Dumbledore, Moody, and Fudge have a brief look at the grounds where Crouch was found. Harry spies a Pensieve, a shallow stone basin that can store one's memories; in this case, the memories belong to Dumbledore. He peers in and is sucked into Dumbledore's memories of years ago, specifically the trials of Death Eaters, including Karkaroff, who, in hopes of a less harsh punishment, names many of the Death Eaters for the council, including Snape, for whom Dumbledore vouches as innocent. In a second memory Bagman is charged with passing information to Voldemort, but instead the Wizengamot clears him. A third memory shows Crouch sentencing the Lestranges and his son to Azkaban. Back in Dumbledore's office the headmas-ter returns and shares another memory of Bertha Jorkins as a teen. Harry tells Dumbledore about his dream, and the headmaster speculates Harry's scar hurts when Voldemort is near and very angry. He notes that Voldemort's previous ascension to power was accompanied by disappearances and finds Jor-kins's disappearance worrisome. Harry learns that Neville's parents were tortured by the Lestranges, and before the close of the conversations, Dumb-ledore reasserts his belief in Snape's loyalty.

Chapter 31: "The Third Task"
Harry shares the details of his conversations with Dumbledore with Hermione, Ron, and Sirius. They see Malfoy outside looking mysteriously as if he is talking into his hand. Sirius sends an owl encourag-ing Harry to stay focused on the tournament. A *Daily Prophet* story by Skeeter calls Harry "Disturbed and Dangerous" and is based on his nightmare in Divi-nation. Again, Hermione tries to figure out how the journalist acquired access to that information. She suddenly has a brainstorm and rushes to the library.

The champions meet in a separate chamber after breakfast to greet their families. Harry plans not to attend this gathering but sees Mrs. Weasley and Bill have arrived to serve as his substitute family. After dinner everyone heads to the maze, formerly the Quidditch field. The champions may send up red sparks using their wands if they get into trouble and need assistance. The champions enter the maze. Cedric encounters a Blast-Ended

Skrewt. Harry comes upon a number of obstacles including a boggart taking the shape of a Dementor, a skrewt, and an actual Dementor, all of which he defeats. He hears Fleur scream but cannot get to her. Then he hears Krum inexplicably attempt to use the Cruciatus Curse on Cedric, so Harry stuns the Durmstrang champion, saving Cedric. The two Hogwarts champions go their separate ways, and Harry successfully answers a riddle posed by a sphinx. Subsequently, he and Cedric stumble on the cup at the same time, but a giant spider thwarts them. The spider seriously injures Harry's leg, but he and Cedric eventually defeat the spider together and then agree to share the victory, grabbing the Triwizard Cup simultaneously. They quickly realize it is a Portkey (the same object used to transport Harry, Hermione, and the Weasleys magically to the Quidditch World Cup), which transports them away from Hogwarts.

Chapter 32: "Flesh, Blood, and Bone"
Harry lands on his injured leg, which was pinched by the spider. They are in a graveyard, clearly far from Hogwarts. A figure—Wormtail (Peter Pettigrew)—approaches and uses the Avada Kedavra spell on Cedric, killing him instantly. Harry's scar bursts into excruciating pain. Wormtail binds Harry to the marble headstone of Tom Riddle, Sr.'s grave. Nagini, the snake that assisted Voldemort in the opening of the novel, also waits there. Wormtail carries a bundle in which a small, repulsive creature almost like a human baby with flat red eyes rests. Wormtail drops the bundle into a cauldron and utters an incantation, adding dust from Riddle, Sr.'s grave; his own amputated right forearm; and a vial of Harry's blood. These mysterious ingredients simmer together, and, shockingly, Lord Voldemort—now in human form—arises from the smoke that shrouds the cauldron.

Chapter 33: "The Death Eaters"
Voldemort examines himself, tests his wand, and looks at Wormtail's left arm, where a tattoolike version of the Dark Mark emerges. Voldemort discusses his family history, and soon hooded and masked Death Eaters Apparate, genuflecting before him. Voldemort accuses them of treachery as they beg

for forgiveness. He magically replaces Wormtail's bleeding stump of an arm with a shiny silver arm. Voldemort enumerates the present Death Eaters, including Lucius Malfoy and some who are missing, including the Lestranges, imprisoned in Azkaban.

Voldemort boasts that he returned from death and that the power of Lily's sacrifice has now been negated by his use of Harry's blood in his resurrection. He explains that Wormtail found him after Wormtail's escape from Hogwarts at the close of the third novel. Voldemort also recounts his journey back to full embodiment over the last four years and how Bertha Jorkins was instrumental in getting him the information he needed to set up the Triwizard Tournament as a means to his return. He announces the rest of his plan—to kill Harry, but only after a duel, which he commands of Harry.

Chapter 34: "Priori Incantatem"
Voldemort begins the duel by casting the Cruciatus Curse and taunting Harry. Resisting Voldemort's next attempted curse, the Imperius Curse, Harry dodges behind Riddle Sr.'s tombstone. When they both try to cast a spell simultaneously, a strange phenomenon occurs—the beams of light from the wands meet and connect, casting the two wizards into the air. Harry hears a phoenix song and knows he must not break the connection. *Priori Incantatem* translates roughly to "prior incantation." The mystical event occurs as the two wands connect and produce shadowy images of the previously cast spells, in this case, from Voldemort's wand. Harry sees phantom versions of Cedric, Frank Bryce, and his parents, all of whom urge him on. When Lily tells him to break the connection, Harry grabs Cedric's body and the Portkey while his shadowy protectors hold off Voldemort, and Harry returns to the Hogwarts grounds.

Chapter 35: "Veritaserum"
Harry arrives back at the edge of the maze amid public confusion and his own disorientation. He tells Dumbledore that Voldemort has returned. Moody rushes Harry back to his office and begins asking strange questions about the scene in the graveyard, finally confessing that he put Harry's name in the Goblet of Fire and telling him that all

the ways he helped Harry to win the tournament were planned in order to help Voldemort rise to power again. Harry feels confused about why the former Auror, Moody, would make the trophy a Portkey, put the Imperius Curse on Krum, or refer to Voldemort as the "Dark Lord."

Dumbledore, Snape, and McGonagall burst in just as Moody is about to kill Harry. The headmaster explains that this man whom they have come to know over the past year is not the real Alastor Moody; he then opens a magical trunk in the office to find the real Moody at the bottom, stunned and sleeping. The Polyjuice Potion wears off to reveal the impostor Moody is actually Barty Crouch, Jr., who, under the influence of Veritaserum provided by Snape, confesses he and his mother used Polyjuice Potion to switch places in Azkaban. After her son was sentenced to Azkaban, Mrs. Crouch sunk into a deep depression. Crouch finally decided that (since Mrs. Crouch was dying) he would grant her one final wish and somehow get his son released from prison.

The Crouches worked out a sophisticated plan that amounted to their visiting their son in the wizarding prison, where the mother and son switched places (via use of Polyjuice Potion). Crouch escorted his son to their home, where Barty Crouch, Jr., was controlled through the Imperius Curse by his father and cared for by Winky. However, the plan was not executed as smoothly as the Crouches had hoped. Bertha Jorkins inadvertently discovered Barty Crouch, Jr.'s existence when she stopped by the Crouch home one day. Extra precautionary measures were enacted, but Crouch's son was growing increasingly restless and frustrated. Winky then persuaded Crouch to let his son attend the Quidditch World Cup; at the event Barty Crouch, Jr., started to resist the Imperius Curse, stole Harry's wand, escaped into the surrounding forest, and was able to conjure the Dark Mark, since he remained fiercely loyal to Voldemort.

Voldemort learned from Bertha Jorkins that Barty Crouch, Jr., was still alive, and he and Wormtail liberated him from his prison at home. The young Death Eater took on Moody's identity to prove his loyalty to Voldemort. Wormtail

cared for Crouch, who of course knew of his son's absence, until he escaped Wormtail's guard. Barty Crouch, Jr., waited for his father to go to Hogwarts and, using the Marauder's Map, found and killed him. Obviously quite deranged, Barty Crouch, Jr., rejoiced in the return of Voldemort and in his father's murder.

Chapter 36: "The Parting of the Ways"
Dumbledore makes arrangements for Barty Crouch, Jr. (now a prisoner again), and the abused Mad-Eye Moody. He takes Harry to meet Sirius in the headmaster's office. Dumbledore asks Harry to recount the events that transpired in the graveyard and clarifies for Harry what happened with *Priori Incantatem*: Because Harry's and Voldemort's wands share the same phoenix feather core from Fawkes, the wands do not work properly against each other. One of the wands will force the other to regurgitate its previous spells. The phoenix yet again goes to Harry's aid; Fawkes's tears mend Harry's injured leg. Dumbledore then praises Harry's bravery and sends him to the hospital wing to recuperate, cautioning friends and family to allow him rest.

Harry awakes to a yelling match among Fudge, McGonagall, and Dumbledore over the fact that Fudge let a Dementor enter Hogwarts to administer its fatal kiss to Barty Crouch, Jr., rendering him incapable of testifying to his actions. Fudge argues that Barty Crouch, Jr., was a raving lunatic acting alone, and his testimony is therefore useless. Dumbledore asserts Harry's claim about Voldemort's return, but Fudge remains skeptical and resistant. Dumbledore resolves that if Fudge refuses to act upon Harry's claim (Fudge rejects the headmaster's concern that the Dementors will quickly ally with Voldemort as soon as his return is widely known), they will part ways. Fudge hands Harry the 1,000 galleons in prize money for winning the tournament and then storms out of the castle.

Dumbledore issues a series of orders, one of which concerns reconciling Sirius in human form with Snape, against whom Sirius nurses a boyhood grudge; Dumbledore, however, says they must put their differences aside. Meanwhile, Harry grieves over Cedric's death and receives motherly comfort from Mrs. Weasley, then drifts into a dreamless sleep.

Chapter 37: "The Beginning"

The Diggorys do not blame Harry for Cedric's death and refuse his offer of the tournament prize winnings. Dumbledore instructs students to leave Harry to himself, and he enjoys contemplative times with his friends Ron and Hermione. Dumbledore insists for some mysterious reason that Harry return to the Dursleys' for at least part of the summer.

Hagrid tells Harry, Ron, and Hermione that Dumbledore gave him and Madame Maxime a task to complete over the summer. At the Leaving Feast Harry wonders about Snape's allegiance. Dumbledore pays homage to Cedric and affirms Harry's story to the student body, that Voldemort killed Cedric and that the Ministry of Magic has decided to ignore Voldemort's return. Dumbledore emphasizes the importance of unity and solidarity: "Differences of habit and language are nothing at all if our aims are identical and our hearts are open" (723).

The students from Beauxbatons and Durmstrang depart. On the Hogwarts Express home Hermione reveals that Skeeter is actually an illegally unregistered animagus in the shape of a beetle and Hermione has her trapped in a magically unbreakable jar. She blackmails the journalist into ceasing her writing of slanderous stories. How she gained her information becomes obvious now, including her sitting on the windowsill of Professor Trelawney's Divination classroom to gain details about Harry's dream; she hid herself outside and listened intently while Hagrid revealed his giant heritage to Madame Maxime; and Draco Malfoy (who had been seen looking as if he were talking to his hand) held Skeeter in his palm and gave her details she so longed for.

Fred and George explain that they were blackmailing Ludo Bagman, who paid their World Cup bet in Leprechaun's gold. Harry gives them his Triwizard Tournament winnings, which he has mixed feelings about to begin with, to start their own joke shop, where they plan to sell products they have been developing all school year, including the Ton-Tongue Toffee they gave to Dudley at the start of the novel. Uncle Vernon meets Harry at the station,

and Mrs. Weasley assures Harry that Dumbledore will let him visit the Burrow over the summer.

CRITICAL COMMENTARY

At 734 pages (more than double the size of *Prisoner of Azkaban*) *Goblet of Fire* continues the dark and intense turn begun in the third novel, culminating in a frightening denouement that secured the series' crossover to the adult fiction bookshelves. Introducing complex new themes and social critiques, this fourth novel in the series serves a pivotal purpose in the narrative arc of Harry's story—in his role as a hero, Voldemort's increasing power, and his own emotional maturation.

Harry's Human Flaws

Harry undergoes a number of changes and challenges that propel his development as a protagonist and as a hero of the wizarding world. Following JOSEPH CAMPBELL's "hero's journey" paradigm, Harry once again finds himself the reluctant hero, drawn into the Triwizard Tournament for reasons beyond his comprehension. In participating in the tournament, however, Harry tests his mettle and is once again the realistic and accessible hero whom readers love. He couples courage with a modesty that seems realistic to most readers.

His human flaws may infuriate readers—he procrastinates finding the solution to the second task until well past when he can help himself—but he nonetheless comes through in those moments of drama and danger. For example, when the other champions seemingly fail to appear to rescue their captives in task two, Harry refuses to abandon them. In chapter 26, "The Second Task," Harry's worries reveal his courageous heart: "Harry looked wildly around. Where were the other champions? Would he have time to take Ron to the surface and come back down for Hermione and the others?" (500). When Krum and Cedric finally arrive for their captives, Harry's concern for others means he not only stays to be sure his friends are safe but even helps Krum with his captive (with Krum transfigured as a shark, he is a bit clumsy with his teeth until Harry lends him the jagged rock to free Hermione from her bindings). This scene showcases his characteristic courage in the face of danger, which ultimately defines him as a hero. Perhaps most appealing to readers is his accompanying sense of humility and perhaps even a bit of embarrassment as he receives a tongue lashing from Ron: "Harry, you prat . . . you didn't take any of that song seriously, did you? Dumbledore wouldn't have let any of us drown!" (503). Shortly thereafter, Harry silently berates himself: "Harry's feeling of stupidity was growing. Now he was out of the water, it seemed perfectly clear that Dumbledore's safety precautions wouldn't have permitted the death of a hostage just because their champion hadn't turned up" (505). In the end, however, the judges share what is surely readers' perception that Harry's delay out of concern for the hostages "show[ed] moral fiber" and is yet another illustration of Harry's authentic, instinctive, seemingly unswayable sense of right.

Harry is a typical adolescent in some key ways—he feels afraid to ask a girl to the Yule Ball, for example—and yet demands are placed upon him that his classmates cannot begin to understand. As a result, Harry faces his own mortality in almost every book but never so disturbingly as in the conclusion of *Goblet of Fire*, when the final task of the Triwizard Tournament turns out to be a ploy to lure Harry into Voldemort's clutches. In this grisly graveyard confrontation Harry finds strength that he does not consciously realize he possesses but comes through in the face of danger as he always does. In the chapter "Priori Incantatem," Harry faces Voldemort, surrounded by Death Eaters: "There was a split second, perhaps, when Harry might have considered running for it, but his injured leg shook under him as he stood on an overgrown grave, as the Death Eaters closed ranks, forming a tighter circle around him and Voldemort" (659). Realizing that he is "unprotected" and that the Dueling Club in which he participated in *Chamber of Secrets* has quite inadequately prepared him for this sort of confrontation, Harry nonetheless faces Voldemort as an equal, with integrity and strength. Throwing off Voldemort's Imperius Curse, Harry promises himself that he "was not going to die kneeling at Voldemort's feet . . . he was going to die upright like his father, and he was going to die trying to defend himself, even if no defense was possible" (662). It is this form

of courage—certainly feeling the fear that is natural but acting nonetheless in the service of good and for others—that distinguishes Harry as a hero. Readers also experience Harry's increasing sense of duty and moral obligation to others in this same scene. Even when under attack by Voldemort, the most powerful dark wizard of the age, Harry makes sure to retrieve his classmate Cedric Diggory's body per his ghostly request, knowing Cedric's parents would be devastated not to say good-bye to their son.

Death and Mortality

Harry's direct experience of the death of another young person and his own near-murder by the reincarnated Voldemort place mortality front and center as a theme of the novel and of Harry's own journey. Harry is emotionally changed by the losses and trauma he experiences, rejecting the gold that is his prize for winning the Triwizard Tournament and experiencing survivor's guilt in chapter 36: "The thing which he had been fighting on and off ever since he had come out of the maze was threatening to overpower him. He could feel a burning, prickling feeling in the inner corners of his eyes" (714). With Mrs. Weasley's comforting presence Harry is able to experience his grief fully: "The full weight of everything he had seen that night seemed to fall in upon him as Mrs. Weasley held him to her. His mother's face, his father's voice, the sight of Cedric, dead on the ground all started spinning in his head until he could hardly bear it, until he was screwing his face against the howl of misery fighting to get out of him" (714). Rarely in the series does Harry express his humanity so vividly as in this middle book.

Some reviewers commented on the emergence of death as a theme in the books, but it is clear that, though violent death is portrayed more vividly here in the middle novel of the seven-book series, the books have always been about loss, death, and fear of death, since Harry was orphaned by Voldemort's vicious murder of Lily and James Potter.

Parent-Child Relationships

The parent-child relationship thus consumes a good deal of the book's narrative space, more in this fourth novel than any other perhaps because of the questions it raises about the power and pitfalls of the love between a parent and child—both for Harry and for other characters. Of course, throughout the series Lily's sacrifice of her life for her child is pivotal in explaining Harry's defeat of Voldemort in every book. But in this fourth novel Harry once again manages to defeat Voldemort and his band of evil minions in the graveyard confrontation because of the protection that his mother's sacrifice has conferred upon him. Dumbledore later explains that the *Priori Incantatem*—or the "Reverse Spell Effect"—was at work in the graveyard. When two wands that share a core meet in battle, they will malfunction, with the peculiar effect of "force[ing] the other to regurgitate spells it has performed—in reverse" (697). Harry's parents, even in spectral form, again issue a protective charm for their son that enables him to escape Voldemort and the graveyard battle, and Harry is profoundly moved and saddened by this "visitation."

It is not just the relationship between Harry and his parents that the book uses to dramatize the importance and power of the parent-child bond, and the Crouches represent its dark side. At the end of the novel we learn the secret of Barty Crouch, Jr.'s escape from Azkaban, which was facilitated by his mother's sacrifice of her own life with the aid of Polyjuice Potion: "We took on each other's appearance. . . . The dementors are blind. They sensed one healthy, one dying person entering Azkaban. They sensed one healthy, one dying person leaving it" (684). She dies in Azkaban, having taken on Barty, Jr.'s, appearance. Rowling's repeated use of this plot device invites speculation; does Mrs. Crouch's sacrifice differ significantly from Lily Potter's sacrifice of her own life, throwing herself in front of her baby rather than let him be killed by Voldemort? Though Harry was a young innocent and Barty, Jr., a convicted criminal, certainly the maternal impulse to save her child recurs in the series.

Barty Crouch, Sr., remains ostensibly responsible for the imprisonment of his own son (though the junior Crouch has earned his punishment for his affiliation with the Death Eaters). Harry witnesses through the Pensieve the dramatic trial of Barty Crouch, Jr., confronted by his father as a ministry official. Though later confessions from the son sug-

gest he was indeed a hardened devotee of the dark arts, the courtroom confrontation Harry witnesses heartbreakingly illustrates Crouch, Sr.'s plight, as his son both pleads his innocence ("Father, I didn't! . . . I swear it, Father, don't send me back to the Dementors") and begs his mother to save his life ("I didn't do it, I didn't know! Don't send me there, don't let him!") (595). Barty, Jr., begs his father to spare him, but Crouch, Sr., only avers, "You are no son of mine!" (596). However, despite his callous dismissal of his offspring during the first wizarding war, Crouch, Sr., clearly spends the rest of his life regretting his role in Barty, Jr.'s imprisonment, to the extreme of hiding his fugitive son despite the latter's increasingly erratic and violent behavior. As Barty, Jr., recalls in chapter 35, under the influence of Veritaserum, he was a victim of the "Imperius Curse . . . I was under my father's control" (685). In the end, the father cannot seem to find any redemption for his past sins and is murdered by his son on the grounds of Hogwarts, as his son confesses in chapter 35: "When everyone was gone, I transfigured my father's body. He became a bone . . . I buried it, while wearing the Invisibility Cloak, in the freshly dug earth in front of Hagrid's cabin" (690–691). That Crouch, Sr., takes on a desiccated and lifeless form is perhaps fitting because of the sadness, loss, and regret that seemed to take up the latter part of his life.

Institutional Corruption

A key theme introduced in *Goblet of Fire* that takes on significantly more importance in *Order of the Phoenix* and the rest of the series is that of institutional corruption, especially the bureaucracies of the legal and judicial system. Though Rowling's critique of inept administrators is not fully fleshed out until the Ministry of Magic systematically fails to protect the public from Voldemort's growing influence, this fourth novel introduces characters whose inaction and weakness of character enable Voldemort to gain power: Bartemius Crouch, Sr.; Cornelius Fudge; and Ludo Bagman. Crouch, Sr., and Minister of Magic Fudge are more obsessed with power than with justice, and this manifests itself in *Chamber of Secrets* when Fudge, as minister, moves swiftly to arrest Hagrid in order to be seen taking action rather than taking correct and meaningful action. Harry's revisiting of the trials of the Death Eaters in the first wizarding war also reinforce Crouch, Sr's obsession with punctilious adherence to the letter of the law over justice, compassion, and reparation.

Bagman, though less influential in his role as the head of the Department of Magical Games and Sports, takes on an important role in coordinating the Quidditch World Cup, but his buffoonery and illicit gambling activities mar his affable facade. In the end George Weasley reveals to Harry that Bagman is "in big trouble with the goblins" because of unpaid debts, that he backs out of money he owes the Weasley twins after a wager on the Quidditch World Cup, and that "he's lost everything gambling. Hasn't got two Galleons to rub together" (732). Along with being a poor sport and demonstrating a lack of integrity in his book-making, Bagman's attempting throughout the narrative to help Harry win the tournament, is self-serving, motivated by the desire to make a successful wager on Harry as the tournament winner.

Cornelius Fudge, as well, shows cowardice and incompetence in chapter 36, "The Parting of the Ways," the title of which refers to the split between the Ministry of Magic and Dumbledore, representative of both Hogwarts and the soon-to-be-reconstituted Order of the Phoenix. Fudge loses authority with Dumbledore when he bypasses the headmaster and lets a Dementor in to administer the Dementor's kiss to Barty Crouch, Jr., as Harry speculates, "It had sucked his soul out through his mouth. He was worse than dead" (703). Because Fudge prefers to see Barty Crouch, Jr.'s actions as isolated acts of a maniac rather than a coordinated effort to resurrect Voldemort, Fudge's authority is sorely compromised, and he loses credibility with each utterance: "You-Know-Who . . . returned? Preposterous. Come now, Dumbledore," he blusters (704). Rowling profitably uses Fudge as a "doubting Thomas" whose value of administrative efficiency trumps common sense and truth telling. As the central character, Harry is of course the sympathetic central consciousness of the story, and Fudge—set up as, in some ways, a straw man—is bound to play the fool when

he rejects Harry's narrative whereas Dumbledore accepts it at face value. These are just three of the characters in leadership roles who fail to live up to the expectations of their offices and in whom Harry quickly loses his faith.

Loss of Innocence

This loss of innocence reflects the increasingly adult world that the characters occupy and Rowling's movement toward a mixed readership of children, adolescents, and adults. In their fourth year the students are exposed to a disturbing curriculum in their Defense Against the Dark Arts class, with the impostor Mad-Eye Moody not only discussing but actually performing the three Unforgivable Curses. Chapter 14, "The Unforgivable Curses," has Mad-Eye Moody introducing the students to the Imperius Curse, the Cruciatus Curse, and *Avada Kedavra*, casting all three on some spiders he has taken to class for this express purpose. Readers begin fully to understand the implication of these wizarding crimes, partly because both Harry and Neville Longbottom continue to suffer the results of the performance of these Unforgivable Curses on their parents; Mad-Eye only stops the demonstration as a result of Hermione's pleading because she sees that "Neville's hands were clenched upon the desk in front of him, his knuckles white, his eyes wide and horrified" (214–215), clearly imagining his parents suffering the same fate as the spider that is being tortured in front of him.

Beyond the more demanding curriculum, Harry and his friends are moving from children to young adults, and the Yule Ball at Christmas requires a new level of maturity. As a Hogwarts champion Harry is required to have a date, and teenage romance and dating—natural parts of adolescence—are introduced into the narrative. Indeed, critics have commented that Harry seems to agonize more over asking Cho Chang out on a date than he does over the tasks of the Triwizard Tournament. His friendship with Ron takes a similarly dramatic turn as Ron's resentment about Harry's financial resources and his constant limelight sparks envy that results in a temporary falling out between the two friends. As their bitter exchange plays out in chapter 17, Ron accuses, "I don't know why you're bothering to lie, you didn't get in trouble for it, did you?" and "You want to get to bed, Harry. I expect you'll need to be up early tomorrow for a photo-call or something" (287). Though Hermione tries to explain in the next chapter that "he's jealous! . . . it's always you who gets all the attention, you know it is. I know it's not your fault" (289), Harry still feels stung and betrayed that his best friend thinks he is a glory hound and a liar. Until Harry survives his battle with the Hungarian Horntail Ron cannot put aside his hurt feelings and reestablish their friendship.

Social Justice

Though interspecies tensions have appeared throughout the first three books, they reach new heights in *Goblet of Fire*, as Hermione raises questions of social justice and Voldemort's campaign of terror intensifies. Harry's vision of the wizarding world becomes more global as the Quidditch World Cup introduces him to new species of creatures such as the Veela and the social plight of such species as giants, house-elves, goblins, and merpeople. Harry's growing awareness of wizards as the dominant social group that exerts influence over policy, practice, and social treatment of other species mirrors the plotline of the Death Eaters and Voldemort's social philosophy based on blood status. Though Voldemort's worldview, one in which blood status dictates civil and social rights, is meant to be repugnant to the wizarding community, wizards' own contemptuous attitudes are equally disturbing. For example, Hermione and Harry discover that Winky and Dobby are working in the Hogwarts kitchen. In visiting them, they learn that Dobby—an anomaly—is thrilled to have been freed, exclaiming, "Professor Dumbledore says he will pay Dobby, sir, if Dobby wants paying! And so Dobby is a free elf, sir, and Dobby gets a Galleon a week and one day off a month!" (379). When Hermione complains indignantly that this is actually quite little, Dobby explains that he talked Dumbledore down; as the emblem of social justice and equality, Dumbledore's treatment of the house-elves is part of introducing the prevailing magical attitudes that wizards promote and that most house-elves embrace.

Winky reflects the most dominant belief system the house-elves have adopted: "Winky is a disgraced

elf, but Winky is not yet getting paid! . . . Winky is not sunk so low as that! Winky is properly ashamed of being freed!" (379). As Dobby explains, "Tis part of the house-elf's enslavement, sir. We keeps their secrets and our silence, sir. We upholds the family's honor, and we never speaks ill of them" (380). Deprived of compensation, autonomy, and voice, house-elves nonetheless participate in their oppression despite the efforts of Hermione's campaign for their liberation, raising important questions about the relationship between dominant and subordinate groups and some questions about whether the oppressed can or should reject efforts to liberate them from their oppression. Thus, "creature rights" begin to emerge as a central issue in this novel because of Hermione's (oft-maligned) campaign for house-elf liberation.

Further, Harry becomes aware of how hybrids like Rubeus Hagrid are social pariahs and werewolves like Remus Lupin experience ostracism because of their difference. These narrative concerns are central to Rowling's philosophical and aesthetic vision and become especially important in this fourth novel because of the introduction of the global magical community through the Quidditch World Cup and the international magical cooperation sponsored by the Triwizard Tournament. Many critics have been especially interested in Rowling's treatment of "difference" and have seen it as a proxy for such diverse concerns as acquired immunodeficiency syndrome (AIDS), gay and lesbian rights, and colonialism. Dumbledore's claim at the farewell banquet that "differences of habit and language are nothing at all if our aims are identical and our hearts are open" (723) seems to set the tone for the rest of the books in the series, where collaboration across species becomes even more important and hard to negotiate.

Loyalty

More narratively central to *Goblet of Fire* than other works is the theme of loyalty—to friends, social groups, family, or political and ideological causes. Readers first see loyalty become an issue when the Goblet of Fire expels Harry's name; Ron immediately assumes that Harry has found some advanced magic to hoodwink the goblet and has chosen not to confide in him. As his best friend Ron is deeply hurt, and their friendship goes through a cooling-off period until the completion of the first task. Ron's "tantrum" over his perception that Harry does not trust him enough to take him into his confidence about entering his name humanizes Ron, but it also raises the very real specter of envy that occurs in many friendships.

Family loyalty is also explored in *Goblet of Fire,* primarily through the Crouches. Though Rowling does not reveal the full extent to which loyalty has been tested until well into the plot of the novel, the sacrifices that the Crouches made—or failed to make—out of loyalty to each other drive much of the plot. Rowling suggests that Crouch, Sr.'s overcommitment to his career led to neglect of his family life and that this neglect created an environment in which the passion and power of Voldemort's cause were especially appealing to the young Barty Crouch. His father's loyalty to his institution and to bureaucracy over family ties also is dramatized as Harry witnesses the trial of Death Eaters in Dumbledore's office through the Pensieve. Though Barty Crouch, Jr., clearly shows allegiance to the "wrong side" of the moral and social battle that is being fought throughout the series, there is also something poignant about his mother's love for him and her sacrifice of her own life so that he might live free of Azkaban. That he used that freedom to work toward violent ends is, of course, supposed to be disturbing for readers; however, the bizarre family dynamics of the Crouches does invite speculation about Rowling's use of Mrs. Crouch's sacrifice—her loyalty and love for her son clearly eclipse those of her husband, whose cold dismissal and neglect of his child are diametrically opposed to the sorts of family relationships the books seem to value and endorse (the Weasleys and the Potters, for example).

Ideological loyalty becomes a more significant theme in this fourth book because of Voldemort's return to a corporal body. Blind adherence to Voldemort's belief system—in blood status and social purity—is a criterion by which the dark wizard judges the Death Eaters who return to his service

at the novel's climax. Though Pettigrew clearly stays with his "master" out of fear rather than loyalty, Voldemort rewards those who show abject devotion and punishes those who appear to have left his service. From the earliest chapter, Voldemort refers to Barty Crouch, Jr., as his "*faithful* servant," someone whose "loyalty has never wavered" (10). Peter Pettigrew/Wormtail receives a magical, powerful silver hand to replace the one he cuts off as part of the spell to restore Voldemort to full life, and Barty Crouch, Jr., ostensibly would have received a similarly valuable reward had he managed to return to his master's side. Voldemort invokes the notion of loyalty when he berates the returned Death Eaters in chapter 33 after he has regained bodily form: "I see you all, whole and healthy, with your powers intact—such prompt appearances!—and I ask myself . . . why did this band of wizards never come to the aid of their master, to whom they swore eternal loyalty?" (647). Later, this clear tension between the set of values embraced by Voldemort and his followers and their actual motives becomes more vivid: Addressing Pettigrew/Wormtail, Voldemort accuses, "You returned to me, not out of loyalty, but out of fear of your old friends. You deserve this pain, Wormtail" (649). Demanding loyalty and inspiring fear, Voldemort displays a remarkable lack of self-awareness that only draws closer attention to the seemingly instinctive execution of the virtues of love, loyalty, and friendship that those fighting against Voldemort demonstrate. Similarly, fear, intimidation, and violence are infertile grounds for producing loyalty, and Voldemort's graveyard punishment of his adherents highlights this contradiction between his professed desire for loyalty and the sorts of acts he commits to attain it. And, of course, the truth of Snape's loyalties has, since the first book, been a question of passionate interest to readers and one that is not fully resolved until well into *Deathly Hallows.*

Finally, the plight of the house-elf is also related to questions of loyalty, as Winky's actions are motivated entirely by her loyalty to the Crouches. The house-elves are bound to their owning families by both magical obligation and a code of loyalty that guides their service, as Dobby explains in chapter

21: "Winky forgets she is not bound to Mr. Crouch anymore; she is allowed to speak her mind now, but she won't do it" (380). Even though Winky was callously tossed aside after years of loyal service to the Crouch family, she still laments her banishment, sobbing, "Poor master, poor master, no Winky to help him no more!" (382). This distorted sense of loyalty—one created from servitude rather than love—seems a target of Rowling's critique in the portrayal both of the house-elves and of the Death Eaters. The book's plot is set into motion primarily by Winky's sense of loyalty to her family and Barty Crouch, Jr.'s, imprisonment in his home. It is Winky's urging that motivates his father to let Barty, Jr., attend the Quidditch World Cup. Winky's misery is a central subplot of the novel after she is banished from the Crouches' service, and she does not reveal even after she has been "freed" that Barty Crouch, Jr., is indeed responsible for the Dark Mark at the Quidditch World Cup and that he was freed from Azkaban when his mother exchanged places with him. As the second major house-elf character introduced by Rowling, Winky is also important because she helps dramatize the conflicts over house-elf "slavery" that Hermione fights against and that surfaces in the fourth novel as a substantive subplot (though *Chamber of Secrets* introduced Dobby to the series).

Good versus Evil
As in the early books the conflict of good and evil that is a staple of the fantasy tradition is in full force in this book. Though *Goblet of Fire* is more simplistic in its addressing of this conflict than subsequent novels (which introduce such "evil" or at least disturbing characters as Dolores Umbridge), the main characters, and readers, continue to root for the side of good as the side of evil seems to be a gathering storm. Beginning with the appearance of the Death Eaters at the Quidditch World Cup and their tormenting of the Muggle campsite manager and his family, Rowling introduces new and increasingly portentous manifestations of dark magic: the ambushing of Mad-Eye Moody (the significance of which is not revealed to readers until the novel's end), the introduction of characters such as Igor Karkaroff, Snape's mysteriously ambiguous alle-

giances, and, of course, the final, climactic graveyard battle that a number of book reviewers called too dark for young readers (though the opening chapter is similarly gory). Even subtler forms of evil such as Crouch's powermongering and his neglect of and subsequent sacrifice of his son (in the name of justice) to the cause of his career give readers pause, as do Minister of Magic Fudge's inability to take action in the face of imminent threats and Ludo Bagman's affable incompetence. None of these instills faith in the power of institutions to respond to threats and initiate change; that lack of faith is further supported by subsequent novels.

Critiques of Sensationalism
Another theme that has garnered some questions from critics and reviewers about its autobiographicality is the scathing indictment of inflammatory and sensationalist media that crops up in *Goblet of Fire*, specifically in the character of Rita Skeeter, whose reckless journalistic license sows drama and spite. Skeeter's *Daily Prophet* stories—for example, "Further Mistakes at the Ministry of Magic," documenting the ministry's failures at the Quidditch World Cup (202); "Dumbledore's Giant Mistake," assailing Dumbledore for his employment of Hagrid as a teacher, citing giants' vicious nature (437); and "Harry Potter's Secret Heartache," accusing Hermione of toying with Harry's and Viktor's affections (511)—become a framing technique and a plot device as a number of new conflicts are introduced through *Daily Prophet* stories throughout the novel. This technique allows Rowling to present to readers developments happening outside the central narrative of Harry's experiences at Hogwarts (for example, changing public opinion about the ministry or Harry, Hagrid, or Dumbledore). The muckraking, borderline slanderous, nature of Skeeter's stories is also used strategically by Rowling to propel the action, both through Skeeter's interviewing of Harry and the other champions (her focus on Harry to the exclusion of the others becomes a source of tension in the book) and through Skeeter's use of the power of the pen to incite negative public opinion about whoever is her target du jour.

The novel's conclusion remains significant in relation to the topic of sensationalism since Rowling reveals Skeeter's status as an illegal animagus (deduced by Hermione), and Skeeter is then literally "caged" in her insect form in a shatter-proof jar and controlled by Hermione. If, indeed, as Rowling has suggested, Hermione is based on an adolescent version of Rowling herself, then this plot twist suggests a bit of wish fulfillment, considering that some critics have viewed Skeeter as a caricature of the growing media frenzy surrounding Rowling's personal life and career. As the series grew in popularity—along with film adaptations, merchandising, theme parks, ad infinitum—so did Rowling's fortune, and speculation about the upcoming novels and their plotlines reached a fever pitch. Rowling's personal life became difficult to protect from intrusion, and as Harry Potter became a cottage industry, interest also grew in Rowling's fascinating personal narrative (the rags-to-riches story of the "single-mom-on-the-dole"). Perhaps Skeeter's distasteful conduct and nonexistent professional ethics are in part a parody of the journalists whose relentless interest in her life and work was a constant intrusion for Rowling. Hermione's successful outwitting of Skeeter in the final chapters may be something of an inside joke for the books' author, especially as the next novel, *Order of the Phoenix*, finds Hermione manipulating Skeeter into making her press connections work *for* Harry instead of against him in the eyes of the public.

Goblet of Fire represents Rowling's first full-fledged transition to a mixed readership; though *Prisoner of Azkaban* is a darker foray into Harry's world, it serves as a transition for the novelist from an adolescent reading public to an adult audience. This middle book in the series fully realizes that transition, as reflected by the exploration of darker themes and the more graphic violence that opens and closes the novel. Harry's steady foray into the world of adult responsibility—from the lighthearted teen romance to the burden of heroism to blood sacrifice and attempted murder—ushers readers into troubled times for Harry and the readers who love him.

INITIAL REVIEWS

Released on July 8, 2000, the fourth book in the series was hotly awaited. The book's release kicked off the tradition of midnight book release parties, with Harry Potter–costumed kids and adults lined up for blocks for first crack at the novel. Expectations ran high for the book, and for the most part, according to reviewers, Rowling lived up to those expectations. Reviewers praised it as inventive, readable, entertaining, and funny while a few reviews criticized the novel's pacing and writing quality.

Multiple reviewers began by noting their concern over potential disappointed expectations, given the hype surrounding the novel and the short interval between the release of the third and fourth books in the United States; further, tight security and the prohibition on advance review copies concerned reviewers, who thought these could be ploys to camouflage low quality rather than measures designed to maintain excitement about the book. Charles De Lint in *Fantasy and Science Fiction* and Yvonne Zipp in the *Christian Science Monitor* both commented on the enormously high expectations for the fourth book and De Lint conceded, "I was wrong on all counts" (27). Amanda Craig of the *New Statesman* and Joan Acocella of the *New Yorker* both also praised the book as living up to the hype, Acocella admitting, "After all that, I would love to tell you that the book is a big nothing. In fact, it's wonderful, just like its predecessors." Most reviewers praised it, some calling it "thrilling" (*Publishers Weekly*, "Forecasts" 195), "enchanting" (Papinchak 43), and "well-wrought" (*Sunday Herald*). The *San Francisco Chronicle* critiques the book as "spotty" and "ungainly," while Deirdre Donahue calls it "mediocre," even though she acknowledges in the major mainstream newspaper *USA Today* that "the story has its moments" (1D).

The novel's plot, pacing, themes, and writing quality attracted the most attention from reviewers, while a number also remark positively on the features of Rowling's work most frequently praised: her inventiveness, humor, and use of details.

Reviewers had mixed assessments of the book's plotting and pacing, with some finding the story complicated and slow but riveting; others criticized the novel as plodding. *Publishers Weekly* noted that the book's gripping introduction falters, regaining sure footing a good bit into the novel, while Robert

Papinchak in *People* claimed, "The fuse is lit from the first paragraph, and nonstop action follows for the next 734 pages" (43). Martha Parravano in *Horn Book Magazine* astutely captures these contradictory evaluations when she observed that *Goblet of Fire is* "what you call a wallow—one that some will find wide-ranging, compellingly written, and absorbing; others, long, rambling, and torturously fraught with adverbs." The *Guardian* (London) praised the book's "storytelling" of the highest order" (McCrum), a compliment echoed by the *Times Educational Supplement* reviewer, Geraldine Brennan, who concurred that the book showed Rowling "in control, rationing out just enough of the much-discussed-love-and-death interest." Julia Briggs in the *Times Literary Supplement* agreed that the narrative is controlled and "well-constructed." Several reviews faulted the book for its reliance on what Parravano called in *Horn Book Magazine* a "complicated explanation" and a preposterous denouement echoed by Acocella in *New Yorker*, who noted, "Rowling is a great showoff when it comes to surprise endings, and this, I think, is actually a fault of the books." Donahue claimed that the plots were "wearing thin" by the fourth novel, though Sarah Johnson's review in the London *Times* commended Rowling for paring away some of the "boring reiterative material" in the opening that detracted from the quality of *Chamber of Secrets* and *Prisoner of Azkaban*. Acocella agreed with some reviewers who found the pace slower than those in the previous books but did not call this a flaw, instead finding the "energy more dispersed."

Reviewer evaluations of Rowling's development of key characters and introduction of new characters were also mixed. While Karl Miller in *Raritan* called the protagonists "likeable and sprightly," Parravano believed that the lead character of Dumbledore was "reduced to a caricature of geniality." Amanda Craig, of *New Statesman*, complimented Rowling's introduction of "several inspired new creations" and found her weaving in of characters from previous novels admirable (54). Robert McCrum in the *Guardian* found Harry lacking subtlety and depth, a judgment Brennan echoed in the *Times Literary Supplement*: "Characterisation remains

less impressive." Kristen Baldwin in *Entertainment Weekly* disagrees, claiming that the author "gives her character complex new dimensions."

Consistently praised by reviewers of *Goblet of Fire* were Rowling's imagination and sense of humor. Miller admired the "resiliently inventive and explosive" spells, and Penelope Lively in her London *Independent* review commended the author's "rich seam of inventiveness" (5). Craig's *New Statesman* review praised Rowling's "genius" in the "extraordinarily detailed world" her books create (54), a point also noted by *Publishers Weekly*, which called the book's details as "ingenious and original as ever" (Forecasts 195). Rowling's use of humor and parody, some of the most appealing features to young readers, did not escape comment: Johnson's London *Times* review specifically identified the "delicious parodies" as part of the book's strengths, and Baldwin admired the book's "cauldron of inspired images."

Almost universally praised by reviewers are the increasingly ambitious, morally complex, and more disturbing themes that *Goblet of Fire* explores. Charlotte Decker commented on the darker themes, as did De Lint, noting that "mortality and racism and human rights issues" were all treated capably in this fourth volume (27). Baldwin, too, favorably remarked upon Rowling's treatment of weightier political issues such as prejudice and racism, particularly her authorial decision to keep Dumbledore in charge of "lesson teaching" rather than employ the heavy hand of a chiding narrator. Acocella's review in the *New Yorker* commented, as well, on the ambitious thematic aspirations of this fourth book, adding "cynicism of government officials, injustice of the law courts, the vagaries of international relations, the mendacity of the press" to the list of weightier questions the book introduces to its readers.

Some reviewers concerned with the book's impact on religious readers such as Zipp in the *Christian Science Monitor* and Michael Maudlin in *Christianity Today* focused on the graphic final confrontation scene in the graveyard, which Zipp found "just too scary for kids under 12," or the allegation that the books are morally ambiguous, with Maudlin concluding that "good and evil are clear and absolute in the books, just not fully explained—yet" (117). Craig's review, as well, noted that the terrifying conclusion of the novel, may very well be troubling for younger readers, calling it the "stuff of nightmares" (54). Baldwin confirmed this assessment when she called the ending "a spectacle of violence, wrenching emotion, and horror." Parravano's *Horn Book* review departed from these otherwise admiring assessments in her critique of the slight emotional impact of Cedric's death, given the lack of investment that readers have had in him as a minor character.

Finally, Rowling's writing style received attention. Reviewers were more likely to find fault with her prose than to comment positively on it, though this could be, as Amanda Craig explained, that "her style is so transparent that it is easy to miss its skill." More common, though, were claims that the book's prose was "flat" and unimpressive.

SCHOLARSHIP

Several articles address *Goblet of Fire* in isolation, including looking at the book's literary lineage, translation issues, legal questions, and leadership. See the "Scholarship on the Harry Potter Series" and "Additional Resources on the Harry Potter Series" sections for more critical assessments of the series as a whole.

Manda Rosser's essay "The Magic of Leadership" in *Advances in Developing Human Resources* examines the book as an exemplar of three leadership theories: base of social power, situational leadership model, and transformational and transactional leadership. Rosser pulls out specific plot points (primarily from the film adaptation) that are illustrative of the various theoretical models and describes ways of using the film as an educational tool.

Two essays explain the literary heritage of *Goblet of Fire*. Kathryn Jacobs argues in "Harry—Is that Potter, Percy, or Plantagenet?" that the book abandons earlier narrative conventions typical of the "British schoolboy" genre and adopts a new paradigm, WILLIAM SHAKESPEARE's multiplay historical epic. She compares the book most closely to Shakespeare's *1 Henry IV*, primarily through structural parallels. Karl Miller's article "Harry and the

Pot of Gold" in *Raritan* identifies *Goblet of Fire* as literary heritor of the gothic, the school story, and the orphan story. He also finds comparable features to Shakespeare's works and to a 19th-century work of British fiction, James Hogg's *The Three Perils of Man*.

As a number of articles have, Laetitia Bedeker and Ilse Feinauer's "The Translator as Cultural Mediator" takes up the question of the politics and influence of translation, of particular interest and relevance to the Harry Potter series because of the number of languages into which the books have been translated. The authors are primarily interested in "the mediating role of the translator and the importance of cultural awareness during the process of translation" (133). Bedeker and Feinauer argue for a "functionalist" approach to translation, one that takes into account the cultural function of those words, concepts, and phrases in the "target text" (one being translated) and their role in the "target culture" (the translation's readership).

Finally, William MacNeil's essay "'Kidlit' as 'Law-and-Lit'" in *Cardozo Studies in Law and Literature* engages in the kind of analysis more typically found in scholarly assessments of *Order of the Phoenix* or later novels, an examination of Rowling's representation of the legal system. Comparing the trial of Death Eaters that Harry views in the Pensieve to the Nuremberg trials of Nazi war criminals, MacNeil is also interested in Rowling's treatment of injustice in the form of house-elves, whose bondage as employees of Hogwarts and wizarding families is introduced fully in this fourth novel, and in racial prejudice dramatized by Hagrid's "outing" as a half-giant.

CHARACTERS

Sirius Black Harry's godfather and best friend of Harry's father, James Potter. Readers see significantly more of Sirius in the fourth novel, even though he now is in hiding from wizarding officials. Primarily, he serves as a confidante for Harry, a trusted adult friend and surrogate parent. As Harry encounters more and more confusing new circumstances that challenge his developing moral compass, his regular owls to Sirius become a central part of the story.

Our introduction to Sirius as a character remains somewhat partial: Readers know he was unjustly accused of a crime and lives in hiding; we also know he was a good friend of the Potters and is somewhat embittered by Wormtail's betrayal, which led to the Potters' death and his own imprisonment in Azkaban. *Goblet of Fire* demonstrates this caring side of Sirius as he relocates from parts unknown in the world to a cave in Hogsmeade, traveling mainly in his animagus form as a shaggy black dog for Harry's benefit and safety. As does Dumbledore as a store of historical knowledge, Sirius serves an important role in the narrative by explaining how the events of Voldemort's first rise to power are informing the present, such as the insights he shares about Crouch's ignominious behavior and fall from political stardom during the Death Eater trials.

Barty Crouch, Jr.   Former Death Eater, escaped Azkaban prisoner, and son of the ministry head of the Department of International Magical Cooperation. Barty Crouch, Jr., remains a shadowy character introduced to readers only through Pensieve flashbacks and secondhand stories from Sirius (until the end of the novel). This contrasts with the film version of *Goblet of Fire*, which was adapted to include an early introduction to Barty Crouch, Jr., in an opening scene to help viewers make more sense of his appearance as the Moody impostor at the film's denouement. In the novel Barty Crouch, Jr., is a flat character—seemingly insanely devoted to Voldemort, willing to make any sacrifice to bring about the Dark Lord's rise to power. It is only in Pensieve flashbacks and from stories that readers are able to detect a hint of something else in Barty Crouch, Jr. Sirius's recollection of the events of his own capture suggests that Crouch's cold, callow sentencing of his son to Azkaban and disowning of him compounded an increasingly chilly public sentiment toward his political leadership; some believed that his careerism and fanatical devotion to what could be perceived either as justice for victims or punishment of Death Eaters alienated his family and partially led to his son's attraction to the dark side. In this light we are invited to have a small bit of sympathy for Barty Crouch, Jr., as the

"neglected son." His actions in the book, however, are calculating and baldly in the service of evil so that limited sympathy is not cultivated throughout the story.

Barty Crouch, Sr.   Ministry head of the Department of International Magical Cooperation; former head of the Department of Magical Law Enforcement; and former judge in the Wizengamot. Crouch, Sr. plays a significant role in the plot of *Goblet of Fire*. As a ministry official involved in the coordination of the Triwizard Tournament, he serves as a tournament judge and works on the logistics for the Quidditch World Cup. However, Rowling portrays Crouch as obsessed with details and rules; he appears as a career climber, perhaps to the detriment of an impulse toward humaneness and compassion. A significant development in his character occurs when in *Goblet of Fire* readers become privy to Dumbledore's memories of the trials of Death Eaters during Voldemort's first reign of terror, largely because of the lack of emotion Crouch shows at the sentencing of his own son. He is seemingly more bothered by the social reprobation this causes than by the reasons for his son's turn to the dark arts.

In *Goblet of Fire* it is Crouch's absence that readers should take note of more than his presence, as throughout the novel it creates an increasing sense of concern over his many duties either going undone or turned over to underlings such as Percy Weasley. Ultimately we learn that his wife's sense of loss at the sentencing of Barty Crouch, Jr., overwhelmed his father's sense of duty. The transferring of Mrs. Crouch to her son's place in the prison has the function of revealing two things about his character: The sense of reason and order he has previously been defined by is vulnerable to the pull of emotion, and his judgment about his son in the end is gravely wrong. The damage he has done to his son's moral compass was wrought early and is irrevocable. Even Crouch realizes this in the end, and it is perhaps symbolic that in the last chapters Barty Crouch, Jr., reveals that he murdered his father and transfigured his corpse into a bone that he buried, emblematic of his father's desiccated spirit and inability truly to love his son.

Fleur Delacour Triwizard Tournament champion from Beauxbatons. Fleur is a stunningly attractive girl who is part Veela, mysterious and seductive she-creatures who also serve as the Bulgarian mascots at the Quidditch World Cup. As the only female entrant in the Triwizard Tournament Fleur performs disappointingly, finishing last in the first task of procuring the golden egg from the dragon; dropping out of the second task, necessitating Harry's saving of her sister, Gabrielle, from the merpeople; and becoming victim to Viktor Krum, who, under the Imperius Curse, stuns her, removing her from the third task.

Emphasis on her appearance and sexual attractiveness serves to reinforce one of the major themes of *Goblet of Fire*: adolescent romance. Many of the male students become preoccupied when she passes them in the halls; Ron transforms into a bumbling teenager who can barely speak intelligibly when he encounters her. The feelings of some of Hogwarts' male students, as well as strong tides of jealousy experienced by some of the Hogwarts' female students, reinforce that the main characters (Hermione, Ron, and Harry, all at least 14 if not 15 years old during the course of the novel) are no longer children. All of them are now experiencing puberty and the range of emotions, many of which are romantic and sexual in nature, that influence their actions in this, and later, novels.

Cedric Diggory Hogwarts Triwizard Tournament champion and a Hufflepuff sixth-year. While readers have been introduced to Cedric in passing during previous novels in the series, he takes on new importance in the fourth book. We first encounter him when the Weasleys, Harry, and Hermione take the Portkey to the Quidditch World Cup, where they join Cedric and his father, Amos, at the departure location. Some insensitive comments from Amos reveal he is intensely competitive and relishes his son's victory over Harry, whose widespread fame makes a good target for Amos's spirit of competitiveness, a spirit Cedric does not share. After Harry is compelled to participate in the tournament and is considered an "illegitimate" tournament champion, Hufflepuffs, Ravenclaws,

and Slytherins alike show their displeasure with buttons that say, "Support Cedric Diggory: The Real Hogwarts Champion" and general social snubbing of Harry; Cedric, however, does not participate in this protest, confirming Dumbledore's comments, at the end of the novel, on Cedric's nature as a quintessential Hufflepuff: intensely loyal (in this case, to his friend Harry) and hardworking. Midway through the novel as Harry develops an attraction to the Ravenclaw Quidditch Seeker Cho Chang, he also develops a resentment toward Cedric, who he learns is escorting Cho to the Yule Ball. Nonetheless, Harry and Cedric develop a sort of grudging respect and camaraderie for each other throughout the tournament as they share hints about the tasks and, in the novel's denouement, share the trophy—the Portkey that takes them to Tom Riddle's grave.

Cedric's death in the series is in some ways a safe one that serves the narrative function of cementing Voldemort's fundamentally evil character (his charge to "kill the spare" when Harry and Cedric transport to the graveyard reflects the gross lack of value he attributes to human life). At the same time, Rowling preserves young readers from emotional trauma by killing off a minor, yet likable, character and still fulfills some of the goals of the story, such as helping readers contemplate the impact of Cedric's death on Harry.

Albus Dumbledore Hogwarts headmaster and Harry's mentor. Dumbledore serves, in this novel as well as the previous ones, as the moral leader of both Hogwarts and the political institutions of the wizarding world. He continues in this role as a touchstone for Harry and for the narrative as a whole—in times of conflict, distress, or trouble, all characters turn to Dumbledore to determine the right course of conduct, whether it is the unexpected emergence of Harry's name from the Goblet of Fire or the appearance of a delirious Crouch on the school grounds. Dumbledore serves as a moral compass for the series thus far, almost to the point of infallibility. His encouraging and continued remarks about the value of friendship (whether it be insisting that Snape and Sirius put aside their differences or reminding students and staff that uniting as one will prove Cedric's death was not in vain) highlight one of Rowling's major themes: the importance, necessity, and joy of friendship.

Hermione Granger   Harry and Ron's best friend; a capable Muggle-born witch. Several major developments occur in *Goblet of Fire* in the character of Hermione Granger. First, readers begin to appreciate new aspects of Hermione's personality as she takes on the role of romantic interest for Ron Weasley and Viktor Krum. Until this point adolescent flirting has been almost absent from the series, but as the Yule Ball, a formal dance, requires its attendees to have dates, relationships start evolving in new directions. Ron's denial of his interest in Hermione as more than a friend is part of the plot tension in this book—even though, as usual, Rowling is able to use Hermione's keen perception of social dynamics to reveal to readers the source of Ron's hostility at the Yule Ball.

Second, Hermione's characteristic regard for truth and justice finds a new outlet in this novel in her formation of the Society for the Protection of Elfish Welfare, or S.P.E.W. Though Rowling makes it almost impossible for anyone—readers or classmates—to take the organization seriously because of the laughable acronym, Hermione's campaign for house-elf liberation advances what we have known about her from previous novels. While she has developed an increasing disregard for what she perceives as useless or unjust rules, S.P.E.W. is her first active campaign against what she perceives to be a corrupt system. However, the society does reinforce one of her historically irritating qualities, the know-it-all attitude that alienates others, namely, her belief that she knows better than house-elves what is good for them.

Third, Hermione continues in her role as a confidante for Harry, especially during his rift with Ron. Loyal and supportive, Hermione never wavers in her belief in Harry's claim that he did not enter his name into the Goblet of Fire, and her sage advice and listening ear are central in getting Harry through both the academic demands of the year and the three tasks of the Triwizard Tournament.

Finally, Rowling spotlights Hermione's defining characteristic, her quest for knowledge and valuing of truth, in Hermione's tangle with the sensationalist journalist Rita Skeeter, who seems to represent everything Hermione despises—the journalist manipulates people, words, and public opinion; she misrepresents the truth; and she shows a callous disregard for others along with a self-serving thirst for social drama. Hermione brings to bear all her best resources—the library, her insight, her problem-solving skills, and her magical abilities—to discover that Rita Skeeter is an unregistered animagus in the form of a beetle; she sets out to capture the liar and in doing so finally puts an end to her rumormongering.

Rubeus Hagrid   Half-giant gamekeeper and Care of Magical Creatures teacher at Hogwarts. Hagrid, as does Sirius, serves one of Harry's confidantes and also has a close relationship with Ron and Hermione. In this novel in the series the greatest developments in his character are his increasing commitment to Dumbledore and the cause of good, his romantic interest in Madame Maxime, and the wounding of his heart and ego by the vicious story published by Rita Skeeter in the *Daily Prophet*. Because Hagrid's love of animals is ubiquitous, he rules out no creature, however dangerous, as appropriate for the Care of Magical Creatures class. It is because of this love for all creatures great and small that the Hogwarts students are able to enjoy exposure to Blast-Ended Skrewts, repugnant hybrids bred by Hagrid and the product of cross-breeding between fire crabs and manticores that look like shelless lobsters. They make an appearance in the third task of the tournament as obstacles in the maze.

Hagrid is especially hurt by Skeeter's story because of his strong belief in judging an individual on character rather than blood or species, a theme echoed throughout the novels and by many characters. After Skeeter's story skewers him as vicious, violent, and with total disregard for the health and well-being of his students (as well as accurately reporting that his mother was a barbaric giantess named Fridwulfa), Hagrid feels deeply saddened.

Only Dumbledore's encouragement, coupled with the support of his young friends Hermione, Harry, and Ron, helps him see that he will only be surrendering to Skeeter's hateful tactics if he stops teaching.

Igor Karkaroff Headmaster of Durmstrang and traitorous former Death Eater. Karkaroff is introduced in this novel and makes few notable appearances later it. For the purposes of the story he serves as an example of a Death Eater who lacked the intestinal fortitude of the more devoted of them such as the Lestranges and Barty Crouch, Jr. Unwilling to show his true colors, Karkaroff recants his affiliation with the Death Eaters and blames the Imperius Curse for his actions. Karkaroff made an enemy of Moody during Voldemort's first rise to power, and his betrayal of his fellow Death Eaters alienated him from both his former patron Lord Voldemort and those Death Eaters who remained loyal to the fallen wizard.

Rowling portrays Karkaroff as weak-willed and imperious, a person who sees perfidy and treachery everywhere and who takes great offense at petty insults. Concerned throughout the tournament that his champion and his school are being treated unfairly, he is frequently at odds with Dumbledore in this novel. Karkaroff serves another important role because of the nervous relationship he develops with Snape in *Goblet of Fire*; as a former suspected Death Eater for whom Dumbledore repeatedly vouches, Snape is sought out by Karkaroff when the Dark Mark symbol begins to appear on Death Eaters' arms, signaling Voldemort's returning strength. In this way Rowling uses Karkaroff to raise reader suspicions of Snape, on ongoing question the series refuses to resolve until the very end.

Viktor Krum Durmstrang Triwizard Tournament champion and Seeker for the Bulgarian Quidditch team. Viktor Krum is a flat character whose limited role is as Hermione's love interest and idol for many of the young men at Hogwarts. Accompanying Hermione to the Yule Ball, he also becomes a confusing source of tension for Ron Weasley as it becomes increasingly apparent that Ron is romanti-cally interested in his friend Hermione. Krum is already a celebrity because of his role as Seeker on the Bulgarian professional Quidditch team; Ron has also cultivated an intense celebrity admiration for him. This admiration makes the subsequent plot developments more complex as Ron grapples with his adoration of Krum as a professional athlete and his feelings of jealousy toward him as a romantic rival. Krum receives little real development as a character; he spends time in the library pursuing Hermione and confronts Harry at one point in the book over concern that Harry might be Hermione's boyfriend; he is also Karkaroff's star student, but beyond these minor plot points, Krum remains a fairly undeveloped character in this and the rest of the novels in the series.

Neville Longbottom Harry's friend and fellow Gryffindor. Neville appears sporadically throughout the novel, and while he does not contribute significantly to the plot, readers and Harry learn more about his background. It is common knowledge that he lives with his intimidating grandmother and that his magical powers are less than impressive, but Harry's visits to Dumbledore's office Pensieve disclose that Neville's parents, Frank and Alice, were Aurors (dark wizard hunters), who were tortured into insanity by Death Eaters, specifically the nefarious couple Rodolphus and Bellatrix Lestrange. Neville's parents currently reside in St. Mungo's Hospital for Magical Maladies and Injuries, unable to recognize their son except as someone of whom they are fond. In *Goblet of Fire* Neville has a role of minor significance when the impostor Moody attempts to manipulate his interest in plants as a way of helping Harry with the tournament's second task. The film adaptation does use Neville's character in this fashion rather than using the book's mechanism, which is to have Dobby steal Gillyweed on overhearing Moody's recommending it.

Draco Malfoy Harry's fellow Hogwarts student, teen archnemesis, and Slytherin. Though Harry and Draco have several magical duels in this fourth novel in the series, Rowling provides little other substantive information about him as a character except continued confirmation of his elitism; this elitism, inherited from his parents, can be traced to his father Lucius's allegiance to Lord Voldemort. Malfoy remains a two-dimensional character, though subsequent novels develop him more fully.

Madame Olympe Maxime   Headmistress of Beauxbatons (a European wizarding school); a half-giantess. Madame Maxime has an obvious romantic interest for Rubeus Hagrid. She appears to have an amicable history with the other institutional leaders of the wizarding world and is initially receptive to Hagrid's amorous advances, even if she perhaps uses them to gain access to tournament information to pass on to the Beauxbatons champion, Fleur Delacour. Maxime's character remains fairly undeveloped in this novel; the only truly significant detail Rowling reveals about her is her outrage at Hagrid's suggestion that she, like him, is also racially part giant. Rowling suggests in the novel's conclusion that Madame Maxime has admitted her parentage and is willing to work with Hagrid on behalf of the side of good as an ambassador to the exiled community of giants.

Minerva McGonagall   Deputy headmistress, Transfiguration professor at Hogwarts, and head of Gryffindor House. As Dumbledore's trusted and reliable colleague and mentor to Harry and his friends, Professor McGonagall plays a role that is both central and somewhat two-dimensional. She is steadfastly on the side of right but appears in the narrative mostly doing the will of Dumbledore. Aside from chastising Moody for turning Malfoy into a ferret, announcing the Yule Ball will be held, and expressing outrage over Fudge's use of the Dementor against Barty Crouch, Jr., McGonagall's appearances in the story are fairly limited.

Alastor "Mad-Eye" Moody   Battered former Auror and Defense Against the Dark Arts teacher. Readers are not actually introduced to the real Mad-Eye Moody until the closing chapters of the book. As Barty Crouch, Jr., has taken on Moody's appearance and role before readers even encounter him, very few conclusions can be drawn about his

character, except from what is revealed in flashbacks or by other characters. He is a grizzled survivor: a devoted—almost fanatical—dark wizard hunter, or Auror, who becomes paranoid because of his work during Voldemort's first rise to power. Flashbacks via the Pensieve reveal he suffered and sacrificed much in order to defeat the powers of evil. However, the narrative of *Goblet of Fire* reveals very few real details about Moody because he spends the book trapped in a magical trunk, put there by the impostor Barty Crouch, Jr.

Harry Potter   Protagonist, a Gryffindor, and second Hogwarts champion in the Triwizard Tournament. Harry grows in a number of ways in this middle book of the series even as he struggles with some of the same kinds of adolescent pettiness as his friends.

Harry's relationship with Ron and the Weasleys deepens in this novel. Staying at the Burrow during the summer, attending the Quidditch World Cup, and befriending Fred, George, and Ginny (as well as Ron) continue to build Harry's intimacy with the Weasley family. Molly and Bill's appearance at the third task and Molly's comforting of Harry after the death of Cedric stress again her role as surrogate mother to Harry. Ron and Harry's friendship emerges stronger after they resolve Ron's jealousy and bitterness over Harry's participation in the Triwizard Tournament.

As do many entering the beginning of the adolescent years, Harry suffers crises of confidence that are both paralyzing and empowering, whether evading dragons or asking a girl on a date. Though Ron also struggles with some of these problems, the difficulties Harry faces as our central protagonist form the centerpiece of the novel. Harry's strategies of procrastination as he avoids having to deal with the challenge of decoding the golden egg's confusing message or his deferral of figuring out how he will get past the dragon in the first task resonate with teen (and adult) readers who have ever faced, or avoided facing, something unpleasant. At the same time, Harry's confidence starts to grow as he meets these challenges and succeeds—both at the tournament and romantically (even if his success rests in just securing a date for the

Yule Ball). And yet, Harry's emotional development is not complete or free of trouble; he has a tendency toward pettiness when Cho and Cedric start dating, to the point of rejecting useful advice from his fellow Hogwarts champion simply because he is a romantic rival for Cho's affections. His last-minute "solutions," which are often simply good luck or the help of others, also make him a realistic hero rather than an infallible one.

Finally, Harry's traumatic confrontation with Voldemort in the graveyard, even as it scars him emotionally as well as literally (when Wormtail takes his blood for the resurrection ceremony), forces him to gain a level of maturity that most adolescents will never have to experience. While his impulse is to run away from Voldemort, in the end he faces him in an epic duel. Even as he is wracked with grief over Cedric's death, he also becomes fortified to ensure that he will take his friend's body back to Hogwarts for the Diggorys' sake. Already having experienced loss and grief through his parents' deaths and his life as an orphan, Harry seems faced with unspeakable levels of fear and tragedy, but this is partly what makes him such a likable, identifiable, and admirable hero: When faced with challenges that seem insurmountable, he always draws upon the best in himself to meet them and, with the help of his friends and mentors, defeat them even if he encounters loss along the way. At the end of the novel, he achieves a sense of confidence and hope that whatever the challenges he will face in the future—now that Voldemort has returned—he has the inner strength and the support of loved ones that will help him through the struggle.

Rita Skeeter   A sensationalist journalist and unregistered animagus (beetle). As a writer for the *Daily Prophet* and freelancer for other wizarding publications such as *Witch's Weekly*, Skeeter employs unscrupulous journalistic tactics that are largely responsible for the public's perceptions of events at Hogwarts over the academic year. Skeeter's stories infuriate Hermione since one of Hermione's central character traits is valuing truth and knowledge; that Rita so cavalierly plays with the truth and violates her subject's trust and right to privacy send Hermione into a frenzied quest to stop Rita Skeeter's irresponsible publishing. Using journalism as a weapon, Skeeter misrepresents and tries to exploit Harry's orphanhood, sensationalizes Arthur Weasley's encounter at Mad-Eye Moody's house, publicly faults the ministry for the Dark Mark at the Triwizard Tournament, and eventually causes Hermione to receive hundreds of hate letters via owl post because of her magazine article portraying Hermione as a scheming vixen. In the end Skeeter seems to symbolize the power of the free press and language to shape public opinion as well as serve as Rowling's scathing critique of an irresponsible use of such power.

Skeeter is eventually revealed to be an unregistered animagus who uses her animal form, a beetle, unethically to acquire sources for her stories, a method Hermione eventually exploits for Harry's benefit.

Severus Snape   Potions Master and nemesis of Harry and Sirius. During *Goblet of Fire* readers gain access to important information about the Potions professor, learning that he was an accused Death Eater and that Dumbledore steadfastly defended his loyalty to the cause of good. Despite suspicion by Sirius, Harry, Ron, and Hermione, and despite a flashback accusation from Igor Karkaroff during the Death Eater trials, the headmaster consistently rejects any suggestion that Snape still feels an allegiance to Voldemort. At the same time *Goblet of Fire* serves as an important turning point both in the story and for Snape because of Voldemort's return to bodily form and the Dark Mark that appears on Snape's arm. Nevertheless, Snape's assumed allegiance to Dumbledore appears to have no effect on his treatment of the Gryffindor protagonists: He persists in mocking and unfairly punishing them for reasons not entirely understandable yet.

Ron Weasley   Harry's best friend and fellow Gryffindor. Like Harry, Ron grows in this book as he moves toward adolescence and starts to feel the growing pains of developing romantic interest in the opposite sex. Similarly, Ron starts to feel more deeply the pains of his economic status, and his bitterness about it simultaneously erodes and strengthens his friendship with Harry.

One of the major plotlines of *Goblet of Fire* is the rift between Ron and Harry over Harry's participation in the tournament. This seems a natural evolution of their friendship as Ron has often served as Harry's sidekick, and this development of a sense of resentment over Harry's constant "starring role" in both the social and existential dramas of their lives seems inevitable. Envious of both Harry's financial security and his public attention, Ron struggles to make sense of these undesirable feelings that conflict with his regard for and friendship with Harry. While he does to some degree resolve these feelings, this underlying tension continues to develop in later books. At the close of this novel Ron's role is primarily as a source of consolation and comfort for Harry after his traumatic graveyard battle.

Lord Voldemort/Tom Riddle, Jr. Harry's archnemesis; a power-hungry, evil, half-blood wizard and former Hogwarts student. *Goblet of Fire* is important to readers' developing understanding of Voldemort because Rowling demonstrates the extent of his cruel nature as well as the lengths to which he will go for power.

Aside from the opening chapter of the novel, where Voldemort callously strikes dead an innocent Muggle, and his resurrection in the graveyard, readers' primary exposure to Voldemort throughout the rest of the narrative is in Harry's dreams. Through these dreams readers see how pitiless and punishing Voldemort can be even to his most loyal supporters, such as his use of Unforgivable Curses on Wormtail, who has nourished him and sacrificed to restore him to bodily form. During the graveyard confrontation, when Voldemort rises again, he mirthlessly ponders his family history, musing to Harry about his half-Muggle parentage, an important revelation hinting at the ensuing fuller exploration of Voldemort's inner turmoil and the source of his quest for both power and immortality.

Readers' introduction to the corporeal Voldemort fulfills expectations of him as one without mercy or regard for human life, as his first command in the graveyard is to strike Cedric dead with no chance at defending himself, even referring to him as a "spare," as though he were an object instead of a person. Voldemort uses the Cruciatus Curse on a penitent Death Eater who begs for forgiveness for not remaining loyal, and he promises death to those of his followers who have not returned to his service. He remains a somewhat mysterious figure.

Wormtail/Peter Pettigrew Former school friend of James Potter, Sirius Black, and Remus Lupin, and previously Ron's pet rat, Scabbers. Pettigrew is characterized as a weak and spineless parasite whose relationship with his trio of teenage friends at Hogwarts was largely based on their pity for him rather than a true sense of camaraderie or respect shared by the other three. At the end of *Prisoner of Azkaban* Pettigrew escapes for parts unknown, and at the beginning of this novel we see he has sought out and now assists the incapacitated Voldemort with his nefarious plan to return to bodily form and to power. Wormtail is Rowling's example of a person whose decisions are motivated by fear and who lets his low self-regard and quest for a sense of importance drive his moral decisions. Unlike our hero, Harry, who acts for the cause of good and for the good of others in spite of his fears and anxieties, Pettigrew appears self-serving and hungry for attention; these qualities cultivate in him an interest in and attraction to the Dark Arts. Pettigrew's role in the novel is important because if it were not for his cowardly retreat to Albania, where he sought out the disembodied Voldemort, and his chance encounter with Bertha Jorkins (the gossipy and wayward ministry employee), Voldemort would not have been able to orchestrate the manipulation of the Triwizard Tournament to gain access to Harry.

FILM ADAPTATION

The fourth installment of the Harry Potter series, *Harry Potter and the Goblet of Fire*, premiered in London on November 6, 2005, and in New York City on November 12, 2005; it opened for nationwide release to the rest of the United States on November 18. This film (as had its predecessor, *Prisoner of Azkaban*) earned a PG-13 rating, mostly due to violent and disturbing scenes including the murder of Cedric Diggory and Voldemort's return to human form. In stark contrast to the reaction to the first two Disneyesque Harry Potter films, critics such as Shawn Levy of the *Oregonian* cautioned that "parents of young Potter-heads and their even younger siblings should take special care; this is truly grisly stuff" because Harry and Voldemort's confrontation is "as terrifying a scene as you can imagine." Similarly, Frank McNally of the *Irish Times* described the film as "brilliant but scary."

Running for a total of 157 minutes, the film promised to keep viewers entertained and wary with taglines like "Dark and difficult times lie ahead" and "On November 18, everything will change." Like the *Prisoner of Azkaban*, *Goblet of Fire* was released on both regular and IMAX screens, helping to solidify ticket sales. In a severely slumped movie market *Goblet of Fire* surpassed WARNER BROTHERS executives' sales estimates. *USA Today's* Scott Bowles reported that "despite its darker themes and a PG-13 rating, *Harry Potter and the Goblet of Fire* enjoyed the fourth-largest movie opening ever with $101.4 million. . . . The debut is the largest of the Potter series and made the franchise Hollywood's fourth-largest ever. The series has raked in about $930 million domestically, behind only the *Star Wars*, *James Bond* and *Lord of the Rings* franchises." Similarly, Greg Hernandez of the Los Angeles *Daily News* wrote that "online ticket seller Fandango reported Sunday that it was selling an average of 10 tickets per second on opening day Friday, the heaviest advance ticket demand for any film ever besides [*Star Wars: Revenge of the*] *Sith*." While IMAX screens sold out continuously, the other factor in the film's success was the population of adults attending the movie. Bowles noted that "roughly 40% of *Goblet's* audience is non-family adults, compared with a little more than 30% for the previous films." In his review Bowles also included comments from Dan Fellman, head of distribution at Warner Brothers, who said, "Audiences are growing up with Potter, and even more people are relating to the issues in the story." Even though Harry Potter's character is only 14 years old in *Goblet of Fire*, adults could relate to and appreciate many of the situations Harry (and his classmates) endured, including the feelings of excitement associated with young love, the nerve-wracking experience of ask-

ing someone on a date for the first time, and, more seriously, coping with the death of a friend.

Critics and fans alike responded positively to Mike Newell in the role as director. Newell was the first British person to direct a Harry Potter film and is rumored to have been chosen partly because of his success with romantic comedies like *Four Weddings and a Funeral*. *Goblet of Fire* showcased similar comedy with respect to the interactions of Harry, Cho, Hermione, Viktor Krum, and, of course, Ron and the striking French student, Fleur Delacour. Several critics suggested that as a native Brit Newell was able to capture the essence of Hogwarts more tangibly than the non-British directors who preceded him. Shawn Levy awards Newell perhaps the highest praise, writing that "from the start [of the film] the air is heavier, the use of special effects more pointed, the close-ups of the young stars' eyes more probing and purposeful, the pacing more assured, the grim reality more plainly faced. It's the first Harry Potter movie that is a really good film."

The screenplay writer Steve Kloves also received praise from critics, including Richard Corliss of *Time*, who argued that Kloves "put *Goblet's* 734-page bulk on a severe diet that slimmed the plot without starving it" (99). In an interview with Kloves Corliss asked him about how he managed to "slim the plot." Kloves described the task as "by far the most difficult thing [he'd] ever done in [his] life," adding that "it took two years to make that work—mostly trying to decide what to leave behind" (99). Corliss argued that the movie is better than the book because, thanks to Kloves, the film "telescopes the book's first 100 pages into a thrilling 20 minutes. The whole movie zips through the narrative like the Hogwarts Express, transporting viewers from the mundane to the magical in no time flat" (99). Bowles, however, again cites the Warner Brothers executive Fellman, who said, "We are really trying not to stray from the original story [. . .] since that audience is so large and so devoted, there's no need to change things." Even though some scenes viewers looked forward to seeing on screen were cut (such as when Fred and George Weasley give Dudley Dursley a batch of Ton-Tongue Toffee), accelerating immediately to the Quidditch

World Cup and its incredible special effects did not displease many viewers.

Reviews of *Goblet of Fire* were overwhelmingly positive, and critics agreed that the film was darker and scarier than those preceding it. British reviewers shared their opinions first. James Christopher from the London *Times* called the film "a considerable triumph," and David Edwards of London's *Daily Mirror* described the film as "the best yet." In the States the positive reviews continued. Anthony Breznican of *USA Today* gave the film "two wands up" (5D), and the *Chicago Sun-Times*'s Roger Ebert claimed that even though the movie was "more violent" and "less cute" than the three preceding films, "the action is not the mindless destruction of a video game; it has purpose, shape and style." Bowles headlined his review with "*Goblet of Fire* keeps wizard tales hot," explaining that "he may be getting older and struggling with love, but Harry Potter hasn't lost his magic touch in theaters." Levy backhandedly insults the first three films of the series while praising the fourth: "After three films laced with enough sugar to make a career for a firm of dentists, Harry Potter all of a sudden has grown up with a bloody bang. *Goblet of Fire* . . . is a mature, tense, frightening and altogether masterful film. It is easily the best in a quartet that, to now, has been more successful financially than artistically."

There were no completely negative reviews, but several critics responded unenthusiastically to the computer-generated special effects. Kyle Smith of the *New York Post* argued that "the story so often stops its forward motion to take us on long detours into the land of CGI effects that it amounts to a $150 million magic show." M. Price of the *Fort Worth Press* critiqued the film in writing that "generally convincing character portrayals—even if the recurring players are fast outgrowing the roles—help to prevent the film from becoming merely a pageant of special-effects gimmickry. Or maybe it's the special-effects gimmicks that keep the fans lining up for more and more of the same" (20).

While "gimmicks" probably were not the sole cause of *Goblet of Fire*'s enormous success, fans were impressed by them, including the Quidditch World Cup, the arrival of the students from Durmstrang and Beauxbatons, and the first and second tasks of the Triwizard Tournament. The structure of the Quidditch stadium wowed viewers; fans were also delighted with Viktor Krum's dramatic (and dangerous) entrance and the enormous Irish mascot. The arrival of the Durmstrang men and the Beauxbatons women also delighted fans. Madame Maxime's gigantic carriage pulled by winged horses made for a grand entrance, and the Durmstrang ship rising magnificently from the Black Lake added to the mystery of Hogwarts' "friends from the north." A full-scale dragon—capable of blowing fire—was constructed for the film, and the Hungarian Horntail's pursuit of Harry kept fans anticipating its next move anxiously. Perhaps the most impressive special effects concerned the second task of the Tri-Wizard Tournament, during which Harry and his fellow competitors had to swim past magical creatures and merpeople to rescue someone important to each of them. Filmmakers constructed an enormous aquarium specifically for this scene. According to the Internet Movie Database, this aquarium was one of the largest underwater sets ever constructed, capable of holding 132,000 gallons of water. A set source also added that "safety divers swam in with scuba regulators to allow them to breathe without having to surface. These scenes were shot in a huge purpose-built tank with a blue-screen background. Daniel Radcliffe alone logged around 41 hours, 38 minutes underwater during the course of filming. At one point during training he inadvertently signaled that he was drowning, sending the crew into a huge panic to bring him back up to surface."

The cast of *Goblet of Fire*, as had that of the movies before it, continued to please both fans and critics. Newcomers included the following: Robert Pattison as Cedric Diggory, Stanislav Ianevski as Viktor Krum, Roger Lloyd-Pack as Barty Crouch, Katie Leung as Cho Chang, Clémence Poésy as Fleur Delacour, Predrag Bjelac as Igor Karkaroff, and David Tennant as Barty Crouch, Jr. Fans were pleased with Tennant's technique of flicking his tongue rapidly to demonstrate his connection to the reptilian Voldemort. When Brendan Gleeson (as Mad-Eye Moody) mimicked this movement, a clear connection was established between the two characters. This connection was fitting since Barty Crouch, Jr., takes Polyjuice Potion to appear as Mad-Eye Moody. Two other additions to the cast received particular praise for their performances: Brendan Gleeson as Mad-Eye Moody and Miranda Richardson as Rita Skeeter. Levy congratulated them, writing, "Along with Gleeson's ferocity as the very moody Moody, Miranda Richardson as the unctuous gossip columnist Rita Skeeter adds new layers of wit to the enterprise." Likewise, *USA Today*'s Claudia Puig wrote that "Brendan Gleeson does a fine job as the enigmatic 'Mad Eye' Moody, and Miranda Richardson is appropriately eccentric as journalist Rita Skeeter" (1D).

Perhaps the movie's most anticipated performance, however, was executed by Ralph Fiennes as Lord Voldemort. Fans waited nervously for Voldemort to appear in human form. Until *Goblet of Fire* all viewers had glimpsed of Harry's nemesis was the face plastered on the back of Quirrell's head in *Sorcerer's Stone*. Fiennes surpassed all expectations. Breznican of *USA Today* called Fiennes "scene-stealing" (5D), and his colleague Puig agreed, describing Fiennes's portrayal of the Dark Lord as "terrifying" (1D). Joe Neumaier of New York's *Daily News* interviewed Fiennes about playing Voldemort. Fiennes explained, "One of the hardest things to play [is] the personification of evil! It's a full-on villain turn. You have to find a certain style or tone, you don't want to be either too campy or too understated. I thought of that old (standard) about Voldemort having an unhappy childhood." In turn, Fiennes truly grasped Voldemort's nature.

Filmmakers opted to delete the presence of house-elves in the movie entirely. Viewers unfamiliar with the novel were unable to meet Winky—who plays a crucial role in the novel's plot—the troubled house-elf spurned by Barty Crouch, Sr. Not including Winky or Dobby in the film severely downplayed the plight of these servants. The novel acquaints readers with the debate about house-elves, mainly that they prefer servitude; in the book Rowling also reveals that house-elves are responsible for staffing the Hogwarts kitchen. Though the deletion of these characters leaves viewers less informed

about an important aspect of the wizarding world, the removal of their presence from the story also led to viewers' knowing less about Hermione, who in the fourth novel forms S.P.E.W. (the Society for the Promotion of Elfish Welfare). In creating S.P.E.W., Hermione annoys many of her classmates, who, like Ron, think the elves are happy in their current social station. Her tireless efforts to start the society, recruit and maintain members, and even sneak into the Hogwarts kitchen and speak to Winky herself truly showcase Hermione's passion for justice. Removing the house-elves from the film may have aided in streamlining the plot, but the decision also diminished Hermione's character.

Filmmakers not only decided to downplay Hermione's passion for social justice: Once again, they decided to hyperfeminize her as well (see the discussion of the film adaptation of *Prisoner of Azkaban*). When Hermione attends the Yule Ball, she walks down the stairs slowly in a pink dress. According to the Internet Movie Database, "Costume designer Jany Temime considered Hermione's dress for the Yule Ball as the most important [costume], comparing it to that of Cinderella. The design of the dress was changed several times before the designers were satisfied with the results. Emma Watson was very careful not to wear it more than necessary because she was afraid that she would wreck it." In the book Hermione wears a periwinkle blue dress. Perhaps the change in dress color seems unimportant; the color pink is associated with femininity while the color blue is associated with masculinity. The desire to hyperfeminize Hermione becomes more troubling, however, at the close of the Yule Ball scene. In the novel Harry returns to the Gryffindor common room to find Hermione and Ron in the middle of a shouting match. Essentially, the chapter ends with Hermione's scolding Ron for waiting until the last possible moment to ask her to be his date to the ball, capitalizing on the jealousy he felt after seeing her there with Krum. In the film, however, Hermione and Ron have a rather public disagreement on a stairway in Hogwarts. Ron attempted to make matters between Hermione and Krum difficult during the ball itself, and during their confrontation, it is Hermione who bursts into tears and who tells Ron that he "ruined everything." Hermione is depicted as the weepy, spurned lover rather than a strong female, who, in the novel, retains autonomy. The film, on the other hand, awards all the power to Ron.

Another aspect of the film deserving critical exploration is the appearance of the Death Eaters and the destruction they create at the Quidditch World Cup. When the Dark Lord's followers appear, they are dressed in long black robes with tall, pointed hats and skull masks on their faces. Viewers often compare their appearance and accompanying destruction with the Ku Klux Klan, known for terrorizing those they despise while robed and masked, too afraid to show their own faces. As do members of the Klan, the Death Eaters commit hate crimes by attacking those they consider inferior to them, in terms of family heritage or, more specifically here, blood status. Their behavior at the Quidditch World Cup mirrors that of a terrorist attack. They leave the campgrounds in tatters, with shredded tents standing miserably and smoke still rising from fires finally distinguished. This image of destruction haunts viewers and serves as yet another example of why critics classified *Goblet of Fire* as an amazing but scary film that greatly affected so many fans, children and adults alike.

WORKS CITED AND FURTHER READING

Acocella, Joan. "Under the Spell." *New Yorker*, 31 July 2000, 74–78.

Bedeker, Laetitia, and Ilse Feinauer. "The Translator as Cultural Mediator." *Southern African Linguistics and Applied Language Studies* 24, no. 2 (2006): 133–141.

Black, Sharon. "Harry Potter: A Magical Prescription for Just about Anyone." *Journal of Adolescent and Adult Literacy* 46, no. 7 (April 2003): 540–544.

Bowles, Scott. "Bewitched Adults Keep Potter's *Fire* Blazing." *USA Today*, 28 November 2005, p. 1D.

———. "*Goblet of Fire* Keeps Wizard Tales Hot." *USA Today*, 21 November 2005, p. 1D.

Brennan, Geraldine. Review of *Harry Potter and the Goblet of Fire*. *Times Educational Supplement*, 14 July 2000.

Breznican, Anthony. "*Harry Potter* Fans Are Screaming with Delight." *USA Today*, 21 November 2005, p. 5D.

Briggs, Julia. "Fighting the Forces of Evil." Review of *Harry Potter and the Goblet of Fire*. *Times Literary Supplement*, 22 December 2000.

Bruce, Iain. "Wizard Read Lives Up to Hype J. K. Rowling Deserves Credit For." *Sunday Herald*, 9 July 2000.

Christopher, James. Review of *Harry Potter and the Goblet of Fire*. *Times* (London), November 2005.

Corliss, Richard. "*Harry Potter and the Goblet of Fire*." *Time*, 5 December 2005, 99.

Craig, Amanda. "Magical Boy." *New Statesman*, 17 July 2000, 54.

De Lint, Charles. Review of *Harry Potter and the Goblet of Fire*. *Fantasy and Science Fiction*, December 2000, 27.

Decker, Charlotte. Review of *Harry Potter and the Goblet of Fire*. *Book Report* 19, no. 3 (November 2000): 62.

Donahue, Deirdre. "*Goblet of Fire* Burns Out; Lengthy Fourth Books Lacks Spark of Imagination." *USA Today*, 10 July 2000, p. 1D.

Edwards, David. *Review of Harry Potter and the Goblet of Fire*. *Daily Mirror* (London), 14 November 2005.

"Forecasts: Children's Books." *Publishers Weekly*, 17 July 2000, 195.

Gleick, Peter. "Harry Potter, Minus a Certain Flavour." *New York Times*, 10 July 2000.

Gray, Paul, and Andrea Sachs. "Harry's Magic Is Back Again." *Time South Pacific* (Australia/New Zealand Edition), 24 July 2000, 75.

Hernandez, Greg. "Three-Day *Potter* Opening Fourth Largest Ever." *Daily News* (Los Angeles), 21 November 2005.

Jacobs, Kathryn. "Harry—Is That Potter, Percy, or Plantagenet? A Note on Shakespeare's *1 Henry IV* in the Transitional Novels of J. K. Rowling." *Borrowers and Lenders: The Journal of Shakespeare and Appropriation* 2, no. 1 (Spring/Summer 2006). Available online. URL: http://www.borrowers.uga.edu/cocoon/borrowers/request?id=781415. Accessed August 25, 2009.

Johnson, Sarah. Review of *Harry Potter and the Goblet of Fire. Times* (London), 8 July 2000.

Kipen, David. "Trouble with Harry." *San Francisco Chronicle,* 10 July 2000.

Levy, Shawn. "A More Potent Potion Fills *Goblet of Fire.*" *Oregonian,* 17 November 2005.

Lively, Penelope. "Thursday Book: Harry's in Robust Form, Although I'm Left Bug-Eyed: *Harry Potter and the Goblet of Fire* by J. K. Rowling." *Independent* (London), 13 July 2000, p. 5.

MacNeil, William. "'Kidlit' as 'Law-and-Lit': *Harry Potter and the Scales of Justice.*" *Cardozo Studies in Law and Literature* 14, no. 545 (Fall 2002): 545–561.

Maudlin, Michael. "Virtue on a Broomstick." *Christianity Today,* 4 September 2000, 117.

McCrum, Robert. "Plot, Plot, Plot That's Worth the Weight." *Guardian,* 9 July 2000.

McNally, Frank. "Wizard's Latest Adventure 'Brilliant but Scary.'" *Irish Times,* 14 November 2005.

Miller, Karl. "*Harry and the Pot of Gold.*" *Raritan* 20, no. 3 (2001): 132–140.

Neumaier, Joe. "Ralph Fiennes Glad to Be Bad in Latest *Harry Potter* Movie." *Daily News,* 13 September 2005.

Nye, Lesley. "Editor's Review." *Harvard Educational Review* 71, no. 1 (2001): 136–145.

Papinchak, Robert. Review of *Harry Potter and the Goblet of Fire. People,* 24 July 2000, 43.

Parravano, Martha. "*Harry Potter and the Goblet of Fire.*" *Horn Book Magazine* 75, no. 6 (November 2000): 762–763.

Price, M. "*Harry Potter and the Goblet of Fire.*" *Fort Worth Press,* 21 November 2005, p. 20.

Puig, Claudia. "Harry and Gang Stoke Fantasy of Fire." *USA Today,* 17 November 2005, p. 1D.

Rosser, Manda. "The Magic of Leadership: An Exploration of *Harry Potter and the Goblet of Fire.*" *Advances in Developing Human Resources* 9, no. 2 (May 2007): 236–250.

Smith, Kyle. "Trivia for Harry Potter and the Goblet of Fire." Internet Movie Database. URL: http://www.imbd.com/title/tt6336373/trivia. Accessed August 25, 2009.

Zipp, Yvonne. Review of *Harry Potter and the Goblet of Fire. Christian Science Monitor,* 13 July 2000.

Harry Potter and the Order of the Phoenix (2003)

SYNOPSIS

Chapter 1: "Dudley Demented"

Shabbily attired, Harry eavesdrops on the Muggle TV news, wondering why there have been no announcements related to Voldemort's return. Hearing someone apparating or disapparating, Harry leaves for a walk. With no news from the *Daily Prophet* nor owls from Ron or Hermione, he feels abandoned in Little Whinging, mulling over his nightmares about Cedric's murder by Voldemort. While at the park Harry ponders how the dynamics between him and Dudley have changed; unafraid of the bullying Dudley, Harry feels avenged that Dudley now fears Harry's magical abilities. As he walks to Number Four, Privet Drive, Harry runs across Dudley, or "Big D," as his gang calls him, who taunts Harry about his muttering, "Don't kill Cedric!" in his sleep. Harry pulls out his wand as a mock threat when suddenly a stillness falls over the evening. Shockingly, two Dementors attack Dudley, and Harry, who has to attempt his Patronus three times before he can drive them off, barely saves his cousin from the dementor's kiss. Mrs. Figg arrives; as he moves to hide his wand, he is startled to realize that she is no Muggle when she tells him to keep it out for protection.

Chapter 2: "Peck of Owls"

Mrs. Figg reveals that she is a Squib. With Dudley in shock Harry and Mrs. Figg begin to carry him home when Mundungus Fletcher belatedly Apparates. After a tongue lashing Mrs. Figg dispatches him to tell Dumbledore about the Dementors and Harry's Patronus Charm before the ministry charges him with violating the Reasonable Restrictions of Underage Sorcery. Mrs. Figg leaves the two boys at the house of the Dursleys, who are horrified by Dudley's condition. As they begin accusing Harry of magical misdeeds, a series of owls arrive, first expelling him from Hogwarts and ordering his wand destroyed, then rescinding the order. During the commotion Aunt Petunia unexpectedly reveals her knowledge of Dementors, shocking her husband. A third owl orders Harry to appear for a hearing at the Ministry of Magic on August 12. A fourth owl from Sirius tells him not to leave the house. Harry finds himself unable to answer his uncle's question about why Dementors are after him. After Harry tells his uncle that Voldemort has returned, Vernon kicks him out under the guise of protecting his family, when a fifth owl with a Howler arrives for Aunt Petunia, the explosive letter shrieking, "Remember my last, Petunia!" (40). She is visibly shaken and asserts that Harry must stay with them.

Chapter 3: "The Advance Guard"

Filled with self-pity, Harry sends owls to Ron, Hermione, and Sirius apprising them of his circumstances but hears no response. Harry ponders his future possibilities if he is indeed expelled from Hogwarts. On the fourth day while the Dursleys are out, Harry hears a loud crash—a group of wizards including Remus Lupin and Mad-Eye Moody have appeared and tell him he is leaving immediately with them. Nymphadora Tonks, an Auror, helps him gather his belongings and reveals she is a Metamorphmagus, who can change her appearance at will. After Lupin leaves a note for the Dursleys, Moody performs a disillusionment charm to camouflage Harry, and they leave by broom following Moody's ominous set of instructions. They arrive at Number Twelve, Grimmauld Place, London, the headquarters of the Order of the Phoenix.

Chapter 4: "Number Twelve, Grimmauld Place"

The unplottable house is invisible to Muggles and guarded by many magical enchantments. Mrs. Weasley directs Harry upstairs and sends the group of wizards to a separate room. Upstairs Hermione and Ron are excited to see Harry but apologetic over their Dumbledore-ordered silence. Hermione and Ron explain to him that the order is a group of wizards poised to combat Voldemort and the Death Eaters. Suddenly, Fred and George Apparate, and Ginny enters the bedroom. The twins reveal Snape is attending a meeting for the order. Their older brother, Bill Weasley, has been working a desk job at Gringotts; he has begun dating Fleur Delacour, the Beauxbatons competitor in the Triwizard Tourna-

ment. Charlie Weasley is also serving the order but is still abroad in Romania making contacts with foreign wizards. Ron reports that Percy's political ambitions have created a rift with their parents. Ron and Hermione point out that Percy shares the views of many in the wizarding world that Harry is unstable and that Voldemort has not returned. Hermione tells Harry that the *Daily Prophet* has been subversively undermining his credibility.

Mrs. Weasley arrives, ending their conversation, and she mentions Kreacher, the Black family's disturbed house-elf. As they move to the kitchen for dinner, Tonks trips over the umbrella stand, awakening the portrait of Sirius's mother, whose piercing shrieks startle Harry.

Chapter 5: "The Order of the Phoenix"

Sirius reports that he offered the house, his family estate, to Dumbledore as headquarters but feels bitter because he cannot contribute in other ways he considers more useful, such as networking with other wizards or spying. Snape exacerbates Sirius's feelings by taunting him about his "supervisory cleaning duties" over the doxy-infested house while Snape is serving as a double agent. Over dinner the group notes the goblins have refused to declare their allegiances in the potential wizarding war, while Mundungus tells an off-color story about his shady dealings. As a small-time crook he is useful to the order, but Molly disapproves of him.

It is clear the members of the order do not all agree on how much information Harry needs about Voldemort's activities. They do tell him that Voldemort has not killed anyone, but both the Death Eaters and the order have been marshaling forces. Fudge's resistance to admitting Voldemort has returned has influenced the *Daily Prophet* to downplay Harry's and Dumbledore's claims, so the order has recruited Kingsley Shacklebolt and Nymphadora Tonks as ministry insiders—Aurors, dark wizard hunters. They allude to a secret weapon Voldemort may be after, but Molly interrupts the conversation and sends the kids to bed.

Chapter 6: "The Noble and Most Ancient House of Black"

Ron, Hermione, and Harry retire upstairs to bed, with Ron locking the door to keep Kreacher out of their room. They conclude they have not really learned anything they did not already know about Voldemort and the Death Eaters. Fred and George Apparate into the room, and the group discusses the magical weapon that Sirius mentioned. The next morning Molly charges the kids with ridding the drawing room of doxies. Harry learns that Sirius has been keeping Buckbeak in his mother's bedroom. During their cleaning the kids happen upon a locket that becomes important later in the series, but in this chapter they take no notice of it. Fred and George update Harry on their prankster inventions and tell him they are still hoping to open a joke shop with the money he gave them from the Triwizard Tournament. Mundungus arrives with some stolen cauldrons, further inciting Molly's anger at his involvement in the order. During their cleaning Kreacher periodically attempts to smuggle out Black family treasures, including the tapestry with the "noble and most ancient house of Black" family tree and its family motto, *Toujours pur*, or "always pure." Sirius tells Harry that his mother burned his name off after he ran away at age 16; his brother, Regulus, joined the Death Eaters, a decision his parents supported, though when Regulus defied one of Voldemort's orders, he was murdered. Sirius points out several of his distant relatives, noting that all pureblood wizards are related in some way: He is a distant cousin of Tonks and related to both Bellatrix Lestrange and the Malfoys.

Chapter 7: "The Ministry of Magic"
Harry begins the day of his hearing with breakfast with the Weasleys, Tonks, and Lupin, who are discussing Tonks's night shift for the order and Scrimgeour's recent suspicious questioning of her and Kingsley. Mr. Weasley tells Harry that the hearing will be on his office floor in Amelia Bones's office, and they set out early on foot for the ministry. They enter the building through the visitor's entrance, an unused telephone booth, and readers are introduced to a description of the majestic hall that will figure prominently later in the novel; a fountain featuring golden statues of a witch, wizard, centaur, goblin, and house-elf is at the center of the hall. Harry is required to surrender his wand to a security guard. They take the elevator to Mr. Weasley's

floor—the Improper Use of Magic Office shares the floor with the Auror Headquarters—where Arthur and Kingsley have an artificially polite conversation to camouflage their actual relationship. Harry and Mr. Weasley reach his office; the latter is reviewing his memos when a wizard informs them that Harry's hearing has been rescheduled for an earlier time in an obscure corner of the building. They race to the faraway courtroom, already five minutes late.

Chapter 8: "The Hearing"
Harry enters a dungeon and realizes he has seen it before: in Dumbledore's Pensieve, when the Lestranges were sentenced to Azkaban. Fifty wizards, including Minister of Magic Cornelius Fudge and Percy Weasley, are there. As the hearing is called to order, Dumbledore makes an entrance as witness for the defense, unsettling Fudge. Fudge reads the charges of Harry's conjuring of a Patronus, and Amelia Bones, head of the Department of Magical Law Enforcement, marvels at Harry's ability to perform such an advanced charm. Fudge continues to read off the charges until Harry interrupts, justifying his magical use because of the dementor attack. Fudge attempts to discredit Harry's accusation by pointing out he has no other witnesses to support his story since Muggles cannot see dementors, but Dumbledore presents Mrs. Figg to testify on Harry's behalf. She describes the attack despite the minister's skepticism of her Squib status and appears to convince some members of the Wizengamot. When Fudge tries to attribute the Dementors' attack to coincidence, Dumbledore makes a pointed suggestion that they were deliberately sent to Little Whinging to attack Harry, accusing the ministry of either incompetent handling of the creatures or deliberate malfeasance. A tense verbal battle ensues between Dumbledore and Fudge, setting the stage for larger conflicts that the book explores between the governing body and the educational institution. The Wizengamot votes by a majority to clear Harry of all charges.

Chapter 9: "The Woes of Mrs. Weasley"
Harry is shocked both by the abrupt clearance of charges and Dumbledore's hasty exit from the chamber. He meets Mr. Weasley, and they spy Fudge

in conversation with Lucius Malfoy. Harry wonders whether Fudge could be under the Imperius Curse, but Arthur says Dumbledore believes Fudge to be acting voluntarily. They return to Number Twelve, Grimmauld Place, where everyone celebrates Harry's exoneration, but his scar starts to hurt; later, Harry suspects Sirius is not entirely happy about his returning to Hogwarts. They receive their book lists, and Hermione receives a prefect badge, as does Ron, who is shocked at the responsibility given to him; Harry reflects on his mixed emotions. He is embarrassed about his surprise at Ron's prefect badge, feeling jealousy as well as guilt about not being genuinely happy for Ron. He also feels hurt about being slighted by Dumbledore.

Mrs. Weasley sets up a celebratory party in honor of Ron and Hermione's new posts. Harry feels less disappointed about being overlooked for prefect when he hears neither Sirius, Tonks, nor his father was a prefect. Fred and George purchase Venomous Tenacula seeds from Mundungus, and Harry starts to feel bad that he is funding the career that Molly does not support. Moody pulls out a photo of the first Order of the Phoenix and chronicles their fates, ranging from those murdered by Voldemort to those who are current members of the order. Moody seems nostalgic, but Harry finds him morbid, so he sneaks upstairs, where he finds Mrs. Weasley weeping over Ron's dead body in the drawing room. He realizes she is dispatching a boggart, and Ron's body takes the shape of the corpses of her other children, her husband, and Harry. Lupin, Sirius, and Moody arrive and try to reassure the sobbing Molly about her fate and that of her children. Harry retires to bed feeling aged, marveling that he spent the day worrying about prefect badges and joke shops.

Chapter 10: "Luna Lovegood"
Harry awakens late for the Hogwarts Express after a night of bad dreams. He, Hermione, and Ron scramble to get to the station. As Padfoot (Sirius's animagus form of a dog), Sirius accompanies them despite Dumbledore's wishes, along with Tonks, Lupin, Moody, and Mrs. Weasley. Sturgis Podmore fails to show up for his escort duty. Once aboard the train Ron and Hermione have to go to the prefect's carriage, though Ron goes out of his way

to note that he is not "enjoying it," unlike the officious Percy. The train cabins are full, but Ginny finds them a cabin with Luna Lovegood, a slightly dotty Ravenclaw fourth-year student, whose father edits the tabloid *The Quibbler*, which Luna is reading. Neville exclaims that he got a *mimbulus mimbletonia* for Christmas and pokes it, causing it to erupt stinksap all over the compartment. At that moment, Cho Chang greets Harry, who is mortified at his stinksap-covered appearance. When Ron and Hermione arrive after an hour, they tell the group that Draco is the Slytherin prefect.

Harry reads a *Quibbler* story about Sirius that asks the question "Notorious Mass Murderer OR Innocent Singing Sensation?" and another about Cornelius Fudge's goblin hatred, illustrating the salacious nature of the newspaper. New prefect Malfoy enters their compartment and taunts Harry. His claim that he will be "dogging [Harry's] footsteps" (194) worries Harry, who suspects Draco identified Sirius in his animagus form at Kings Cross. When they arrive at the station, Hermione and Ron disappear for prefect duties, and Harry is disappointed to find Professor Grubbly-Plank instead of Hagrid welcoming first years. Harry is also surprised to find winged, batlike horses pulling the carriages that take them to Hogwarts from Hogsmeade station. When he asks Ron and Hermione about them, they look at him strangely, revealing that, indeed, they cannot see any strange creatures. Luna reassures Harry that he is not crazy—she can see them as well, news that is not at all reassuring since her nickname is *Loony*.

Chapter 11: "The Sorting Hat's New Song"
When they arrive at the Great Hall, Harry, Ron, and Hermione notice that Hagrid is not at the staff table but Umbridge, whom Harry recognizes from his hearing, is. The new Sorting Hat song gives a history of Hogwarts and each house's values but also claims that unity is needed within Hogwarts, not division. Nearly Headless Nick confirms that in periods of great danger, the hat has similarly admonished students and staff, but Harry cannot imagine befriending Slytherins. Shockingly Umbridge interrupts Dumbledore's speech to advocate a preservation of tradition, which Hermione translates later for Ron and Harry as the ministry's interfering at Hog-

warts. Harry notices that his classmates frequently point and whisper at him, but this social ostracism is most noticeable in the Gryffindor common room; his dorm mate Seamus Finnegan confesses his mother did not want him to return to school because she believes the *Daily Prophet*'s allegations about Harry and Dumbledore's mental instability. Ron has to threaten Seamus with detention to resolve the row, and Harry worries that others share Seamus's doubts.

Chapter 12: "Professor Umbridge"
The next morning Ron and Harry meet up with Hermione in the common room, where Fred and George have posted an ad for joke shop product testers. At breakfast Angelina Johnson tells them that she has been made Quidditch captain and that the team needs a new Keeper. Fred and George stop by to offer Ron Skiving Snackboxes and allude to debating whether or not to return for their seventh year. Hermione and Ron are curious about how the twins plan to finance a joke shop, but Harry deflects their questions. In Potions Snape torments Harry, dashing his hopes that his membership in the order might improve Snape's disposition toward Harry. In Defense Against the Dark Arts Umbridge orders the students to put away their wands. Hermione refuses to obey Umbridge's order to read the first chapter in class, "Basics for Beginners," and Harry angers Umbridge by insisting that real-world knowledge is more useful than theoretical knowledge. Refusing to rescind his claim that Voldemort has returned, Harry is sent with a note from Umbridge to see McGonagall, who cautions him about antagonizing Umbridge, as "you know where she comes from and to whom she is reporting" (248).

Chapter 13: "Detention with Dolores"
News of Harry's disagreement with Umbridge sweeps the school, but Hermione suspects many fellow students do not believe him. Before bed Hermione sets out two camouflaged hats in her campaign to free house-elves, who win their liberty by accepting clothing from their owners. The next day Professors Flitwick and McGonagall both emphasize the importance of Ordinary Wizarding Level examinations. During Care of Magical Creatures at least two students, Luna and Ernie McMillan, publicly declare

their support for Harry despite skepticism from others. Angelina berates him for having detention during Keeper tryouts, but Umbridge flatly rejects his request to do a makeup detention, stating it "ought to reinforce the lesson" (266). Each night of his week's detention she forces him to write "I will not tell lies" using a magical quill that carves the words in his hand even as it writes them on the paper in his blood. Ron is mysteriously tired throughout the week; he later reveals that he is tired because he is practicing for the Gryffindor Keeper position, which he eventually wins. During Harry's Friday detention his scar hurts, and Hermione urges him to talk to Dumbledore about the matter, but his resentment prevents him from doing so.

Chapter 14: "Percy and Padfoot"
Harry writes a coded letter to Sirius asking about Hagrid and telling him about his scar's hurting. While sending it from the Owlery, he meets Cho Chang, and when Filch accuses Harry of sending an order for Dungbombs, Cho steps to his defense; Harry feels happy about their newfound intimacy. At breakfast Hermione reads the *Daily Prophet*, which reports that Sirius is in London; they speculate worriedly that Lucius Malfoy recognized him at platform nine and three-quarters. Ron and Harry spend Saturday practicing Quidditch despite Hermione's warnings that they are gravely behind in their homework. Ron performs poorly as Keeper, exacerbated by the Slytherins' mocking them from the stands.

Sunday an owl arrives with a letter from Percy to Ron. Besides congratulating him on his prefect appointment, Percy cautions Ron against associating with Harry and alludes to a coup at Hogwarts. Even though Ron rejects Percy's advice, Harry cannot help but worry about public opinion reflected in Percy's words. That night in the common room Sirius daringly appears in the fire. Sirius suspects that his scar's painfulness is similar to the psychic connection with Voldemort Harry felt throughout his fourth year. He tells them their weak, non-magical-use curriculum for Defense Against the Dark Arts is in response to Fudge's paranoid fears that Dumbledore is forming an army. He also tells them that Dumbledore is not worried about

Hagrid's welfare, and neither should they be. He ends by guilting Harry about not being enough like his father, James, to risk a meeting in Hogsmeade.

Chapter 15: "The Hogwarts High Inquisitor"

Hermione, Ron, and Harry read the *Daily Prophet* front page story, "Ministry Seeks Educational Reform: Dolores Umbridge Appointed First-Ever 'High Inquisitor.'" A new law allows the Ministry of Magic to appoint candidates to teaching posts at Hogwarts, also allowing the high inquisitor the power to evaluate other educators. That day Harry is disturbed when Professor Trelawney is "inspected" by Umbridge. In Defense Against the Dark Arts Harry earns detention again. In Transfiguration McGonagall dismisses Umbridge's "inspection," as does Grubbly-Plank. After detention with Umbridge Harry returns to the common room, where Hermione and Ron are waiting. Hermione suggests that they teach themselves the practical skills they need; she suggests that Harry should teach them Defense Against the Dark Arts privately, and she and Ron laugh when he modestly ascribes all his successes to luck, guts, or help from others. Eventually Harry becomes angry about their dismissal, feeling misunderstood because they do not know what it is like to have fought Voldemort. They apologize and reassure him that it is exactly this knowledge and experience that make him a good candidate and urge him to consider it.

Chapter 16: "In the Hog's Head"

Harry reluctantly agrees to teach a small group of students practical Defense Against the Dark Arts. They plan to meet at Hogsmeade. Harry worries that Sirius, who has been silent since their fireplace exchange, will show up despite Dumbledore's warnings. At the next Hogsmeade weekend a group of students meet at a "dodgy" pub called the Hog's Head, and Harry is shocked and slightly annoyed when two dozen students show up for the group. Harry fears students have arrived because they want to hear the story of Cedric's death and warns them to leave if that is the case, and everyone stays. They sign a parchment as a pact of secrecy about the club and its mission despite the reluctance of a few students. Hermione tells Ron that Ginny is dating Michael Corner, much to Ron's brotherly consternation.

Chapter 17: "Educational Decree Number Twenty-Four"

Harry's week begins with Umbridge's declaring, "All Student Organizations, Societies, Teams, Groups, and Clubs are henceforth disbanded" (351). Fearing Umbridge has gotten wind of their group, Harry and Ron tell Hermione, who says she jinxed the parchment and any traitor would be immediately identified. During History of Magic an injured Hedwig appears at the window, and Harry takes her to Professor Grubbly-Plank since Hagrid is still absent. The note, from Sirius, says, "Today, same time, same place." Umbridge inspects Snape's class, questioning him about his repeated applications for the Defense Against the Dark Arts position. In Divination Professor Trelawney implies that she is on probation because of her visit from Umbridge. That night Harry, Ron, and Hermione meet Sirius in the fire; he already knows about the Defense Against the Dark Arts group because Mundungus Fletcher was in disguise at the Hog's Head. He bears a message from Mrs. Weasley against pursuing it, but Sirius himself heartily endorses it. Umbridge unceremoniously interrupts their conversation via Floo Network but does not know it was Sirius talking to Harry, Ron, and Hermione.

Chapter 18: "Dumbledore's Army"

During Transfiguration Hermione, Ron, and Harry speculate that Umbridge has Filch reading Harry's mail. Gryffindor's Quidditch team gets permission to re-form, only after intervention by Dumbledore. Hermione starts to have doubts about the Defense Against the Dark Arts group—or the D.A., Dumbledore's Army, as they name it—because of Sirius's endorsement, worrying he has become reckless and seems to be living vicariously through them. The night's Quidditch practice takes place in rainy weather, and Harry has a flash of pain in his scar; he realizes he is channeling Voldemort's moods. That night he falls asleep and has a dream about a door at the end of a long corridor. Dobby wakes him, returning Hedwig, and admits he has been taking all Hermione's hats for himself. Dobby wants to help Harry and tells him about the Room of Requirement as a location for D.A. meetings. At the group's first meeting Harry is elected leader, and they begin practicing the disarming charm. Their successful session leads to another scheduled for the following week.

Chapter 19: "The Lion and the Serpent"

The D.A. continues meeting under Harry's successful guidance. Hermione bewitches fake galleons for the members to signal them when meetings will be held. The upcoming Gryffindor-Slytherin Quidditch match causes hallway tensions. The day of the match the Slytherins all wear badges that say, "Weasley Is Our King!" to complement the offensive song they have created to psych out the Gryffindor team: They praise Ron as their king because they know he will perform poorly as Keeper and enable them to win the match, and they are right. But Harry guarantees the team's victory by catching the Snitch. After the match Malfoy insults Harry's mother and the Weasleys' parents, and George and Harry brawl with several Slytherins. McGonagall is set to give them detention when Umbridge interrupts; Educational Decree 25 now gives her the power to alter punishments of students, and she bans Fred, George, and Harry from Quidditch for life. While lamenting their punishment in the common room, Hermione sees Hagrid has returned.

Chapter 20: "Hagrid's Tale"

Under the Invisibility Cloak Ron, Harry, and Hermione head to Hagrid's house, where they find Hagrid battered and bruised. Reluctantly he admits he and Madame Maxime have been talking with the giants on Dumbledore's orders. Their attempts to make them allies failed as the Death Eaters were also wooing the giants. Hagrid also learned his mother is dead, and he is evasive about where he has been the three days since Maxime has returned. Umbridge arrives unannounced, and though the kids hide under the Invisibility Cloak, she suspects they are there. She leaves after notifying Hagrid she will be inspecting his class soon. Hagrid tells the kids that he has some "really special" animals planned for their Care of Magical Creatures class.

Chapter 21: "The Eye of the Snake"

Hermione frets that Hagrid will not listen to her advice about playing his Care of Magical Creatures

class a little safer. Further, Hagrid's injuries mysteriously appear to be fresh each day. Hagrid announces their class will take place in the Forbidden Forest. Harry is relieved to see the batlike horses he and Luna saw in chapter 10; Hagrid explains that they are visible only to those who have witnessed death. Umbridge arrives, unsettling Hagrid as she intimidates and condescends to him and grills students. Later, a furious Hermione chalks up Umbridge's attack as rooted in her hatred of half-breeds. Ron invites Harry to spend Christmas at the Burrow, even though Harry feels sorry he will not be seeing Sirius. Harry learns that Ginny Weasley has replaced him as Seeker. At their last D.A. practice Cho gets becomes emotional about Cedric's death, and she and Harry share a kiss as he comforts her. Hermione explains later to Ron and Harry about Cho's conflicted feelings. That night Harry dreams he is attacking Arthur Weasley in the form of Voldemort's snake, Nagini.

Chapter 22: "St. Mungo's Hospital for Magical Maladies and Injuries"

Harry and Ron go to Dumbledore's office to explain what Harry has just seen concerning Arthur. Dumbledore sends two former Hogwarts headmasters from their portraits to other "important magical institutions" (469). A former headmaster, Everard, confirms Mr. Weasley has been injured, and Dumbledore fashions a Portkey to send the Weasley children and Harry to Number Twelve, Grimmauld Place. They wait impatiently for news and finally learn Arthur will be okay. Meanwhile, Harry agonizes over his fear that the snake lurking inside him will cause him to do harm to someone he cares about.

The next morning Tonks and Moody escort them to St. Mungo's. Arthur is in a cheery mood but is evasive about where he was when attacked by the snake. When Harry and the Weasleys eavesdrop on the adult conversation, they hear Moody express concern that Harry is being "possessed" by Voldemort.

Chapter 23: "Christmas on the Closed Ward"

After hearing Moody's terrifying prediction Harry begins to fear that he is the weapon that Voldemort is after. To protect the others, he prepares to return

to the Dursleys', when the portrait of Phineas Nigellus delivers a message from Dumbledore that Harry
should stay where he is; Harry reacts with frustration and anger at not being let in on Dumbledore's
plans. When Hermione arrives unexpectedly back
from skiing with her family, a frank conversation
with Ron, Hermione, and Ginny (who was actually possessed by Tom Riddle in year two) reassures
Harry that he is not being possessed. Percy sends
his Christmas sweater back to Mrs. Weasley, who
is crushed. Hermione makes a quilt for Kreacher,
but they cannot seem to locate him. They all visit
Arthur on the closed ward. Harry and the others
wander around the hospital, where they run across
a memory-impaired Gilderoy Lockhart injured in
their second year and visit him briefly. While in the
long-term ward they meet Neville and his grandmother, who are visiting Neville's parents and have
an uncomfortable exchange; the kids learn that the
Longbottoms were tortured by Bellatrix Lestrange
with the Cruciatus Curse.

Chapter 24: "Occlumency"
Kreacher seems mysteriously in better spirits after
Sirius locates him in the attic, a change in mood that
will be key later in the book. Snape informs Harry he
will be studying Occlumency, the magical defense of
the mind against external penetration. Snape antagonizes Sirius about his confinement at Grimmauld
Place, almost generating a wand duel. Arthur returns
to the Black home, completely cured. Before Harry,
Ron, and Hermione leave to go back to Hogwarts,
Sirius gives Harry a small package and tells him to
open it later. When they arrive back to Hogwarts,
Harry invites Cho to go to Hogsmeade with him on
the Valentine's Day trip. Harry reports to Snape's
dungeon for his first Occlumency lesson and learns
that Voldemort is skilled in Legilmency, or the ability to extract feelings and memories from another
person's mind. The usual rules of Legilmency—often
requiring eye contact or close contact—do not seem
to apply to Harry and Voldemort because of the connection that was forged between them when Voldemort attempted to kill him.

Snape tells Harry that Voldemort is now aware
of Harry's access to his thoughts and feelings. Snape
removes several silvery wisps of thought and places

them in the Pensieve before beginning their lesson;
it goes poorly because Harry is unable to control his
emotions, a process Snape says is central to resisting Voldemort's penetration. During their practice
Harry realizes the corridor he has been dreaming
about is in the Department of Mysteries. Snape
refuses to answer Harry's questions about what is
there. That evening Harry feels the sensation that
Voldemort is very, very pleased about something.

Chapter 25: "The Beetle at Bay"
The *Daily Prophet* reports that 10 Death Eaters, including Bellatrix Lestrange, have escaped
from Azkaban. In the article Fudge links the
breakout with Sirius and suggests Black has
become the ringleader of a Death Eater gang.
They also read about the mysterious death of
Broderick Bode, killed by a Devil's Snare disguised as a houseplant at St. Mungo's. Hagrid
tells the kids he is on probation. The tone at
school changes, with greater credence given to
Harry and Dumbledore's claims in light of the
Azkaban breakout. Occlumency lessons do not
improve, though the D.A. continues successfully,
and Harry's scar hurts frequently. On Valentine's
Day Harry escorts Cho to Hogsmeade, but their
coffee date is ruined by a jealous tantrum by Cho
over his agreement to meet Hermione for lunch.
They meet up in the Three Broomsticks, where
Hermione is sitting with Luna Lovegood and Rita
Skeeter. Hermione wants Skeeter to write Harry's
story and Luna's father to publish it as a way of
getting the truth out to the wizarding public. Rita
agrees to do it mainly because Hermione knows
she is an unregistered animagus and uses this
information to blackmail Skeeter.

Chapter 26: "Seen and Unforeseen"
Ron, Harry, and Hermione are all eager to read
Harry's published story. Hermione translates
Cho's strange behavior in Hogsmeade for Harry,
and Ron's Quidditch practice goes terribly. Gryffindor loses to Hufflepuff in Quidditch. At breakfast Harry receives numerous owls with letters
and the *Quibbler* story by Rita Skeeter. Umbridge
is outraged that Harry has given the interview,
taking 50 points from Gryffindor and banning

the *Quibbler* from Hogwarts. Many students and teachers confirm they believe Harry's story. Harry has several dreams about the mysterious corridor, including one in which he sees from Voldemort's perspective and interrogates two Death Eaters.

Harry begins to lose faith in the value of Occlumency, but he continues lessons with Snape and makes enough progress to break into Snape's mind and see Snape's disturbing and sad childhood memories. Their lesson is interrupted by Professor Trelawney's shriek; she is fired publicly in the entrance hall by Umbridge, though Dumbledore asserts his reserved right to allow her to remain in residence there. He also introduces the new Divination teacher he has procured, the centaur Firenze.

Chapter 27: "The Centaur and the Sneak"
Harry and Ron have their first Divination lesson with Firenze. He dismisses Professor Trelawney's use of astrology and other "human nonsense" and instead directs their attention to the "impersonal and impartial" wisdom of the centaurs. They look to the skies for larger patterns rather than simple fortune-telling. After the lesson Firenze sends Harry to Hagrid with an ambiguous message that his attempts are not working and he should abandon them, but Hagrid neither clarifies the meaning nor concurs with it.

Harry gathers comfort from the D.A. meetings; at an April meeting Dobby arrives to warn Harry that Umbridge is approaching even though the house-elves have been forbidden to tell. Harry is caught by Umbridge and Draco though everyone else escapes. Umbridge takes him to Dumbledore's office, where he finds McGonagall and several Ministry of Magic representatives, including Fudge. Dumbledore controls the conversation and falsely confesses to having ordered the students to form the group after Umbridge produces the list of names Harry posted in the Room of Requirement and labeled *Dumbledore's Army*, confirming Fudge's paranoid fears. A magical skirmish ensues, and Dumbledore hexes the ministry people. He emphasizes to Harry the importance of sticking with his Occlumency lessons before riding away holding Fawkes's tail.

Chapter 28: "Snape's Worst Memory"
The story of Dumbledore's escape spreads through school, and Umbridge takes over as head of Hogwarts. Draco docks Gryffindor points, newly empowered as a member of the "Inquisitorial Squad," certain students handpicked by Umbridge who have been loyal to the ministry. Umbridge calls Harry to her office and tries to induce him to reveal Sirius's and Dumbledore's whereabouts. They are interrupted by a loud explosion; Fred and George have set off fireworks throughout the school. That night Harry dreams once again of the mysterious corridor and advances farther than ever through the doors in his dreams. Harry clashes with Cho over her friend Marietta's betrayal of the D.A. His Occlumency lesson is cancelled midway through when Snape goes to help Draco, but Harry, suspecting perhaps Snape is trying to keep knowledge of the Department of Mysteries from him, recklessly plunges into the Pensieve and sees Snape, his father, Lupin, Peter Pettigrew, and Sirius taking their O.W.L. examinations. Harry sees a confrontation in the courtyard, where his father torments Snape with various hexes and jinxes until Lily Evans, Harry's mother, intervenes, though Snape shows no gratitude to her. Snape returns to the dungeon, interrupting Harry's viewing, and his rage is visible; he orders Harry never to return to his office. Harry feels horrified at seeing just how arrogant and conceited his father was, just as Snape has always claimed.

Chapter 29: "Career Advice"
With six weeks left until exams Harry, Ron, and Hermione buckle down on their studies. Harry is still haunted by the memory from the Pensieve—it challenges all of his beliefs about his father's goodness, and he struggles to make sense of it. Meanwhile, the fifth years are expected to attend a meeting with their head of house regarding career trajectories. This conversation with McGonagall is supervised by Umbridge, who attempts to dissuade McGonagall from encouraging Harry's aspirations to become an Auror after graduation. Fred and George arrange a diversion for Harry to talk with Sirius, and despite Hermione's dire warnings, Harry breaks into Umbridge's office to ask Sirius about

Snape's memory. Harry is clearly anguished about his father's behavior, and Remus and Sirius, both at Grimmauld Place, try to reassure him that they were all immature and showed bad judgment at that age and that at heart James was a good person. Harry returns to the Great Hall, where Umbridge and the Inquisitorial Squad have cornered Fred and George, who promptly conjure their brooms, quit school, announce the opening of their new shop, and fly away.

Chapter 30: "Grawp"

Hogwarts students carry on Fred and George's troublemaking by causing problems for Umbridge. Harry confesses that Fred and George are financing their joke shop with the Triwizard Tournament winnings he gave them. Hermione pressures Harry to resume his Occlumency lessons with Snape, and Harry lies to her about the content of his dreams. In fact, he now can see in the corridor, through the door, to a room full of shelves with dusty glass spheres.

During the final Quidditch match of the season between Gryffindor and Ravenclaw Hagrid pulls Hermione and Harry aside and asks them to go into the Forbidden Forest with him. He tells them the centaurs are angry with him because he intervened in their attack on Firenze when he agreed to teach at Hogwarts. Hagrid leads them to his giant half brother, Grawp, whom Hagrid has been keeping restrained in the forest. He asks Hermione and Harry to visit Grawp once in a while when Hagrid is on a mission for Dumbledore, since he is about to be fired by Umbridge. On their way back to school they encounter the centaurs, led by Magorian and Bane. They threaten Hagrid but let him pass because, as Hermione and Harry are accompanying him, they do not believe in harming the young and innocent. When they return to Hogwarts, they realize that, mystifyingly, Gryffindor has won the Quidditch match.

Chapter 31: "O.W.L.S"

Harry and Hermione confess to Ron that they did not see his winning saves in the Quidditch game and tell him about Grawp. Their courses are now focused on reviewing for O.W.L. examinations, and McGonagall informs them the tests will be spread over two weeks. A group of ancient wizards from the Wizarding Examination Authority arrive to conduct the O.W.L. examinations. Harry, Ron, and Hermione take written and practical examinations in Charms, Transfiguration, Herbology, Defense Against the Dark Arts, Potions, Care of Magical Creatures, Astronomy, and Divination. Hermione also takes exams in Arithmancy and Ancient Runes. During their Astronomy examination Harry sees several figures, including Umbridge, approaching Hagrid's cabin. A magical duel breaks out, and in the midst McGonagall, approaching from the castle, is hit with several Stunning Spells. Hagrid hauls away a Stunned Fang as Umbridge attacks him; he escapes into the Forbidden Forest. Harry, Ron, and Hermione speculate he has gone to join Dumbledore. The next morning Harry falls asleep during his History of Magic examination and in his dream sees Sirius being tortured in the mysterious room filled with glass spheres.

Chapter 32: "Out of the Fire"

Abandoning his History of Magic examination, Harry tracks down Hermione and Ron and urges them to help him find a way to get to the Ministry of Magic to save Sirius. Hermione tries to help him see reason, but Harry will not be deterred. Ginny and Luna overhear Harry's yelling and offer help; the group plans to use Umbridge's fire a second time to check whether Sirius is still at Grimmauld Place. Harry and Hermione use the Floo Network and find Kreacher, who claims Sirius has gone to the Department of Mysteries. Umbridge catches them, and the Inquisitorial Squad hauls Ron, Ginny, and Luna into the office as well. Umbridge calls in Snape to request a bottle of Veritaserum to interrogate Harry, but Snape tells her that making it takes a month. Harry realizes he had forgotten that Snape is a member of the order and tries to communicate in code that Sirius is being tortured. Snape pretends not to understand and leaves. As Umbridge is about to use the Cruciatus Curse on Harry, Hermione falsely confesses she will show Umbridge where the secret weapon is, and they lead her into the Forbidden Forest.

Chapter 33: "Fight and Flight"

Hermione leads Harry and Umbridge into the Forbidden Forest, talking loudly to attract the attention of the centaurs. A group of about 50 centaurs surround them; when Umbridge insults them, they bind her and take her away. Despite their previous assertions about not hurting the innocent, they are about to attack Harry and Hermione when Grawp stumbles upon them, asking for Hagrid. In the ensuing melee Harry and Hermione escape. They run into Ron, Luna, Ginny, and Neville, who have jinxed the Inquisitorial Squad, and the group argues over who will go, to the ministry. Harry finally concedes they can all go and they fly away on the Thestrals (scaly winged creatures that can only be seen by those who have witnessed death) that have been attracted by Harry and Hermione, covered in drops of Grawp's blood from the centaurs' bow-and-arrow attack.

Chapter 34: "The Department of Mysteries"

The six young wizards fly to London on the Thestrals and arrive at a seemingly empty ministry for the rescue mission. They go to the Department of Mysteries and face a labyrinthine path to the room Harry sees in his dreams. After several wrong turns, including a room with a glass tank filled with miniature brains and one with an unsettling stone archway on a raised dais, they enter the room with the glass spheres but find no one there. Ron finds a glass sphere with Harry's name on it, so Harry takes it off the shelf. Just then a group of Death Eaters confronts them.

Chapter 35: "Beyond the Veil"

Lucius Malfoy and Bellatrix Lestrange lead a group of a dozen Death Eaters, who command Harry to give them what they explain is a prophecy and mock him for his "weakness for heroics." It is obvious they want the sphere, which Harry realizes is a prophecy explaining why Voldemort tried to kill him. He stalls for time to try to escape. Malfoy explains the only ones who can retrieve a prophecy from the Department of Mysteries are those about whom it was made. Harry orders his friends to smash the glass orbs on the shelves, and they scramble to escape, battling Death Eaters throughout the

many rooms. Hermione is attacked, as is Neville, and Ginny's ankle is broken.

Clutching the prophecy, Harry is cornered in the room with the stone archway, his friends immobilized and injured, when members of the order arrive—Sirius, Lupin, Moody, Tonks, and Kingsley battle the Death Eaters as Harry and Neville try to escape. In the chaos the prophecy smashes, and to Harry's immense relief Dumbledore arrives. Bellatrix's spell hits Sirius, who falls through the stone archway, much to Harry's horror.

Chapter 36: "The Only One He Ever Feared"

Lupin and Neville try unsuccessfully to comfort Harry over Sirius's death in the midst of the battle. When Bellatrix Lestrange turns to run, Harry chases her into the atrium of the ministry. She taunts him as he tries unsuccessfully to use an Unforgivable Curse on her. During their battle the Fountain of Magical Brethren is damaged. Voldemort appears and casts *Avada Kedavra* at Harry, but Dumbledore intervenes. An epic magical battle ensues; Voldemort briefly possesses Harry but evaporates from Harry's body when Harry longs to see Sirius. When Harry returns to himself, Fudge and several ministry officials are there, startled but no longer able to deny Voldemort's return. Dumbledore forges a Portkey and sends Harry back to school.

Chapter 37: "The Lost Prophecy"

Harry arrives back at Hogwarts at Dumbledore's office. He agonizes over Sirius's death, faulting himself for not listening to Hermione's admonitions. Harry flies into a rage at Dumbledore's attempts to comfort him. Dumbledore takes responsibility for Sirius's death by admitting he should have been franker with Harry about how Voldemort might use his connection with Harry. Dumbledore explains that he believed he was protecting Harry by distancing himself, that Voldemort might have used their connection to destroy Dumbledore. Still working through his emotions, Harry makes many accusations at Dumbledore, who feels only regret for the way he has mishandled his relationship with Harry this year.

Dumbledore finally confides to Harry that he left him with the Dursleys because of the protection of his mother's sacrifice, which remained in their home and thus had the bond of blood. Dumbledore shows Harry in the Pensieve the prophecy that Trelawney made to him 16 years earlier, that the one "with the power to vanquish the Dark Lord approaches" (841). Dumbledore explains that the prophecy did not specifically identify Harry but that Voldemort's choice to "mark him as his equal" was the deciding factor—Voldemort did not hear the entire prophecy that suggested to attack the boy would mean the possibility of transferring his powers. Harry asks about the part of the prophecy that states, "Neither can live while the other survives" (841); Dumbledore confirms this means that one of them has to kill the other.

Chapter 38: "The Second War Begins"

The chapter begins with a *Daily Prophet* story announcing Voldemort's return. Ron, Hermione, Luna, Ginny, Neville, and Harry are all recovering in the hospital wing, none with permanent damage. Umbridge, who was rescued from the centaurs by Dumbledore, is also in the hospital wing. The group discusses the lost prophecy, but Harry does not tell them that he knows what it was. A confrontation with Malfoy reveals that Lucius is in Azkaban. Harry visits Hagrid's cabin, but talking about Sirius upsets Harry. He reflects on how alienated he feels from his friends because of his status as a "marked man." While packing on the last night of classes, he finds the present Sirius gave him, a two-way mirror that he could use to communicate. Of course, when he tries it, it does not work, but it gives him an idea. He wants to know more about death, so he seeks out the Gryffindor ghost, Sir Nicholas, who tells him that Sirius will not be back as a ghost; only those too afraid to cross over stay in the wizarding world as ghosts. He talks to Luna, who tells him her mother died when Luna was nine and confirms that she also heard the voices in the stone archway. On the train ride home Ginny reveals that she is dating Dean Thomas and that Cho has now started dating Michael Corner. Moody meets them at the station along with the Weasleys, Tonks, and Lupin, who have a stern talk with the Dursleys, and Molly reassures him they will see him at the Burrow over the summer.

CRITICAL COMMENTARY

The fifth book of Rowling's Harry Potter series is most concerned with issues of power. While the book follows the same structure as all works in the series—Harry's journey from the Dursleys' to Hogwarts and back over the course of an academic year—*Order of the Phoenix* departs from previous installments by adopting a grimmer tone and is widely regarded as the darkest of the seven books. In addition to questions of agency and legitimacy Rowling explores philosophical questions about free will and identity, as well as internal conflict.

Power

Rowling is interested in two types of power, institutional (or political) and personal, as well as legitimate and illegitimate forms of these two kinds of power. The most significant example of political illegitimacy in the novel is the unseating of Dumbledore from his position of headmaster by the Ministry of Magic's Dolores Umbridge. As the senior undersecretary to the minister Umbridge is the ideal bureaucrat, her obsession with control overshadowed only by her sadism. In coupling Umbridge's brutal tendencies with her ultrafeminine behavior, Rowling reveals her own fondness for irony. The mewing kittens on the flowered plates that adorn her office, her pink cashmere sweaters, and her high-pitched voice contrast starkly with the satisfaction she gets from tormenting the students physically and mentally—from her magical method of carving lines into students' hands to her gradual deprivation to students of everything they love, Rowling relishes the pairing of opposites. Umbridge gradually infiltrates the Hogwarts administration by moving from teacher and inspector to Hogwarts high inquisitor, an advancement made possible only by corruption at the ministry that circumvents Dumbledore's authority and uses magical decrees to increase its influence at Hogwarts. Umbridge's character is Rowling's most scathing indictment of political agendas influencing educational institutions.

As Fudge's minion Umbridge has authority that is fundamentally questionable since her assuming the position of Defense Against the Dark Arts teacher does not follow Hogwarts' usual hiring protocol—namely, Dumbledore's approval. The many decrees she writes for Hogwarts students such as "Teachers are hereby banned from giving students any information that is not strictly related to the subjects they are paid to teach" and "No student organisations, societies, teams, groups and clubs may exist without the knowledge and approval of the High Inquisitor" do not serve the welfare of the students; indeed, they seem specifically designed to inflict suffering upon students by depriving them of some of their most beloved activities and crippling their relationships with their teachers. It is this sadism that most vividly characterizes Umbridge and that serves to illustrate a kind of evil—not malevolence but misguided moral efforts—that Harry has up until this point not encountered. As Sirius tells Harry, "The world isn't split into good people and Death Eaters" (302), a claim that tests Harry's previously adolescent concept of good and evil. Umbridge and Fudge can be viewed as Rowling's effort to complicate Harry's worldview and challenge his ideas about good and evil.

The interference from the Ministry of Magic in the form of Umbridge's installed dictatorship serves the ministry's political agenda, an agency deeply invested in covering up Voldemort's return in the interest of preventing public panic. Instead of earning the trust or respect of those she serves (in contrast with Dumbledore), she spies on students, forces them to do her will, and cruelly punishes them if they do not adhere to her beliefs. Umbridge's—and inherently Fudge's—conviction that Voldemort has not returned drives her vindictive actions; students who support Harry's claims by joining the D.A. are severely punished.

Umbridge's political agendas spill over into her classroom, further undermining her legitimacy as an authority figure. Her teaching philosophy demonstrates both a lack of concern for student well-being and a lack of passion for learning, preferring to cultivate her students' obedience rather than their intellects. She denies her Defense Against the Dark Arts students practical knowledge, instead lecturing only on topics included on the Ordinary Wizarding Level exams. Harry asks Umbridge about actually practicing defensive magic in class so the students are prepared for the "real world." Umbridge responds, "This is school, Mr. Potter, not the real world" (244). When other students, including Hermione, Dean, and Parvati, also ask about practicing spells in class, Umbridge reassures them that "as long as you have studied the theory hard enough, there is no reason why you should not be able to perform the spells under carefully controlled examination conditions" (244). She teaches directly to the test, completely ignoring her students' desire to find practical connections with her curriculum in their lives. She forces her students to memorize and recite passages from outdated textbooks, foreshadowing the ministry's weak attempt in subsequent books to prepare the wizarding community for Voldemort's return through the widespread distribution of pamphlets useless for self-protection.

Public Policy and Subversion

Some critics have suggested these themes in *Order of the Phoenix* comment critically on U.S. public and foreign policies. Umbridge's "teaching to the test" approach resembles criticisms launched at the No Child Left Behind Act, a federal law passed in 2001. Similarly, her stifling of student speech, activities, and curriculum has been viewed by critics as an exaggerated version of the United States's post-9/11 political and cultural backlash toward critics of George W. Bush's policies on terrorism. Political and public debate emerged in the years immediately after the 9/11 attack over the constitutionality of the USA PATRIOT Act and increasing restrictions on civil liberties, ranging from lack of due process to questions about the legality and ethics of torturing terrorist suspects, wiretapping, and general concern about increasing centralization of power in the executive branch of the U.S. government.

Throughout the novel Umbridge's reign of terror is resisted through subversion—and finally ended—by open rebellion, which has been read as Rowling's affirmation of the possibility of social change, calling to mind the anthropologist Margaret Mead's famous claim that we should "never doubt that a small group of thoughtful, committed citizens can change the world. Indeed, it is the only thing that ever has." Even though Rowling's novel does not advocate radical social restructuring, it does affirm the power of individual and small groups to effect social change within the existing system.

Personal Empowerment

Further, Rowling explores the notion of personal agency and empowerment through the roles that Harry takes on. New roles challenge Harry to accept new responsibilities and leadership tasks. Harry, as the teacher-leader of Dumbledore's Army, takes on (reluctantly) the responsibility of educating his peers; his willingness to lead the club demonstrates his personal agency in the face of an oppressive institution, while the other student members take action by flouting unjust school rules and equipping themselves for a magical world on the verge of open warfare. All the members of the D.A. openly disregard unfair school policies in an effort to train themselves in self-defense. Another example—albeit much more humorous—concerns the Weasley twins, Fred and George. They work tirelessly to perfect their joke products (ignoring rules about testing products on younger students and, more significantly, selling the products to fellow students). Their career aims reflect their concern for the state of their wizarding community: As they say themselves, a world threatened and eventually plagued by war will have a dire need for laughter, which is what they hope to provide with their Weasley Wizarding Wheezes.

Further, the formation of Dumbledore's Army provides an opportunity for Rowling to develop the character of Hermione, who until this point in the series has been accused of valuing academics over action. In direct contrast to Umbridge's unearned authority (which nearly destroys Hogwarts), then, is Hermione's development. Throughout the series Hermione's defining characteristic has been her compliance with rules and regulations. In *Order of the Phoenix*, though, it is Hermione who suggests the students disregard school policy and take the initiative to gain the practical knowledge they need about Defense Against the Dark Arts, knowledge sorely lacking in Umbridge's "by the book" curriculum. In the act of forming the D.A., Hermione's personal agency is established by the painstaking steps she takes to ensure the secrecy of the organi-

zation, including performing an advanced Protean charm to communicate between members and jinx traitors. Hermione's claim partway through the novel that the meetings of the D.A. are "more important than homework!" shocks Ron and Harry and demonstrates that she has moved from dutiful student to revolutionary; her concern shifts from her small group of friends to the greater good of the wizarding community as a whole.

Fate and Free Will

While questions of power are undeniably central to the novel and to Rowling's series, *Order of the Phoenix* extends one of the series's central tensions—the relationship between fate and free will. As Harry learns more about the prophecy that has, unbeknownst to him, governed his life, it becomes clear that Sybill Trelawney's prediction about the rise of Voldemort is Rowling's way of inviting readers to consider the relationships between destiny and choice. Whether readers have a religious worldview defined by divine intervention and human free will or a materialist philosophy that ponders the role of nature versus nurture, the fifth book challenges them to contemplate the powerlessness and the agency that humans experience. In the second book Dumbledore tells Harry, "It is our choices that show what we truly are, far more than our abilities." *Order of the Phoenix* advances this thematic concern of Rowling's by revealing that, rather than the cosmos, it is Voldemort's choice to mark Harry instead of Neville that has determined the course of events. Free will is, if not more important, at least as important as the prophecy that has guided Voldemort's actions in Rowling's cosmology.

Umbridge's decision to target Trelawney for termination is significant because it illustrates Rowling's interest in these questions of free will versus predestination. As the Divination teacher Trelawney has expertise that is constantly questioned. At the same time the novel's resolution suggests that Rowling puts a great deal of stock in fate. When Firenze assumes the post of Divination teacher in chapter 27, readers learn more about the varieties of Seeing. Distinguishing Seeing from "fortune-telling," Firenze gives a cosmic perspective to the study of the universe as a backdrop for human events. As Firenze states, "We watch the skies for the great tides of evil or change that are sometimes marked there" (603). Even as he affirms the necessity of careful self-examination, he challenges the assumption that we can ever know anything about ourselves for certain, whether that is the fate of our species or our own personal mortality.

Death

Rowling has explained that the entire Harry Potter series is centrally concerned with the concept of death. The death of her own mother affected her profoundly, and the ways in which humans process and move on from the death of a family member or friend are especially important in *Order of the Phoenix,* though certainly the whole series explores this theme. In the beginning of the novel Harry is plagued by nightmares of Cedric's murder during the Triwizard Tournament at the end of *Goblet of Fire.* The novel's first scene finds Dudley teasing Harry for waking him at night with screams and pleas for his classmate's life. This opens up one layer of Harry's confrontations in the narrative—as much with Voldemort and the Death Eaters or Umbridge and the incompetent and corrupt Ministry of Magic as with his own survivor guilt. Ultimately, if not for Harry, Cedric might still be alive, or so he fears. While it is a coincidence that both the boys reach the trophy in the center of the maze at the same time, it is only because of Harry's importance to Voldemort that the trophy is a Portkey. In this way Harry feels responsible for Cedric's untimely death, and his emotional conflict over his guilt is emphasized by Rowling early in the fifth novel.

As Harry is called upon by others—mainly curious classmates—to explain Cedric's last moments and Voldemort's return to human form, Harry takes on what critics have called the "witnessing" function, compounding his anguish over surviving that night in the cemetery. Harry, however, refuses to share any details with students seeking gossip; the only information he gives is to his close friends and mentors, who are able to help him work through his grief. Harry's refusal to explain how Cedric died is Rowling's way of promoting respect for those whom we have lost. Harry has never been an attention seeker, but at this crucial time he is doubted by

many and could build more credence for Dumbledore, his story, and himself by revealing more of the intimate details, but he does not. Harry respects the dead—he respects his friend—and Rowling reminds us to do the same.

However, this moral admonition is not the only aspect of death that Rowling hopes to explore in *Order of the Phoenix.* While the beginning of the novel addresses the repercussions of Cedric's earlier death, the end of the novel presents readers with a new tragedy: the death of Harry's godfather, Sirius Black. Rowling admitted to crying for days after writing the scene in which Sirius dies. His death is made even more tragic by the fact that Harry had some promise of a pleasant life outside school if he were able to visit or even live with Sirius. When Sirius dies, then, Harry is doubly destroyed because he has lost not only a friend and mentor, but the possibility of leaving the Dursleys to be with someone about whom he truly cares.

Although a great tragedy, Sirius's death begs readers to consider the cause of his demise: Does he bear some responsibility for his death because of his very human flaws, emphasized throughout the novel, such as his impetuosity, quickness to incite conflict, and tendency to sullenness? From the flashback included in the novel (see "Snape's Worst Memory"), readers can conclude that Sirius is feisty and daring. He enjoys activities that give him a thrill, whether it be teasing "Snivellus" as a teen or fighting for the order at the Ministry of Magic. A former prisoner who had been locked away for over a decade surely grows restless and desires his freedom; there is nothing unnatural about this feeling. But, Sirius is also too rash. After escaping in *Prisoner of Azkaban,* he must still live in hiding since his name has not yet been cleared in the wizarding community. In *Goblet of Fire* he still must disguise himself as Padfoot and be sure not to be seen in the open. Two years after his freeing from prison, two long years of living in hiding, Sirius is very impatient. He feels passionately about the order and wants to fight for what he believes in, but he now becomes a prisoner of his childhood home, forced to endure the epithets unleashed by an ancient portrait of his mother. Once again Sirius is caged, and he is further enraged by seeing other order members, such as Snape, fighting actively for their cause. When the battle with Voldemort occurs near the end of the novel, Sirius is more than ready finally to leave the dark and dreary house of Black at Number Twelve, Grimmauld Place. He joins the battle at the ministry without thinking and during the great battle in the Department of Mysteries falls through the veil. The character of Sirius and his death invite readers to consider his very human foibles and frailties. Because he is a sympathetic character, readers identify with him; at the same time, he is flawed, he often makes poor choices, and he relates in adolescent ways to his godson, such as when he emotionally punishes Harry for being unwilling to risk additional conversations in the Gryffindor common room fire after they are almost caught by Umbridge.

The guilt Harry suffered from Cedric's death was survivor guilt; at the beginning of the novel readers see him in a more advanced stage of grief than they do at the end, over Sirius's death. By the end of *Order of the Phoenix* Harry is still in the earliest stages of grief, at first suffering from disbelief that Sirius could actually be gone. He moves immediately to the stage in which anger consumes him for the death of his godfather; this is evidenced when he uses an Unforgivable Curse on Bellatrix Lestrange. Rowling is careful to follow the first few recognized six stages of grief (disbelief, anger, bargaining, depression, acceptance, and hope) identified by Elizabeth Kübler-Ross while Harry processes Sirius's death. She captures the stage of bargaining poignantly, through Harry's emotional encounter with Sir Nicholas. This is the first novel of the series in which a major character dies, and Rowling is sure to address the major grief experienced by both characters and readers alike, realistically.

Thematically Rowling uses the death of major characters as a way of not only expanding Harry's emotional range as a character but also challenging readers to consider their own emotional control and the limits to which grief can push us. The death of Sirius does make Harry angrier than readers have ever before witnessed; no one would ever consider that it was possible for Harry to use the Cruciatus Curse on another human being, even an enemy (in contrast with his refusal to let Sirius and Lupin kill Peter Pettigrew even after he learned the truth that Pettigrew led to the deaths of his parents in *Prisoner of Azkaban*). Harry, although suffering from teen angst, usually masters his violent emotions. Nonetheless, in the climactic scene in the ministry foyer, Harry attempts to use the unforgivable curse on Bellatrix Lestrange, who mocks him for its failure, shrieking at him that he has to "mean it." In some ways this is comforting for readers, who may be shocked at this lapse by Harry, the character who has always had a firm and unshakeable moral compass.

Fallibility

Order of the Phoenix is perhaps notable for this development—the way that Harry's previously unassailable sense of moral rightness becomes unstable in the midst of his tremendous internal conflicts and his grappling with loss. For example, at the very end of the novel Harry speaks alone with Dumbledore about the prophecy. As Harry has always respected Dumbledore, it is unsettling to read of Harry screaming at his mentor and destroying objects in the headmaster's office. The anger Harry unleashes is a direct contrast to Dumbledore's unwavering personal control and in part exists to give Dumbledore's character the chance to evolve. The denouement of the novel is particularly interesting because of the opportunity it affords readers to learn more about Dumbledore, and the opportunity it gives Rowling to humanize the headmaster.

Dumbledore is a sort of god figure throughout the series, seeming to possess an omniscience and omnipotence that increasingly stretch credulity. Dumbledore not only seems to possess an infallible foresight that contributes to Harry's perception of him as a godlike figure but also holds tight control over the information he dispenses to Harry. Readers have been critical of Dumbledore for the type of control he has taken over Harry and the path of Harry's life. Some fans, in fact, have even questioned whether Dumbledore is a master manipulator. By concealing important information from Harry, is Dumbledore protective or secretive? Whose interests does Dumbledore's control over information really serve? Having known what the prophecy said all along, Dumbledore knows Harry must fulfill his destiny or all could be lost. Not telling Harry and giving him the option of turning from the path he is on could lead to Voldemort's rise to power and the fall of the wizarding world. Conversely, Harry is still young (as Dumbledore himself admits freely), and because of this Dumbledore may only be acting in a way that is best for Harry, which is to spare this boy who has had such a traumatizing past from information that is even more traumatic: He must either become a murderer or be killed.

While this certainly engenders questions about Dumbledore's motivation, it may be seen as a mechanism for Rowling to develop the character of Dumbledore and a precursor to the additional knowledge readers will gain about him in *Deathly Hallows*. Until this point his infallibility is admirable but unrealistic; at the end of the novel Dumbledore recognizes his missteps and admits he has erred in his conduct over the academic year. In the chapter "The Lost Prophecy" he acknowledges that his attempt at maintaining distance from Harry as part of a strategy to prevent tempting Voldemort was a mistake and that he, not Harry, is to blame for Sirius's death. His failing to mentor Harry—and knowing Harry's impulses—resulted in the tragic events at the end of the novel. This admission of failure by Dumbledore is the first real growth readers have seen him experience in the Harry Potter series. Narratively Dumbledore's recognition gives the novelist an opportunity to evolve the character; thematically it suggests that there is a fine line between protection and manipulation.

Social Justice

Another question the novel raises is racial injustice. Rowling has emphasized class differences and blood status in earlier books and has dealt with the issue of racism metaphorically in a general sense. For example, Lupin resigns in *Prisoner of Azkaban*, he tells Harry, because parents would not want their children to be taught by a werewolf. Further, Hermione's mission for S.P.E.W. (Society for the Protection of Elfish Welfare) is in essence based on the premise that racial oppression is fundamentally unjust, even if the oppressed race participates in its oppression.

In previous novels these are subplots rather than major narrative concerns, and *Order of the Phoenix* changes that focus through the introduction of the character of Umbridge and the figurative emphasis placed on the statues in the atrium of the Ministry of Magic. An impressive fountain that fills the atrium is described as follows: "A group of golden statues, larger than life-size, stood in the middle of a circular pool. Tallest of them all was a noble-looking wizard with his wand pointing straight up in the air. Grouped around him were a beautiful witch, a centaur, a goblin, and a house-elf. The last three were all looking adoringly up at the witch and wizard" (127). The hypocrisy suggested with this sculpture is obvious: The witch and wizard, the humans, reign above all other species. Similarly the sculpture suggests that the subordinate species admire the humans and look to them for guidance. This portrayal of the species is meant to trouble readers, and Rowling makes an important statement at the end of the novel when the fountain is destroyed in the epic battle at the ministry. The status of the different species is literally and symbolically destroyed and foreshadows the major conflicts in *Half-Blood Prince*, in which all creatures must learn to work together to survive Voldemort and his followers. The destruction of the statues also implies that Umbridge's repugnant worldview—and, it is hinted, a worldview shared by the Ministry of Magic and its administration—is untenable in the face of this new threat to the wizarding world.

In *Order of the Phoenix*, however, racism is surfaced by Rowling metaphorically and literally—most specifically at Hogwarts itself. First, Umbridge's belief system is based on contempt for nonhumans and, specifically, nonwizards. Her views are most clearly illustrated by her deprecatory comments on the centaurs, especially once Firenze receives a teaching post at Hogwarts, calling them "filthy half-breeds." Umbridge uses similarly eugenic and supremacist language to describe Remus Lupin, a werewolf, and repeatedly attempts to dislodge Rubeus Hagrid, a half-giant, from his post as Care of Magical Creatures professor.

Rowling eventually makes an example of Umbridge, suggesting to readers that views like

Umbridge's are morally repugnant. Readers may feel some sense of triumph when Umbridge is carried off deep into the Forbidden Forest by the herd of furious centaurs. No one can be sure of what happens to Umbridge when she is alone with the centaurs, but it should be assumed it is unpleasant. While Umbridge's getting her comeuppance is an event readers can appreciate, Rowling makes an even more important point by having Dumbledore rescue her, single-handedly, from the centaur herd. Because Umbridge has attempted to orchestrate Dumbledore's downfall since her arrival at Hogwarts, it is in some sense poetic justice that Dumbledore rescues her. Rowling reminds readers that no matter what evil people commit, it is not appropriate to sit idly by while evil is done to them, reinforcing a moral system that values human life no matter how despicable.

Like Dumbledore, Hermione embodies the philosophy of acting in the pursuit of justice and for noble aims. In *Order of the Phoenix* one instance in which she refuses simply to talk about or wait for change but instead becomes actively involved is with the house-elves. Her interactions with the house-elves—namely, Dobby—in the fifth novel build directly on her campaigning for house-elf rights in the fourth novel (recall she started S.P.E.W.: The Society for the Promotion of Elfish Welfare). Hermione's passion for house-elf rights is obvious, especially when readers learn she has taught herself to knit and has been making small pieces of clothing for the elves over the summer; she has given up precious study time, in the year in which she must take her O.W.L. examinations, for the sake of the elves. She leaves her knitted gifts in the hope that elves may acquire them and then be set free.

Authority and Autonomy

The novel's treatment of Hermione and the house-elves, while a subplot, advances larger novelistic concerns about authority, autonomy, and legitimacy. While Hermione's intentions are positive, Hermione's actions are somewhat deceptive and are unappreciated by the house-elves at Hogwarts. Hermione is stalwart in her conviction that the elves are unaware of how poorly they are treated,

and if they were only exposed to a different way of life, they might all desire freedom. It seems unthinkable that the elves would not lead more rewarding lives if they were not slaves, but Rowling makes an important comment here with Hermione's behavior and attitude. What the house-elves, as slaves, have been denied is choice: They serve their masters, never themselves. Hermione, although wanting to improve their status of life, also denies them choice. She does not offer the elves clothing, asking them whether they would like to be freed from their obligations as servants. She uses trickery and attempts to force freedom on them, a course that is not all that different from Umbridge's trying to enforce her new sets of rules on the community of Hogwarts. The elves, Rowling seems to offer, deserve the right to choose what path they will take. Then they are not slaves, but creatures who have authority over themselves.

The question of authority also affects the women in the novel, most specifically McGonagall, Trelawney, and Umbridge. McGonagall, the epitome of proper behavior (she carries herself with grace and authority and models and encourages manners), is pushed to the limit by Umbridge, who irritates McGonagall on both professional and personal levels. McGonagall is disgusted by the outrageous way in which Umbridge punishes her students (her methods are abusive, as when she forces Harry to write, and continuously rewrite, "I must not tell lies" into his own hand, leaving him with a serious injury).

McGonagall is also disturbed by the lack of faith Umbridge has in her students' abilities. Not only does Umbridge supply her students with an outdated curriculum and encourage rote memorization rather than learning, she also discourages them from following their passions. When Harry tells McGonagall he wants to be an Auror, Umbridge argues openly with McGonagall, in front of Harry, that he can never succeed. Even though McGonagall may have some reservations because of some of Harry's grades, she is incited to defend him staunchly. Her defense springs from her love for Harry but is escalated by Umbridge's blatant disrespect for his abilities and interests. McGonagall may occasionally make an example of a student, but she would never attack his or her character. She works to find ways to support her students; perhaps the best example of this behavior is the way in which she constantly reassures Neville of his talents when he suffers from self-doubt perpetuated by his grandmother. With the characters of Umbridge and McGonagall Rowling differentiates between two very different types of authority: assumed and earned. Umbridge assumes authority but does not deserve it; she assumes authority by lowering others, including squashing a student's dreams. McGonagall, on the other hand, has earned her authority. She is a master teacher and administrator at Hogwarts (because of her talents and dedication, not empty allegiance like Umbridge's). Even though Harry and Neville may feel sad about Umbridge's claims, they remain confident because someone whom they respect—McGonagall—sympathizes with them. Personally McGonagall is annoyed by Umbridge's hyperfemininity. Umbridge's pink suits, obsession with kittens, and passive-aggressive throat clearing represent McGonagall's antithesis.

Umbridge embodies all the behavior and habits McGonagall rails against in order to be taken seriously and respected as a female teacher. Her masculine assertiveness, her strict personality, and her tartan colors make McGonagall the conservative yet admired teacher she is. For the most part McGonagall is unemotional in comparison with other women, such as the wildly emotional Sybill Trelawney. Instead, she has a commanding but caring demeanor. For example, she calmly handles Harry's report that Arthur has been attacked at the ministry. In the eye of tragedy she remains composed and serves her students' needs, making sure Harry and the Weasleys are comfortable. In her classes she is authoritative and keeps her students focused, rejecting teachings by colleagues she feels are unacceptable or "woolly," as when she sighs and asks the students who it is Professor Trelawney has predicted will die during their third year, dismissing the nonsense without hesitation. And, finally, one could consider McGonagall's profession as Transfiguration professor a more traditionally masculine job than those held by other women at Hogwarts.

She is not the librarian, the nurse, or the teacher of Divination: Her subject concerns magical science (examining and understanding the properties of objects); further, Dumbledore, the most respected wizard in the community, once taught Transfiguration—McGonagall's job, then, immediately has higher status. McGonagall's reputation as a stern but caring teacher is unquestioned.

Conversely, Trelawney's reputation is questioned. Her reputation precedes her: She remains holed up in her tower reading tea leaves and crystal balls, looking like a giant, glimmering insect. Trelawney represents traditionally feminine qualities as Umbridge does, but Umbridge's serve as a mask for her officiousness while Trelawney's affiliation with historically feminine qualities such as intuition, timidity, and a sort of emotional frailty marks her as a natural target for Umbridge's illegitimate authority. Trelawney, as a Seer, is governed by intuition. She is characterized by her lack of emotional control (in contrast with Dumbledore). For years McGonagall, appalled by Trelawney's predictions and behavior, has only been slightly cordial to her colleague. But, finally, in the face of a threat to their roles at Hogwarts, McGonagall and Trelawney band together. When Umbridge dismisses Trelawney from her post, McGonagall offers her comfort and warmly escorts her back into the building (a scene that is particularly moving in the film adaptation). The dynamics of authority among these women shifts significantly by the close of the novel: Umbridge's authority is dissolved, McGonagall's authority never wavers, and Trelawney's authority, interestingly, becomes more legitimate when readers learn she made the prophecy that will, in fact, determine the course of not only Harry's life but that of the entire wizarding world.

Teen Angst

Trelawney's prophecy becomes the catalyst for great internal conflict for Harry. The gravity of its contents—essentially, that he must be killed or become a killer—does not fully affect him until the story resumes in *Half-Blood Prince*. However, Harry is wracked by other internal struggles throughout the fifth novel that presage those he will wrestle with in the last part of the series. One of the most prominent is his first romantic relationship with Cho Chang. Even though Harry lives under the constant threat of Voldemort's vengeance, Rowling devotes portions of the novel to addressing Harry's inner turmoil over his involvement with Cho, making Harry—the hoped-for hero of the wizarding world—an authentic teenage male as well. The danger of Voldemort is very real, but Harry's worries over Cho and her feelings are also scary. Harry's romantic relationship with Cho represents the unknown: Much as in his interactions with Voldemort, Harry has to strategize his next move with Cho and ultimately must be prepared with some system of defense if matters go badly. This romantic involvement is a stressor for Harry, but a refreshingly lighthearted one in comparison to the other battles Harry must endure. Rowling creates an effective balance in her hero: Giving him other important dimensions, such as concerns about romance and rejection, makes Harry a character with whom readers can identify.

Another internal conflict plaguing Harry and his fellow fifth-year classmates is academic in nature: the Ordinary Wizarding Level examinations. These examinations establish the course of each student's life since the marks they receive on the exams determine what classes they can take in the following years and ultimately, then, what professions they are best suited to adopt. Someone like Hermione, who is undecided in her career path, has the pressure to do well in every exam she takes. Harry, who finds being an Auror attractive, must do well on exams in several subjects he does not necessarily excel in, including Potions. Rowling's focus on the importance of the exams here provides both the students and readers with a sense of continuity, much needed in a world on the brink of open warfare. The exams represent their future: The students are looking ahead, even though their world could be destroyed at any time by a dark wizard and his minions. Although the Hogwarts fifth years are anxious, the attention they devote to the exams is symbolic of their optimism that their world will continue as it did before when Voldemort and his followers were not gaining power, were not threatening to unleash dark magic, and were not

marshaling forces that foreshadow social unrest. The students do not allow their power to pursue lives past the walls and years of Hogwarts to be taken from them.

The book's tension escalates throughout the narrative to culminate in the last chapter, in which readers are told the second war has begun. The darkest of the Harry Potter books to this point, *Order of the Phoenix* treats complex themes, with power (whether personal or political), identity, and internal conflict as the most important among them. However, while subsequent novels in the series continue Rowling's exploration of dark themes such as death, fate, and prophecy, they also reflect an unflagging faith in the power of friendship and loyalty to challenge the forces that menace them.

INITIAL REVIEWS

Released on June 21, 2003, *Order of the Phoenix* was hotly anticipated by readers and very favorably reviewed by most major periodicals; one dissenting reviewer, the English novelist Philip Hensher in the *Spectator*, echoed the literary critic Harold Bloom's harsh treatment of the series as a whole. Bloom has commented that the books will be gathering dust in a few short years. Even though reviewers had been overwhelmingly admiring of Rowling's most ambitious work to that point, the initial reviews of this book nonetheless point out several flaws. Many claim that the book is overlong, introduces unnecessary new characters, and is slowly paced, but most admit these do not undermine its overall aesthetic quality, noting specifically the gripping narrative, stylistic craftsmanship, and increasing complexity.

Reviewers generally concede that the novel is darker and certainly longer than previous installments. Diane Roback et al. echo others in their *Publishers Weekly* review when they argue "there is little action until the end" though this critique seems aimed specifically at the belated magical battles. Julian Sanchez of *Reason* sees *Order of the Phoenix* as Kafkaesque both perhaps in its increasing complexity and in its targeted thematic critique of bureaucracy. Sanchez's allusion to FRANZ KAFKA refers specifically to the Prague writer's works *The*

Trial and *The Metamorphosis*, which disorient readers through narratives about protagonists who are suddenly thrust into bizarre and confusing situations. *The Trial* bears particular relevance since its main character, Josef K., is subject to a distorted and bureaucratic version of the justice system when he is arrested and imprisoned for reasons never explained or revealed to the reader. Rowling's representation of the wizarding world's Wizengamot is paralleled here. Sanchez also sees *Order of the Phoenix* as concerned with what the historian HANNAH ARENDT called the "banality of evil," or the thesis that the great evils of history are executed not by sociopaths or dictators but by the regular people who participate in state-sanctioned injustice. Sanchez applies Arendt's thesis to the powermongering Ministry of Magic bureaucrat Dolores Umbridge.

Other observations in the book's initial reviews are concerned with Rowling's thematic development. Some reviewers such as Lev Grossman of *Time* argue that death has in previous installments been a subtext, and this fifth book adopts a much more explicitly dark tone, especially on the heels of Cedric Diggory's death at the end of *Goblet of Fire*. In contrast, Robert Hughes of the *Wall Street Journal* believes the series has always been dark; in a series about a battle between good and evil, the books have always been concerned with death. Most reviewers concede that both the novel and its protagonist become more complex in the fifth book.

Reviewers comment positively and specifically on Rowling's storytelling abilities: her graceful narrative craftsmanship and the pacing and plotting of the novel. Calling it a "fine novel, and a compelling one" (W13), the *Wall Street Journal*'s Hughes echoes *People* magazine's claim that *Order of the Phoenix* is Rowling's "strongest outing yet" (Daly 45) and Malcolm Jones of *Newsweek*'s assertion that *Order of the Phoenix* is the best book in the series. The *Wall Street Journal* comments on the moral complexity of the work, arguing that it is a "humane and morally interesting tale" (Hughes W13). The *New York Times*, *Booklist*, and *Time* reviews emphasize Rowling's ability to plot her novel effectively, taking special note of Rowling's "bravura storytelling skills and tirelessly inventive imagination," as character-

ized by Michiko Kakutani. *Time*'s Grossman calls her a "virtuoso plotter, a master of snappy pacing" (60). This affirmation of her increasing skillfulness with plotting is described as a "natural storyteller's gift for pacing and surprise" by the *Newsweek* reviewer Jones.

Reviews on the whole acknowledge minor flaws in the novel including some critiques of clichéd use of language and characters; this includes suggestions that the character of Dobby is annoying in the same vein as Jar Jar Binks from the *Star Wars: Phantom Menace* and that Draco Malfoy is a cardboard villain. There are other frequent assessments that the novel is too long, including the *Wall Street Journal*'s claim the book is in need of "a slimming regimen" (Hughes W13). Amanda Craig and Lisa Allardice of the *New Statesman* identify several minor problems, claiming that new characters such as Nymphadora Tonks and new places such as the Room of Requirement are wholly unnecessary but concur that these extraneous additions do not mar the overall effect of the work. *Booklist* and the *New York Times* agree that the novel "gets off to a ponderous start," as Kakutani states, and could be shorter, but the majority of reviews agree that despite these minor flaws, *Order of the Phoenix* is "rich and satisfying in almost every respect," as John Leonard of the *New York Times Book Review* claims. Grossman, of *Time*, as do Craig and Allardice, enumerates what could be considered picky defects, but these detract only in small ways from the novel's overall success, according to Grossman.

Of the major reviews only the English novelist Philip Hensher's review in the *Spectator* assaults Rowling's overall aesthetic quality. While Hensher believes the series to "please and satisfy simple readers," he makes a point of arguing that he "strongly resist[s] claims for its literary merit." Calling it in turns banal, lacking in subtlety, Scooby Doo-ish, and tiresome, Hensher's review concedes that *Order of the Phoenix* and the series itself are entertaining for children but rejects their value as works of literature. While much less strident than Hensher, Michael Atkinson of the *Village Voice* offsets his complimentary assessment of the work with his assertion that Rowling's Harry Potter series is "100 percent cliché and cliché byproducts, even beyond the obvious Grimm and Tolkien gyps" (48). These two reviews stand almost alone, however, in identifying the series, and *Order of the Phoenix* specifically, as novelistic failures.

SCHOLARSHIP

The majority of scholarly work on *Order of the Phoenix* appears in a special issue of *Topic: The Washington and Jefferson College Review*, very soon after the novel's publication in 2003. Scholars in that issue focus on *Order of the Phoenix*'s exploration of such themes as witnessing, disillusionment, women's empowerment, and the nature of information. However, other scholars have separately examined Rowling's scathing critique of authoritarian governance, bureaucracy, and legal institutions.

Several critical examinations in legal journals have commented on what they call Rowling's satire of Western democracy and view the novel as a lampoon of the inefficiencies and corruption of the state through her portrayal of the Ministry of Magic. Benjamin Barton observes in "Harry Potter and the Miserable Ministry of Magic," in the *Texas Wesleyan Law Review*, that the system of governance of the magical world is distinguished by its essentially nondemocratic nature and its lack of a democratic lawmaking function—for example, policy changes seem to be handed down by divine fiat rather than a democratic process that reflects the will of the people. Paul Joseph and Lynn Wolf echo these claims in their "The Law in Harry Potter," in the *University of Toledo Law Review*, providing evidence that *Order of the Phoenix* is especially adept in illustrating a governing structure that lacks both ethics and competent execution, for example, in laws that are enforced both nondemocratically and inconsistently. They note Cornelius Fudge's absolution of Harry's underage use of magic in *Prisoner of Azkaban*, in contrast with the full-scale criminal trial deployed in *Order of the Phoenix* as one example and the frequent proclamations issued by Fudge through Umbridge in *Order of the Phoenix* as other instances of nondemocratic governance. Similarly, while wizards are prohibited from enchanting Muggle objects, Arthur Weasley regularly does so with

few real legal repercussions. Further, the criminal law system is inhumane and disturbing, and the authors compare Azkaban, the wizarding prison, with the California Pelican Bay Prison, which uses "isolation, deprivation of natural light and air, and strong-armed tactics when moving prisoners" (197). In Joseph and Wolf's assessment the book presents important social issues regarding human rights and justice to readers. On a similar note Bill McCarron discusses in "Power vs. Authority in *Harry Potter and the Order of the Phoenix*" in *Notes on Contemporary Literature* the contrast between power and authority evident in the novel, observing that power such as that imposed by Fudge or Umbridge from above is treated contemptuously by Rowling in the novel when contrasted with the authority earned by Dumbledore and granted from his followers in the wizarding community.

Noah Chevalier's "The Liberty Tree and the Whomping Willow: Political Justice, Magical Science, and Harry Potter" offers an exhaustive and historicized analysis of *Order of the Phoenix*, reaffirming Barton's and Joseph and Wolf's focus on the book's critique of governance institutions. However, Chevalier contributes a new scholarly perspective by arguing that Harry functions as a "radical" whose individual heroism challenges the corrupt infrastructure. Rowling establishes Harry's heroism both by his role in the fight against Voldemort as the battle between good and evil and by his resistance to the authoritarian structures of the ministry and the ministry-controlled press, the *Daily Prophet*. Drawing upon Jacobin writers of the 1790s such as William Godwin and Mary Shelley (most noted for her novel *Frankenstein*) and French Revolution concerns over the "place of social and political justice within the context of a burgeoning industrial economy" (402), Chevalier's detailed assessment places *Order of the Phoenix* in the literary and philosophical contexts of Godwin and Shelley. Godwin, according to Chevalier, critiqued the political theorist and philosopher Edmund Burke's views emphasizing the goodness of governing institutions. Godwin's 1798 tract *Enquiry Concerning Political Justice* challenged the notion that political justice could be achieved through institutional mechanisms as long as social inequalities persisted. As a strong advocate of the power of human reason, Godwin expressed views that can be categorized as philosophical anarchism, or the belief in the inherent power of human reason to achieve self-governance, rejecting moral legitimacy of institutions to rule. Finally, Chevalier's essay makes an important connection between the novel *Frankenstein*, which "considers the effects of modern technology on the natural body" (409), and the character of Sirius's house-elf, Kreacher, both despised creatures who are the victims of social contempt.

A special issue of *Topic* in 2005 focused on *Order of the Phoenix*, with particular attention paid to themes of witnessing, truth telling, and control of information. Three related essays have explored these thematic concerns of the novel, including "You Survived to Bear Witness'" Heather Debling's analysis of the figure of the witness in the novel and what she argues is Rowling's valorization of truth telling. Acknowledging that modern media have created a culture of confession, Debling argues that witnessing is an extension of trauma and has value when transformed into testimony; essentially, Debling claims that Rowling destabilizes the role of the witness and the definition of what is true (citing Dumbledore's false confession in *Order of the Phoenix* to organizing Dumbledore's Army and Marietta's true confession altered by Kingsley Shacklebolt's memory charm). In the end, however, asserts Debling, Rowling is not interested in undermining the witness figure, but the novel does endorse critical reading and assessment of witnessing.

Rowling's commentary on knowledge, information, power, and control is also of interest to critics, such as in Jennifer Flaherty's "Harry Potter and the Freedom of Information: Knowledge and Control in *Harry Potter and the Order of the Phoenix*." Critically related to Debling's analysis of witnessing (how we know what is true), Flaherty contends that the novel's central concern is information—which is, in reality, power—that all of the characters attempt to control. As other writers and reviewers have acknowledged, the battle Harry faces in *Order of the Phoenix* is not against Voldemort but against the corrupt bureaucracy and bloated institution of the Ministry of Magic that tries to camouflage—and control—the truth about Voldemort's return. Flaherty cites Minister of Magic Cornelius Fudge's use of disinformation disseminated through the *Daily Prophet* and his attempts to manipulate the judicial system during Harry's hearing for the use of underage magic as evidence of her claim. Umbridge, as well, serves to illustrate Flaherty's thesis; as the high inquisitor, Umbridge is interested primarily in staunching the flow of information (her attempts to inspect all communication by owl post and prohibiting teachers from discussing the Azkaban breakout with students), and as a teacher, she denies her students practical information about Defense Against the Dark Arts.

Flaherty explains Hermione's character evolution in the novel from devoted rule follower to rebel. As the most dedicated student in the novels, Hermione has unquenchable intellectual curiosity and passion for education, which inspire her resistance to Umbridge's powermongering. Further, Flaherty cites the ubiquity of this theme of knowledge and control as central to the novel's concluding conversation between Dumbledore and Harry and the ways knowledge of the prophecy about Harry and Voldemort have been denied to him. Because Harry's understanding of knowledge is immature—he fails to see the consequences of his knowing—the novel explores the ramifications of seeking knowledge as well as a failure to anticipate the possible outcomes of having it, such as Harry's snooping into Snape's memories, which results in his disturbing glimpse into his father's teenage character flaws. Harry fails to become invested in the study of Occlumency, the magical science of blocking Legilmency (a version of mind reading), because his concept of knowing is not tempered by judgment. Flaherty argues that the novel's final comment is that ignorance and safety are not the same, but that too much knowledge can be painful. In the end, Flaherty notes, the novel strips away secrecy and lies from Harry and from the wizarding community.

Finally, Flaherty and Debling's theses are synthesized by Marla Harris's essay "Is Seeing Believing? Truth and Lies in *Harry Potter and the Order of the Phoenix*," which argues that Harry's public labeling at the beginning of the novel—as storyteller, liar, and madman—is systematically transferred to other characters throughout the novel. Rowling's novel quietly moves authority from, for example, "credible" texts such as the *Daily Prophet* to the tabloidesque *Quibbler*, one example of the way she invites readers to examine the nature and quality of "truth" and how we define it and recognize it. "Fact" and "fiction" come under fire as the series itself has blurred the line between them—the reality of the allegedly mythical Chamber of Secrets and Sorcerer's Stone in the first two books illustrates this blurring. As Harris writes, "The novels repeatedly dramatize the fallibility of sight, that what characters claim to see may not be real or, as in the case of Mrs. Figg, they may claim to see things they do not" (86). She refers here to the example of Arabella Figg's testimony at Harry's hearing at the ministry, where readers have every reason to believe that, as a Squib, she is not being truthful when she comes forward to testify that she saw the Dementor attack on Harry and Dudley. Rowling further challenges her readers' assumptions about reality versus appearance in her use of characters whose sanity is questionable (Mad-Eye Moody and Luna Lovegood, for example), but whose keen insights and perception eventually emerge as correct. As Debling does, Harris confirms that the novel advocates a kind of "critical viewership," exhorting readers to adopt a critical stance toward texts and people and the claims they make.

Continuing the gender-focused approach that has occupied many critics of the Harry Potter series, Karley Adney, in "From Books to Battle: Hermione's Quest for Knowledge in *Harry Potter and the Order of the Phoenix*," explores Hermione's battle for knowledge; Adney is particularly interested in challenging claims such as Elizabeth Heilman's assertion in "Blue Witches, Pink Wizards: Representations of Gender Identity and Power" that Rowling's female characters are weak. Adney argues that Hermione's campaign for house-elf justice, her actions as prefect, and her subversive resistance to Umbridge are all evidence of her leadership qualities. Critical discussion of *Order of the Phoenix*, then, has focused primarily on the potential legal and governmental satire the novel

offers, the thematic concerns of truth versus lies or reality versus appearance, and gender analysis of the female characters.

CHARACTERS

Sirius Black Member of the order and Harry's godfather. Although he escaped life as a prisoner in the wizarding jail Azkaban and was able to live somewhat freely "on the run" in *Goblet of Fire*, Sirius literally becomes reimprisoned in *Order of the Phoenix*. He is forced to remain at Number Twelve, Grimmauld Place, the Black family home, in order to avoid calling attention to the order; he offers this home (although haunted by his fanatical purebred-loving mother and her loyal house-elf Kreacher) to the order to use as headquarters. Rowling emphasizes one of Sirius's important characteristics in *Order of the Phoenix*: his estrangement from his fanatical family. Sirius explains how he could not tolerate the behavior of his family because of their obsession with blood status. He shows Harry the family tapestry from which his name has been excised because he did not share their zealous pureblood mania. Sirius has always been an outsider in the wizarding community, but in *Order of the Phoenix* Rowling also stresses his outsider status within his own family. He represents the rebel and eventually pays for his rebellious nature.

Sirius feels that giving his home to the cause of the order is one of the only useful things he has done since he is otherwise confined. The novel tests his already restless nature, and in the novel's final battle Sirius jumps at the chance to fight, paying little (if any) attention to possible consequences of his actions. Sirius's death is quick, unexpected, and mysterious. No one can be sure of what happened to Sirius—where he has gone or where he will go, after falling through the veil. With his passing Rowling raises questions and emphasizes the uncertainty associated with his death, which echo the loss and confusion experienced after the death of a loved one.

Albus Dumbledore Headmaster of Hogwarts. Dumbledore for a time must relinquish his post as headmaster (which Dolores Umbridge then fulfills).

Always a caring mentor Dumbledore shocks Harry with the distance he puts between them in *Order of the Phoenix*, contrasting the close relationship he and Harry have had since the first book in the series. Even when Dumbledore arrives to defend Harry at the ministry hearing, he makes little contact, especially eye contact, with Harry. We learn later in the book that Dumbledore perceives Voldemort's strong mental connection with Harry and may be able to read his thoughts. Since Dumbledore is the leader of the order, he believes it best to limit his direct contact with Harry.

Dumbledore does not, however, cease to be Harry's mentor, despite Harry's feeling that the headmaster has abandoned him. Dumbledore asks Severus Snape to teach Harry Occlumency (the art of blocking someone from accessing one's mind), and so, albeit indirectly, Dumbledore still protects Harry's well-being. Dumbledore continues to protect Harry from difficult knowledge. Dumbledore has known all along that Harry would either have to become a murderer or die, according to Sybill Trelawney's prophecy, but has kept this information secret in order to preserve Harry's innocence just a little longer, even as he recognizes the irrationality and possible danger in this act. Dumbledore's true growth in the course of *Order of the Phoenix* is his realization that this judgment has been in error, and that emotionally and physically abandoning Harry has been an irrational decision.

Dumbledore's position as master of the Hogwarts universe is nearly undone, however, by Umbridge, another important development in the fifth novel. She seeks to undermine Dumbledore while providing the ministry with insider information on the wizarding school. She is given the authority to dismiss members of Dumbledore's staff, but when she fires Sybill Trelawney and orders her to leave school grounds, Dumbledore reasserts his power and protects his staff, students, and school. He allows Trelawney to remain in her tower, reminding Umbridge she has no authority to force teachers to leave the premises, and before Umbridge can even process the act, Dumbledore hires a new Divination teacher, the centaur, Firenze. While Dumbledore knows hiring Firenze will upset Umbridge (because

she despises nonhuman or part-human creatures), he still acts with the best interest of his school at heart: Firenze takes his job seriously and is gifted in the art of Divination. In these acts Dumbledore's most consistent character features—his wisdom, ability to anticipate trouble, and compassion for the greater good—are reinforced. This compassion for others is best demonstrated when he rescues Umbridge from the pack of centaurs in the Forbidden Forest. No matter what horrible acts someone has committed, Dumbledore always acts in accordance with the golden rule.

At the novel's denouement at the Ministry of Magic Dumbledore fights Voldemort in a spectacular battle, an emotionally powerful experience for Dumbledore because Voldemort takes possession of Harry's body and then taunts Dumbledore to kill him, thus destroying Harry as well. Although he may not have acted because of preexisting knowledge about how Voldemort must be defeated, readers can be certain that the main reason Dumbledore did not act on this opportunity was that he would have destroyed Harry, whom he has come to love.

Cornelius Fudge   Minister of Magic. He refuses to believe that Voldemort has returned. Part of this refusal stems from his feeling threatened by Dumbledore (past books comment on Dumbledore's aptness as a choice for Minister of Magic). Fudge exploits the public's wariness of Harry and Dumbledore's claims about Voldemort and in turn leaves the wizarding community unprepared for war. His desire to establish ministry presence (and rule) at Hogwarts further demonstrates his need to subvert Dumbledore and substantiate himself as a legitimate leader. Fudge, true to his last name, mishandles nearly every situation in which he is involved.

Hermione Granger   Harry's and Ron's best friend, founding member of Dumbledore's Army, and student leader. In this book Hermione is made a prefect, a post that affirms her responsibility and ability to care for others. Ron Weasley is also made a prefect and uses the opportunity to tease some of the younger students; Hermione, on the other hand, sees her role as ensuring younger students' safety and dignity (that means Fred and George Weasley are banned from testing their products on them). As always Hermione's prime concern is education—but not only for herself. In this installment of the series Hermione works tirelessly to educate other members of the wizarding community. She continues her efforts to advance the welfare of the house-elves, she seeks to educate the general wizarding public about Harry's encounter with Voldemort, and, most important, she wants to teach her classmates to defend themselves so they will be prepared if the need arises.

The other most important way in which Hermione helps to educate others in *Order of the Phoenix* occurs when she rebels against her Defense Against the Dark Arts professor, Dolores Umbridge. For Hermione education (and a solid one, at that) is the most important priority, and Umbridge does nothing to provide education for Hogwarts students. Hermione has always pursued knowledge, and until this book the most familiar image of her is that of a girl reading in a library with her nose buried in a book. It is in *Order of the Phoenix* that Hermione transforms from a bookworm to a fighter, using her "book knowledge" as a springboard for action. She fights against Umbridge's injustice of denying her students a useful education by taking matters into her own hands.

In the process Hermione becomes more fearless. She flouts school rules by attending Dumbledore's Army meetings since Umbridge, as Hogwarts high inquisitor, has ruled that no student organizations may meet without her approval. Hermione lies blatantly to a teacher—Umbridge—telling her that Dumbledore has hidden a secret weapon in the Forbidden Forest. Her growing independence is also demonstrated by her new willingness in the novel to speak Voldemort's name out loud. As a character Hermione grows immensely in comparison to the girl she was in *Sorcerer's Stone*, where her worst fear was being expelled. Education was her only priority then, and while it remains one in this novel, she has others: her friends, their welfare, and the greater good of the wizarding world.

Rubeus Hagrid Groundskeeper of Hogwarts. Hagrid does not appear in *Order of the Phoenix* until well into the narrative. He has been with Olympe Maxime, negotiating with giants. His role as a liaison between Dumbledore and the giants illustrates yet again the high degree of trust placed in Hagrid by the order. In *Goblet of Fire* Hagrid's status as an outsider was emphasized once Rita Skeeter uncovered the story that he was half-giant. In this book Hagrid's outsider status proves to be a valuable connection that serves his side well. His role as peacemaker reminds readers one should not "judge a book by its cover." Hagrid may be the easily befuddled gentle giant, but in this book Rowling illustrates the depth of his intelligence through the way he interacts with the giants during his trip.

Hagrid meets his half brother Grawp, a full-blooded giant. Hagrid reminisces about his family with Madame Maxime in the preceding novel, demonstrating that although he has no family left (his father passed away and his mother abandoned her husband and child), he still desires one. In this way Rowling grants Hagrid's wish with the appearance of Grawp, even though the young giant physically harms Hagrid on the journey back to Hogwarts. Regardless, Hagrid finds a family outside Hogwarts, of which he has been deprived for so long. Through his relationship with Grawp Hagrid's role as caretaker is further emphasized. He provides for his brother (whom he keeps hidden in the Forbidden Forest), and once he realizes Umbridge will probably fire him from his teaching post, he enlists Harry, Ron, and Hermione to watch over Grawp. Hagrid has always been a caring friend; in this book readers also see him as a loving big brother.

Bellatrix Lestrange Voldemort's loyal follower. She was imprisoned along with other Death Eaters after Voldemort's downfall prior to the beginning of the first novel. She gladly went to prison as a statement of her unwavering allegiance to the Dark Lord. With the help of the Dementors she and some of her fellow Death Eaters escape from Azkaban in *Order of the Phoenix* to rejoin Voldemort. She is characterized as a hateful woman who seeks nothing more than the status of Voldemort's most dedicated servant. During the first war she helped torture Frank and Alice Longbottom, Neville's parents, to a state of insanity by means of the Cruciatus Curse. Her appearance at the novel's final battle in the Department of Mysteries infuriates Neville, who can think of nothing in her presence but avenging his parents. When Sirius dies, Bellatrix gloats. In the film version she also uses the Killing Curse on Sirius before he falls through the veil, emphasizing her ruthlessness. As ringleader for the Death Eaters in the epic battle at the ministry, Bellatrix fears Voldemort's wrath since the prophecy is destroyed, meaning she has failed in her mission.

Neville Longbottom Member of Gryffindor and founding member of Dumbledore's Army. Neville experiences important personal and emotional growth, including increased self-confidence, in *Order of the Phoenix*. Readers first see Neville carrying a special plant onto the Hogwarts Express. He is clearly proud of his interest in Herbology and plans to pursue his passion. But, where he shows most faith in himself concerns his involvement in Dumbledore's Army. As usual, spells do not come naturally to Neville. Instead of being discouraged by his progress (which seems slow compared to that of other members of Dumbledore's Army), Neville focuses his energy on succeeding, and his hard work yields great rewards. The defensive spells he acquires serve him well when he accompanies Harry and his other close friends into the heart of the Ministry of Magic at the end of the novel. His journey to the ministry is symbolic. The Neville of *Sorcerer's Stone*, who refused to join Harry, Ron, and Hermione on their quest to rescue the Sorcerer's Stone from Quirrell/Voldemort, contrasts starkly with the Neville of *Order of the Phoenix*. Neville has grown more confident and invested in his friends to the point that he is willing to risk his life.

Neville also develops emotionally in *Order of the Phoenix*. It is in this novel that his classmates (and Rowling's readers) learn the fate of Neville's parents: They remain at St. Mungo's after being tortured into insanity by means of the Cruciatus Curse by Bellatrix Lestrange and her husband. Neville's throwing himself into Dumbledore's Army

and the battle at the ministry is a way for him to seek vengeance for the wrongdoings suffered by his parents. His strength stems from his deep love for his family. Neville is also extremely important to this novel because of the prophecy on which the whole book (and the fate of the wizarding world) ultimately hinges. Being born near the end of July and to parents who thrice attempted to defeat the Dark Lord, Neville had a malleable fate until Voldemort chose to mark Harry instead of Neville. By penning the prophecy in such a manner, Rowling asks readers to consider Neville's importance in the series: He has always been one of the students featured in the plots, but the prophecy's implication is that Neville is more vital to the series than readers may have originally imagined.

Luna Lovegood Founding member of Dumbledore's Army and a Ravenclaw. Luna is the daughter of the editor of the *Quibbler*, a wizarding tabloid; as such, she is viewed by other students as quirky and eccentric. She remarks that she is teased and does not have any friends, and that may be true, but by the end of *Order of the Phoenix* she has many close friends because of her simple wisdom and her loyalty. She is one of the few members of Dumbledore's Army who accompany Harry to the ministry in search of Sirius. Her character functions as a reminder to readers that it is unwise to judge someone on the basis of rumor or outward appearance. Her nickname may be *Loony* Lovegood, and she may wear earrings she made herself out of radishes, but she is a complex girl who is teased by those who are unaware of the tragedies of her past, including the death of her mother only a few years earlier.

Luna identifies with Harry because they have both encountered death. Almost from the moment she meets him, Luna offers Harry some comfort. When Harry is alarmed by the Thestrals, Luna educates him. She comforts him after the passing of Sirius. It is no coincidence her last name is *Lovegood*: She cares strongly for her friends. Further, Luna has more social power than it may initially seem. Since her father is the editor of the *Quibbler*, she is able to help Harry have the truth of what happened with Voldemort, Cedric, and the Death Eaters distributed to the public. Essentially, without Luna Harry's story would not have been told.

Draco Malfoy   Harry Potter's major nemesis besides Voldemort. As usual, there is great animosity between Harry and Draco, but in *Order of the Phoenix* the tension is heightened since Harry knows that Draco's father, Lucius Malfoy, is definitely a Death Eater. In his interview with Rita Skeeter published in the *Quibbler* Harry reveals the names of the Death Eaters he saw the night Voldemort returned and Cedric was killed, and Lucius Malfoy's is among those printed for all to see. At the end of the novel when even the Minister of Magic himself realizes that Voldemort has returned, the Death Eaters named by Harry are taken to Azkaban and Draco's animosity toward Harry grows exponentially.

Draco becomes a prefect in his fifth year and is one of the first members of Dolores Umbridge's Inquisitorial Squad, a group of students who spy on other students in Umbridge's service. This role gives him the power to insult students and instill fear, traits he has always admired in others. This newly conferred power allows Draco to award and dock house points, a privilege formerly reserved only for Hogwarts staff. The other method by which Draco feels power is bullying other students, whether it be in his role as prefect when he is rude to the younger children or as a fifth-year student picking on his classmates. At a Quidditch match an enraged Draco starts a nasty fight with the Weasley twins by insulting their family—specifically their mother. Draco is simultaneously power-hungry and weak, and in him Rowling seems to suggest children's responsibility either to adopt unquestioningly the belief system of their parents or to break away from it.

Minerva McGonagall   Member of the Order of the Phoenix, Transfiguration professor, and deputy headmistress of Hogwarts. McGonagall's character is truly tested in *Order of the Phoenix* because of her new colleague, Dolores Umbridge. McGonagall has a spotless reputation and is known for being serious, mindful, and caring toward her students.

Umbridge represents the complete opposite: petty, mean, and abusive. Umbridge's passive-aggressive throat clearing and giggling contrast with the assertive and respected reputation McGonagall has established for herself at Hogwarts. McGonagall's patience is further tested in *Order of the Phoenix* when Umbridge is awarded authority in the role of Hogwarts High Inquisitor.

McGonagall resists Umbridge in many ways, both in the classroom and out. A prime example of this would be when Harry discusses his career opportunities with McGonagall, and Umbridge interjects disparaging comments, reminding Harry only of reasons why he can never be an Auror. McGonagall, on the other hand, assures Harry loudly that he can and will be successful as long as he works hard. McGonagall's reaction to Trelawney is an even clearer example of both McGonagall's compassion and her strength: Umbridge fires Trelawney and waits smugly for her to leave the building, but McGonagall goes to the flighty teacher's rescue. This act is significant, considering McGonagall has always responded dismissively to Trelawney's field of study, Divination. McGonagall's allying herself with Trelawney demonstrates just how at odds she is with Umbridge.

As a member of the order McGonagall engages in the final battle at Hogwarts and is stunned multiple times in the chest, a set of injuries that, at her age, may be fatal. McGonagall survives and the attack reminds characters and readers alike that McGonagall is resilient. Hogwarts will benefit from her leadership and stability the next year.

Harry Potter   The protagonist and founding member of Dumbledore's Army. In *Order of the Phoenix* Rowling masterfully captures Harry's teen angst, a driving narrative force in the novel. This angst is his defining feature throughout the book, whether it be his anger at Dumbledore for avoiding and ignoring him or his resentment at having been deprived of information about the prophecy that defines his fate.

While Harry wrestles with complex emotions throughout the novel (ranging from his first romantic relationship with Cho Chang to utter fury at being banned from Quidditch and mental stress to do well on his O.W.L. examinations), no emotion he experiences is as powerful or consuming as the grief he feels from Cedric's death and, later, the loss of Sirius (the full repercussions of which are not explored until *Half-Blood Prince*). Another cause for turmoil for Harry is visions he has of what Voldemort orchestrates to do, is doing, or has done, including Arthur Weasley's being attacked at the ministry by Nagini or Sirius's being tortured in the Department of Mysteries.

Rowling's cleverness is obvious here: By allowing Harry and Voldemort to see into each other's minds, she demonstrates how connected and similar these two characters are, drawing upon the literary tradition of doppelgangers, often dark doubles used to antagonize or emphasize some dimension of the protagonist. Both are orphan half-bloods with great power—one representing good; the other, evil. The statement Rowling may be trying to make (and has done so before) is that all characters have choices. Each person makes his or her own path, and this point can be made no more clearly than in *Order of the Phoenix*. Harry feels angry and betrayed in the novel, and if there were a time for him to succumb to despair, it would be now. But, he does not: He chooses to pursue good, and the most obvious way in which he does this is by rebelling against the oppressive force of Umbridge and founding Dumbledore's Army. Victimized by Umbridge in many respects (denied an education, physically abused, his feelings dismissed, deprived of his hobby, Quidditch), Harry is proud to lead Dumbledore's Army and so teach his classmates to protect themselves from harm, and to fight back. Although hesitant at first, leading the club gives Harry a great sense of satisfaction (which does not stem wholly from the fact that he is successfully deceiving Umbridge). He is a natural teacher, offering consistent praise to his students and giving them constructive lessons from which they learn both theory and application.

When the battle in the Department of Mysteries is finished, Harry is given an opportunity to process all that he has learned about friendship and loyalty, fate and free will. Key to Harry's development in this novel is his new awareness of the secret weapon

Voldemort sought—the prophecy, which foretells Harry's future: He must either become a killer or be killed. This revelation is monumental, and Harry must wrestle with his future, a future void of Sirius. However, his small victories in the novel (defeating the Death Eaters and destroying the prophecy) suggest that as the series continues, greater victories will be had. He has seen his friends grow into able soldiers for the cause of the Order of the Phoenix, promising that as the conflicts become increasingly difficult, their newfound skills will serve them well. Most important, and what affects Harry most heavily, is that Harry's mission is now clear. He is no longer simply fighting against Voldemort. He must find a way to destroy him once and for all.

Severus Snape Potions professor and member of the order. Snape's allegiance to the order is questioned and questionable since he is suspected by many of his fellow order members to be secretly working for Voldemort. Rowling revealed in *Goblet of Fire* that Snape was, in fact, a former Death Eater; in the fifth book readers gain new information about Snape's history and allegiances. In *Order of the Phoenix* Rowling reveals that it is Snape who told Voldemort of the prophecy on which the entire plot of the novel hinges. He overheard Trelawney's telling Dumbledore the prophecy and rushed to tell Voldemort the valuable information he had acquired; this further calls into question Snape's loyalties.

In *Order of the Phoenix* Snape and Harry spend a good amount of time alone together because Dumbledore has asked Snape to train Harry in Occlumency, the art of blocking another person from entering, reading, or toying with one's mind. Snape is a renowned Occlumens and is frustrated by Harry's repeated failures to master the art. When Harry is left alone in Snape's office and views some of Snape's memories, Rowling gives us a glimpse into Snape's life as a child and student at Hogwarts, offering some rationale for his bitter attitude. More important, we are granted access to Snape's "worst memory," in which he is teased and tortured by Sirius Black and James Potter. After Harry sees this portion of the memory, Snape ends his Occlumency lessons. The symbolism in the terminating of these lessons is crucial: Snape appears as if he had been helping Harry but is quick to end it. This abandonment parallels Snape's involvement with the order, leaving readers to wonder whether he is truly dedicated to the cause or only pretending to be.

Finally, in *Order of the Phoenix* Snape cannot and will not let go of the grudge he has against Sirius for his past transgressions and childhood taunting, and the animosity between the characters mounts in *Order of the Phoenix*. Snape flaunts his freedom and ability to do whatever is asked of him by the order, wherever that may be, because unlike Sirius, he is not a prisoner of his own home. These digs rile Sirius because they are true, and Snape knows that. Snape's comments serve as a catalyst for Sirius's rash behavior at the end of the novel (when he rushes off to the ministry to aid the order), and therefore, some readers hold him at least partly responsible for Sirius's death.

Nymphadora Tonks An Auror and Metamorphmagus. She is a clumsy, accident-prone Metamorphmagus and a member of the Order of the Phoenix. She is a pureblood, but she and her parents have been shunned by other members of her family (such as the Malfoys) for her association with and support of half-bloods and Muggles. Tonks is determined and hopeful and, as such, embodies the spirit of the order. Her Metamorphmagus abilities are important to her role as protector; since she is able to change her appearance at will, she dons disguises that allow her to offer protection to her charges without being detected. She is distinguished by her ability to manipulate her appearance and clumsy nature, in contrast to the male Aurors such as Kingsley Shacklebolt and Mad-Eye Moody, who are known for their stealth and seriousness. She forcefully rejects femininity. She refuses to answer to the feminine and sprightly name *Nymphadora*, instead preferring to be called by her last name, *Tonks*.

Dolores Umbridge Senior undersecretary to the Minister of Magic, Defense Against the Dark Arts professor, Hogwarts High Inquisitor, and eventually headmistress of Hogwarts for a brief period. The name *Dolores* is linked etymologically to the Latin word *dolor*, meaning "pain" or "sorrow." True to her name Umbridge is the catalyst for great pain—mental, emotional, and physical—in the novel. She is Fudge's stooge and as such refuses to acknowledge that the wizarding world is in any danger. She is a staunch supporter of the ministry and is the ministry's means of direct interference at Hogwarts. She begins her post at Hogwarts as the new Defense Against the Dark Arts professor; this assignment is ironic since Umbridge fiercely asserts that there is no manifestation of the Dark Arts threatening her or any other member of the wizarding community. Her curriculum requires students to memorize and regurgitate information rather than learning about defensive theories or even practicing actual spells. She teaches her students only what will appear on their exams, reassuring that school is only about taking and passing exams.

Rowling's fondness for irony is demonstrated by her decision to make Umbridge the High Inquisitor of Hogwarts: This job requires Umbridge to evaluate the staff and practices of Hogwarts. As a teacher who cares nothing for student learning, Umbridge in her role as High Inquisitor is ludicrous. This irony directly parallels the beliefs of the ministry and its stance on Dumbledore's return.

Whether in her role as a teacher or administrator at Hogwarts, Umbridge's sadistic nature thrives. An example of her abusive punishments of students is Harry's detention for claiming that Voldemort has returned in front of his classmates: She makes him write "I must not tell lies" with a quill that, when used, engraves the message in the writer's skin. When Umbridge discovers Dumbledore's Army and summons Marietta to Dumbledore's office, she shakes the girl when she is unable to speak.

In perpetuating this cycle of violence, she eventually becomes a victim. Mastered by her desire for complete control over Hogwarts and desire to provide Fudge with more information on Dumbledore, Umbridge foolishly falls for Hermione's lie that Dumbledore has hidden a secret weapon in the Forbidden Forest. When she understands that she has been tricked, her anger mounts; simultaneously, the centaurs appear. Umbridge is a racist who believes in status based on blood rank (pureblood, half-blood, and Mudblood), and she also subscribes to the notion that humans rank far above all nonhuman creatures, some of the lowest classifications including half-breeds such as the centaurs. At the end of the novel Umbridge's abduction by the centaurs and ultimate rescue by Dumbledore seem to serve as Rowling's form of poetic justice. When she appears again in the narrative, she is visibly shaken and recovering from shock.

Voldemort/Tom Marvolo Riddle, Jr. Harry's nemesis, the antagonist of the series. He is hardly present himself in the novel, but the entire plot focuses on Voldemort's attempts to retrieve the prophecy. Voldemort believes this prophecy is key to his victory, although he is not entirely aware of its contents (having heard only sections of it from Severus Snape, who overheard the prophecy being described by Trelawney to Dumbledore). As a master of Legilmency (the practice of being able to penetrate, read, and control another person's mind) Voldemort is able to enter Harry's mind and gather information in order to strategize: An important example of this would be when Voldemort implants the image of Sirius being tortured at the ministry, because the image is fake but entices Harry to the ministry, and that is Voldemort's goal.

Voldemort's appearance at the end of the book is monumental. He has not been seen in the flesh since the close of *Goblet of Fire*. Voldemort appears in the atrium of the ministry, followed shortly by Dumbledore. The battle between the two wizards is epic and demonstrates what an enormous and real threat Voldemort has become. During his battle with Dumbledore Voldemort physically possesses Harry's body and taunts Dumbledore to kill him while he is enjoying it. His total occupation of Harry symbolizes the enormity of his power: Mocking Dumbledore during this battle suggests what is absent from his character, including his lack of respect for life and an absence of love, true loyalty, and friendship. The battle being staged in the ministry also illustrates Voldemort's confidence: The ministry is a public place and

wizards—especially Aurors—have easy access to the building. Voldemort's appearance here shows that he is ready to be witnessed and that he has acquired great strength. In the end he disappears from the ministry, not to be seen again until *Half-Blood Prince*.

Arthur Weasley Member of the Order of the Phoenix, employee of the Ministry of Magic, husband to Molly Weasley, and father to Bill, Charlie, Percy, Fred, George, Ron, and Ginny Weasley. Arthur is a vital member of the Order of the Phoenix, offering his insight and leadership. In the fifth novel he takes on the dangerous role of staying at the Department of Mysteries in the Ministry of Magic to protect the prophecy. While he is on duty, Nagini the snake attacks him, wounding him badly. Arthur recovers from this brutal attack, but this threat to his life encourages readers to think more seriously about the current, grave situation in the novel: Voldemort has gained a good deal of power and is a real threat. In almost dying for the order, Arthur shows himself to be a committed leader of the resistance in *Order of the Phoenix*.

One might expect Arthur to be a dedicated member of the order who plays an important role in its success because of the symbolism of his name. Rowling alludes to many well-known British literary traditions, including Arthurian mythology. Rowling's Arthur resembles the king of Arthurian folklore, a king whose knights were powerful and always questing (for example, for the Holy Grail). The knights of the Round Table—Arthur's knights—are like the order in that they face challenges that only the strong and dedicated complete. Rowling's Arthur has his own knights in his children; they all, at one time or another, join him and fight for his cause, which becomes their own. It is no coincidence that Rowling names one of Arthur's sons *Percy*, which is also the name of one of King Arthur's most famous knights, even as Percy abandons his familial obligations officially in this novel in the series.

Fred and George Weasley Twin sons of Arthur and Molly Weasley. In *Order of the Phoenix* they arrive at the legal age in the wizarding world (17) and in turn are eligible for an apparition license. Fred and George are good-hearted, loyal friends, founding members of Dumbledore's Army, and devoted to their family. When Malfoy insults their mother, Molly, at a Quidditch match, the twins instigate a physical fight. Known for their practical jokes and mischievous behavior, Fred and George give comic relief to the novel's dark war-threatened world. Their development of Weasley's Wizard Wheezes demonstrates they are bright entrepreneurs who value laughter and happiness: They create, test, and sell their own products, which become invaluable to the students at Hogwarts not only because some products have side effects that provide excuses to miss class but because the students of Hogwarts enjoy a good laugh.

Dropping out of Hogwarts is their most profound act since they know their mother (whom they love and respect) will completely disapprove. As members of Dumbledore's Army, they leave the school as a statement against Umbridge's tyranny; as people who appreciate the value of laughter they leave only after convincing Peeves to "give [Umbridge] hell" for them. Through the Weasley twins Rowling suggests that one does not need a formal education to be creative and successful. As long as they have good intentions (as do the Weasley twins), people can accomplish their goals.

Ginny Weasley   Founding member of Dumbledore's Army and the youngest of the Weasley children. As Arthur and Molly Weasley's only daughter, Ginny has always felt the protection of not only her parents but her six older brothers as well. Having been raised in a house of playful boys, she has also learned to hold her own and is gifted at cursing others, especially when she uses the Bat-Bogey Hex. Her talent with this hex in particular saves her and other members of Dumbledore's Army when members of the Inquisitorial Squad imprison her and some fellow D.A. members in Dolores Umbridge's office.

Being a member of the Weasley family also provides her with another important skill: the ability to play Quidditch. With so many brothers who love the sport Ginny also learns to play and to play extremely well. As her brother Ron does, she tries out for the Quidditch team and plays the position of Seeker after Umbridge bans Harry, Fred, and George from playing Quidditch. Rowling's choice for Ginny's Quidditch position is significant, since it aligns her with Harry and foreshadows the dynamics of their relationship in following books (where one seems to always be seeking the other). The position of Seeker is also, arguably, the most important position on a Quidditch team, so Rowling's giving Ginny this role signifies that women are an equally important part of the sport.

The novel also includes Ginny and some of her romantic encounters, demonstrating her maturity and growth from the young girl who merely stood speechless when seeing Harry in *Chamber of Secrets*. As does Ron, she goes into battle at the ministry. She suffers an injury during the battle, but her ability to fight, dedication to her friends, and passion for the order's mission are clear and continue to establish her as an increasingly significant character in the series.

Molly Weasley   The wife of Arthur Weasley and mother of the seven Weasley children. She is a member of the Order of the Phoenix and functions as a surrogate mother to Harry. In *Order of the Phoenix* readers learn the true depth of her fears (see the chapter "The Woes of Mrs. Weasley"). Though she is usually very controlled, Molly's composure breaks when she experiences significant terror at the thought of losing any of those whom she loves. Her experience with the Boggart in Number Twelve, Grimmauld Place, explicitly demonstrates her love for her family and, likewise, the fear she feels at possibly losing one of them.

Molly follows the straight and narrow; she criticizes those who break the rules and is especially disapproving of the petty crook Mundungus Fletcher throughout the novel. She feels heartbroken by Percy's official disowning of his family and feels especially betrayed because he is an extreme manifestation of an important element of her character—respecting the rules. She also disapproves of the Muggle world and its practices, highlighted in her annoyance with Arthur for getting the Muggle remedy of stitches after Voldemort's snake Nagini attacks him in the Department of Mysteries. Because she is a rule follower, Molly's disapproval of the Muggle world can be translated into one of her more general characteristics: fearing the unknown. As a woman living in a world where her family, friends, home, and safety are threatened by dark wizards, she has a natural fear. Regardless of this fear, however, Molly soldiers on and continues to serve as a caretaker and host for many characters, providing them with a home, safety, and love.

Percy Weasley The Weasleys' third-oldest son and employee of the Ministry of Magic. Percy has always been known for his desire to succeed and his strict obedience to rules. In *Order of the Phoenix* his job at the ministry supersedes even his allegiance to his family. He disowns them and does not even acknowledge his own father at work, treating Arthur as if he feels ashamed of him. Percy's love of power sways him, and his devotion to the ministry strengthens while his commitment to his family lessens.

Percy's name warrants analysis since *Percy* is a derivation of *Percival*. Percival, a legendary figure in Arthurian literature, was a knight at King Arthur's court. Legends of Percival are many and varied, but his connection to King Arthur's quest for the Grail remains evident. Although Percy strays from his family in the fifth Harry Potter book, considering his name as well as his father's (*Arthur*) in light of the British literary tradition from which Rowling borrows, Percy is very likely to see the error of his ways and once again become loyal to his family.

Ron Weasley Harry's and Hermione's best friend, founding member of Dumbledore's Army, and student leader. In *Order of the Phoenix* Ron is thrust into positions of leadership and into the limelight, a departure from previous novels: He becomes a prefect, Keeper on the Gryffindor Quidditch team, and a founder of Dumbledore's Army. Molly Weasley feels ecstatic that Ron has been chosen to be a prefect in his fifth year. She remarks that now he,

too, participates in the great tradition of leadership in the Weasley family. This fulfillment of tradition is exactly why Rowling's choice to make Ron a prefect is significant: Ron sometimes feels as though he cannot live up to the glorious reputation of his older brothers and discovers that he can and will. As one of the youngest of seven siblings, Ron faces enormous pressure to succeed.

While Ron may doubt himself, Rowling's and Dumbledore's confidence in Ron's role as prefect shows that readers should not. Ron's execution of this assignment seems mixed: He sometimes does not want to act on the difficult aspects of his job, such as reprimanding his brothers for their inappropriate behavior. He calls the younger students names like *midgets*, appalling Hermione. All things considered, however, Ron makes a good prefect because of his caring and dedicated nature.

Ron finds himself in another role of leadership when he becomes a Keeper for the Gryffindor Quidditch team. Ron's Quidditch position is significant: He prevents the other team from scoring, and so when they do, he feels much worse than the rest of the team since he is directly responsible for not stopping the Quaffle. Late in the novel Ron basks in his victory against Slytherin because he has become successful at another activity most of his brothers excelled in, and Ron lives up to the Weasley family tradition (and the vision he saw as a first year in the Mirror of Erised seems to be coming true).

Like Hermione, Ron encourages Harry to lead Dumbledore's Army so that he and his fellow students might be better prepared to defend themselves if they find themselves in a position of being attacked. As a founding member of this student organization Ron helps lead his fellow students into battle at the Ministry of Magic. In the Department of Mysteries Ron falls victim to a mysterious, tentacled brainlike creature that severely affects his mental abilities. Even though impaired during the battle Ron is still willing to support his friend Harry in this battle, demonstrating his character's growth from bystander to leader. Charlie and Bill Weasley are members of the order; Fred and George have left school to start their own business; Percy serves as an assistant to the minister. One could argue all the Weasley children are leaders, but it is Ron and the only female sibling, Ginny, who help Harry combat Voldemort and his followers. All members of the order fight in their own ways, playing to their own strengths to help the cause of the order, but Ron's engagement in the actual battle foreshadows his leadership in the subsequent books since the rest of his family will join him on the battlefront eventually.

FILM ADAPTATION

While the film adaptation of Rowling's fifth novel specially premiered in Tokyo on June 28 and in the United Kingdom on July 3, the rest of the world waited until July 11, 2007, for this installment of the Harry Potter movie series; the movie made more than $330 million its opening weekend. Fans of all sorts lined lobbies and streets for midnight showings, with the lines remaining throughout the weekend. The longest of the first five books, the movie was, in fact, the shortest of all the films with a runtime of 138 minutes.

The director, David Yates, knew portions of the book would have to be sacrificed for a successful translation of the story onto the screen. The adaptation omits some key subplots, such as Percy Weasley's estrangement from his family, Hermione's manipulation of Rita Skeeter, Neville Longbottom's personal tragedy, and Harry's encounters with the centaurs. The movie's focus remains on Harry's inner turmoil, emphasized by the movie's most well-known tagline, in which Voldemort tells Harry, "You will lose everything." The movie chronicles Harry's struggles at the beginning of the Hogwarts term—when fellow classmates and members of the wizarding community doubt him—to the end of the school year, when Harry realizes that without his closest friends he has no chance to withstand Voldemort. As such the movie highlights the meetings of the D.A., suggested by the movie's other taglines, "Evil must be confronted" and "The rebellion begins."

In an effort to include as many details of the novel as possible, however, the filmmakers worked to find a creative and effective way to incorporate segments of the narrative into mere seconds-long clips in the film. Building upon the important role newsprint plays in the development of the plot in Rowling's book, the movie capitalizes on the use of headlines to account for important events that are not otherwise awarded time in the movie. To reflect the doubt over Harry's claims about Voldemort in the beginning of the film, the headline "Potter or Plotter?" is displayed on the front page of a newspaper. Once Umbridge becomes High Inquisitor of Hogwarts, headlines splash across the screen: "Ministry Seeks Educational Reform," "Parents Endorse Ministry Move," and "Minister Fudge Puts Education in the Front Line," in order to demonstrate the ministry's interference at Hogwarts. Later in the film it is necessary for viewers to know how angry the centaurs have become since the centaurs' conflict with the wizarding community and ensuing attack on Umbridge are key to the plot. The filmmakers pay little attention to the centaurs (the scene from the novel in which Firenze becomes the new Divination teacher is entirely cut), and in order to account for these developments, the headline "Ministry Angers Centaurs" appears. Hagrid also makes a passing comment that he has never seen the centaurs "so riled up before." The end of the film must explain the change in atmosphere after Harry's battle with Voldemort at the ministry. In an effort to encompass the new climate of the wizarding community, snapshots of newspapers are shown declaring: "Dumbledore, Potter Vindicated," "Umbridge Suspended Pending Investigation," "He Who Must Not Be Named Returns," "Hogwarts Headmaster Reinstated," and "Minister to Resign?"

The newspaper as a narrative device in the film is reinforced by the newspaper clippings' tone: They are all a sepia shade. This bland color is fitting, as the film has a dull palette. Compared with the first four Harry Potter films, the fifth film is most like *Prisoner of Azkaban*, which is known for its darker hues. The lack of color in the fifth film amplifies Harry's own emotional state as well as the general mood of the wizarding community. At 15, Harry struggles with teen angst, emphasized by the drab colors used throughout most of the film. The headquarters for the Order of the Phoenix—Number Twelve, Grimmauld Place—is worn and dark, symbolizing not only the mania of the avid purebloods who once lived there (the Blacks with their family motto of *Toujours pur*—meaning "always, or forever, pure"), but the collective mood of the order, who are worried and tired from continuous strategizing against Voldemort and his legion of followers.

Similarly Hogwarts itself is nearly devoid of color; the one exception is Umbridge herself. Her pink suits contrast with the mournful Hogwarts landscape. Her office walls, drenched in chalky pink and dotted with plates featuring mewing kittens, mock the gravitas of the academic office she holds even as they mirror the feminine facade that masks her malevolence. Umbridge lovingly caresses the portrait of Fudge she keeps on her desk throughout the movie, illustrating her devotion to the ministry. Her adamant denials that Voldemort has returned and the way Yates stages these moments (with Umbridge's hands in fists and her voice rising shrilly) establish Umbridge's status as an outsider in the Hogwarts community. While others worry over or are at least suspicious of Harry and Dumbledore's claims, Umbridge's appearance emphasizes her status as an outsider, dressed ironically in cheerful colors.

Harry Potter fans anxiously anticipated the scene in which Harry has his first kiss with his love interest, Cho Chang. True to the novel Yates stages the scene after the close of a D.A. meeting. Harry and Cho stand alone, conveniently, under a bloom of mistletoe. Filmmakers lessen the romantic tension by having Harry mention Nargles (magical creatures that may not even exist and that are frequently referenced by Luna Lovegood); the mention of Nargles highlights Harry's entry into unknown territory—romance—with this kiss. Knowing this relationship will not progress any further, the filmmakers hint at the developing attraction between Harry and Ginny. When Hermione tells Harry that Cho "could not take her eyes off [him]" at a D.A. meeting, the camera pans to Ginny's face, which shows slight shock and disappointment. And later, before Harry and Cho kiss, the scene focuses on

the other members of the D.A. leaving the meeting. The camera focuses briefly on Ginny, who notes that Harry wants to be left alone with Cho: She looks at him a bit longingly and then walks off, crestfallen. Yates lays the foundation for the love relationship that becomes quite evident in the rest of the Harry Potter series.

New cast additions for this film include Natalie Tena as Nymphadora Tonks, George Harris as Kingsley Shacklebolt, Evanna Lynch as Luna Lovegood, Imelda Staunton as Dolores Umbridge, and Helena Bonham Carter as Bellatrix Lestrange. Evanna Lynch won the role over 15,000 girls and handmade the signature radish earrings her character wears in the film. Imelda Staunton became known for playing the part of Umbridge perfectly, pegging the annoying clearing of the throat and sweet but sinister, girlish giggle. As Voldemort's most loyal follower, Helena Bonham Carter in the role of Bellatrix Lestrange is unsettling and masterfully evil. Her unwavering devotion is obvious in her somewhat erotic response to the Dark Mark pulsing on the inside of her forearm, which she smells and practically licks. When she mocks Neville (whose parents she tortured into insanity), she captures Bellatrix's cruel nature.

The critical reception for the film was mixed. For instance, A. O. Scott claims in the *New York Times* that *Order of the Phoenix* "is not a great movie, but a pretty good one." Roger Ebert in the *Chicago Sun-Times* contends that the movie is "a well-crafted entry" in the series. With the exception of praising the phenomenal British cast, reviewers typically responded negatively to the film. The major criticism of the movie was the lack of magic and special effects so abundant in all the other Harry Potter installments. There are no adventurous trips down Diagon Alley, no great monsters to be fought, no dragons to outdo or complex puzzles to solve. Kenneth Turan pronounced that "the magic is gone: As the story gets darker, the momentum gets muddier" in the *Los Angeles Times*. The well-known critic Ebert asked, "Whatever happened to the delight, and, if you'll excuse the term, the magic in the Harry Potter series?" An even more striking review was that of Carrie Rickey (in the *Philadelphia*

Inquirer), who hoped that "book no. 7 is better than movie 5, a slog that might induce Potter fatigue even among stalwarts." But Bob Logino suggested otherwise, writing prophetically that *Order of the Phoenix* "will be another surefire box-office wonder" in the *Atlanta Journal-Constitution*.

WORKS CITED AND FURTHER READING

Adney, Karley. "From Books to Battle: Hermione's Quest for Knowledge in *Harry Potter and the Order of the Phoenix*." *Topic: The Washington and Jefferson College Review* 54 (2004): 103–112.

Atkinson, Michael. "The Broom of the System." *Village Voice*, 25 June–1 July 2003, p. 48. ProQuest Newsstand. Available online by subscription. Accessed December 30, 2007.

Barton, Benjamin. "Harry Potter and the Half-Crazed Bureaucracy." *Michigan Law Review* 104 (May 2006): 1,523–1,538.

———. "Harry Potter and the Miserable Ministry of Magic." In *Harry Potter and the Law,* edited by Jeffrey Thomas. *Texas Wesleyan Law Review* 12, no. 1 (2005): 441–443.

Carney, John, and Todd DeMitchell. "Harry Potter v. Muggles: Literary Criticism and Legal Challenge." *International Journal of Educational Reform* 14 (2005): 2–16.

Chevalier, Noah. "The Liberty Tree and the Whomping Willow: Political Justice, Magical Science, and Harry Potter." *Lion and the Unicorn* 29, no. 3 (2005): 397–415.

Cooper, Ilene. "Reading Harry." *Booklist*, July 2003. Academic Search Elite. Available online by subscription. Accessed December 30, 2007.

Craig, Amanda, and Lisa Allardice. "Cold Comfort at Hogwarts." *New Statesman*, 7 July 2003, 49–50. Academic Search Elite. Available online by subscription. Accessed December 30 2007.

Daly, Sean. Review of *Harry Potter and the Order of the Phoenix*. *People*, 7 July 2003, 45. Academic Search Elite. Available online by subscription. Accessed December 30, 2007.

Debling, Heather. "'You Survived to Bear Witness': Trauma, Testimony, and the Burden of Witnessing in Harry Potter and the Order of the Phoenix." *Topic: The Washington and Jefferson College Review* 54 (2004): 73–82.

Ebert, Roger. "Review: *Harry Potter and the Order of the Phoenix*." 10 July 2007. Available online. URL: http://rogerebert.suntimes.com/apps/pbcs.dll/article?AID=/20070709/REVIEWS/70620005. Accessed November 22, 2009.

Flaherty, Jennifer. "Harry Potter and the Freedom of Information: Knowledge and Control in Harry Potter and the Order of the Phoenix." *Topic: The Washington and Jefferson College Review* 54 (2004): 93–102.

Grossman, Lev. "That Old Black Magic." *Time*, 30 June 2003, 60. Academic Search Elite. Available online by subscription. Accessed December 30, 2007.

Harris, Marla. "Is Seeing Believing? Truth and Lies in Harry Potter and the Order of the Phoenix." *Topic: The Washington and Jefferson College Review* 54 (2004): 83–92.

Heilman, Elizabeth. "Blue Wizards and Pink Witches: Representations of Gender Identity and Power." In *Harry Potter's World: Multidisciplinary Critical Perspectives*. Edited by Elizabeth Heilman. New York: Routledge, 2003.

Hensher, Philip. "A Crowd-Pleaser but No Classic." *Spectator*, 28 June 2003, 30–31. Opposing Viewpoints Resource Enter. Available online by subscription. Accessed December 30, 2007.

Hughes, Robert. "Wizard's Return." *Wall Street Journal*, 27 June 2003, p. W13. Proquest. Available online by subscription. Accessed December 30, 2007.

Jones, Malcolm. "Something about Harry." *Newsweek*, 13 July 2003. MasterFILE Premier. Available online by subscription. Accessed December 30, 2007.

Joseph, Paul, and Lynne Wolf. "The Law in Harry Potter: A System Not Even a Muggle Could Love." *University of Toledo Law Review* 34, no. 2 (2003): 193–202.

Kakutani, Michiko. "For Famous Young Wizard: A Darker Turn." *New York Times*, 21 June 2003.

Logino, Bob. "Movie Reviews: *Harry Potter and the Order of the Phoenix*." 10 July 2007. Available online. URL: http://www.imdb.com/title/tt0373889/news?year=2007;start=21. Accessed November 22, 2009.

McCarron, Bill. "Power vs. Authority in *Harry Potter and the Order of the Phoenix*." *Notes on Contemporary Literature* 34, no. 5 (2004): 8–10.

Rickey, Carrie. "Harry Potter and the Lack of Focus." *Philadelphia Inquirer*, 9 July 2007. Available online.

URL: http://www.philly.com/inquirer/columnists/carrie_rickey/20070709_With_the_fifth_install ment_of_the_Harry_Potter_films_in_theaters_ tonight_and_the_seventh__and_final__tome_due_ in_bookstores_on_the_21st__Potter_fever_is_epi-demic_.html. Accessed November 22, 2009.

Robeck, Diane, et al. Review of *Harry Potter and the Order of the Phoenix. Publishers Weekly*, 30 June 2003. Academic Search Elite. Available online by subscription. Accessed December 30, 2007.

Sanchez, Julian. "Eichmann in Hogwarts." *Reason* 35, no. 6 (2003): 51–54. Academic Search Elite. Available online by subscription. Accessed December 30, 2007.

Scott, A. O. "Hogwarts under Siege." *New York Times*, 10 July 2007. Available online. URL: http://movies.nytimes.com/2007/07/10/movies/10harr.html. Accessed November 22, 2009.

Strimel, Courtney B. "The Politics of Terror: Rereading 'Harry Potter.'" *Children's Literature in Education* 35, no. 1 (2004): 35–52.

Turan, Kenneth. "*Harry Potter and the Order of the Phoenix*: The Magic Is Gone." *Los Angeles Times*, 10 July 2007. Available online. URL: http://www.latimes.com/entertainment/news/movies/la-et-harry10jul10,0,3170191.story. Accessed November 22, 2009.

Woodford, Donna C. "Disillusionment in Harry Potter and the Order of the Phoenix." *Topic: The Washington and Jefferson College Review* 54 (2004): 63–72.

Harry Potter and the Half-Blood Prince (2005)

SYNOPSIS

Chapter 1: "The Other Minister"

The hour nears midnight, and the Muggle prime minister considers the string of tragic events that have recently occurred in his world. Just when he thinks matters could not be any worse, he receives a visit from Cornelius Fudge, the former Minister of Magic (equivalent to the prime minister of the Muggle world). The Muggle prime minister feels apprehensive about this meeting, especially since whenever he has an encounter with Fudge, the news is never pleasant: The last time he met with Fudge, in fact, it was only to learn that Sirius Black, a convict, had somehow escaped from the wizarding world's best-guarded prison, Azkaban.

The Muggle prime minister's suspicions are confirmed when Fudge informs him that "He-Who-Must-Not-Be-Named" is responsible for many terrible events that have occurred recently (including the collapse of the Brockdale Bridge, several gruesome murders, and a rash of violence). When the Muggle prime minister asks what Fudge plans to do next, Fudge informs him that he has been "sacked" and that someone else has assumed the position of Minister of Magic; his name is *Rufus Scrimgeour*. Scrimgeour arrives, looking "shrewd" and "tough." He informs the Muggle prime minister that for his safety wizards—incognito—will be stationed in the Muggle ministry. The Muggle prime minister is appalled at this idea, but his concerns are somewhat quelled when he learns that one of his best employees, Kingsley Shacklebolt, is actually a wizard who has been working undercover for sometime already. Dismayed at the state of looming doom, the Muggle prime minister tells Scrimgeour and Fudge just to use magic to "sort out" the problems, to which Scrimgeour replies, "The other side can do magic, too" (18).

Chapter 2: "Spinner's End"

In a run-down industrial neighborhood there is a sudden popping noise, which yields a robed figure standing on a riverbank. Within moments another figure appears, and suddenly both are moving quickly, one chasing the other. The woman in the lead is Narcissa Malfoy (Draco Malfoy's mother), and she is followed closely by her sister, the dreaded Bellatrix Lestrange (one of Voldemort's most adamant and cruel supporters). Bella begs her sister to slow down as the two maneuver through the dingy neighborhood; Narcissa makes veiled references to finding a man whom Voldemort trusts, who lives in the dodgy village in which they have appeared. Bella, on the other hand, thinks Narcissa is making a mistake in seeking this gentleman and that Voldemort himself has made a mistake in trusting this man as well.

Once they arrive at the man's house, the door opens, and Severus Snape welcomes them into his home. Bellatrix distrusts Snape, and she begins to interrogate him, all the while questioning his loyalty to Voldemort. She asks a range of questions, including why Snape did not kill Harry so long ago, if Snape is, as he claims, loyal to Voldemort. Snape answers by explaining that working at Hogwarts for so many years has allowed him to gain Dumbledore's trust, and in doing so, Snape has proven himself to be one of Voldemort's most valuable assets. Narcissa, no longer able to keep silent, reveals how distraught she is because of the plan involving Draco (what exactly this plan concerns, however, is not revealed at this point in the narrative). Narcissa says that Draco is too young to be involved in the plan. Bellatrix, ever loyal to Voldemort, interrupts and tells Narcissa that she should be proud that her son has been chosen directly by the Dark Lord to be involved in the task. Narcissa responds that Voldemort chose Draco only to punish Lucius Malfoy (who was captured at the end of *Order of the Phoenix*). Snape says that it is not in his power to change Voldemort's mind about Draco's involvement; Snape also says that Draco must try to follow through with his orders, even though he feels Voldemort intends that Snape carry out the plan in the end.

This news causes Narcissa to break down completely, and Snape says there might be something he can do to help. Narcissa asks Snape to make an Unbreakable Vow to protect Draco. Bellatrix taunts Snape, still very doubtful of his loyalty, when Snape suddenly kneels next to Bellatrix and makes the vow, astonishing Bellatrix with his seriousness. The vow requires Snape to protect Draco and to carry out Draco's mission if the boy cannot.

Chapter 3: "Will and Won't"

The scene shifts to Privet Drive, where Harry sits waiting at his window. Dumbledore had written to Harry earlier in the summer to tell him he would personally pick him up that evening, at precisely 11 o'clock P.M. In the letter Dumbledore tells Harry he will escort him to the Burrow after Harry assists him with a "small matter." Distracted by the news of Dumbledore's arrival—and thinking that perhaps

the news was too good to be true—Harry has not yet cleaned him room or even finished packing. In the utter mess of his room papers lie everywhere, broadcasting various types of news. One article refers to Harry as "the chosen one" while summarizing his battle in the Hall of Prophecy in the Ministry of Magic; another chronicles Scrimgeour's taking office and "rumors of a rift" between the new minister and Dumbledore; yet another article informs Hogwarts students of how to guard their safety; and another piece is a pamphlet of instructions to help readers protect themselves from dark forces.

At exactly 11 P.M. a streetlamp goes out, signifying Dumbledore's arrival. Thinking that Dumbledore may not arrive as promised, Harry had neglected to inform the Dursleys of the possible arrival of his special visitor, news that, unsurprisingly, causes them great annoyance. Once Harry welcomes Dumbledore, they sit together with the Dursleys (against Vernon's wishes), and Harry notices that one of Dumbledore's hands is black and withered. Dumbledore launches into some important business: Harry's inheritance. Sirius Black (Harry's godfather) bequeathed all his belongings to Harry. Dumbledore assumes that Sirius's house (and the former headquarters of the Order of the Phoenix), Number Twelve, Grimmauld Place, is now also in Harry's possession, and a quick test will confirm this notion. Dumbledore tells Harry he must summon Kreacher (the Black's house-elf); if the elf responds to Harry's commands, then Harry is indeed the new owner of the home. Dumbledore summons the elf, and it arrives, screaming. When Harry tells Kreacher to "shut up," he does, proving that Harry owns not only the elf but the house as well. Harry commands Kreacher to go work at Hogwarts with the other house-elves in the school kitchen. Buckbeak, whom Harry also inherited, will stay with Hagrid.

Before leaving, Dumbledore reprimands the Dursleys for their poor treatment of Harry. He asks for their assurance that Harry may return to Privet Drive at least once more to make sure the magic Dumbledore evoked 15 years ago continues to work until Harry is of age (at age 17 in the wizarding world). Then Harry and Dumbledore walk into the night to, as Dumbledore explains, "pursue that flighty temptress, adventure" (56).

Chapter 4: "Horace Slughorn"

To complete their mission it is necessary for Harry and Dumbledore to Apparate to another location. Apparating feels like "being pressed hard from all directions" (58) and suffocating all at once. They arrive in a village by the name of *Budleigh Babberton*, where Harry learns one of Dumbledore's oldest friends is staying; Dumbledore hopes to persuade this old friend to return to Hogwarts. While walking, Harry questions Dumbledore about some of the information the ministry has posted concerning the Death Eaters and other allies of Voldemort. Harry is especially concerned about something called Inferi, which Dumbledore explains are corpses that have risen to do Voldemort's bidding.

When Harry and Dumbledore reach the house where Dumbledore's old friend stays, Harry is shocked. The front door hangs ajar, and once they enter the house, they are further worried because it is a complete disaster: Destroyed furniture, shards of glass, and even blood litter the home. Harry is shocked when Dumbledore does not seem overly concerned and instead starts poking around the furniture, stopping at a large armchair that, when poked, answers with an "Ouch!" The man whom they have come to find is Horace Slughorn, and he is disappointed that Dumbledore did not react more excitedly at the destruction of the house they are in, but the headmaster explains that had the Death Eaters really attacked, the Dark Mark would have been hanging grimly over the house.

Dumbledore asks his friend whether he will return to Hogwarts, but Slughorn says that he will not return to the school (he fears too much for his safety in these troubling times). When Dumbledore introduces Slughorn to Harry, the old man says he will not be persuaded simply by meeting this famous boy (although readers soon learn Slughorn has an affinity for famous people—he likes the benefits these connections provide, whether it be free candy or prime Quidditch tickets). Slughorn reveals that he was a former head of Slytherin and that he loved Harry's parents, but especially Lily Potter, since

she had a fantastic talent for Potions, the subject Slughorn used to teach. Slughorn reflects on some of the great tragedies of the war with Voldemort, and as Dumbledore and Harry prepare to leave, Slughorn decides he will go back to Hogwarts. After leaving, Dumbledore tells Harry that Harry would be "the jewel of [Slughorn's] collection" (75) of famous friends. Dumbledore and Harry talk about the loss of Sirius, the prophecy, and another interesting subject: Dumbledore plans to give Harry private lessons in the coming school year. Without revealing what the lessons will concern, Dumbledore accompanies Harry to the Burrow.

Chapter 5: "An Excess of Phlegm"

When they arrive at the Burrow, Molly is talking with Tonks, who looks upset and leaves almost immediately after their arrival. Dumbledore assures Harry he will see him at Hogwarts, and after he leaves, Molly provides a warm meal for Harry. During their visit Molly informs Harry that Arthur Weasley has been promoted to the head of the Office for the Detection and Confiscation of Counterfeit Defensive Spells and Protective Objects. Molly explains that the terror accompanying the war provides an opportunity for dodgy people to take advantage of vulnerable members of the wizarding community by creating fake (and sometimes even dangerous) spells and objects that promise to provide additional protection and safety. Arthur arrives home safely (even though all nine hands on the famous Weasley family clock are pointing toward "mortal peril").

Harry goes to sleep, but morning arrives quickly and Harry wakes up as Ron and Hermione enter his room, followed soon by Ginny. She starts griping about an annoying woman in the house, and Hermione joins in complaining; Harry feels shocked that the girls would talk so negatively about the only woman he knows of in the house, Mrs. Weasley. Harry discovers rather quickly there is another woman in the Burrow, however, when Fleur Delacour enters his room, carrying a breakfast tray. Fleur (the Beauxbatons champion in *Goblet of Fire*) and Bill Weasley are engaged; Fleur had an internship at Gringotts bank to practice her English and, while she was there, she and Bill (a curse breaker for the same bank) fell in love. All of the women in the home feel irritated by not only Fleur, but also the way most of the men behave in her presence. Because of her thick French accent Ginny has taken to calling Fleur "Phlegm."

The friends discuss other matters, including Tonks's obvious depression and then the prophecy, which Harry informs Ron and Hermione he heard, since the prophecy destroyed in the battle at the ministry was not the only copy. He reveals to his friends that he appears to be the only one who can destroy Voldemort and quotes the part of the prophecy that says, "Neither can live while the other survives." After revealing this information to Ron and Hermione, Harry suddenly feels much better. The O.W.L. results the students have been waiting for all summer finally arrive, and everyone is relatively happy with his or her score except Hermione and Harry. Hermione received only 10 "Outstandings" instead of 11, and Harry received only an "Exceeds Expectations" in Potions. Snape requires an "Outstanding" rank on the Potions exam to continue studying the subject during one's sixth year at Hogwarts, and Potions is required for one to become an Auror, which is Harry's ideal career.

Chapter 6: "Draco's Detour"
People continue to disappear, including Florean Fortescue and Mr. Ollivander. When the letters from Hogwarts arrive with book lists, Harry learns that he has been made Gryffindor Quidditch captain. The family and Harry and Hermione plan to make a trip to Diagon Alley, but the usually joyful anticipation leading to the trip deteriorates into anxiety due to the state of security and the coming war. When they arrive at Diagon Alley (via security cars provided by the ministry), they meet Hagrid, who is also sent to protect them as they gather their school supplies. Hagrid is overjoyed to see Harry and thanks him for letting him keep Buckbeak (now known by the name of *Witherwings*). In an effort to complete their shopping in a timely manner, the group splits up, with Harry, Ron, Hermione, and Hagrid shopping together. Their first stop is Madam Malkin's robe shop, where Hagrid waits outside, knowing the small shop will already be cramped enough without him.

Draco Malfoy is already trying on robes in the shop, accompanied by his mother. An argument ensues, during which Draco insults Hermione and Harry taunts Draco that Lucius (Draco's father) is held at Azkaban Prison. The skirmish ends with Narcissa's stating she and Draco will buy their goods at a shop that does not serve clients like Hermione, whom she calls "scum." Harry, Ron, Hermione, and Hagrid rejoin the others and soon find themselves in front of Fred and George's shop, Weasleys' Wizard Wheezes. In a time of sadness and worry the Weasleys' shop provides a place of laughter and lightheartedness. While they all enjoy themselves in the store, Harry becomes distracted when he sees Draco walking down Diagon Alley, his mother nowhere in sight. Harry, Hermione, and Ron sneak after him, watching him turn onto Diagon Alley. They follow him to Borgin and Burkes and then use a set of Extendable Ears to eavesdrop on the conversation between Draco and Borgin. Only hearing snippets of the conversation, they are unable to piece together exactly why Draco is in the shop, except that he needs Borgin to tell him how to do something with an object that he will not be able to take into the store. They also see Draco threaten Borgin, while mentioning Fenrir Greyback explicitly. Before leaving Draco also reminds Borgin to "keep that one safe" (125). Wondering what Draco could possibly have been talking about, Hermione enters the store once he leaves, attempting to discover what it was Draco was discussing; Borgin makes her leave the store.

Chapter 7: "The Slug Club"
Harry becomes obsessed about what Draco is doing, and his constant speculations annoy his friends, Hermione in particular. When Harry tells them his theory that Draco may have been initiated as a Death Eater, he feels extremely irritated that Hermione and Ron do not agree with him. As is traditional, the group travels to King's Cross Station to take the Hogwarts Express to school for the start of term. Before boarding the train, however, Harry tells his theories about Draco to Arthur, who also doubts that Draco, as a 16-year-old, would have been initiated as a Death Eater. On the train Harry searches for a compartment

(since as prefects, Ron and Hermione have other duties to attend to); he asks Ginny to sit with him, but she declines, saying she needs to meet Dean Thomas. Harry feels even more annoyed at this news. Instead, he sits with Neville and Luna, who are both happy to see him. A rude girl named Romilda Vane enters the compartment, telling Harry he does not have to sit with people like Neville and Luna, but loyal as always, Harry explains coldly to her that they are his friends.

While on the train Harry and Neville receive an invitation from Professor Slughorn to join him for lunch. When they arrive at Slughorn's compartment, they are met by other Hogwarts students, including Blaise Zabini, Cormac McLaggen, Marcus Belby, and Ginny. These students will form the newly reinstated "Slug Club," a group of students handpicked by Slughorn for their talents that might make them famous, their connections to famous people, or their own current fame. After the meeting and still curious about Draco's intentions, Harry follows Blaise (a Slytherin) back to his compartment. Wearing his Invisibility Cloak, Harry slips into the Slytherin compartment and climbs onto the luggage rack. Draco reveals nothing in his conversation except that he does not see the purpose of continuing or succeeding in his school exams since he is sure Voldemort will rise to power and all that will concern Voldemort is how devoted a person was to his cause, not the type or quality of that person's education.

When Hogwarts comes into view, all the students prepare to exit the train, but Malfoy stays behind in the compartment. Without warning Draco performs the body-binding spell on Harry; Draco must have realized Harry entered the compartment because of a few signs, including Harry's gasping uncomfortably when Goyle's trunk happened to hit him in the head as Goyle removed it from the luggage rack. Harry, his body completely frozen, falls from the rack, and Draco approaches him and then stomps on his face, breaking Harry's nose. He then covers Harry with his Invisibility Cloak and exits the train, leaving Harry bleeding profusely, with no one questioning his whereabouts.

Chapter 8: "Snape Victorious"

Harry worries about who, if anyone, will find him, since Ron and Hermione will assume he exited the train without them. As his anxiety reaches a peak, the compartment door slides open, and Tonks enters. She tells Harry that when she did not see him leave the train, she boarded the train to look for him. Tonks cleans up Harry as best she can and then sends a Patronus to the school to inform the staff that Harry is safe; the Patronus is a four-legged creature. Someone makes his way from the school toward Harry and Tonks, and once the figure is closer, Harry realizes in disgust that it is Snape. He badgers Harry all the way to the Great Hall, where Harry takes his seat at the Gryffindor table. Everyone is relieved to see him and stunned by the blood covering his face. Hermione helps him clean up.

Dumbledore makes his annual "welcome back" speech, including important announcements for the term. The most shocking announcement the headmaster makes is that Professor Slughorn will be the new Potions master, and that Severus Snape will now be the Defense Against the Dark Arts instructor. Harry is enraged. Dumbledore reminds the students to guard themselves carefully in their current situation, telling them, "Lord Voldemort and his followers are once more at large and gaining in strength" (168). After dinner Harry starts discussing his theories that Draco and Voldemort have formed a contact within the school and becomes irritated when others dismiss him. On the way to his dormitory Harry encounters Hagrid, who says he looks forward to seeing him, Ron, and Hermione in class the next day. After saying goodbye, Ron and Harry contemplate Hagrid's reaction when, tomorrow, none of his three closest and most beloved students will be in his class because none of them is registered for Care of Magical Creatures any longer.

Chapter 9: "The Half-Blood Prince"

The next morning the students receive their class schedules during breakfast in the Great Hall. Professor McGonagall helps get the students situated, and when Neville doubts himself because of his grandmother's remarks, McGonagall provides him with confidence. Harry worries about attending Potions because, assuming he would not be allowed to study the subject another year because he did not achieve an "Outstanding" in last year's exam, he did not buy the necessary supplies or textbooks for the course. McGonagall assures him that Slughorn will lend him supplies until he can acquire his own.

During their lesson with Snape, the Defense Against the Dark Arts professor, Snape cautions the students about the gravity of the subject they will be studying, especially considering the current situation. The first Defense Against the Dark Arts lesson concerns the study of nonverbal spells. Harry earns a detention after speaking during class and then responding to Snape in an antagonistic manner. After leaving the class Jack Sloper stops Harry in the hall with a message from Dumbledore: Their first private lesson will be Saturday night, the same night Harry is supposed to serve detention with Snape.

Later Harry, Ron, and Hermione find themselves in Slughorn's Potions class, where three potions are already brewing. Harry borrows some supplies from Slughorn, and then the names of the mysterious brewing potions are revealed (thanks to Hermione). The potions are Veritaserum, Polyjuice Potion, and Amortentia (a highly powerful love potion). Slughorn is impressed by Hermione's knowledge and upon learning her name asks whether she is related to a famous "Granger," to which she answers that she is Muggle-born. Shortly thereafter the class commences work on their assignment for the day, which is to make the Draught of Living Death. The person who completes this task best will be awarded a prize: a vial of a fourth mystery potion that Hermione correctly identifies as liquid luck, the formal name of which, as Slughorn explains, is *Felix Felicis*.

The students set about their task of making the draught, and Harry is annoyed with the book Slughorn has lent him: The pages are scribbled over with recommendations for making the potions. In some cases the directions are changed entirely. Harry decides to take the advice left by the previous book owner. When Slughorn informs the class that time has run out, Harry's potion is by far the

best sample in the room. Slughorn awards Harry the vial of Felix Felicis, and afterward Harry reveals to his friends that his potion was so successful because he followed the helpful notes left in the textbook. Ginny questions Harry about why he would obey the advice in the book, especially considering the debacle with Tom Riddle's diary from years before. Hermione performs a spell to see whether the book is cursed, but nothing happens, so Harry keeps it. He notices an inscription on the back cover: "This Book Is the Property of the Half-Blood Prince."

Chapter 10: "The House of Gaunt"
Dumbledore arranges matters so that Harry can still attend his first private lesson with the headmaster; Harry's detention with Snape will be served at a later date. Harry wonders what the lesson could possibly concern, since Dumbledore's office looks the same as usual. When Dumbledore explains that their lessons will involve some guesswork, Harry asks Dumbledore whether he thinks what he guesses will be correct. Dumbledore responds, "I make mistakes like the next man. In fact, being— forgive me—rather cleverer than most men, my mistakes tend to be correspondingly huger" (197). Dumbledore then explains that he and Harry will literally be taking a trip down memory lane: They will visit one of Bob Ogden's memories. Bob used to work for the Department of Magical Law Enforcement, and his memory involves an encounter with the Gaunt family. After dumping the memory into the Pensieve, Dumbledore and Harry join Bob on his journey.

Bob makes his way to the town of Little Hangleton, then takes a path through the darkening woods, stopping in front of a house that Harry is surprised to find inhabited. A man stands before them; he is extremely dirty, missing teeth, and "his eyes were small and dark and [staring] in opposite directions" (201). The man speaks, but Ogden does not understand him. Harry does, however, since the man, whose name is Morfin, speaks Parseltongue. An elderly man walks out of the house, annoyed at the presence of Ogden. He tells Morfin to get in the house. Ogden tells Mr. Gaunt he is at their house because Morfin committed a serious offense against wizarding law: He attacked a Muggle. Begrudgingly,

Mr. Gaunt allows Ogden into his home, where Ogden, Dumbledore, and Harry notice Merope, Gaunt's daughter. Gaunt presents himself as a pure-blood snob, making his feelings of disgust for those with less than pureblood status painfully obvious. At one point Gaunt even shows Ogden a family heirloom, a ring with the Peverell coat of arms. He also nearly suffocates his daughter while he yanks on a locket hanging from her neck; the locket was once Salazar Slytherin's, and Gaunt owns it now because he and his family are Slytherin's last living descendants.

Suddenly they hear a horse and carriage passing, and they can hear a girl talking to a young man named Tom, who says the house they are passing does not belong to his father, but most of the other land does. The boy and girl laugh and are disgusted by a snake they see nailed to the Gaunts' door. The carriage passes and the noise fades away. Morfin begins taunting his sister about the Muggle boy who just passed the house in the carriage and how she likes to wait in the yard just to catch a glimpse of him. Mr. Gaunt is angered severely by his daughter's taking such an interest in a Muggle. Gaunt becomes so enraged, he attempts to attack his daughter, but Ogden stops him. Ogden runs away, and Harry and Dumbledore leave his memory. Dumbledore explains that Ogden returned shortly thereafter with other officers to seize Morfin, who was later convicted for his crimes and sent to Azkaban. Dumbledore then also reveals that Mr. Gaunt, whom he refers to now as Marvolo, also served a short sentence in Azkaban for attacking some wizarding officials. Harry understands, then, that Mr. Marvolo Gaunt is Voldemort's grandfather and that the poor, frightened, terrorized girl—Merope—is Voldemort's mother. Another piece of the puzzle soon becomes clear: The young man in the carriage admired by Merope was Tom Riddle, Sr.

Harry asks Dumbledore whether Merope and Riddle married. Dumbledore says no and speculates that Merope must have used a love potion on Riddle. Dumbledore further explains that when Marvolo Gaunt was released from Azkaban, he returned home expecting to find Merope there, but instead all that awaited him were the decrepit

house and a letter from Merope chronicling what she had done. Harry wrestles with making sense of how Voldemort lived in an orphanage if Merope was using a love potion on Riddle. Dumbledore shares another theory with Harry: He supposes that since she truly loved Riddle, Merope eventually stopped using the love potion. She no longer wanted to trick Riddle into staying with her. When he discovered the truth, Riddle abandoned Merope, even though she was pregnant. Alone and destitute Merope gave birth to her son and then died. After these revelations Harry asks Dumbledore whether he really believes it is important to know about Voldemort's past, to which Dumbledore answers, "Very important, I think." Before leaving Harry notices that the ring Dumbledore wears is indeed the same ring he just saw on Marvolo Gaunt's hand in Ogden's memory. When Harry asks Dumbledore to tell him how he acquired the ring, Dumbledore ushers Harry out of his office, saying that time has grown short and their lesson has ended.

Chapter 11: "Hermione's Helping Hand"
Harry, Ron, and Hermione agree to go speak to Hagrid since they know he probably feels hurt by their no longer pursuing Care of Magical Creatures. While reading the *Daily Prophet*, Harry is particularly surprised by an article stating that Stan Shunpike (the Knight Bus conductor) has been arrested after being overheard talking about a plan involving Death Eaters. Hermione wonders whether Stan made this plan while placed under the Imperius Curse. The students make their way to the pitch for Quidditch tryouts.

Cormac McLaggen (a member of the "Slug Club") introduces himself and tries out for the position of Keeper, the same position as Ron. When Keeper tryouts begin, McLaggen performs very well. Nervous, Ron prepares for his turn when a girl's voice calls "Good luck" from the stands. Harry turns toward the voice, expecting to see Hermione, but instead sees Lavender Brown, who acted suspiciously earlier that morning when he and Ron passed her in the hall. Ron saves all five penalty shots, whereas McLaggen saves only four. McLaggen insists that Ron's tryout was unfair and demands that they both try out again. Ron saves all five penalties again, and McLaggen again misses one of the five. Ron secures the position of Keeper and comments that McLaggen was quite good and almost looked confounded when he missed the final shot; at this observation "Hermione turned a very deep shade of pink" (227).

Harry, Ron, and Hermione then go to visit Hagrid. At first, Hagrid refuses even to open his door to them, but eventually he lets them in. Hagrid seems annoyed and suddenly begins crying. He informs them that Aragog (his gigantic pet spider in the Forbidden Forest) is very ill. After this confession Hagrid is nicer to the students as they offer him comfort and apologize for not being able to take his course. After returning to the castle, they cross paths with Slughorn, who invites Harry and Hermione to dinner. Harry has his detention to serve with Snape, so his night is already committed.

Chapter 12: "Silver and Opals"

Halfway through October the students' first opportunity to visit Hogsmeade presents itself. The morning of the trip Harry wakes up early and pages through his (and the Half-Blood Prince's) copy of *Advanced Potion-Making* while in bed. Harry notices a spell scribbled on a page: "*Levicorpus* (nvbl)." Harry understands this to mean the spell is a nonverbal one. He begins repeating the spell in his mind, and suddenly Ron is jerked out of bed and finds himself hanging upside down in the air. Harry finds the counterjinx (*Liberacorpus*), repeats it to himself, and Ron falls back onto his bed. Hermione reprimands Harry for continuing to use the book and its added spells, but Harry ignores her.

While walking through Hogsmeade, Harry, Ron, and Hermione cross paths with Mundungus Fletcher (a wizard known for his thievery). Mundungus seems to be selling things, and as Harry approaches, he gathers his wares quickly. Enraged, Harry pins Mundungus against a wall: The thief is selling some of Sirius's belongings. Mundungus Disapparates, and the students go to the Three Broomsticks and try to calm Harry. After leaving the pub they find themselves walking behind Katie Bell and her friend Leanne. Katie holds something in her hand and seems to be arguing with Leanne. Suddenly, Katie floats into the air and then

begins screaming in horror. When Leanne, Ron, Harry, and Hermione pull her down, she continues screaming in pain. Harry goes for help, and Hagrid arrives and carries Katie back to the castle. Leanne tells Hermione that Katie went to the bathroom in the Three Broomsticks and returned holding a mysterious package; Leanne says that Katie said she had to deliver it to someone at Hogwarts.

Harry argues that the necklace must have been placed in the bathroom by Draco. He speculates that Draco must have bought the necklace the day they followed him into Borgin and Burkes. Harry even mentions this theory to McGonagall, who says there is not enough proof to accuse Malfoy. She adds further that Malfoy was not even in Hogsmeade since he was serving detention with her. They leave McGonagall's office with Harry still trying to convince Ron and Hermione that Malfoy is to blame, but neither of them believes Harry's theories.

Chapter 13: "The Secret Riddle"

Harry meets Dumbledore for his second private lesson of the year. The foundation of this lesson is formed by two memories: one from Caractacus Burke and the other from Dumbledore himself. Caractacus's memory is of Merope's visiting Borgin and Burkes and offering to sell her locket—Slytherin's heirloom. Completely destitute and alone, she is eager for any money, so Burke offers her 10 galleons, referring to the exchange as the "best bargain . . . ever!" Harry feels disgusted by the way Burke exploited Merope's situation.

The next memory is of Dumbledore's visit to the orphanage where Voldemort was raised. Dumbledore speaks with Mrs. Cole, the head of the orphanage. After a few drinks of gin she is willing to share some private information with Dumbledore about the mysterious Riddle boy. Mrs. Cole says that one night Merope arrived at the orphanage, and shortly thereafter, her baby was born, and within an hour after his birth, Merope passed away. Before she died, though, Mrs. Cole says, Merope said she hoped the boy would look like his father and that he should be named *Tom* (after his father) *Marvolo* (after his grandfather) *Riddle*. Mrs. Cole also adds that the boy seems to be a bit of a bully.

When Dumbledore introduces himself to the boy, the young Voldemort suspects that Dumbledore is a psychologist sent to evaluate him. When Dumbledore assures Tom that he is not there to inspect him, Tom answers Dumbledore rudely, demanding he tell the truth. Dumbledore explains calmly he is from a school that has a spot for young Voldemort if he would like to attend. Once again the boy thinks that he is being tricked and that Dumbledore is really from an asylum. Dumbledore reassures the boy and explains that the school he is from—Hogwarts—is a place where one studies magic. At this revelation young Voldemort explains that he can also do magic; he always knew he was much different from all the other children he had ever known. Suspicious again, the boy demands that Dumbledore prove himself to be a wizard. Dumbledore ignites a dresser on fire and, just as quickly, extinguishes the flames.

Dumbledore informs the young Voldemort that at Hogwarts (and in the wizarding world) certain laws and codes must be followed. He also instructs the boy to return anything he has stolen from his fellow orphans; Dumbledore says he will know whether the boy has followed his instructions and reminds young Voldemort that stealing is not allowed at Hogwarts. Dumbledore gives the boy more information about preparing for term, and before the headmaster leaves, young Voldemort informs him that snakes talk to him. As the memory nears its end, Harry and Dumbledore return to the present. Harry and Dumbledore discuss young Voldemort's personality and how, from even such a young age, he seemed to rely only on himself and knew he was "special." Dumbledore also draws Harry's attention to the way the young Voldemort "liked to collect trophies" (277). Dumbledore calls this to Harry's attention now, saying that the habit will also be important to the Voldemort they encounter in later years.

Chapter 14: "Felix Felicis"

Slughorn decides to host a Christmas party for members of his "Slug Club" only. Ron, clearly jealous that Harry and Hermione are both invited, says Slughorn's party sounds stupid. Hermione says that Ron's feelings are unfortunate because she was going to ask him to attend; after this revelation Ron's attitude brightens. Harry wonders what would happen if Ron and

Hermione became romantically involved. Later that evening Harry sees Dean and Ginny kissing on his way back to the Gryffindor common room. Harry is suddenly consumed with "a savage urge to jinx Dean into jelly" (286).

An impending Quidditch match between Gryffindor and Slytherin causes a lot of anxiety, for Ron, in particular. He threatens to resign as Keeper, worried about how poorly he will perform in the match. At breakfast Hermione says she sees Harry slip something into Ron's drink. Ron finishes his drink and then the team makes their way to the pitch. Gryffindor plays amazingly well, with the team scoring repeatedly, and Ron defending the Gryffindor goal brilliantly. Harry catches the Snitch, and Gryffindor is victorious. After the game Hermione confronts Harry, accusing him of pouring Felix Felicis into Ron's drink at breakfast. Using the liquid luck potion in any competition is illegal, and Hermione is furious with Harry for breaking the rules. But, much to Hermione's astonishment, Harry explains he only pretended to pour the potion into Ron's drink; he knew Hermione would see and say something at breakfast that would cause Ron to think he had been given the potion, and, in turn, he would play more confidently.

At a victory celebration later that day Harry and the rest of the Gryffindors are subjected to watching Ron and Lavender Brown kissing feverishly, their arms entangled. Harry leaves the common room, and ducking into a nearby classroom, he finds Hermione practicing spells alone. She has seen Ron with Lavender. Suddenly, the door opens, and Ron and Lavender also enter the classroom. Lavender leaves the room, and Ron says that he has been looking for Harry. The two boys stand quietly as Hermione walks toward the classroom door. Upon reaching it, she turns around and fires a spell at Ron that sends a pack of birds at Ron's head, where they attack him instantly. Hermione ducks out the door, and Harry thinks he hears her crying as she leaves.

Chapter 15: "The Unbreakable Vow"

Ron and Lavender are seen kissing constantly. Ron says Hermione should not be upset; he acknowledges that they were going to attend Slughorn's Christmas party together, but only as friends, and that really he is "a free agent" and Hermione "can't complain." Harry wonders whether his two best friends will ever speak to each other again. Hermione speaks to Harry about another romantic matter: She overheard Romilda Vane talking about slipping Harry a love potion. Harry, still without a date for Slughorn's Christmas party, asks Luna to be his guest. Later Hermione and Parvati stage a conversation in front of Ron in an effort to make him jealous. Hermione tells Parvati that she and Cormac McLaggen are dating and that she really enjoys dating a "good" Quidditch player.

At Slughorn's party Harry feels uncomfortable when Slughorn forces him into a conversation with Snape about Harry's talent for making perfect potions. Moments later Filch enters the party, dragging Draco behind him; Draco claims to have been trying to sneak into the party. Slughorn tells Draco he can stay at the party, even though he was not invited. Snape tells Draco he wants to speak with him alone. Suspicious, Harry leaves the party, puts on his Invisibility Cloak, finds Snape and Malfoy, and eavesdrops on their conversation. Snape admonishes Draco, saying that they "cannot afford mistakes." Draco defends himself against the accusation that he was somehow involved with Katie Bell's accident. When Snape tries to read Draco's mind for the truth, he realizes that Bellatrix has been teaching Draco Occlumency. Harry learns that Draco has been avoiding Snape and that Snape made the Unbreakable Vow to protect Draco. Draco refuses to tell Snape any of his plan and instead says Snape only wants to help him so he can take the credit for what will be accomplished. When Snape suggests that Draco is so upset because Lucius has been captured, Draco storms out of the office.

Chapter 16: "A Very Frosty Christmas"
Ron is shocked that Snape made the Unbreakable Vow, since, as Ron explains, if a person breaks the vow, that witch or wizard will die. During Christmas Eve dinner Mr. Weasley explains to Harry that Stan Shunpike may have been arrested so officials look as if they have "made some progress" in the war against Voldemort. In response to Harry's new suspicions about Snape Lupin reminds Harry that Dumbledore trusts him, and, in turn, others should trust Snape as well. Lupin says that he has been working undercover with the werewolves, trying to gain any information useful to the order. Lupin explains that the werewolves have sided with Voldemort because if he is victorious, the werewolves believe they will have a better quality of life. Lupin also provides some important information on the werewolf Fenrir Greyback: Unlike other werewolves, Greyback carefully plans every one of his attacks. Greyback is the wolf who attacked the young Lupin. Harry asks Lupin whether he knows anything about the Half-Blood Prince. Harry explains some of the spells he found in the used textbook, such as *Levicorpus*, and Lupin admits the spell was popular while he was at school with James Potter, Sirius Black, and Peter Pettigrew.

For Christmas Ron receives a necklace from Lavender with a charm reading "My Sweetheart" hanging from it. He is appalled. Later in the day Percy suddenly arrives at the Burrow, escorting the Minister of Magic, Rufus Scrimgeour. Mrs. Weasley is overjoyed at seeing her estranged son. The minister asks Harry to accompany him on a walk. The minister tries to wheedle some information from Harry about Dumbledore, but Harry remains tight-lipped. When the minister asks Harry (perceived by the public as the "Chosen One") to "stand alongside the ministry" to raise the wizarding community's confidence, Harry understands that Scrimgeour wants Harry to present himself as if he were working for the Ministry of Magic. Harry refuses, especially since the ministry did not act as Harry's ally when he told them Voldemort had returned. When Scrimgeour asks Harry whether he knows what Dumbledore is up to, Harry refuses to say anything and demonstrates his unfailing allegiance to the headmaster.

Chapter 17: "A Sluggish Memory"
After the students return to Hogwarts from winter break, they receive news about Apparition lessons; halfway through their sixth year at Hogwarts they are now old enough to learn the technique. Dumbledore and Harry have another lesson, which begins with Harry's questioning Snape's intentions. Irritated by Harry's asking whether he trusts Snape, Dumbledore says simply that he has already answered that question for Harry. One of the memories Harry will soon gain access to is Slughorn's, which concerns

Voldemort as a student at Hogwarts. Dumbledore explains that Tom Riddle was a very talented student and was liked by the staff. Tom Riddle also gained a following of very loyal friends who assisted him in many tasks (including the death of the girl who has become known as "Moaning Myrtle").

Before accessing Slughorn's memory, however, Dumbledore shares another with Harry. The memory shows a teenage Voldemort at the Gaunts' house, where he experiences a confrontation with Marvolo Gaunt (Voldemort's maternal grandfather). Marvolo tells the teenage Voldemort he looks exactly like the Muggle boy Merope fancied. Marvolo then refers to his own daughter as a "slut," and moments later the scene goes dark and Harry and Dumbledore leave the memory. Dumbledore explains that the day after the events in this memory transpired, the bodies of the Riddle family were found dead in their home (as is depicted in the opening chapter of *Goblet of Fire*).

The next memory Harry and Dumbledore visit is one of Slughorn's: It involves him and several male students, one of whom is the teenage Voldemort. The memory is stranger than any other Harry has seen: Every so often, the memory becomes cloudy and Slughorn's voice booms. In the memory the teenage Voldemort asks Slughorn about something called Horcruxes. Once teenage Voldemort poses this question, it is clear to Harry and Dumbledore that the memory has been altered and that Slughorn's answers, such as "I don't know anything about Horcruxes and I wouldn't tell you if I did" (371), are not what Slughorn originally said to his student. Dumbledore suggests that the memory has been altered because Slughorn is "ashamed" of what really happened. Dumbledore tells Harry he must find a way to get the actual memory from Slughorn, since the contents of the memory will be invaluable to them in gaining an understanding of how finally to defeat Voldemort.

Chapter 18: "Birthday Surprises"
When Harry mentions Horcruxes to Hermione, she has no idea what the objects might be. In Potions class the students are responsible for finding anecdotes for potions that each have poison in them. As Hermione points out, the prince's copy of the spell

book will not be of any use to Harry since he must first identify the potion with the poison. Harry performs miserably during the class but then realizes that the prince has left an important note about an effective antidote for victims who have ingested poison: "Just shove a bezoar down their throats" (377). Harry retrieves a bezoar from the supply closet, hoping to pass the lesson. Slughorn rewards Harry for his quick thinking, and Hermione is disgusted. After the lesson Harry asks Slughorn whether he remembers anything else about Horcruxes, upsetting the professor.

The students begin Apparition lessons, and during one lesson Harry overhears Draco talking to Crabbe and Goyle about something suspicious. Over the next few weeks Harry tries in vain to figure out Draco's plan. When Ron's birthday arrives, he eats a box of chocolates containing a love potion: The sweets were originally intended for Harry from Romilda Vane. After Ron insults Lavender, Harry takes Ron to see Slughorn in the hope that the professor can provide an antidote for Ron's lovesickness. Slughorn remedies the problem and then offers the boys a drink. Ron, strangely, falls to the ground and appears to have a seizure. Harry understands that Ron has probably been poisoned, darts to Slughorn's store cupboard of ingredients, grabs a bezoar, and shoves it down Ron's throat.

Chapter 19: "Elf Tails"
Ron's family and friends gather around his bed in the hospital wing; he will make a full recovery and while sleeping mumbles incoherently. One of these mumblings sounds like Hermione's name. Hagrid bounds in and, as usual, lets slip some information that should be confidential. This time he reveals that for some unknown reason Dumbledore is angry with Snape. Hagrid says he heard Snape tell Dumbledore that the headmaster "took too much for granted" (405) and that Snape sounded as if there was something he no longer wanted to do (but Hagrid has no idea what that might be). During the following days Cormac McLaggen takes Ron's spot as Keeper on the Quidditch team, and Lavender becomes a nuisance, always pestering Harry about Ron and what, if anything, is going on between him and Hermione.

At a Quidditch match Harry finds himself injured and then in the hospital wing. Suspicious of an encounter with Malfoy earlier that day, Harry has an idea. He summons Kreacher to the hospital wing; Kreacher arrives, wrestling with Dobby. Harry commands Kreacher to follow Draco and asks Dobby to follow Kreacher to see that the mischievous house-elf does as Harry has commanded.

Chapter 20: "Lord Voldemort's Request"

Harry learns that Ginny and Dean have had a major argument; he is quite interested in the details but quickly pretends his curiosity stems from the effect the situation might have on the Gryffindor Quidditch team. Harry hurries off to another appointment with Dumbledore. Dumbledore asks Harry whether he has obtained the unaltered memory needed from Slughorn in order to understand Voldemort better. Harry feels ashamed of not making retrieval of the memory more of a priority and promises Dumbledore he will get the memory for him. Before accessing another memory to learn more about Voldemort, Dumbledore informs Harry that Voldemort—after graduating from Hogwarts—desired a teaching job at Hogwarts. Dumbledore theorizes this desire stemmed from Voldemort's wanting to remain in his first true home and that if he were to become a teacher, Voldemort would have a lot of influence and power over young wizards.

When Dumbledore refused Voldemort a teaching job, Voldemort took a post at Borgin and Burkes, persuading people to sell valuable artifacts. One such example of this concerns Hepzibah Smith, whom the young Voldemort charmed. Hepzibah owned Helga Hufflepuff's goblet and Slytherin's locket. Two days after Voldemort's visit Hepzibah died; Voldemort had modified Hepzibah's house-elf's memory so that it would claim that it had killed its mistress. After a while Hepzibah's family realized two of her most valuable possessions had gone missing. No one saw Voldemort after that incident for many years. After viewing this memory, Dumbledore reinforces for Harry that Voldemort has a passion for collecting trophies.

Dumbledore shows Harry another memory: This one concerns Dumbledore and Voldemort, 10 years

after Hepzibah's death. Again, Voldemort asks for a post at Hogwarts. Dumbledore refuses him and questions Voldemort about his practices with magic and his loyal but troublesome followers. Once they leave the memory, Dumbledore confirms Voldemort wanted the post of professor of Defense Against the Dark Arts, proven by the fact that after Dumbledore refused Voldemort's request, the teaching position became cursed: No teacher has served in the role of Defense Against the Dark Arts professor for more than a year.

Chapter 21: "The Unknowable Room"

Ron explains that he is unhappy with Lavender and compares dating her to "going out with the giant squid" (450). Kreacher and Dobby arrive to give Harry a report on Draco: Dobby says that Draco keeps visiting a room on the seventh floor while other students stand guard. Harry has an epiphany, realizing that Draco has been visiting the Room of Requirement. Harry tries, without success, to access the room. Students continue to prepare for their Apparition tests by taking practice lessons in Hogsmeade while Harry remains at Hogwarts. Harry spends his time in the castle trying to track down Draco, and as he attempts to access the Room of Requirement without success, Tonks appears behind him. When Ron and Hermione return from Hogsmeade, they discuss the oddity of Tonks's leaving her post as guard of the school to search for Dumbledore in the castle.

Chapter 22: "After the Burial"

Hagrid informs Harry, Ron, and Hermione that Aragog the spider has died; Hagrid asks them to attend the funeral. Hermione convinces Harry to use his vial of Felix Felicis when attempting to gain access to Slughorn's memory about Horcruxes. Harry drinks the potion and instead of making his way to Slughorn's office gets a hunch that instead he should attend Aragog's funeral. On his walk to Hagrid's Harry encounters Slughorn and mentions his reason for heading to the groundskeeper's hut. Slughorn is immediately interested, since Acromantula venom (which Aragog possessed a great deal of) is very valuable. After the ceremony the men share some drinks. Realizing that both the adults are highly intoxicated, Harry seizes his opportunity to manipulate Slughorn into giving him the memory that concerned Horcruxes. Before cooperating, Slughorn admits he is ashamed about what the actual memory contains. Then Slughorn raises his wand to his head, removes the memory, and gives it to Harry.

Chapter 23: "Horcruxes"

Harry rushes to the office of Dumbledore, who is overjoyed with Harry's acquisition. The two dive into the memory to uncover the mystery of what exactly a Horcrux is. The teenage Voldemort asks Slughorn for information on Horcruxes, which Slughorn reveals constitutes practicing very dark magic. Slughorn explains that a Horcrux is "an object in which a person has concealed part of their soul" (497). If one creates a Horcrux, Slughorn continues, "even if one's body is destroyed, one cannot die, for part of the soul remains earthbound and undamaged" (497). Young Voldemort asks how one could even split the soul; Slughorn explains it involves unnatural magic that can only occur after one commits a murder. Voldemort then suggests that the more pieces one's soul is divided into, the more powerful one might become. He asks Slughorn whether splitting a soul into seven parts would confer the most power, since 7 is the most powerful number by magical standards. Slughorn becomes upset and asks Voldemort whether he is inquiring about Horcruxes only for academic purposes, and Voldemort confirms that he is.

After exiting the memory, Dumbledore thanks Harry for giving this information to him since it confirms his suspicion that Voldemort must have made several Horcruxes. The first Horcrux, which had already been destroyed—Dumbledore confirms—was Tom Riddle's diary (which appeared and was destroyed in *Chamber of Secrets*). Dumbledore had always assumed that Tom's lack of concern after the destruction of this first Horcrux signified that other Horcruxes existed. Since Voldemort would have wanted to become as strong as possible, Dumbledore assumes he split his soul into seven parts. And, since one of those parts remains with Voldemort in the body he now inhabits, there are five other Horcruxes to be accounted

for. Dumbledore reveals he has also destroyed a Horcrux himself: Marvolo Gaunt's ring, which caused Dumbledore's arm to wither and turn black. Dumbledore explains that he found the ring among the ruins of the Gaunt house while searching for information about Voldemort's past.

Harry and Dumbledore theorize about the remaining four objects that might house a piece of Voldemort's soul. They agree that, as one who favored precious objects of great importance, two of the other Horcruxes would probably be Hufflepuff's cup and Slytherin's locket. Dumbledore suggests that Voldemort would also have wanted to use objects important to Ravenclaw and Gryffindor. After some discussion Dumbledore proposes another theory that perhaps Voldemort's beloved snake Nagini may also serve as a Horcrux. If all the Horcruxes can be destroyed, so can Voldemort. Harry questions his ability first to find and then to destroy the Horcruxes, but Dumbledore assures him he will succeed because, unlike Voldemort, he is "pure of heart."

Chapter 24: "Sectumsempra"

The next day Ron informs Harry and Hermione that he and Lavender have split up; similarly, so have Ginny and Dean. Harry debates whether he should pursue his romantic feelings for Ginny, especially since Ron is his best friend and dating Ginny could complicate his relationship with Ron. Harry's pursuit of Draco continues, and one day he spies Draco crying. He overhears Draco telling Moaning Myrtle that he "can't do it" and that if he does not follow through soon, someone will kill him. Suddenly, Draco sees Harry spying via a bathroom mirror. The two engage in a battle, during which Harry screams, "*Sectumsempra*," causing blood to spill from Draco's face and chest.

Hearing Moaning Myrtle's screams, Snape rushes into the bathroom, tells Harry not to move, and takes Draco to the hospital. When Snape returns, he asks Harry where he learned such a spell. When Harry says he found the spell in a library book, Snape commands that Harry give him his schoolbooks. Harry convinces Ron to give him his spell book, and then, in dire need of a place to hide his own Potions book, Harry finds himself with access to the Room of Requirement. When Harry returns to the bathroom, Snape does not believe the book Harry shows him is Harry's and sentences him to detention. Harry misses a Quidditch match, but the Gryffindors are victorious without him. When Harry enters the Gryffindor common room, Ginny runs to tell him the good news, and without hesitation Harry seizes her and kisses her. After the kiss Harry meets eyes with Ron, who silently gives Harry approval to date Ginny.

Chapter 25: "The Seer Overheard"

Hermione tells Harry she wants to have a conversation with him about the Half-Blood Prince. Tired of her rebukes, Harry wants to avoid the conversation and merely laughs at her when she produces a picture from some time ago about Hogwarts athletics. The picture references the captain of the team, Eileen Prince. Harry gets an invitation to Dumbledore's office, and on his way, he runs into Professor Trelawney, who has just been in the Room of Requirement. After overcoming the shock that Harry—a student—knows about the room, Trelawney tells Harry she heard a male's voice in the room. Harry convinces Trelawney to tell Dumbledore about what she just heard, and as they walk to his office together, Trelawney reminisces about her first interview with Dumbledore. She mentions that her conversation with the headmaster was interrupted by Snape. At this news Harry realizes that it must have been Snape who informed Voldemort of the prophecy's contents.

But when Harry enters Dumbledore's office, he becomes distracted: Dumbledore tells Harry he believes he knows the location of a Horcrux, and he wants Harry to travel with him immediately to destroy it. First, however, Harry shares his frustration with Dumbledore in trusting Snape, especially since Snape was listening during Trelawney's account of the prophecy. Dumbledore tells Harry he believes Snape felt overwhelming regret for informing Voldemort of the prophecy's contents and reiterates, again, his complete trust in Snape to Harry. Dumbledore instructs Harry to get his Invisibility Cloak. When Harry retrieves his cloak, he begs Ron and Hermione to keep careful watch on Snape and Draco since Dumbledore will be out of

the castle that evening. He returns to Dumbledore, who rushes him out of the castle, and they Apparate to the vicinity of the Horcrux.

Chapter 26: "The Cave"

Harry and Dumbledore appear on a rocky shore with the sea below. Dumbledore assumes that as children some orphans from Voldemort's orphanage were allowed near here for some fresh air. Harry follows Dumbledore's lead by jumping into the sea and swimming to a rock with a slit in it. Upon climbing through the slit in the rock, Harry realizes they are at the opening of a large cave. After Dumbledore offers some of his own blood as payment, Harry and Dumbledore enter the cave, which houses a great black lake. A green light emanates from the center of the lake, where, Dumbledore suspects, the Horcrux is being kept. Harry and Dumbledore board a boat probably left by Voldemort when he hid the Horcrux and make their way to the middle of the lake. Harry notices that there are bodies under the lake surface; Dumbledore assumes that these bodies will not remain so still once they retrieve the Horcrux.

When Harry and Dumbledore reach a small island in the middle of the lake, they find something like a basin on a pedestal filled with a green liquid. They assume the Horcrux lies in the liquid. Because they are unable to stick their hands into the potion, Dumbledore deduces that they must drink the potion to retrieve whatever rests underneath it. Dumbledore tells Harry that he will drink the potion and that, no matter what happens, he must make sure that Dumbledore drinks all of the potion so Harry can retrieve the Horcrux. Dumbledore drinks the potion and soon is miserable and crying for mercy. Pained at the sight of Dumbledore in agony, Harry tries to comfort him as Dumbledore finishes all of the potion in the basin even while begging for death. Dumbledore collapses begging for water, and Harry uses a spell to conjure some water in a goblet, but just as quickly as the goblet fills with water, it disappears before Dumbledore can drink any of it. Harry attempts to get some water from the lake; when the water's surface is disturbed, the bodies come to life and start to attack. Dumbledore creates a magnificent ring of fire around himself and Harry, scoops the locket (the presumed Horcrux) out of the basin, and leads Harry back to the boat. They make their way back to the mouth of the cave, and Harry assures Dumbledore they will succeed in their mission.

Chapter 27: "The Lightning-Struck Tower"

Harry takes hold of Dumbledore, and they Apparate to Hogsmeade. Harry suggests they ask Madam Rosmerta for help, but Dumbledore asks for Snape. Within minutes Madam Rosmerta appears, explaining she saw Harry and Dumbledore from her window. Dumbledore realizes something is wrong, and his suspicions are confirmed when Madam Rosmerta points to the Dark Mark hanging in the air above Hogwarts. She provides them with brooms, and they fly to the castle and land on a tower. Dumbledore commands Harry to go get Snape, and as Harry heads to the door leading inside, he hears voices. The door thrusts open. Someone screams a disarming spell, and simultaneously Harry's body goes rigid and falls propped against a tower wall, covered with his Invisibility Cloak.

Dumbledore's wand goes flying from his hand and off the tower as Draco steps onto the tower roof. Harry gathers that Dumbledore has immobilized him to protect him. Draco explains that members of Voldemort's forces have already invaded the castle and are engaged in battle. Draco used a discarded Vanishing Cabinet to help dark wizards infiltrate the castle. One of the cabinets is stationed in the Room of Requirement, the other at Borgin and Burkes (so finally Harry realizes what it was Draco spoke with the shopkeeper about before the start of the school year: the set of Vanishing Cabinets). Dumbledore speaks to Draco, telling the boy that he is not a killer and that he does not have to follow through with any mission set upon him by Voldemort. Dumbledore even offers Draco and his mother amnesty if he chooses to go over to the side of the order.

Suddenly, several others join Harry, Draco, and Dumbledore on the tower, including Fenrir Greyback and some Death Eaters. They command Draco to kill Dumbledore, but he falters. The tower doors burst open again, and Snape appears. The Death Eaters continue arguing over who should kill Dumbledore when a voice interrupts: Dumbledore

whispers Snape's name. Snape makes his way to the front of the crowd, and Dumbledore pleads with Snape, begging "Severus . . . please . . ." At this plea Snape draws his wand and shouts, "*Avada Kedavra!*" and Dumbledore's lifeless body—with the force of the killing curse—is lifted from the tower and flung over the edge into the darkness.

Chapter 28: "Flight of the Prince"

Although stunned into disbelief, Harry realizes he can move again. He removes his Invisibility Cloak and makes his way down the steps into the heart of the castle. Harry sees Ginny, Neville, McGonagall, and others engaged in battle but remains in pursuit of Snape. Finally within reach of him, Harry fires a curse at Snape. Harry misses and hears Snape command Draco to run. As Harry continues trying to attack Snape, someone places the Cruciatus Curse on Harry; seeing this, Snape screams, "No!" and suddenly Harry's pain vanishes. Undeterred, Harry follows Snape and attempts the *Sectumsempra* spell. At this Snape becomes enraged and tells Harry he will not use one of Snape's own spells on him. Snape reveals that he is the Half-Blood Prince. Harry calls Snape a coward, and now furious, Snape sets a spell on Harry; in the wake of the spell's effects Snape escapes.

Hagrid appears and refuses to believe what Harry tells him: Snape has killed Dumbledore. When they find Dumbledore's body, Harry realizes he is kneeling on the locket he and Dumbledore recovered earlier that evening. But when Harry examines the locket, worry overcomes him: It is very different from the one he saw in the memory of Hepzibah Smith's showing the young Voldemort the object. Inside the locket is a scrap of paper from R.A.B. with a message for the Dark Lord. The message explains that R.A.B. knows he will be dead before Voldemort ever sees the locket, and that R.A.B. stole the real Horcrux and planned to destroy it. Harry feels more discouraged than ever, believing that Dumbledore weakened himself and then died for nothing.

Chapter 29: "The Phoenix Lament"

Once back in the school Harry confronts the remains of the battle. Bill Weasley was attacked by Fenrir Greyback, but since Greyback was not transformed into a werewolf at the time, Bill will not turn into a werewolf later. Harry informs some of the others of Dumbledore's death. Most of them question Dumbledore's trust for Snape, and McGonagall feels personally responsible for Dumbledore's death because she asked Professor Flitwick to find Snape and help them during the battle in the castle. Harry also reveals that Draco was able to sneak Death Eaters inside Hogwarts.

While they are discussing the logistics of the battle, Molly and Arthur Weasley arrive to visit Bill. Molly is distraught, especially since, as she puts it, Bill "was going to be married!" (622). Fleur is outraged and asks Molly whether she thinks Fleur would no longer marry Bill simply because he was attacked by a werewolf; Fleur adds that she is "good-looking enough" for both of them and then tends to Bill. Suddenly, Molly tells Fleur that a family member has a tiara that would look beautiful on Fleur the day of their wedding. Fleur understands this is Molly's way of offering a truce, and the two embrace each other.

Tonks then cries, "You see . . . she still wants to marry him!" (623). To which Lupin responds, "It's different." Finally, the root of Tonks's misery is discovered: She is in love with Lupin, but he has rejected her advances because he thinks he is too old and poor for her, and he is a werewolf. Saddened by Dumbledore's death, Lupin tries to deflect the conversation, but McGonagall reminds him that Dumbledore would be happy two people had found love. She escorts the group to Dumbledore's office, where a new portrait already hangs with Dumbledore sleeping inside it. The heads of house—along with other staff—discuss the future of Hogwarts, debating whether the school will even be open next year. It is agreed (albeit reluctantly by some) that the students should remain on the Hogwarts campus for Dumbledore's funeral, if they so desire.

Chapter 30: "The White Tomb"

Wizards and witches arrive in droves for Dumbledore's funeral. As Harry thinks obsessively about the identities of the true Horcruxes, Hermione gives him some news about Snape. She found some interesting information while further researching Eileen

Prince, who she assumed once owned the Potions book. Eileen Prince married Tobias Snape. Eileen was Snape's mother, and Hermione discovers in an article in an old issue of the *Prophet* that Tobias Snape was a Muggle, making Snape a half-blood.

Dumbledore's funeral is held on a beautiful day. Before the ceremony begins, strange music begins to sound: It is the song of the merpeople, paying their respects to their good and loyal friend Dumbledore. Harry feels consumed with grief for Dumbledore, regretting that he had not known the headmaster better. Harry also contemplates how one by one, people who love him have sacrificed themselves for his sake: He resolves that now he will confront Voldemort himself and seek justice.

Without warning towering white flames encase Dumbledore's body and the table he rested on. When the fire disappears, a white tomb is left in its place. As other people and creatures pay tribute, Harry tells Ginny they should no longer be involved with each other since Voldemort could use her or harm her in an effort to hurt Harry. Moments later Scrimgeour approaches Harry again. The minister desperately wants some information concerning Dumbledore, but Harry refuses, remaining "Dumbledore's man, through and through" (649). Harry tells Ron and Hermione that he plans to return to Privet Drive once more, since Dumbledore wanted him to; after that Harry plans to visit Godric's Hollow. Hermione and Ron vow to accompany Harry wherever he plans to go, reminding him they could have bowed out of their adventures together long ago. Ron reminds them all that their summer will include a trip to the Burrow for Bill and Fleur's wedding. With danger looming Harry relishes this future day of peace with his friends.

CRITICAL COMMENTARY

Half-Blood Prince follows the series's darkest novel, *Order of the Phoenix*. Umbridge's reign of terror and Voldemort's return ignited pain, suspicion, and doubt in all members of the wizarding community, and many of those doubts concern allegiance and whether characters such as Snape are loyal to Dumbledore or Voldemort. Class consciousness and elitism continue to plague Rowling's world and serve as the basis for Voldemort's pureblood fanaticism. This novel also provides readers with a better understanding of Voldemort through glimpses into his personal history, during which he transforms from an orphan into the terrible Dark Lord. Readers learn that Voldemort—and men such as Slughorn and even Dumbledore—have a passion for collecting, and Rowling explores the dynamics and implications of emotional attachment to material things. The most important theme Rowling treats in *Half-Blood Prince*, however, is love. She examines how love becomes vital in times of despair and depicts love as the strongest type of magic.

Suspicion and Doubt

The wizarding community, threatened by Voldemort's return to power, is plagued in this sixth novel with constant suspicion and a climate of fear: Death Eaters potentially linger behind every corner, and once-trusted friends may be acting under the Imperius Curse—as was Madam Rosmerta, whose enchantment was critical to Dumbledore's death and the battle at Hogwarts at the end of the novel. A major theme of *Half-Blood Prince* is the consuming nature of suspicion and doubt, illustrated by characters including Harry Potter, Draco Malfoy, and, of course, Severus Snape.

Harry is a cause for suspicion, but also a doubter himself. Building on the events in *Order of the Phoenix*, during which much of the wizarding community views Harry with suspicion for claiming that Voldemort has returned, Rowling opens *Half-Blood Prince* by confronting those suspicions. Aware of a battle in the Department of Mysteries at the Ministry of Magic, people wonder about the contents of the prophecy and wonder whether Harry Potter can provide their path to survival: As a *Prophet* reporter writes, "Some are going as far as to call Potter 'the Chosen One,' believing that the prophecy names him as the only one who will be able to rid us of He-Who-Must-Not-Be-Named" (39). A writer of another article in the *Prophet* reveals suspicion of Harry in the title "Harry Potter: The Chosen One?" Even though Harry's claims that Voldemort has returned are completely vindicated by the beginning of *Half-Blood Prince*, people still question and suspect Harry; Rowling suggests that even if one

can be believed—as Harry eventually is—in times of great fear, suspicions cloud even the clearest minds. Rowling also suggests that although this dramatic reversal of public opinion exonerates Harry of accusations of insanity or attention seeking, it also reveals the fickle nature of public perception.

For the majority of the novel Harry suspects Malfoy of wrongdoing and finds himself preoccupied with discovering every detail of Malfoy's whereabouts and his actions. Hermione and Ron scoff at Harry's ideas, figuring they are rooted in Harry's intense personal dislike for Malfoy rather than a genuine threat. Concerned that Malfoy has been initiated as a Death Eater, Harry tries to convince his friends of the validity of his theories while riding the Hogwarts Express to the school: "She didn't touch him, but he [Draco] yelled and jerked his arm away from her when she went to roll up his sleeve. It was his left arm. He's been branded with the Dark Mark" (130). Ron and Hermione tire quickly of hearing Harry's elaborate theories. Their quick dismissal of Harry's ideas demonstrates that they have lost some of their vigilance (despite the urgings of Mad-Eye Moody that they maintain it constantly). Even if Harry desperately searches for ways to assign guilt to Malfoy, their refusal to entertain Harry's theories about the son of a confirmed Death Eater is on some level ironic, since Harry's doubts and theories are completely founded.

Perhaps the case arousing the most suspicion and doubt in readers is Dumbledore's unwavering belief in Snape's allegiance to the Order of the Phoenix. Since his arrival in the wizarding world, Harry has questioned Dumbledore's trust in Snape, partly because he himself is treated so viciously by Snape and partly because he quickly learns about Snape's past associations with Voldemort. Harry's skepticism of Snape's loyalties is always addressed immediately by Dumbledore: When Harry refers to the Potions master as "Snape," Dumbledore rebukes Harry and tells him to call his teacher "*Professor* Snape," stressing that Snape deserves respect (79). Snape's repeatedly saving Harry's life (as when Quirrell attempted to jinx Harry's broom in *Sorcerer's Stone* and when he protected Harry from the massive Dementor attack in *Prisoner of*

Azkaban) has done nothing to curb Harry's doubts about Snape and, consequently, Dumbledore's continued trust in the former Death Eater. Dumbledore does not calm Harry's doubts when he says: "I make mistakes like the next man. In fact, being—forgive me—rather cleverer than most men, my mistakes tend to be correspondingly huger" (197). If Snape's allegiance lies with Voldemort instead of Dumbledore, the consequences would be catastrophic, and as a result, despite his confidence in Dumbledore's judgment in nearly all other matters, Harry cannot and does not trust Dumbledore's judgment concerning Snape. Harry even broaches the subject with Lupin, who responds, "People have said it, many times. It comes down to whether or not you trust Dumbledore's judgment. I do; therefore I trust Severus" (332). Snape's murder of Dumbledore seems to confirm Harry's doubts, but Dumbledore's colleagues remain in shock. They had never known Dumbledore to make such an egregious error in judgment. Dumbledore's belief in and death at the hands of Snape foreshadow the themes of *Deathly Hallows*, in which more of Dumbledore's questionable decisions shock readers.

Allegiance

Most suspicions in the novel arise from questions surrounding a given character's allegiance, which serves as another major theme in the novel. The most important cases of questionable allegiance concern Snape, the Malfoy family, and Harry. Snape's allegiance to Voldemort seems obvious after he murders Dumbledore, but Rowling incorporates details throughout the entire novel, well before the climactic murder scene, that communicate to readers his allegiance to the Dark Lord. Narcissa Malfoy tells her sister, Bellatrix, that she believes in Snape's loyalty to Voldemort because Voldemort himself believes Snape is loyal to him. Bellatrix answers, "The Dark Lord is . . . I believe . . . mistaken" (21). Snape defends himself carefully to Bellatrix and Narcissa: He tells the women, "I have played my part well. . . . And you overlook Dumbledore's greatest weakness: He has to believe the best of people. I spun him a tale of deepest remorse when I joined his staff, fresh from my Death Eater days, and he embraced me with open arms" (31). Shortly after

this confession Snape renders Bellatrix speechless when he agrees to make the Unbreakable Vow with Narcissa: His decision to make this vow seemingly confirms his support of the Dark Lord. Furthermore, Rowling reveals that Snape overheard Sybill Trelawney tell Dumbledore the original prophecy. Snape then informed Voldemort of the prophecy's prediction. Harry considers this betrayal as the most damning evidence of Snape's guilt, even though Dumbledore explains that the remorse Snape felt for telling Voldemort the prophecy serves as the basis for his allegiance to the order.

Almost all evidence throughout this novel signals that Snape's loyalty lies with Voldemort. A few details, however, cast doubt on this theory and suggest that Snape's allegiance may actually be to Dumbledore, ambiguity upon which the author capitalizes. One such detail concerns a conversation Hagrid overhears between Dumbledore and Snape. Hagrid tells Harry, "I jus' heard Snape sayin' Dumbledore took too much fer granted an' maybe he—Snape—didn' wan' ter do it anymore" (405). Perhaps Dumbledore devised an elaborate plan in which Snape must *appear* to have betrayed Dumbledore; the apparent betrayal would, in fact, help lead to Voldemort's downfall. Some readers think that Hagrid's saying Snape no longer wanted "ter do it anymore" refers to a plan by Dumbledore. The major challenge to this theory is that Snape murders Dumbledore, an act that seems to confirm his betrayal of the order. But killing Dumbledore would convince anyone—even Voldemort—that Snape's allegiance is to the Dark Lord. Some readers continued to believe that Dumbledore's murder was, in fact, part of the plan he devised in an effort to portray Snape as loyal to Voldemort while Snape actually continued to work as a double agent for the order. Such a theory, however, could not be fully proven until the conclusion of *Deathly Hallows*. The other problem with this theory is what Dumbledore says to Snape before Snape murders him: "Severus . . . please . . ." (595). These words show Dumbledore pleading for Snape to spare his life; on the other hand, these words may be Dumbledore's way of begging Snape to follow through with Dumbledore's plan in which Snape must murder him.

Snape's allegiance cannot be determined on the basis of his actions in this novel. Even though most evidence indicates that Snape's allegiance is to Voldemort, Rowling includes details (such as the conversation Hagrid overhears between Dumbledore and Snape) that allow readers to interpret Snape's allegiance in multiple ways. Perhaps Rowling's point in raising some suspicion, however small, about Snape's allegiance is that allegiance is truly fragile and that all are susceptible to being swayed—for good or for bad.

The Malfoys also present readers with a poignant example of the complicated dynamics associated with the concept of allegiance. In this book Narcissa demonstrates unflagging allegiance to her son. She tells Bellatrix, "There is nothing I wouldn't do anymore!" to protect Draco (21). Narcissa's devotion to Malfoy is executed beautifully in the film version of *Half-Blood Prince,* in which Narcissa, dressed in elegant robes, her face stained with tears, begs Snape to protect her son. The Unbreakable Vow made between Snape and Narcissa also requires that Snape murder Dumbledore if Draco fails to kill him. Rowling in her depiction of Narcissa implies that a mother must do whatever is necessary to protect her child, even if it involves turning an ally (Snape) into a murderer; this trope reinforces some of the series's larger themes about parental protection and maternal sacrifice, such as Lily Potter's sacrifice of her own life for her son's.

Draco's allegiance, unlike his mother's, wavers. He believes himself a follower of Voldemort, bragging to his classmates that he may not complete his Hogwarts education so he can serve the Dark Lord instead. His aunt Bellatrix remarks of her nephew: "I will say this for Draco: He isn't shrinking away from his duty, he seems glad of the chance to prove himself, excited at the prospect" (33). He assists the Death Eaters in entering the castle, precipitating the novel's explosive final battle between the Order of the Phoenix and a group of Death Eaters, but cannot perform the specific task assigned to him by Voldemort of murdering Dumbledore. Even when Draco has a perfect opportunity to execute the headmaster, who has been rendered defenseless, he cannot make himself use the Killing Curse.

Dumbledore tries to exploit this failure of nerve, recognizing it for what it is—an ambivalence over fully committing himself to the Dark Arts: "You have been trying, with increasing desperation, to kill me all year. Forgive me, Draco, but they have been feeble attempts. . . . So feeble, to be honest, that I wonder whether your heart has really been in it" (585). Draco's vacillating over murdering Dumbledore shows that he is torn over this task and, likewise, uncomfortable with the future he faces: living as a murderer and as a follower of Voldemort. Malfoy, now almost of adult age in the wizarding world, yearns to make his own choices, to determine his own fate instead of blindly following the beliefs and actions of his parents. Perceptive as always, Dumbledore verbalizes Draco's struggle for him in suggesting his heart does not support his actions. That Draco cannot follow through with the task assigned him by Voldemort suggests that Draco will turn away from the Death Eaters.

Though Harry is suspicious about Dumbledore's belief in Snape, he remains staunchly loyal to the Hogwarts headmaster; this loyalty is showcased vividly in *Half-Blood Prince.* Desperate for a mascot to raise morale, the new Minister of Magic, Rufus Scrimgeour, appeals to Harry several times to support the ministry publicly. Harry catches on to Scrimgeour's plot easily, asking, "So basically . . . you'd like me to give the impression that I'm working for the Ministry?" (345). Knowing that the ministry staff wrongfully imprisons people such as Stan Shunpike just to appear that they are making progress in the war against Voldemort, Harry refuses to support the ministry, just as his mentor Dumbledore does. Harry tells Scrimgeour that he does not "like some of the things the Ministry's doing" (346). Furious, Scrimgeour responds, "Dumbledore's man through and through, aren't you Potter?" (348); Harry proudly supports Dumbledore. Harry has only known two Ministers of Magic, Fudge and Scrimgeour, and Harry never argued about the ministry's actions with Fudge, incompetent as he was. Harry's openly criticizing the practices of the ministry to Scrimgeour testifies to his allegiance to Dumbledore.

The other instance that best stresses Harry's fierce loyalty to Dumbledore concerns the retrieval of the locket, which they both believe to be a Horcrux. Dumbledore gives Harry strict orders not to be swayed by anything Dumbledore might say. They reach the locket in the cave, which can only be retrieved by drinking a toxic potion; as Dumbledore drinks, he pleads madly with Harry to stop giving him the potion. Even when Dumbledore screams in pain and begs for death, Harry follows Dumbledore's initial commands and forces the headmaster to keep drinking. Harry undoubtedly would have preferred to end Dumbledore's pain rather than inflict it but instead obeys Dumbledore's orders, forcing himself to witness the agonizing battle his mentor undergoes to acquire a piece of Voldemort's soul—essential to the larger battle of good and evil that Harry knows is of foremost importance to Dumbledore. Rowling demonstrates Harry's allegiance to Dumbledore in this moving scene, suggesting that true loyalty means following through on even difficult, painful, and perhaps seemingly impossible promises, especially when in service of the greater good.

Class-Consciousness

For some characters in the Harry Potter novels allegiances are based entirely on one's class. As do novels preceding it in the series, *Half-Blood Prince* explores concepts inextricably linked to class-consciousness including pureblood mania, the servant class, and the mistreatment of the lower class.

Rowling provides readers with a striking and unsettling portrait of pureblood fanaticism in two families: the Malfoys and the Gaunts. In *Half-Blood Prince* Draco again (as in *Chamber of Secrets*) publicly humiliates Hermione by insulting her Muggle status. When the students meet in Madam Malkin's while shopping for school supplies in Diagon Alley, Draco's elitism is clear: Draco tells his mother, "If you're wondering what the smell is, Mother, a Mudblood just walked in" (112). Draco adopts this attitude from his parents. His mother, Narcissa, says, "Now I know the kind of scum that shops here. . . . we'll do better at Twilfitt and Tatting's" (114). This statement reflects Narcissa's nature as someone obsessed with appearance and standing;

her name, after all, is a derivative of *Narcissus*, the name of the man who fell in love with his own reflection. This scene recalls images of the Civil Rights movement, in which racist whites refused to drink from water fountains black citizens used. The Malfoys flaunt their high social standing and their financial resources.

The Gaunts, quite conversely, cling to their elite pureblood heritage as a way of compensating for the complete squalor in which they live. In striking contrast to the perfectly kempt, white-blond Malfoys, Morfin Gaunt is described as follows: "The man standing before them had thick hair so matted with dirt it could have been any color. Several of his teeth were missing. His eyes were small and dark and stared in opposite directions" (201). Morfin's serpentine appearance clearly links him to his pureblood relative, Salazar Slytherin (and seems almost a deliberate antithesis to the Aryan Malfoys). Bob Ogden questions Morfin for attacking a Muggle, another habit of pureblood fanatics. Morfin's father, Marvolo, unsurprisingly supports both elitist and patriarchal views. He mistreats his daughter, Merope, forcing her to cater to him and his son; when she drops a pan, Marvolo humiliates her, and even Ogden involves himself in the situation, asking Marvolo to control his temper. Merope's romantic interest enrages Marvolo above all else. Morfin, who descends from "generations of pure-bloods, wizards all" (208), cannot bear his daughter's loving a Muggle: "My *daughter—pureblooded descendant of Salazar Slytherin—hankering after a filthy, dirt-veined Muggle?*" (210). Marvolo's chauvinism prevents his daughter from pursuing the man she loves without retribution: Instead, Merope lives in fear and turns to deception (the use of a love potion) to secure Tom Riddle's affection.

Members of pureblood families are not the only proponents of elitist and classist values, however, as the novel's title emphasizes. Snape, obsessed with blood status in his youth, created such a title for himself to emphasize his pureblood heritage. When Hermione discovers Eileen Prince was Snape's mother, and a pureblood, Harry deduces the following about Snape: "He'd play up the pure-blood side so he could get in with Lucius Malfoy and the rest of them. . . . He's just like Voldemort. Pure-blood mother, Muggle father . . . ashamed of his parentage, trying to make himself feared using the Dark Arts, gave himself an impressive new name" (637). Coupled with Snape's calling Lily Potter a "Mudblood," Snape's attachment to his pureblood heritage and internalized self-hatred for his half-blood status are both baleful and sad. Rowling proves that regardless of one's class or financial resources pureblood fanatics live miserable lives, dominated by their obsessions.

Another way Rowling explores the concept of class in *Half-Blood Prince* is through the actions of servants in the novel, specifically of the house-elves Dobby and Kreacher. Rowling first focused attention on the plight of the house-elves in *Chamber of Secrets* and further explored their social situation with Hermione's championing of their rights in both *Goblet of Fire* and *Order of the Phoenix*. Sirius's death leaves Kreacher without a master until Harry assumes control of the elf. When Kreacher appears in the Dursleys' home, Dumbledore tells Harry, "Give him an order. . . . If he has passed into your ownership, he will have to obey. If not, then we shall have to think of some other means of keeping him from his rightful mistress" (52). Some critics believe Dumbledore's commands reflect his class: The elves, he feels, are meant to receive orders; if an elf disregards commands, Dumbledore also suggests taking other actions to ensure the elf's obedience. Others argue that Dumbledore's actions here simply reflect his recognition of the social and functional reality of house-elves and their material relationships to their masters, not an endorsement of or comfort with it, supported by his insistence on paying Dobby fair wages and time off when he hires him to work at Hogwarts.

Harry, accustomed to being treated as a servant for the Dursleys during his time in their home, takes on the role of master in *Half-Blood Prince*. Unlike Dumbledore, Harry feels somewhat uncomfortable with an elf in his charge. Perhaps more empathetic than most to the life of servitude, Harry assigns both Kreacher and Dobby the menial and hardly taxing task of trailing Malfoy. Regardless, the presence of the elves in the novel requires readers to think

about class and whether the house-elves should be bound to serve masters without compensation or the right of refusal. For instance, Dobby expresses his feelings toward Harry as follows: "Dobby is a free house-elf and he can obey anyone he likes and Dobby will do whatever Harry Potter wants him to do!" (421). The irony Rowling weaves into Dobby's statement (that he is free to *obey*) causes readers to question the state of the elves, free or not. Similarly, readers should question the treatment of the elves after Kreacher says, "Kreacher will do whatever master wants . . . because Kreacher has no choice, but Kreacher is shamed to have such a master, yes" (421). Most readers strongly dislike Kreacher (since his lies in *Order of the Phoenix* lead to Sirius's death, even if indirectly) and care little about his comfort and wishes. Kreacher's real loyalty lies with Bellatrix, a criminal. Kreacher's being forced to serve Harry, however, is no different from Dobby's being forced to serve the Malfoys: Both elves were subject to respecting commands from people who care little, if anything, about them and see them as instruments in service of their needs and desires. In turn Rowling continues to emphasize the mistreatment of the elves by those of higher class.

Rowling also draws attention to questions and consequences of social inequality. One of the most obvious examples of the suffering of a subordinate or oppressed group caused by the dominant group is the destruction of the Brockdale Bridge. The Muggles on the bridge at the time of its collapse may belong to all social and economic groups, but to the Death Eaters who cause the destruction, all Muggles are unworthy of regard or respect. Voldemort's quest for domination, after all, stems from his obsession with blood status and, by suggestion, social status.

Another keen example of class elitism involves Draco Malfoy. Malfoy, a member of the upper class, threatens Borgin—a shop owner—in order to make him help him prepare the Vanishing Cabinets: Malfoy mentions his friend Fenrir Greyback the werewolf, who would be angry if Borgin did not help Malfoy. The pressure Malfoy applies is effective because of his class status, reinforced with the threat of violence. Interestingly, however,

Borgin and his colleague Burke exploit members of the class lower than theirs. Merope Gaunt provides an example of this exploitation. Desperate, starving, and pregnant, Merope hopes to receive money for some of her family heirlooms, including Salazar Slytherin's locket. When she agrees to sell Borgin the locket, he gives her only 10 galleons for it (261). Harry is troubled by the way Borgin and Burke swindled Merope. Borgin shows no shame or remorse for taking advantage of Merope, illustrating the way in which those in power can exploit the powerless. Rowling suggests that class-consciousness affects members of all classes and species and that the institution of strict class stratifications and the perpetuation of classist attitudes—beliefs important to Voldemort—serve as the catalyst for many societal problems.

Memory and the Influence of the Past

Rowling strongly stresses the importance of personal history in *Half-Blood Prince*. The novel provides readers with insights into key events in Voldemort's past that help explain his choices and values. In doing so, Rowling suggests that the past is vital to understanding a person's present; Rowling's work also indicates that multiple perspectives are necessary to understand a historical moment or movement clearly.

Preparing for yet another confrontation with Voldemort, Dumbledore and Harry gather and view memories from various perspectives—ranging from that of a ministry official to a shopowner to a Hogwarts professor—to understand Voldemort's past better. Rowling's use of characters of different professions and social classes demonstrates that one's past is inextricably bound up with the history of many others; Voldemort, who has influenced the lives of many, is no exception. The events in Voldemort's past relayed by those who have been affected by him provide readers with some explanation for his refusal to trust in or depend on others, his quest for power, and his obsession with blood status and hatred of Muggles.

Raised in an orphanage, Voldemort felt abandoned and alone. Voldemort learns later that his mother welcomed death after giving birth to him; even though she might have used some form of

magic to transform her disposition and supply her with the will to live, Merope preferred to die because she was heartbroken by her rejection by Tom Riddle, Voldemort's father. Rowling shows what a devastating effect Merope's choice to abandon her child had on him: Accustomed to being abandoned and refusing self-pity or friendship, Voldemort completely isolates himself in bitterness. Merope's abandoning Voldemort may be the catalyst for his refusal to trust anyone other than himself. Even when Dumbledore arrives at the orphanage to share good news with the young Tom Riddle, Jr., the orphan suspects Dumbledore is not a headmaster of a school but a doctor from an asylum. Voldemort yells, "She wants me looked at, doesn't she? Tell the truth!" (269). His abandonment causes Voldemort, from a very young age, to behave guardedly, viewing even adults as trustworthy and caring as Dumbledore with suspicion.

He refuses to let anyone grow close to him and instead terrorizes the other children so they learn to fear him. This fear makes him feel powerful. Voldemort prefers to be alone and seizes a form of control—wielded by fear—over the other orphans. Rowling explores the potentially tragic consequences of parental abandonment. The stark contrast between Voldemort and Harry as orphans vividly illustrates this: Voldemort instills fears while Harry combats it. Harry understands, however, that he was not willingly abandoned, and he thus evolves into a much different man from Voldemort.

Readers also better understand Voldemort's obsession with blood status once they learn more about his personal and familial past. Voldemort is obsessed with status, so naturally he would desire that his followers be of the highest blood status possible in the wizarding world: pureblood. Voldemort's pureblood fanaticism (ironic as it is since he is a half-blood), however, stems from his hatred for his father, a Muggle. The disastrous relationship between Merope and Tom Riddle led to Merope's devastation, giving birth at an orphanage after being abandoned. Rowling demonstrates Voldemort's hatred of Muggles clearly in *Chamber of Secrets* and emphasizes it again in *Half-Blood Prince*; Dumbledore explains to Harry that even in the orphanage Voldemort "wished to be different, separate, notorious. He shed his name, as you know, within a few short years" (277). His father's actions shaped Voldemort's perception of the entire Muggle world.

As Harry develops an understanding of Voldemort's past, he also grows to appreciate his own personal story. While readers typically view Harry and Voldemort as extreme opposites, *Half-Blood Prince* emphasizes how alike the two characters truly are. Both are orphans who, provided with an opportunity to enrich themselves by studying at Hogwarts, are plagued with doubts. Voldemort says he always thought he was different from the other children: "I knew I was special. Always, I knew there was something" (271). Harry, likewise, seemed to suspect he was different from all the other children: His hair grew faster, he found himself on school rooftops, and he could even talk to snakes. Harry may not have voiced his suspicions of his difference as clearly as Voldemort, but he knew he was capable of doing things his classmates could not. Readers also witness Voldemort's reaction to hearing about Hogwarts, which mirrors Harry's: Both boys feel excited but worry about how they will pay for school since they have no money of their own or how they will acquire school supplies. Dumbledore informs the penniless Voldemort that Hogwarts helps students in need; conversely, Harry does not need monetary support from the school because his parents provided for him by leaving him a vault full of money. Once again, Rowling emphasizes how the choices parents make shape their children's lives. Merope dies thinking only of herself; in stark contrast, James and Lily Potter die thinking only of their son.

Voldemort, like any other person, is responsible for his choices, however. This novel in the Harry Potter series invites readers to consider that though children are usually subject to their parents' values and experiences (or consequences thereof), they eventually must make their own choices and establish themselves as individuals. Both Harry's and Tom Riddle's stories reflect this theme, but another example is Draco Malfoy's. Bred to believe in the Dark Lord's supremacy, Draco distinguishes himself from his parents' belief system when he is unable

to make himself murder Dumbledore at the end of the novel. By contrast, Voldemort, abandoned by his family, could have chosen to trust others again and flourish in the community of Hogwarts: He is invited often to develop such a sense of belonging and community; he perpetuates the feelings of isolation and despair so evident in his family history instead.

More than any novel preceding it in the series, *Half-Blood Prince* encourages readers to understand the importance of the past. Harry tells Hermione and Ron that he does not understand why Dumbledore believes knowing Voldemort's past is so important. Hermione, in response, says, "I think it's fascinating. . . . It makes absolute sense to know as much about Voldemort as possible. How else will you find out his weaknesses?" (280). Indeed, Harry and his friends discover Voldemort's weaknesses by studying his past. They eventually view Voldemort as the self-doubting and self-loathing fraud he is—self-doubting (or perhaps just arrogant) because he divides his soul into seven parts (suggesting he knows he could not take over the wizarding world on his first attempt without being destroyed) and a fraud because he touts pureblood mania even though he is a half-blood himself. Rowling emphasizes the importance of history, reminding readers the only way to determine the course of the future is to consider the events of the past carefully.

Collecting

Rowling draws significant attention to the behavior of collecting and its implications in *Half-Blood Prince*. Characters such as Slughorn, Voldemort, and Dumbledore fixate on their collections and often apply pressure, without remorse, on others to aid them in completing their respective collections.

Voldemort and Dumbledore pursue objects (including heirlooms and even memories), whereas Slughorn collects people. When Harry meets Slughorn, the former Hogwarts Potions professor tells Harry he was also the head of Slytherin House and adds, "The whole Black family had been in my House, but Sirius ended up in Gryffindor! Shame—he was a talented boy. I got his brother Regulus, when he came along, but I'd have liked the set" (70). Rowling even subtly critiques Slughorn's habit of amassing people when she compares his disappointment that Sirius was not a member of his house to that of "an enthusiastic collector who had been outbid at an auction" (70). Slughorn collects people by inviting students to attend events of his infamous "Slug Club," a group of students hand-picked by him, particularly students he feels will acquire eventual fame. Dumbledore explains that Slughorn does not desire fame for himself but prefers to boast about his relationships with those who are famous: "Horace formed a kind of club of his favorites with himself at the center, making introductions, forging useful contacts between members, and always reaping some kind of benefit in return" (75). Essentially, Slughorn collects people who provide him with connections. He obviously cares more about his own status than the welfare of his students, for one can imagine the embarrassment and disappointment students suffer if they are not invited to join the Slug Club (as in Ron's resentment of Slughorn's private Christmas party, to which only club members and their guests are invited).

By contrast, Voldemort collects objects, beginning during his stay at the orphanage. Dumbledore knows that the strange boy he visits has stolen objects from many of his fellow orphans and demands that Voldemort return the objects to their rightful owners. These stolen items, Dumbledore understands, Voldemort considers trophies; stealing is another way for Voldemort to instill fear in his fellow orphans, and the more objects he collects, the more powerful he feels. They serve the additional function of reminding him of his power over others. His obsession with collecting refines itself with age. Instead of stealing random objects, his mission becomes acquiring objects of great importance. As Slughorn does, Voldemort applies pressure to others to gather items for his collection; unlike Slughorn, however, Voldemort gracefully—and deceptively—charms others in his quest to collect. His encounter with Hepzibah Smith is an example of such manipulation. Voldemort as a young man flatters Hepzibah by visiting her personally, charming her over tea, and feigning interest in the old woman's stories. Hepzibah believes Voldemort's interest is genuine, but he cares only for the ancient objects she possesses, such as Helga Hufflepuff's goblet. Objects that belonged to Helga Hufflepuff, Rowena Ravenclaw, Godric Gryffindor, and Salazar Slytherin carry status and significance, and acquiring these objects is a way for Voldemort to gain status and power since the objects themselves are so highly coveted. Voldemort's preserving sections of his soul in these objects is his way of symbolizing his domination over the wizarding community by connecting himself to some of the most powerful and ancient wizards in the world.

Dumbledore similarly "collects" in *Half-Blood Prince*: He works tirelessly to collect memories pertaining to Voldemort's past. Harry endures pressure from Dumbledore to help him collect a memory that would provide information vital not only to battling but also to defeating Voldemort. Although Dumbledore's collecting serves to benefit not only him but the entire wizarding community, his need to complete his connection parallels the need Slughorn and Voldemort share. Rowling suggests that all men, whether self-obsessed like Slughorn or wise and serene like Dumbledore, can develop a need to amass, organize, and preserve. But in a world plagued by chaos like the wizarding world in which they live, readers can appreciate why collecting becomes a common way of restoring order to characters' lives and serves as a recurring motif in *Half-Blood Prince*.

Love

Arguably, the most prominent theme in *Half-Blood Prince* is love. Developing romantic relationships, romantic entanglements, ensuing marriages, and those already happily married fill the pages of Rowling's sixth novel, emphasizing its importance. There are two primary reasons for the flood of romantic details included in this book. First, Harry and his classmates are 16 and 17 years old, so naturally romance and love become important elements in their lives. Second, the war against Voldemort causes people to look for and find comfort in being loved and loving another; in short, on the brink of imminent war members of the wizarding community celebrate the joy of love as they face fears of destruction and death.

The two most notable romances to develop between students in *Half-Blood Prince* are the relationships between Ron and Lavender and Ginny and Harry. The two romances are strikingly different: Ron and Lavender's relationship develops out of entirely physical attraction, whereas Ginny and Harry's relationship is built on a sound emotional and intellectual connection. Readers might question what drives Ron to become romantically involved with anyone, let alone Lavender, and rightfully so. Early in the novel Ron rebukes Ginny for kissing a classmate, and Ginny argues that Ron is simply jealous because he is the only one of his group of friends who has not yet kissed someone (Hermione kissed Krum, Harry kissed Cho, and Ginny kissed several boys she has dated). Shortly after this confrontation Ron finds a means of catching up to his schoolmates in the romantic arena: "There, in full view of the whole room, stood Ron wrapped so closely around Lavender Brown it was hard to tell whose hands were whose" (300). Students witness Ron and Lavender kissing constantly, and Ron admits to Harry that his relationship with Lavender consists of nothing more than the physical aspect.

Hermione's reaction to Ron and Lavender's relationship keenly demonstrates fickle, jealous young love. Saddened, angered, and disappointed by seeing Ron kiss Lavender, Hermione goes to an empty classroom to be alone. Within minutes Ron and Lavender stumble in, causing Hermione to send an angry flock of gold birds at Ron's head. Hermione's actions, usually composed, show that a broken heart can cause anyone to behave irrationally, including magically attacking a best friend. Hermione continues to behave immaturely when she attempts to hurt Ron's feelings by insulting his Quidditch skills. In a conversation staged clearly to irritate Ron Hermione tells Parvati Patil that she and Cormac McLaggen will attend Slughorn's Christmas party together. When Parvati remarks that Hermione seems inclined to date Quidditch players, Hermione admits she likes Quidditch players, but "*Really good* Quidditch players" in particular (313). This is a strategic dig intended to hurt Ron, as he is highly sensitive about his Quidditch abilities. Rowling captures the stereotypical passive-aggressive behavior of a young woman, as is Hermione, jilted in the game of love.

While Ron and Lavender's attraction is merely physical, Rowling provides readers with a relationship based on a more substantive connection in the romance between Ginny and Harry. Rowling has hinted at Ginny's attraction to Harry over several years, beginning with her flustered behavior when Harry arrives unexpectedly at the Burrow in *Chamber of Secrets*. *Half-Blood Prince* shows Harry reciprocating Ginny's feelings. Harry witnesses Dean and Ginny kissing and has an unexpected reaction: "It was as though something large and scaly erupted into life in Harry's stomach, clawing at his insides: Hot blood seemed to flood his brain, so that all thought was extinguished, replaced by a savage urge to jinx Dean into a jelly" (286). Harry, unlike Hermione, does not act on his jealousy, partly out of respect for his best friend, Ron. Harry and Ginny share a passionate, long-awaited kiss only after Harry receives approval from Ron, since Harry does not want to jeopardize his relationship with Ron by pursuing a relationship with Ginny. The Weasleys have always provided Harry with a home and a family, so the love Harry has for Ginny grows out of emotional bonds that have existed for years. Rowling demonstrates the love Ginny and Harry share is genuine, especially in the last chapter of the book. Harry tells Ginny that Voldemort will probably come after her in an effort to hurt him, and out of respect—and more important love—for each other, Harry and Ginny agree to remain apart while Harry embarks on his final adventure to destroy Voldemort. His request that Ginny remain behind demonstrates Harry's selfless love and concern for Ginny's safety, while Ginny's agreement to wait patiently for Harry's return testifies to her love and commitment. Ginny and Harry spend only a short time together before they must part. In turn, Rowling argues that even though the time lovers might share is fleeting, their feelings can be true and lasting.

Love and romance are also primary themes in *Half-Blood Prince* because of Voldemort's return: In the face of great crisis members of the community seek, find, and celebrate love. As reflected in the images and stories of soldiers marrying before going off to World War II, Voldemort's first rise to power caused people to fall in love and marry quickly. Molly and Arthur Weasley were married in such a fashion: When Ginny asks her mother about that, Molly responds by saying, "Yes, well your father and I were made for each other, what was the point in waiting?" (93). Similarly, Bill Weasley and Fleur Delacour plan to marry: Though Molly and Arthur eloped during Voldemort's first reign of terror, Molly feels uncomfortable with her son's marrying, arguing that Bill and Fleur have nothing in common and that "they've hurried into [their] engagement" (92). Molly's feeling threatened by another woman playing the role of caretaker for her son reflects the discomfort many mothers feel in such a situation. After Greyback attacks Bill and Molly swabs his face, Fleur interposes herself and says that she can take care of her husband herself. Molly's first priorities have always been the care and safety of her family, however, so one comment by Fleur changes Molly's perception of her: When Fleur sees how Bill looks after the attack, she says, "What do I care how he looks? . . . All those scars show is zat my husband is brave!" (623). Fleur's dedication to Bill, even after he is mauled by a werewolf, proves to Molly that the love of her son and future daughter-in-law is genuine. The feud between the women is suddenly settled through shared grief over Bill's accident and Molly's promise to lend Fleur a goblin-made tiara for the wedding. Although Molly suspects her son's marriage proposal is a rash response to Voldemort's return, she understands that the two deeply love each other and that love like theirs, especially in such a dire time, should be celebrated rather than questioned.

Rowling also emphasizes the theme of the redemptive power of love with the character of Dumbledore, whose knowledge of the importance of love reminds Harry of love's power. Dumbledore explains to Harry that Voldemort does not understand the power of love, and failing to understand this power would be Voldemort's greatest weakness. Dumbledore furnishes a memory for Harry in an effort to teach his pupil more about Voldemort's past. The memory showcases Dumbledore and

Voldemort's discussing the powerful ancient magic of love. In the memory Dumbledore calls Voldemort still "ignorant" in certain types of magic, to which Voldemort responds, "The old argument. . . . but nothing I have seen in the world has supported your famous pronouncements that love is more powerful than my kind of magic, Dumbledore" (444). Further, Dumbledore confirms to Harry that the "power the Dark Lord knows not" mentioned in the prophecy refers to love (509). Dumbledore also verifies that the power that will continue to protect Harry in his battles with Voldemort is his "ability to love" (511). Dumbledore, until his death, encourages people to care for and love one another, knowing that the concept of love—so foreign to and disregarded by Voldemort—could lead to the destruction of the Dark Lord. Rowling's emphasis on the theme of love in *Half-Blood Prince* reminds us of Dumbledore's message to Harry at the end of *Sorcerer's Stone*: Love remains the most powerful magic.

INITIAL REVIEWS

On July 16, 2005, the sixth volume of the Harry Potter series was released; expectations were high after the generally well-reviewed fifth novel, *Order of the Phoenix*. Reviews of *Half-Blood Prince* overwhelmingly found the book praiseworthy, with special admiration reserved for the book's complex and inventive fantasy world and the increasingly streamlined storytelling. Only a few outliers deviated from the consensus that the book was an engaging, dramatic, impressive, and thematically complex addition to the series.

Reviewers overall noted the sixth book's darker tone, a similar assessment to initial reception of its predecessor, *Order of the Phoenix*. Rowling is widely regarded to have taken a more ambitious and thematically complex approach to Harry's story by the middle of the series, and *Half-Blood Prince* continues that trajectory. Jabari Asim's *Washington Post* review specifically notes the "increasing violence" in this volume but concedes that it "fits within the storyline and never seems gratuitous." Lev Grossman's review in *Time* also confirms that the series's "mood is darkening," as does Michiko Kakutani in the *New York Times,* who calls it the "darkest and most unsettling installment yet." Peter Lambert's review in the *Times Literary Supplement* goes so far as to say that the book is "deeply distressing" (20), largely because he sees the series as rejecting readers' desires for neat resolutions and escapism in favor of plot surprises that develop more complex themes than the previous volumes. By contrast, the growing darkness of the series's tone was viewed with dismay by John Mullan, who wrote in the *Guardian* (London) that the "odd glumness of this novel is partly a consequence of its loss of a satisfying plot, its lack of shape." Others, including the *Boston Globe's* Liz Rosenberg note the book's "new charge of gloom and darkness" but see it less as a symptom of narrative failure and more as a function of the "transitional" function the book seems to fulfill. But this reviewer seemed to suggest that the book's primary function was to "set up" the plot for the final volume in the series and that it had a lot of "narrative logistics" to establish before the series's conclusion. *Salon's* Laura Miller also comments on the book's "transitional" feel, though on the whole this assessment seems more descriptive than critical.

Referred to most frequently with something like awe in reviews of the sixth novel is the skillful way Rowling ties together plot threads from previous books. Yvonne Zipp in the *Christian Science Monitor* finds it "exciting to see the tapestry take shape," and Faith Wallace phrases her similar admiration as praise for the way "Rowling masterfully weaves in long-awaited answers to questions from previous books while presenting new clues to those that remain unanswered." *Publishers Weekly* echoes this admiration, commenting on the novel's accomplishment of "pulling together threads from all the previous titles and expertly poising readers for the planned finale" (Review 77). Kakutani calls the series a "giant jigsaw puzzle of an epic" and commends Rowling's clever and careful assembling of it. Grossman, as well, lauds Rowling's weaving of her "narrative threads into a complex, moving, and elegantly balanced whole, without any apparent effort." Reviews in *Horn Book Magazine* and the *London Independent* made

similar observations about Rowling's demonstration of remarkable narrative control in this book

Similarly, many reviews use adjectives such as *engaging, dramatic, intense, riveting,* and *spellbinding* in describing the sixth installment's pacing and structure. Besides complimenting Rowling's ability to tie together plot threads from previous novels, reviewers speak of the novel's storytelling in glowing terms, such as Sue Corbett's claim that the book "delivers a dramatic punch that matches the frenzy surrounding its release" while also calling the novel "intense" and "absorbing" (43). Anita Burkam in *Horn Book Magazine* tells readers there is "plenty of engaging mystery and suspense," while Peter Lambert less loftily praises Rowling's "efficient" storytelling (20). On the hyperbolic end of the spectrum in *Entertainment Weekly* the fantasy novelist Christopher Paolini, echoing Kakutani, calls Rowling's work "epic" and characterizes the book as one of the "great achievement[s] in fantasy literature" (72). Similarly adulatory is Liz Rosenberg's *Boston Globe* review, which declares, "Rowling's powers are startling, beautiful, original, wholly inimitable. The book bears the mark of genius on every page. Even in her occasional moments of awkwardness, the force of her imagination bears us up." Faith Wallace in the *Journal of Adolescent and Adult Literacy* concurs with this assessment, calling *Half-Blood Prince* "riveting and complex", as does *Booklist,* describing Rowling as "at the top of her game" in the sixth novel (Cooper 1,948). Fiona Lafferty concedes that the book "takes a while to get going," but despite this, "it is a cracking good read" (31). *Magpies's* Lyn Linning was also impressed with Rowling's storytelling, asserting that Rowling is able to maintain "intrigue and suspense" while the book "integrates action, relationships, the past and the present in an intriguing plot rising to a moving, exciting climax" (33).

As with previous volumes in the series, reviewers consistently comment on Rowling's gifted imagination and her creativity and inventiveness in the crafting of the wizarding world. Nicole Sperling begins her review in *Entertainment Weekly* marveling, "Rare is the series that remains so imaginative, so consistent, and so beguiling this late in its cycle" (31). Liesl Schillinger's *New York Times Book Review* also praises the alternate world Rowling has created, writing that Rowling has "succeeded in delivering another spellbinding fantasy set in her consummately well-imagined alternate reality." Kakutani agrees, adding that it is not simply the "richly imagined and utterly singular world" that enchants readers, but that it is as "detailed, as improbable and as mortal as our own," an observation other critics and scholars have made in explaining the series's enormous popularity. Linning explains that it is the "pleasure of re-entering that imaginative space" that keeps readers returning to the series in vast numbers with each new volume (33). Meghan Cox Gurdon in the *Wall Street Journal* calls Harry Potter's environs a "brilliantly clever parallel world" that we learn significantly more about in this sixth entry in the series. Particularly in this book of the series, Ross Douthat comments, the wizarding world is a "marvelously complex place, thick with tangled family trees, buried secrets, parallel pasts, and double agents." Throughout the publication of the Harry Potter series Rowling's powers of imagination have favorably impressed most of her readers and critics.

Another aspect of Rowling's writing that critics have generally responded positively to is the way she develops the series's characters. Douthat clarifies that Rowling excels "not in plumbing the depths of the self, but in dancing nimbly on the surface of personalities, relying on archetype and caricature in ways that call to mind the best of Dickens," and he is not the first to compare Rowling's work with that of Charles Dickens for this reason. Schillinger, as well, calls characterization "Rowling's gift." Wallace praises the novel's "realistic adolescent emotion and behaviors, capturing first love, jealousy, and humiliation in realistic ways," important achievements for a writer working in the fantasy genre. As does the fully fleshed out alternative world Rowling has created, her characters, notes Boyce in the *Independent,* "behave like we do," and though Rowling's characters experience fears and suspicions specific to wizards and witches, Muggle readers recognize in them their own frailties and faults.

Several reviews of this sixth novel mention the increasing thematic complexity of this volume, extending the foray into some of the darker themes Rowling introduced in *Order of the Phoenix.* Zipp, for example, observes that Rowling "raises some interesting questions about the perils of believing the best in others and whether the possibility of redemption is always worth the cost." Angie Schiavone in the *Sydney Morning Herald* notes that Rowling's examination of the power of love is more powerful than ever in this sixth book. Rosenberg treats Rowling's "unswerving dedication to these two primal elements"—love and death—with admiration, as *Half-Blood Prince* advances these themes in new and high-stakes ways.

A few reviewers found fault with *Half-Blood Prince,* but they tended to be out of sync with the majority of other reviewers. For example, Deirdre Donahue in *USA Today* claims the book is "slow-paced" but admires other elements such as the creation of engaging new characters. David Kipen in the *San Francisco Chronicle* completely panned the novel, calling it "dull," lacking in freshness, and a "brick." Mullan's *Guardian* review pillories the dialogue as "unlifelike"; Tasha Robinson's review in the comedy magazine the *Onion* critiques the book as "formulaic" though finding other features to praise—describing it as a "slick novel that reads effortlessly and intensely." A number of reviewers also observe what they believe to be the usual flaws in the series, such as the *New Statesman's* Kate Saunders's appraisal of the book as "hobbled by paragraphs of waffle that could have easily been cut" (38). This observation is affirmed by Schiavone, who less critically calls them "necessary explanatory lulls." Douthat writes a mixed evaluation in the *National Review,* quick to point out the book's demonstration of the "usual faults of the series" including pedestrian prose style and Harry's clichéd interior development; Douthat does, however, acknowledge "Rowling's genius for plotting," her careful craftsmanship, and her "talent for moralizing without polarizing." In the end, these critiques are very much in the minority.

Oddly, few reviews comment on Rowling's prose in this book; many reviews of the next book in the series, *Deathly Hallows,* almost always take Rowling to task for a less-than-graceful use of language, overreliance on adjectives, and unnecessary exposition. Few, if any, reviews of *Half-Blood Prince* make the same critique.

SCHOLARSHIP

Few scholars address the novels in the series independently. For scholarly works that discuss more than one novel or the series as a whole, see "Scholarship on the Harry Potter Series" as well as "Additional Resources on the Harry Potter Series," charting the academic and popular analyses of the series. The two essays that address *Half-Blood Prince* on its own focus on the images of alcohol consumption and on the legal system Rowling presents.

The lengthiest treatment of *Half-Blood Prince* is Benjamin Barton's "Harry Potter and the Half-Crazed Bureaucracy," published in the *Michigan Law Review.* Barton explores Rowling's treatment of the legal system through a close analysis of the "nature, societal role, and legitimacy of government" (1,525). Barton asserts that Rowling's treatment of three features of government—its functions, structure, and bureaucrats—is both scathing and effective; Rowling's satire of the failures of government structures lampoon elements of both the British and U.S. governments. Arguing that Rowling's books present a disdain for government and promote libertarianism, Barton draws upon political theory, current events, and Rowling's biography to chart the book's attitude toward governmental legitimacy.

Christopher Welsh's article "Harry Potter and the Underage Drinkers: Can We Use This to Talk to Teens about Alcohol?" in the *Journal of Child and Adolescent Substance Abuse* examines the portrayal of alcohol consumption in the Harry Potter series, focusing specifically on *Half-Blood Prince* because of Horace Slughorn's habit of both consuming alcohol and serving it to minors. Though there is an insignificant amount of alcohol in this beverage, it does lead to intoxication in house-elves; Welsh identifies in the sixth novel instances of underage students' consuming both Butterbeer and mead and of teachers' imbibing ostensibly alcoholic drinks. Welsh wonders whether the

books can provide a springboard for conversation with teens about alcohol use. He questions Rowling's portrayal, suggesting that "children and adolescents might read this and think that drinking alcohol is funny," and "more concerning is the message that it is appropriate for adults, particularly teachers and mentors, to serve alcohol to adolescents and drink to obvious intoxication with them" (122). Welsh sees this representation of alcohol consumption as presenting an opportunity for educators to engage adolescents in conversations about the theme in the books and how it might translate to decision making in their own lives. The question Welsh poses has been relevant since the inception of the series with *Sorcerer's Stone* when Harry, newly acquainted with the fact that he is a wizard, must sit and wait for Hagrid in the Leaky Cauldron before he can obtain his school supplies in Diagon Alley. To access the wizarding world, interestingly, Harry must travel through a pub. In addition, scenes of both adults' and teens' consuming alcoholic beverages appear throughout the series.

CHARACTERS

Sirius Black Harry's dead godfather; former member of the Order of the Phoenix. Although Sirius fell in battle in the previous novel, *Order of the Phoenix,* he plays a meaningful role in the sixth installment of the series. He serves as a reminder of those who have been lost in the war against Voldemort; Tonks's appearing sad and depressed leads several characters to assume that her feelings have been caused by the loss of her cousin, Sirius, whose death leaves Harry, in particular, with a feeling of loss.

Though Sirius functions primarily as a reminder of the costs of war, memories of him also emphasize Harry's movement through the different stages of grief. In the previous novel readers witness Harry as he progresses through the stages of denial such as anger and bargaining—anger at himself for falling victim to Voldemort's scheme, questioning Hogwarts' ghosts about the afterlife out of a desperate need to reconnect with his godfather. In the sixth novel Harry both experiences depression and later moves on to acceptance. Rowling shows her ability to depict the universal human experience of losing a loved one accurately through Harry's range of emotion captured during Rowling's brief mentions of Sirius.

Fleur Delacour   Bill Weasley's fiancée. Known for her stunning appearance and thick French accent, Fleur functions as a source of tension for several women in the novel—namely, Ginny, Mrs. Weasley, and Hermione—who find her annoying and, to some degree, competition for the affection of the men in their lives. In *Goblet of Fire* Rowling confirms during the Triwizard Tournament that Fleur is part Veela, a seductive species of creature that is the team mascot for the Bulgarians at the Quidditch World Cup. Her uncanny ability to secure the undivided attention of the men in her vicinity becomes an increasingly threatening and annoying quality. Accustomed to being the only woman at the Burrow besides her mother, Ginny Weasley feels unsettled and irritated by Fleur's presence, to which all the men respond positively (and nearly obsessively, as in Ron's case). Similarly, Hermione (whose romantic interest in Ron is hinted at and finally made explicit at the close of the novel) feels aggravated by Ron's interest in Fleur, as when he fawns over Fleur at Christmas dinner.

Molly Weasley is also annoyed by Fleur. Molly feels threatened by Fleur since, as Bill's future wife, Fleur will take on a very significant role in his life. Molly's maternal protectiveness at times metamorphoses into jealousy, but when Fleur remains at Bill's side after Fenrir Greyback's gruesome attack, Molly welcomes Fleur to the family and the women bond over caring for Bill. Buried under Fleur's irritating beauty is a dedicated heart. Molly grows to appreciate her future daughter-in-law's unconditional love for her son during the novel's conclusion, when Fleur, in her French accent, says, "You thought I would not weesh to marry him? Or per'aps, you hoped? . . . What do I care how he looks? I am good-looking enough for both of us, I theenk! All these scars show is zat my husband is brave!" (623). Fleur's commitment to Bill despite his wounds and scars reveals a new dimension of a character whom up until this point fellow characters (and readers) have viewed as either vain or, at the very least, moderately self-involved.

Albus Dumbledore   Hogwarts School of Witchcraft and Wizardry headmaster and mentor to Harry. Aware of the struggles awaiting Harry in his future, Dumbledore has as his highest priority preparing Harry as well as he can for those struggles, whether magical, internal, or personal. One of the greatest lessons Dumbledore teaches Harry is to consider a person's past in devising a strategy for victory. Showing Harry glimpses of Voldemort's history in *Half-Blood Prince* through the Pensieve, teaches Harry key facts about the Dark Lord, enabling him to use his knowledge to understand his opponent, knowing that an epic battle to the death between them is foretold. Though Dumbledore appears already to have gained a great deal of knowledge of Tom Riddle's childhood and adolescence, most of the information is new to Harry, and, as readers discover, Dumbledore places great faith in Harry's ability to acquire information that even he, one of the most powerful wizards in the world, is not able to retrieve (Slughorn's memory).

In this sixth novel Rowling continues to emphasize Dumbledore's wisdom. By threading together even the most seemingly unimportant pieces of information, Dumbledore is able to confirm what he long suspected—how Voldemort learned to harness the dark power of the Horcrux to evade death—and after Harry helps him confirm that Voldemort has, indeed, created a series of Horcruxes, Dumbledore goes about both retrieving and destroying some of those Horcruxes. In the process of doing so, Dumbledore sacrifices not only his time and energy, but his health (his arm, withered and black, is never restored to a healthy condition). His willingness to endanger his own well-being emphasizes Dumbledore's selfless nature, without which the wizarding community would know very little about Voldemort and his weaknesses and, as a result, how ultimately to defeat him.

Dumbledore's death at the hands of Severus Snape at the climax of *Half-Blood Prince* stunned readers at the book's publication and continues to present points of contention. Although Snape murders him, it is unclear whether Dumbledore's last words "Severus . . . please" are deliberately ambiguous—Dumbledore's asking Snape to spare his life or his request that Snape execute him as part of some larger plan. Even the clarifying narrative voice does not reveal much: "Snape gazed for a moment at Dumbledore, and there was revulsion and hatred etched in the harsh lines of his face" (595). Whatever the motivation for Dumbledore's words and Snape's ensuing actions, Dumbledore falls in battle, leaving readers questioning the future of Hogwarts, the institution Dumbledore held so dear and worked tirelessly to protect. When his funeral is held, scores of witches, wizards, and creatures of countless species arrive to mourn the loss of this man. With such a showing of support Rowling confirms the positive impact and influence Dumbledore had on not only on Hogwarts but on the wizarding world as a whole, with "all lessons . . . suspended, all examinations postponed," and "wizards and witches . . . pouring into the village, preparing to pay their last respects to Dumbledore" (633). Even the merpeople and centaurs turn out to pay homage to the headmaster at his funeral, highlighting again Dumbledore's appreciation of all species.

Marvolo Gaunt Direct descendant of Salazar Slytherin; patriarch of the Gaunt household. In her depiction of the Gaunts—Marvolo in particular—Rowling illustrates the epitome of pureblood fanaticism. Gaunt's personal philosophy is shaped entirely by his beliefs about blood status. Even though his ancestors left Gaunt with very little in the way of material inheritance, he clings desperately to his lineage as a way of asserting his superiority, status, and power. With his character Rowling suggests the dangers of becoming obsessed: He is a selfish man who serves as a catalyst for his daughter Merope's demise. He ignores his modest, unassuming daughter's needs and happiness and treats her as a servant but praises his half-mad son for perpetuating the belief that blood status is one's most important quality. Gaunt, carried off to Azkaban, expects to return home to find Merope prepared to cater to his needs; perhaps as his comeuppance his daughter is

nowhere to be found, and the old, decrepit patriarch dies completely alone.

Merope Gaunt Daughter of Marvolo Gaunt, Tom Riddle, Sr.'s lover, and, most important, Voldemort's mother. As a young woman who is forced to serve her father and brother, Merope is taken with the handsome Tom Riddle, even though he is a Muggle and she lives in a house with men who value blood status above all else. Merope uses any means necessary to win the love of the handsome Tom Riddle. Desperate to experience love (which neither her father nor brother seem to feel for her), Merope resorts to duping Riddle with a love potion. More conscientious than her father and brother, though, Merope eventually stops employing the use of a love potion on Riddle (according to Dumbledore's conjectures), a choice that distinguishes her from the rest of her family. Regardless, the result of Merope and Riddle's union through deception is catastrophic: Tom Riddle, Jr./Voldemort is brought into existence.

At first glance, Merope appears weak. She suffers abuse at the hands of her ill-tempered father, and she is described as "a girl whose ragged gray dress was the exact color of the dirty stone wall behind her. . . . Her hair was lank and dull and she had a plain, pale, rather heavy face. Her eye's, like her brother's, stared in opposite directions" (204–205). When Harry saw Merope in the Pensieve, he "thought he had never seen a more defeated-looking person" (205), and in many respects she remains so; however, she is willing to defy the father she has served all her life to pursue a relationship (even if forced) with a Muggle.

Interestingly, the only time Merope asserts herself concerns love, specifically romantic love. She may have also loved her son, but she does not assert herself and fight to survive for his benefit. In this sense Merope is very much like her father: selfish. Rowling more fully explores the ramifications of Merope's choice to abandon her child in the memories Dumbledore obtains about Voldemort's character development from a young boy into a man, but one can safely assume that Merope is part of the literary tradition of the "monstrous mother," who puts her own needs and feelings before those of her child or children.

Morfin Gaunt   Son of Marvolo Gaunt; obsessed with blood status as his father, Marvolo, is. Rowling demonstrates Morfin's obsession with blood status most poignantly when readers learn he is to be carted off to Azkaban for harming some Muggle children. Morfin's fanaticism governs his life and influences almost all of his behavior, regardless of the consequences. Similarly to Draco, Morfin not only accepts his father's beliefs but goes to great lengths to preserve those beliefs. Rowling describes Morfin as being quite snakelike in appearance; this description aligns with the creature Morfin's nephew—Tom Riddle, Jr.—will become: Voldemort.

Hermione Granger   Harry's and Ron's best friend and fellow Gryffindor. In *Half-Blood Prince* Hermione's character wavers between two wildly different aspects of the human being: reason and emotion (primarily an uncharacteristic jealousy). Hermione's constant concern over Harry's using the Half-Blood Prince's potion book also stems from jealousy: Her sense of reason and rightful skepticism question whether the prince—whoever it may be—can or should be trusted. The greater catalyst for Hermione's jealousy about Harry's using the book, however, is that with the Half-Blood Prince's book's assistance Harry continuously outperforms her in Potions class. Hermione even tells Harry that without the prince's book, Harry would "never have . . . got a reputation for Potions brilliance you don't deserve" (530).

Simultaneously, however, Hermione's jealousy serves as a motive for questioning the use of the prince's textbook. She questions Harry passionately, asking, "Was this spell, by any chance, another one from that potion book of yours?" and then persists, "So you just decided to try out an unknown, handwritten incantation and see what would happen?" (240). She also showcases some of the classic, rule-abiding Hermione readers see in the earlier novels with her admonition that "it's probably not Ministry of Magic approved" (240). Regardless of her motivation, Hermione's dedication to discovering

the truth leads to the revelation that Snape is the Half-Blood Prince. Without Hermione's passion for research and willingness to explore the Hogwarts archives, Harry would not have learned about Eileen Prince, Snape's mother. Early in the novel she believes "this Prince character was a bit dodgy" (240), and after Harry receives detention for using the gory *Sectumsempra* spell on Malfoy, she cannot resist shaming Harry by implying that if he had heeded her advice, he would not have found himself in such a difficult situation.

Although Rowling suggests in earlier novels that Hermione and Ron will become romantically linked (Harry notes the romantic tension between his best friends on several occasions), their romance is stalled, and Hermione's jealousy consumes her when Ron decides to become involved with Lavender Brown. Known for being reasonable and thoughtful, Hermione in her show of jealousy suggests, perhaps obviously, that when scorned, people are capable of behaving irrationally—even the usually composed Hermione. For example, the slighted Hermione sends a flock of canaries to attack Ron after she sees him kiss Lavender. Similarly, Ron purposely kisses Lavender in Hermione's presence to upset Hermione. With Hermione and Ron's childish behavior, Rowling proposes that Hermione and Ron are too immature for a serious romance with each other. Both of them recognize their immaturity, especially in light of Dumbledore's murder, and Rowling shows readers that later they are ready for a relationship, primarily through Ron's comforting a weeping Hermione at Dumbledore's funeral.

Rowling also shows that Hermione becomes more daring as she grows up while maintaining her respect for rules and regulations. Near the start of the novel and almost without thinking, she questions Mr. Borgin about his earlier conversation with Draco; a younger Hermione would not have been capable of such a confrontation since it requires questioning a figure of authority. Hermione's respect for rules based on fairness remains strong. When Harry feigns mixing Felix Felicis potion into Ron's drink the morning of a major Quidditch match, Hermione confronts Harry aggressively, chastising him for his behavior (even though Harry had only tricked Ron into thinking he had consumed some of the luck-inducing potion). Though Hermione's character has undergone significant development since readers met her on the Hogwarts Express in *Sorcerer's Stone,* her obsession with rules has not abated.

Rubeus Hagrid   Hogwarts professor and grounds-keeper; close friend of Harry, Ron, and Hermione. As with almost every other installment in the series the character of Hagrid encourages readers to respect all forms of life, even those that seem strange or dangerous; he also—as always—reveals important clues about his fellow characters. Hagrid is incredibly saddened by Aragog's illness and ensuing death. Holding a funeral for the gigantic spider may seem somewhat strange—or even silly—but with this action, Hagrid reminds characters and readers alike that all life, even that of spiders, should be respected and honored.

Hagrid also divulges information that others prefer to remain confidential, but the details Hagrid shares allow readers to understand the series and its major characters better. Hagrid's informing Harry that he overheard a conversation in which Dumbledore appeared to be angry with Snape may not help readers understand the events of the sixth book better—namely, Dumbledore's death—but Hagrid's shared detail becomes especially important when Snape's actions and motivations for killing Dumbledore are explored in more detail in *Deathly Hallows.*

Bellatrix Lestrange   Fanatical supporter of Voldemort; sister of Narcissa Malfoy; Draco's aunt. Though Bellatrix played the role of Voldemort's fiercely dedicated Death Eater in *Order of the Phoenix,* in this novel Rowling depicts Bellatrix as suspicious of Snape's intentions and, by association, Voldemort's. In *Half-Blood Prince* their open confrontation at Snape's home on Spinner's End begins, "I don't trust you, Snape, as you very well know!" and many accusations by Bellatrix about Snape's level of commitment to the Dark Lord (25). Snape's response—"Do you really think that the Dark Lord has not asked me each and every one of

those questions? And you really think that, had I not been able to give satisfactory answers, I would be sitting here talking to you?" (26)—manages to deflect but not really fully alleviate Lestrange's suspicions. She has gone from blindly following the Dark Lord to questioning his decisions; as a result, her wavering suggests creeping doubt about Voldemort's omnipotence.

On one level, Bellatrix's doubt signifies a character fault shared by most Death Eaters: the lust for power. Snape quickly subverts her suspicion by exploiting Bellatrix's growing doubts: "You think he is mistaken or that I have somehow hoodwinked him? Fooled the Dark Lord, the greatest wizard, the most accomplished Legilmens the world has ever seen?" (26). When Snape explains that he is privy to plans about which Bellatrix knows very little, her jealousy ignites; thus, Rowling uses her as a device to remind readers of the consequences linked with corruption and the desire for ultimate power. Bellatrix's doubt of Voldemort also foreshadows the Dark Lord's impending fall. When a follower (as previously unquestioning as Bellatrix) begins to doubt her master, the doubt can be suggestive of the decline of the master's reign. Even though Voldemort may appear to gain power throughout the novel, the character of Bellatrix suggests to readers that Voldemort's ascent to domination is not inevitable but fraught with challenges that may very well be insurmountable.

Remus Lupin   Werewolf and member of the Order of the Phoenix. In *Half-Blood Prince* Lupin is not a central character. But, as with many other characters, his self-sacrificing behavior emphasizes the struggle the order faces in combating Voldemort's return to power. He puts himself at risk by working undercover and infiltrating the werewolf community in an effort to gather any information that might be helpful to the order. By putting himself at risk in this manner, Lupin places the well-being of all others in the wizarding community before his own.

The person for whom he sacrifices most is Tonks. Although plainly aware of Tonks's feelings for him, Lupin refuses to become romantically involved with her because he fears he is too old and too different (as a werewolf) from her; his refusal to become romantically involved is rooted in his desire to protect her both from the physical jeopardy she could be placed in by being associated with him and from the social stigma that will inevitably result from involvement with him. However, after Dumbledore's murder and the knowledge that the fallen headmaster would be happy for them, Lupin pursues a romantic relationship with Tonks. Through Lupin Rowling suggests that putting others before one's self is indeed a noble act, but one should not deny himself or herself happiness in doing so.

Draco Malfoy   One of Harry's nemeses; a member of Slytherin House. In *Half-Blood Prince* Draco's classism and the mysterious task he is engaged in throughout the book play central roles in the plot. As in all of Rowling's other novels Draco Malfoy and his parents are characterized by their pureblood mania and contempt for half-bloods and Muggles. When Draco threatens Mr. Borgin (of Borgin and Burke's shop in Diagon Alley), he does so by dropping names of powerful people and creatures with whom he has connections, noting, "Tell anyone . . . and there will be retribution. You know Fenrir Greyback? He's a family friend" (125). His reference to the sadistic werewolf who serves Voldemort instills fear in Borgin immediately. Draco's behavior, in this instance, is consistent with his preoccupation with rank and power, even if that status or power is attained by association only.

Draco remains secretive throughout the novel, lending *Half-Blood Prince* the feel and contours of a detective story, more so than the other novels in the series. For much of the plot Harry preoccupies himself with discovering Draco's secret plans; Harry's fruitless search causes anxiety and suspicion about Draco in some of his classmates, and in Rowling's readers as well.

Ironically this upper-class young man is thrust into the role of servant in this installment of the series. The pressure to carry out the horrific task Voldemort assigns is difficult for Draco to bear. Even though Narcissa and Lucius are also loyal followers of the Dark Lord, they, too, have difficulty with Draco's assignment. Narcissa feels especially disturbed by Draco's assignment, as her emotionally charged conversation with Snape at Spinner's End illustrates. Similarly to Orestes in AESCHYLUS'S *Oresteia*, Draco finds himself in a situation in which he must avenge his father. Because Lucius did not succeed in the task assigned to him by Voldemort, now Draco must be triumphant, or the consequences will be dire. When Draco is unable to fulfill his orders—to kill Dumbledore—Rowling hints to her readers that Draco is not fully committed to the Dark Lord's cause and that, someday, he might escape the cycle—and pureblood mania—passed from one generation to the next in his family.

Minerva McGonagall   Transfiguration professor and head of Gryffindor House. Even though McGonagall plays a more minor role in *Half-Blood Prince* than in earlier novels, her actions are significant. Traditionally McGonagall, as head of house, is responsible for supplying students with their school schedules. When she discusses Neville's schedule with him and he doubts his abilities because of comments made by his grandmother, McGonagall gives him confidence. She continues to provide support for Hogwarts students; as the characters central to the story mature, McGonagall's role in their lives also changes. She served as a mother figure in their early years in reminding students of quiet hours and bed times, but in later years she protects them by offering support as they mature and grapple with difficult decisions such as choosing and pursuing career paths.

Very much as her students do, in *Half-Blood Prince* McGonagall finds herself thrust into a role with new responsibilities: With Dumbledore gone, she must temporarily oversee the school. In the figure of McGonagall Rowling reminds readers that even some of the most confident characters can be confronted with questions for which they do not have immediate answers. McGonagall, shocked completely by Snape's murdering Dumbledore, finds herself questioning Dumbledore's trust in Snape. Usually completely confident about Dumbledore's decisions, McGonagall begins to wonder whether Dumbledore made a terrible mistake in defending and believing in Snape. Interestingly, McGonagall's wavering faith in Dumbledore's omniscience could be paralleled to Bellatrix Lestrange's growing mistrust of Voldemort's assessment of Snape, each the faithful disciple whose previously unquestioning admiration for her mentor begins to wane. Thrust into the sole position of authority after Dumbledore's death, McGonagall with the other heads of house must decide the future of Hogwarts, but her first priority remains the students' safety.

Cormac McLaggen   Seventh-year student, member of Gryffindor House, and member of the Gryffindor Quidditch team after Ron is hospitalized. McLaggen is the stereotypical "jock": He is concerned mostly with Quidditch and his superior performance on the field. When he is not chosen for the Gryffindor team at the beginning of the year, he demands another tryout after accusing Harry of favoring Ron. Narratively McLaggen's role is small, but it does highlight the growing importance of romance for the adolescent students. His interest in Hermione confirms her growth into an attractive young woman who is increasingly of romantic and sexual interest to her male classmates.

As a result, McLaggen serves Hermione's interests in helping her make Ron jealous. Hermione invites McLaggen to Slughorn's Christmas party. Hermione's plot backfires, however: McLaggen pursues Hermione physically in ways with which she grows increasingly uncomfortable; rejoining Harry at the party after admitting she "just escaped—I mean, I've just left Cormac . . . under the mistletoe," even confessing that she chose him because she "thought he'd annoy Ron most" (317). Though McLaggen is a minor character in the novel, his hormone-induced behavior suggests the thick sexual tension clouding the narrative.

Harry Potter   Protagonist. Throughout most of *Half-Blood Prince* we see little of Harry and his classmates's attending actual classes or participating in extracurricular activities. While there are important Quidditch practices and Harry and his class-

mates practice apparating, Harry occupies himself with two major activities: attempting to discover Draco's plans and spending time with Dumbledore exploring Voldemort's life before, during, and after the Dark Lord's time at Hogwarts.

In this way, as with *Order of the Phoenix* and since *Goblet of Fire*, Rowling moves away from the typical narrative pattern she followed in the first three books, tracing Harry and his friends through their school year, setting numerous scenes in their classrooms and dorms doing homework, and focusing on their interpersonal relationships. With each subsequent novel Rowling moves Harry's story away from his academic work and outward toward the wizarding social and political milieu. With the addition of the Triwizard Tournament in *Goblet of Fire* Harry's mental interaction with Voldemort and trips to the Ministry of Magic in *Order of Phoenix*, and now his forays into the memories of Voldemort's past in *Half-Blood Prince*, Harry's journey becomes less embedded in his life as a student at Hogwarts and more tied to the fate of the world outside the school.

As is typical for Harry, he suspects Draco of being involved with Voldemort, and even more significantly, he believes that Draco intends to carry out a plan that will lead only to death and destruction, but of whom he is unsure. Harry becomes preoccupied with discovering Draco's scheme, with entire chapters ("Draco's Detour" and "The Unknowable Room") devoted to his following his Slytherin classmate. Even Hermione and Ron dismiss Harry and his endless theories, behavior that suggests Harry is no longer thinking clearly since his two best friends almost always trust his intuition. This may be in part because of the tragic ending to his heroic efforts the previous spring when Voldemort exploited his connection with Harry in order to lure him to the Department of Mysteries. Though the wizarding public at the start of *Half-Blood Prince* recognizes the validity of Harry's assertions about Voldemort, Ron and Hermione could not help but be hesitant to jump once again into Harry's sometimes too-enthusiastic efforts at saving people. Harry's suspicions prove correct, however, and the doubt his friends may have had about Harry's judgment vanishes when Hogwarts is infiltrated by Voldemort's supporters thanks to Draco's clever idea to use a set of Vanishing Cabinets (one placed in Borgin and Burke's on Diagon Alley, and the other in the Room of Requirement in Hogwarts).

In this novel in particular, Harry's defining characteristic is his loyalty. He is, as he tells Scrimgeour, "Dumbledore's man." His devotion to the headmaster is unwavering and demonstrates itself poignantly when Harry and Dumbledore leave to retrieve the locket Horcrux in the cave. Dumbledore insists that no matter how he responds, Harry must force him to finish the potion in the basin at the bottom of which rests the supposed Horcrux. Harry keeps his word to Dumbledore, who begs Harry to help him when pain wracks him as he drinks the potion. Harry keeps his promise to Dumbledore, however excruciating it may be, while watching the headmaster he has grown to love being tortured by the very potion Harry continues to give him.

More significant, however, is the way Harry demonstrates a growing commitment to Dumbledore as well as the maturity to carry out difficult tasks. He offers support and does not stray from the mission at hand, largely because he knows Dumbledore is already in a fragile condition and is depending on Harry for strength. When Harry reassures Dumbledore that they will make it through this trial, even Dumbledore tells Harry he is not afraid, simply because Harry is accompanying him on this difficult task. The loyalty Harry feels toward Dumbledore provides the headmaster with confidence, a significant feat considering the battles Dumbledore has already endured, including his defeat of Grindelwald many years earlier.

Most important, Harry learns a very significant lesson from Dumbledore: It is necessary to know the past in order to prepare for the future. Seeing snapshots of the young Tom Riddle, Jr., on the verge of transforming into Voldemort teaches Harry how to prepare himself for the ensuing battles with the Dark Lord. In turn Rowling reminds readers that history cannot be ignored, and knowing one's history is necessary for not only surviving the present but also moving into the future.

Horace Slughorn Potions professor and longtime friend of Albus Dumbledore. Each year Rowling introduces at least one new professor to the Hogwarts faculty: Horace Slughorn joins the school staff, returning to an institution at which he taught years earlier. Though Slughorn held a post at Hogwarts previously, Rowling suggests early in *Half-Blood Prince* that he is not entirely trustworthy: Although Dumbledore invites him to return to the school, he clearly has reservations about Slughorn but feels pressure to fill the post, noting that Hogwarts is "one member of staff short" (60). Dumbledore informs Harry of one of Slughorn's suspicious qualities, explaining evenhandedly to him that Slughorn "likes his comfort. He also likes the company of the famous, the successful, and the powerful" (74). That these qualities are so antithetical to Dumbledore's own generous nature immediately instills in both Harry and readers an instant dislike of the unctuous Slughorn. Throughout the novel Slughorn exhibits ethically questionable behavior, including showing favoritism toward particular students and an obvious fixation on status and celebrity.

Slughorn invites students to become members of the Slug Club, a group of students he selects on the basis of their talents or affiliations with famous people. He hopes that these students will go on to hold positions of power or receive fame and praise for their accomplishments; if these students achieve success, Slughorn parasitically brags about his connections with them. In some cases Slughorn's desire for power or status through association has clouded his judgment, especially in the case of Tom Riddle, Jr. Slughorn's informing Riddle about Horcruxes and Slughorn's ensuing shame for doing so may be Rowling's way of suggesting that hunger for status causes people to act without considering the consequences. It is the information about Horcruxes that Slughorn reveals to the young Tom Riddle, Jr., that makes defeating Voldemort such a difficult task.

Rowling also uses Slughorn to teach readers about the importance of the past, which cannot be escaped. Even though Slughorn desperately tries to alter his memories, Rowling proves that they cannot simply be erased even through magical tampering. To help solve the crises he aided in creating, Slughorn must confront the truth of the past and eventually reveal it to Harry. Rowling also stresses the importance of the past with Slughorn's character through his connection with Harry's parents, especially his mother, Lily. Because of Slughorn Harry learns more about his mother and her talents, including her gift for making potions, and finds out that she, too, was a member of the Slug Club. These memories give Harry new insight about his mother. In turn Rowling demonstrates that while the past may be difficult to address, it can also provide answers and connections to those no longer with us.

Severus Snape/the Half-Blood Prince Defense Against the Dark Arts professor; head of Slytherin House; Dumbledore's murderer; and the Half-Blood Prince. While Rowling has caused readers to question Snape's loyalty because of his unclear motives throughout the first five novels, she supplies readers with a stunning detail that seems to make his allegiance to Voldemort clear: Snape murders the man who has trusted him and defended him throughout the series, Dumbledore. Though this murder seems to be a definitive demonstration of where Snape's loyalties lie, readers cannot help but question whether this outcome is all part of a larger strategic plan by Dumbledore, who has never been wrong yet about the maneuverings of the Death Eaters.

For example, some of the details about the murder are ambiguous, and the dialogue during the scene particularly contributes to this sense of ambiguity: "Somebody else had spoken Snape's name, quite softly" (595). It is Dumbledore, who, as Harry observes, "for the first time, . . . was pleading" (595). With "revulsion and hatred" etched on Snape's face (595), he nonetheless executes his contemptible responsibility to execute Dumbledore (a task originally assigned to Draco) and casts *Avada Kedavra*.

An aspect of Snape's character made strikingly clear in *Half-Blood Prince* is his desire to protect Hogwarts students, Draco in particular. He finally receives the post he has coveted since first joining the Hogwarts staff, the position of Defense Against the Dark Arts professor. Snape takes his responsibility very seriously, however, and stresses that his students must think carefully about the nature of the dark arts and the danger inherent in them. By warning his students that dark magic is "ever-changing," constantly mutating, he encourages them to be aware and ready to defend themselves. Consequently, Rowling gives readers an insight into Snape's character, suggesting that even though he does not always respect them, he does care about them. Snape places special importance on Draco's safety and demonstrates how much he cares for the young man when he makes the Unbreakable Vow with Narcissa Malfoy. Perhaps Snape feels so strongly about protecting Draco because he sees a lot of himself in the young Malfoy: Both serve Voldemort, both want to please Voldemort, and both must fulfill the orders Voldemort gives them or face the dire consequences.

Since Snape is the Half-Blood Prince, Rowling clarifies for readers just how important blood status was and may still be to Snape; this obsession with blood status provides another similarity between Snape and Draco. Snape, a half-blood, remains ashamed of his heritage. He posits himself as a pureblood, insulting those who have the same or lower rank of blood status. Snape's obsession with blood status made him act rashly; in *Order of the Phoenix* Snape called Lily Evans a "Mudblood" even though she was attempting to save him from James and Sirius's taunting. The consequences of that action are not fully revealed until *Deathly Hallows,* but regardless, Snape's concern with blood status was the catalyst for many of his most serious personal tragedies. Likewise, Draco has found himself in some very troubling situations, such as being assigned the task of murdering Dumbledore, based on his family's dedication to Voldemort and the Dark Lord's views about blood status. In an effort to spare Draco pain like that which Snape endured, the former Potions master takes a special interest in protecting Draco.

Nymphadora Tonks Member of the Order of the Phoenix. In this installment in the series Tonks continues to serve in the role of protector, especially for Harry. Officially Tonks works in her professional capacity as an Auror for the Ministry of Magic (the same role in which she served when introduced to readers in *Order of the Phoenix*). When Draco breaks Harry's nose and leaves him in a train compartment, Tonks rescues Harry; with her character Rowling stresses that thinking quickly and being observant are necessary, especially considering the state of crisis in the wizarding world. And while Tonks seems to have especially keen powers of observation, most of the other characters seem to lack these skills when considering Tonks and her behavior: They realize she is depressed but assume it is because she has lost her cousin, Sirius. Instead, her depression grows from pining over Remus Lupin because he refuses to become romantically involved with her. Tonks, then, suffers from unrequited love. In this sense she functions as a foil to Merope Gaunt. Merope loses hope and magically enchants Tom Riddle, Sr., so that he will love her, eventually losing him when she can no longer tolerate the artificial relationship. Tonks, on the other hand, waits patiently for Lupin, who eventually reciprocates her feelings.

Voldemort/Tom Riddle, Jr. Harry's nemesis and one of the most powerful dark wizards of all time. In this novel (which Rowling herself claims serves, in a way, as a prequel to her other books) Rowling provides readers with insight into Voldemort's past. Through the Pensieve she exposes readers (along with Harry and Dumbledore) to the events that shaped Tom Riddle, Jr., into the Dark Lord. His difficult childhood most directly influences the adult Tom Riddle, Jr., becomes.

Riddle had a painful and traumatic childhood, and in considering the orphan's circumstances, some readers even feel sympathy for Voldemort. Tom was first raised by the grim orphanage's alcoholic matron, his childhood characterized by poverty, squalor, illness, and the stark, sterile atmosphere specific to institutions. In turn, Tom Riddle, Jr., develops a kind of reflexive suspiciousness that leads him to conclude first that when Dumbledore arrives at the orphanage, the headmaster intends to take him to an asylum.

In the figure of adolescent Riddle Rowling argues that putting one's needs before those of his/her children will not only harm but devastate the child who is neglected. Riddle learns his mother could have stayed alive for the sake of her son but did not try to, or, as the young Tom says offhandedly to Dumbledore, "My mother can't have been magic, or she wouldn't have died" (275). When he learns his father also abandoned him, he is doubly wounded.

Riddle is an angry and—although he claims otherwise—lonely child, who torments his fellow orphans for sport, steals others' possessions, and revels in the secret magical powers he has always had. Socially disempowered and robbed of the status and prestige he so desperately craves, Riddle is almost gleeful when Dumbledore reveals to him that he really belongs in a hidden parallel world where his magical ability will be treated as admirable rather than strange. When Dumbledore says to him, "You are a wizard," Rowling describes Riddle's face as "transfigured: There was a wild happiness upon it" (271). This behavior foreshadows his ensuing fascination with dark magic and the pain and torture commonly associated with such magic, which Voldemort delights in performing.

As Dumbledore explains, one of the only places (if not the only place) where Riddle felt he truly belonged was Hogwarts. Shortly after Riddle graduated, Dumbledore confides to Harry, Voldemort "approached Professor Dippet and asked whether he could remain at Hogwarts as a teacher," partly, Dumbledore speculates, because he was attached to Hogwarts as "the first and only place he had felt at home" and because Hogwarts is a "stronghold of ancient magic" (431). There is even something pathetic about his return to Hogwarts and his attempt to convince Dumbledore (now in tenure as headmaster) to let him be a teacher: "Will you let me return? Will you let me share my knowledge with your students? I place myself and my talents at your disposal. I am yours to command" (444). Riddle's request is especially disingenuous since while he was a student at Hogwarts, the staff nurtured Riddle and helped him develop his talents. Riddle became not only a gifted wizard but a school leader as well. His career at Hogwarts also demonstrates another important element of Voldemort's character: his desire to remain solitary. Even as a young man Riddle did not desire the companionship of friends but nevertheless acquired a devout following. This situation hints at Voldemort's nature as well: He has many devout followers, but none he would trust implicitly or put before his own needs.

Half-Blood Prince is essential to the series in that it fully develops Riddle/Voldemort as a character; until this point he is essentially two-dimensional, lacking depth or any rationale for his motivations and his unrelenting quest for power. As a somewhat "cardboard" villain who represents a supernatural and unstoppable evil, Voldemort is in *Half-Blood Prince* "humanized," or at least it is partly explained how he evolved into the figure who becomes so sadistic and seemingly without any redeeming quality.

Perhaps the most valuable piece of information Rowling imparts to readers concerning Voldemort is his interest in the concept of Horcruxes. The way Voldemort achieves immortality is significant. As someone abandoned by those who should have provided for and loved him, Riddle seeks to create as many small selves as possible so that his presence is preserved and cannot be ignored again. Of all the magical methods Rowling might have devised as a means for Voldemort to flee death, this choice in particular emphasizes Riddle/Voldemort's obsession with control and power and reflects his traumatic childhood, in which his parents abandoned him.

Arthur Weasley Ron's father, employed by the Ministry of Magic. Arthur previously worked in the Misuse of Muggle Artifacts Office but was promoted to the head of the Office for Detection and Confiscation of Counterfeit Defensive Spells and Protective Objects. Arthur's promotion affirms for readers that he is a trustworthy, honest, and responsible man. More important, however, Rowling emphasizes that Arthur cares for the welfare of others, above all else. This need to protect not only his family but members of the community in general shines when the family (along with Harry, Hermione, and Hagrid) visit Diagon Alley to purchase school supplies for the coming term. When Arthur sees a stand where a wizard sells counterfeit protection objects, he becomes upset and neglects to address the question-

able wizard only because he and his family must run their errands as quickly as possible. Though Arthur Weasley does not play a major role in the sixth novel, he is a core member of the Order of the Phoenix, the coalition of good wizards who have vowed to protect Harry and fight Voldemort.

Fred and George Weasley Ron Weasley's older twin brothers. As in all other novels in the series Fred and George are a source of comic relief, especially in the midst of the dismal and relentless exposure of Voldemort's grim childhood and the present-day anxieties of the rapidly declining social stability brought on by Voldemort's increasing strength. The Weasley twins' presence in *Half-Blood Prince* is especially important, considering the bleak forecast for the wizarding community. While the twins function as a source of humor, Rowling makes a more significant and serious statement concerning their success at the store: Pursuing one's goals, even in a nontraditional manner, can lead to success with hard work. Though their mother would prefer they follow a traditional academic path as their highly successful older brothers Bill and Charlie did, Fred and George, who quit school (making a glorious exit in *Order of the Phoenix*), now own and run a successful business, Weasley's Wizarding Wheezes. Their passion for making others happy combined with their dedication to their business fuels their success. With the Weasley twins Rowling suggests that innovative ideas do not arise from formal education alone but also from a spirit of fun and love for one's profession.

Ginny Weasley The youngest Weasley sibling and Harry's love interest. In this sixth installment of the series Rowling depicts Ginny as a young woman who has matured and developed an interest in her fellow male students. Building on Ginny's romantic involvements in *Order of the Phoenix*, Rowling suggests that Ginny is, to a degree, a heartbreaker. She is popular with the young men and is unafraid of moving on to new romantic pursuits when one becomes stale. When she and Harry finally kiss, Rowling's foreshadowing from previous volumes becomes obvious. Throughout the novel Harry feels extremely jealous when Ginny is dating one of his classmates. Their long-delayed opportunity to be with each other finally arrives when "without thinking, without planning it, without worrying about the fact that fifty people were watching, Harry kissed her" (533). Rowling suggests that, unlike Ron and Lavender's shallow and physical relationship, Harry and Ginny's is an intimacy that goes beyond their mutual physical attraction.

Filmmakers and Rowling have given audiences clues that foreshadow Harry and Ginny's relationship; these take on new significance, ranging from Ginny's frantic blushing when she sees Harry at the kitchen table in *Chamber of Secrets* to Ginny's lingering look at Harry in *Order of the Phoenix* as she leaves a D.A. meeting while Harry stays behind, alone with Cho. Ginny also respects Harry's difficult situation and, in doing so, shows how she truly cares for Harry. When Harry tells Ginny he thinks it is best if they part because Voldemort might use her as a weapon against him, Ginny accepts his decision. Although these characters are young, Rowling suggests that their romance is mature, especially in comparison to Lavender and Ron's.

Molly Weasley Mother to Bill, Charlie, Percy, Fred, George, Ron, and Ginny; married to Arthur Weasley. In this novel Molly Weasley continues to protect fiercely and love her family, including Harry. Rowling emphasizes her role as a surrogate mother to Harry when he first arrives at the Burrow. Even though everyone else has gone to bed, Molly waits for Harry to arrive, and when he does, she makes him a meal. Molly's behavior supports Rowling's suggestion that one does not have to be related by blood to be considered family. Molly makes few dramatic changes over the course of the sixth novel and appears only sporadically. Nonetheless, she remains a consistent figure in the series and, notably, in Harry's life as he grows from the young, curious boy wizard in *Sorcerer's Stone* into the heavy-hearted young man in *Half-Blood Prince*.

Ron Weasley Harry's and Hermione's best friend and fellow Gryffindor. In this novel Ron's character helps emphasize two very important themes: the

longing for a romantic relationship and the looming threat of death. Ron, previously unattached, becomes seriously involved with Lavender Brown. One can fairly question just how true his feelings for Lavender are. He mysteriously becomes romantically linked with her after seeing Ginny kiss a boy, remembering that Harry has kissed Cho, and learning that Hermione has even "snogged" Viktor Krum. After a particularly targeted taunt from his younger sister, Ginny, Ron rather suddenly begins a physical relationship involving frequent public embraces with Lavender Brown.

Like many teenagers, Ron feels as if he is too romantically inexperienced in comparison to his fellow students, and in an effort to reach a level of experience comparable to that of Ginny, Harry, and Hermione, he finds himself a willing partner. Clearly Lavender feels more strongly about Ron than he does about her, a fact evidenced by the "Sweetheart" necklace Lavender gives Ron for Christmas, which he refuses to wear. Ron behaves immaturely simply to frustrate Hermione, who obviously cares for him as well. Rowling traces the development of his romance with her, moving from childish bickering to genuinely caring for and comforting each other by the end of the novel.

Ron's nearly dying after drinking the mead that Slughorn offers him and Harry also emphasizes how fragile life is. Readers, arrested with fear when Ron starts foaming at the mouth from the poison in the mead (intended originally for Dumbledore), realize that as the Harry Potter saga continues, more characters will inevitably die. Readers expect that Ron will naturally have to survive to help Harry finish his quest and are unsettled by knowing how close he comes to dying. The threat of death haunts all characters and readers alike, and Ron's experience serves to emphasize that threat. Further, Harry's saving Ron's life by shoving a bezoar into his throat stresses Harry's role as savior for not only his friends but for the wizarding community in general.

FILM ADAPTATION

After directing *Order of the Phoenix*, David Yates returned to direct the next film in the series, *Half-Blood Prince*. In an interview with *Entertainment*

Weekly's Jeff Jensen Yates describes his excitement about working on his second Harry Potter film: "What I love about the movie is that it has many different parts—comedy, romance, suspense, good versus evil—but it also sets up the final chapter that is *Deathly Hallows*. . . . It really is the beginning of the end." Colin Covert of the Minneapolis/St. Paul *Star Tribune* admires the way Yates was able to take another lengthy novel and "[trim] Rowling's doorstop of a book to its essentials, goosing the action along briskly." The credit for such trimming, however, belongs rightfully to Steve Kloves, responsible for writing yet another screenplay for the series. The *New York Times*'s Manohla Dargis describes Kloves's final product as "surgically adapted" from Rowling's novel, and Kenneth Turan of the *Los Angeles Times* calls Kloves "a good steward of the material who is respectful of the novels but not overly reverential." Conversely, the London *Times*'s Kevin Maher writes that "the movie plays fast and loose with J. K. Rowling's overstuffed source novel, and excises several needless flashback sequences while controversially adding an opening gobsmacker of its own." The "gobsmacker" to which Maher refers is the devastating destruction of London's Millennium Bridge (in the book Death Eaters destroy Brockdale Bridge). But, the deletion of what Maher calls "needless" flashbacks severely disappointed legions of fans since those flashbacks help explain Voldemort's history and a way the Dark Lord might ultimately be defeated.

The deletion of seemingly crucial source material was not the first disappointment fans experienced concerning *Half-Blood Prince*. Though scheduled for initial release on November 21, 2008, the film did not premiere until July 2009. Some sources claim that the postponement of the film's release was due to the writer's strike of 2007–08. WARNER BROTHERS executives, realizing that the aftermath of the strike would have the greatest effect on their 2009 box office sales, decided to release the predicted blockbuster film in 2009 even though it was ready for release in 2008. *Entertainment Weekly*'s Jensen asked Yates about the problems with the film's release, and Yates said, "The studio needed to fill a slot for 2009. That was really the

only reason why it was moved. But we could have released it [in 2008]. The movie was ready." The film finally premiered in Tokyo on July 6, 2009, in London on July 7 in New York on July 8 and opened for regular release on July 15. The Motion Picture Association of America rated the film PG for "some scary images and sensuality." This rating surprised some viewers, however, since scenes including the possession of a female student (Katie Bell cursed by a necklace), the Inferi attack (when Harry and Dumbledore retrieve a supposed Horcrux), and a hormonal student licking his finger suggestively (Cormac McLaggen does so while flirting with Hermione) seemed to warrant a PG-13 rating.

Critical reviews seem to agree that the months between November 2008 and July 2009 fans were forced to endure were definitely worth the wait. Unsurprisingly critics in Harry's homeland award the film very high praise. Maher of the London *Times*, although more than pleased with the preceding films in the series, writes, "The strangest thing about the new Harry Potter movie is not that it's unusually good, which it is, but that it unequivocally illustrates just how poorly we've been served by the previous five instalments in the franchise." The London *Daily Mirror*'s Mark Adams adds that "the Harry Potter films just get better and better. . . . *Half-Blood Prince* is a wonderful wizarding adventure, brimming with action, love, drama, humour and dazzling performances. It is cracking stuff and bound to be the hit of the summer." On the other side of the pond critics echoed the remarks of their British colleagues. The *Chicago Sun-Times*'s Roger Ebert speaks to both the quality of the film and the fact that prior knowledge of the series is required for true appreciation of the cinematic adaptation of *Half-Blood Prince*: "I admired this Harry Potter. It opens and closes well, and has wondrous art design and cinematography as always, only more so. . . . The middle passages spin their wheels somewhat, hurrying about to establish events and places not absolutely essential." Even though Ebert acknowledges some viewers may find the film to be "padded," he also concedes that "those scenes may be especially valued by devoted students of the Potter saga. They may also be the only ones who fully understand them; ordinary viewers may be excused for feeling baffled some of the time."

Other critics comment that in a film brimming with danger and death happiness is still present. Dargis of the *New York Times* says, "That any sense of play and pleasure remains amid all the doom and dust, the poisonous potions and murderous sentiments, is partly a testament to the remarkable sturdiness of this movie franchise, which has transformed in subtle and obvious fashion, changing in tandem with the sprouting young bodies and slowly evolving personalities of its young, now teenage characters." The *Los Angeles Times*'s Turan credits the *Half-Blood Prince* with "demonstrat[ing] the ways that the Potter movies have become the modern exemplars of establishment moviemaking. We don't turn to these films for thrilling or original cinema, we look for a level of craft." And, Covert of the Minneapolis/St. Paul *Star Tribune* reflects on the level of the craft to which Turan refers: "Unlike most film series, the Potter movies haven't weakened along the way. The films have done justice to J. K. Rowling's complicated mythology, speaking confidently to the fan base while remaining accessible to the general public."

Filmmakers shot the movie over a nine-month period in England with a blockbuster cast, which Turan of the *Los Angeles Times* calls "a comprehensive guide to contemporary U.K. acting." The additions to the cast were roundly complimented for their skills. Adams of London's *Daily Mirror* comments of Jim Broadbent as the reluctant but endearing Professor Slughorn: "Broadbent is a perfect addition to the magical teaching staff: wonderfully witty and whimsical." Hero Fiennes-Tiffin and Frank Dillane also joined the cast as Voldemort at ages 11 and 16, respectively. Fiennes-Tiffin is Ralph Fiennes's nephew, and the similarity in appearance presents itself easily on screen. Dargis of the *New York Times* argues that both Fiennes-Tiffin and Dillane are "excellent young actors" and adds that Dillane, in particular, "conveys the seductiveness of evil with small, silky smiles he bestows like dangerous gifts." Another newcomer, Jessie Cave, provides comic relief as the Ron Weasley–obsessed Lavender Brown. More than 7,000 young women auditioned for this role,

highly coveted by many females because of Lavender's countless kissing scenes with Rupert Grint (as Ron Weasley) who, with his legions of female fans, has achieved heartthrob status.

Critics also reflected on the performances of returning cast members. Many viewers were shocked by McGonagall's appearance and the way she seemed much more worn and elderly than in the *Order of the Phoenix*. Dame Maggie Smith was undergoing treatment for breast cancer during the filming of *Half-Blood Prince*. Helena Bonham Carter also drew critical attention in her returning role as Bellatrix Lestrange. The *Chicago Sun Times*'s Ebert calls her a "destructive vixen," and Adams of London's *Daily Mirror* describes Carter as "astonishingly evil and mesmerising." Carter says that "pretending to be a witch has great appeal" to her and that she also finds Bellatrix interesting because she is, simply put, an "anarchist." When playing this rebel, Carter says that she finds her role to be "very therapeutic" since, as one of the Dark Lord's most dedicated followers, she unleashes her fury on the wizarding world and destroys sets and props in many scenes. An example of Carter's capturing Bellatrix's rampant desire for destruction occurs near the end of *Half-Blood Prince* when she jumps onto a table in the great Hall and runs from one end to the other, smashing and kicking dishes the entire length of the table.

Two other characters viewers and readers both love to hate received special attention for their performances in the film: Tom Felton as Draco Malfoy and Alan Rickman as Severus Snape. The *Star Tribune*'s Covert says that the in *Half-Blood Prince*, "Character growth is deftly sketched," citing Felton's performance as Malfoy as an excellent example. Felton says that he truly loves playing the part of Malfoy, especially in the sixth Harry Potter film. In a *TV Guide* special made to promote the film Felton discusses how, though he auditioned for the roles of Harry and Ron, he takes pride in the role of Malfoy the Slytherin, even if, as he says, Draco is "a wimp, straight through and through." Performing in the role of Slytherin head of house, Alan Rickman as Severus Snape continues to receive positive reviews. The *New York Times*'s Dargis claims that Rickman's performance remains so strong and engaging because Rickman "invests his character . . . with much-needed ambiguity, drawing each word out with exquisite luxury, bringing to mind a buzzard lazily pulling at entrails." Turan praises Rickman for "dripping disdain when he eviscerates Harry with lines like, 'How grand it must be to be the chosen one.'" Rickman's careful execution of his role also receives Ebert's commendation, which the critic says Rickman "invests . . . with such macabre pauses."

Some critics had less pleasing things to say about Daniel Radcliffe, Rupert Grint, and Emma Watson. Dargis calls the teen actors "prettily manicured bores"; similarly Ebert offers an unpleasant review of Radcliffe: "[his] Potter is sturdy and boring, as always." Conversely, Maher claims that "Radcliffe, perhaps emboldened by his stage time in *Equus*, has leavened his formerly plank-like turn with smart self-deprecating shrugs and sighs." Covert found Watson's performance impressive and a genuine depiction of a spurned lover, writing, "Watson's Hermione huffs and scowls in romantic frustration as her two childhood pals steadfastly ignore her almost-adult charms." In an interview with *Movie Magic* Emma Watson explains that "Hermione's part in the *Half-Blood Prince* has very much to do with Ron. . . . It's very comic, and also quite sad for Hermione. It's very kind of Ron-based, her part" ("*Half-Blood* Wizards"). But of the trio Grint received the best reviews. Maher says that "Grint especially is becoming something of an accomplished comic actor," and Covert adds, "As the love-bedazzled Ron, Grint delivers the film's standout comic performance."

As usual this Harry Potter film included amazing special effects. Filmmakers treat viewers to some of the most incredible effects implemented thus far in the series. When Dumbledore and Harry visit the cave to retrieve one of Voldemort's Horcruxes, the Inferi attack, and Dumbledore battles them. As the Internet Movie Database reports, the VFX supervisor Tim Alexander explains that creating the attack took months, adding that it was "much bolder and scarier than we imagined that they'd ever go in a Potter movie. David Yates was really cautious of not making this into a zombie movie. . . . A lot of

it came down to their movement—they don't move fast, but they don't move really slow or groan and moan. We ended up going with a very realistic style." Some viewers believed the Inferi were very similar to the portrayal of Gollum/Smeagol in Peter Jackson's *Lord of the Rings* trilogy; regardless, the attack is unsettling. Dumbledore's counterattack is undeniably impressive. The production designer Stuart Craig and a team of designers traveled the world examining caves to serve as inspiration for this scene. After visiting Switzerland and Mexico, they traveled to Frankfurt, Germany, and found a salt crystal cave, after which they modeled the set for *Half-Blood Prince*. Craig and his team only built small parts of the cave set; the rest of the set was computer generated. One part of the set they did physically build was the island with the podium holding the Horcrux. The Inferi attack that island and capture Harry, pulling him into the depths of the lake in the cave. Gambon, noticeably exhausted, summons his remaining strength, and the fire he unleashes crowds the entire screen. Rings of flames rise up as he guards Harry protectively, a gesture that hearkens back to the start of the film, when Dumbledore lovingly pats Harry's hand before they embark on their mission to secure Slughorn as a member of the Hogwarts staff.

The film version of *Half-Blood Prince* also introduced some new sets while reintroducing some crowd favorites. For instance, *Half-Blood Prince* is the first film in which viewers see the Astronomy Tower, the site of Dumbledore's confrontation with Malfoy, followed by his murder at the hands of Snape. Quidditch also makes its first appearance since the film version of *Prisoner of Azkaban*. Fans were delighted to see Ron at work as a Keeper, and perhaps the Quidditch tryouts were so entertaining because the cast loved filming these scenes. Rather than just following the dizzying pursuit of the Snitch or of a chaser trying to score, *Half-Blood Prince* devotes screen time to the Gryffindor House's Quidditch team tryout. The way Ron blocks Quaffles by kicking them or while hanging upside down on his broom, struggling not to fall, provides an example of Grint's comic talent at work. Rupert Grint, in an interview with the publication *Movie Magic*, reflects on filming the

Quidditch scene: "I was happy to do the Quidditch scene. . . . There was one shot where I had to save a series of Quaffles, and there was one shot where they were throwing 350 of those rubber Quaffles. They pelted me and I did actually fall off the broom and was hanging by a wire" ("*Half-Blood* Wizards"). Fans appreciated his dedication to the scene and his comic craft at work.

As Covert mentions in his review, Felton as Malfoy demonstrates significant character growth, and, indeed, Malfoy's personal struggles form an important strand of the film. While the film simplifies the novel's more complex plot concerning his use of a set of Vanishing Cabinets to provide a point of entry for Voldemort's followers into Hogwarts, filmmakers do complicate Malfoy's emotions and allegiance to Voldemort. Felton engages viewers as he breaks down emotionally in a bathroom before a tense encounter with Harry. Gripping the sink with his hands, Malfoy stares into a mirror, a keen choice by filmmakers that emphasizes Malfoy's internal struggle as one forced to demonstrate allegiance to Voldemort out of fear. Perhaps the greatest use of symbolism for Malfoy's struggle concerns a spherical cage housing two birds, one black and one white. The two birds arguably represent Draco's struggle between good and evil. Tellingly he takes the white bird out first and uses it to experiment with the Vanishing Cabinets. The bird twitters happily as Draco places it inside the cabinet located in the Room of Requirement in Hogwarts. After an encounter with some Death Eaters with the other cabinet in Borgin and Burke's, the bird returns, dead. The symbolism here suggests that Draco has sacrificed his goodness to pursue a future with the Death Eaters but also functions as a red herring. Viewers unfamiliar with the books may assume Malfoy's allegiance remains with the Dark Lord; readers, on the other hand, know better.

Filmmakers also capitalize on the romance in *Half-Blood Prince*. Rowling's novel emphasizes developing relationships involving scores of characters, but for obvious reasons the details of some relationships are altered. Bill and Fleur's story is deleted entirely, and Lupin and Tonks are already in love when viewers first see them. Tonks's depression after Lupin denies

her is lost, but this is probably due to time constraints. On the other hand, some romance is added. In the beginning of the film Harry waits in an underground station, reading an issue of the *Daily Prophet* in a small café. The waitress and Harry quickly decide to go on a date but not before Dumbledore whisks Harry off to recruit Slughorn. Some viewers questioned why filmmakers would include this scene at the cost of sacrificing details about more important characters such as Tonks, Lupin, Fleur, and Bill. Harry's potential date and its quick cancellation (without an explanation to the woman Harry will be meeting) emphasize the uncertainty in the wizarding community due to Voldemort's return: Plans are always subject to revision since a crisis can strike at any time, at any moment. On a similar topic many fans were upset by the scene in which a flock of Death Eaters appear during Christmas at the Weasley home and burn the Burrow to the ground. While this decision begs some logistic questions (if it is shown, where will Bill and Fleur's wedding take place?), it emphasizes the destructive power of Voldemort and his followers.

Many fans also eagerly awaited the romantic encounters between Harry and Ginny. Ginny's interest in Harry has been clear since the second film, *Chamber of Secrets*, in which the young girl becomes befuddled and darts from the Burrow's kitchen after first seeing Harry. Filmmakers foreshadowed their impending romance with moments like Ginny's tying Harry's shoelaces or offering Harry her hand as they walk to the Room of Requirement to dispose of the Half-Blood Prince's potion book. Interestingly Ginny and Harry share their first kiss in the Room of Requirement, in comparison to their kiss after a Quidditch match in the novel. Staging the kiss in this location foreshadows the path their relationship will take: Harry (in the novel) leaves Ginny behind to pursue Voldemort and, as with anything placed in the Room of Requirement, finds her again when he truly needs her.

Half-Blood Prince ends much as *Goblet of Fire* does, with Harry, Ron, and Hermione standing together, alone, looking out on the Black Lake. At the end of the fourth movie Hermione utters the famous lines "Everything's going to change now, isn't it?" To end the sixth movie in the same manner as the fourth asks viewers to recall Hermione's words and realize that in the final chapters of the Harry Potter film saga the ultimate battle between Harry and Voldemort will occur and everything will change, once and for all.

WORKS CITED AND FURTHER READING

Adams, Mark. "Film Review: *Harry Potter and the Half-Blood Prince.*" *Daily Mirror,* 12 July 2009.

Asim, Jabari. "Harry VI: The Plot Darkens, but Our Hero Grows Brighter in Response." *Washington Post.* 18 July 2005. Available online. URL: http://www.washingtonpost.com/wp-dyn/content/article/2005/07/17/AR2005071701016.html. Accessed September 1, 2009.

Barton, Benjamin. "Harry Potter and the Half-Crazy Bureaucracy." *Michigan Law Review* 104, no. 6 (May 2005): 1,523–1,538.

Blasingame, James, and Faith H. Wallace. "Harry Potter and the Half-Blood Prince." *Journal of Adolescent and Adult Literacy* 49, no. 3 (November 2005): 250–251.

Bonamici, Kate. "By the Numbers." *Fortune* 152, no. 2 (July 25, 2005): 28–28.

Bryce, Frank Cottrell. Review of *Harry Potter and the Half-Blood Prince. Independent* (London), 22 July 2005. Available online. URL: http://www.independent.co.uk/arts-entertainment/books/reviews/harry-potter-and-the-halfblood-prince-by-j-k-rowling-499657.html. Accessed August 25, 2009.

Burkam, Anita L. Review of *Harry Potter and the Half-Blood Prince. Horn Book Magazine* 81, no. 5 (September 2005): 587–588.

Casteel, Shandy. "As His World Returns." *Pop Matters,* 1 August 2005. Available online. URL: http://popmatters.com/books/reviews/h/harry-potter-half-blood-prince.shtml. Accessed August 25, 2009.

Chapman, Jeanine. Review of *Harry Potter and the Half-Blood Prince. Horn Book Magazine* 81, no. 6 (November 2005): 744.

Cooper, Ilene. Review of *Harry Potter and the Half-Blood Prince. Booklist* 101, no. 22 (August 2005): 1,948.

Corbett, Sue. Review of *Harry Potter and the Half-Blood Prince. People,* 64, no. 5 (August 2005): 43.

Covert, Colin. "Dark Brew." *Star Tribune,* 15 July 2009, pp. E1, E6.

Dargis, Manohla. "In Latest *Harry Potter,* Rage and Hormones." *New York Times,* 15 July 2009.

Decker, Charlotte. Review of *Harry Potter and the Half-Blood Prince. Library Media Connection,* February 2006, 68.

"Designing Hollywood." In *Movie Magic.* San Antonio, Tex.: Bauer, 2009.

Donahue, Deirdre. "'Harry' Does Some Serious Growing Up." *USA Today,* 17 July 2005. Available online. URL: http://www.usatoday.com/life/books/reviews/2005-07-17-harry-potter_x.htm. Accessed August 25, 2009.

Douthat, Ross. "Redemption at Hogwarts." *National Review,* 12 September 2005, 49–49.

Ebert, Roger. "*Harry Potter and the Half-Blood Prince.*" *Chicago Sun-Times,* 12 July 2009.

"Fantastic Fiction!" *Scholastic Scope,* 9 May 2005, 26–26.

"Fiction Reprints." *Publishers Weekly,* 17 July 2006, 160–160.

Grossman, Lev. "Love Potions and Tragic Magic." *Time,* 25 July 2005, 62–63.

Gurdon, Meghan Cox. "The Author Still Possesses Magical Powers." *Wall Street Journal.* 19 July 2005. Available online. URL: http://online.wsj.com/article/SB112172580409888779.html. Accessed September 1, 2009.

"The *Half-Blood* Wizards Have Their Say." In *Movie Magic.* San Antonio, Tex.: Bauer, 2009.

Jensen, Jeff. "This Magic Moment." *Entertainment Weekly,* 17 July 2009, 24–31.

Kakutani, Michiko. "Harry Potter Works His Magic Again in a Far Darker Tale." *New York Times.* 16 July 2005. Available online. URL: http://www.nytimes.com/2005/07/16/books/16choc.html. Accessed August 25, 2009.

Kipen, David. Review of *Harry Potter and the Half-Blood Prince. San Francisco Chronicle.* 17 July 2005. Available online. URL: http://www.sfgate.com/cgi-bin/article.cgi?f=/c/a/2005/07/17/MNGKQDPCNS1.DTL&type=books. Accessed September 1, 2009.

Lafferty, Fiona. "Beyond the HP Source." *Times Educational Supplement,* 2 September 2005, 31.

Lambert, Peter. "With a Merciless Pen." *Times Literary Supplement,* 29 July 2005, 20.

Linning, Lyn. "Harry Potter and the Half-Blood Prince." *Magpies* 20, no. 4 (September 2005): 33.

Maher, Kevin. "*Harry Potter and the Half-Blood Prince.*" *Times* (London), 16 July 2009.

Miller, Laura. "Heroes and Hormones." Salon.com. 17 July 2005. Available online. URL: http://dir.salon.com/story/books/review/2005/07/17/rowling/index.html. Accessed August 25, 2009.

Mullan, John. Review of *Harry Potter and the Half-Blood Prince. Guardian.* 23 July 2005. Available online. URL: http://www.guardian.co.uk/books/2005/jul/23/booksforchildrenandteenagers.harrypotter. Accessed September 1, 2009.

Paolini, Christopher. "'Prince' of Darkness." *Entertainment Weekly,* 29 July 2005, 72.

Review of *Harry Potter and the Half-Blood Prince. Publishers Weekly,* 25 July 2005, 77.

Review of *Harry Potter and the Half-Blood Prince. Library Media Connection* 24, no. 5 (February 2006): 68.

Robinson, Tasha. Review of *Harry Potter and the Half-Blood Prince. Onion AV Club.* 2 August 2005. Available online. URL: http://www.avclub.com/content/node/25314. Accessed August 25, 2009.

Rosenberg, Liz. "'Prince' Shines among Growing Darkness." *Boston Globe.* 18 July 2005. Available online. URL: http://www.boston.com/ae/books/articles/2005/07/18/prince_shines_amid_growing_darkness/. Accessed September 1, 2009.

Saunders, Kate. "Great Escape." *New Statesman* 134, no. 4,751 (August 2005): 38.

Schiavone, Angie. Review of *Harry Potter and the Half-Blood Prince. Sydney Morning Herald.* 23 July 2005. Available online. URL: http://www.smh.com.au/news/books/harry-potter-and-the-halfblood-prince/2005/07/22/1121539138363.html?oneclick=true. Accessed September 1, 2009.

Schillinger, Liesl. "*Harry Potter and the Half-Blood Prince*: Her Dark Materials." *New York Times Book Review,* 31 July 2005. Available online. URL: http://www.nytimes.com/2005/07/31/books/review/31SCHILL.html?ei=5089&en=09eade2310dd851a&ex=1280462400&pagewanted=print. Accessed August 25, 2009.

Serrill-Robins, Mira, and Dan Beucke. "Harry Potter and the Cyberpirates." *Business Week,* August 2005, 9.

"Smothered in HP." *Economist,* 3 September 2005, 75.

Sperling, Nicole. "*Harry Potter and the Half-Blood Prince.*" *Entertainment Weekly,* 3 August 2007, 31.

Turan, Kenneth. "Review: *Harry Potter and the Half-Blood Prince.*" *Los Angeles Times,* 14 July 2009.

"2005 Editors' Choice." *Booklist* 102, no. 9/10 (January 2006): 6–20.

Wallace, Faith H. Review of *Harry Potter and the Half-Blood Prince. Journal of Adolescent and Adult Literacy* 49, no. 3 (November 2005): 250–251.

Welsh, Christopher. "Harry Potter and the Underage Drinkers: Can We Use This to Talk to Teens about Alcohol?" *Journal of Child and Adolescent Substance Abuse* 16, no. 4 (2007): 119–126.

Wysocki, Barbara, and Phyllis Levy Mandall. Review of *Harry Potter and the Half-Blood Prince. School Library Journal* 51, no. 9 (August 2008): 78.

Zipp, Yvonne. "There's Still Every Reason to Be Wild about Harry." *Christian Science Monitor.* 18 July 2005. Available online. URL: http://www.csmonitor.com/2005/0718/p11s01-bogn.html. Accessed September 1, 2009.

Harry Potter and the Deathly Hallows (2007)

SYNOPSIS

Chapter 1: "The Dark Lord Ascending"

The Hogwarts Potions master Severus Snape meets a fellow Death Eater, follower of Lord Voldemort, on a dark road. They proceed to the home of Lucius Malfoy and enter a dark room where a group of people are seated around a table. A shadowy figure is suspended above the table. Snape reports to Voldemort and the group that Harry Potter will be moved from his current location on Saturday night. Another Death Eater, Yaxley, disagrees and claims an alternative plan is in place, citing another source, as well as suggesting that the ministry may be on its way to falling and that the head of Magical Law Enforcement is now under his Imperius Curse. Voldemort asserts that Harry Potter's continued existence is due only to luck and chance and announces that he must be the one to kill Harry—but he needs someone's wand, as his last chance to kill Harry was foiled by a wand malfunction. He takes Lucius Malfoy's wand without exchanging his own; Voldemort taunts Lucius about his discomfort with the Dark Lord and his occupancy of the Malfoy manor. Despite Bellatrix Lestrange's (Lucius's sister-in-law) assertion that the Malfoys are delighted to have him at their family home, Voldemort mocks their family, revealing that Nymphadora Tonks, one of the Aurors who have protected Harry Potter throughout the last two books and niece of Bellatrix, has just married Remus Lupin, former Defense Against the Dark Arts teacher; friend of Harry's father, James; and a werewolf since childhood.

Voldemort comments on the corruption of pure-blood family lineage and draws Snape's attention to the hovering figure. Readers learn that she is Charity Burbage, formerly a teacher of Muggle studies at Hogwarts School of Witchcraft and Wizardry. Because she has published a defense of Muggles and attack on wizard chauvinism, Voldemort uses the killing curse *Avada Kedavra* on her, leaving her body for his giant snake, Nagini.

Chapter 2: "In Memoriam"

Cleaning out his school trunk, Harry cuts himself on a fragment of glass that is part of a two-way mirror that his godfather, Sirius Black, now dead, gave him in the fifth novel of the series, *Order of the Phoenix*. Harry is pulling out all the items he plans not to use this year—including his academic materials, as he does not plan to return to school. Items he keeps in his traveling trunk include the gold locket that Dumbledore injured his hand—and ultimately died—to obtain. He also takes a photo album of his dead parents, his Invisibility Cloak, and an assortment of other items that might be useful along his journey.

Harry reviews the stack of newspapers, in particular the wizarding publication the *Daily Prophet*, to read a story that eulogizes Dumbledore. Read-

ers learn from Elphias Doge that Dumbledore has always been a friend to outsiders. Further, the story reveals that Dumbledore's father was accused of an attack on three Muggles; Dumbledore admits that his father was guilty of the crime and that, in a seeming contrast to his father, Dumbledore was a staunch supporter of Muggle rights. Dumbledore distinguished himself in his school years for his brilliant magical abilities and his scholarly publications. Aberforth, his brother, also attended Hogwarts but traded in duels rather than books. After school Dumbledore experienced two major tragedies: the death of his mother and sister; for the latter he ambiguously felt personally responsible. Doge's article alludes to Dumbledore's major life accomplishments including the epic wizarding duel with Grindelwald in 1945. Harry ponders this life of Dumbledore's before he knew him and regrets not having learned more about his mentor before Dumbledore's death at the end of *Half-Blood Prince*.

The most recent edition of the newspaper reveals a forthcoming book by the noted sensationalist journalist Rita Skeeter called *The Life and Lies of Albus Dumbledore*. An interview in the paper suggests Skeeter's book alleges that Dumbledore dabbled in the dark arts and had a "murky past," along with skeletons in his family closet. Rita Skeeter also implies that she has developed a close relationship with Harry and that Harry's accusations against Snape as Dumbledore's murderer are false. While he continues packing, Harry swears he sees a flash of a blue eye in the broken mirror shard.

Chapter 3: "The Dursleys Departing"

The Dursleys arrive home dressed for traveling. Harry has told them they are in danger because Harry lives there and knows Voldemort or one of his followers could very well appear in Little Whinging, ready to execute Harry and anyone else nearby. Vernon refuses to believe Harry's claims despite Harry's reminder that Kingsley Shacklebolt and Arthur Weasley, both representing the Ministry of Magic, visited to warn them that the protective charm that currently keeps him safe from Voldemort will break when he turns 17, in four days. The Dursleys are reluctant to accept "government" protection from the ministry. Harry tries to convince them that various catastrophic events that have happened in the Muggle world are being caused by Voldemort and the Death Eaters. Harry finally convinces Dudley of the potentially horrible fate that could befall them if Death Eaters, Dementors, or Inferi find them; they agree to go with the members of the order who are soon arriving.

Dedalus Diggle and Hestia Jones arrive to escort the Dursleys from their home, informing them that they will drive several miles before Disapparating. The original plan for Harry to set off with Mad-Eye using Side-Along Apparition has apparently changed. As the Dursleys start to leave, Dudley expresses an uncharacteristic concern for Harry's well-being, wondering why he is not accompanying them and where he is going to go, as well as expressing a changed perception of Harry that borders on affection. The Dursleys leave with Diggle and Jones.

Chapter 4: "The Seven Potters"

Harry collects his possessions and feels a surprising sense of wistfulness about leaving Privet Drive. A group of wizards led by Mad-Eye Moody, the former Auror, arrives, interrupting his memories. They have had to devise an alternative plan because they know that Pius Thicknesse, acting under the Imperius Curse, has made it an imprisonable offense to use magical means to leave one's house; under the Imperius Curse Thicknesse has essentially cornered Harry. Harry realizes that the guard's plan is problematic because it involves 13 of the people he cares about (six disguised as him to thwart Voldemort and the Death Eaters), who will all be leaving Privet Drive and flying to seven different locations. Even though the Order of the Phoenix, the subversive group battling Voldemort's Death Eaters, has leaked a fake trail to the ministry, Harry still feels greatly concerned for the safety of his friends. Moody produces Polyjuice Potion, telling him that seven Harry Potters will be leaving with a companion via brooms, thestrals, or Hagrid's motorbike, to which Harry strenuously objects because of his reluctance to put people in danger. However, all of them are of age and prepared to make him comply with the plan by force if they have to.

Harry's friends Ron Weasley, Hermione Granger, Fred and George Weasley, and Fleur Delacour step up immediately to take the Polyjuice Potion while the less noble but useful Mundungus Fletcher has to be coerced by Hagrid. They drink the potion and suddenly it seems as if seven Harry Potters stand in the Dursley home. They mount their forms of transport and leave, only to be surrounded by 30 hooded figures. In the chaos Harry drops Hedwig's cage and sees her fall lifeless to the bottom of the sidecar. Harry wants to go back to battle, but Hagrid asserts that his job is to get Harry to safety and they continue on, pursued by four Death Eaters. Despite numerous magical additions to Hagrid's motorcycle, the sidecar splits away from the motorbike for a terrifying moment; the sidecar remains afloat only through Harry's quick thinking and use of the *Wingardium Leviosa* spell. Plucked from the falling sidecar by Hagrid, they evade Death Eaters until Stan Shunpike, driver for the Knight Bus and apparently under the Imperius Curse, identifies Harry as the real version of himself, drawing Voldemort after them. As Hagrid launches himself off the bike to attack a Death Eater, Harry struggles to maintain control of the motorbike and fend off Voldemort. He and Hagrid both crash-land into a pond.

Chapter 5: "Fallen Warrior"

Harry finds himself in a pond of muddy water, disoriented and trying to awaken a still Hagrid. He next finds himself tended to by Tonks's parents—Ted and Andromeda—who reassure Harry that Hagrid is alive and fine. Andromeda is Bellatrix Lestrange's sister, the one Voldemort taunted Bellatrix about earlier in the novel (since Andromeda married a nonpureblood and her daughter married a werewolf). Harry and Hagrid confess that they were attacked by Death Eaters and do not know where anyone else is. The Tonkses fret over their daughter's safety. Harry and Hagrid take the Portkey back to the Burrow, but they are the first to arrive. The order's plan has gone awry, and two pairs of Harry's protectors have missed their Portkey. Lupin and George arrive, George covered in blood, missing an ear. Lupin and Harry deduce that the Death Eaters knew it was he because he used *Expelliarmus*, the disarming spell, against Stan Shunpike (whom he knows, likes, and knew to be Imperiused) rather than an attacking spell. When Lupin chastens him for not attacking with a more serious Stunning Spell, Harry retorts, "I won't blast people out of my way just because they're there.... That's Voldemort's job" (71).

Hermione and Kingsley appear. They confirm that Voldemort can fly and that they barely escaped the group of Death Eaters who chased them. Shunpike and Travers, both of whom were identified by members of the order as Death Eaters, are supposed to be in Azkaban, leading them to conclude that there has been a prison escape covered up by the Ministry of Magic.

Fred and Arthur Weasley arrive next, followed by Tonks and Ron. The group still waits for Bill and Fleur and Mad-Eye and Mundungus. When Bill and Fleur arrive, they announce that Mad-Eye has been killed and that Mundungus abandoned them. They immediately suspect he is the traitor, but Bill suggests that because Mundungus suggested the "Seven Harrys" trick, which surprised Voldemort and the Death Eaters, he probably did not betray the order's plan to the Death Eaters. Harry affirms that he trusts everyone in the room and does not believe anyone would betray him. Bill and Lupin go to retrieve Mad-Eye's body. Harry feels an impulse to leave, despite all that has been wagered and lost trying to get him to the Burrow safely; he worries about endangering his friends. He is also upset as he reports that his wand did magic without his intending for it to, even though Mr. Weasley tries to assure him that wizards often produce magic in high-pressured situations that they are not normally capable of doing.

As he heads outside for a moment alone, his scar begins to throb, and he sees Voldemort tormenting the wand maker Ollivander about the connection between Voldemort's and Harry's wands. When he tells Ron and Hermione about this vision, they beg Harry not to let Voldemort inside his head and to practice Occlumency.

Chapter 6: "The Ghoul in Pajamas"

Mad-Eye is missed; Harry plans to mount his search for the Horcruxes—the magically bewitched objects that hold the pieces of Voldemort's soul—as soon as possible, but he has to wait until the Trace—the magical tracking placed on each minor wizard until he or she is of age 17—disappears. Ron warns him that his mother plans to find out what he, Harry, and Hermione are doing, including what mission Dumbledore has set them on that involves their dropping out of Hogwarts, something Harry readily admits to her when she confronts him. He insists that he must fulfill Dumbledore's request and that Ron and Hermione do not have to accompany him. Mrs. Weasley abruptly changes the subject to the upcoming wedding of Bill and Fleur, enlisting him, Ron, and Hermione in completing preparations for the ceremony.

Dinner discussion turns to the role of the Secret Keeper in keeping hidden the location of Number Twelve, Grimmauld Place, the former headquarters of the Order of the Phoenix. Harry struggles with the strain between him and Ginny, their formerly affectionate relationship now tested by his upcoming mission. Mad-Eye's body is not recovered, the ministry appears to be covering up the battle, and Scrimgeour, the current Minister of Magic, is more interested in public relations spin than the cause of right.

Ron, Hermione, and Harry share a brief moment alone in Ron's bedroom, mourning for Dumbledore and Mad-Eye. Ron and Hermione's romantic relationship continues subtly to evolve. Harry once again tries to convince them not to go with him; Hermione confesses tearfully that she modified her parents' memories to induce them to move to Australia and forget about her, so their abandoning his cause is out of the question. Ron has enlisted their house ghoul to pose as Ron with spattergroit, an unpleasant skin condition, as a cover story for his absence.

They briefly discuss their plan of action. Hermione wants to hunt Horcruxes, while Harry thinks they should go to Godric's Hollow, where his parents are buried and where he survived the first Killing Curse. Hermione suggests Voldemort might anticipate their plan. Their conversation turns to the locket they recovered from the cave at the end of *Half-Blood Prince*, including the thief's claim in a note that he or she planned to destroy the real Horcrux. Hermione notes she has found books on destroying Horcruxes. *Secrets of the Darkest Art,* one that young Tom Riddle may have used to make his initial Horcruxes, reveals the danger of splitting one's soul at all, let alone into seven pieces, as Voldemort does. They only way to reverse it is to feel true remorse for one's evil acts. The only way to destroy a Horcrux, they learn, is with a strong force such as the basilisk fang that Harry used in *Chamber of Secrets* to destroy Riddle's diary.

Hermione explains that the piece of the soul can inhabit a Horcrux but can "flit in and out of someone if they get too close to the object" (105), as with Ginny Weasley and Riddle's diary in *Chamber of Secrets.* Harry wonders why he did not ask Dumbledore how he destroyed the other Horcrux in *Half-Blood Prince,* Voldemort's maternal grandfather Marvolo Gaunt's gold ring with a black stone.

Mrs. Weasley interrupts their conversation to set them doing more errands. Fleur's parents arrive for the wedding. They have to use a Portkey to enter since the ministry and the order have placed magical enchantments on the Burrow, Mrs. Weasley asks Harry whether he would like a birthday celebration, and he discourages her from going to any trouble but eventually agrees to a celebratory dinner with Tonks and Lupin.

Chapter 7: "The Will of Albus Dumbledore"
Harry awakens on his 17th birthday after having a dream in which he mutters the name *Gregorovitch.* The name seems familiar, and Harry feels as if he has heard it before somewhere. The Weasleys give him the traditional wizarding coming-of-age gift, a watch. Hermione gives him a Sneakoscope. Ginny calls him into her room, and they share a kiss, which is interrupted by Ron and Hermione. Ron later admonishes Harry for having dumped Ginny and now kissing her, and Harry feels devastated at imagining Ginny's future with a man other than him.

At Harry's birthday dinner Hagrid gives him a mokeskin pouch in which the owner can hide anything and be the only one allowed to retrieve it. Arthur is late but sends a Patronus to warn them that the Minister of Magic, Rufus Scrimgeour, is arriving with him. When Arthur eventually arrives with the minister, Scrimgeour asks for a private

moment with Ron, Harry, and Hermione. He is there because of Dumbledore's will, and Hermione explains cynically that the delay since Dumbledore's death is due to the Decree for Justifiable Confiscation—the ministry has examined the items Dumbledore left them and Scrimgeour interrogates them about why Dumbledore has left them specific possessions: to Ron, a Deluminator, a magical object that has the power to suck all the light from a place and restore it with a click; to Hermione, a copy of the *Tales of Beedle the Bard,* a book of wizarding folktales; and to Harry, the Snitch he caught in his first Quidditch match at Hogwarts. Scrimgeour suggests that Dumbledore left Harry the Snitch to hide something in it because, as Hermione reveals, Snitches have "flesh memories," the ability to remember the touch of the first human to lay hands on them. Though he fears something will happen when he takes it, nothing does. Dumbledore also leaves Harry the sword of Godric Gryffindor, but Scrimgeour claims that Dumbledore had no right to leave the sword to anyone because it qualifies as an important historical artifact.

Harry accuses the ministry of failing to take real action against the Death Eaters and Voldemort. After a confrontation Scrimgeour leaves angrily. Harry enjoys a birthday dinner with the Weasleys and then joins Hermione and Ron in the attic room to discuss Dumbledore's mysterious gifts. Harry reveals that he captured this Snitch in his first Quidditch match in his mouth, not with his hand; placing the Snitch in his mouth reveals writing on the small golden ball, "I open at the close," but no matter how they ponder, they cannot deduce the phrase's meaning, nor why Dumbledore would have willed Harry the sword. Hermione has never heard of her gift, *The Tales of Beedle the Bard,* but Ron explains that the work is a collection of old fairy tales told to wizard children—something Hermione and Harry, raised as Muggles, would know nothing about.

Chapter 8: "The Wedding"
Harry, Ron, and the Weasley twins wait to greet wedding guests. Harry uses Polyjuice Potion to take on the appearance of a local village boy, hoping to

be passed off as "Cousin Barny" in order to protect the secrecy of his location. A variety of friends and relatives arrive, including Xenophilius Lovegood, Luna's father and editor of the wizarding tabloid the *Quibbler*. Luna also attends and mysteriously recognizes Harry from "his expression"; her ability to recognize Harry in this manner is consistent with her strangeness. Auntie Muriel, a crotchety old witch, arrives and insults various guests. Viktor Krum (a former Triwizard Tournament champion in *Goblet of Fire*, Durmstrang student, and rival of Ron's for Hermione's affections) arrives and causes a stir.

The wizard who presided over Dumbledore's funeral also marries Fleur and Bill Weasley. At the reception Krum confides angrily to "Barny" that Luna's father is wearing a strange image of a triangular eye that is the symbol of Grindelwald, the dark wizard Dumbledore defeated. In talking with Krum, Harry also remembers where he has heard the name *Gregorovitch* before when he sees Krum's wand at the reception: During the wand-weighing ceremony of the Triwizard Tournament, Ollivander identified Gregorovitch as the maker of Krum's wand. He realizes Voldemort must be searching for a wand maker because of the malfunctioning that occurs when Voldemort and Harry's wands duel.

Harry reveals himself to Elphias Doge, the writer of Dumbledore's obituary. Doge tries to assuage Harry's concern that Dumbledore was involved with the Dark Arts. Muriel joins them, praising Rita Skeeter's journalistic skill and indicating her eagerness to read Skeeter's new biography of Dumbledore. She implies that Dumbledore murdered his sister, Ariana, who was a Squib, or person born into a wizarding family without magical powers. Muriel claims that Ariana was locked in the cellar, that few knew she existed until she died, and that Dumbledore's mother was an arrogant and proud woman who was ashamed of her daughter. Doge attempts to deny all Muriel's accusations. She also recalls that Aberforth Dumbledore (brother of the Hogwarts headmaster) broke his brother's nose during Ariana's funeral service, according to Bathilda Bagshot, a magical historian (and, as Harry remembers, the author of his textbook *A History of Magic*). Muriel additionally reveals that the Dumbledores

and Bagshot lived in Godric's Hollow, where Harry's parents were murdered by Voldemort. Harry feels betrayed that Dumbledore never revealed these commonalities with him.

Suddenly Kingsley Shacklebolt's silvery lynx Patronus appears, disrupting the happy wedding celebration. The Patronus announces, "The Ministry has fallen. Scrimgeour is dead. They are coming" (159).

Chapter 9: "A Place to Hide"
Chaos erupts, and Hermione grabs Ron and Harry and Disapparates to Tottenham Court Road, a Muggle Street. Hermione has cast an "Undetectable Extension Charm" on her small beaded handbag, allowing her to store the essentials they need for a quick getaway (including changes of clothes for all of them, books, and Harry's Invisibility Cloak) in her purse. They slip into an all-night café to get their bearings, but two Death Eaters are waiting, and a magical battle erupts. They Apparate to Grimmauld Place, the Black ancestral home, because they are not sure where else to go; they feel safer at Grimmauld Place since the order has reassured them that jinxes have been placed upon it to keep Snape away. Many of the rooms in the house show signs of having been searched.

Harry's scar begins to hurt; Voldemort is angry. Arthur Weasley's Patronus appears to report that the family is safe but that they are being watched. When Harry retreats to the bathroom, he fully feels Voldemort's anger and sees him order Draco to torture the Death Eater they stunned in the café.

Chapter 10: "Kreacher's Tale"
Harry awakens the next day and ponders the mission Dumbledore has left him—to destroy the Horcruxes. Muriel's accusations leave him feeling as though he did not really know the headmaster. He enters Sirius's old bedroom and finds an old photograph of Harry's father, James, with Sirius, Lupin, and Peter Pettigrew, as well as a letter from his mother to Sirius written near Harry's first birthday revealing his parents socialized with Bathilda Bagshot. Harry tells Hermione what he learned about Dumbledore, and she tries to dissuade him

from going to Godric's Hollow, frightened that the Death Eaters found them so easily.

They find the room of Sirius's brother, Regulus Arcturus, and realize he must be the R.A.B. who signed the letter left in the locket Horcrux that Harry and Dumbledore found at the end of *Half-Blood Prince*. A reformed Death Eater, he was murdered by Voldemort. Like the other rooms in the house, it appears to have been searched. They try to summon the locket to no avail and realize that in *Order of the Phoenix*, when they cleaned out the house, a locket was discarded; Harry considers the possibility that Sirius's house-elf Kreacher could have taken it as he often hid Black heirlooms. Harry, as current owner of Grimmauld Place, is his master, and he calls Kreacher, who tells them that Mundungus Fletcher stripped the place of items of value, including the locket.

Kreacher tells them how the locket came into his possession: Regulus pressed Kreacher into service for Voldemort, who required an elf's service. Kreacher tested the magical enchantments Voldemort placed on the locket—including drinking the poison Dumbledore drank in *Half-Blood Prince* and being pulled under the water by the Inferi, the zombielike creatures under the lake. Harry wonders how the house-elf escaped the dire situation, and Ron comments that house-elf magic is not like wizard magic; they can Apparate and Disapparate out of Hogwarts, whereas wizards cannot. Voldemort's disdain for all creatures that are not pureblood wizards prevented him from considering the house-elf a threat to his agenda. Because the house-elf's highest law is his master's bidding, when Regulus summoned Kreacher, he returned.

Kreacher also reveals in a moving tale that Regulus, obviously having had a change of heart, had Kreacher take him to the cave and sent him back with the locket to destroy it. Regulus drank the potion himself while Kreacher watched, horrified, as his master was dragged under the surface of the lake by the Inferi. Hermione's sympathy is repulsed by the house-elf, who embraces his family's elitist beliefs about purebloodedness. Kreacher reveals he could not destroy the locket, nor tell Regulus's mother what happened to her son.

Hermione's claims that wizards "would pay for how they treat house-elves" (198) explains why Kreacher betrayed Sirius to Voldemort and was loyal to Narcissa Malfoy and Bellatrix Lestrange, who treated him with kindness while Sirius treated him with contempt. Harry, in a moment of sympathy, gives Kreacher the fake locket they recovered from the cave and asks him to fetch Mundungus Fletcher and take him to Grimmauld Place.

Chapter 11: "The Bribe"

Kreacher does not return for several days, and two Death Eaters begin to loiter outside the house. Cabin fever sets in as Harry, Ron, and Hermione do not receive any contact from the order. Remus Lupin arrives and relates the events at the Burrow after they Disapparated. He shares their worries at how quickly the two Death Eaters found them on Tottenham Court Road, asserting that it would be impossible for Harry still to have the Trace on him. Lupin reports that most guests were able to Disapparate before the ministry officials and Death Eaters arrived, though the latter have infiltrated the former almost entirely. They did not know Harry was there despite rumors that they tortured Scrimgeour, the Minister of Magic, trying to learn Harry's location.

Because they have control of the ministry, the Death Eaters are being allowed to resort to cruel and brutal tactics and have the cooperation of the *Daily Prophet*, which is running stories that Harry is wanted for questioning in Dumbledore's death as a cover for their violent acts. Lupin reports the coup has been silent, and Thicknesse has replaced Scrimgeour; because Voldemort is acting as a puppet master, he has cleverly accessed all the institutional power while promoting public fear and uncertainty. Planting public distrust of Harry, formerly a symbol of the anti-Voldemort movement, is all part of Voldemort's plan to change ministry policy and public sentiment, including the formation of a new committee, the Muggle-Born Registration Commission, alleging that Muggle-borns with no close wizarding relative will be found guilty of obtaining their magical powers by theft or force.

Lupin asks Harry to confide in him the mission Dumbledore assigned, but Harry refuses. He offers to accompany them, but the three teens are confused about why he would want to abandon his wife, Tonks, who Lupin reveals is pregnant. Harry accuses him of wanting to abandon his son. Lupin confesses he made a grave mistake marrying Tonks and reproducing because he has made them outcasts. Harry antagonizes Lupin over his offer to join them on their "adventure" despite Lupin's claims that he is not interested in personal glory. Lupin draws his wand, stuns Harry, and races out. Reflective and remorseful, Harry reviews the copy of the *Daily Prophet* Lupin left, reading an excerpt from Rita Skeeter's biography of Dumbledore; it includes more accusations that Dumbledore's mother, Kendra, forced his sister, Ariana, to hide the shameful fact that she was a Squib. Kreacher returns with Mundungus, who reveals that the locket was extorted from him by Dolores Umbridge.

Chapter 12: "Magic Is Might"
Time passes, and at the end of August an increasing number of Death Eaters loiter outside Grimmauld Place, seemingly waiting for someone to make a mistake. The house now has been transformed to a bright and clean place, and Kreacher is friendly and accommodating. Harry takes home a copy of the *Daily Prophet*, which reports that Severus Snape has been confirmed as headmaster of Hogwarts. A brother and sister, Alecto and Amycus Carrow, will fill the Muggle Studies and Defense Against the Dark Arts positions. Hermione remembers that the portrait of Phineas Nigellus Black hangs in the house—and in Dumbledore's office—allowing Black to wander back and forth between them; she takes the Grimmauld Place portrait and hides it in her magically expandable handbag.

Harry, Ron, and Hermione discuss their plans to infiltrate the ministry to get the locket from Umbridge. They have been taking turns staking out the entrance to get a sense of the rhythms, personnel, and routines, and Harry proposes they make their move the next day, since they have now been planning for a week. Harry's scar hurts, and he sees Voldemort searching for Gregorovitch and murdering a woman and two children who claim Gregorovitch is not with them. Hermione continues to berate Harry for not practicing Occlumency, for ignoring the danger that Dumbledore warned about because of Harry's connection with Voldemort.

Harry asserts that he plans to use it since he is not good at blocking Voldemort out of his mind anyway. The three of them discuss why Voldemort would want Gregorovitch—and whether Harry's wand did act on its own in the duel after they escaped Privet Drive early in the novel.

They gather their needed supplies and Disapparate to the ministry. Their plan involves disabling three ministry workers whose movements they have been tracking and then transforming into them using Polyjuice Potion. They follow their coworkers to the public toilets, which are also secret entrances to the building. Upon arriving, they see that the magical fountain that formerly occupied the center of the atrium has been replaced with a black stone statue of a witch and wizard on top of piles of humans supporting them, the phrase "Magic Is Might" engraved on the base.

Ron, in the guise of Cattermole, is confronted by Yaxley, the Death Eater who is now head of the Department of Magical Law Enforcement. Yaxley asks about the rain in his own office, which Cattermole, as a member of the Department of Magical Maintenance, is slow to address; Yaxley threatens him, stating loudly that Cattermole's wife is currently under interrogation about her blood status. The three friends are about to split up as Ron goes to take care of the meteorological problem with spell-casting advice from Hermione. As the elevator doors open, Dolores Umbridge, Harry's old nemesis and now head of the Muggle-Born Registration Commission, steps on with the new minister, Pius Thicknesse.

Chapter 13: "The Muggle-Born Registration Commission"
Umbridge hijacks a startled Hermione/Mafalda Hopkirk into heading to the Muggle-Born Registration Commission hearings and Harry/Runcorn gets off the elevator, dons the Invisibility Cloak, and makes his way through the ministry, intending to search Umbridge's office. He comes upon a group of workers assembling pamphlets entitled "Mudbloods and the Dangers They Pose to a Peaceful Pureblood Society." He sees also that Umbridge has attached Moody's magical eye to her door as both a gross act of contempt and a useful means of surveilling her staff. Harry creates a distraction and sneaks

into the office. He searches for the locket and finds Arthur Weasley's file, in which Harry is referred to "Undesirable No. 1." While Harry is distracted by a copy of the Rita Skeeter biography of Dumbledore, Thicknesse enters, though Harry is able to don the Invisibility Cloak in time to avoid being spotted.

Harry decides their first order of business must be leaving the ministry without being caught. With Ron occupied in Yaxley's office, Harry descends in the elevator to the floor of the Department of Mysteries and the dungeon where interrogations are taking place with no clear plan to extricate Hermione. Harry encounters Dementors who wait in the dingy dungeons, keeping watch over Muggle-borns who await their "interviews." As Mary Cattermole enters the small interrogation room, Harry slips in behind her, under his cloak. He is able to communicate his presence to Hermione, and both of them notice that Umbridge is actually wearing the locket they are looking for. When Hermione inquires about it, Umbridge fabricates a lie that the S stands for "*Selwyns*," pureblood relatives, which infuriates Harry, who stuns Yaxley and Umbridge. Hermione replaces the Horcrux with a fake, and the two of them free Mrs. Cattermole, warning her and the other Muggle-borns to leave the country and go into hiding as they deter the Dementors with Patronuses, escorting the crowd of 20 Muggle-borns ahead of them. They encounter Ron, who warns them the ministry is aware of intruders. At the atrium level, the group encounters wizards sealing off the exits, whom Harry, as Runcorn, orders to let them through. When the real Reg Cattermole appears, chaos ensues, but they manage to escape and Disapparate to Grimmauld Place.

Chapter 14: "The Thief"
Harry awakens in a forest; Ron is "splinched," meaning he left a piece of himself behind in the Apparation. Hermione heals the wound, explaining to Harry that Yaxley held on to her during the Apparation and now has access to Grimmauld Place, meaning they can never return. Harry reveals he took Mad-Eye's eye from Umbridge's door, it was the reason they knew about the intruders. They decide to camp at their current location, the woods where the Quidditch World Cup was held, and set up a tent and some protective enchantments.

Because they do not yet know how to open the mysterious locket or destroy it, Harry puts it on, and he and Hermione share watch duty. Harry ponders the locket Horcrux and the fate of Kreacher and whether he will betray them to the Death Eaters. He has a dream where he sees Voldemort kill Gregorovitch, who confesses that some unnamed item Voldemort wants was stolen years ago; Voldemort obtains this information in a vision he sees by looking into Gregorovitch's mind. Harry sees the image of a laughing blond thief and can only conclude that the thief is the one in danger now.

Chapter 15: "The Goblin's Revenge"
Harry buries Mad-Eye Moody's eye at the foot of a resilient old tree. The three friends agree to move continuously, so they pull up camp and Disapparate to the outskirts of a town to get some food. When Harry ventures into town, he encounters Dementors and cannot conjure a Patronus because he wears the Horcrux locket. They realize that whoever wears the Horcrux—along with an ongoing lack of access to regular meals—becomes surly, and they agree to rotate it. The trio begins to feel frustrated by their exile and lack of direction and cannot decide where to go next, feeling as though they have no clear sense of where to find the other Horcruxes. They check the Muggle orphanage where Tom Riddle was raised but decide the dreary corner of London it once occupied does not reflect the grandeur that the dark wizard envisioned as a hiding place for his soul. Harry argues they should look at Hogwarts, but Ron and Hermione disagree.

During a fight over the poor quality of their dinner, the three friends hear someone approach: a makeshift band of travelers on the run from the new regime, which includes their friend and fellow Gryffindor Dean Thomas; Tonks's father, Ted; two goblins; and another man, named Dirk. Using Extendable Ears—one of Fred and George's joke shop products—they eavesdrop on the conversation, as their magical enchantments prevent their tent from being perceived. They learn the goblins are neutral in the war of the wizards, and the bank is no longer solely under goblin control. Griphook tells a story, not appearing in the *Daily Prophet*, that Ginny Weasley and some other students tried to steal the sword of Gryffindor from Snape's office; however,

The Forest of Dean, where Harry, Ron, and Hermione spend portions of *Harry Potter and the Deathly Hallows* camping out in order to evade the Death Eaters   *(Photo by Robert Hindle/Used under a Creative Commons license)*

they did not succeed, and for safety Snape had it put in Gringotts—where Griphook realized it was a fake since goblin-made armor possesses certain properties unable to be replicated by wizarding craftsmanship. The group of men and goblins debates whether Harry is credible, and Ted suggests that the others read the *Quibbler* rather than the *Daily Prophet.*

As the group heads off to find a place to sleep, Hermione realizes the portrait of Phineas Nigellus Black they took from Grimmauld Place could tell them whether the sword was actually stolen from Dumbledore's office, as his portrait hangs there, and the former Hogwarts headmaster can travel between portraits of himself. Black tells them Neville Longbottom and Luna Lovegood helped in the attempt to steal the sword. While Black refuses to tell them

when the sword was replaced, he does tell them that Dumbledore used it to break open Marvolo Gaunt's ring, another of the Horcruxes; the sword, they learn, is impregnated with basilisk venom. Dumbledore swapped the sword because he knew that if Harry inherited it, the ministry would have rights to inspect it. They try to determine where the real one might be hidden. Ron picks a fight (and is wearing the Horcrux) about Harry's lack of a solid plan. After a nasty argument he Disapparates.

Chapter 16: "Godric's Hollow"
Harry and Hermione pack and leave; both avoid mentioning Ron's name. The journey starts to feel hopeless as Dumbledore seems to have left Harry with very little information to find and destroy the

Horcruxes. They take to propping up the portrait of Phineas Nigellus Black, who visits every few days, hoping to find out where Harry is; they relish the opportunity to hear tidbits of how life at Hogwarts is going. Hermione continues to study *The Tales of Beedle the Bard* and observes Grindelwald's symbol, the one Lovegood wore at Bill and Fleur's wedding, in the corner of a page. Harry proposes they go to Godric's Hollow, and Hermione agrees. Because Bathilda Bagshot, author of *A History of Magic*, still lives there, they wonder whether Dumbledore might have entrusted the sword to her.

Using Polyjuice Potion the duo transform into Muggles from the local village and enter the village, realizing that, oddly, it is Christmas Eve. They come upon the memorial for Harry's parents and go to the graveyard where they are buried. A phrase on Dumbledore's sister's and mother's grave, "*Where your treasure is, there will your heart be also*" (325), puzzles them. When they find his parents' grave, Harry is startled to see their epitaph reads, "*The last enemy that shall be destroyed is death*" (328), which Hermione interprets as, not a Death Eater idea, as Harry fears, but life beyond death. They place a Christmas wreath at the Potters' graves and leave.

Chapter 17: "Bathilda's Secret"

Hermione and Harry sense someone lurking in the graveyard, so they hurry out and don the Invisibility Cloak. They come across the Potters' former house, the place where they died. A commemorative sign is in place, and dozens of visitors have added graffiti, the newest of which is supportive of Harry. A heavily muffled old woman approaches and beckons them to follow her; she can see the Potters' house, which should be invisible to her. Since they should also be invisible to her while wearing the cloak, they decide to follow her and find out more about her. Harry asks whether she is Bathilda, and she nods and gestures that they follow her. They enter her bad-smelling house, and she removes her shawl, revealing an extremely old woman. Harry spies a photograph of the merry-faced thief among several empty frames he saw in his vision and tries to persuade Bathilda to identify him, but she looks at him uncomprehendingly. She asks Harry to follow

her upstairs, and once he identifies himself, she collapses and the snake Nagini emerges from her body. A frantic battle ensues, Hermione going to his rescue, and Harry senses Voldemort's approaching. They manage to Disapparate. In pain Harry is also able to experience Voldemort's view of Harry's parents' murder replayed in his mind. He also sees Voldemort find the photograph of the thief he seeks.

Harry awakens in the tent; Hermione has tended to a snakebite wound and used a Severing Charm to separate the Horcrux from his chest, where it had attached itself. She tells him that his wand was broken beyond repair in the struggle in Bathilda's house.

Chapter 18: "The Life and Lies of Albus Dumbledore"

Harry is inconsolable about the loss of his wand, which offered him the protection of the twin cores against Voldemort. Hermione has a copy of Skeeter's biography of Dumbledore, thinking they can look for the photo of the thief in it; she took it from Bathilda's house. They find that the thief is Gellert Grindelwald, the dark wizard Dumbledore defeated in an epic battle in 1945. Harry and Hermione learn that Skeeter alleges Dumbledore returned to Godric's Hollow to care for his sister and brother after his mother's death. Skeeter reports that Bagshot is Grindelwald's great-aunt and that he stayed with her for a time after being expelled from Durmstrang for his out-of-control behavior. Dumbledore and Grindelwald became fast friends, and Skeeter alleges the former shared his friend's chauvinistic views of Muggles, reprinting a letter from the 17-year-old Albus to Gellert. Skeeter alleges the two teen wizards had a falling out two months into their friendship after Ariana's death, never meeting again until their legendary duel. She also alleges Aberforth Dumbledore blamed his brother for their sister's death.

Harry feels disappointed about the letter Dumbledore wrote using the phrase "For the Greater Good," which later became the basis for Grindelwald's atrocities against Muggles. Hermione argues that Dumbledore was young and that he changed, accusing Harry of being upset that Dumbledore did not tell him this himself, and he had to learn it from Skeeter. Harry feels betrayed and lost.

Chapter 19: "The Silver Doe"

They agree to leave their campsite early because of the feeling that they can hear someone outside. Harry takes watch and sees a silver doe Patronus that feels familiar and welcoming. He follows her to a frozen pool, in which the sword of Gryffindor lies. Harry is stunned and wonders how this came to be. Remembering how he pulled the sword from the Sorting Hat in his second year at Hogwarts, he knows he must immerse himself in the pool since true Gryffindors are daring and brave. He plunges into the pool and clasps the sword, when the Horcrux tightens itself around his neck, choking him. Only Ron's sudden arrival saves him; his friend pulls him out of the pool. Ron says he has returned, if they will have him. They sense someone else's presence but do not see anyone. Ron had pulled the sword from the pool, and they decide the only way to know whether it is the real sword of Gryffindor is to try to destroy the locket Horcrux with it; Harry feels strongly that Ron is the one who is supposed to do it. Harry asks the locket to open in Parseltongue; two living eyes blink out from behind the golden doors of the locket. Shadow versions of Harry and Hermione appear, taunting Ron about his worst fears, but Ron is able to destroy the locket with the sword.

Harry reassures Ron that Hermione's affections are for Ron, not Harry, and when they return to the tent, Hermione's outraged reaction at Ron's return—and her anger at his absence—seems to confirm this. Ron apologizes and explains he wanted to return immediately but was accosted by a gang of Snatchers—gangs trying to earn gold by rounding up Muggle-borns and "blood traitors"—who prevented him from returning and one of whom he disarmed, getting back his own wand in addition to the Snatcher's in the process. He explains he found them with the Deluminator, which transmitted their conversation when they first used Ron's name again, which they had been avoiding since his departure. The Deluminator worked as a transporter to take him to the right spot in the woods. They still cannot explain who

cast the silver doe Patronus. Ron gives Harry the spare wand from the Snatcher.

Chapter 20: "Xenophilius Lovegood"

Hermione is still angry, but as a group they feel cheered by their success and the sense that someone is on their side. Ron tells them about the Taboo—the ministry has jinxed even pronouncing Voldemort's name; this way the ministry can track anyone who utters it, and that is how they found the three friends on Tottenham Court Road. Ron and Harry speculate whether the doe Patronus could have been cast by Dumbledore, but Harry assures Ron that Dumbledore is definitely dead. Ron starts to put more stock in Dumbledore's foresight at giving Ron the Deluminator and thinks that while Dumbledore's vision may not be clear, it is not absent.

Harry struggles to feel comfortable with his new wand. Ron tells them about a new radio program that is the only one resisting the ministry's "line," but listeners need a password to tune in. Hermione tells them they should go see Xenophilius Lovegood because she sees the triangular symbol again in Dumbledore's signature in the letter in Skeeter's book, and Lovegood is the only one still alive who can tell them what it means. Ron and Hermione

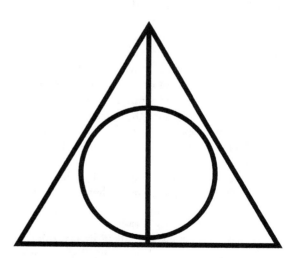

The symbol of the three Deathly Hallows becomes important to the defeat of Voldemort in the seventh Harry Potter novel.

outvote Harry, who is afraid of another conflict like the one he and Hermione recently encountered in Godric's Hollow. The Lovegoods live near the Weasleys, and Ron confesses that when he abandoned them he stayed with his brother Bill and Fleur rather than return home to his parents.

They Disapparate and locate the Lovegoods' strange-looking house. Xenophilius, looking disheveled and distracted, ushers them up to the second floor, where a press is printing issues of the *Quibbler*. Lovegood claims that the horn of a Crumple-Horned Snorkack hanging in the room is actually an Erumpent horn, a highly dangerous and potentially explosive artifact, according to Hermione, though Lovegood rejects her claim. They ask him for help, but he seems reluctant and nervous as well as evasive about Luna, who he claims is down by the stream outside their house. He leaves to call her and returns with refreshments. When they ask about the symbol, he says it is the sign of the Deathly Hallows.

Chapter 21: "The Tale of the Three Brothers"
Xenophilius explains the Deathly Hallows is a mythology that has few believers, all of whom seek to obtain the hallows. He refers them to a well-known wizarding fairy tale, "The Tale of the Three Brothers," about three brothers who cheat death out of three prizes: a powerful wand, a stone that can resurrect the dead, and a cloak that makes the wearer invisible. These three treasures are the Deathly Hallows: the Elder Wand, the Resurrection Stone, and the Cloak of Invisibility, representations of which make up the strange symbol they keep seeing. Xenophilius claims the objects actually exist and allow their possessor to become "master of Death." The trio realizes that the Invisibility Cloak Lovegood has described is Harry's, but they reject his claim that the other Hallows exist. He explains that the Elder Wand is most easily traced because the possessor must capture it from its previous owner in order to be its master and lists a number of epic wizarding duels that allegedly involved the wand. Hermione asks whether the Peverells were involved with the legends; she asks this question because she and Harry saw the Peverell grave at Godric's Hollow, upon which the symbol was marked. Xenophilius confirms that the three original brothers in the tale were Antioch, Cadmus, and Ignotus Peverell.

While Xenophilius prepares dinner, they debate the existence of the Hallows including which of the three is the best to possess. Harry investigates Luna's room, where she has painted a large mural of Harry, Ron, Hermione, Ginny, and Neville with a necklace using the word *friends*. He notices the room is dusty and is alarmed that she is not there and appears not to have been in the house for some time. Confronted, Xenophilius confesses to Luna's being held by the ministry, her whereabouts withheld because of the subversive stories he prints in the *Quibbler*. He attempts to stop them from leaving as Death Eaters arrive, but his spell hits the Erumpent horn. A giant explosion leaves them buried in debris. The Death Eaters Selwyn and Travers taunt Lovegood, accusing him of lying about Potter's being there. Hermione blasts out the floor so they crash into the sitting room. They have a glimpse of Harry before the three friends Disapparate.

Chapter 22: "The Deathly Hallows"
Setting up the tent, they wonder whether Luna is dead or alive in Azkaban. Hermione insists the Hallows cannot be real, while Ron and Harry are more open to the idea. Hermione explains that the Peverell name was one of the first pureblood lines to become extinct, at least the male line, so that the name no longer existed though descendants might. Harry realizes he heard the name *Peverell* when he saw Voldemort's father, Tom Riddle, Sr., in the Pensieve, and that perhaps the sign of the Hallows was engraved on Gaunt's ring, the Horcrux Dumbledore destroyed. Harry's mind races, and he suspects that the stone in the ring could be the Resurrection Stone and that he is descended from the third brother, and that is why he is in possession of the cloak, which Dumbledore kept for Harry after his parents died. He suspects the ring shards are in the Snitch Dumbledore left him and realizes that Voldemort must be after the Elder Wand. Hermione accuses Harry of getting carried away with the story as a way of explaining events.

Weeks go by, and Harry is as obsessed with finding the Hallows as Ron and Hermione are with the Horcruxes, convinced they must continue on the path set by Dumbledore for them.

Ron tunes the radio to *Potterwatch,* the subversive, antiministry, password-protected radio show. They report the "real news" about Death Eater activities including the murder of Ted Tonks, Gornuk, and Dirk Cresswell, members of the traveling party they encountered in the forest, and the murders of Muggles committed by Death Eaters. Lupin and Kingsley Shacklebolt are also on the show, and updates on Harry Potter's friends and supporters reveal that Xenophilius Lovegood has been imprisoned but is still alive and that Hagrid escaped arrest and is on the run. Harry is heartened by connecting with others who are resistant to Voldemort's reign. Unthinking, Harry uses Voldemort's name, the Taboo is activated, and wizards immediately arrive outside their tent.

Chapter 23: "Malfoy Manor"
Hermione casts a spell at Harry to swell up his face so the Death Eaters do not recognize him. They give fake names to the group of Snatchers led by Fenrir Greyback, the Death Eater werewolf who attacked Bill at the end of *Half-Blood Prince.* Harry claims to have been stung to explain his swollen face. He provides enough fake details to convince them that he is actually a Slytherin pureblood. Harry, Ron, and Hermione learn that Dean Thomas has also been captured.

A copy of the *Daily Prophet* with Hermione's picture in it undoes their ruse. They recognize Harry and decide to take him to Malfoy Manor. Harry can see Voldemort's vision intruding on his own and knows Voldemort is someplace far away but suspects not for long. Narcissa asks Draco to identify Harry, but Draco is unsure; whether he answers sincerely or not is unclear. Bellatrix Lestrange is thrilled when they identify Ron and Hermione but alarmed that they possess the sword of Gryffindor. She orders them, except Hermione, to be locked in the cellar until she figures out what to do. Ron and Harry find Luna, Dean, Griphook, and Mr. Ollivander in the cellar with them, and they struggle to free themselves while they hear Hermione being tortured upstairs as Bellatrix assumes they have stolen the fake copy from her vault at Gringotts. Harry pulls everything out of the mokeskin purse Hagrid gave him and in the shard of the glass Sirius gave him thinks he sees Dumbledore's blue eye.

Draco arrives to fetch Griphook so the goblin can confirm whether Harry and his friends stole the sword from Bellatrix's vault. When they relight the Deluminator, Dobby is there, having Apparated. He takes Luna, Dean, and Mr. Ollivander to Bill and Fleur's cottage, but the noise rouses suspicion. Wormtail comes down to check, and Harry and Dobby tackle him. His silver hand (granted by Voldemort at the end of *Goblet of Fire*) grasps Harry's neck, but Harry reminds him that he saved his life in *Prisoner of Azkaban,* and in a moment of surprising pity, Pettigrew relents. Unfortunately Voldemort's silver gift betrays Pettigrew and strangles him as punishment for his mercy. They creep upstairs, where Griphook has honored their request to pretend that the fake sword is the real one. Bellatrix is about to give Hermione to Greyback the werewolf when Ron bursts in to save her. Bellatrix threatens to kill Hermione unless they give up their wands, and they do. Their certain death is interrupted by Dobby, who smashes the chandelier onto the floor. Grabbing Griphook and Dobby, Harry Disapparates to Bill and Fleur's residence, Shell Cottage. When they arrive, Harry sees that the silver knife Bellatrix brandished is now lodged in Dobby's chest. The house-elf dies.

Chapter 24: "The Wandmaker"
The others have arrived safely, but Dobby's death fills Harry with inconsolable grief. They work to bury him, and Harry realizes that he can fully close his mind to Voldemort and that the sorrow he feels is an antidote to Voldemort's mental intrusion. His friends help him give Dobby a proper grave and makeshift funeral; he leaves him a grave marker stating, "Here Lies Dobby: A Free Elf."

Returning to the cottage, Harry overhears that the Death Eaters have targeted the Weasley family but that they are safe at Aunt Muriel's. Harry feels a new authority and insists that he talk to Ollivander and Griphook before they are also sent to Aunt Muriel's for protection. He realizes that Dumbledore's admonition "Help will always be given at Hogwarts to those who ask for it" partly explains how Dobby knew their location when he pleaded desperately for help and saw the gleam of the blue eye in the mirror shard. Harry asks Ron and Hermione to join him in his conversation with Griphook

when he chooses to speak with him first before Ollivander; significantly Harry chooses to discuss Horcruxes with the goblin rather than discuss the Hallows with Ollivander. Griphook was the goblin who
showed Harry to his own vault the first time he visited
it in *Sorcerer's Stone* with Hagrid. Griphook calls him
an unusual wizard because of his treatment of house-
elves and goblins. Harry tells him he wants to break
into a well-protected vault in Gringotts, something
the goblin claims is impossible. Griphook says he
will consider their request. Harry explains to Ron
and Hermione why he thinks Voldemort would have
asked the Lestranges to hide a Horcrux in the vault.

The three friends visit Ollivander, who, having been held captive for almost a year, is infinitely
grateful for having been rescued. He identifies the
two wands Harry took from the manor as Bellatrix's
and Draco's. Ollivander explains that the manner
of taking can influence the way the wand interacts
with the wizard; defeating the opponent means the
wand will often change allegiance. Harry asks him
about the Elder Wand and what Voldemort wanted
to know about wandlore in order to defeat the connection that had been forged between the twin cores
of his and Harry's wands. Ollivander confesses that
Voldemort has been asking about the wand known
variously as the Elder Wand, the Death Stick, and
the Wand of Destiny throughout wizarding history.
The Death Eaters will also know that Harry's wand
is broken because of *Priori Incantatem,* a spell that if
performed on Hermione's wand (which they left at
Malfoy Manor) will reveal the wand is hers and not
Harry's. Harry confirms from Ollivander that he told
Voldemort that Gregorovitch had the Elder Wand, a
fact that was only a rumor previously.

Harry explains to Ron and Hermione that Grindelwald took the Elder Wand from Gregorovitch
years ago. When Grindelwald used it to rise to
power, Dumbledore defeated him and took possession of it. Harry says that the wand is at Hogwarts,
but that Voldemort is already there and that the
Horcruxes were the most important task because
that is what Dumbledore set for them to do. Harry
can see Voldemort at Hogwarts, talking to Snape,
opening Dumbledore's tomb, and taking possession
of the Elder Wand.

Chapter 25: "Shell Cottage"
Harry ponders the enormity of his decision not to
race Voldemort to the Elder Wand. Ron wonders
whether Dumbledore is actually still alive. Griphook
agrees to help them in exchange for the sword of
Gryffindor, a price Harry is at first unwilling to pay.
The three friends debate the request and especially
Griphook's claim that Gryffindor stole the sword
from a goblin named Ragnuk the First. They try to
understand the goblin resentment over their perception of wizarding arrogance, including wizardkind's
assertion that only they are entitled to carry wands.
Harry finally decides that they will tell Griphook
he can have the sword after he helps them get into
the vault but that Griphook will not be able to take
possession of the sword until after he, Ron, and
Hermione have used it to destroy all the Horcruxes.
Hermione is uncomfortable with this sleight of word,
but they all agree they have no choice.

Their plan to enter the Lestranges' vault stretches
into weeks. Bill returns Ollivander—and Muriel's
tiara borrowed from the wedding—to Muriel's house.
Lupin arrives suddenly to announce the birth of his
and Tonks's son, Ted, named after Tonks's father, who
was killed. They name Harry Ted's godfather. Bill
pulls Harry aside to warn him about whatever sort of
deal they have made with Griphook; having worked
with goblins at Gringotts, Bill is concerned Harry
does not fully understand goblin notions of ownership,
treasure, and property and warns Harry to be careful.

Chapter 26: "Gringotts"
Harry, Ron, and Hermione prepare Polyjuice Potion
for Hermione so she can successfully impersonate Bellatrix Lestrange. They borrow a tent from Bill since
they plan not to return and leave the comforts of Shell
Cottage, even after their Gringotts quest is finished.
Harry fears that something will go wrong despite their
careful planning. The next morning Hermione, with
the aid of the Polyjuice Potion, transforms into Bellatrix; she magically alters Ron's appearance (hoping
that being her companion will be enough to get him
into the bank); meanwhile, Harry and Griphook plan
to enter under the Invisibility Cloak.

They Disapparate to Charing Cross Road and
into the Leaky Cauldron. Travers, another Death
Eater, approaches Bellatrix and reports that those

In *Deathly Hallows* Bill Weasley and Fleur Delacour settle at Shell Cottage after their marriage. Their home overlooks a beach and is the eventual site of Dobby's grave. This version was constructed for the film adaptations. *(Photo by Russ Hamer/Used under a Creative Commons license)*

who let Harry escape have been confined to Malfoy Manor. Hermione manages to rationalize her appearance out-of-doors. Unfortunately Travers is also heading to Gringotts, and they walk together to the bank. When Bellatrix is asked for identification, Griphook implores Harry to act quickly with the Imperius Curse, asserting that the guards must know Bellatrix's wand had been stolen. Harry casts the Imperius Curse on the goblin inspecting Hermione's wand and on Travers, who quickly realizes Bellatrix could not have had a new wand made. Harry sends the Imperiused Travers to hide while the rest of them board a cart. Setting off through a passageway, they find themselves restored to

their normal appearance when they go through a waterfall Griphook calls the "Thief's Downfall." Since the goblins became suspicious, they activated defensive charms, including the enchanted waterfall, which removes all magical concealment.

They come upon a giant dragon tethered to the ground and guarding the deepest vaults. Griphook uses the Clankers, a small metal instrument, to discourage the dragon from attacking them; it retreats, obviously expecting pain (as the scars on its face reveal) when it hears the noise. They enter the vault and suspect they are looking for Helga Hufflepuff's cup, but if some other Horcrux lies hidden in the vault, they realize that they do not know what it would look like. As Hermione touches a golden cup, Griphook explains that the goblins have added the Gemino and Flagrante Curses, which cause everything touched to burn and multiply. They spy the cup up on a shelf but are at a loss about how to retrieve it. The dragon roars from outside the door, and they hear goblins approaching. Hermione uses her wand to levitate Harry, and he reaches the cup, using the sword of Gryffindor to grab it.

Adrift on the burning treasure, Harry manages to grab the cup as Griphook claims the sword and the vault opens, sending them into the outer chamber. Goblins attack them as Griphook abandons them; Harry, Ron, and Hermione battle them with spellwork, and then Harry frees the dragon and they clamber onto it. With a combination of Gouging Spells and the dragon's breath of fire, Harry, Ron and Hermione make their way out of the passageway and into the sky.

Chapter 27: "The Final Hiding Place"
The dragon takes them high above the countryside. Harry wonders how long it will be until Voldemort realizes they are hunting Horcruxes. As the dragon flies over a small lake, they agree to jump once it gets close enough. Climbing to the shore, they treat their burns from the vault and regroup.

Harry feels the intrusion of Voldemort penetrating his mind once again and sees a goblin reporting the loss of the golden cup to Voldemort; Harry then sees Voldemort callously murder the bearer of bad news and those unlucky enough to hear it. Voldemort cannot believe Harry knows about the Horcruxes but feels compelled to investigate the safety of the others; he acknowledges that he did not feel when the diary, one of the Horcruxes, was destroyed but believes his inability to feel the Horcrux's destruction was due to his disembodiment at the time. Voldemort cannot imagine Harry could know about the ring at the Gaunt shack, the locket in the cave, or another Horcrux at Hogwarts. Voldemort decides to take Nagini with him to confirm the other Horcruxes are still safe and intact.

When Harry returns to consciousness, he affirms they need to go to Hogwarts immediately, figuring Voldemort will check that one last. They Disapparate to Hogsmeade and hope to find some point of access to the castle when they arrive.

Chapter 28: "The Missing Mirror"

They arrive at Hogsmeade and are immediately set upon by a group of Death Eaters. They hide in a side street and debate their course of action. The Death Eaters set the Dementors after them, and Harry conjures a Patronus in order to save himself and his friends. Suddenly, a door opens on the side of the narrow street and ushers them in. The barman from the Hog's Head challenges the Death Eaters, yelling out the window and laying claim to the Patronus by conjuring his own antlered version, a goat.

The barman reveals himself as Aberforth Dumbledore; his blue eye has been appearing in the mirror shard, and he admits he sent Dobby to assist Harry and the others when they were being held prisoner in Malfoy Manor. Aberforth feeds them, chastises them for jeopardizing their lives by coming, and says he will send them on their way in the morning. Harry refuses, saying he needs to complete the task Dumbledore set for him. Aberforth's sarcasm reveals he does not think much of his brother's penchant for visions and plans and the delegation of difficult duties to others. Aberforth prods Harry—does he believe Albus was forthcoming with him? Harry thinks about how he has made a mental commitment to trust in Albus Dumbledore's intentions; he made this decision while he was digging Dobby's grave and decided to continue with the mission Dumbledore set for him. Aberforth claims that Albus did not have enough consideration for those loved ones who were hurt by his quest for justice and truth. He tells them the

story of their sister, Ariana, who was attacked by three Muggle boys when she was six. Traumatized by the event, Ariana was not able to control or rid herself of her magical abilities; their father went after the attackers and was imprisoned though he did not reveal his motives because of the potential that Ariana would be imprisoned if her madness was discovered. In turn, the Dumbledore family attempted to camouflage her condition.

Aberforth bitterly recalls that in a rage Ariana inadvertently killed their mother, Kendra. Albus returned home to help, an event Aberforth speaks of contemptuously. An argument over Aberforth's impending return to Hogwarts—and Albus's conspiring with his friend Grindelwald for wizarding domination—resulted in Ariana's accidental death. Aberforth continues to question Albus's love for Harry, but Harry reinforces his commitment to the greater good—to self-sacrifice as part of combating evil. Aberforth seems moved by this argument and approaches Ariana's portrait, which is revealed to be a passageway into Hogwarts. She disappears down a passageway behind her and returns with Neville Longbottom.

Chapter 29: "The Lost Diadem"

Neville greets them all enthusiastically, though he looks battered. He tells Aberforth that a "couple more" people will be apparating into the bar and to send them down the passageway. Neville informs Harry, Ron, and Hermione of developments at Hogwarts focusing on the Carrows; Amycus Carrow teaches the Dark Arts (formerly Defense Against the Dark Arts), and during classes students practice the Cruciatus Curse on disobedient classmates. Alecto, his sister, teaches a distorted version of Muggle studies, painting nonwizarding people as stupid, dirty, and cruel.

Neville explains that he, Luna, and Ginny were carrying on a subversive resistance until Luna was taken from the train at Christmas and Ginny failed to return after Easter break. Their resistance was tempered by threats to their families, including Neville's grandmother. They use the tunnel to access Hogwarts and then emerge into a strange room, the Room of Requirement, where 20 or so members of Dumbledore's Army wait. One day when Neville was getting hungry, he wished for food and the passageway to the Hog's Head opened. Since that fateful day the D.A. has used the room for their safe place to gather and discuss strategies for fighting Voldemort and his Death Eaters.

Harry's scar pains him, and he sees Voldemort has discovered the loss of the ring Horcrux. Harry realizes they need to move quickly, and his supporters are dismayed and upset when they realize that Harry is not there to organize an overthrow of the Death Eaters in power at Hogwarts. Reluctant to involve the group, Aberforth remembers Albus's penchant for secrets and lies and realizes that his friends are there to help. He enlists them to search for the object that belonged to Rowena Ravenclaw. Luna describes the lost diadem—a crown—that belonged to Ravenclaw but has been missing for centuries; however, the statue in the Ravenclaw common room wears a version of it. Luna offers to take Harry to see it.

They use the Marauder's Map to find their way there. When Harry approaches the statue to read the inscription, "Wit beyond measure is man's greatest treasure" (588), Alecto Carrow appears and summons Voldemort.

Chapter 30: "The Sacking of Severus Snape"
Harry senses Voldemort knows where he is. Luna stuns Carrow, and Harry hides under the cloak again. McGonagall arrives outside the door, where Amycus Carrow is trying to enter; he becomes panicked that his sister has called for Voldemort when they no longer have Harry in their possession. He also reveals that Voldemort warned them Harry might try to get into Ravenclaw Tower. Speculating that they can blame some students for the false alarm, Amycus responds to McGonagall's rejection of this plan by spitting in her face. Harry performs the Cruciatus Curse on him. McGonagall offers to help Harry by fortifying the castle against Voldemort and the Death Eaters—along with ushering students out of the passageway into the Hog's Head.

They leave the common room, and Snape appears, questioning McGonagall's presence in the hallways at night. A duel ensues, and only when Professors Flitwick, Sprout, and Slughorn appear does Snape flee. They round up the underage students and begin setting up magical defenses to keep

Voldemort out of the castle. McGonagall sends Slughorn to gather the Slytherins and warns that each professor must decide where his or her loyalties lie once and for all.

Harry and Luna return to the Room of Requirement and find members of the order and Dumbledore's Army there, ready to fight, including Percy (who admits he has been behaving like a pompous moron for the last few years). The Weasleys agree to let Ginny stay in the Room of Requirement rather than sending her away because she is underage. Harry notices Ron and Hermione are gone.

Chapter 31: "The Battle of Hogwarts"
They gather in the Great Hall. Voldemort's magically enhanced voice resonates in the castle; he claims that if they turn over Harry Potter, he will leave those at Hogwarts alone. When McGonagall sends the student out, all the Slytherins leave, though students of age from the other three houses remain.

Kingsley Shacklebolt maps out the battle plan, and McGonagall sends Harry to look for the diadem. He realizes that no one living knows where the diadem is but that the Ravenclaw ghost might know. The ghost is reluctant to help but eventually reveals her identity as Helena Ravenclaw, Rowena's daughter. When Harry emphasizes the diadem will help him defeat Voldemort, she tells the story of having stolen it from her mother and then running away. Rowena sent the Baron (now the Bloody Baron, the Slytherin ghost) after her; he killed her when she refused to return with him—and then killed himself in regret. She hid the diadem in a hollow tree in a forest in Albania, a location she revealed to Tom Riddle, who was flattering and empathetic. Harry concludes that Voldemort hid the diadem, now a Horcrux, at Hogwarts the night he asked Dumbledore for a job.

As he wanders back to the Great Hall, he realizes it is midnight and the battle has begun. Harry thinks of the statues of Ravenclaw he has seen—and then recalls a room he has been in but most professors have not—the Room of Requirement. He meets Ron and Hermione along the way; both carry an armload of basilisk fangs. They have been in the Chamber of Secrets, which Ron opened by mimicking the Parseltongue he heard Harry speak when they smashed the locket.

They head to the Room of Requirement, now empty, meeting Ginny, Tonks, and Neville's grandmother along the way. Ron expresses his concern for the house-elves, and Hermione rewards his empathy with a passionate kiss. Harry begs, *"I need the place where everything is hidden"* (627), and the door opens. He finds the tiara just as Crabbe, Goyle, and Malfoy emerge from the aisles of miscellany. Ron and Hermione happen upon them, and a magical duel ensues; the diadem flies into a pile of objects. Malfoy shouts at Crabbe and Goyle not to kill Harry as Voldemort wants to do it, but to no avail. Suddenly a wall of fire appears; Crabbe has conjured it but has no control over it. Harry, Ron, and Hermione find some old broomsticks in the pile and decide to fly their way out, though Harry is reluctant to abandon his Slytherin classmates to this terrible death. Hermione and Ron rescue Goyle while Harry rescues Malfoy from the flames. Before leaving the inferno, he spies the tiara being tossed about by the animal-shaped flames and manages to grasp it before finding the exit.

Ginny is missing, and Crabbe is dead. Hermione recognizes the strange fire as Fiendfyre because the tiara crumbles in Harry's hands; this special type of fire is one of the substances that destroy Horcruxes but are dangerous and unpredictable. The three return to the fight, and an explosion sends them flying, along with Fred, Percy, and two Death Eaters. Harry emerges from a pile of debris to see Ron and Percy mourning their brother Fred's death.

Chapter 32: "The Elder Wand"
Giant spiders—Aragog's descendants—begin to penetrate the walls of Hogwarts. Hermione has to prevent Ron physically from chasing after Death Eaters who have every intent to continue murdering anyone in their path. She reminds them they need to find Nagini, the snake, who they believe is another Horcrux. Harry sees into Voldemort's mind: He is in the Shrieking Shack; Lucius Malfoy is begging Voldemort to disclose his son's whereabouts. He tells Malfoy to fetch Snape. Nagini is in the room with a magical protection around it. They don the Invisibility Cloak and enter the battle in the halls of Hogwarts again.

A troop of spiders enters the front door, and Hagrid disappears into the band of arachnids, yelling, "Don't hurt' em!" Several giants join the fray, including Grawp, who is, by all accounts, comparatively small in stature compared to his fellow giants. Dementors approach, and it is only when Luna, Ernie, and Seamus cast Patronuses that Ron, Hermione, and Harry are able to shake off the specter of despair. The three of them head to the Whomping Willow in order to escape the giants. Knowing the passage underneath the tree leads to the Shrieking Shack, Harry pauses momentarily to wonder whether he is actually playing into Voldemort's trap but realizes the only way to defeat the evil wizard is by killing the snake. They sneak within earshot of the room where Voldemort and Snape are talking, Snape begging Voldemort to let him seek out Harry. Voldemort ignores his request, confident Harry will come to him, and asks Snape why the Elder Wand does not work for him. Snape's paling complexion reveals he knows why: Voldemort is not its proper master since it was Snape, not Voldemort, who defeated Dumbledore in a duel. Realizing that Snape must be killed so Voldemort can gain control of the wand, Voldemort sets Nagini on Snape, who collapses after wounds to the neck, and his master leaves to take charge of the battle. Harry is compelled to approach the dying Snape, who puts his silvery wisps of memories into a flask produced by Hermione. Snape looks searchingly into Harry's eyes before dying.

Chapter 33: "The Prince's Tale"
Voldemort announces to Hogwarts that he will give Harry one hour to meet him in the forest and that he is merciful, wishing to avoid the spilling of magical blood. Harry, Ron, and Hermione enter the Great Hall and see the wounded and dead, including the remaining Weasleys mourning over Fred and the bodies of Tonks and Lupin. Harry cannot stand the pain and flees to the headmaster's office, where he pours Snape's thoughts into the Pensieve. He sees Snape's history before him: the young Snape watching Lily Evans, Harry's mother, doing magic tricks for her chiding sister and rejecting Snape's first extension of friendship; Snape and Lily, before entering Hogwarts, discussing the magical world; Lily bidding a turbulent farewell to her

sister at platform nine and three-quarters, including the revelation that Petunia's hostility toward wizards is rooted in her envy of her sister's abilities; Snape, Lily, James, and Sirius in a confrontation on the Hogwarts Express, and then their sorting. Harry sees Snape and his mother arguing over their increasing divide—she a Gryffindor and he a Slytherin—and their eventual estrangement when he calls her a Mudblood in the scene Harry witnessed in *Order of the Phoenix* during an Occlumency lesson with Snape. A tense conversation between the adult Snape and Dumbledore shows Snape approaching the headmaster panicked over the prospect that Voldemort is going to murder Snape. He pledges Dumbledore his unwavering allegiance if Dumbledore will agree to protect him.

A subsequent scene in Dumbledore's office shows Snape heartbroken over Lily's death. Dumbledore claims that if he truly loved her, Snape must help Dumbledore protect her son. Briefer memories recast Snape for readers—fulfilling his promise to Dumbledore and remaining true to his love of Lily as he struggles over his wounded pride at Lily's rejection. Nonetheless, he clearly risks his life as a double agent for the order, tending to Dumbledore's injured hand when he was cursed by Marvolo Gaunt's ring. Readers learn that the blackened hand he suffered in *Half-Blood Prince* was only part of a curse Snape managed to contain but could not cure and that Dumbledore, in actuality, had less than a year to live; he elicits Snape's promise to murder him in place of Draco Malfoy; Voldemort plotted to murder Malfoy as a way of torturing Malfoy's parents (since Lucius failed Voldemort on other important tasks).

In another memory Snape is questioning Dumbledore's trust in him, why Dumbledore confides in Harry but not in Snape; the memory also shows Snape's struggling with the difficult position he occupies. The memory relays Dumbledore's message: After Dumbledore has been killed, there will be a time when Voldemort will fear for Nagini's life. At this future time Harry must know that when Voldemort tried to kill him as a baby, a fragment of his soul implanted itself in the only living thing in the building, Harry. It is this fragment that gives him the power to talk to snakes and to

see into Voldemort's mind. In order for Voldemort to be killed, that part must also die. Snape is horrified to realize that Dumbledore is suggesting they have been protecting Harry all this time so he might be sacrificed, or sacrifice himself, in order to kill Voldemort. Dumbledore suggests that perhaps Snape has grown to care for Harry, and Snape casts a Patronus, a silver doe, confessing his love for Lily (who is represented clearly in the doe Patronus) persists.

The next memory shows Dumbledore's portrait in the headmaster's office instructing Snape to organize Harry's liberation from the Dursleys and insisting Snape take every step to remain in Voldemort's good graces. We also learn that Snape, through Phineas Nigellus, learned Harry's location and managed to get him the sword of Gryffindor, even though Dumbledore never confided in Snape the reason for the sword's usefulness to Harry.

Chapter 34: "The Forest Again"
Harry returns from the memories of Snape realizing he will not survive this final battle since part of Voldemort's soul resides in Harry and must be destroyed. Harry contemplates the beauty of life and feels fearful of death. He realizes he was a part of Dumbledore's larger plan. It seems inevitable that he must die in order to prevent the further loss of life. Harry puts on the Invisibility Cloak and exits the castle, passing his friends, who are carrying dead bodies in from the battlegrounds outside. He stops Neville to tell him that Voldemort's snake must be killed no matter what.

Harry heads toward the forest and remembers the golden Snitch Dumbledore left him with its magical words "*I open at the close.*" He whispers to it, "I am about to die," and the enchanted Snitch opens, revealing the Resurrection Stone with the mysterious image representing the Deathly Hallows engraved on its surface. As he turns it over three times, it calls to him ghostly versions of his dead friends and family—his father, Sirius, Lupin, his mother—all reassuring him about death and that they will be with him at the end. Harry runs into two Death Eaters, who lead him to a clearing in which Voldemort and his followers are gathered. Harry reveals himself to the crowd; Hagrid is there, tied to a tree. A few moments of tense silence precede a curse cast by Voldemort and a flash of green light.

Chapter 35: "King's Cross"

Harry awakens in a timeless space, not sure where he is, and finds himself on a white floor. He hears a strange soft thumping of a pitiful creature he cannot yet identify. The space seems to take shape before his eyes, as does the creature, which is like a small naked child left shuddering under a seat. Dumbledore suddenly appears, walking toward him. Harry asks whether they are both dead, but Dumbledore says that Harry's voluntary submission to Voldemort's attack—allowing Voldemort to kill him—has made the difference. Harry's soul is completely his own and the piece of Voldemort's soul that has resided in him for so many years has died. As the seventh Horcrux, one that Voldemort never intended to make, part of Harry also remained inside Voldemort, and they are indelibly tethered together, even more so because Voldemort took Harry's blood in their battle in the graveyard in *Goblet of Fire* when Voldemort returned to corporeal form.

Dumbledore also guesses that Harry's wand broke Voldemort's borrowed wand because Harry and Voldemort were joined in a way no two other wizards in history have been joined before. The wand was imbued with Harry's courage and Voldemort's magical skill and could not withstand its battle with Harry's wand.

Harry looks around and realizes not only that he is not dead, but that they are in King's Cross, the train station, or some version of it, cleaner and emptier than usual. Harry asks about the Deathly Hallows, and Dumbledore asks his forgiveness for not being forthright about the Hallows and admits that their search for the Deathly Hallows is what drew him and Grindelwald together. He confesses he had one of the Hallows, the wand. Dumbledore realized that James Potter, a descendant of the original Peverell brothers of the tale, held another of the Hallows—the Invisibility Cloak. Dumbledore feels bitter, and even fearful, that somehow the Hallow could have prevented the Potters' deaths.

Dumbledore is also self-critical of his youthful arrogance and resentment of his sister's demands on their family. He berates himself for his selfishness.

He tells Harry the story of the fateful night of his sister's death and the way he fooled himself about Grindelwald's true worldview and intentions. He explains he never took the post of Minister of Magic because he feared he could not be trusted with the immense power, since, he admits, the notion of obtaining power was his weakness. When he finally met Grindelwald again in battle, he defeated him and won the Elder Wand; Harry tells him that Grindelwald denied to Voldemort that he ever had it, perhaps a sign of regret for his former repugnant actions.

Dumbledore's location of the Hallow he desired most of all, the Resurrection Stone, led him to act rashly, putting on the ring without considering the curse. Dumbledore confesses his weaknesses and calls Harry the worthier man, who uses the Hallows as they were intended—the cloak to protect others and the Resurrection Stone to allow his own self-sacrifice. Dumbledore explains that Voldemort did not know about the Hallows and their power but would have been interested only in the power of the wand to dominate others; since Voldemort does not love anyone and there is no one he would wish to revive from the dead, Voldemort would reject the idea that he needed the cloak.

Harry looks back at the moaning creature behind them and realizes that he has to return to Hogwarts for the battle, that he has the choice to go on. He knows he must go back to prevent more loss and death and perhaps to finish Voldemort once and for all. Before leaving, Dumbledore reassures Harry that the conversation they just shared is both real and inside Harry's head.

Chapter 36: "The Flaw in the Plan"

Harry awakens on the forest ground and remains still, hearing hushed murmuring around him. He still has his wand and the Invisibility Cloak. Opening his eyes slightly, he concludes that Voldemort also has collapsed. Voldemort sends Narcissa Malfoy over to verify whether Harry is dead; she whispers to him, asking whether Draco is alive. Harry verifies that he is and she lies to trick Voldemort and to protect Harry, announcing that Harry Potter is dead. Voldemort bids Hagrid to carry Harry back to the castle, and even when they pass Dementors, Harry remains unaffected.

Voldemort tells the Hogwarts fighters that Harry is dead, that he was a coward who was running away from the battle, and that they should surrender or they will all be slaughtered. Harry continues to feign death, difficult in the face of his friends' grief. He hears Neville attempt to attack Voldemort, who disarms him immediately. He summons the Sorting Hat from the headmaster's office and places it on Neville's head, as Voldemort announces there will be no more sorting into houses, only Slytherins. The hat bursts into flames, and Neville is on fire, until all at once a tremendous force emerges— Harry dons the Invisibility Cloak, the centaurs erupt from the forest, giants stamp forward to enter the fray, and the Hogwarts fighters make one last attack. Neville pulls out a sword and beheads Nagini. Harry casts a Shield Charm to protect him from Voldemort's wrath. An army of the friends and family of the Hogwarts students who stayed to fight seems to arrive from nowhere along with a horde of house-elves led by Kreacher.

The Death Eaters quickly begin to lose the battle; Mrs. Weasley takes on Bellatrix Lestrange and kills her. Harry steps out from the cloak to cast a protective charm over Mrs. Weasley as Voldemort attempts to curse her as revenge for Bellatrix's death. Voldemort and Harry face off, and the crowd is silent and afraid. Voldemort insists Harry's continued survival is an accident. The two wizards engage in a battle of words and wit, Harry defending Dumbledore and revealing Snape's true allegiance. Harry asks Voldemort to try to feel remorse, but Voldemort is incapable of feeling regret, even when Harry reveals to him that Snape never defeated Dumbledore because they colluded to plan the headmaster's death. Further, Harry explains that the Elder Wand is not truly Voldemort's and that is why it has been magically ineffective; the true master is actually Draco, since it was his spell that disarmed Dumbledore, and since Harry defeated Draco and took his wand, Harry is the true master of the Elder Wand. Voldemort, disbelieving Harry's tale, casts a Killing Curse, but because the Elder Wand is indeed Harry's, it rebounds and strikes Voldemort dead.

Voldemort's defeat rouses joy in the crowd of wizards at Hogwarts and across England. The innocent are released from prison and the Imperiused are returning to their senses. As the ghosts, wizards, centaurs, and house-elves sit together in the Great Hall, Harry slips away for some peace and quiet, beckoning Ron and Hermione to go with him. When they enter the headmaster's study, the portraits applaud him. Harry approaches Dumbledore, who is tearful and proud. Harry tells Dumbledore the fate of the Hallows: Harry dropped the stone in the forest, he plans to keep the cloak, and he decides to give up the Elder Wand since he feels it wields too much power to keep in his possession. Harry uses the Elder Wand to mend his own wand and reveals his plans to return it to Dumbledore's tomb.

Epilogue: "Nineteen Years Later"

The epilogue introduces readers to a scene at platform nine and three-quarters. Ginny and Harry, now married, accompany their two sons, Albus and James, to the Hogwarts Express while their daughter, Lily, complains about being too young. Hermione and Ron, also married, are there with their two children, Rose and Hugo. Draco Malfoy is there, sending his son Scorpius off to school at Hogwarts as well. Teddy Lupin has begun a romantic relationship with Victoire Weasley, the daughter of Fleur and Bill. Young Albus Severus confesses his fear of being sorted into Slytherin, and Harry reassures him that one of his namesakes was a Slytherin and the bravest man he knew.

CRITICAL COMMENTARY

Rowling's final novel, *Deathly Hallows*, furthers themes significant to each of the novels in the Harry Potter series, including allegiance, love, respect, sacrifice and loss, truth, power, and control. More obvious than in previous novels, Harry's role as a Christ figure also warrants analysis. Finally, Rowling's choice to include front and back matter in *Deathly Hallows* (material she does not include in any other novel in the Harry Potter series) is significant.

Allegiance

Rowling furthers her series's theme of allegiance in *Deathly Hallows*; in this final installment she explores the concept of allegiance pertaining to both objects and people. In her exploration and explanation of how wands become a wizard or witch's ally, Rowling suggests that allegiance can be compelled by force, but that true loyalty cannot be compelled. People form true allegiance in only one manner: through love.

The issue of wand allegiance has been clear since the inception of the Harry Potter series, with Mr. Ollivander's telling words "The wand chooses the wizard. . . . That much has always been clear to those of us who have studied wandlore" (494). Harry, whose wand is destroyed in Godric's Hollow while he is visiting Bathilda Bagshot's house, acquires a new wand by force at Malfoy Manor. Concerned about how the wand will perform under his assumed command, Harry asks Ollivander more about the nature of wand allegiance. Ollivander tells him, "Of course, the manner of taking matters. Much also depends upon the wand itself. In general, however, where a wand has been won, its allegiance will change" (493). This comforts Harry somewhat but unnerves him as well: He wonders how well his new wand will function, especially in times of need; he thinks carefully about the fate of the Elder Wand and what horrors will occur when Voldemort finds the wand and demands its allegiance. Wands honor their owners, but one wand might change hands several times. In turn Rowling demonstrates that objects can be bent to allegiance to a new master. Humans, however, are not so easily coerced.

Scores of Rowling's characters in *Deathly Hallows* demonstrate unwavering allegiance to Harry—an allegiance never demanded but offered out of pure respect and love (in contrast to objects like wands, incapable of loving). Likewise characters such as Percy Weasley and Severus Snape demonstrate, wholeheartedly, that true allegiance arises from feelings of love. Characters (whether close friends of Harry or not) demonstrate their loyalty to him in various ways. For instance, even though those hosting the show *Potterwatch* run the very serious risk of being jailed and, quite possibly, killed, a group of Harry's friends writes and airs *Potterwatch*, a program that entertains its listeners, provides hope for those fighting against Voldemort and his Death Eaters, and, most important, proves the allegiance of those involved with the show's production to Harry. Others of Harry's friends risk their lives in more threatening situations, as in the episode of the "Seven Potters" (when members of the order transport Harry—and

six of his friends disguised as Harry—from Privet Drive to a safe location). Indeed the risk of protecting Harry remains high, and during this maneuver George loses an ear and Mad-Eye Moody loses his life. This injury and death reinforce this theme.

Further, Rowling reminds readers of the allegiance characters who have already died had, and still have, to Harry. One such example concerns Dumbledore. Having completed his mission in the transporting of the "Seven Potters," Kingsley Shacklebolt tests to see whether Lupin (who arrives at the safe location) really is Lupin. Kingsley asks Lupin to tell him what was the last thing Dumbledore said to them both, and Lupin answers, "Harry is the best hope we have. Trust him" (72). This response stresses the allegiance Dumbledore had and still has to Harry, especially coupled with the detail that Dumbledore wills Harry the shards of the Resurrection Stone, another choice that demonstrates his faith in him (since Dumbledore has faith that Harry, unlike him, will not be swayed by the ultimate power of the Hallows), as their exchange in the supernatural King's Cross illustrates.

One of the most moving instances of a character's loyalty to Harry is Hermione's. Hermione's respect and love for her parents are apparent throughout the series, so her choice to modify her parents' memories so that she can help destroy the Horcruxes (and prevent her parents from worrying about her safety) reveals her faith and confidence in Harry, Dumbledore, and the cause of the order. Hermione modifies the memories of her parents, formerly the Grangers, so they think they are Wendell and Monica Wilkins. The Wilkinses now live in Australia and are completely unaware that they have a daughter named Hermione. With tears in her eyes Hermione tells Harry, "Assuming I survive our hunt for the Horcruxes, I'll find Mum and Dad and lift the enchantment" (97). Always focused on her education and future, Hermione in her choice not to attend Hogwarts during her final year of school also speaks volumes about her loyalty to Harry. Hermione, however, is only one character of many who consistently show allegiance to Harry; she, as do the others who risk their lives for Harry's sake, does so out of respect and love, which Harry has earned over the course of the previous six novels.

The Weasley family provides another example of Rowling's consideration of allegiance as a theme. The final battle with Voldemort looms, and the Weasleys arrive at Hogwarts, prepared to fight. Suddenly, Percy Weasley bursts into the room where his family waits, begging their forgiveness: "'I was a fool!' Percy roared, so loudly that Lupin nearly dropped his photograph. 'I was an idiot, I was a pompous prat'" (605–606). Having rejected and neglected his family for several years in favor of a promising position in the ministry, Percy finally realizes that his family is his priority and that the ministry (which has rarely appreciated Arthur's work there) has made a grave mistake. The cause of Percy's allegiance is, as with those who fight bravely for Harry, a reacknowledgment of the importance of familial love.

Perhaps the most serious questions regarding allegiance are raised by the character of Severus Snape. Since *Sorcerer's Stone* Rowling has challenged readers to puzzle out Snape's allegiance; though he seemed loyal to Dumbledore, Snape's murder of Dumbledore at the end of *Half-Blood Prince* jolted readers and forced them, yet again, to debate where Snape's allegiance truly lay. Time and again readers witness Snape's telling Voldemort variations of the phrase "My lord knows I seek only to serve him" (654) throughout the novel. His hateful treatment of the students at Hogwarts combined with his actions throughout the novel strongly suggest that he truly serves Voldemort and not the order. However, Snape's loyalty is to one person, and one person only: Lily Potter, the love of his life. Harry confirms this fact when he tells Voldemort during the epic battle at Hogwarts, "Snape was Dumbledore's, Dumbledore's from the moment you started hunting down my mother" (740). Sworn to right the wrong he committed in telling Voldemort about the prophecy that eventually leads to Lily's death, Snape becomes a double agent for the Order of the Phoenix to protect Lily's son, Harry. The details of "The Prince's Tale" reveal Snape's allegiance to Lily—and therefore Dumbledore and Harry—very clearly. Though Rowling cleverly provided reasons for readers to doubt Snape's commitment to the order, Snape never wavered in his dedication from the moment he pledged his service to Dumbledore after the Potters' deaths. Snape's

devotion, like Percy's, arises from one emotion only: love. One cannot be forced to love or to be loyal (as Rowling demonstrates deftly with such characters as Dobby and the Malfoys): In humans and magical creatures alike, allegiance can in no way be commanded but instead springs from love.

Love

As in all other novels in the Harry Potter series, the power of love remains one of Rowling's central themes. In *Sorcerer's Stone* Rowling implies that love is the most powerful magic; Rowling's message about love in *Deathly Hallows* is the same. The book's plot centers on romantic love, including the relationships of Hermione and Ron, Ginny and Harry, and Snape and Lily, but Rowling also includes examples of familial love, reminding readers that regardless of the context, real love requires sacrifice and forgiveness.

One example of familial love that shocks both Harry and readers involves Dudley Dursley, who in his final good-bye to Harry admits he cares about his wizard cousin. Harry mentions that the Dursleys have always considered him a "waste of space," to which Dudley responds, "I don't think you're a waste of space. . . . You saved my life" (40). Though these words do not explicitly translate to feelings of love, Harry acknowledges that hearing these words from Dudley is almost like hearing Dudley say, "I love you" (41). Dudley sacrifices his pride and his parents' approval to let Harry know he cares about him. Harry, tortured and bullied by Dudley all his life, forgives Dudley in acknowledging his cousin's apology. In turn, though it may not appear to be traditional familial love, Harry and Dudley reach an understanding of the important role each has played in the other's life and recognize that familial bonds result from the inevitable intimacy that emerges from shared space and history.

The Weasley family is also illustrative of this theme. Percy's decision to reunite with his family before the epic battle of Hogwarts not only reveals his allegiance but also reveals Rowling's belief in the power of love to transform individuals. As must Dudley, Percy must forgo his pride: For years he has considered his family lacking in judgment and embarrassing; in *Deathly Hallows* Percy realizes he has been the one acting foolishly. Percy's sacrifice is not unnoticed: His family, who truly love him, forgive him immediately and welcome him generously back into the Weasley fold.

Now "of age" in the wizarding world Harry, Hermione, and Ron find themselves entering into serious romantic relationships rooted in true, deep love. While Harry and Ginny do not spend much time with each other during *Deathly Hallows*, their romantic relationship (which finally started in *Half-Blood Prince*), though stifled, eventually flourishes (as Rowling reveals in the novel's epilogue). Having told Ginny that for her own safety she should no longer be involved with him at the end of *Half-Blood Prince*, Harry feels overwhelmed when he sees Ginny at the Weasleys' Burrow while preparing for Bill and Fleur's wedding. Harry, at the Burrow during his birthday as well, finds himself alone with Ginny, who tells him she wanted to give him something special for his 17th birthday (when a wizard comes of age). Ginny gives Harry a passionate kiss: "She was kissing him as she had never kissed him before, and Harry was kissing her back, and it was blissful oblivion, better than firewhisky; she was the only real thing in the world, Ginny, the feel of her, one hand at her back and one in her long, sweet-smelling hair" (116). Ginny and Harry, although in love with each other, sacrifice being together so that Harry can pursue and finally conquer Voldemort, demonstrating a maturity that reflects the depth of their love. Harry, who longs for Ginny constantly, seems to ask her forgiveness for his choices before even leaving on his mission, and she grants it. Reunited after the battle of Hogwarts, the two obviously take up their relationship again, since, as Rowling reveals in the epilogue, 19 years later they are happily married and have three children: James, Albus, and Lily.

Rowling has long foreshadowed Hermione and Ron's romantic involvement, which blooms fully in *Deathly Hallows*. They share glances, embraces, and kisses, but the love they feel for each other is most clearly demonstrated when Ron leaves Hermione and Harry while camping, and when Bellatrix Lestrange tortures Hermione in Malfoy Manor. When Ron disappears, Hermione's fury is the flip side of her love for him. Though she feels emotionally crushed, Hermione sacrifices searching for Ron and braves the diffi-

cult journey with Harry alone rather than follow him. At Ron's return Hermione is livid because he abandoned them, but she ultimately forgives him for his absence. What reveals her love for Ron most clearly is not only her constant worry about his safety while he was gone but her hurt feelings that perhaps she and Harry had been injured or killed and that Ron either would not have known or, worse, did not care.

Ron's reciprocal love for Hermione is revealed in Malfoy Manor when Bellatrix tortures Hermione. Ron can hardly control himself when he hears her screams and eventually risks his life to save her from further punishment at Bellatrix's hands. Ron's sacrificing himself to protect the girl whom he once considered annoying and bossy suggests Rowling's optimism about the power of human love—as the two have grown, weathered conflicts and dramas together, and shared confidences and intimacies, their previously conflict-fraught friendship has blossomed into a deep affection.

The greatest demonstration of love, however, is made by Severus Snape in honor of the woman he has loved since he was a boy: Lily Potter. "The Prince's Tale" reveals Snape's great love for Harry's mother, a love he nurtured for decades by consistently sacrificing his own well-being in the hope that his actions would honor Lily and posthumously gain him her forgiveness. Devastated by the consequences of his choice to betray Lily by informing Voldemort of the contents of the prophecy, Snape tells Dumbledore he wishes he were dead; Dumbledore replies simply, "If you loved Lily Evans, if you truly loved her, then your way forward is clear" (678). The "way" to which Dumbledore refers is life as a double agent, Snape's continuously risking his life in order to further the cause of good—the cause that Lily Potter would have advanced herself. Voldemort kills Snape, but before Snape dies, he transfers his memories concerning Lily to Harry; in doing so, Snape gives Harry the knowledge necessary to understand Snape's hostility of the past seven years. Witnessing Snape's great love for his mother, Harry recognizes Snape's sacrifice and forgives him since his mother cannot. Ginny and Harry's choice to name their second son after Snape (Albus Severus Potter) also illustrates a gratitude and appreciation—perhaps even love—for Snape without whose great sacrifice conquering Voldemort would not have been possible.

Respect

The theme of respect presents itself in all of Rowling's seven novels, ranging from the troubling way in which the Dursleys treat Harry to the plight of the house-elves to the way Merope Gaunt suffers from her father's insults. In most general terms Rowling advocates respect for all forms of life, which manifests itself in multiple forms—whether it is human dignity, cherishing those we love, or the right to self-determination. This theme reaches its peak in *Deathly Hallows:* Specifically with the species of house-elves and goblins, Rowling illustrates the importance of respecting and valuing all forms of life and the dire consequences of refusing to do so.

This theme underpins Voldemort's contempt toward the house-elves, a contempt that contributes directly to his downfall. When Kreacher unveils his tale of horror for Hermione, Harry, and Ron, explaining that Voldemort left him to die in the cave where the locket Horcrux was (supposedly) hidden, they are horrified that Regulus, the "master," would leave his loyal servant to such a fate. But, Kreacher's loyalty to Regulus (who plants the fake locket in place of the real Horcrux) immediately puts one of Voldemort's Horcruxes in jeopardy. Hermione comments on Voldemort's mistake in not respecting all forms of life: "Of course, Voldemort would have considered the ways of house-elves far beneath his notice, just like all purebloods who treat them like animals" (195). Voldemort's failure to notice the power of the house-elves (and of Kreacher in particular) costs him dearly, one way this plotline reinforces this larger theme in the series.

Conversely Harry's respect for all forms of life contributes directly to his victory over Voldemort. House-elves and goblins assist Harry repeatedly because they know Harry values them and does not consider his life more important than their own. Annoyed and angered by Kreacher's behavior since *Order of the Phoenix*, in *Deathly Hallows* Harry takes a different tactic with the grumpy house-elf: He chooses to be kind to him. When Harry gives Kreacher Regulus's old locket, the house-elf is overcome with emotion; Harry's acknowledgment of Kreacher's dedication and service to Regulus causes a dramatic shift in the house-elf's behavior. Harry found himself commanding Kreacher to behave and respect his friends in earlier novels; by respecting Kreacher (who was more lonely than mean-spirited), Harry finds himself with a new ally who wants to care for him and fight on his behalf. Several examples illustrate the power of respect. First, Kreacher assumes control of Grimmauld Place and takes pride in his home, which was formerly dark, dank, and miserable. Harry arrives home one day to a completely new setting: "Nothing in the room, however, was more dramatically different than the house-elf who now came hurrying toward Harry, dressed in a snowy-white towel, his ear hair as clean and fluffy as cotton wool, Regulus's locket bouncing on his thin chest" (225). The respect Harry shows Kreacher causes the house-elf to take pride not only in his home but also in his appearance, evidenced by his clean garment and sudden passion for hygiene.

Harry's respect for all forms of life (in stark contrast to the attitude of his archnemesis Voldemort) also contributes to his victory over the Dark Lord because of the support of house-elves and goblins. Once Harry shows compassion for Kreacher, the house-elf reciprocally cares deeply for Harry's well-being as well. Instead of leaving them to fend for themselves, Kreacher begins cooking for Harry, Hermione, and Ron: "Kreacher came bustling to the table with a large tureen in his hands, and ladled out soup into pristine bowls, whistling between his teeth as he did so" (227). Dobby, the other house-elf, whom Harry has always respected (Harry outwitted Lucius Malfoy in *Chamber of Secrets* to earn Dobby his freedom), rescues Harry from the bowels of Malfoy Manor before Bellatrix Lestrange can turn him over to Voldemort: When Bellatrix rebukes Dobby for using a wand, Dobby says, "Dobby has no master! . . . Dobby is a free elf, and Dobby has come to save Harry Potter and his friends!" (474). In the end Dobby sacrifices his own life to save Harry's, largely because Harry has shown him something he has known little of: respect for his dignity. Similarly Kreacher goes to Harry's assistance in the final battle at Hogwarts: "The house-elves of Hogwarts swarmed into the entrance hall, screaming and waving carving knives and cleavers, and at their head, the locket of Regulus Black bouncing on his chest, was Kreacher, his bullfrog's voice audible even above this din: 'Fight! Fight! Fight for my Master, defender of the house-elves! Fight the Dark Lord, in the name of brave Regulus! Fight!'" (734). Rowling skillfully weaves this theme into the plotline as part of demonstrating that Voldemort should have been more wary of the house-elves, who brand a powerful magic of their own; they make helpful allies, but to Harry Potter, of course.

The goblin Griphook serves also serves as a very powerful ally as he helps Harry, Ron, and Hermione obtain one of Voldemort's Horcruxes (Helga Hufflepuff's goblet). Griphook (although seeking some treasure for himself—the sword of Gryffindor, originally the goblin Ragnuk the First's sword) ushers Harry, Ron, and Hermione into the depths of Gringotts bank, into the Lestrange vault. Voldemort naturally assumed one of his Horcruxes would remain safe because of the bank's reputation but never considered the allegiance of the goblins, which shifts often and without mercy (as illustrated by Griphook when he steals the sword of Gryffindor from Harry while in the Lestrange vault). Harry, however, earns the respect of Griphook, who calls him "an unusual wizard" (486). When Harry asks him why, he says that Griphook explains that Harry is a bit curious because of his behavior toward house-elves and goblins: Harry digs Dobby's grave himself and rescues Griphook, acts that in the goblin's worldview make him "very odd" (486). Griphook expounds on this initial observation by adding, "Goblins and elves are not used to the protection or the respect that you have shown this night. Not from wand-carriers" (488). The goblin's statement reflects that most of the wizarding community champions Harry because of his respect for and valuing of life in all forms, a trait Voldemort does not and cares not to possess.

This theme of respect for life is further underscored not simply by the other species that go to Harry's rescue during the final epic battle against evil, but by the rewards Rowling bestows upon Harry because of his consistent consideration for all life—even when difficult. In the climactic battle with the Slytherins in the Room of Requirement over Rowena Ravenclaw's diadem—when

the Fiendfyre consumes the room's contents and Harry and his friends must scramble desperately to escape sure destruction—Harry's concern for all life plays a fundamental part in his ultimate victory over Voldemort. Though he could easily have abandoned Draco Malfoy to certain death in the Room of Requirement, even though Ron berates Harry for risking their own lives to save Draco and Goyle's, Harry's impulse toward good prevails, and he scoops Draco up and out of the room. In the end Harry could not have been more justly rewarded for his selfless actions in saving Draco's life. When Harry regains consciousness in chapter 36 after the final confrontation with Voldemort, it is only because Harry can honestly answer Narcissa's question about whether Draco is still alive that he is able to hoodwink Voldemort, with Narcissa's deception, into believing his death, a central tactic in the final attack on the Death Eaters. Thus, Rowling's narrative world further rewards respect for life.

Sacrifice and Loss

Naturally more characters die in *Deathly Hallows* than in any of the other Harry Potter novels. Some characters, including Hedwig and Mad-Eye Moody, die during the carefully plotted transfer of Harry from Privet Drive to the Tonkses' house. These losses early in the novel, although hard to bear, brace readers with the knowledge that indeed many more beloved characters will be lost during the wizarding community's final battle with Voldemort.

Characters of varying degrees of importance to the story lose their lives in this last novel of the series, including Bathilda Bagshot, Colin Creevey, Dobby, Lupin, Tonks, and Snape. Although never a main character in the series, Bathilda Bagshot in her death—and Voldemort's ensuing desecration of her corpse—emphasizes the horrific lengths to which Voldemort will go in order to achieve ultimate power. Although Bagshot was respected in the wizarding world as a renowned historian, the abuse to which Voldemort subjects her lifeless body (to function as a suit to hide Nagini) also accentuates Voldemort's disrespect for not only the living but the dead.

Colin Creevey, the boy who since his arrival at Hogwarts has admired Harry, loses his life in the final battle of Hogwarts. Even as a minor character, however, Colin in his death carries important significance. Colin's death deserves special attention because of his heritage: He is one of the only Muggleborns (mentioned by name) to die in the final battle against Voldemort and his Death Eaters. Rowling's choice to have Colin die demonstrates the sacrifices made by those under the greatest threat from Voldemort. The Dark Lord's regime (coupled with Umbridge's unceasing effort to excise the wizarding world of people with any degree of Muggle heritage) would have punished Colin severely for his Muggle-born status. Colin, as does Hermione, fights actively to destroy the forces keen to destroy them.

Dobby's death resounds powerfully with Rowling's readers and characters alike. A lovable character who made his mission to protect Harry from any harm, Dobby dies shortly after rescuing Harry and the other prisoners held hostage in the basement of Malfoy Manor. Dobby died doing what he considered his greatest work: protecting people—most specifically, Harry—from harm. Though Dobby's death upset readers, their sadness at the house-elf's death could not match Harry's; Harry digs Dobby's grave himself, refusing to use magic to do so. However, Dobby's death is fitting and necessary to the story line. No epic battle occurs without tragic loss. As a key character in the overarching conflict with Voldemort, Dobby sacrifices his own life in order to save Harry's; it is a loss necessary to create a sense of verisimilitude. The epitaph Harry leaves on Dobby's headstone, "Here Lies Dobby: A Free Elf," speaks to Harry's relationship with Dobby. Harry, responsible for Dobby's being freed from his vicious masters the Malfoys (in *Chamber of Secrets*), was honored that Dobby in his freedom chose to protect Harry. It also reinforces important themes of the books: dignity, respect, and autonomy for all creatures.

The deaths of characters such as Lupin and Tonks, two of the most important characters who die, remind readers, as does Dobby's death, that the tolls of battle are great. Perhaps the most tragic aspect of Lupin and Tonks's dying in the final battle of Hogwarts is that they were newly married and, more significantly, new parents, to Teddy Tonks.

Readers question why Rowling would have both Lupin and Tonks lose their lives, especially with a newborn waiting for them, to be raised by them and loved by them. Though their deaths reinforce the magnitude of the costs of war, Rowling may have left Teddy without parents also to stress that, in a good and healthy community, there is no such thing as an orphan: Harry, in the same situation as Teddy, found love and nurturing in friends and a surrogate family, the Weasleys. Teddy undoubtedly will find the same comfort (and seems to have found that comfort already when Rowling shows him flirting happily with Victoire, Bill and Fleur's daughter in the epilogue).

Perhaps the one to make the greatest sacrifice in the battle against Voldemort is Snape. Though his life is not worth more than that of any other character in the series, Snape risked it continuously by working as a double agent for the order and was forced to play this role in increasingly artful and dangerous ways as the series progressed. Directly confronted with the dark ways that he once found so appealing, Snape masters his former desire for power and sacrifices himself completely out of love, a sacrifice that allows Harry to make to peace with the teacher he once so violently hated. Rowling, in the novel's epilogue, confirms that even Harry feels Snape made one of the greatest sacrifices in helping the order and its supporters conquer Voldemort. Harry, while bidding his children farewell and good luck for the coming school year, has some private words with his youngest son, Albus Severus, whom he tells, "You were named for two headmasters of Hogwarts. One of them was a Slytherin and he was probably the bravest man I ever knew" (758). These words are high praise from Harry, considered one of the bravest men in the wizarding community himself.

Truth

Rowling furthers one of her most important themes —the importance of recognizing and affirming truth—in her final novel of the series. She raised important questions about the concept of truth in *Prisoner of Azkaban*, specifically, the importance of truth's being revealed, no matter the cost (though Harry feels discouraged that Pettigrew escapes at the end of the third novel, Dumbledore reassures him that revealing the truth about Sirius's innocence is more important). Harry, finely attuned to the importance of truth after the events with Sirius and Pettigrew, finds himself confronted with a difficult situation and the truth about the person involved, Albus Dumbledore. Rowling reveals truths about many characters in *Deathly Hallows* (Snape's allegiance, the power of love over the Malfoys, the existence of the Hallows), but the most important truths exposed concern Dumbledore. Harry always assumed he knew the truth about Dumbledore, that he was a good and honorable man, always fighting for the protection of and welfare of the entire wizarding community. Instead, however, Harry only really learns the truth about Dumbledore in the final installment of Rowling's series, and he learns that truth is perhaps more complicated than it might initially seem.

Harry first finds himself unsettled by what he reads in the *Daily Prophet* about Dumbledore's past, a past he soon learns is murky and dark. Harry realizes that he "had never thought to ask Dumbledore about his past" (21), and after reading the obituary Elphias Doge wrote about Dumbledore, Harry "had been forced to recognize that he had barely known [Dumbledore] at all" (21). Harry feels betrayed that he knew nothing of Dumbledore's family life, but he feels troubled and mad that he knew nothing of Dumbledore's former desire to reign over Muggles, a goal he shared with Gellert Grindelwald, another detail that angers Harry. Once Harry learns more about Dumbledore's past with Grindelwald, Harry, furious, says, "He shared a damn sight more of what he was really thinking with Gellert Grindelwald than he ever shared with me" (362). Shocked, Harry exclaims, "The Dumbledore we thought we knew didn't want to conquer Muggles by force!" (361). Seeing Harry's faltering faith in Dumbledore's judgment, Hermione attempts to reassure Harry by telling him, "Harry, he changed! . . . Dumbledore was the one who stopped Grindelwald, the one who always voted for Muggle protection and Muggleborn rights, who fought You-Know-Who from the start, and who died trying to bring him down!" (361). Harry cannot deny that Hermione is speaking the truth, but feelings of doubt and mistrust about Dumbledore still plague him.

As Harry discovers more about Dumbledore's past, Hermione realizes that Harry's anger toward Dumbledore stems less from the headmaster's former beliefs about dominating Muggles and more from Dumbledore's decision not to confide the truth of his past—or his plans for the future about how to conquer Voldemort—in Harry himself. Desperate and upset, Harry feels as though Dumbledore never confided in him, instead using him as a pawn in Dumbledore's scheme to conquer Voldemort. The truth, Harry realizes painfully, is that Dumbledore manipulated Harry to fulfill the mission of destroying the Horcruxes, knowing Harry would do whatever was necessary to defeat Voldemort once and for all. Harry sees (via the Pensieve and Snape's memories) Dumbledore tell Snape, "Harry must not know, not until the last moment, not until it is necessary, otherwise how could he have the strength to do what must be done?" (685). Readers may view this revelation in one of two ways: Some may consider Dumbledore's decision not to tell Harry that he must sacrifice his life to defeat Voldemort admirable, recognizing that Dumbledore's youthful adherence to "the greater good" stood with him even into this final battle with evil. Dumbledore maintained his focus on the benefit of wizardkind rather than succumbing to the emotional attachment to Harry that he had developed. By contrast, other readers might view this decision as yet another example of Dumbledore's manipulative nature (a characteristic he admits to feeling troubled about after withholding information from Harry during *Order of the Phoenix*). Harry maintains a certain confidence early in the novel, thinking that Dumbledore set him on a special mission (characters including Molly Weasley and Lupin ask Harry what Dumbledore has asked him to do, but Harry refuses to reveal any information about the plan simply because Dumbledore, whom he trusted, told him the knowledge should not be shared). Harry learns the difficult truth that Dumbledore has foreseen the difficult choice Harry has to make; simultaneously, he tries to make sense of the fact that Dumbledore trusted he would fulfill the mission set him: to die in order to destroy Voldemort. Whether readers view Dumbledore as an omniscient patriarch or a manipulative master chess player, they will continue to contemplate questions about fate, free will, and trust long after reading this final novel in the series.

Dumbledore, after Harry's death, tells Harry the truth about his past and his quest for power, and Harry's trust in his mentor is restored fully. Harry learns the truth about Dumbledore's past and the truth that Voldemort would not have been defeated without Dumbledore's careful manipulation and weaving together of strands of an incredibly intricate plan.

Power and Control

The lust for power and control serves as one of the driving forces of the Harry Potter series: Voldemort's quest for ultimate power and immortality, after all, is the direct cause of the Potters' deaths and Harry's battle against the Dark Lord. Voldemort is not the only figure with an insatiable hunger for power, however. Characters such as Gellert Grindelwald and Albus Dumbledore and institutions such as the Ministry of Magic also seek ultimate power and control. Readers have long been aware of the name *Grindelwald*: In *Sorcerer's Stone* Harry learns that Dumbledore defeated the dark wizard Grindelwald in an epic battle. Not until *Deathly Hallows* does Harry—with his readers—learn that Grindelwald's crimes concerned the domination of Muggles while seeking the Hallows and, inherently, ultimate power. Grindelwald is so consumed with his desire for power that he even adopts the Hallows symbol as his own. Hermione informs Harry that in his quest to dominate Muggles Grindelwald also adopted a slogan: "For the greater good." Hermione explains, "'For the Greater Good' was even carved over the entrance to Nurmengard [. . . t]he prison Grindelwald built to hold his opponents" (360). Grindelwald's motto may cause readers to recall the phrase *Arbeit macht frei*, a German phrase that loomed over the entrance gates to many Nazi concentration camps that translates literally as "Work makes [a person] free." Both For the greater good and *Arbeit macht frei* promise those who must live by the mottoes—those in the prison or the camps—that their sacrifices are beneficial, either to the community at large or to them. His unyielding quest for power ends only when Dumbledore overpowers Grindelwald. Though the wizarding

world rejoiced at Dumbledore's victory, few knew the Hogwarts headmaster also agonized over his own desire for power and the weak will that led him ultimately to avoid opportunities that would grant him too much power: Dumbledore did not trust himself to assume those responsibilities honorably.

Readers probably are not surprised by Grindelwald's lust for domination; Dumbledore's similar aspirations, however, are shocking and unsettling. Even though Dumbledore's similarity to Grindelwald in his worldview (about dominating Muggles) lasts only the summer of his 17th year, Dumbledore's grave lapse in judgment causes the destruction of his remaining family: Ariana dies during the battle among Albus, Aberforth, and Grindelwald, and after her funeral Aberforth decides to sever his relationship with his older brother. When Betty Braithwaite interviews Rita Skeeter about her forthcoming book *The Life and Lies of Albus Dumbledore*, Skeeter says, "I can promise that anybody who still thinks Dumbledore was white as his beard is in for a rude awakening! Let's just say that nobody hearing him rage against You-Know-Who would have dreamed that he dabbled in the Dark Arts himself in his youth!" (25). Skeeter then adds that "for a wizard who spent his later years pleading for tolerance, he wasn't exactly broad-minded when he was younger!" (25). In only the second chapter of *Deathly Hallows* Rowling provides readers with these details (via Rita Skeeter), which raise suspicion about Dumbledore's conduct and history concerning dark magic. Much more damning is the letter Dumbledore wrote to Grindelwald and what it says about their shared worldview. Dumbledore tells Grindelwald, "Your point about Wizard dominance being FOR THE MUGGLES' OWN GOOD—this, I think, is the crucial point. Yes, we have been given power and yes, that power gives us the right to rule, but it also gives us responsibilities over the rules" (357). A glimmer of the Dumbledore Harry and readers have come to admire and respect reveals itself in Dumbledore's point about responsibilities over the rules, suggesting that while Dumbledore may have supported wizard supremacy, he still advocated that wizards behave responsibly. Even so, this is a troubling attitude of paternalism that Rowling carefully constructs as part of capturing the human frailties that all characters in her works have. Though Dumbledore frequently sought to orchestrate events for the greater good, the tragic death of his sister—the direct result of his human failings—in the end led him to take greater care in his decision making and cultivated a cutting awareness of his own failures.

Similarly, when Dumbledore tells Grindelwald, "We seize control FOR THE GREATER GOOD. And from this it follows that where we meet resistance, we must use only the force that is necessary and no more" (357), his phrase "we must use only the force that is necessary and no more" demonstrates both Dumbledore's desire for power and his restraint and unwillingness to harm when unnecessary. Regardless, these telling statements indict Dumbledore: He is just as guilty as Grindelwald of searching for power over others. Unlike Grindelwald, however, Dumbledore redeems himself in his later years with his unwavering support of and protection for not only Muggle students such as Hermione, but students such as Lupin, as well, who would never have been granted access to Hogwarts because of his lycanthropy. Elphias Doge, one of Dumbledore's closest friends, offers, "As anybody who knew Albus would attest, he revealed the remotest anti-Muggle tendency. Indeed, his determined support for Muggle rights gained him many enemies in subsequent years" (17). Once Dumbledore confronts his own flaws, he dies honorably and somehow fittingly in a battle against another dark wizard, who supports values eerily similar to those Dumbledore defended heartily as a young wizard.

The Ministry of Magic, under the control of Voldemort and his Death Eaters, clearly depicts the careful distinction that must be made between an institution and the people who occupy it. For example, the Ministry of Magic in the earlier novels, while not particularly capable (as in the case of Cornelius Fudge), is also relatively benign. Once it is infiltrated by Death Eaters, the ministry's new motto is "Magic Is Might," reflective of Voldemort's philosophy that those born with magical abilities—purebloods, that is—have power over all others. Supporting the ministry's motto is the implementation of the Muggle-Born Register, which states, "Recent research undertaken by the

Department of Mysteries reveals that magic can only be passed from person to person when wizards reproduce. Where no proven wizarding ancestry exists, therefore, the so-called Muggle-born is likely to have obtained magical power by theft or force" (209). The name of any person found to be without wizarding ancestry automatically appears on the register; further, all who appear on the register must "present themselves for interview by the newly appointed Muggle-Born Registration Commission," headed by none other than the sadist Dolores Umbridge (209). Though earlier incarnations of the ministry do Harry no favors, as more and more followers of Voldemort assume positions of power within the ministry, the institution itself changes, and that power is marshaled in the service of darker ideologies. For example, Harry witnesses the Muggle-Born Registration Committee at work after sneaking in to the ministry: He sees a pamphlet with a cover that reads, "Mudbloods and the Dangers They Pose to a Peaceful Pure-Blood Society" (249), and he witnesses as several people are tortured by Umbridge. Harry overhears someone professing wizarding heritage to Umbridge. Unbelieving of the poor soul, Umbridge tells the man, "This is your final warning. . . . If you struggle, you will be subjected to the Dementor's Kiss" (258). Stunned, Harry realizes that as the most powerful institution within the wizarding community the ministry is indeed sponsoring a genocide of nonwizarding people if they refuse to obey ministry orders, only because those who are in the service of Voldemort have managed to grab the reins of institutional power. Harry rescues Mary Cattermole from Umbridge's insults and attacks and tells Mary, "Go home, grab your children, and get out, get out of the country if you've got to. Disguise yourselves and run. You've seen how it is, you won't get anything like a fair hearing here" (263). Infuriated, Harry deduces that the ministry is more corrupt than ever; this corruption, however, stems from Voldemort's desire for complete pureblood power.

Similarly, Voldemort's adherents clearly understand that the way to gain formal social power is to overtake the institutions that most influence the populace. In addition to the Ministry of Magic, they gain control over the primary educational institution in the wizarding world, Hogwarts. Perhaps to get revenge on Dumbledore, Voldemort takes over Hogwarts in order to poison the minds of young wizards and witches, thus assigning him control over the wizarding population from a very young age. Lupin explains Voldemort's tactic of requiring that all wizarding children attend Hogwarts (a newly instated rule) to Harry: "This way, Voldemort will have the whole Wizarding population under his eye from a young age. And it's also a way of weeding out Muggle-borns, because students must be given Blood Status—meaning that they have proven to the ministry that they are of Wizard descent—before they are allowed to attend" (210). Hogwarts, an institution once known for its inclusive environment, experiences radical and disturbing changes under Voldemort's supervision, including the gruesome execution of Charity Burbage, Hogwarts Muggle studies professor. Voldemort claims that Burbage "taught the children of witches and wizards all about Muggles . . . how they are not so different from us" (11–12). He adds, "Last week Professor Burbage wrote an impassioned defense of Mudbloods in the *Daily Prophet*. Wizards, she says, must accept these thieves of their knowledge and magic. The dwindling of the purebloods is, says Professor Burbage, a most desirable circumstance. . . . She would have us all mate with Muggles" (12). Alecto Carrow replaces Burbage, and under Snape's headmastership Muggle Studies becomes a mandatory course for all students (it had been only an elective before). Neville explains that in Carrow's class "We've all got to listen to her explain how Muggles are like animals, stupid and dirty, and how they drove wizards into hiding by being vicious toward them, and how the natural order is being reestablished" (574). This philosophy of "reestablishing the natural order" stems directly from Voldemort's vicious quest for power. Appropriately the Dark Lord's quest ends in Hogwarts, the school he overthrew, the same school that gave him knowledge of the wizarding world and, most important, a home.

Christian Influences

Some critics have long considered Harry a Christ figure, but whether or not Harry is viewed as such, Christian influences resound in *Deathly Hallows*

more than in any other novel in the Harry Potter series. Rowling depicts Harry as a Christ figure because of the young wizard's willingness to die to save those he loves. Similarly Rowling admits that the Harry Potter series largely concerns the concept of death, accepting death, and life after death. Various moments in *Deathly Hallows* suggest that many of Rowling's characters (and inherently, Rowling herself) believe in a spiritual afterlife akin to that of the Christian belief system.

Harry's role as a Christ figure is supported by Lupin and Tonks's naming Harry as their child's godfather and Harry's final conversation with Dumbledore in King's Cross Station. Rowling first posits Harry as a spiritual leader in *Deathly Hallows* when Lupin asks him to be Teddy's godfather. This position, in the traditional sense, places Harry in the role of spiritual guide. Harry's position as a Christ figure becomes most obvious in Harry's conversations with his mentor, Dumbledore. Harry tells Dumbledore, "I should have died—I didn't defend myself! I meant to let him kill me!" to which Dumbledore responds, "And that . . . will, I think, have made all the difference" (708). As did Christ, Harry sacrifices himself willingly, as Dumbledore acknowledges when he tells Harry the following: "You are the true master of death, because the true master does not seek to run away from death. He accepts that he must die, and understands that there are far, far worse things in the living world than dying" (720–721). Furthermore, and perhaps most significantly, this conversation between Harry and Dumbledore takes place in King's Cross (Station). The decision to have Harry discuss his willingness to sacrifice himself to save others could have happened in any location, but Rowling's choice to place it in a place whose name alludes to Jesus Christ as the "King of Kings" he is referred to in the Bible and the "Cross," or the Crucifixion by which he was sacrificed, seems to reinforce even more strongly Harry's role as a savior.

Rowling never refers explicitly to heaven in the Harry Potter series, but she suggests, quite strongly, that those who die continue to "live on" even after their life on earth ends, a belief Christians share. This notion of "living on" presents itself when Harry, visiting Dumbledore in King's Cross, asks Dumbledore whether he—Harry—is dead. Dumbledore responds: "That is the question, isn't it? On the whole, dear boy, I think not" (707). Harry realizes during this important conversation that he must "go back" to the battle. Dumbledore tells him that "if you decided not to go back, you would be able to . . . let's say . . . board a train" (722). When Harry asks Dumbledore where this train would take him, Dumbledore answers simply, "on" (722). In all of these exchanges Dumbledore implies that Harry still lives, even though he died in the forest while sacrificing himself to Voldemort. Similarly Harry confirms the belief that after death people "live on." When Ron theorizes that Dumbledore may be assisting Harry, Hermione, and him on their quest to destroy the Horcruxes in the form of a ghost, Harry answers, "'Dumbledore wouldn't come back as a ghost. . . . He would have gone on'" (504). Throughout the series Rowling has reinforced that the characters who have died live on in our memories and our hearts, even though she does not specifically state that the eternal soul persists in a separate place beyond the material plane.

Finally, although Rowling does not say specifically that her characters hold Christian beliefs (thus suggesting those who die then go to heaven with Christ), she does quote directly from the Bible: Harry and Hermione read the epitaph on the Potter's gave, which reads "The last enemy that shall be destroyed is death" (328), a passage taken directly from 1 Corinthians 15:26. The influence of Christian philosophy on *Deathly Hallows* is indisputable.

Front and Back Matter

Deathly Hallows is the only installment of the Harry Potter series to include front matter (two epigraphs) and back matter (an epilogue). The inclusion of these signifies Rowling's desire to contextualize her final novel (by means of the epigraphs) and to take the series—to which she devoted so much time, energy, passion, and love—to its close, the way she feels is most appropriate.

The first epigraph is from AESCHYLUS's *Oresteia*, a trilogy of Greek tragedies. The lines belong to the Chorus, which says:

> Oh, the torment bred in the race,
> the grinding scream of death
> and the stroke that hits the vein,

> the hemorrhage none can staunch,
> the grief,
> the curse no man can bear.
> But there is a cure in the house
> and not outside it, no,
> not from others but from *them,*
> their bloody strife. We sing to you,
> dark gods beneath the earth.
> Now hear, you blissful
> powers underground—
> answer the call, send help.
> Bless the children,
> give them triumph now.

The quote appears in the second tragedy of the trilogy, *The Libation Bearers,* a tragedy that focuses on Orestes and the way he avenges his father Agamemnon's death. Rowling's selection of a quotation from *The Libation Bearers* is appropriate, then, since Harry, too, avenges not only the death of his father but also that of his mother and all those who have died in the war against Voldemort in *Deathly Hallows.* The quote itself, however, also deserves explication. The first five lines reflect Orestes' fate: He must carry the pain of his father's death, coupled with the knowledge that he will have to avenge that death by killing others himself. Harry, as does Orestes, suffers from such "torment," a pain that "none can staunch." Similarly Harry suffers from the "curse no man can bear" in avenging his parents; it is not a curse to avenge them, but Harry's being marked specifically by Voldemort is Harry's curse.

The next lines, "But there is a cure in the house / and not outside it, no, / not from others but from *them,*" refer to the fact that Orestes, a member of Agamemnon's house, is the only person who can avenge his father's death. Likewise, Harry (since he was marked by Voldemort so long ago) must, as the only one left living in the Potters' house in Godric's Hollow, and as a member of the House of Gryffindor (the antithesis of Slytherin House), be the person who slays Voldemort.

The final lines of the epigraph are more difficult to explicate, partly because of the translation of *The Oresteia,* Rowling uses. Other translators interpret the final lines of this passage as appealing to the gods of the earth, rather than the "blissful powers underground." The final lines of this passage can generally be read as an appeal for help to assist the children planning to avenge Agamemnon's death. Fittingly Harry has been fighting actively against his parents' murderer since he was a child only 11 years old. Even more significant, these lines belong to the Chorus. Perhaps Rowling chose an excerpt quote from the Chorus to emphasize the pleading of nearly the entire wizarding world that Harry save them from the Dark Lord.

The second epigraph is from William Penn's *More Fruits of Solitude* and reads as follows:

> Death is but crossing the world, as friends do the seas; they live in one another still. For they must needs be present, that love and live in that which is omnipresent. In this divine glass, they see face to face; and their converse is free, as well as pure. This is the comfort of friends, that though they may be said to die, yet their friendship and society are, in the best sense, ever present, because immortal.

Penn, known for his compassionate personality, composed his *Fruits of Solitude* to impart the wisdom that helped him lead a fulfilling life. One example is the second epigraph Rowling includes in *Deathly Hallows,* which originates in a section entitled "Union of Friends." While the quotation may cause readers to think of Dumbledore and Harry's friendship, the passage actually bears relevance to Harry's friendships with anyone he lost in the battle with Voldemort, including his parents and Sirius, whom he sees and talks with before making his journey into the forest to sacrifice himself to Voldemort. Penn's passage in particular emphasizes the infallibility of real friendship, of which Rowling provides many examples throughout the series.

Rowling's decision to include an epilogue in *Deathly Hallows* both delighted and enraged fans. Many readers rejoiced in the knowledge that Harry and Ginny married and named their children after Harry's parents (James and Lily), and that they named their youngest son *Albus Severus,* a fitting tribute to both Albus Dumbledore and Severus Snape; some fans were also pleased to learn Hermione and Ron also married and had two children, Hugo and Rose. Rowling also reveals that Draco has a son, Scorpius, and that matters between Draco and Hermione, Ron, and Harry are resolved. Rowling's choice to name Neville the Herbology professor also seemed fitting, considering his talents in the subject at Hogwarts. Fans felt validated when their predictions about the future of Rowling's central characters aligned with Rowling's decisions; it is rewarding to feel that they knew the characters well enough to predict their fates in the wizarding world.

Contrarily, Rowling upset many fans by including an epilogue and, in doing so, clearly determining the future of Harry, Ron, Hermione, Ginny, and Neville. Harry Potter fans who are also FAN FICTION writers felt that their creativity was stifled by Rowling: Those who thought Hermione and Harry belonged together were especially annoyed by the novel's epilogue. Regardless, Rowling, as the series's creator, had the right to reveal the future of the characters as she always envisioned. Rowling wanted to share the fates she had outlined for these creations so dear to her long ago (as she had numerous times in interviews, including repeatedly quashing the idea that Hermione and Harry would end up married). Though some fans wished that Rowling would have left the series open-ended and ripe for interpretation, one cannot deny that Rowling has the right to end the series as she sees fit, a series in which she invested nearly two decades of her life, and that ultimately changed reading habits, bookstore sales, and the lives of readers across the world.

INITIAL REVIEWS

The level of public interest in the conclusion of the seven-book series grew to frenetic proportions by the time *Harry Potter and the Deathly Hallows* neared its release date of July 21, 2007. Published simultaneously in 90 countries across the globe, the book broke the sales record of *Half-Blood Prince* by selling 11 million copies in the first 24 hours. The breathless anticipation for the closing book in the series consumed readers, book reviewers, scholars, and booksellers, all wondering whether the final novel would meet the expectations of anxious readers. The critical question for reviewers across the globe seemed to be "Will this book be worth the wait?" For readers who had been invested in the series since its initial publication—1997 in Britain and 1998 in the United States—it hardly seemed possible that this final volume could provide a successful resolution for this story and these characters, one that would satisfactorily meet the expectations of millions of fans. Most reviewers, however, believed the book succeeded in meeting those expectations as well as any novel possibly could.

Though few reviewers offered uncategorical praise, the majority believed Rowling had succeeded in meeting or at least neared meeting the almost unattainable hopes of Harry Potter enthusiasts; most reviewers praised Rowling's storytelling ability, inventiveness, and rich characterization while a few commented with varying degrees of dissatisfaction on Rowling's "clunky" prose style and lack of subtlety.

Rowling's plotting and pacing earned both praise and critique, consistent with reviews of the previous novels. Some reviewers, such as Sue Corbett of *People*, find that the book's plot "careen[ed] nearly nonstop from one scrape to the next" (45); Barbara Wysocki in *School Library Journal* observes that "the high-tension adventures of Harry assisted by Hermione and Ron will immediately draw everyone into the question to vanquish Voldemort" (74). *Newsweek*'s Malcolm Jones remarks that "Rowling hits the accelerator and never takes her foot off the floor for the next 500 pages" and that she has a "true storyteller's knack for incident and plot twists" (60). Karen Coats in *Bulletin of the Center for Children's Books* also acknowledges Rowling's "meticulous plotting" echoed by Claire Gross's note that Rowling "obviously had a long eye for plotting" (109). Reviewers were consistently impressed that the final novel integrated minor characters from all the previous novels, integrated carefully planted details from the rest of the series, and wrapped up loose ends in a satisfying way. The renowned *New York Times* book critic Michiko Kakutani sums up this admiration for execution of Rowling's vision, calling the book a "monumental, spellbinding epic." Rowling impressed Kakutani and many other reviewers with the foresight and complexity of her narrative unfolding simply because of her ability, as Schiffren states, to "plot intricately detailed stories seven books out." The London *Times* reviewer Alice Fordham is equally laudatory of Rowling's successful fitting of "every piece of the puzzle together,"

though she acknowledges that some readers (and indeed, some reviewers) would "find the lengthy explanations tedious." MeghanGurdon in the *Wall Street Journal Asia* calls the book a "skillfully plotted drama" (12). Even reviewers who found other flaws with the novel, such as Jenny Sawyer in the *Christian Science Monitor*, could not avoid praising the novel's "multilayered narrative."

Though many reviewers were entranced by the novel's engaging narrative and its pacing, a smaller number found the plot uneven and, at times, plodding. John Peters in *Kirkus Reviews* comments on the "slow stretch" in the middle (810), which Stephen King's candid *Entertainment Weekly* commentary also humorously critiques: "There's an awful lot of wandering around and camping in that tent." Both the *School Library Journal* and *Publishers Weekly* characterize the novel's plotting as "wandering" (Wysock: 74) and "meandering ("*Harry Potter*" 83)" and *Newsweek*'s Jones makes note of the novel's "leisurely start" (60). Other plot critiques are targeted less at the structure and pacing and more at the narrative integrity, as in Claire Gross's *Horn Book Magazine* review, which faults Rowling's addition of "certain plot devices" that seemed "hasty" and "scenes of conceptual exposition" that are "poorly integrated." The reviews overall seemed mixed about the quality of Rowling's narrative structure, with some finding it well paced and others judging it uneven.

Rowling's development of major and minor characters in this final novel was well received by critics, especially her handling of the final revelation of Severus Snape's allegiance and his tragic backstory as well as the complexity she added to Albus Dumbledore's character. The London *Times*'s Fordham praises "Rowling's genius," specifically her "quieter skill of creating characters that bounce off the page, real and flawed and brave and lovable." Lisa Schiffren, in the *Weekly Standard*, also uses the word *lovable*, and Gross in *Horn Book Magazine* acknowledges the novel's "deepening character complexities [that] match Harry's evolving recognition of life's shades of gray." *Publishers Weekly*, as well, emphasizes Rowling's "skill at portraying characters," calling it her constant and "great virtue." A few reviewers fault Rowling for lack of "subtle characterization," such as Jones in *Newsweek* and Schiffren in *Weekly Standard* ("Rowling rarely paints central characters in moral shades of gray"); this lack of consensus about Rowling's ability to draw her characters seems to produce critical tensions that may in fact suggest she has achieved at least some degree of success in her aesthetic vision.

Finally, less focused on Rowling's achievements in characterization are reviewers such as Jenny Sawyer in the *Christian Science Monitor,* who lament not the quality of characterization but the focus: for example, that the series did not center more heavily on Snape, even as Elizabeth Hand's *Washington Post* review observes, "Snape's fate, more than Voldemort's, perhaps more than even Harry's, is the most heartbreaking, surprising, and satisfying of all Rowling's achievements." Most reviewers seem to agree that Rowling's crafting of endearing, engaging characters whom readers of all ages really care about makes the series so popular, even as a few reviewers criticize the three main protagonists as flat or one-dimensional.

Thematically the series's concern with complex, dark, and important moral questions develops in natural and inevitable ways in this final installment, the majority of reviewers note. Peters in *Kirkus Review,* calls it a "grand finish," despite a "simplistic . . . treatment of race and class" (810), a claim that the London *Times*'s Fordham also comments on: "The message of tolerance and consideration is not especially subtle," but this flaw does not, in her estimation, undermine the books' pointed "ethical dimension." It is not just the moral and ethical themes that reviewers find perhaps overly simplistic yet important. *Newsweek*'s Jones finds *Deathly Hallows* to be "darker" as well as "deeper" (60). Sam Anderson, for example, calls the books "death-obsessed," as does Philip Hensher in the *Spectator,* who more vividly describes the seventh book as "extraordinarily keen on violent death." However, this emphasis on death does not seem misplaced or inappropriate. Roz Kaveney's more moderate *Times Literary Supplement* review balances her observation that the seventh volume is a "dark book which may upset younger readers" with the concession that "it will also instruct them in the cost of what is valuable" (19). Specifically Ilene Cooper explains in *Booklist* that the final novel "embellishes

on the hallmark themes of the series: the importance of parental influences, the redemptive power of sacrifice, and the strength found in love." Gurdon summarizes the book's themes in more religious terms as "free will, the power of love, and the sanctity of the soul" (12), seeming to reinforce Karen Coats's assessment in *Bulletin of the Center for Children's Books* of Harry's discovery of the Deathly Hallows as "a genuinely challenging, morally complex problem to work through" (109). Sawyer, on the other hand, complains in the *Christian Science Monitor* that the story lacks a foundation, a "hero's moral journey"; Sawyer charges that Harry's disillusionment and skepticism about Dumbledore are inauthentic and argues that Snape faces a more "compelling inner crisis" than does Harry. Yet, Sawyer seems to be in the minority in claiming that the final volume is thematically undernourishing.

Perhaps most consistently drubbed by the majority of reviewers is Rowling's prose style, in *Deathly Hallows* specifically, but throughout the series as well. *Publishers Weekly* bemoans Rowling's editors' failure to do "their jobs more actively," wishing they had "helped her build tension with more devices than the use of ellipses and dashes" ("Harry Potter" 83). Reviewers seem especially annoyed by her overuse of punctuation as a form of mechanical emphasis. Hensher's *Spectator* review includes this critique: "Her main means of ratcheting up excitement is through punctuation, and some hectic pages are mad thickets of exclamation marks." The *New Statesman*'s Lyn Hanley, too, comments on what he sees as a shocking "artlessness" of Rowling's writing. Charles De Lint in *Fantasy and Science Fiction* concedes in his otherwise glowing review that her prose is "sometimes clunky" an adjective also used to describe Rowling's prose by Liz Rosenberg in the *Boston Globe* and Elizabeth Hand in the *Washington Post.*

By contrast, reviewers in major publications such as the *New York Times*'s Kakutani and *New York Review of Books*'s Alison Lurie remark favorably on the style, as in Lurie's assessment that "Rowling writes extremely well" and Kakutani's lack of mention of style. The *Chicago Sun-Times* reviewer Matt Zakosek, too, claims Rowling's prose in *Deathly Hallows* is the "strongest" of all the volumes. In the middle ground stand Kaveney's evaluation of Rowling's prose as "rarely more than adequate" (19) and Salon.com's Laura Miller's assertion that Rowling's "prose style has never been especially graceful or beautiful." The *Telegraph*'s Tabor Fischer agrees, remarking wryly that "J. K. Rowling won't be vying for the title of the greatest stylist working in the English language." In the end, however, reviewers who are critical of Rowling's prose style are generally critical of multiple elements of the books, while favorable reviews place little emphasis on the stylistic sophistication of the books: Descriptors like *sturdy* and *workmanlike* are common.

Typical of the reviews of Rowling's earlier works, most of the praise is reserved for her ability to imagine fully a rich, textured, and inventive alternate universe, a feat she continues in this important final volume. It is this aspect of the series that leads such reviewers as Tina Jordan and Anna Belle Hindenlang in *Entertainment Weekly* to claim that "these books will be read years from now by generations yet to be born," and Lyn Linning to announce in the Australian journal *Magpies,* "The series will be included in all school and children's library collections as long as libraries exist" (32). Kakutani reserves high praise for the magical world of the Harry Potter series, calling it as "fully detailed as L. Frank Baum's Oz or J. R. R. Tolkien's Middle Earth, a world so minutely imagined in terms of its history and rituals and rules that it qualifies as an alternate universe." Salon.com's Miller reinforces this admiration, noting colorfully that "the texture and color of her imaginary world is earthy (but not lusty), homely, grounded, irreverent, antic, perfectly suited to the audience of 10-year-olds she first devised it for 10 years ago." Despite the critiques of her prose style or her story structure, Rowling's ability to imagine fully a detailed alternate universe is overwhelmingly recognized by reviewers, critics, and readers alike.

A few reviews, often by well-known or even celebrity reviewers with a history of criticizing the entire Harry Potter series, savaged the seventh novel in the series for various reasons. Rowling's fellow British children's novelist Philip Hensher, writing for the *Spectator,* is one example of this. His review of *Deathly Hallows* is tamer than his reviews

of the others in the series, as he acknowledges that "this last volume did draw me in with its redemptive passions in a way its predecessors haven't always succeeded at doing" and he prefers "this last volume to the previous two or three in the series." Hensher has consistently charged Rowling with lack of originality and a ham-handed, weak command of prose style, charges he also levels at this installment but with less vitriol.

Hensher's treatment is complimentary compared with pans by Lynsey Hanley in the British current affairs magazine *New Statesman* and Sam Anderson in the lifestyle magazine *New York.* Hanley views the series as symptomatic of cultural infantilization and targets the "artlessness" of Rowling's writing, calling it a "clunky and clichéd non-style." The narrative, as well, does not escape Hanley's scathing critique, as she calls the first half of the book both "dull" and "repetitive and inconsequential." Anderson's review praises the book's "charm and immense power" but finds that "even by pulp standards, her storytelling is ridiculous." Charging that Rowling has "trouble with the basic mechanics of plot," he calls the novel "ponderous, overactive, dangerously clotted with characters, and confusing," primarily in terms of what he assesses as the book's flawed "narrative logic." Besides assailing Rowling's prose style, as many other reviewers have, Anderson ends by calling the book "strangely forgettable."

Few other reviews of *Deathly Hallows* are as uniformly unfavorable as Hensher's and Anderson's, though some reviews in specialty publications targeted perceived thematic implications, and failures, of the book. Lakshmi Chaudhry's review in the American political magazine the *Nation* unfavorably reviews the book from a political perspective while Christopher Hitchens, polemicist, author, intellectual, and atheist, is especially critical of, in his estimation, Rowling's flawed worldview. Chaudhry reflects the publication's emphasis on social responsibility by faulting Rowling for a "take on evil [that] is politically evasive" and a protagonist who "shows little compassion for anyone outside his immediate circle of friends". Chaudhry's perspective echoes some scholarly articles that have charged Harry with a myopic and individualistic motivation for challenging Voldemort and have argued that Hermione serves as a stronger model of heroism because of her campaign for liberation and equality for house-elves motivated by a passion for justice and not a personal grudge. Chaudhry is especially critical of the book's epilogue, which she calls "vapid" and a confirmation that Harry's motivations are superficial.

Hitchens's critique in the *New York Times Book Review* is directed largely at the quality of Rowling's moral vision, finding her narrative choices derivative, unoriginal, and internally inconsistent. As do other reviewers, Hitchens charges Rowling with use of the deus ex machina, or, in Latin, "a god from a machine." Critics have in the past claimed that Rowling relies too heavily on coincidence to do narrative work for her, and Hitchens focuses on, especially, her overuse of this tactic but believes it is particularly absurd for, in his view, a largely secular literary universe (though other writers have argued for the series's inherent Christian themes). Beyond this allegation Hitchens, as do others, finds Voldemort a cardboard villain and the plot and characters "thin and derivative."

SCHOLARSHIP

As of press time, no scholarly work has been published specifically addressing the final book in the series. For works that discuss the series as a whole, including *Deathly Hallows*, see "Scholarship on the Harry Potter Series" and "Additional Resources on the Harry Potter Series."

CHARACTERS

Sirius Black   Harry's godfather, killed at the conclusion of *Order of the Phoenix*. Sirius continues to be an influence on teenage Harry as he struggles with feelings of alienation and loneliness and continues his self-examination.

Because Harry, Ron, and Hermione spend part of their exile at Number Twelve, Grimmauld Place, memories of Sirius are pervasive. Harry gains some access into the history of his dead godfather: As he explores Sirius's room he can see the way his godfather defined himself in contrast to his pureblood Slytherin family. When Harry sees Sirius's room, he appreciates his godfather's decorating taste: "Sirius seemed to have gone out of his way to annoy his parents. There were several large Gryffindor banners, faded scarlet and gold, just to underline his difference from the rest of the Slytherin family" (178). Harry also finds comfort in recognizing his father in many of the pictures he finds in Sirius's room.

While staying at Number Twelve, Grimmauld Place, Harry comes to terms with one of his godfather's major shortcomings: his reprehensible treatment of Kreacher the house-elf. The contempt Sirius displayed toward Kreacher largely shaped their relationship and certainly contributed to Sirius's death, as Kreacher cooperated with the Death Eaters by lying to Harry about Sirius's being away from Grimmauld Place at the end of *Order of the Phoenix*.

As Harry discovers the Resurrection Stone inside the Golden Snitch at the climax of the novel, Sirius is one of the four figures who reappear to him to offer him consolation as he walks toward what he believes is sure death, reassuring his godson that dying does not hurt, and that it is "quicker and easier than falling asleep" (699). When Harry sees Sirius, he looks "tall and handsome, and younger by far than Harry had seen him in life. He loped with an easy grace, his hands in his pockets and a grin on his face" (699). Harry's seeing Sirius before facing Voldemort in the forest is significant because it gives him peace and confidence and allows him to face his fate bravely.

Dobby   Loyal house-elf who dies after assisting Harry in his escape from Malfoy Manor. Dobby, who tried so desperately to save Harry from danger in *Chamber of Secrets* and who played a key role in Harry's success in the Triwizard Tournament, emerges as an important character in this final book in the series. Dobby is both a savior and a martyr, as well as a free elf who relishes his liberation, a counterexample to the elves that all the wizards, unsupportive of Hermione's Society for the Protection of Elfish Welfare, use as examples to claim that elves enjoy their oppression.

It is significant that when Harry and his friends are trapped in the Malfoys' cellar Dumbledore's statement that "help will always be given to those at Hogwarts who ask for it" is answered by Dobby. If one of the series's major themes is the value of freedom, choice, and autonomy, as well as the value of all creatures, then there can be no better choice than Dobby to go to Harry's aid when help seems least likely to arrive. Dobby has grown over the seven novels from a masochistic, oppressed house-elf of the Malfoys to a fully realized individual who is devoted to Harry but also relishes his new freedom and rights to work for pay. As 19th-century antiabolitionists argued about African-American slavery in the United States, those wizards who support house-elf slavery believe house-elves not only enjoy serving others with no compensation but would be lost without the benevolent patronage of their masters. Dobby's ready embrace of his newfound freedom and rights is a direct refutation of these sorts of arguments.

Dobby sacrifices his life in this final book; if it seems unfitting, it is at least unsurprising that the house-elf who showed such tireless devotion to Harry should be forever remembered by readers for his selfless heroism, which is equivalent to any of Harry's own sacrifices. His epitaph, "Here Lies Dobby: A Free Elf" (481), commemorates one of Harry's most significant accomplishments in the series, securing Dobby's freedom from his oppressive masters, the Malfoys, at the end of *Chamber of Secrets*. Similarly Harry's decision to dig Dobby's grave by hand (rather than have it prepared magically) signifies that Harry values the elf's friendship and, more important, his life.

Albus Dumbledore Hogwarts headmaster and Harry's mentor. In some ways all of *Deathly Hallows'* narrative emerges from the vision of Albus Dumbledore, either confirming or challenging the perceptive headmaster's predictions about the nature of particular characters. The book is as much about Dumbledore's carefully plotted posthumous plans as it is Rowling's imagination or Harry's emotional and spiritual journey to maturity. The novel not only reveals whether Dumbledore's predictions are correct but also provides insight into Dumbledore's tragic past and how that past shaped his actions and beliefs during his later years in life.

The items Dumbledore wills to Harry and his friends offer readers initial insight into the prescience that the headmaster is renowned for and

reassures readers that despite whatever doubts Harry has or Rita Skeeter plants, Dumbledore's powers of perception are still impressive. His gift of the Deluminator to Ron, who is prone to short-term panic but given to long-term dedication, shows Dumbledore's talent for character judgment. As Dumbledore understands not only Hermione's studious nature but her doggedness and powers of observation, the volume of *Tales of Beedle the Bard* speaks to his faith in his young student's intellect. Finally, that Dumbledore confers upon Harry the cracked Resurrection Stone reveals his confidence that his young protégé will be able to navigate the temptations of the Hallows' power in ways that Dumbledore himself could not.

However, *Deathly Hallows* takes a more realistic turn than the rest of the series in that Dumbledore's judgment, while often accurate, is not infallible. While his observation in *Prisoner of Azkaban* that Peter Pettigrew (Wormtail/Scabbers) would owe Harry a debt after Harry prevents Sirius and Remus from murdering him is accurate, Pettigrew's paying his debt to Harry has catastrophic consequences. The brief moment of mercy that Wormtail shows Harry is a betrayal to Voldemort that is not unpunished; Voldemort's gift of the silver hand to his servant Pettigrew turns against him when Pettigrew responds to Harry's beseeching for mercy. As in the case of Snape, a reformed dark wizard whose risk taking for Dumbledore ultimately means his death, Pettigrew in willingness to be merciful ultimately causes his own death. That Dumbledore's ability to see every possible outcome of his elaborate plans is fallible adds a human element to his character that renders him more three-dimensional than in previous books.

At the same time Dumbledore is very accurate about two other characters: Draco Malfoy and Tom Riddle/Lord Voldemort. Knowing that despite their repugnant philosophies the Malfoys still cherish the one powerful value that the series overwhelmingly endorses—unconditional human love—Dumbledore recognizes that the Malfoys are salvageable in ways that Voldemort is not. Narcissa does everything in her power to prevent Draco from becoming a murderer, because murder, in the narrative's worldview, would irreparably damage his soul; similarly, at the close of this novel, Lucius begs Voldemort for permission to seek his son in the castle while Narcissa directly lies to Voldemort about Harry's being dead after his encounter with Voldemort in the forest when she learns Draco is still alive inside Hogwarts. Though allied with dark magic, the Malfoys still have their unconditional love for their son, and Dumbledore's plan to defeat Voldemort accounts for this likelihood.

By the same token Dumbledore counts on Voldemort to fail to recognize any virtue embraced by the protagonists of the series: loyalty, love, sacrifice, bravery, the value of life (whether human life or creature life), humility, and fair play. The character of Dumbledore stands in for all of these virtues just as Voldemort stands in for their opposites: selfishness, cowardice, greed, imperiousness, and betrayal in the name of self-serving objectives. As the chapter "King's Cross" reveals, Dumbledore not only admires these virtues, he models them—and his sense that Voldemort not only does not value them but cannot even recognize them empowers Harry to defeat the dark wizard.

Readers also learn a great deal about Dumbledore's character and the important life events that shaped his path to leadership. In *Deathly Hallows,* Harry's emotional and psychological journey is as much about his quest to destroy Horcruxes and unseat Voldemort from power as it is to learn more about and come to terms with Dumbledore's past and his mentor's human flaws. Rita Skeeter's biography, *The Life and Lies of Albus Dumbledore,* raises many questions about the essential nature of the former Hogwarts headmaster, questions that eat at Harry's already fragile trust in Dumbledore's judgment concerning his fight against Voldemort.

Beginning in *Order of the Phoenix* Harry's relationship with Dumbledore undergoes significant changes. He learns that Dumbledore often protects him from unpleasant realities that might have better prepared the young Harry to face the challenges he encountered had he known about them. In this way Dumbledore admits he made errors in judgment, such as in his reluctance to tell Harry about Sybill Trelawney's prophecy about Voldemort and a child born on July 31, 1980, who was a threat to him.

Dumbledore rectifies his tendency to withhold information from Harry to some degree in *Half-Blood Prince* when he spends many evenings at the Pensieve with Harry, tracing the life of Tom Marvolo Riddle in an effort to understand better the dark wizard's lifelong obsession with power and evil. The trust Dumbledore places in Harry in asking him to accompany him to the cave where Voldemort hid the locket Horcrux solidifies their relationship, but the revelations in *Deathly Hallows* destabilize their bond because Harry places so much value on trust and honesty in his friendships. Both readers and Harry learn the explanation for Dumbledore's withholding of certain kinds of information from Harry, namely, the shame he feels about the immaturity he showed in his young life after his sister's tragic death. Dumbledore must live with the choices he made: selfish resentment over his mother's death and the care he and Aberforth were required to extend to Ariana, his failure to recognize the real repugnance of his friend Grindelwald's ideologies, and, ultimately, that if he had shown a stronger moral center, his sister's death might have been prevented. These are dark moments from Dumbledore's past that he concealed from Harry out of shame, not secrecy. Dumbledore asks Harry's forgiveness for not being more honest in the past: "Can you forgive me? . . . can you forgive me for not trusting you? For not telling you? Harry, I only feared that you fail as I had failed. I only dreaded that you would make my mistakes. I crave your pardon, Harry. I have known, for some time now, that you are the better man" (713).

At the same time *Deathly Hallows* adds a rich dimension to Dumbledore that readers have not previously viewed. Until this novel Dumbledore has had omniscience—a wisdom and deep knowledge of human nature that gives him an almost preternatural ability to predict people's behavior. *Deathly Hallows* humanizes him by revealing some of his very human flaws, such as the appeal power held to him and his subsequent lifelong resistance to being put in positions of political authority that would be tempting to misuse. Similarly, extratextually Rowling announced at a gathering of readers that Dumbledore's relationship with Grindelwald was more than just a friendship; in revealing the headmaster as a gay man, she adds another layer of narrative complexity and, indeed, believability to the appeal that a charismatic young man such as Grindelwald—whose chauvinistic and elitist worldviews formed the justification for violence toward Muggles—could have swayed the otherwise egalitarian-minded Dumbledore to his philosophy.

Though shocked by some of Dumbledore's choices and former beliefs, readers feel at peace with Dumbledore's past after realizing that he did, indeed, fight "for the greater good" by placing faith in Harry, a selfless man who, unlike his mentor, had the power to master temptation of uniting the Hallows and defeat Voldemort. Dumbledore's faith in Harry's character seems to redeem Dumbledore from the poor choices he made in his past.

Hermione Granger   Harry's close friend and fellow Gryffindor. Hermione, who has always been a faithful friend to Harry throughout the series, plays a central but somewhat passive role in this last book of the series. Hermione's organizational and research skills have always been crucial to Harry's success in his quests, whether participating in the Triwizard Tournament, figuring out the purpose and location of the Sorcerer's Stone, or saving his godfather Sirius's life. *Deathly Hallows* is no exception, as Hermione accompanies him on his exile and searches for the Horcruxes as well as puzzling out as many of the clues as Harry does; her meticulous planning and foresight are key to helping the trio succeed in their quest to destroy the Horcruxes. Hermione also serves in the stereotypically female role of the caretaker of her two male friends, marshaling resources and preparing for their travels with her magically enhanced handbag. Aware of her stereotypical role as the caretaker, though, Hermione confronts Ron about her position by saying, "I notice I'm always the one who ends up sorting out the food, because I'm a *girl,* I suppose!" (293). Ron assures her she is responsible for cooking because she is best with magic, but regardless, Rowling illustrates Hermione's dissatisfaction with her continuing role as the caretaker of the threesome.

Hermione grows in the most significant ways in her relationship with Ron. While the two friends have throughout the series become increasingly intimate, this final novel reveals them fully emerging as a romantic couple. Whether it is the lover's spat when Ron returns to their tent home base in the forest after abandoning them or his headlong rush into the Malfoys' sitting room in order to rescue Hermione from Bellatrix Lestrange's magical torture, the romantic relationship between Hermione and Ron becomes a strong subplot of *Deathly Hallows.*

Hermione's evolution as a character is less important in this last book. She develops a more sensitive moral compass defined by right conduct rather than rules in *Goblet of Fire* as she begins to resist the "listen to authority" model of behavior, and especially in *Order of the Phoenix,* when she recognizes the illegitimate power Dolores Umbridge tries to exert over Hogwarts. As founder of S.P.E.W. (Society for the Promotion of Elfish Welfare), Hermione is deeply committed to social justice. However, over the course of the series and culminating in this final novel, Hermione is much more willing to take risks and challenge social norms in order to agitate for social justice, whether infiltrating the Ministry of Magic or breaking into Gringotts, whereas early in the series she would have resisted these sorts of bold gestures.

Griphook   Goblin employed by Gringotts; assists Harry, Ron, and Hermione in the recovery of a Horcrux. Though Griphook appears in the first book in the series, readers learn little about him until this last novel. Griphook primarily stands in as an exemplar of the goblin species and the tense relationship they have with wizards. As a narrative necessity Griphook's encounter with Harry, Ron, and Hermione—and their dramatic rescue of him from Malfoy Manor—serves to reinforce Harry's good-hearted regard for all creatures regardless of species or blood status. Griphook acknowledges that Harry is an "unusual wizard" (486), since Harry saved Griphook's life and dug the grave for a house-elf. Though Rowling emphasizes that goblins cannot be trusted, Griphook's comments to Harry concerning his regard for the welfare of goblins and house-elves are genuine.

Griphook's presence also provides an entrée into the plot to break into Gringotts. Further, when

Harry asks Griphook to aid them in their plot to rob the Lestranges' vault, Rowling has an opportunity to elucidate not only the tensions between wizards and goblins but also the short distance between Voldemort's hateful and offensive worldview and the attitudes widely held by wizardkind about who is and who is not entitled to the rights to use magic and carry wands: The goblins have no such rights.

At the same time Griphook serves as more than a plot device; as, according to Bill Weasley, a somewhat typical example of goblin values, Griphook convincingly makes claims upon the reader's sympathies because of the clear ways that wizards have committed atrocities against goblins (according to Hermione, with her encyclopedic knowledge of wizarding history). In this way the whole of mainstream wizard society has participated in this injustice. Bill Weasley's perspective, however, makes a compelling counterpoint as he cautions Harry about the goblins' reputation for greed and entitlement. Readers are exposed to this side of Griphook when he makes off with the sword of Gryffindor when the group is trapped by the approaching goblin guards and quickly abandons them at the first opportunity. In this way Rowling conveys the complexity of such sectarian conflicts in examples that mirror real-world tensions.

Kreacher House-elf; servant to Harry. Kreacher remains important in this final book because, like Griphook, he is a representative of another magical species that has been oppressed or mistreated by wizards and thus serves to contrast the worldview of Voldemort—chauvinistic, elitist, xenophobic—with the less obvious but still hierarchical underpinnings of wizarding society. Perhaps the most poignant example of Voldemort's ideology concerning creatures such as house-elves involves Kreacher. Voldemort, who needed a house-elf's assistance, forced Kreacher to go to the cave in which the locket Horcrux was to be kept. Voldemort unflinchingly forced Kreacher to drink the potion in the basin on the island in the middle of the lake (the same potion Dumbledore was forced to drink on his visit to the cave with Harry). Kreacher, as did Dumbledore, experienced extreme pain in doing so. Seeing the basin empty, Voldemort put the sup-

posed Horcrux in the empty basin and then left, abandoning Kreacher alone in the cave. Kreacher explains one of the more harrowing memories associated with the incident as follows: "Kreacher needed water, he crawled to the island's edge and he drank from the black lake . . . and hands, dead hands, came out of the water and dragged Kreacher under the surface" (194). Only after Regulus Black commanded Kreacher to return home was the tortured house-elf allowed to escape the depths of the cave lake in which he had been held prisoner. Voldemort's disregard for Kreacher's life clearly illustrates the suffering house-elves have had to endure at the hands of wizards.

While Voldemort endorses a hierarchy based on blood status, wizard society is organized by a similar hierarchy based on species. This hierarchy is targeted for critique by Rowling, whose series places high value on egalitarianism and democracy. For example, Sirius's death can indirectly be traced back to his inhumane treatment of Kreacher the house-elf. In *Deathly Hallows* it is only when Hermione's campaign for house-elf rights comes to fruition in Harry's conversion to her point of view that this message is made most clearly. Harry's development of empathy for Kreacher results in a transformation not only in the life of the exploited and oppressed creature—Kreacher—but in the life of Harry and his friends, who ultimately benefit from Kreacher's improved disposition and loyalty.

Bellatrix Lestrange Voldemort's most faithful servant; Death Eater; Narcissa Malfoy's sister and Draco's Malfoy's aunt. Bellatrix Lestrange is somewhat two-dimensional as a character because of her unflagging devotion to the Dark Lord. Her abject devotion to Voldemort drives her actions throughout the series but, most significantly, in this book fuels her torture of Hermione in Malfoy Manor. Bellatrix evolves very little throughout this book or the series as a whole; she seems to have little ambivalence about the subject of blood status or her affiliation with dark magic. In this way her death at the end of the novel in a duel with Molly Weasley is met by readers and fellow characters with little regret.

Bellatrix's firm belief in blood status as a measure of worth is constantly challenged by her family tree: Voldemort, who delights in the pain of others, likes to remind her of the genealogical mistakes of her relatives such as Tonks's marrying Lupin, a werewolf, and her sister Andromeda's marriage to a Muggle-born. In turn Bellatrix spends a great deal of time trying to convince her "master" of her allegiance to his cause.

Neville Longbottom   Close friend of Harry's and fellow Gryffindor; a pureblood wizard. Neville, as a pureblood wizard, has nothing to fear from the policy and regime changes implemented by Voldemort and the Death Eaters. Neville Longbottom serves as a powerful example of the uninvested bystander in a position of power within a social structure who has no personal interest in social change but whose commitment to the cause of equality and right overrides self-interest. Early in the series Neville's magical powers were questionable, but Rowling has always made his integrity and character evident, as in *Sorcerer's Stone* when he stands up to his friends Harry, Ron, and Hermione, who sneak out of the Gryffindor dormitory after curfew. Dumbledore rewards Neville for his courage in doing so, thus granting Gryffindor enough points to win the coveted House Cup.

Though he is a subsidiary character in the novels, he plays a central role in this last book, leading a resistance against Headmaster Snape through a subversive campaign of high jinks and magical tomfoolery along with more serious minded protection of his nonpureblood classmates. Neville has nothing to gain by resisting Death Eater rule; in this way Rowling uses him as an admirable emblem of commitment to moral conduct in the face of immoral systems. Neville distinguishes himself most notably in his fulfillment of Harry's request that he kill Voldemort's snake, Nagini, no matter what happens to Harry. Neville's success in this task despite Voldemort's enticement to join the Death Eaters (because of his pureblood origins) reflects his increasing confidence, leadership, and courage. Significantly, Rowling reveals in the novel's epilogue that Neville serves in the role of Herbology professor at Hogwarts. This choice by Rowling emphasizes, yet again, Neville's growth in confidence and

brings to fruition the future Rowling hinted at for Neville beginning in *Goblet of Fire* when Mad-Eye Moody acknowledges Neville's talent for the subject. Likewise Neville's success confirms Neville's grandmother's comments about him in *Deathly Hallows*, that Frank and Alice Longbottom would be proud of their son and that, after many years of thinking otherwise, Neville's grandmother was finally proud of her grandson also.

Luna Lovegood   Harry's close friend; unusual student whose father publishes the wizarding newspaper the *Quibbler*. Like Ginny and Neville, Luna is one of the corps of students in Dumbledore's Army who continue the subversive resistance after Harry, Ron, and Hermione leave on their quest for the Horcruxes. Luna's role is subsidiary to that of her father, Xenophilius, who is important as the source of information about the Deathly Hallows and the Peverell brothers. The antiestablishment worldview that both Xenophilius and Luna have embraced throughout the series lays the foundation for Luna's father to reveal the tale of the Deathly Hallows, which is not widely subscribed to by the wizarding world.

Abducted by the Death Eaters to leverage Xenophilius's cooperation with their nefarious plans, Luna has the role in the narrative of illustrating how the Death Eaters, and evildoers in general, exploit people's intimate relationships to achieve their goals. Luna is also a true friend and unfailingly believer in Harry: Harry finds himself especially taken by the mural Luna painted in her room. The mural shows the faces of many students involved in Dumbledore's Army with a golden chain linking them together. The links of the chain, Harry realizes, all spell the word *friends*. Luna's lovable and quirky ways make her comic relief but also extend the theme of social tolerance explored by the books since she and her father are considered, by most, as social outcasts for their strict adherence to their belief in the existence of outrageous creatures and events.

Remus Lupin   Member of the order; part werewolf. In *Deathly Hallows* Lupin plays a small role, but his narrative purpose is undeniable. As a werewolf who has long been the victim of social ostracism from the wizarding community, Lupin in his personal situation reflects some of the larger social questions that the book explores. Once the Death Eaters are in power, Muggle-born wizards now begin to experience the sort of alienation and fear that Lupin feels all the time. These feelings are explored to some degree in *Prisoner of Azkaban* and *Half-Blood Prince* but are addressed in more depth in this final novel when the reluctant marriage he enters into with Tonks results in her pregnancy. Lupin feels a tremendous amount of guilt for potentially subjecting his offspring to the sort of judgment and pain that he himself experiences because of his condition. When Harry confronts Lupin for abandoning Tonks, the guilt Lupin feels for binding Tonks and their future child to his fated condition is clearly revealed.

When Lupin dies in the final battle of Hogwarts, Rowling suggests that his pain and shame die with him: Since the order and its supporters are victorious in battle, the brutal treatment and prejudiced actions toward werewolves such as Lupin are at an end. Lupin, as a beloved character, thus mirrors the larger social questions that the battle between the Death Eaters and the rest of the wizarding world invites readers to consider.

Draco Malfoy Member of Slytherin House, a Death Eater, and one of Harry's archnemeses. As Harry's rival, Draco is established early in the series almost as Harry's diametric opposite. Where Harry is giving, conscientious, concerned with the welfare of others, and humble, Draco is arrogant, self-serving, and elitist. However, the final book emphasizes the books' themes of redemption, sacrifice, and the power of love, as Dumbledore's death in *Half-Blood Prince* is essentially about preserving what little good is left in Draco Malfoy. Knowing that Voldemort is pressuring Draco to orchestrate Dumbledore's death in order to exert control over his anxious parents, Lucius and Narcissa, Dumbledore elicits a promise from Severus Snape that should it be required, Snape will murder the headmaster rather than let Voldemort succeed with his

evil machinations; in this way Dumbledore spares Draco from experiencing the awful act of having his soul violently split after committing a murder.

Deathly Hallows unravels the implications of this act in a number of ways. The Malfoys—including Draco's parents—become less and less committed to the cause of domination and power embraced by Voldemort even though they lend their homestead as a base where Voldemort and his followers congregate. Lucius, when readers encounter him, is subjected to humiliation and contempt from Voldemort and seems only to want to ensure the safety of his family. Narcissa, as well, in the end betrays Voldemort because of her concern for her son. Draco, as well, clearly becomes less invested in the objectives of Voldemort and the Death Eaters. When Harry, Ron, and Hermione are captured by Greyback and his Snatchers, Draco is reluctant to confirm Harry's identity, even though it is obvious he is aware the man they have captured is, indeed, Harry.

The actions of the Malfoys reinforce Rowling's primary theme, the power and importance of human, especially parent-child, love. From Lily Potter's sacrifice of her life to save her son's to Narcissa's betrayal of Voldemort by lying about Harry's death in the forest, Rowling continuously creates plot points that reinforce the notion of love as a powerful tool in defeating evil, largely because evil is often blindsided by love.

In the end Draco and Harry seem to arrive at an uneasy resolution, and even 19 years later in the book's epilogue readers see that the relationship between the now fully grown men (and fathers) is chilly yet respectful.

Harry Potter Protagonist. More than any other character Harry grows in important ways in *Deathly Hallows*; he not only wins his battle with Voldemort but also works through struggles with personal relationships and assumes a mature new authority that enables him finally to resist the hold that Voldemort has had over him since he became the "Boy Who Lived."

In this final book in the series Harry has to come to terms with the ways his epic battle with Voldemort puts pressure on his romantic relationships, his friendships, and even, posthumously, his mentor, Dumbledore. Having broken up with Ginny Weasley primarily to protect her from being put in harm's way, Harry still harbors feelings for her evidenced at his birthday celebration at the Burrow. Harry and Ginny clearly long for each other, as Rowling demonstrates powerfully in a passionate kiss they share. Because of the threat that Voldemort may harm Ginny in order to get to Harry, however, Harry forces himself to leave Ginny behind when he sets out on his journey to destroy the Horcruxes.

His friendship with Ron and Hermione is tested throughout the book as well. They both expect Harry to have the insight, leadership, and courage that he has demonstrated in previous adventures and are challenged and often frustrated by Harry's lack of direction in their collective pursuit of the Horcruxes: Ron tells Harry, "We thought you knew what you were doing! . . . We thought Dumbledore had told you what to do, we thought you had a real plan!" (307). At the same time his and Ron's friendship deepens into a lifelong bond after they destroy Salazar Slytherin's locket. Similarly, Hermione's help during the quest to destroy the Horcruxes remains invaluable, whether she is saving him from the Dark Lord's beloved snake, Nagini, at Bathilda Bagshot's house or thinking quickly as Death Eaters advance upon the Lovegood residence. Without the assistance of his loyal friends Harry, once again, would not have been successful on his journey to destroy the Horcruxes and, ultimately, Voldemort.

Harry's relationship with Dumbledore also evolves since Harry gains a new understanding of his mentor. Before Dumbledore's death, Harry believed that they had a close relationship, largely because of the trust Dumbledore showed to his young protégé and the important tasks he set Harry about doing. However, Rita Skeeter's salacious book and the bitterness that Aberforth Dumbledore has toward his brother both color Harry's perception of his old friend. Part of the major journey that he takes as the protagonist of the novel is through the process of coming to terms with his previous idealization of Dumbledore and the recognition that he was human, with flaws, though perhaps not as serious or devastating as his adversaries would allege.

In the final chapters of the novel Harry's exchange with the phantom Dumbledore at King's Cross is a means of not only revealing key plot information to the reader but also resolving his ambivalence about the role Dumbledore played in his sister's death, his imperfections as a teenager, and his life's missteps. Dumbledore explains to Harry that he "wanted to escape" from his situation as caretaker of his siblings after the deaths of his parents and that he "resented" the role as well (715). Dumbledore also resolves some of Harry's concerns about Dumbledore's support for Grindelwald's scheme to obtain complete power over all other species. Dumbledore tells Harry that he "had few scruples" (716) and that he realized, eventually, he "was not to be trusted with power" (717). Harry realizes and appreciates Dumbledore as a human, just as capable of making mistakes as any other person, and finds peace in realizing his mentor was as human as he. This realization allows Harry and Dumbledore to smile warmly at each other as Harry tells Dumbledore, sitting comfortably in his portrait in the Hogwarts headmaster's office, that he is putting an end to the quest for the Hallows, once and for all.

Beyond his close circle of friends Harry also grapples throughout the book with the important role he plays in the resistance to the Death Eaters' rule and the necessary sacrifices that are made not just on his behalf but on behalf of the cause of good. This feeling of guilt—that others are suffering because of him—is often manipulated by Voldemort, who knows the suffering of those he loves is Harry's greatest fear. When Harry realizes that those of his friends who have arrived to take him from the Dursleys' to a safe location will be risking their lives to save him, Harry responds adamantly, "If you think I'm going to let six people risk their lives . . ." (48). Harry must accept that for him to find the Horcruxes and defeat Voldemort many of those about whom he cares very deeply must risk their lives. This acceptance, however, does not make the injuries or deaths of his friends and loved ones any easier for Harry to bear. The death of Dobby, George's injuries, Fred's death, and the wounds his friends suffer all drive Harry to his final confrontation with Voldemort in the forest; in the end, this compassion and love for others are his greatest qualities. It is a range of human emotion that Voldemort cannot feel, and it is what makes Harry a hero.

Dobby's death is also important in the novel to Harry's development as a character. The loyal house-elf, who jeopardized Harry's life and enrollment in Hogwarts out of concern for his safety, has gone to Harry's aid more than once: feeding him information in *Chamber of Secrets* from the Malfoys, giving him the Gillyweed in *Goblet of Fire* that allows him to succeed in the second task, and finally rescuing Harry and his friends in the last novel as they are locked in a cellar of Malfoy Manor. Dobby's death cements both the series's important thematic advancement of the power of love, loyalty, and redemption and Harry's commitment to dethroning Voldemort from power. Harry's reciprocal loyalty to Dobby demonstrates itself when he buries his friend. Harry acquires a spade and considers it an honor to prepare Dobby's grave: "He dug with a kind of fury, relishing the manual work, glorifying in the non-magic of it, for every drop of his sweat and every blister felt like a gift to the elf who has saved their lives" (478). Harry emerges from digging Dobby's grave filled with a new confidence and authority that translate into decisive action and incisive planning.

Most important, Harry grows to understand his relationship with Voldemort. Though he exploits the psychic connection he has with Voldemort in ways that help him early in the novel, he cannot seem to help but feel the lure of this connection even though it can be disturbing and is counter to Dumbledore's warnings. Eventually, Harry not only learns to close his mind to Voldemort's but also rids himself of the desire to make that connection. As his friendships become close knit and he feels the support and love of those around him more deeply, he loosens the hold that Voldemort has over him. When Dumbledore tells him in shadow version at King's Cross that the part of Voldemort's soul that was unwillingly transferred to him when he was a baby—and the part of Lily's sacrifice that Voldemort unwillingly absorbed during their confrontation in the graveyard at the end of *Goblet of Fire*—

has died, Harry becomes liberated in spirit and body from the unholy power of Voldemort. Indeed, when Harry returns to his body (if he ever left it) in the Forbidden Forest, he is a stronger Harry. Voldemort's magic cannot touch him, and Harry has no trouble mustering the composure and bravery required finally to vanquish Voldemort from power. This same confidence, readers learn, leads Harry to a career as an Auror later in life.

Kingsley Shacklebolt   Auror and devoted member of the Order of the Phoenix, later Minister of Magic. Kingsley Shacklebolt seems to illustrate Rowling's themes of authority, power, and moral rectitude. Most, if not all, of the institutional leaders in the series are corrupted by power: Cornelius Fudge fears the loss of his power more than he does the threat of evil, Rufus Scrimgeour is similarly motivated, Pius Thicknesse is weak and susceptible to the Imperius Curse, Dumbledore himself admits he rejected all offers to serve as Minister of Magic because of the corrupting influence of power on his character. Shacklebolt takes over as minister at the end of the series, and readers are left to assume that his sterling character and fight on the side of right throughout the wizarding war predict his success in the role of Minister of Magic in ways that previous leaders have failed. Significantly Kingsley also repeatedly risks his life to protect Harry. Unlike Scrimgeour, who pleaded with Harry to stand as a mascot for the ministry, Kingsley considers Harry and the rest of the wizarding community's safety far more important than his image or the image of the ministry.

Severus Snape   Headmaster of Hogwarts; ally and spy for the Order of the Phoenix. No character in *Deathly Hallows*, with the possible exception of Albus Dumbledore, becomes more fully elucidated than Severus Snape, whose true nature is finally revealed at the end of the novel. Entire critical books have been written, prior to the publication of this final novel, about Snape's potential allegiance. After *Half-Blood Prince*, when Snape murders Dumbledore (seemingly in cold blood), readers could only assume that Dumbledore's assessment of Severus Snape's character had been wrong and that he was, indeed, on the side of the Death Eaters. However, the final novel reveals that Snape's double-agent status had been maintained and that in the end he sacrificed his own life for Harry because of his lifelong love of Lily Evans, Harry's mother (a love revealed in detail during the chapter "The Prince's Tale").

Rowling has portrayed Snape throughout the series as a hateful, unctuous, and petty man; early in the series this behavior is more annoying than dangerous, but in the last two novels determining Snape's true loyalties takes on weightier dimensions. As he assumes the role of headmaster of Hogwarts upon Dumbledore's death (and avoids responsibility for the murder), Snape seems to be acting in the interest of Voldemort and as his servant. At the same time we have Dumbledore's assurances that Snape is loyal to the order to consider. Not until readers learn that Dumbledore arranged for his own murder by Snape in order to cement Voldemort's faith in Snape as his servant and to save Draco Malfoy from the fate of becoming a murderer is Snape fully redeemed in both Harry's and readers' eyes. Snape becomes the ultimate hero who risked his life in order that good might triumph. When Harry explains to his son Albus Severus that his middle name is that of a Slytherin who, Harry says, "was probably the bravest man I ever knew" (758), even Harry confirms Snape's status as the greatest hero in the series.

More important, though, Snape as a character and his plotline reinforce one of Rowling's most important themes, which is the power of human love to redeem and transform. While readers might think of this theme primarily in the act of Harry's mother's sacrifice of her life for her son's, Snape's character, as well, contributes to this narrative message. Even Dumbledore feels shocked by the depth of Snape's love for Lily: When Snape performs the Patronus spell and a doe erupts from Snape's wand, Dumbledore asks, impressed, "After all this time?" (687), suggesting that after so many years, even Dumbledore thought Snape's love for Lily (who is represented in the form of the doe) would have faded. As Snape passes on the story of his work as

a double agent—and his childhood and adolescent love for Lily Evans—through his bottled thoughts on his deathbed, his last wish is to look into Harry's eyes, the eyes that throughout the series readers have been reminded look just like his mother's.

Nymphadora Tonks Member of the order; married to Remus Lupin. Though Tonks plays a minor role throughout *Deathly Hallows*, she illustrates some of the major themes of the series, including unconditional love, commitment to social justice, and self-sacrifice.

Her marriage to Lupin and willingness to have a child with him illustrate the difference between her and the other pureblood wizards who have joined with Voldemort in the quest for dominance. Tonks, who shares Black family lineage, sees only Remus Lupin's kindness, intelligence, and commitment and not his unfortunate lycanthropy; she sees and believes in their love even more than Lupin does. Further, even though she is of pureblood status and could benefit from that social privilege, Tonks fights valiantly on the side of right from her work as an Auror to her dedication to protecting Harry. Finally, Tonks makes the ultimate sacrifice of her life in the battle of Hogwarts, along with her husband. Even though Rowling clearly suggests that Lupin and Tonks were committed to something greater than themselves in their determination to defeat Voldemort, readers cannot help but wonder about the impact of leaving their son, Teddy Lupin, an orphan to be raised by his grandmother. Similar to Frank and Alice Longbottom, Tonks and Remus demonstrate that personal sacrifice is sometimes necessary and that, as has Neville, Teddy will grow to become a capable wizard who finds love and support from extended family and friends, as illustrated during Rowling's epilogue when readers see Teddy enjoy himself at platform nine and three-quarters flirting with Fleur and Bill's daughter, Victoire.

Voldemort Harry's archnemesis; the Dark Lord. Readers learn more about Voldemort that reinforces his viciousness and complete lack of regard for the life of either his enemies or his loyal followers; the notion of friendship is beyond his experience or value system. He is also incapable of recognizing or acknowledging the concept of love, which, ultimately, leads to his downfall.

Though readers have always known that Voldemort lacked the basic human emotions of compassion, loyalty, and selflessness, they see very clearly just how devoid of humanity Voldemort is in the last book in the series. Though the child and adolescent obviously harbored the bitterness and malice that led him to become the greatest dark wizard that ever lived, the splitting of his soul into the seven Horcruxes completes his transformation into something beyond human and unspeakably evil. Dumbledore's tracing for Harry in *Half-Blood Prince* of Tom Riddle's disturbing evolution sets the stage for the individual and political acts of cruelty Voldemort commits in *Deathly Hallows*.

This last novel opens with Voldemort's murder of Charity Burbage, the Muggle studies teacher, who embraces a viewpoint he despises. Not only does he casually have her killed, but he mentally torments her as well; it is this sadistic love of other people's pain that seems to distinguish him in this book from most of his followers. Similarly he continually humiliates even his most devoted followers, including Bellatrix Lestrange, whom he taunts about her "Mudblood" relative (Tonks); he displays clear contempt for the Malfoys and their attachment to their son, which he simply cannot understand, and punishes other Death Eaters for any lapse in devotion or performance.

The ultimate example of Voldemort's suspicious and cruel nature is the murder of Peter Pettigrew (Wormtail). Though Wormtail demonstrates a weakness of character throughout the series, he stops short of killing Harry in the cellar at Malfoy Manor where he is trapped with his friends, largely because he recognizes that Harry showed him mercy during their confrontation at the Shrieking Shack in *Prisoner of Azkaban*. This slight show of mercy by Wormtail, however, is met immediately with destruction; the silvery, magical replacement hand that Voldemort graced Wormtail with at the end of *Goblet of Fire* turns on its owner, revealing either Voldemort's omniscience or his inherent belief in the treachery of others.

The chapter entitled "King's Cross" is perhaps most important in revealing some of the fundamental qualities of Voldemort. Harry and Dumbledore discuss the fatal flaws that have led Harry and Voldemort to their final confrontation. Because Voldemort so strongly lacks all of the defining features Harry possesses, he can anticipate but cannot understand those qualities; this lack of understanding ultimately, according to Dumbledore, leads to Voldemort's defeat, his falling "backward, arms splayed, the slit pupils of the scarlet eyes rolling upward. Tom Riddle hit the floor with a mundane finality, his body feeble and shrunken, the white hands empty, the snakelike face vacant and unknowing. Voldemort was dead" (744). Voldemort's entire turn toward dark magic was rooted in his quest for eternal life, for immortality; his fear of death and thirst for power are his only allegiances. Conversely Harry's love for others and values of love, charity, and commitment are powerful weapons precisely because they are not self-serving. Harry's willingness to sacrifice himself is another extension of the series's larger theme—the importance of concern for others beyond the self and the willingness to suffer for the collective good beyond one's own needs.

Arthur and Molly Weasley Parents of the Weasley children; members of the order. Both Weasley parents survive the second wizarding war to see their grandchildren born (Rose, Hugo, Albus, James, and Lily), but not without surviving devastating losses including Bill's mauling by the werewolf Fenrir Greyback in *Half-Blood Prince*, George's disfigurement during the transfer of Harry from Privet Drive to safety in *Deathly Hallows*, and the death of Fred during the final battle of Hogwarts. Their joint leadership in the Order of the Phoenix culminates in Molly's rage-filled duel with Bellatrix Lestrange while defending her daughter, Ginny, as Harry battles Voldemort nearby; by making the battles simultaneous and side by side, Rowling suggests that Molly's battle with Bellatrix is as important to Molly as Harry considers his battle with Voldemort. Reinforcing Rowling's emphasis on the value and possibility of unconditional love, Molly and Arthur become surrogate parents for Harry and show their willingness to risk sacrificing their lives in order to fight on the side of right in the epic battle on which the fate of wizarding society hinges.

Fred and George Weasley Twin brothers; members of the order; owners of Weasley's Wizard Wheezes. As the jester/prankster figures in the series, the Weasley twins (who are a year older than Ron) manage to maintain their image as jokesters while remaining committed to the cause of fighting dark magic. The Weasley twins are so committed, in fact, that one suffers serious injuries and the other dies while fighting on behalf of the order. Even though George has his ear severed in the battle against the Death Eaters when moving Harry from Privet Drive, he rebounds with a witticism about feeling "saintlike" because he is "holey," a reference to the ear he has lost in battle (74). Fred's death in the battle of Hogwarts serves, as does the death of some significant minor characters, to emphasize the series's message that any war against wicked forces requires some sacrifice and loss. Rowling's choice to make Fred and George twins deserves analysis. Though the loss of Fred is terrible, readers may feel some comfort that George, one of the Weasleys famous for giving lightness and laughter to the wizarding world in times of great trouble, lives on.

Ginny Weasley Youngest of the Weasley family; member of Gryffindor House; Harry's romantic interest and, eventually, his wife. Ginny's primary role in the last three books of the series is as Harry's love interest. In the final novel we see very little of her except to know that Harry has broken off their relationship in order to save her the suffering of his absence. Further, as a member of Dumbledore's Army, she is part of the core group of Harry's supporters remaining at Hogwarts who subversively resist the occupation of the school by Death Eater philosophies and faculty. Though Ginny has evolved over the series from a shy preteen to a confident young woman, she does not display the depth of development that some of the other characters do; she is an activist in her support of Harry but does

not initiate change in the same way as Hermione; she distinguishes herself on the Quidditch field but is no competition for Harry; she challenges Snape's illegitimate rule but as part of a small group along with Luna and Neville. At the same time Ginny's positive qualities as an autonomous young woman who stands by her beliefs and makes her own decisions have appealed to readers.

Ron Weasley Harry Potter's best friend; the youngest Weasley son. Ron's foremost quality throughout the series is his steadfast friendship with Harry. Even though he struggles to grapple with some feelings of jealousy over Harry's notoriety and the public attention he receives for his role as "the Boy Who Lived" as well as Harry's superior financial situation, Ron always comes through for Harry, and his family serves as a stabilizing and supportive force in Harry's life. In this last novel Ron evolves in two major ways: His romantic relationship with Hermione, which has been developing over the last three novels, is finally realized, and Harry and Ron's relationship is tested by Ron's exile, but they are reconciled and are closer friends than they were before.

Ron is a somewhat immature and adolescent character and handles his romantic interest in Hermione in childish ways. Though his qualities of being playful and lighthearted are some of his best, these traits also render him unable to admit his feelings for Hermione, and instead he resorts to game playing and petty torments rather than facing his feelings for her. In this last novel Hermione and Ron take their relationship to the next level, largely because of Ron's willingness to examine his feelings and be forthright about them. In the end Hermione's torture by Bellatrix Lestrange in Malfoy Manor forces Ron to confront the depth of his love for Hermione and compels him to lead the attack on the Death Eaters in the Malfoys' living room: When he hears Hermione screaming in pain, "Ron was half sobbing as he pounded the walls with his fists" (466).

Ron also grows in important ways as a friend to Harry in *Deathly Hallows*. When Ron is tested by the added stress of the locket Horcrux, his natural tendency toward moroseness and self-pity is exacerbated, leading him eventually to abandon his two friends. The fact that he immediately wishes to return (but is prevented by the Snatchers) is consistent with his previous behavior—and one of the reasons, perhaps, that Dumbledore willed him the Deluminator. In the end Ron's continued desire to return to and aid his friends is what takes him back, and this notion of the power of friendship, loyalty, and commitment is another of Rowling's important messages about human relationships, which Ron demonstrates fully.

Wormtail/Peter Pettigrew Classmate of Harry's father and loyal servant of Voldemort. When Dumbledore reassured Harry about the correctness of his decision to prevent Sirius and Lupin from killing Pettigrew in revenge for the deaths he caused, he also predicted that Pettigrew would be indebted to him. In this last novel Dumbledore's prediction is realized. Unfortunately Dumbledore's prediction about Voldemort's merciless nature and total lack of regard for any life-form (even his dedicated followers) also holds true when Voldemort murders Pettigrew for not killing Harry in Malfoy Manor. Pettigrew is as unctuous as he was in past novels, but the moral debt he owes to Harry is one of the ways Rowling affirms that the preservation of life is an important value. Rowling emphasizes the importance of protecting life just as Pettigrew's silvery arm, a gift from Voldemort, instantly betrays its owner when his loyalty to Voldemort falters. Pettigrew's death—along with Snape's—paints Voldemort more vividly as devoid of the ability to form attachments to others and as obsessed with abject obedience rather than true loyalty like that Harry engenders in his friends and followers.

FILM ADAPTATION

Deathly Hallows, unlike its predecessors, was adapted into two movies; at press time neither of these films had been released. *Deathly Hallows, Part I*, is scheduled to be released on November 19, 2010, and *Deathly Hallows, Part II*, is scheduled to be released on July 15, 2011. The following information, based on interviews given by filmmakers and cast members, provides the foundation for the critical analysis of these films.

One of the major sources of information on the *Deathly Hallows* films is Jeff Jensen's "This Magic Moment" in the July 17, 2009, edition of *Entertainment Weekly*. The director David Yates revealed to Jensen that, compared to *Half-Blood Prince*, he is "planning a more complex, contemporary, 'intense' take on adolescence in *Deathly Hallows*." Yates also added that "part one of *Deathly Hallows* is the rawest and most real-world of the films I've made in the series so far. I've very consciously run away from Hogwarts. I'm trying to find a reality that we haven't explored to this extent before. . . . It's very much the real world and that's quite fun and brings its own dynamic". Yates's decision to "run away" from Hogwarts for *Deathly Hallows, Part I*, seems natural, however, since the focus of most of the novel is on Harry, Ron, and Hermione's quest to find Voldemort's Horcruxes.

Movie Magic's staff also conducted some anticipated and crucial interviews with Yates, who added to the information he shared with *Entertainment Weekly*'s Jensen: Many of the characters in *Deathly Hallows, Part I* "are refugees, ultimately, in the first part, running for their lives and pursued at every turn. They're on a mission, so there's definitely this sense of magical refugees on the road." Though Yates revealed few particulars about *Deathly Hallows, Part II*, he did state that the second film causes filmmakers and cast members to "get very operatic and very expressive again. And oddly elegiac." Yates was somehow able to balance the last three Harry Potter films at once: While completing the final editing for *Half-Blood Prince*, he was also shooting both parts of *Deathly Hallows*. Although the schedule was tiring, Yates told the staff of *Movie Magic* that the work had been "amazing, but it's fun, actually, and fortunately, because this is my third in a row at the moment, it feels very natural and normal to be working at this pace [very fast-paced, crazy schedule]."

Since it was announced, the decision to split the story of *Deathly Hallows* into two films has excited fans and aroused suspicion in critics. The producer David Heyman revealed that after many discussions with Rowling it was decided that *Deathly Hallows* deserved two films because so much transpires in the last novel. The screenwriter, Steve Kloves, highly favored adapting Rowling's novel into two films: "I intuited—almost from the first moments I began reading it and certainly once I'd finished—that to realize the story in a single film was going to be a tall order. . . . Ultimately everyone felt that despite the challenges it would present, it was the most sound creative decision." *Goblet of Fire* filmmakers had also debated making the fourth book into two films, but decided against it. Kloves argued that *Deathly Hallows* filmmakers could preserve more plot details with two films devoted to the seventh novel. "I'm really excited about it because it should allow us to stretch a bit with the characters and give them the proper send-off. . . . We want to give them [the fans] the best and most complete experience possible." Dan Radcliffe (who plays the beloved role of Harry Potter) also championed the idea of making two films based on the last novel: "I think making two movies is the only way you can do it, without cutting out a huge portion of the book. . . . There have been compartmentalized subplots in the other books that have made them easier to cut—although those cuts were still to the horror of some fans—but the seventh book doesn't really have any subplots. It's one driving, pounding story from the word 'Go'."

Fans, cast members, and filmmakers seemed only to feel grateful that Rowling's final novel would be made as two films so a thorough adaptation might be rendered. The *New York Times*'s Manohla Dargis, however, feels that the decision to make two films based on *Deathly Hallows* was not made out of consideration for the story or those who love the series, but for money: "Considering that the take for Harry Potter and His Big Pot of Cinematic Gold now totals almost $4.5 billion in international box office, the studio's reluctance to embrace the end is touchingly obvious." Dargis is not the only voice to express cynicism about the studio's explanation that aesthetic and creative concerns justified the splitting of the book into two films—certainly extending the film

releases will also increase incredible profits for the filmmakers and for Rowling herself.

Much as in the fervor surrounding the other Harry Potter films, fans have hypothesized the contents of the final films; more details about what the movies will lack have been made public than details about what they will retain. Filmmakers did confirm that viewers would learn more about Voldemort's history, an element compressed severely in *Half-Blood Prince*. Voldemort's personal story, filmmakers realized, naturally complements Dumbledore's former belief system, so the more fitting place for these revelations was in the *Deathly Hallows* films. Filmmakers, however, have been keen to reveal what the *Deathly Hallows* films will not include, leaving viewers to wonder about what the films will actually contain. For instance, *Deathly Hallows* (both the first and second parts) will not have the primary setting at Hogwarts. Similarly, with little action transpiring at Hogwarts, viewers will not see the principal characters in their familiar Hogwarts robes and accompanying uniforms. Rupert Grint (who plays Ron Weasley) told *Entertainment Weekly*'s Jensen that he stole a Gryffindor tie from the set. Grint appeared as the only one of the three main characters to feel sentimental at all about the Hogwarts uniform; Radcliffe and Emma Watson (the actress who plays Hermione Granger), as Jensen reports, wanted the Hogwarts uniforms burned. Radcliffe said, "When you're 18, one of the worst things to be wearing while trying to chat up a girl on the set is a school uniform. You look like you're a kid! You're not going to score dressed like that!"

Filmmakers also experienced some challenging situations while filming the final installments of the Harry Potter saga, ranging from scheduling conflicts to filming of challenging scenes. Yates recalls that he filmed about 10 percent of the second part of *Deathly Hallows* while working on the first part because of the demands on several actors in the films: Some of the cast had to balance other projects with filming the Harry Potter films, so scheduling for filming became quite hectic. Rupert Grint was prevented from filming for a period of time—not because of participation in other projects, however: Unfortunately, he had swine flu.

In an interview with *Entertainment Weekly*'s Jensen, the three main stars—Rupert Grint, Emma Watson, and of course, Daniel Radcliffe—discussed which scenes posed the most difficulty for them in filming *Deathly Hallows*. Legions of fans who think little of the personal relationships between the actors offscreen were somewhat surprised by a revelation made by Grint and Watson. Jensen reported that "for Grint and Watson, their hardest scene. . . . was a kiss between Ron and Hermione that shapes their destiny. 'I remember being inches away from her lips and thinking, "Good Lord, this is going to be strange,"' says Grint. Adds Watson: "'Rupert is like a brother to me, and our relationship couldn't be more platonic. So kissing him—well, it felt like incest, to be honest. But I think it's going to be very sweet.'" Radcliffe believes the scene that will be most difficult for him concerns facing Voldemort in the forest outside Hogwarts: "As for Radcliffe, the scene he's most dreading is scheduled to be filmed right around Christmas [2009]. It's the emotionally-charged climactic moment when Harry walks alone and afraid through a dark wood toward a fateful confrontation with Voldemort. . . . Ask Radcliffe about it, and he shuts you down. 'No, please, I'm trying not to think about it. I still have no idea how I am going to do that,' he says. 'That'll be a tricky one.'"

Filmmakers and fellow actors mourn finishing the finale but also appreciate the incredible opportunities and experiences filming the Harry Potter series has allowed them. When the staff of *Movie Magic* asked the director David Yates about his reactions to filming the final installment of the series, he answered, "It's a great opportunity, it really is. A wonderful one. And I'm quite excited about it, because I think it's really kinetic but moving at the same time. There's not a pressure. I'd say it's more of a responsibility than a pressure to deliver something special." The producer, David Heyman, looks forward to the freedom to explore new projects but added that he will feel "great sadness, because this has been a remarkable gift in so many ways, working with people who are the very best at what they do, in an environment that is without ego. Great pride, but without ego. . . . The studio has been so remarkable and given us remarkable freedom to make the films that we do. It's been great and I will miss this environment."

Watson shares Heyman's feelings. In an interview with *Movie Magic* she reported that filming the Harry Potter series has "been half of our lives. . . . It's made us, it's formed us. It's such a big part of my life, so it will be really sad [to leave the stories]—and so much of the crew who have been there since the beginning are like my family. We will always be very important to each other . . . . But, at the same time, after eight Harry Potter films, we'll be ready to go and do other things, and be other people, and have time for ourselves." In the same interview Grint said, "I've really enjoyed it and part of me will miss it. But it'll also be good to be free. Ron Weasley has become a big part of my life, and not just because we've both got ginger hair! I've been so proud to play him and loved every second of being part of this world. I'm really looking forward to filming the last two films and being back with my 'Weasley family' and, of course, to seeing my good friends Emma and Dan." As did his costars and friends, Radcliffe reflected on his experiences of bringing the beloved Harry Potter to life on screen: "I'm sort of clinging on to every moment that there is now in a way, because this is the beginning of the end, but I'm not really thinking about that. I'm not thinking too far ahead. I'm just enjoying the moments and hanging on to them while I've got them." Filming the Harry Potter series may have drawn to a close, but the appreciation and gratitude audiences feel for embodying the characters portrayed (especially by Radcliffe, Grint, and Watson) live on.

WORKS CITED AND FURTHER READING

Anderson, Sam. "Harry Potter and the Ignominious Cop-Out." *New York*, August 13, 2007, 70–71.

Cart, Michael. "Carte Blanche." *Booklist* 1, 15 January 2008, 54.

Chaudhry, Lakshmi. "Harry Potter and the Half-Baked Epic." *Nation,* 13 August 2007, 5–6.

Coats, Karen. Review of *Harry Potter and the Deathly Hallows. Bulletin of the Center for Children's Books* 61, no. 2 (October 2007): 109.

Cooper, Ilene. Review of *Harry Potter and the Deathly Hallows. Booklist,* August 2007.

Corbett, Sue. "A Glorious End for the Potter Books." *People,* 6 August 2007, 45.

"Daniel Radcliffe: Coming to Terms with Harry Potter." In *Movie Magic.* San Antonio, Tex.: Bauer, 2009.

Dargis, Manohla. "In Latest *Harry Potter,* Rage and Hormones." *New York Times,* 15 July 2009.

"David Heyman Faces the Final Chapter." In *Movie Magic.* San Antonio, Tex.: Bauer, 2009.

De Lint, Charles. "Books to Look For: Charles De Lint." *Fantasy & Science Fiction,* January 2008, 30–33.

"Directing the Magic." In *Movie Magic.* San Antonio, Tex.: Bauer, 2009.

Fischer, Tabor. "Harry Potter Review: Is All Well in the End?" *Telegraph.* 23 July 2007. Available online. URL: http://www.telegraph.co.uk/news/uknews/1558079/Harry-Potter-review-Is-all-well-in-the-end.html. Accessed August 25, 2009.

Fordham, Alice. Review of *Harry Potter and the Deathly Hallows. Times* Online (London). 21 July 2007.

Gross, Claire E. "*Harry Potter and the Deathly Hallows.*" *Horn Book Magazine* 83, no. 5 (September 2007): 551–553.

Gurdon, Meghan Cox. "The Finale Is Magical, Even for Muggles." *Wall Street Journal Asia,* 26 July 2007, p.12.

Hand, Elizabeth. "Harry's Final Fantasy: Last Time's the Charm." *Washington Post,* 22 July 2007. Available online. URL: http://www.washingtonpost.com/wp-dyn/content/article/2007/07/21/AR2007072101025.html. Accessed August 25, 2009.

Hanley, Lynsey. "The Wizard of Us." *New Statesman,* 30 July 2007, 54–55.

"*Harry Potter and the Deathly Hallows.*" *Booklist* 104, no. 9/10 (January 2008): 18.

"*Harry Potter and the Deathly Hallows.*" *Booklist* 104, no. 9/10 (January 2008): 12.

"*Harry Potter and the Deathly Hallows.*" *Publishers Weekly,* 30 July 2007, 83.

"*Harry Potter and the Deathly Hallows.*" *Booklist* 104, no. 13 (March 2008): 10.

Hensher, Philip. "No More School." *Spectator,* 25 July 2007.

Hitchens, Christopher. "The Boy Who Lived." *New York Times Book Review,* August 12, 2007, 10–11.

Jensen, Jeff. "This Magic Moment." *Entertainment Weekly,* 17 July 2009, 24–31.

Jones, Malcolm. "Harry Potter: The End Is Here." *Newsweek,* 30 July 2007, 60.

Jordan, Tina, and Anna Belle Hindenlang. *Entertainment Weekly,* August 3, 2007, 72–73.

Kakutani, Michiko. Review of *Harry Potter and the Deathly Hallows. New York Times.* 19 July 2007. Available online. URL: http://www.nytimes.com/2007/07/19/books/19potter.html. Accessed September 1, 2009.

Kaveney, Roz. "The End Game." *Times Literary Supplement,* 27 July 2007, 19.

King, Stephen. "J. K. Rowling's Ministry of Magic." *Entertainment Weekly,* 11 July 2007 Available online. URL: http://www.ew.com/ew/article/0,,20044270_20044274_20050689,00.html. Accessed August 25, 2009.

"Life with—and after—Ron Weasley." In *Movie Magic.* San Antonio, Tex.: Bauer, 2009.

Linning, Lyn. Review of *Harry Potter and the Deathly Hallows. Magpies* 22, no. 4 (September 2007): 32.

Lotto, Mark. "Harry Potter and the End of Enchantment." *New York Observer.* 23 July 2007. Available online. URL: http://www.observer.com/2007/harry-potter-and-end-enchantment. Accessed September 1, 2009.

Lurie, Alison. "Pottery." *New York Review of Books,* 27 September 2007, 32–35.

Meister, Beth L. "*Harry Potter and the Deathly Hallows.*" *School Library Journal* 53, no. 9 (September 2007): 206–207.

Miller, Laura. "Goodbye, Harry Potter." Salon.com. 20 July 2007. Available online. URL: http://www.salon.com/books/review/2007/07/20/harry/print.html. Accessed September 1, 2009.

Mullan, John. "A Shapely Plot and No Loose Ends." *Guardian.* 21 July 2007. Available online. URL:

http://www.guardian.co.uk/uk/2007/jul/21/harry potter.books. Accessed August 25, 2009.

Parravano, Martha. *"Harry Potter and the Deathly Hallows." Horn Book Magazine* 83, no. 6 (November 2007): 705.

Peters, John. "Grand Finale." *Kirkus Reviews,* 15 August 2007, 810.

Rosenberg, Liz. "The End." *Boston Globe.* 23 July 2007. Available online. URL: http://www.boston.com/ae/books/articles/2007/07/23/the_end/. Accessed August 25, 2009.

Sawyer, Jenny. "Missing from *Harry Potter*—a Real Moral Struggle." *Christian Science Monitor.* 25 July 2007. Available online. URL: http://www.csmonitor.com/2007/0725/p09s02-scoop.html. Accessed September 1, 2009.

Schiavone, Angie. "Rowling Holds Us Spellbound to the End." *Sydney Morning Herald.* 23 July 2007. Available online. URL: http://www.smh.com.au/news/books/rowling-holds-us-spellbound-to-the-end/2007/07/22/1185042949545.html. Accessed August 25, 2009.

Schiffren, Lisa. "Magic Alert: The Last Installment in the Harry Potter Saga." *Weekly Standard,* 13 August 2007.

"Sneak Peak at *Harry Potter and the Deathly Hallows.*" In *Movie Magic.* San Antonio, Tex.: Bauer, 2009.

Wysocki, Barbara. *"Harry Potter and the Deathly Hallows." School Library Journal* 53, no. 9 (September 2007): 74.

Zakosek, Matt. "'Hallows: Grim yet Poetic." *Chicago Sun-Times.* 22 July 2007. Available online. URL: http://www.suntimes.com/potter/478998,CST-BOOKS-potterbook22.article. Accessed August 25, 2009.

Scholarship on the Harry Potter Series

The Harry Potter series grew in popularity among both young readers and adults concurrently with the publication of the third book, *Prisoner of Azkaban,* in 1999. Since then both the series and the Harry Potter phenomenon garnered a great deal of attention in scholarly journals and from academic presses in the early 2000s. Both scholars and armchair analysts began publishing interpretive work on the series about a range of topics—Rowling's aesthetic choices and the merits of her work; historical, cultural, and literary contexts; and analysis through lenses as diverse as religious, philosophical, and mythological. For a discussion of nonscholarly treatments of the series, see "Additional Resources on the Harry Potter Series" section.

Articles and books that focus on individual novels within the series can be found with each entry in this book, and the present section deals with work that discusses more than one of the Harry Potter novels. All author citations are references to the Works Cited and Further Reading that follows this entry.

LITERARY, NARRATIVE, AND THEMATIC CONCERNS

Many scholars have been interested in analyzing the thematic and literary dimensions of Rowling's books. The notion of "transformation" is the center of two scholarly essays. Kate Behr in "'Same as Difference': Narrative Transformations and Intersection Cultures in Harry Potter" uses the question "What makes the Harry Potter books so readable and so popular?" as a starting point for exploring narrative transformation. Behr claims that Rowling's narrative structure of using particular settings or props for comic and then dramatic effect is part of her craftsmanship. For example, the Room of Requirement mentioned in *Goblet of Fire* is the subject of Dumbledore's bathroom joke (it is full of chamber pots) but then becomes the site of subversion and resistance as a practice room for Dumbledore's Army in *Order of the Phoenix*; similarly, the comic use of Polyjuice Potion by Harry, Ron, and Hermione in *Chamber of Secrets* becomes an instrument of torture for Mad-Eye Moody in *Goblet of Fire*. This theme of transformation, according to Behr, persists in both the magical curriculum in the form of the Transfiguration course and in character development, where moral transformation occurs when characters who are thought to be good can turn out to be bad, or vice versa (such as Sirius

Black and Cornelius Fudge). Further, the characters themselves go through metaphorical or literal transformations: Harry and Hermione both grow personally throughout the series, while characters such as Lupin and Sirius undergo literal physical transformations. It is this literal transformation that interests Amy Green in her article "Interior/ Exterior in the 'Harry Potter' Series: Duality Expressed in Sirius Black and Remus Lupin." Her analysis focuses on the ways that Lupin and Black's physical transformations serve to reveal character features. Further, Green provides historical contexts on lycanthropy (werewolves) and discusses the relevant social issues, such as AIDS and homophobia, that Rowling could be commenting on with the struggle these two characters face.

Other writers have discussed the series in light of particular themes or motifs they see developed. For example, Deborah DeRosa's "Wizardly Challenges to and Affirmations of the Initiation Paradigm in Harry Potter" explores the "initiation paradigm" and Rowling's use of the journey Harry undertakes as he becomes acculturated to the wizarding world, while Leigh Neithardt has engaged in similar analysis in her essay "The Problem of Identity in *Harry Potter and the Sorcerer's Stone*." Neithardt, as does DeRosa, traces Harry's literal and metaphorical journeys in the novels as he faces Voldemort and wars with his own fears, anxieties, and insecurities. John Kornfeld and Laurie Prothro's essay "Comedy, Conflict, and Community: Home and Family in *Harry Potter*" takes up this theme by contrasting the mundane and the magical worlds that Harry occupies and the ways that Rowling conceptualizes such institutions as family and home in her rejection of the notion of blood as determinant of family groups. Other scholars, including Charles Elster, have studied the books' treatment of related institutions such as Hogwarts and the sorts of learning Rowling privileges. Elster's article, "The Seeker of Secrets: Images of Learning, Knowing, and Schooling" examines the types of learning Harry and his friends engage in, including heroic knowledge, real-world learning,

gendered learning, and living and learning in a wizarding school. "'If Yeh Know Where to Go': Vision and Mapping in the Wizarding World" by Jonathan Lewis also focuses on the initiation of Harry into the wizarding world though framed in the lens of Rowling's use of maps and hidden places. Lauren Berman's "Dragons and Serpents in J. K. Rowling's *Harry Potter* Series: Are They Evil?" considers the mythological, folkloric, and biblical implications of dragons and serpents and traces the role of each within Rowling's narrative and moral framework.

Loyalty and identity as illustrated by the school's sorting process into the four houses are explored by Chantel Lavoie in "Safe as Houses: Sorting and School Houses at Hogwarts." A related essay, "Crowning the King: Harry Potter and the Construction of Authority" by Farah Mendlesohn, examines the ideologies of authority, specifically the social structures and assumptions about power that are unchallenged in Rowling's novels, including the passive validation of social hierarchies. Karin Westman's "The Weapon We Have Is Love," published in the *Children's Literature Association Quarterly*, explores the twin themes of love and desire in the series, primarily in the characters of Harry and Dumbledore.

Other themes or features of the series that have been examined by scholars include representations of such arenas as athletics or the law. For example, Terri Toles Patkin's "Constructing a New Game: J. K. Rowling's Quidditch and Global Kid Culture" takes the invented game of Quidditch as an opportunity for examining the role of games in society, arguing that defining "play" also defines "culture." Patkin believes that Quidditch can be "understood as a metaphor for the complex and interlocking roles within wizarding society." Though her approach might be said to be informed by psychoanalytic approaches (such as her discussion of the broomstick as a phallic symbol) or materialist lenses (for her discussion of the commercialization of Quidditch within the wizarding world), her analysis cannot be placed within one theoretical tradition.

Though many of the essays focusing on Rowling's critique of corrupt institutions and the government and legal organizations in the series focus on *Order of the Phoenix,* William MacNeil draws attention in "Kidlit as 'Law-and-Lit': Harry Potter and the Scales of Justice" to Rowling's "thematic of legalism," specifically through the use of the Pensieve in *Goblet of Fire,* which provides a glimpse into the system of jurisprudence in the magical world: the Death Eater trials in the first wizarding war and the conviction of Barty Crouch, Jr. The legal system seems to cry out for reform as soon as we are introduced to it, says MacNeil. Injustice in the unequal treatment of criminals and accused criminals is rampant. Brycchan Carey, as does MacNeil, considers the question of house-elves as part of Rowling's consideration of the boundaries of equality and access to civil rights in "Hermione and the House-elves: The Literary and Historical Contexts of J. K. Rowling's Antislavery Campaign." James Landman similarly explores the "rule of law," in "Using Literature to Teach the Rule of Law," where he [argues that the books are concerned with "the rules of fair play that form our notion of due process" or the "quality of justice it delivers" in the Potter series (165), as does Susan Hall in "Harry Potter and the Rule of Law: The Central Weakness of Legal Concepts in the Wizard World."

Literary Merit

A number of scholars have demonstrated interest in challenging the series's literary merit, in terms of elements such as structure, theme, plotting, genre convention, and language. One of the earliest critiques was that of one of the foremost literary scholars in the United States, Harold Bloom, whose July 11, 2000, column in the *Wall Street Journal* (though not in a scholarly venue, the opinion piece offered a scholarly perspective) outlines the "inadequacies," "aesthetic weaknesses," and "crucial liabilities" of the first book. Bloom critiques the book primarily on what he sees as a failure of imaginative vision and an overuse of clichéd writing, including stylistic ordinariness. A chapter in Jack Zipes's 2001 book *Sticks and Stones: The Troublesome Success*

of Children's Literature from Slovenly Peter to Harry Potter, "The Phenomenon of Harry Potter, or Why All the Talk?" is often cited by other critics and, as does Bloom's essay, outlines what Zipes believes to be the artistic failures of Rowling's work. Zipes argues that the book's success is fueled by its adherence to popular myths like the "rags to riches" story and that the books are conventional, "cute and ordinary." His primary critiques are that Rowling's novels are both formulaic and sexist. John Pennington's essay "From Elfland to Hogwarts, or the Aesthetic Trouble with Harry Potter" in *The Lion and the Unicorn* the following year (2002) further charts Rowling's aesthetic failures including concurring with Bloom's assessment of the series's lack of imagination and inventiveness. Pennington also finds the books to have narrative, structural, and thematic failures, charging that they are derivative, lack distinct voices for each character, and promote reader passivity. In addition, he believes the books use sloppy language and do not tackle large philosophical questions.

In contrast, Philip Nel's 2005 essay "Is There a Text in This Advertising Campaign? Literature, Marketing, and Harry Potter" in the *Lion and the Unicorn* responds to Pennington's critique, rejecting Pennington's argument that Rowling's failure to adhere to fantasy literature definitions set out by J. R. R. TOLKIEN (whom Pennington and others view as an archetype for fantasy literature) is an aesthetic failure and asserting the importance of separating the Harry Potter phenomenon (POTTERMANIA) from the Harry Potter series. Nel documents what he believes are examples of Rowling's literary craftsmanship including her use of satire. He praises what he calls "third-person narratives that are closely aligned with first-person perspective—a technique known as free indirect discourse" (246). Nancy Knapp, as does Nel, makes a three-pronged argument in her article "In Defense of Harry Potter: An Apologia" that the books are valuable as great children's literature because they are intensely engaging (that is, children love and show enthusiasm for them). She claims that they have significant literary worth, citing the number of awards the books have received and arguing that they meet the American Library Association's Newbery Award standards, though Rowling is not eligible for the award because she is not an American citizen. Finally, Knapp argues that the books raise questions of "deep significance to children's social and ethical development." Other essays do not respond directly to Pennington but to general attacks on the Harry Potter series's aesthetic value, including Amanda Cockrell's "Harry Potter and the Secret Password" and Kathleen McEvoy's "Aesthetic Organization: The Structural Beauty of J. K. Rowling's *Harry Potter* Series."

Literary Traditions

Pat Pinsent's "The Education of a Wizard" nicely dovetails the Harry Potter scholarly enterprises of both identifying the literary traditions that Rowling draws upon and defending Rowling against claims that her work is derivative. Pinsent contends that "Rowling's originality is in no way diminished by not being first in the field," and the essay places the Potter series in the context of other fantasy works for children that employ similar devices, characters, or plotlines.

A hefty number of critical essays have traced the Harry Potter books' place in a number of literary traditions (including the BILDUNGSROMAN, or coming-of-age stories; fantasy; and children's literature) or the intertextual relationships between the series and the other literary works Rowling draws upon in her writing of the novels; in addition, some critics have offered work that points out the literary allusions in the series. Countless critics have observed the relationship between Rowling's school story and the classic British boarding school text, Thomas Hughes's *Tom Brown's Schooldays* published in 1857 and also wildly popular during its era. In "Harry Potter's Schooldays" Alexandra Mullen argues that the two texts are similar because they both reflect what a culture expects an education to do. Mullen's comparisons also pose a provocative question about what source of worldview each book uses as its foundation, as Hughes's book is ultimately undergirded by faith in a Christian god while the Potter

series seems to affirm not a supernatural source of comfort but the value of human love. Lucy Rollin, as well, argues that Hughes's Tom Brown is Harry Potter's literary ancestor, and her article "Among School Children: The Harry Potter Books and the School Story Tradition" makes stricter and more focused comparisons between the two than Mullen's. Rollin's article also adds the dimension of tracing the paternalistic and masculine plotting and characterization in the two stories. David Steege contends in "Harry Potter, Tom Brown, and the British School Story" that the series belongs to the school story tradition of *Tom Brown's Schooldays* but contends that Rowling "transform[s] the genre so significantly that the books have been able to cross borders with unprecedented success" (141). Nicholas Tucker, as well, has written on the parallels between the two books in "The Rise and Rise of Harry Potter." Tucker differs in one major way from Rollin and Mullen, in his characterization of Hogwarts as socially exclusive (because its exclusive nature as a school for wizards makes it selective), while the latter view the school as democratized (in that it accepts students of all blood status). Karen Manners Smith's essay "Harry Potter's Schooldays: J. K. Rowling and the British Boarding School Novel" places Harry Potter's boarding school experiences within the context of literary representations and cultural discussions of the British boarding school.

Beyond the school story scholars have analyzed the series and its place in a number of other literary traditions. Anne Alton, Evelyn Perry, Steven Barfield, and Amy Billone have all discussed the series as an entry in the fantasy or children's fantasy tradition. For example, Alton argues in "Generic Fusion and the Mosaic of Harry Potter" that the series's fusion of multiple genres ranging from fantasy to bildungsroman to the school story and sports story is what creates its appeal to readers. Similarly, Sarah Meier makes a stronger case in "Educating Harry Potter: A Muggle's Perspective on Magic and Knowledge in the Wizard World of J. K. Rowling" for the books as Tolkienesque fantasy because of the artful creation of a "secondary world" of the sort Tolkien describes in his landmark essay "On

Fairy Stories." (See also Miranda Yaggi's "Harry Potter's Heritage: Tolkien as Rowling's Patronus against the Critics" for a similar discussion of Rowling and Tolkien and DawnEllen Jacobs's article "Tolkien and Rowling: Reflections on Receptions" for a comparison of the initial reception of Tolkien's *Lord of the Rings* novels with that of the Harry Potter novels.)

Meier, as does Alton, sees the Harry Potter books as classic bildungsroman narratives. Perry's and Billone's discussion of the books as children's fantasy are more critical than explanatory: Perry advocates considering the series as literature rather than "fandom" or "hype" and conducting an extended analysis of the parallels between Harry Potter's journey and the account of the young king Arthur in T. H. WHITE'S *The Sword and the Stone* and *The Once and Future King.* Billone, however, uses a wider literary and feminist lens in "The Boy Who Lived: From Carroll's Alice and Barrie's Peter Pan to Rowling's Harry Potter" to discuss the story in the context of children's fantasy tradition, such as *Peter Pan* and *Alice in Wonderland,* arguing for the centrality of dream sequences to propel the narrative in Rowling's books and for a more conscientious reading of the books' gender dynamics. Rebecca Whitus Longster's essay reads the Weasley brothers in the tradition of the Shakespearean jester figure. Jan Lacoss's "Of Magicals and Muggles: Reversals and Revulsions at Hogwarts" argues that the series can be read as a folktale, identifying features of the series that resemble folktales, including garb, social groupings, a specialized lexicon, rites of passage, food, boundary crossing, taboos, social folkways, and other aspects of custom and culture.

Critics have charted the influence of particular literary figures on Rowling as demonstrated in her books. Bill McCarron, for example, in "Literary Parallels in *Harry Potter and the Chamber of Secrets*" sees Rowling as operating in the tradition of the British poets John Milton and John Donne and the mysterious American postmodernist Thomas Pynchon. At the same time Tucker in "The Rise and Rise of Harry Potter" and others have seen traces of ROALD DAHL and Cinderella in the series, while, Lesley Nye in the *Harvard Educational Review* puts the series "into historical perspective" by documenting the many classics in children's fantasy literature the books draw upon, ranging from Robin Hood to Beowulf to Mary Poppins to LEWIS CARROLL's *Alice* stories. Judith Saltman, as well, undertakes a critical overview in "Harry Potter's Family Tree," positioning the books within the context of other canonical works by British and fantasy writers such as Dahl, Lemony Snicket, CHARLES DICKENS, URSULA LE GUIN, and C. S. LEWIS (see Joy Farmer, "The Magician's Niece," 2001, for an extended discussion of the relationship between Rowling and Lewis). Christopher Routledge maintains in "Harry Potter and the Mystery of Ordinary Life" that the major appeal of the books is not that they offer magic and mystery but rather that they are detective stories à la Sherlock Holmes, asserting that the main aim of detection in both Holmes and the Harry Potter novels is "finding justice for the wrongly accused" (205). Westman draws parallels in her article "Perspective, Memory, and Moral Authority: The Legacy of Jane Austen in J. K. Rowling's Harry Potter" in the journal *Children's Literature* between the narrative perspective and characterization of Harry Potter and several of the heroines in JANE AUSTEN novels, including *Emma* and *Mansfield Park.*

Comparisons between the Harry Potter series and other literary works as diverse as the *Chronicles of Narnia* (Ernella Fife), the romantic/Byronic hero (Maria Nikolajeva), and the *Mahabaratha* and *Ramayana* (V. S. K. Chellammal and Chitra Lakshimi) have also been undertaken by critics. Roni Natov, for example, looks at the books within the tradition of the "orphan hero" tradition found in *Jane Eyre* and novels by Dickens.

Themes and Imagery
Finally, literary scholarship has examined the role of Rowling's use of particular kinds of imagery or themes in the series. Peggy Huey and Sarah Gibbons each delineate the role of mythology—primarily Greek—in Rowling's books. Huey's essay, "A Basilisk, a Phoenix, and a Philosopher's Stone: Harry Potter's Myths and Legends" is a minien-

cyclopedic overview of the mythological creatures the series incorporates—centaurs, Cerberus, the phoenix, unicorn, and basilisk—while Gibbons in "Death and Rebirth: Harry Potter and the Mythology of the Phoenix" discusses in more depth the literary symbolism of Rowling's use of the phoenix in the books. Gibbons focuses specifically on the phoenix as a symbol of immortality and peace.

A unique but valuable approach to the series is "Sentences in Harry Potter, Students in Future Writing Classes," Edward Duffy's systematic and well-supported challenge to claims by well-known critics of the series such as William Safire and Bloom who have trounced the books' writing style. In *Rhetoric Review* Duffy uses Richard Lanham's *Revising Prose* as a basis for examining Rowling's sentences for liveliness, rhythm, and cohesiveness. Rhetorical analysis of Rowling's prose reveals her fascination with the written word and with the power of reading as well as an admirable "style and rhythm, fluidity and sparkle" (185) that Duffy offers as counterevidence to Rowling's detractors. Similarly useful for readers interested in language study is "Naming Tropes and Schemes in J. K. Rowling's Harry Potter Books," by Don L. F. Nilsen and Alleen Pace Nilsen which traces various tropes and schemes used by Rowling throughout the series.

The series has also earned attention from writers interested in its therapeutic value, usually through the books' themes of healing, trauma, and terror. Sharon Black in "Harry Potter: A Magical Prescription for Just About Anyone" describes her "prescription" of the Potter books as a remedy for depression and illness, claiming that Rowling's books have a therapeutic power and that Rowling's purpose is not just "teaching people how to put spells on corridors and staircases; she's teaching them that they can deal with unpredictability and change" (542). Seth Lerer takes a broader approach in "'This Life to Mend, This Book Attend': Reading and Healing in the Arc of Children's Literature" focusing on the relationships between reading and healing. He assents that the Harry Potter series specifically offers a moral about literacy's power. Rowling uses books as props and

tropes—whether Tom Riddle's diary, Hermione's hours in the library, the *Monster Book of Monsters*, or Harry's habit of reading late into the night while at the Dursleys'.

Two essays are particularly concerned with the use of the books in addressing themes of terror and trauma. Maureen Katz's "Prisoners of Azkaban: Understanding Intergenerational Transmission of Trauma Due to War and State Terror (with Help from Harry Potter)" uses the third book in the series as a springboard for personal reflection. As a psychiatrist and descendant of Holocaust survivors, Katz talks about the experiences of children of victims of terror and the way Harry's encounter with Dementors may model the sort of feelings of hopelessness those children of survivors experience. Courtney Strimel, as well argues in "The Politics of Terror: Rereading *Harry Potter*" that the books reach children because they tackle themes of terror that many readers experience on a day-to-day basis, whether it is large-scale national terror or the attack on Muggles in *Goblet of Fire's* Quidditch World Cup, which represents "extreme social instability and danger" (39).

Finally, the collection *Heroism and the Harry Potter Series* examines the various conceptions of heroism evident in the Harry Potter series in the context of the ways fictional heroism in the 21st century challenges the idealized forms of a simplistic masculinity associated with genres such as epic, romance, and classic adventure story. The authors argue that the Harry Potter novels propose new and genuine models of heroism based on responsibility, courage, humility, and kindness.

Moral and Ethical Concerns

Scholars across disciplines such as Strimel have been interested in considering the question of the moral implications of the series and have used diverse frameworks for doing it, as in Strimel's article "The Politics of Terror: Rereading Harry Potter." Lauren Binnendyk and Kimberly Schonert-Reichl, for example, approach the books by using the noted psychologist Lawrence Kohlberg's schema for moral development as a way of placing characters from the series—Draco, Dobby, Hermione, Ron, and

Harry—at different places on Kohlberg's scale in their essay "Harry Potter and Moral Development in Pre-Adolescent Children." They also generate ideas for potentially using the series for classroom purposes to promote moral development of students (see also Lana Whited and Katherine Grimes for a discussion of the Harry Potter series as an illustration of Kohlberg's theories of moral development). By contrast, Catherine Deavel and David Deavel are more interested in the moral recommendations the series makes; their article "Character, Choice, and Harry Potter" targets a skeptical audience who may believe the series's moral implications are questionable or undesirable; the primary purpose of the essay is to outline, in their judgment, Rowling's implied moral recommendations. By tracing the dilemmas Harry faces, Deavel and Deavel argue Rowling promotes values such as freedom, truth, and choice, as well as sacrifice and love.

Likewise, essays by William Wandless and by Rebecca Skulnick and Jesse Goodman analyze the moral questions the series poses and the choices its hero makes, as Skulnick and Goodman focus more specifically on the notion of civic leadership in "The Civic Leadership of Harry Potter: Agency, Ritual, and Schooling." Strimel, as well, addresses this issue, rejecting the claim that the series's moral ambiguity is damaging to young readers and asserting that because, for example, characters who initially seem good turn out to be bad, and vice versa, young readers are encouraged to sort out behavior from overall worth; they can practice deciphering character judgments in light of Dumbledore's admonition to Harry in *Chamber of Secrets:* "It is our choices, Harry, that show what we truly are, far more than our abilities" (332–333). A similar examination is undertaken by Perry Glanzer in "Harry Potter's Provocative Moral World: Is There a Place for Good and Evil in Moral Education?" asserting that public schools can legally and usefully take on moral education.

Finally, Westman's critical analysis "Perspective, Memory, and Moral Authority: The Legacy of Jane Austen in J. K. Rowling's Harry Potter," in the scholarly journal *Children's Literature* has placed the books within literary contexts by consider-ing the relationship between several works by the British novelist Jane Austen and the Harry Potter books; Westman is particularly interested in Rowling's and Austen's characterization and thematic development using memory, sympathy, imagination, and perspective as narrative tools for promoting the moral growth of their characters.

The series's implications for reader discussions of compelling moral and ethical issues have also received scholarly attention. Binnendyk and Schonert-Reichl use Kohlberg's theories to suggest the books can be of use for prompting conversation about moral development both of the characters and of readers, while Amanda Cain uses the Aristotelian theory of moral development outlined in the *Nicomachean Ethics* as a context for analyzing the role of reading in making a transition from childhood to moral maturity in her essay "Books and Becoming Good: Demonstrating Aristotle's Theory of Moral Development in the Act of Reading." The educational utility of the series is explored in Donna Gibson's "Empathizing with *Harry Potter*: The Use of Popular Literature in Counselor Education," which describes a classroom exercise using *Sorcerer's Stone* to help counselor education students cultivate and talk about empathy. A more theoretical approach is taken by Veronica Schanoes, whose anthologized essay "Cruel Heroes and Treacherous Texts: Educating the Reader in Moral Complexity and Critical Reading in J. K. Rowling's Harry Potter Books" explores Rowling's use of moral ambiguity in her presentation of good versus evil and the stability of meaning in written texts, especially the interrelationship between moral judgment making and the power narratives have to subvert our assumptions about right and wrong.

OTHER CRITICAL APPROACHES

Contemporary (post-1960s) literary critics have moved away from critical approaches that examine only the text itself and toward a literary theory informed by diverse contexts. The critical body of work on the Harry Potter series is no different, as scholars examine Rowling's work through a variety of lenses, including race, class, gender, psychology, history, and culture.

Materialist and Marxist Readings

Andrew Blake's book *The Irresistible Rise of Harry Potter* takes what could be called a materialist or Marxist approach in that Blake examines the economic and global contexts of the Harry Potter series both as a set of books and as a phenomenon. Blake argues that a massive and systematically coordinated marketing campaign partially explains the series's success as well as the way the books address "many of the anxieties in our changing political and cultural world" (4). Blake argues that the national boundaries of Great Britain began to dissolve in major ways around the same time the series appeared, setting up Harry Potter as a concept around which an "imagined community" could emerge. Blake also targets his analysis at the political implications of the series, offering interpretations on a broad range of topics including the series' images of gender, its relationship to other forms of popular culture, economics and politics in 1990s Britain, and the literary-prize industry. While focusing heavily on culture and history, Blake's book-length study also tackles the theme of consumerism, maintaining that the books became part of a consumer culture that commodifies appealing British heroes such as Sherlock Holmes and James Bond and translates them into blockbuster box office profits.

Other critics have used a materialist approach by examining the ideological messages the books carry about social order and the role of adolescents within it. For example, in "Harry Potter and the Functions of Popular Culture" Dustin Kidd outlines the reasons popular culture is necessary for the United States and places his analysis in the context of "commodity capitalist economies," or the ways culture becomes one of many products. Kidd, like Blake, places the Harry Potter books in a cultural context by arguing that the book is powerful in shaping norms, produces cultural innovation (such as the creation of a separate children's best-seller list so that the adult *New York Times* best sellers would not be outsold by Rowling's novels), and has the potential to promote social change through its impact on and emphasis on literacy. A related analysis is taken on by Georgii Tse-

plakov, who uses the Harry Potter novels as exemplars for his larger discussion of "project literature" in his article "Talent and the Widow's Mite of Project Literature." Tseplakov is interested in examining the way that literary production has adopted some of the tactics of the business models of "project management," a process that, he argues, does not necessarily translate into a loss in aesthetic value.

Roberta Seelinger Trites's "The Harry Potter Novels as a Test Case for Adolescent Literature" looks more directly at the ideologies of adolescence promoted by the series as part of distinguishing adolescent from children's literature, particularly the role of literature such as the Harry Potter series in teaching adolescent readers "their role in the power structure" (473).

Psychoanalytic Approaches

Literary scholars have also examined the series from psychoanalytic perspectives, including those of Carl Jung, Sigmund Freud, Jacques Lacan, JOSEPH CAMPBELL, and Julia Kristeva. Mary Pharr argues in "In Medias Res: Harry Potter as Hero-in-Progress" for a reading of Harry as a hero through the lens of Campbell's "monomyth," arguing that Harry is a "hero-in-progress." Sharon Black in "The Magic of Harry Potter: Symbols and Heroes of Fantasy" also uses the psychoanalytic perspectives of Campbell's famous treatise *The Hero with a Thousand Faces* and Bruno Bettelheim's *The Uses of Enchantment* to discuss the psychological impact of the books through case studies of two young readers and to examine the series from the perspective of Campbell's motif. Black and Pharr both trace the notion of the "child of destiny" through diverse children's fantasy and science fiction, including *Charlotte's Web,* the *Chronicles of Narnia,* and *Star Wars* as well as Harry Potter. M. Katherine Grimes's essay "Fairy Tale Prince, Real Boy, Archetypical Hero" also draws upon Campbell's and Bettelheim's theories in addition to literary history and genres such as realist literature and fairy tales.

In addition to the myth criticism of Campbell, several critics have used Freudian frameworks for opening up the series. Mary Eagleton's "The Dangers of Intellectual Masters: Lessons from Harry Potter and Antonia Byatt" makes similar analytical comparisons, interrogating the concept of the erotic relationship between teacher and master, specifically the relationship between Hermione and the Defense Against the Dark Arts teacher Gilderoy Lockhart in conjunction with an analysis of A. S. Byatt's book *Possession*. Eagleton draws upon the work of Freud, the father of modern psychoanalysis, as does Alice Mills, whose focused article "Harry Potter and the Terrors of the Toilet" uses some Freudian theories and the work of the French philosopher Julia Kristeva as a lens for discussion of Rowling's narrative use of the bathroom, whether as a site for conflict (the defeat of the troll in *Sorcerer's Stone*), magical potion making and bodily transformation (Polyjuice Potion in *Chamber of Secrets*), or Moaning Myrtle's misery (see also Lisa Damour for a use of Freud's developmental theories as applied to the series). Mills argues specifically that the Harry Potter books are highly traditional in their treatment of the toilet and that usual uses of the bathroom (bodily excretions) are substituted with more socially palatable sorts (tears, vomit). In another article, "Archetypes and the Unconscious in *Harry Potter* and Diana Wynne Jones's *Fire and Hemlock* and *Dogsbody*," Mills uses Jungian concepts of the archetype and unconscious to "read" the books through the lens of the psychological concept of "wish fulfillment." Benoit Virole in "Harry Potter's Cauldron: The Power of Myth and the Rebirth of the Sacred" takes a more explicitly Jungian approach to the series; Virole believes we need to look at the psychoanalytic appeal and use of narrative and character archetypes by Rowling in order to explain the extraordinary appeal of the series, though he does not discount the huge, global, and multipronged marketing campaign that also explains its commercial success.

Less theoretically grounded are Peter Gottesman's and Maureen Katz's essays, both of which are concerned with the psychological utility of the books and their impact on readers. Gottesman in "Harry Potter and the Sorcerer's Stone," published in the *Teachers College Record*, speculates on the psychological needs that the books fulfill for young readers including imagination, relevance, justice, subversion of authority, and sympathy.

Historical Lenses
In addition to psychoanalytic frameworks, some critics have used historical lenses—either contemporaneous with the publication of the novels or retrospective—through which to view the series. For example, Noel Chevalier's perceptive and exhaustively researched article "The Liberty Tree and the Whomping Willow: Political Justice, Magical Science, and Harry Potter" draws upon the political philosophies of William Godwin, an 18th-century English intellectual, and the work of Godwin's granddaughter, Mary Shelley, specifically the novel *Frankenstein*, to examine the moral implications of technology (in Rowling's work, magic). More important to Chevalier is his analysis of Harry as a radical who recognizes the corruptness of the institutions governing the wizarding world even as he preserves (versus destroys) the basic structures that preserve social order (such as the Ministry of Magic and Hogwarts). Chevalier also integrates a discussion of Enlightenment and French Revolution principles to advance his assessment of Harry Potter's heroism. Like Chevalier, Brycchan Carey in "Hermione and the House-Elves: The Literary and Historical Contexts of J. K. Rowling's Antislavery Campaign" argues that Rowling's work is informed by two centuries of children's literature that takes up abolitionist themes and integrates comparisons with Rowling's characterization of the house-elves' psychology and cultural ideologies about Afro-Caribbean slave historically. In contrast to Chevalier and Carey, whose historical framework makes textual connections to important figures in British literary and philosophical traditions, Blake's *The Irresistible Rise of Harry Potter* uses contemporaneous historical contexts—economic, political, cultural, and social changes in Britain during the time the books were written—as a framework for making arguments about British culture. Karin Westman engages in a similar examination in her essay "Specters of Thatcherism," claiming that the books are both an "echo and commentary on . . .

a late capitalist, global consumer culture" (306), specifically on the 1980s prime minister of Britain MARGARET THATCHER.

Postmodern Theory

Two scholarly articles draw on postmodernist theoretical frameworks to analyze the series. Virginia Zimmerman's "Harry Potter and the Gift of Time" employs the theoretical frameworks of Jacques Derrida, specifically his concept of the "trace," or a linguistic device that is "a sign dissociated from its origin . . . [that] conveys meaning even as its very existence reveals the irretrievability of what is signified" (196). Zimmerman applies this concept to the plotline and narrative strategies of the books, discussing Harry's scar and Horcruxes as types of traces and the Time-Turner in *Prisoner of Azkaban* as a subversion of conventions of time. Similarly interested in postmodern theoretical approaches to the books is Drew Chappell, whose essay "Sneaking Out after Dark: Resistance, Agency, and the Postmodern Child in J. K. Rowling's Harry Potter Series" contrasts constructions of modernist childhood such as Dorothy Gale (the main character of *The Wizard of Oz*) and Charlie Bucket (the main character of *Charlie and the Chocolate Factory*) with Harry Potter as an exemplar of postmodernist childhood in which Harry's character invites "young readers to critically engage with power structures in their lives and become architects of their own agency" (282).

Race, Class, and Gender

The politics of gender, race, class, and other social categories of identity—whether racial and gender stereotypes, heteronormativity, or analysis of the series's reinforcement of patriarchal values—has also inspired scholarly debate. A number of writers have advanced the argument that the series is very socially conservative in its character portrayals, reflecting a false veneer of gender equity and reinforcing patriarchal values of male dominance. Amy Billone, for example, argues that this minimal role of women in children's fantasy is in fact historically persistent, comparing Harry Potter with *Alice in Wonderland* and *Peter Pan*. Meredith Cherland's

"Harry's Girls: Harry Potter and the Discourse of Gender" uses feminist poststructuralist theory to analyze the construction of gender within the books. Similar arguments have been made about race and class.

Gender ideologies and sexual orientation frame Elizabeth Heilman's argument in "Blue Wizards, Pink Witches: Representations of Gender Identity and Power" that women are subordinate to male characters, demonstrate stereotypically feminine weaknesses, and rarely hold offices of power benevolently (for example, Dolores Umbridge). This case is mirrored by Tison Pugh and David Wallace, who also argue for the series's ideological conservatism about gender. Their essay, "Heteronormative Heroism and Queering the School Story in J. K. Rowling's Harry Potter Series" also analyzes the novels in terms of the absence of same-sex relationships or same-sex attractions, an implicit promotion of the alpha-male model of masculinity, and a portrayal of gender equity that obscures actual oppression of women. Ximena Gallardo-C. and C. Jason Smith contest this interpretation in "Cinderfella: J. K. Rowling's Wily Web of Gender," arguing that "there are alternative, radical readings of the series" and offering a "proactive feminist interpretation" (191). In "Feminism and Equal Opportunity: Hermione and the Women of Hogwarts" Mimi Gladstein offers a similar defense of Rowling's profeminist characterizations of women in the series, as does Eliza Dresang in "Hermione Granger and the Heritage of Gender." A less activist interpretation is undertaken by Janet Brennan Croft, whose essay "The Education of a Witch: Tiffany Aching, Hermione Granger, and Gendered Magic in Discworld and Potterworld" documents the contrasting worldviews of gender, education, and power of the two fantasy series (Rowling's Harry Potter and Terry Pratchett's Tiffany Aching), partly as a springboard for considering "real world" debates about single-sex and coeducational classrooms.

Masculinity studies is represented by Terri Doughty's "Locating Harry Potter in the 'Boys' Book' Market," where she places the Harry Potter series within the context of several other "realistic" fiction novels aimed at a teen boy readership. Doughty claims that the Potter series "addresses many of the same problems treated in contemporary fiction for boys" (246) but is distinct as a fantasy novel and in its treatment of masculinity.

A shorter essay, Marianne MacDonald's "Harry Potter and the Fan Fiction Phenom," discusses FAN FICTION (stories written using the Harry Potter characters and rewriting the narrative or creating new narratives) and slash fiction (fan fiction with a gay or lesbian focus), outlining the demographics of slash fiction writers and their motivations for producing gay-themed Harry Potter fan fiction. Finally, Pugh and Wallace have published an article in *English Journal*, "Playing with Critical Theory," which provides a fruitful starting point for discussions of race, class, gender, and sexual orientation in the series.

Casey Cothran's essay "Lessons in Transfiguration: Allegories of Male Identity in Rowling's Harry Potter Series" similarly reads social subtexts in Rowling's portrayal of characters, such as interpreting Lupin's lycanthropy as a metaphor for homosexuality with Rowling's underlying message rejecting homophobia because of her positive characterization of him as a protector of children. Cothran finds Freudian dream interpretation useful in understanding Rowling's use of dreams as a narrative tool. Blake's book, as well, devotes a chapter to analyzing the series as gender-conservative in the spirit of liberal feminism that maintains social structures rather than radically challenging gender oppression. Carey's essay "Hermione and the House-elves: The Literary and Historical Contexts of J. K. Rowling's Antislavery Campaign" can also be useful for thinking about issues of gender because of the way his discussion of antislavery activism intersects with discussions of gender, as he notes that Hermione's public advocacy for house-elves is roundly rejected and treated with contempt, reinforcing gender dynamics whereby heroic undertakings by boys are rewarded but activism for social justice by girls is dismissed or mocked.

Issues of race and national identity are also of interest to scholarly writers such as Hollie Anderson, whose "Reading Harry Potter with Navajo Eyes" finds much to identify with in its treatment of Harry as an outsider and the use of boarding schools. Elaine Ostry, in contrast, charges Rowling in her essay "Accepting Mudbloods: The Ambivalent Social Vision of J. K. Rowling's Fairy Tales" with a paradoxical approach to diversity in her books; while the narrative structure in which "racial" outcasts like Hagrid and Lupin are explicitly embraced by the cause of good and an overt message of antidiscrimination runs through the series (the Mudblood, half-blood, and pureblood conflicts that drive the story), the school itself is fairly racially homogeneous and all the main characters are white. Jennifer Sattaur defends the series from accusations of racism, classism, and xenophobia in "Harry Potter: A World of Fear," in the *Journal of Children's Literature Studies,* claiming that that the books are neither consciously nor unconsciously racist, charging that the ambiguity and complexity of the later works actually dismantle racism and classism in ways that are not fully apparent in the first three novels.

Similarly, the books, while demonstrating a distrust or absence of foreign cultures and peoples early in the series, introduce a more global perspective in *Goblet of Fire* with the Triwizard Tournament and the Quidditch World Cup. This theme is explored from an explicitly postcolonial perspective in Giselle Liza Anatol's essay "The Fallen Empire: Exploring Ethnic Otherness in the World of Harry Potter," which traces the books' use of imperialist imagery and subplots. Sattaur argues that Rowling incorporates elements of the real-world "war on terror" and mirrors our contemporary worldview and that the books capture the public's imagination through their fidelity to "real-world" concerns and incorporation of archetypal images.

Scholars in branches of disability studies are also represented in the Harry Potter critical canon. For example, in "Understanding Harry Potter: Parallels to the Deaf World" Todd Czubaek and Janey Greenwald profitably unpack the series's remarkable parallels between wizarding children in Muggle worlds and the experience of deaf children in hearing families, societies, and institutions. They argue that the books can be read as parallel to the experience of many deaf children, who will relate to Harry's experiences of oppression and alienation.

Analysis of social class of both Rowling and the world of Harry Potter is undertaken by Julia Park, who argues in "Class and Socioeconomic Identity in Harry Potter's England" that Rowling's middle-class worldview is revealed throughout the series and that British class structure is "reflected in the wizard world she has created" (180). Suman Gupta provides a book-length examination of the first four novels in *Re-Reading Harry Potter,* with the primary purpose of examining "the political social implications of the Harry Potter books, or the political and social effects that constitute the Harry Potter phenomenon" (7). Gupta's study addresses several aspects of the series through *Goblet of Fire:* readership and reception, economic and social impact, the novels' commercial and literary features, the role of Rowling-as-author within a critical reading, the books as children's literature and fantasy literature, and religious perspectives. Gupta's dense and theoretical approach also examines allusions within the novel and the role of such themes and symbols as blood, servants and slaves, and desire. Social class is also addressed.

Other social contexts explored by scholars include "Harry Potter and the Secret Password: Finding Our Way in the Magical Genre," Amanda Cockrell's examination of why the series is a magnet for detractors, specifically religious zealots, arguing that the books hit too close to home in their lampooning of social intolerance and that their literal "closeness" to home (the wizarding world is adjacent to the human one, in contrast with Tolkienesque secondary worlds that exist outside and separate from the human world) is part of its subversion. Steven Barfield's "Of Young Magicians and Growing Up: J. K. Rowling, Her Critics, and the 'Culture of Infantilism' Debate" takes a different approach, responding to claims that the series panders to an adult nostalgia for childishness and that it is part of a cultural "arrested development" of Generation Xers who are reluctant to adopt the new responsibilities of adulthood. Barfield tackles those arguments by rejecting allegations that the series's affiliation with boarding school fiction and fantasy literature, both of which have been excluded from the literary canon, diminishes its value for readers or for culture.

OTHER CONTEXTS

Capitalism, Commercialism, and Marketing

Extending the critical lenses even further from texts and contexts are those scholarly essays and books that draw upon philosophical, economic, religious, or pedagogical contexts. From a scholarly perspective the marketing of the series and the role of consumer capitalism in its success are of interest across disciplines. Stephen Brown in "Harry Potter and the Marketing Mystery: A Review and Critical Assessment of the Harry Potter Books" explores the metaphors of marketing and the pervasive use of consumerism and consumerist rhetoric throughout the books, specifically focusing on examples from the Quidditch World Cup in the fourth novel, *Goblet of Fire.* Brown argues that not only is marketing part of the Potter corporate machine, but that consumerism and consumer products pervade the book and are central to Rowling's construction of the wizarding world.

Kara Lynn Anderson's "Harry Potter and the Susceptible Child Audience," published in *Comparative Literature and Culture,* is one of the few scholarly essays to take up reception studies and Harry Potter as its topic. Anderson is interested in examining the child, teen, and adult readership of the series as well as expanding the study of the series to include child readers as subjects rather than objects of examination. Anderson's essay fruitfully considers the commodification of the books and the extension of marketing authority over the books' "brand" to WARNER BROTHERS as a separate, "co-owning" entity from the author J. K. Rowling.

The phenomenon of Pottermania, a catchall term for the cultural and consumer explosion of Potter products, is of concern to Philip Nel, who asserts that we need to sort the books from the phenomenon in order to assess their literary value fairly, a claim Sarah Gibbons supports in "Death and Rebirth: Harry Potter and the Mythology of the Phoenix," noting that commodities and culture have historically been intertwined, making it difficult for literary critics to see as valuable a cultural work (book) that is also commercially successful. Blake's book and Tammy Turner-Vorbeck's "Pottermania: Good, Clean Fun or Cultural Hegemony?" both argue that consumerism has played an important role in the series's proliferation and been key to the books' success but also suggest that perhaps Pottermania has even created the new teen consumer.

A more specialized essay is Jarrod Waetjen and Timothy A. Gibson's "Harry Potter and the Commodity Fetishism," an esoteric analysis of the series as a commodity that has been appropriated by a global media conglomerate. The authors examine contradictory messages in the series about the relationship of "class and material life" (4), arguing that the books simultaneously critique materialism and celebrate the *jouissance* of commodities. Waetjen and Gibson position their discussion within the contractual relationship between Rowling and Warner Brothers and examine the representation of class and consumption in the novels. Finally, they critique what they believe to be a strategic move by AOL Time Warner to promote the layers of the text that valorize commodities over readings of the text that critique racism, classism, and materialism. A less scathing discussion of marketing and commercialism related to the Harry Potter books is Iain Stevenson's "Harry Potter, Riding the Bullet and the Future of Books: Key Issues in the Anglophone Book Business," a review of the status of publishing and the impact of Rowling's books on publishing in English and other languages.

A related analysis of the commercial and cultural implications of the books is conducted by Elizabeth Teare in "Harry Potter and the Technology of Magic," where she argues that the books "enact both our fantasies and fears of children's literature and publishing in the context of twenty-first century commercial and technological culture" (329).

Reader Response

In "Writing Harry's World: Children Co-Authoring Hogwarts" Ernest Bond and Nancy Michelson investigate the way young readers and Harry Potter fans have responded not just psychologically and emotionally but also literarily to the series, including the use of the Internet to share their enthusiasm and to create fan fiction about the characters. Rebecca Sutherland Borah in "Apprentice Wizards Welcome: Fan Communities and the Culture of Harry Potter" discusses Harry Potter fan culture more broadly, through investigation of fan message boards and interviews with both young and adult readers of the series, while Catherine Tosenberger's "'Oh my God, the Fanfiction!' Dumbledore's Outing and the Online Harry Potter Fandom" focuses specifically on the revelation of Dumbledore's sexual orientation and its impact on fan fiction online. Sara Beach and Elizabeth Willner similarly use field research (surveys of middle schoolers) in "The Power of Harry: The Impact of J. K. Rowling's Harry Potter Books on Young Readers" to argue that the books' popularity emerges from the richness of her characters and the magical world she creates—as well as the respect she has for her readers by placing demands on their intellects through hefty themes and lengthy tomes.

Scholarly essays targeting teachers and professors appear in a number of peer-reviewed journals and are primarily concerned with impact on young readers, classroom applications, and uses for particular types of students. For example, at least two essays—by Andrew Frank and Matthew McBee in "The Use of Harry Potter and the Sorcerer's Stone to Discuss Identity Development with Gifted Adolescents" and by Sharon Black in "Harry Potter: Enchantment for All Seasons"—are interested in exploring the ways that teachers can use the series to support curricula for gifted adolescents. Recommendations include using the book(s) as a mechanism for talking about development issues, identification with the characters, and imagination with teens. The Harry Potter series has even prompted publications on the use of the books to teach chemistry, genetics, Latin (Alleen Nilsen and Don L. F. Nilsen), and fungi (Tisha Beaton). Others, including Rebecca Butler's "The Literature Continuum: The Harry Potter Phenomenon" provide more general suggestions for using the Harry Potter series in the K–12 setting, while Laura Shearer Bahor offers personal reflections on and an argument for the use of the books in a college classroom. In *"The Sorcerer's Stone*: A Touchstone for Readers of All Ages" Susan Wood and Kim Quackenbush, as well, offer ideas for classroom activities as varied as poetry, journal writing, and fantasy genre. Similarly, Perry Glanzer's *English Journal* essay "In Defense of Harry . . . but Not His Defenders: Beyond Censorship to Justice" presents strategies and rationales for using the books as part of a larger unit of study in which students are exposed to literary works that embrace competing worldviews.

In the less traditional mode of reader response is "Harry Potter and the End of the Road: Parallels with Addition," by Jeffrey Michael Rudski, Carli Segal, and Eli Kallen. Their psychological analysis uses traditional social science methodologies to measure whether devoted readers' dedication to the books could be defined as an "addiction." The authors identify several categories of behavior and criteria for assessing addiction and use online surveys and quantitative analysis to conclude that "self-identified fans of the HP series reported experiencing many of the behavioral correlates of addiction" (272).

Educational Value(s)

Scholars have also been interested in using the Harry Potter series as a springboard for discussing real-world school systems and their values. In "Harry Potter Pedagogy: What We Learn about Teaching and Learning" Renee Dickinson has conducted an analysis of the books in the light of the literary critic Jane Tompkins's advocacy of discussion facilitation rather than the lecture mode of teaching; she assesses several Hogwarts teachers'

methodologies using the psychologist Benjamin Bloom's classic epistemological taxonomy for levels of knowing and understanding, ranking McGonagall the highest for her balance of instruction and practice and Professor Binns, the ghostly teacher of History of Magic, the lowest for his lack of engagement and reliance on lecture as a means of transferring information. Similarly, Jodi Levine and Nancy Shapiro use the books as a springboard for thinking about the first-year college experience, including diversity, exposure to new ideas and sorts of curriculum, and placement (sorting) into particular courses of study. In "But Is He Really Smart? Gardner's Multiple Intelligences Theory in the World of Harry Potter" Alicia Willson-Metzger and David Metzger target learning styles rather than teaching styles in *Popular Culture Review*, drawing upon Howard Gardner's "multiple intelligences" theory to compare Harry and Hermione's differing cognitive gifts.

Mary Black and Marilyn Eisenwine take a related but more literary approach in "Education of the Young Harry Potter: Socialization and Schooling for Wizards," analyzing the books to answer the questions about Rowling's messages about school and education in general. The writers conclude that the educational philosophy is progressive and that messages of social tolerance and diversity are promoted. A related essay addresses not the messages about teaching but those about parenting, analyzing the parent substitutes and images of parenting presented in the first four books in the series. Elisabeth Rose Gruner's "Teach the Children: Education and Knowledge in Recent Children's Fantasy" poses a similar research question but positions her analysis of Harry Potter within other recent children's fiction including Terry Pratchett's Tiffany Aching novels and Philip Pullman's His Dark Materials series.

Janet Seden in "Parenting and the Harry Potter Stories: A Social Care Perspective" uses the titular perspective to examine the relationship between literature and social work and the adequacy of the family structures and the care they offer the children in the series, including the Dursleys, Weasleys, Malfoys, and Grangers.

Translation and Publication Studies

A related essay, "The Travels of Harry: International Marketing and the Translation of J. K. Rowling's Harry Potter Books" by Gillian Lathey, published in one of the many scholarly journals focusing on children's literature, *Lion and the Unicorn*, examines the relationship of translation to stability of meaning, retention of geographical and linguistic idiosyncrasies, and global marketability. Eirlys Davies in "A Goblin or a Dirty Nose? The Treatment of Culture-Specific References in Translations of the Harry Potter Books" more broadly outlines multiple approaches to translation of a text into other languages, specifically examining the techniques used by Harry Potter translators in making culture-specific items appropriate for and relevant to readers in different cultures. The essay is particularly useful in providing specific examples of translator decisions about culture-specific items, whether to transform, localize, omit, or explain them in the target translation (see also Nancy Jensch for a discussion of translator decisions about particular names, places, and wizarding jargon). Katrine Brondsted and Cay Dollerup in their essay "The Names in Harry Potter" in *Perspectives: Studies in Translatology* perform a similar analysis of translation of the books but focus specifically on character names, their origins, and translation into five other languages—Danish, Swedish, Norwegian, German, and Italian; Philip Nel's "You Say 'Jelly,' I Say Jell-O?" explores the question of whether it is possible to create similar literary experiences for children in different countries and whether it is desirable to do so.

A related field looks at the impact of the Harry Potter series on publishing, specifically within the legal system. Shira Siskind's "Crossing the Fair Use Line: The Demise and Revival of the *Harry Potter Lexicon* and Its Implications for the Fair Use Doctrine in the Real World and on the Internet" discusses the conclusions of the court case that initially prohibited RDR books from publishing the *Harry Potter Lexicon* and discusses the legal implications of the decision. Ted Striphas performs a

similar sort of analysis in "Harry Potter and the Simulacrum: Contested Copies in an Age of Intellectual Property," using the concept of the simulacrum (theories about the relationship between originals and copies) to discuss the *Scholastic v. Stouffer* lawsuit; Stouffer's allegations of Rowling's infringement of her intellectual property rights (because of her book *The Legend of Rah and the Muggles*) provides a backdrop for Striphas's argument that the transition from "culture industry" to "copyright industry" is one that "threatens not only to restrict legitimate cultural production to an already enfranchised (and well-attorneyed) few, but also, in the longer term, to create unreasonable terms of access to the cultural commons—the publicly accessible resources by which culture is constantly made over again, anew" (12).

Philosophy, Religion, and Objections

The 2004 scholarly collection *Harry Potter and Philosophy: If Aristotle Ran Hogwarts*, edited by David Baggett and Shawn Klein, offers an array of philosophical approaches to the Harry Potter series. The book includes essays that explore a number of branches of philosophy—moral philosophy, ethics, metaphysics, epistemology—as well as the classical philosophical puzzles that occupy philosophers such as identity, social relationships, time travel, the problem of evil, fate versus free will, and the nature of time and space. A related essay, "Harry Potter and the Acquisition of Knowledge" by Lisa Hopkins, has an epistemological emphasis; Hopkins argues that the books endorse an epistemological approach that knowledge is constructed and acquired rather than inherited, a worldview that is reinforced by characters' and Hogwarts houses' attitudes toward knowledge.

While religious discussions have tended to occur in the sphere of nonscholarly publications (see the "Additional Resources on the Harry Potter Series" section), several scholarly essays have tackled the question of the series's religious implications. Alan Jacobs's reflective essay "Harry Potter's Magic" in the Catholic publication *First Things* meditates for a religious, specifically Christian readership on the ways that Rowling's work mirrors Tolkien's world more than C. S. LEWIS's but that her similarity to a secular writer does not mean the series does not have a moral compass. Jacobs gently rejects concerns among Christian readers about the lack of religiosity of the books and argues that they are stories of character formation that indirectly take on the issue of technology. Similarly, Emily Griesinger's heftier 2002 analysis, "Harry Potter and the 'Deeper Magic': Narrating Hope in Children's Literature" in the scholarly journal *Christianity and Literature,* is aimed at the Christian community, specifically responding to controversies that have arisen about the books' use of magic. Griesinger argues that the fairy tale tradition that Rowling draws upon has a relationship with the Christian supernatural, specifically Christian eschatology. She also challenges the claim that Harry Potter's world is morally neutral or ambiguous. Griesinger makes comparisons with the world of Narnia created by the Christian writer C. S. Lewis and the "secondary worlds" paradigm created by J. R. R. Tolkien. These comparisons are also drawn by Dan McVeigh in "Is Harry Potter Christian?" published in *Renascence,* adding that the series is "no New Age competitor to Christianity . . . it is packed with traditional notions of goodness and vice" (210). Lauren Berman's essay "Rowling's Devil: Ancient Archetype of Modern Manifestation," in contrast, discusses the religious imagery and symbols in the series but does not argue for a religious reading of the text.

In "Pop Goes Religion: Harry Potter Meets Clifford Geertz" a more historically and culturally grounded interpretation is offered by Iver Neumann in the *European Journal of Cultural Studies;* he suggests that the books' appeal to readers is grounded in the interchangeability of religion and magic and reflects the "return of religion to global politics" (83). Francis Bridger's book-length study *A Charmed Life: The Spirituality of Potterworld* bridges philosophy and religion with the author's dual roles as a Christian minister and an academician. Bridger deconstructs the books from several perspectives including moral, theological, and metaphysical, drawing upon extensive textual evidence from the

books, the Bible, and other notable fantasy authors such as Lewis to gird his analysis.

This sort of scholarly work overlaps with some of the nonscholarly publications; for example, writers such as Peter Denton in "What Could Be Wrong with Harry Potter?" tackle from a literary and librarianship perspective the adult objections to Harry Potter and censoring of the works, particularly those movements of the conservative evangelical tradition that use biblical evidence to support their critiques. Barbara Comber and Helen Nixon have made a similar case in "The Harry Potter Phenomenon," published in the *Journal of Adolescent and Adult Literacy,* arguing against the unsubstantiated argument that the books promote Satanism and drawing upon interviews with elementary school age readers to illustrate how intimately students are able to interact with these books despite the depiction of violence and death. In "A Defense of Harry Potter, or When Religion Is Not Religion: An Analysis of the Censoring of the Harry Potter Books," Julia Saric offers a similar apologetic for the series, placing a specific case of a school district's handling of objections to the use of the book in classrooms within the context of fantasy literature as an aesthetic respite. In "Bewitching the Box Office: Harry Potter and Religious Controversy" Rachel Wagner approaches the Harry Potter film adaptations with similar questions in the *Journal of Religion and Film,* analyzing why the "books and films [have] provoked such enthusiastic celebration and simultaneously such harsh scrutiny" (para. 3). Wagner believes three oppositions present problems for Christian objectors to the series: fantasy versus reality, good versus evil, and the secular versus the religious (also see Rebecca Stephens for a discussion of book banning related to the books' subversion of authority). This concern is echoed in "Controversial Content in Children's Literature: Is *Harry Potter* Harmful to Children?" by Deborah Taub and Heather Servaty, whose work is concerned primarily with the appropriateness of the series for young readers; they take up four critical debates, about the issues of dark magic or the occult, the books' addressing of death, children's ability to distinguish between fantasy and reality, and the books' overall tone of scariness.

A comparatively more recent article, "Middle Earth, Narnia, Hogwarts, and Animals: A Review of the Treatment of Nonhuman Animals and Other Sentient Beings in Christian-Based Fantasy Fiction," by Michael Morris, characterizes the Harry Potter books as Christianity-based, using competing frames for examining multiple works by fantasy writers. The frames are the two animal liberationist approaches, belief systems (one secular and one Christian) wherein the "lives of animals require serious moral consideration and have intrinsic value, independent of their use by humans" (344) and welfarist approaches that have "no ethical objections to using animals for food, experiments, or other nonvital purposes, and their moral concern is generally restricted to ensuring that animals do not suffer physically or psychologically" (345). Morris uses these lenses to argue that Tolkien's Middle Earth represents a secular animal liberationist approach to the treatment of nonhuman animals and that Lewis's Narnia books represent a Christian animal liberationist approach. Morris contrasts these two children's fantasy worlds with the ideologies presumed in the Harry Potter series, illustrating that in the wizarding world, there is neither a liberationist nor a welfarist approach, little or no serious moral consideration is given to nonhuman animals, and, indeed, numerous instances of wizards' (both "good" and "evil") "inflicting cruelty on another life form for personal pleasure" (346). Morris is critical of Rowling's world in its treatment of nonhuman animals, concluding that she "has created an overly simplistic world, morally and ethically, in which beasts both magical and mundane have very limited intrinsic value and are enslaved and reduced to sources of food, entertainment, and exploitation for potion ingredients" (348).

Magic, Technology, and Science
Several scholarly articles and at least one full-length book focus on the function and features of magic and science within the Harry Potter series, including the feasibility of many of the magical devices and spells. Michael Ostling's "Harry Potter and the

Disenchantment of the World" bridges a discussion of religion with magic as technology, asserting that "we indeed inhabit a disenchanted world" (4), drawing upon Christian rhetoric and historical and philosophical debates about what constitutes magic as the basis for his argument. Similarly, Peter Appelbaum asserts in "Harry Potter's World: Magic, Technoculture, and Becoming Human" that magic in the Harry Potter series is a "commodified technology" and that the books appeal to readers in their metaphorical use of magic as technology. By contrast, Margaret Oakes argues in "Flying Cars, Flood Powder, and Flaming Torches: The Hi-Tech, Low-Tech World of Wizardry" that the "fundamental distinction" between the Muggle and wizarding worlds is the "different capabilities of Muggles and wizards to first master, and then to manage, the knowledge required to make the technology work" (119). Roger Highfield's *The Science of Harry Potter: How Magic Really Works* offers possible scientific explanations for many of the games, creatures, spells, and other features of Harry Potter's magical world. Highfield also considers scientific principles and their relation to Rowling's work and makes insightful and clear connections for his readers explaining that, in many cases, Rowling's portrayal of the natural world is quite accurate.

WORKS CITED AND FURTHER READING

Alton, Anne Hiebert. "Generic Fusion and the Mosaic of Harry Potter." In *Harry Potter's World: Multidisciplinary Critical Perspectives,* edited by Elizabeth Heilman, 141–162. New York: RoutledgeFalmer, 2003.

Anatol, Giselle Liza. "The Fallen Empire: Exploring Ethnic Otherness in the World of Harry Potter." In *Reading Harry Potter: Critical Essays,* edited by Giselle Liza Anatol, 163–178. Contributions to the Study of Popular Culture 78. Westport, Conn., and London: Praeger, 2003.

Anatol, Giselle Liza, ed. *Reading Harry Potter: Critical Essays.* Contributions to the Study of Popular Culture 78. Westport, Conn., and London: Praeger, 2003.

Anderson, Hollie. "Reading Harry Potter with Navajo Eyes." In *Harry Potter's World: Multidisciplinary*

Critical Perspectives, edited by Elizabeth Heilman, 97–107. New York: RoutledgeFalmer, 2003.

Anderson, Kara Lynn. "Harry Potter and the Susceptible Child Audience." *CLCWeb: Comparative Literature and Culture* 7, no. 2 (2005). Available online. URL: http://docs.lib.purdue.edu/clcweb/vol7/iss2/2. Accessed September 1, 2009.

Appelbaum, Peter. "Harry Potter's World: Magic, Technoculture, and Becoming Human." In *Harry Potter's World: Multidisciplinary Critical Perspectives*, edited by Elizabeth Heilman, 25–51. New York: RoutledgeFalmer, 2003.

Baggett, David, and Shawn E. Klein, eds. *Harry Potter and Philosophy: If Aristotle Ran Hogwarts. Popular Culture and Philosophy*, vol. 9. Chicago: Open Court, 2004.

Bahor, Laura Shearer. "High Brow Harry Potter: J. K. Rowling's Series as College-Level Literature." In *Scholarly Studies in Harry Potter: Applying Academic Methods to a Popular Text*, edited by Cynthia Whitney Hallett, 199–245. Studies in British Literature, vol. 99. Lewiston, N.Y.: Edwin Mellen Press, 2005.

Barfield, Steven. "Fantasy and the Interpretation of Fantasy in *Harry Potter*." *Topic: The Washington and Jefferson College Review* 54 (Fall 2004): 24–32.

———. "Of Young Magicians and Growing Up: J. K. Rowling, Her Critics, and the 'Culture of Infantilism' Debate." In *Scholarly Studies in Harry Potter: Applying Academic Methods to a Popular Text*, edited by Cynthia Whitney Hallett, 175–197. Studies in British Literature, vol. 99. Lewiston, N.Y.: Edwin Mellen Press, 2005.

Beach, Sara Ann, and Elizabeth Harden Willner. "The Power of Harry: The Impact of J. K. Rowling's Harry Potter Books on Young Readers." *World Literature Today* 76, no. 1 (2002): 102–106.

Beaton, Tisha. "Science at Hogwarts." *Science and Children* 43, no. 6 (March 2006): 48–51.

Behr, Kate. "'Same as Difference': Narrative Transformations and Intersecting Cultures in Harry Potter." *JNT: Journal of Narrative Theory* 35, no. 1 (Winter 2005): 112–132.

Berman, Lauren. "Dragon's and Serpents in J. K. Rowling's *Harry Potter* Series: Are They Evil?" *Mythlore* 27, no. 1 (Fall/Winter 2008). 45–65.

———. "Rowling's Devil: Ancient Archetype or Modern Manifestation?" *Journal for Academic Study of Magic* 4 (2007): 163–196.

Berndt, Katrin, ed. *Heroism and the Harry Potter Series*. Surrey, England: Ashgate, 2010.

Billone, Amy. "The Boy Who Lived: From Carroll's Alice and Barrie's Peter Pan to Rowling's Harry Potter." *Children's Literature* 32 (2004): 178–202.

Binnendyk, Lauren, and Kimberly Schonert-Reichl. "Harry Potter and Moral Development in Pre-Adolescent Children." *Journal of Moral Education* 31, no. 2 (2002): 195–201.

Black, Mary, and Marilyn Eisenwine. "Education of the Young Harry Potter: Socialization and Schooling for Wizards." *Educational Forum* 66, no. 1 (2001): 32–37.

Black, Sharon. "Harry Potter: A Magical Prescription for Just about Anyone." *Journal of Adolescent and Adult Literacy* 46, no. 7 (2003): 540–544.

———. "Harry Potter: Enchantment for All Seasons." *Gifted Child Today* 26, no. 3 (Summer 2003): 46–54.

———. "The Magic of Harry Potter: Symbols and Heroes of Fantasy." *Children's Literature in Education* 34, no. 3 (2003): 237–247.

Blake, Andrew. *The Irresistible Rise of Harry Potter*. London: Verso, 2002.

Bloom, Harold. "Can 35 Million Book Buyers Be Wrong? Yes." *Wall Street Journal*. 11 July 2000. Available online. URL: http://wrt-brooke.syr.edu/courses/205.03/bloom.html. Accessed August 25, 2009.

Bond, Ernest, and Nancy Michelson. "Writing Harry's World: Children Co-Authoring Hogwarts." In *Harry Potter's World: Multidisciplinary Critical Perspectives*, edited by Elizabeth Heilman, 309–327. New York: RoutledgeFalmer, 2003.

Borah, Rebecca Sutherland. "Apprentice Wizards Welcome: Fan Communities and the Culture of Harry Potter." In *The Ivory Tower and Harry Potter: Perspectives on a Literary Phenomenon*, edited by Lana Whited, 343–364. Columbia: University of Missouri Press, 2002.

Bridger, Francis. *A Charmed Life: The Spirituality of Potterworld*. New York: Image Books, 2001.

Brondsted, Katrine, and Cay Dollerup. "The Names in Harry Potter." *Perspectives: Studies in Translatology* 12, no. 1 (2004): 56–72.

Brown, Stephen. "Harry Potter and the Marketing Mystery: A Review and Critical Assessment of the Harry Potter Books." *Journal of Marketing* 66, no. 1 (2002): 126–130.

Butler, Rebecca. "The Literature Continuum: The Harry Potter Phenomenon." *School Libraries Worldwide* 9, no. 1 (January 2003): 64–77.

Cain, Amanda. "Books and Becoming Good: Demonstrating Aristotle's Theory of Moral Development in the Act of Reading." *Journal of Moral Education* 34, no. 2 (2005): 171–183.

Carey, Brycchan. "Hermione and the House-Elves: The Literary and Historical Contexts of J. K. Rowling's Antislavery Campaign." In *Reading Harry Potter: Critical Essays*, edited by Giselle Liza Anatol, 103–115. Contributions to the Study of Popular Culture 78. Westport, Conn., and London: Praeger, 2003.

Chappell, Drew. "Sneaking Out after Dark: Resistance, Agency, and the Postmodern Child in J. K. Rowling's Harry Potter Series." *Children's Literature in Education* 39 (2008): 281–293.

Chellammal, V., and S. K. Chitra Lakshimi. "Harry Potter and the Mahabharatha." *Bookbird* 44 (2006): 13–19.

Cherland, Meredith. "Harry's Girls: Harry Potter and the Discourse of Gender." *Journal of Adolescent and Adult Literacy* 52, no. 4 (December 2008/January 2009): 273–281.

Chevalier, Noel. "The Liberty Tree and the Whomping Willow: Political Justice, Magical Science, and Harry Potter." *Lion and the Unicorn* 29 (2005): 397–415.

Cockrell, Amanda. "Harry Potter and the Secret Password: Finding Our Way in the Magical Genre." In *The Ivory Tower and Harry Potter: Perspectives on a Literary Phenomenon*, edited by Lana Whited, 15–26. Columbia: University of Missouri Press, 2002.

———. "Harry Potter and the Witch Hunters: A Social Context for the Attacks on Harry Potter." *Journal of American Culture* 29, no. 1 (2003): 24–30.

Comber, Barbara, and Helen Nixon. "The Harry Potter Phenomenon." *Journal of Adolescent and Adult Literacy* 44 (May 2001): 746–754.

Cothran, Casey. "Lessons in Transfiguration: Allegories of Male Identity in Rowling's Harry Potter Series." In *Scholarly Studies in Harry Potter: Applying Academic Methods to a Popular Text*, edited by Cynthia Whitney Hallett, 123–124. Studies in British Literature, vol. 99. Lewiston, N.Y.: Edwin Mellen Press, 2005.

Croft, Janet Brennan. "The Education of a Witch: Tiffany Aching, Hermione Granger, and Gendered Magic in Discworld and Potterworld." *Mythlore* 27, no. 3/4 (Spring/Summer 2009): 129–142.

Czubak, Todd, and Janey Greenwald. "Understanding Harry Potter: Parallels to the Deaf World." *Journal of Deaf Studies and Deaf Education* 10 (2005): 442–450.

Damour, Lisa. "Harry Potter and the Magical Looking Glass: Reading the Secret Life of the Preadolescent." In *Reading Harry Potter: Critical Essays*, edited by Giselle Liza Anatol, 15–24. Contributions to the Study of Popular Culture 78. Westport, Conn., and London: Praeger, 2003.

Davies, Eirlys E. "A Goblin or a Dirty Nose? The Treatment of Culture-Specific References in Translations of the Harry Potter Books." *Translator* 9, no. 1 (2003): 65–100.

Deavel, Catherine Jack, and David Paul Deavel. "Character, Choice, and Harry Potter." *Logos* 5, no. 4 (Fall 2002): 49–64.

Denton, Peter. "What Could Be Wrong with Harry Potter?" *Journal of Youth Services in Libraries* 15, no. 3 (2002): 28–32.

DeRosa, Deborah. "Wizardly Challenges to and Affirmations of the Initiation Paradigm in Harry Potter." In *Harry Potter's World: Multidisciplinary Critical Perspectives*, edited by Elizabeth Heilman, 163–184. New York: RoutledgeFalmer, 2003.

Dickinson, Renee. "Harry Potter Pedagogy: What We Learn about Teaching and Learning." *Clearing House* 79, no. 6 (2006): 240–244.

Doughty, Terri. "Locating Harry Potter in the 'Boys' Book' Market." In *The Ivory Tower and Harry Potter: Perspectives on a Literary Phenomenon*, edited by Lana Whited, 243–257. Columbia: University of Missouri Press, 2002.

Dresang, Eliza. "Hermione Granger and the Heritage of Gender." In *The Ivory Tower and Harry Potter: Perspectives on a Literary Phenomenon,* edited by Lana Whited, 211–242. Columbia: University of Missouri Press, 2002.

Duffy, Edward. "Sentences in Harry Potter, Students in Future Writing Classes." *Rhetoric Review* 21, no. 2 (2002): 170–187.

Eagleton, Mary. "The Danger of Intellectual Masters: Lessons from Harry Potter and Antonia Byatt." *Revista Canaria de Estudios Ingleses* 48 (2004): 61–75.

Elster, Charles. "The Seeker of Secrets: Images of Learning, Knowing, and Schooling." In *Harry Potter's World: Multidisciplinary Critical Perspectives,* edited by Elizabeth Heilman, 203–220. New York: RoutledgeFalmer, 2003.

Farmer, Joy. "The Magician's Niece: The Kinship between J. K. Rowling and C. S. Lewis." *Mythlore* 88 (Spring 2001): 53–63.

Fife, Ernelle. "Reading J. K. Rowling Magically: Creating C. S. Lewis' 'Good Reader.'" In *Scholarly Studies in Harry Potter: Applying Academic Methods to a Popular Text,* edited by Cynthia Whitney Hallett, 137–158. *Studies in British Literature,* vol. 99. Lewiston, N.Y.: Edwin Mellen Press, 2005.

Frank, Andrew, and Matthew McBee. "The Use of Harry Potter and the Sorcerer's Stone to Discuss Identity Development with Gifted Adolescents." *Journal of Secondary Gifted Education* 15, no. 1 (Fall 2003): 33–38.

Gallardo-C., Ximena, and C. Jason Smith. "Cinderfella: J. K. Rowling's Wily Web of Gender." In *Reading Harry Potter: Critical Essays,* edited by Giselle Liza Anatol, 191–205. Contributions to the Study of Popular Culture 78. Westport, Conn., and London: Praeger, 2003.

Gibbons, Sarah. "Death and Rebirth: Harry Potter and the Mythology of the Phoenix." In *Scholarly Studies in Harry Potter: Applying Academic Methods to a Popular Text,* edited by Cynthia Whitney Hallett, 85–105. Studies in British Literature, vol. 99. Lewiston, N.Y.: Edwin Mellen Press, 2005.

Gibson, Donna M. "Empathizing with *Harry Potter*: The Use of Popular Literature in Counselor Education." *Journal of Humanistic Counseling, Education, and Development* 46 (Fall 2007): 197–210.

Gladstein, Mimi. "Feminism and Equal Opportunity: Hermione and the Women of Hogwarts." In *Harry Potter and Philosophy: If Aristotle Ran Hogwarts,* vol. 9: *Popular Culture and Philosophy,* edited by David Baggett and Shawn E. Klein, 49–59. Chicago: Open Court, 2004.

Glanzer, Perry. "Harry Potter's Provocative Moral World: Is There a Place for Good and Evil in Moral Education?" *Phi Delta Kappan,* March 2008, 525–528.

———. "In Defense of Harry . . . but Not His Defenders: Beyond Censorship to Justice." *English Journal* 93, no. 4 (March 2004): 58–63.

Gottesman, Peter. "Harry Potter and the Sorcerer's Stone." *Teachers College Record* 106, no. 2 (2004): 267–270.

Green, Amy. "Interior/Exterior in the 'Harry Potter' Series: Duality Expressed in Sirius Black and Remus Lupin." *Papers on Language and Literature* 44, no. 1 (Winter 2008): 87–108.

Griesinger, Emily. "Harry Potter and the 'Deeper Magic': Narrating Hope in Children's Literature." *Christianity and Literature* 51, no. 3 (2002): 455–480.

Grimes, M. Katherine. "Harry Potter: Fairy Tale Prince, Real Boy, and Archetypal Hero." In *The Ivory Tower and Harry Potter: Perspectives on a Literary Phenomenon,* edited by Lana Whited, 89–122. Columbia: University of Missouri Press, 2002.

Gruner, Elisabeth Rose. "Teach the Children: Education and Knowledge in Recent Children's Fantasy." *Children's Literature* 37 (2009): 216–235.

Gupta, Suman. *Re-Reading Harry Potter.* London: Palgrave Macmillan, 2003.

Hall, Susan. "Harry Potter and the Rule of Law: The Central Weakness of Legal Concepts in the Wizard World." In *Reading Harry Potter: Critical Essays,* edited by Giselle Liza Anatol, 147–162. Contributions to the Study of Popular Culture 78. Westport, Conn., and London: Praeger, 2003.

Hallett, Cynthia Whitney, ed. *Scholarly Studies in Harry Potter: Applying Academic Methods to a Popular Text*. Studies in British Literature, vol. 99. Lewiston, N.Y.: Edwin Mellen Press, 2005.

Heilman, Elizabeth. "Blue Wizards and Pink Witches: Representations of Gender Identity and Power." In *Harry Potter's World: Multidisciplinary Critical Perspectives*, edited by Elizabeth Heilman, 221–239. New York: RoutledgeFalmer, 2003.

Hopkins, Lisa. "Harry Potter and the Acquisition of Knowledge." In *Reading Harry Potter: Critical Essays*, edited by Giselle Liza Anatol, 25–34. Contributions to the Study of Popular Culture 78. Westport, Conn., and London: Praeger, 2003.

Huey, Peggy. "A Basilisk, a Phoenix, and a Philosopher's Stone: Harry Potter's Myths and Legends." In *Scholarly Studies in Harry Potter: Applying Academic Methods to a Popular Text*, edited by Cynthia Whitney Hallett, 65–83. Studies in British Literature, vol. 99. Lewiston, N.Y.: Edwin Mellen Press, 2005.

Jacobs, Alan. "Harry Potter's Magic." *First Things* 99 (January 2000): 35–38.

Jacobs, DawnEllen. "Tolkien and Rowling: Reflections on Receptions." *Topic: The Washington and Jefferson College Review* 54 (Fall 2004): 46–54.

Jensch, Nancy K. "Harry Potter and the Tower of Babel: Translating the Magic." In *The Ivory Tower and Harry Potter: Perspectives on a Literary Phenomenon*, edited by Lana Whited, 285–301. Columbia: University of Missouri Press, 2002.

Katz, Maureen. "Prisoners of Azkaban: Understanding Intergenerational Transmission of Trauma Due to War and State Terror (with Help from Harry Potter)." *JPCS: Journal for the Psychoanalysis of Culture and Society* 8, no. 2 (2003): 200–207.

Kidd, Dustin. "Harry Potter and the Functions of Popular Culture." *Journal of Popular Culture* 40, no. 1 (2007): 69–89.

Knapp, Nancy Flanagan. "In Defense of Harry Potter: An Apologia." *School Libraries Worldwide* 9, no. 1 (January 2003): 78–91.

Kornfeld, John, and Laurie Prothro. "Comedy, Conflict, and Community: Home and Family in Harry Potter." In *Harry Potter's World: Multidisciplinary Critical Perspectives*, edited by Elizabeth Heilman, 187–202. New York: RoutledgeFalmer, 2003.

Lacoss, Jann. "Of Magicals and Muggles: Reversals and Revulsion at Hogwarts." In *The Ivory Tower and Harry Potter: Perspectives on a Literary Phenomenon*, edited by Lana Whited, 67–88. Columbia: University of Missouri Press, 2002.

Landman, James. "Using Literature to Teach the Rule of Law." *Social Education* 72, no. 4 (2008): 165–170.

Lathey, Gillian. "The Travels of Harry: International Marketing and the Translation of J. K. Rowling's Harry Potter Books." *Lion and the Unicorn* 29 (2005): 141–151.

Lavoie, Chantel. "Safe as Houses: Sorting and School Houses at Hogwarts." In *Reading Harry Potter: Critical Essays*, edited by Giselle Liza Anatol, 35–49. Contributions to the Study of Popular Culture 78. Westport, Conn., and London: Praeger, 2003.

Lerer, Seth. "'This Life to Mend, This Book Attend': Reading and Healing in the Arc of Children's Literature." *New Literary History* 37 (2006): 631–642.

Levine, Jodi, and Nancy Shapiro. "Hogwarts: The Learning Community." *About Campus*, September–October 2000, 8–13.

Lewis, Jonathan. "'If Yeh Know Where to Go': Vision and Mapping in the Wizarding World." In *Scholarly Studies in Harry Potter: Applying Academic Methods to a Popular Text*, edited by Cynthia Whitney Hallett, 43–64. Studies in British Literature, vol. 99. Lewiston, N.Y.: Edwin Mellen Press, 2005.

Longster, Rebecca Whitus. "The Harlequins in the Weasley Twins: Jesters in the Court of Prince Harry (and J. K. Rowling)." In *Scholarly Studies in Harry Potter: Applying Academic Methods to a Popular Text*, edited by Cynthia Whitney Hallett, 107–121. Studies in British Literature, vol. 99. Lewiston, N.Y.: Edwin Mellen Press, 2005.

MacDonald, Marianne. "Harry Potter and the Fan Fiction Phenom." *Gay and Lesbian Review* 13, no. 1 (2006): 28–30.

MacNeil, William. "'Kidlit' as 'Law-and-Lit': Harry Potter and the Scales of Justice." *Law and Literature* 14, no. 3 (2002): 545–564.

McCarron, Bill. "Literary Parallels in *Harry Potter and the Chamber of Secrets.*" *Notes on Contemporary Literature*, 2003, 7–8.

McEvoy, Kathleen. "Aesthetic Organization: The Structural Beauty of J. K. Rowling's *Harry Potter* Series." *Topic: The Washington and Jefferson College Review* 54 (Fall 2004): 14–23.

McVeigh, Dan: "Is Harry Potter Christian?" *Renascence: Essays on Values in Literature* 54 (2002): 197–214.

Meier, Sarah. "Educating Harry Potter: A Muggle's Perspective on Magic and Knowledge in the Wizard World of J. K. Rowling." In *Scholarly Studies in Harry Potter: Applying Academic Methods to a Popular Text*, edited by Cynthia Whitney Hallett, 7–27. Studies in British Literature, vol. 99. Lewiston, N.Y.: Edwin Mellen Press, 2005.

Mendlesohn, Farah. "Crowning the King: Harry Potter and the Construction of Authority." In *The Ivory Tower and Harry Potter: Perspectives on a Literary Phenomenon*, edited by Lana Whited, 159–181. Columbia: University of Missouri Press, 2002.

Mills, Alice. "Archetypes and the Unconscious in *Harry Potter* and Diana Wynne Jones's *Fire and Hemlock* and *Dogsbody.*" In *Reading Harry Potter: Critical Essays*, edited by Giselle Liza Anatol, 3–13. Contributions to the Study of Popular Culture 78. Westport, Conn., and London: Praeger, 2003.

———. "Harry Potter and the Terrors of the Toilet." *Children's Literature in Education* 37, no. 1 (2006): 1–13.

Morris, Michael. "Middle Earth, Narnia, Hogwarts, and Animals: A Review of the Treatment of Nonhuman Animals and Other Sentient Beings in Christian-Based Fantasy Fiction." *Society and Animals* 17 (2009): 343–356.

Mullen, Alexandra. "Harry Potter's Schooldays." *Hudson Review* 53, no. 1 (2000): 127–135.

Natov, Roni. "Harry Potter and the Extraordinariness of the Ordinary." In *The Ivory Tower and Harry Potter: Perspectives on a Literary Phenomenon*, edited by Lana Whited, 125–139. Columbia: University of Missouri Press, 2002.

Neithardt, Leigh. "The Problem of Identity in *Harry Potter and the Sorcerer's Stone.*" In *Scholarly Studies in Harry Potter: Applying Academic Methods to a Popular Text*, edited by Cynthia Whitney Hallett, 159–173. Studies in British Literature, vol. 99. Lewiston, N.Y.: Edwin Mellen Press, 2005.

Nel, Philip. "Is There a Text in This Advertising Campaign? Literature, Marketing, and Harry Potter." *Lion and the Unicorn* 29 (2005): 236–267.

———. "You Say 'Jelly,' I Say Jell-O?: Harry Potter and the Transfiguration of Language." In *The Ivory Tower and Harry Potter: Perspectives on a Literary Phenomenon*, edited by Lana Whited, 261–284. Columbia: University of Missouri Press, 2002.

Neumann, Iver B. "Pop Goes Religion: Harry Potter Meets Clifford Geertz." *European Journal of Cultural Studies* 9, no. 1 (2006): 81–100.

Nikolajeva, Maria. "Harry Potter—a Return to the Romantic Hero." In *Harry Potter's World: Multidisciplinary Critical Perspectives*, edited by Elizabeth H. Heilman, 125–140. New York: RoutledgeFalmer, 2003.

Nilsen, Alleen Pace, and Don L. F. Nilsen. "Latin Revived: Source-Based Vocabulary Lessons Courtesy of Harry Potter." *Journal of Adolescent and Adult Literacy* 50, no. 2 (2006): 128–134.

Nilsen, Don L. F., and Alleen Pace Nilsen. "Naming Tropes and Schemes in J. K. Rowling's Harry Potter Books." *English Journal* 98, no. 6 (2009): 60–68.

Nye, Lesley. "Editor's Review." *Harvard Educational Review* 71, no. 1 (Spring 2001): 136–145.

Oakes, Margaret. "Flying Cars, Flood Powder, and Flaming Torches: The Hi-Tech, Low-Tech World of Wizardry." In *Reading Harry Potter: Critical Essays*, edited by Giselle Liza Anatol, 118–128. Contributions to the Study of Popular Culture 78. Westport, Conn., and London: Praeger, 2003.

Ostling, Michael. "Harry Potter and the Disenchantment of the World." *Journal of Contemporary Religion* 18, no. 1 (2003): 3–23.

Ostry, Elaine. "Accepting Mudbloods: The Ambivalent Social Vision of J. K. Rowling's Fairy Tales." In *Reading Harry Potter: Critical Essays*, edited by Giselle Liza Anatol, 89–101. Contributions to the Study of Popular Culture 78. Westport, Conn., and London: Praeger, 2003.

Park, Julia. "Class and Socioeconomic Identity in Harry Potter's England." In *Reading Harry Potter: Critical Essays*, edited by Giselle Liza Anatol, 179–189. Contributions to the Study of Popular Culture 78. Westport, Conn., and London: Praeger, 2003.

Patkin, Terri Toles. "Constructing a New Game: J. K. Rowling's Quidditch and Global Kid Culture." *Reconstruction: Studies in Contemporary Culture* 6, no. 1 (Winter 2006).

Pennington, John. "From Elfland to Hogwarts, or the Aesthetic Trouble with Harry Potter." *Lion and the Unicorn* 26 (2002): 78–97.

Perry, Evelyn. "Metaphor and Metafantasy: Questing for Literary Inheritance in J. K. Rowling's Harry Potter and the Sorcerer's Stone." In *Scholarly Studies in Harry Potter: Applying Academic Methods to a Popular Text*, edited by Cynthia Whitney Hallett, 241–275. Studies in British Literature, vol. 99. Lewiston, N.Y.: Edwin Mellen Press, 2005.

Pharr, Mary. "In Medias Res: Harry Potter as Hero-in-Progress." In *The Ivory Tower and Harry Potter: Perspectives on a Literary Phenomenon*, edited by Lana Whited, 53–66. Columbia: University of Missouri Press, 2002.

Pinsent, Pat. "The Education of a Wizard: Harry Potter and His Predecessors." In *The Ivory Tower and Harry Potter: Perspectives on a Literary Phenomenon*, edited by Lana Whited, 27–52. Columbia: University of Missouri Press, 2002.

Pugh, Tison, and David L. Wallace. "Heteronormative Heroism and Queering the School Story in J. K. Rowling's Harry Potter Series." *Children's Literature* 31, no. 3 (2006): 260–281.

Rollin, Lucy. "Among School Children: The Harry Potter Books and the School Story Tradition." *South Carolina Review* 34, no. 1 (2001): 198–208.

Routledge, Christopher. "Harry Potter and the Mystery of Ordinary Life." In *Mystery in Children's Literature: From the Rational to the Supernatural*, edited by Adrienne Gavin and Christopher Routledge, 202–207. Houndmills, England: Palgrave, 2001.

Rudski, Jeffrey Michael, Carli Segal, and Eli Kallen. "Harry Potter and the End of the Road: Parallels with Addiction." *Addiction Research and Theory* 17, no. 3 (2009): 260–277.

Saltman, Judith. "Harry Potter's Family Tree." *Journal of Youth Services in Libraries* 15, no. 3 (2002): 24–28.

Saric, Julia. "A Defense of Harry Potter, or When Religion Is Not Religion: An Analysis of the Censoring of the Harry Potter Books." *Canadian Children's Literature* 103, no. 27 (2001): 6–26.

Sattaur, Jennifer. "Harry Potter: A World of Fear." *Journal of Children's Literature Studies* 3, no. 1 (2006): 1–14.

Schanoes, Veronica. "Cruel Heroes and Treacherous Texts: Educating the Reader in Moral Complexity and Critical Reading in J. K. Rowling's Harry Potter Books." In *Reading Harry Potter: Critical Essays*, edited by Giselle Liza Anatol, 131–145. Contributions to the Study of Popular Culture 78. Westport, Conn., and London: Praeger, 2003.

Seden, Janet. "Parenting and the Harry Potter Stories: A Social Care Perspective." *Children and Society* 16 (2002): 295–305.

Siskind, Shira. "Crossing the Fair Use Line: The Demise and Revival of the *Harry Potter Lexicon* and Its Implications for the Fair Use Doctrine in the Real World and on the Internet." *Cardozo Arts Entertainment Law* 27, no. 1 (2009): 291–311.

Skulnick, Rebecca, and Jesse Goodman. "The Civic Leadership of Harry Potter: Agency, Ritual, and Schooling." In *Harry Potter's World: Multidisciplinary Critical Perspectives*, edited by Elizabeth Heilman, 261–277. New York: RoutledgeFalmer, 2003.

Smith, Karen Manners. "Harry Potter's Schooldays: J. K. Rowling and the British Boarding School Novel." In *Reading Harry Potter: Critical Essays*, edited by Giselle Liza Anatol, 69–88. Contributions to the Study of Popular Culture 78. Westport, Conn., and London: Praeger, 2003.

Steege, David. "Harry Potter, Tom Brown, and the British School Story." In *The Ivory Tower and*

Harry Potter: Perspectives on a Literary Phenomenon, edited by Lana Whited, 140–156. Columbia: University of Missouri Press, 2002.

Stephens, Rebecca. "Harry and Hierarchy: Book Banning as a Reaction to the Subversion of Authority." In *Reading Harry Potter: Critical Essays,* edited by Giselle Liza Anatol, 51–65. Contributions to the Study of Popular Culture 78. Westport, Conn., and London: Praeger, 2003.

Stevenson, Iain. "Harry Potter, Riding the Bullet and the Future of Books: Key Issues in the Anglophone Book Business." *Publishing Research Quarterly* 24 (2008): 277–284.

Strimel, Courtney. "The Politics of Terror: Rereading Harry Potter." *Children's Literature in Education* 35, no. 1 (2004): 35–52.

Striphas, Ted. "Harry Potter and the Simulacrum: Contested Copies in an Age of Intellectual Property." *Critical Studies in Media Communication* 26, no. 4 (2009): 1–17.

Taub, Deborah J., and Heather L. Servaty. "Controversial Content in Children's Literature: Is *Harry Potter* Harmful to Children?" In *Harry Potter's World: Multidisciplinary Critical Perspectives,* edited by Elizabeth Heilman, 53–72. New York: RoutledgeFalmer, 2003.

Teare, Elizabeth. "Harry Potter and the Technology of Magic." In *The Ivory Tower and Harry Potter: Perspectives on a Literary Phenomenon,* edited by Lana Whited, 329–342. Columbia: University of Missouri Press, 2002.

Tosenberger, Catherine. "'Oh my God, the Fanfiction!' Dumbledore's Outing and the Online Harry Potter Fandom." *Children's Literature Association Quarterly,* 33, no. 2 (Summer 2008): 200–206.

Trites, Roberta Seelinger. "The Harry Potter Novels as a Test Case for Adolescent Literature." *Style* 35 (2001): 472–485.

Tseplakov, Georgii. "Talent and the Widow's Mite of Project Literature." *Russian Studies in Literature* 45, no. 2 (Spring 2009): 75–93.

Tucker, Nicholas. "The Rise and Rise of Harry Potter." *Children's Literature in Education* 30, no. 4 (1999): 221–234.

Turner-Vorbeck, Tammy. "Pottermania: Good, Clean Fun or Cultural Hegemony?" In *Harry Potter's World: Multidisciplinary Critical Perspectives,* edited by Elizabeth Heilman, 25–51. New York: RoutledgeFalmer, 2003.

Virole, Benoit. "Harry Potter's Cauldron: The Power of Myth and the Rebirth of the Sacred." *Queen's Quarterly* 111, no. 3 (Fall 2004): 371–379.

Waetjen, Jarrod, and Timothy A. Gibson. "Harry Potter and the Commodity Fetishism: Activating Corporate Readings in the Journey from Text to Commercial Intertext." *Communication and Critical/Cultural Studies* 4, no. 1 (2007): 3–26.

Wagner, Rachel. "Bewitching the Box Office: Harry Potter and Religious Controversy." *Journal of Religion and Film* 7, no. 2 (October 2003). Available online. URL: http://www.unomaha.edu/jrf/Vol7No2/bewitching.htm. Accessed August 25, 2009.

Wallace, David L and Pugh, Tison. "Playing with Critical Theory in J. K. Rowling's Harry Potter Series." *English Journal* 96, no. 3 (2007): 97–100.

Wandless, William. "Hogwarts vs. the 'Values Wasteland': HP and the Formation of Character." In *Scholarly Studies in Harry Potter: Applying Academic Methods to a Popular Text,* edited by Cynthia Whitney Hallett, 217–240. Studies in British Literature, vol. 99. Lewiston, N.Y.: Edwin Mellen Press, 2005.

Westman, Karin. "Perspective, Memory, and Moral Authority: The Legacy of Jane Austen in J. K. Rowling's Harry Potter." *Children's Literature* 35 (2007): 145–165.

———. "Specters of Thatcherism: Contemporary British Culture in J. K. Rowling's Harry Potter Series." In *The Ivory Tower and Harry Potter: Perspectives on a Literary Phenomenon,* edited by Lana Whited, 305–328 Columbia: University of Missouri Press, 2002.

———. "The Weapon We Have Is Love." *Children's Literature Association Quarterly* 33, no. 2 (2008): 193–199.

Whited, Lana, ed. *The Ivory Tower and Harry Potter: Perspectives on a Literary Phenomenon.* Columbia: University of Missouri Press, 2002.

Whited, Lana, and Katherine Grimes. "What Would Harry Do? J. K. Rowling and Lawrence Kohlberg's Theories of Moral Development." In *The Ivory Tower and Harry Potter: Perspectives on a Literary Phenomenon*, edited by Lana Whited, 182–208. Columbia: University of Missouri Press, 2002.

Willson-Metzger, Alicia, and David Metzger. "But Is He Really Smart? Gardner's Multiple Intelligences Theory in the World of Harry Potter." *Popular Culture Review* 14, no. 2 (2003): 55–61.

Wood, Susan Nelson, and Kim Quackenbush. "*The Sorcerer's Stone*: A Touchstone for Readers of All Ages." *English Journal* 90, no. 3 (2001): 97–103.

Yaggi, Miranda Maney. "Harry Potter's Heritage: Tolkien as Rowling's Patronus against the Critics." *Topic: The Washington and Jefferson College Review* 54 (Fall 2004): 33–45.

Zimmerman, Virginia. "Harry Potter and the Gift of Time." *Children's Literature* 37 (2009): 194–215.

Zipes, Jack. "The Phenomenon of Harry Potter, or Why All the Talk?" In *Sticks and Stones: The Troublesome Success of Children's Literature from Slovenly Peter to Harry Potter*, 170–189. New York: Routledge, 2001.

Additional Resources on the Harry Potter Series

A wealth of resources written by enthusiasts of the series who are not literary scholars is also available. The work covered in this section, generally published by commercial presses, is likely to be of interest to readers who are looking for additional background and context; those readers interested in scholarly analysis of the series, however, should refer to the previous section, "Scholarship on the Harry Potter Series," which provides a list of works written by academics and literary scholars (published by university or other scholarly presses).

Sources discussed here are still in print and are easily accessible to the general public. These works also focus heavily on Harry Potter; books with minor mentions of the series within larger discus-sions of children's literature, fantasy, and science fiction are not included.

GENERAL INFORMATION ABOUT THE SERIES

Readers looking for a general introduction to the series can choose among several works. In *A Study of the Harry Potter Novels*, Julia Eccleshare provides readers with an introduction to the series, giving summaries of the books and descriptions of the main characters. This work functions primarily as a guide to what happens in some of the novels and can be read as a substitute for the books themselves if one is simply interested in learning about the basic plot elements.

The Definitive Harry Potter Guidebook Series by Marie Lesoway briefly studies the first four novels, providing summaries of the books and explanations of important characters and events. Similarly, in more depth George Beahm's *Magic for Muggles: An Unofficial Guide to J. K. Rowling and the Harry Potter Phenomenon* covers a wealth of general information on J. K. Rowling, the first five novels, the first two movies, as well as Harry Potter merchandise. Beahm's work provides a source for entertainment, as well, since he includes several hundred trivia questions about Rowling's life and the series.

Readers searching for reference manuals on the series also have many options, some addressing several of Rowling's novels and other works much more comprehensive. *The Harry Potter Companion* by Acascias Riphouse supplies a reference manual and explanation for some of the first novels in the series. The work includes details about the Hogwarts castle, a timeline, and maps to help readers better understand Rowling's wizarding universe. A more comprehensive work is Nancy Solon Villaluz's *Does Harry Potter Tickle Sleeping Dragons?* which provides an in-depth analysis of each of the series's novels with insights on the religious undertones in Rowling's series.

An accessible but not necessarily comprehensive resource for readers is the *Greenhaven Press Literary Companion to Contemporary Authors, Readings on*

J. K. Rowling, which has a modest biography, analysis of genre and language, and relatively brief discussions of the series's place in the fantasy, fairy tale, and boarding school traditions. A brief discussion of philosophical implications of the books and critical debate about the series's status as a "classic" and its appropriateness for children are also included. This book discusses the series through the fourth novel, *Goblet of Fire.*

DETAILED REFERENCE GUIDES

Three of the four most exhaustive reference manuals are Colin Duriez's *Field Guide to Harry Potter,* Elizabeth Schafer's *Exploring Harry Potter* (on the first three novels), and Tere Stouffer's *The Idiot's Guide to the World of Harry Potter.* Duriez's work examines Rowling's life, themes in the series, and Rowling's spiritual worldview and considers the series within existing literary traditions. Duriez also includes summaries of the books and a time line for the events in the novels. A major portion of this work is an exhaustive section covering terms from the novels. Duriez incorporates information from many of Rowling's earlier interviews with various other sources in an attempt to authenticate his work (though the interviews were not directly conducted by him). Schafer's reference work, though limited to the first three novels, will be useful to readers who are looking for an exhaustive overview of biography, contexts, teaching ideas, and analysis of literary elements. *Exploring Harry Potter* offers an analysis of literary elements such as characters, themes, and setting; a biography of Rowling; discussions of wizarding culture (food, school life, sports); the geography of Harry's world; mythological and biblical references; history, science, and magic; and a pre-2000 bibliography. Stouffer's *The Idiot's Guide to the World of Harry Potter* is a user-friendly reference work in a series that publishes guides on languages, cooking, hobbies, and cultures. The work explores all seven of the novels, discussing the influences on Rowling's work as well as contextualizing it within traditions of many disciplines, including literature, history, and science.

By far the most exhaustive guide, however, is Steven Vander Ark's *The Lexicon: An Unauthorized Guide to Harry Potter Fiction and Related Materials.* Vander Ark founded the Harry Potter Lexicon Web site, which Rowling praised vigorously until the heated lawsuit that pitted Vander Ark and RDR Books against Rowling; she argued that Vander Ark's work should not be published since its incredible wealth of detail infringed on her creative rights and plans to produce an encyclopedia devoted to the Harry Potter universe. Vander Ark's book was eventually published, with some revisions.

THEORIES ABOUT THE SERIES

A popular activity of Harry Potter enthusiasts has always been theorizing about the books. While the excitement of making predictions about forthcoming books may have faded, reading the works discussed later, specifically on theories about characters and events in the series, is still useful since many of the authors analyze important clues and themes, which provide a richer understanding of the series as a whole.

The Plot Thickens . . . Harry Potter Investigated by Fans for Fans, by Galadriel Waters, discusses the first five books and what she expects to happen in later novels. Waters, together with Astre Mithrandir, and E. L. Fossa wrote a series of three books known as the *Ultimate Unofficial Guide[s] to the Mysteries of Harry Potter.* Their first work offers theories about the first four books; the second provides an analysis of the fifth book while hypothesizing about the contents of the sixth; their last work, a detailed analysis of the sixth book, explores what the authors predict will occur in the last novel. Each of these guides provides a brief summary of each chapter in each book, as well as discussions of clues they think Rowling offers to the contents of the last novel.

In *Unlocking Harry Potter: Five Keys for the Serious Reader* John Granger proposes that Rowling's success as a storyteller is due to what he refers to as "the five keys," including her employment of narrative misdirection to her critique of postmodernism. The last chapter of Granger's book focuses on his predictions of what he thinks will occur in *Harry Potter and the Deathly Hallows.* Granger also edited the collection *Who Killed Albus Dumbledore?* a work that includes essays from six "*Harry Potter* expert detectives" arguing over what truly happened when the headmaster was killed. Similarly, Amy Berner, Orson Scott Card, and Joyce Millman argue Snape's allegiance in *The Great Snape Debate,* published after *Harry Potter and the Half-Blood Prince.* The authors incorporate textual evidence, excerpts from statements Rowling has made, and their own speculations in this collection of essays.

David Langford's *The End of Harry Potter?* offers his theories about what will occur in the last book of the series. Likewise, in *Unauthorized Harry Potter and the Deathly Hallows News: Harry Potter Deathly Hallows and Half-Blood Prince Analysis,* W. Frederick Zimmerman makes predictions about the last book in Rowling's series grounded primarily on what occurs in the sixth novel. Louis CasaBianca's *Defogging the Future: Unauthorized Speculation about the Seventh and Final Book of the Harry Potter Series* and Janet Scott Batchler's *What Will Harry Do? The Unofficial Guide to Payoffs and Possibilities in Deathly Hallows* treat many of the issues and questions also discussed by Langford and Zimmerman, among others. Ben Schoen, Emerson Spartz, Andy Gordon, Gretchen Stull, and Jamie Lawrence compiled their efforts to pen the very user-friendly and readable *Mugglenet.Com's What Will Happen in Harry Potter 7: Who Lives, Who Dies, Who Falls in Love and How Will the Adventure Finally End?*

SOURCES EXPLORING THE MYTHIC TRADITION

One of the most popular topics addressed by enthusiasts of the series continues to be the fantastic and mythical elements Rowling refers to or builds upon in her work. Alan Kronzek and Elizabeth Kronzek's *The Sorcerer's Companion: A Guide to the Magical World of Harry Potter* provides an alphabetized list of elements from the series ranging from amulets and arithmancy to gnomes and goblins to yetis and zombies. Their explanations for each of these entries include brief but detailed descriptions addressing the historical contexts of the subject under study, as well as how the addressed figure, object, or practice appears in Rowling's series.

David Colbert's *The Magical Worlds of Harry Potter: A Treasury of Myths, Legends and Fascinating Facts* and his later, shorter work *The Hidden Myths in Harry Potter* provide insights on the significance of some of the names of characters, creatures, and places in the Harry Potter books; Colbert's *The Hidden Myths in Harry Potter* also includes a fold-out map, indicating important locations in the novels or related to the myths behind the series. Matthew Dickerson and David L. O'Hara's *From Homer to Harry Potter: A Handbook of Myth and Fantasy* places the series within existing literary traditions, exploring connections with Homer's works, Arthurian legends, the tales of JACOB AND WILHELM GRIMM, and several modern fantasy works. The work places special emphasis on the ways a Christian can appreciate Rowling's canon and makes many connections to the work of J. R. R. TOLKIEN and C. S. LEWIS. *Fact, Fiction, and Folklore in Harry Potter's World: An Unofficial Guide* by George Beahm supplies explanations for many of the fantastic creatures, notable magical figures, and practices in Rowling's canon, complemented by a list of resources for exploring further some of the topics he addresses. Similarly, in *Friends and Foes of Harry Potter: Names Decoded* Nikita Agarwal and Chitra Agarwal provide detailed explanations for characters' names, tying Rowling's work into existing literary, mythical, and fantastic traditions. Finally, Fionna Boyle's *An Unofficial Muggle's Guide to the Wizarding World: Exploring the Harry Potter Universe,* as do the Kronzeks' and Beahm's works, offers explanations for many of the creatures, people, and magical traditions in the series; she also includes a section in which she compares and contrasts the books and their film versions, and a section with ideas for hosting a party based on Rowling's work.

RELIGION IN HARRY POTTER

The topic of religion and its representation, or distortion, or lack thereof, in the series has been the foundation for some of the most heated discussions of Rowling's work. Most of the sources with a religious orientation are written from a Christian perspective; only a few sources discuss non-Christians views of and responses to the novels. Two works treat beliefs other than Christianity. The first is Geo Trevarthen's *The Seeker's Guide to Harry Potter*, which explores the series's themes and symbols in detail, paying special attention to the ways in which readers of various faiths can have rewarding reading experiences with the series. The second work, by Dov Krulwich, *Harry Potter and the Torah*, makes positive connections between the series and the Torah, a sacred text in the Jewish faith.

The most outspoken critic of Rowling, who describes her works as recruiting tools for the occult, is Richard Abanes. Abanes's *Harry Potter and the Bible: The Menace behind the Magick* studies the series as a recruitment tool for the occult. He provides a summary of each of the first four books and explains how events and characters suggest Rowling writes specifically to promote the occult. Abanes's other work, *Harry Potter, Narnia, and the Lord of the Rings: What You Need to Know about Fantasy Books and Movies*, addresses the content of each of these series's films, discussing which is "appropriate" material for Christians and which includes "harmful" spiritual content.

John Houghton's *A Closer Look at Harry Potter*, and his follow-up work *The Harry Potter Effect*, examine the Harry Potter novels and the debates that Christians have about the books as well as the impact of Rowling's works on child readers and culture. *The Mystery of Harry Potter: A Catholic Family Guide* by Nancy Carpentier Brown offers support for the series from a Catholic point of view. This book works to prove why Harry Potter is appropriate—and even helpful—reading material for Christians (Catholics in particular). Brown includes lists of questions for discussion and resources for family discussions of the series.

Arguably the best-known writer on the Harry Potter versus religion debate remains John Granger, who has published two books that defend the Harry Potter series against assertions that the books are anti-Christian or support Satanic practices. His *The Hidden Key to Harry Potter: Understanding the Meaning, Genius, and Popularity of Joanne Rowling's Harry Potter Novels* suggests that the series is laden with intense Christian allegories and lessons. His other work, *Looking for God in Harry Potter*, further explores the series from a Christian perspective, topics range from comparing Harry's journey to Christ's to explaining how names in the series have hidden Christian meanings. The title of John Killinger's work, *God, the Devil, and Harry Potter: A Christian Minister's Defense of the Beloved Novels*, makes its content obvious. Killinger argues that Harry is a Christ figure and a character from whom readers can learn powerful lessons. Similarly, both *What's a Christian to Do with Harry Potter?* and *The Gospel According to Harry Potter: The Spiritual Journey of the World's Greatest Seeker* by Connie Neal defend Rowling's works against Christian critics. In another of her works, *Wizards, Wardrobes, and Wookiees: Navigating Good and Evil in Harry Potter, Narnia, and Star Wars*, Neal reflects more on the connections people can make between the events in Rowling's series (and the works of others) and their own spiritual lives. Related very closely to the latter of Neal's books is Russell W. Dalton's *Faith Journey through Fantasy Lands: A Christian Dialogue with Harry Potter, Star Wars, and the Lord of the Rings*; in this work Dalton addresses the criticisms of these three popular fantasy/science fiction series while defending them as tools for exploring and enhancing one's own faith.

RACE, CLASS, AND GENDER

Another important criticism of Rowling concerns her depiction of race, class, and gender issues, among others. Karen Brown's *Prejudice in Harry Potter's World* examines the ways in which different groups within the wizarding community are targeted by prejudice and how the groups (whether based on ranking of species or blood status) contribute to and sustain the social hierarchy in the series. Mercedes Lackey and Leah Wilson's edited collection *Mapping the World of Harry Potter: Science*

Fiction and Fantasy Authors Explore the Bestselling Fantasy Series of All Time provides insights from authors on topics ranging from the social commentary Rowling makes through the Dursley family to the depiction of Hermione Granger.

HARRY AND THE MEDIA

Many critics have been especially fascinated by media response to Rowling's novels. *The Making of the Potterverse: A Month-by-Month Look at Harry's First Ten Years* by Scott Thomas is representative of this critique. The work details the media coverage of the Harry Potter series from the publication of *Sorcerer's Stone* to the release of the fifth film, *Order of the Phoenix*. Thomas includes interviews given by Rowling as well as the film directors to complement the large catalog of other information distributed via various media outlets.

MORALS AND ETHICS IN HARRY POTTER

Clearly the impact of the series on popular culture has garnered a significant amount of attention; another subject intriguing to enthusiasts is the power of the series to shape its readers' morals, ethics, mentalities, and coping mechanisms. Edmund Kern's *The Wisdom of Harry Potter: What Our Favorite Hero Teaches Us about Moral Choices* examines the ways in which Harry's own morality impacts readers of the series. *The Psychology of Harry Potter: An Unauthorized Examination of the Boy Who Lived,* edited by Neil Mulholland, uses a psychological lens to dissect practices and characters of the Harry Potter world, ranging from the classes taught at the wizarding school to Dobby's self-destructive behavior. Similarly, Kathryn Markell and Marc Markell's *The Children Who Lived: Using Harry Potter and Other Fictional Characters to Help Grieving Children and Other Adolescents* serves as a tool to help younger readers cope with issues such as death, fear, and grief by observing how such problems are addressed by Harry himself. The work also discusses other novels with characters in similar situations. The authors include a section on games and crafts related to the novels.

Sections in books devoted to Harry Potter–related art activities or games are not uncommon;

for example, Alison Hansel's *Charmed Knits: Projects for Fans of Harry Potter* provides patterns for some of the popular pieces of clothing and accessories seen in the Harry Potter movies, many of which were knitted by Molly Weasley. One reason for the inclusion of this sort of book is its illustration of the fan community of the series, which has reached proportions (some critics might refer to it as "fanaticism") unseen with any other modern literature. For this reason, Harry Potter fandom itself deserves critical attention.

HARRY AND HIS FANS

One major aspect of fandom concerning Rowling's series is the consistent creation and updating of hundreds of Harry Potter Web sites. *Harry Potter! The Best Websites* by Anthony Swinsinski provides a catalog of what Swinsinski deems the best Web sites about Harry Potter. He lists Web pages, a brief explanation of their content, and the corresponding URL; after each listing there is ample space for the reader to take notes on each site. Other works expand their discussion past fandom on the Web to examinations of readers of the series and the lengths they have gone to in demonstrating their dedication, whether attending "Midnight Madness" parties that honored the release of later novels or being the first in line for each new Harry Potter film. Bill Adler's *Kids' Letters to Harry Potter from around the World* shares young readers' perspectives on the series in the form of letters written directly to Harry, and attests to the devotion and interest of Rowling's fans. Erin Pyne's *A Fandom of Magical Proportions: An Unauthorized History of the Harry Potter Phenomenon* traces the rising popularity of the series since its release. Likewise, Melissa Anelli's *Harry, a History: The True Story of a Boy Wizard, His Fans, and Life Inside the Harry Potter Phenomenon* examines the popularity of the series and its effects on its fans.

LESSONS IN LEADERSHIP

Readers interested in applying lessons and stories from the series to their everyday lives will find interest in Iver B. Neumann and Daniel H. Nexon's *Harry Potter and International Relations,* a work that provides an analysis of the intersection between popular culture and world politics. Related to Neumann and Nexon's work is *If Harry Potter Ran General Electric: Leadership Wisdom from the World of Wizards* by Tom Morris, which uses the series and specific characters and scenarios to teach lessons about leadership.

TRIVIA BOOKS

Many works will engage those interested in testing their knowledge of the details of the series. Racheline Maltese's *The Book of Harry Potter Trifles, Trivia, and Particularities* gives readers a series of puzzles based on Rowling's series to solve. Clive Gifford's *So You Think You Know Harry Potter?* has more than 1,000 trivia questions concerning the first four novels, *The Ultimate Unofficial Trivia Book: Secrets, Mysteries, and Fun Facts Including Half-Blood Prince (Book 6)* by Daniel Lawrence explores the first six novels in the series, and *The Unauthorized Harry Potter Quiz Book: 165 Questions Ranging from the Sorcerer's Stone to the Deathly Hallows* by Graeme Davis includes questions about every book in the series.

RESOURCES FOR FAMILIES AND EDUCATORS

While many Harry Potter enthusiasts provide readers with works addressing how beloved the series has become, giving them ways to make themselves feel part of the wizarding community or experts on Harry Potter's world, others also work to prove the merit of the series both to parents and professional educators.

Gina Burkart's *A Parent's Guide to Harry Potter* is based on her experiences as a mother and a Christian, offering that Rowling's books can serve as a starting point for discussing important life issues. She provides a list of strategies for parents to discuss the books with their children, with a Christian perspective as its focus. Stefan Neilson, Clara B. Allen, and Joe Hutton's *Character Education: The Legacy of the Harry Potter Novels* is geared toward both educators and parents but seems to be a better reference for families. The authors confront the reasons Rowling's series has been attacked and provide parents with strategies for discussing the novels with their children. Also a useful source for parents is Ben Buchanan's *My Year with Harry Potter: How I Discovered My Own Magical World*, which is an inspirational book for parents in that it details the way in which one child was inspired creatively and emotionally. This work serves as a motivator for younger readers as well.

The popularity of the Harry Potter series has not been lost on classrooms from elementary schools to universities. Elizabeth Schafer's *Exploring Harry Potter* is a rich resource for any educator incorporating Harry Potter into the classroom. Schafer addresses the craze over the books, includes a biography of Rowling explores common themes in the books, and discusses illustrations in the books and foreign editions, among many other topics. She includes ideas for teaching elementary students the first three Harry Potter novels, as well as a list of online resources about the series.

Scholastic Professional Books's series of *Literature Guides* to the first four Harry Potter books serve as useful resources for elementary education teachers, in particular. The resources provide brief summaries of each of the books, complemented by a set of discussion questions teachers can pose to their students. These guides also include activity suggestions that address the major themes in each of the novels. A visual resource (a classroom poster) is included with each guide, highlighting major events from the year in Harry's academic career that the guide explores.

Finally, both Eric Randall's The *Pottersaurus: 1,500 Words Harry Potter Readers Need to Know* and Sayre Van Young's *The Unofficial Harry Potter Vocabulary Builder: Learn the 3,000 Hardest Words from All Seven Books and Enjoy the Series More* provide resources that encourage students both to build their vocabulary and to understand the contexts in which difficult words from the series appear.

WORKS CITED AND FURTHER READING

Abanes, Richard. *Harry Potter and the Bible: The Menace behind the Magick.* Bountiful, Utah: Horizon Books, 2001.

————. *Harry Potter, Narnia, and the Lord of the Rings: What You Need to Know about Fantasy Books and Movies.* Eugene, Oreg.: Harvest House, 2005.

Adler, Bill. *Kids' Letters to Harry Potter from Around the World.* New York: Carroll & Graf, 2001.

Agarwal, Nikita, and Chitra Agarwal. *Friends and Foes of Harry Potter: Names Decoded.* Parker, Colo.: Outskirts Press, 2005.

Anelli, Melissa. *Harry, a History: The True Story of a Boy Wizard, His Fans, and Life Inside the Harry Potter Phenomenon.* New York: Pocket Books, 2008.

Batchler, Janet Scott. *What Will Harry Do? The Unofficial Guide to Payoffs and Possibilities in Deathly Hallows.* Morrisville, N.C.: Lulu, 2006.

Beahm, George. *Fact, Fiction, and Folklore in Harry Potter's World: An Unofficial Guide.* Charlottesville, Va.: Hampton Roads, 2005.

————. *Magic for Muggles: An Unofficial Guide to J. K. Rowling and the Harry Potter Phenomenon.* Charlottesville, Va.: Hampton Roads, 2004.

Berner, Amy, Orson Scott Card, and Joyce Millman. *The Great Snape Debate.* Dallas, Tex.: Benbella Books, 2007.

Boyle, Fionna. *An Unofficial Muggle's Guide to the Wizarding World: Exploring the Harry Potter Universe.* Toronto, Canada: ECW Press, 2004.

Bridger, Francis. *A Charmed Life: The Spirituality of Potterworld.* New York: Doubleday, 2002.

Brown, Karen. *Prejudice in Harry Potter's World.* College Station, Tex.: Virtualbookworm.com, 2008.

Brown, Nancy Carpentier. *The Mystery of Harry Potter: A Catholic Family Guide.* Huntington, Ind.: Our Sunday Visitor, 2007.

Buchanan, Ben. *My Year with Harry Potter: How I Discovered My Own Magical World.* Brooklyn, N.Y.: Lantern Books, 2001.

Burkart, Gina. *A Parent's Guide to Harry Potter.* Downers Grove, Ill.: InterVarsity Press, 2005.

CasaBianca, Louis. *Defogging the Future: Unauthorized Speculation about the Seventh and Final Book of the Harry Potter Series.* Santa Monica, Calif.: Flydiver Press, 2006.

Colbert, David. *The Hidden Myths in Harry Potter.* New York: St. Martin's Press, 2004.

————. *The Magical Worlds of Harry Potter: A Treasury of Myths, Legends and Fascinating Facts.* New York: Berkley Books, 2001.

Dalton, Russell W. *Faith Journey through Fantasy Lands: A Christian Dialogue with Harry Potter, Star Wars, and the Lord of the Rings.* Minneapolis, Minn.: Augsburg Books, 2003.

Davis, Graeme. *The Unauthorized Harry Potter Quiz Book: 165 Questions Ranging from the Sorcerer's Stone to the Deathly Hallows.* Ann Arbor, Mich.: Nimble Books, 2008.

Dickerson, Matthew, and David L. O'Hara. *From Homer to Harry Potter: A Handbook of Myth and Fantasy.* Ada, Mich.: Brazos Press, 2006.

Duriez, Colin. *Field Guide to Harry Potter.* Downers Grove, Ill.: InterVarsity Press, 2007.

Eccleshare, Julia. *A Study of the Harry Potter Novels.* London: Continuum International Publishing Group, 2002.

Gifford, Clive. *So You Think You Know Harry Potter?* London: Hodder Children's Books, 2003.

Granger, John. *The Deathly Hallows Lectures: The Hogwarts Professor Explains the Final Harry Potter Adventure.* Allentown, Pa.: Zossima Press, 2008.

————. *The Hidden Key to Harry Potter: Understanding the Meaning, Genius, and Popularity of Joanne Rowling's Harry Potter Novels.* Allentown, Pa.: Zossima Press, 2002.

————. *Looking for God in Harry Potter.* Goodyear, Ariz.: Salt River Press, 2004.

————. *Unlocking Harry Potter: Five Keys for the Serious Reader.* Allentown, Pa.: Zossima Press, 2007.

Granger, John, ed. *Who Killed Albus Dumbledore?* Allentown, Pa.: Zossima Press, 2006.

Hansel, Alison. *Charmed Knits: Projects for Fans of Harry Potter.* Hoboken, N.J.: Wiley, 2007.

Highfield, Roger. *The Science of Harry Potter: How Magic Really Works.* New York: Penguin Books, 2002.

Houghton, John. *A Closer Look at Harry Potter.* Chester, England: Kingsway, 2001.

————. *The Harry Potter Effect.* Chester, England: Kingsway, 2007.

Kern, Edmund. *The Wisdom of Harry Potter: What Our Favorite Hero Teaches Us about Moral Choices.* 2d ed. Amherst, N.Y.: Prometheus Books, 2008.

Killinger, John. *God, the Devil, and Harry Potter: A Christian Minister's Defense of the Beloved Novels.* New York: St. Martin's Griffin, 2004.

Kronzek, Alan Zola, and Elizabeth Kronzek. *The Sorcerer's Companion: A Guide to the Magical World of Harry Potter.* 2d ed. New York: Broadway Books, 2004.

Krulwich, Dov. *Harry Potter and the Torah.* Morrisville, N.C.: Lulu, 2007.

Lackey, Mercedes, and Leah Wilson, eds. *Mapping the World of Harry Potter: Science Fiction and Fantasy Authors Explore the Bestselling Fantasy Series of All Time.* Dallas, Tex.: Benbella Books, 2005.

Langford, David. *The End of Harry Potter?* New York: Tor Books, 2007.

Lawrence, Daniel. *The Ultimate Unofficial Trivia Book: Secrets, Mysteries, and Fun Facts Including Half-Blood Prince (Book 6).* Bloomington, Ind.: iUniverse, 2005.

Lesoway, Marie. *The Definitive Harry Potter Guidebook Series.* Edmonton, Canada: Suggitt Group, 2001.

Literature Guide: Harry Potter and the Chamber of Secrets. Scholastic Professional Books. New York: Scholastic, 2000.

Literature Guide: Harry Potter and the Goblet of Fire. Scholastic Professional Books. New York: Scholastic, 2000.

Literature Guide: Harry Potter and the Prisoner of Azkaban. Scholastic Professional Books. New York: Scholastic, 2000.

Literature Guide: Harry Potter and the Sorcerer's Stone. Scholastic Professional Books. New York: Scholastic, 2000.

Maltese, Racheline. *The Book of Harry Potter Trifles, Trivia, and Particularities.* New York: Sterling & Ross, 2007.

Markell, Kathryn, and Marc Markell. *The Children Who Lived: Using Harry Potter and Other Fictional Characters to Help Grieving Children and Other Adolescents.* New York: Routledge, 2008.

Morris, Tom. *If Harry Potter Ran General Electric: Leadership Wisdom from the World of Wizards.* New York: Doubleday Business, 2006.

Mulholland, Neil, ed. *The Psychology of Harry Potter: An Unauthorized Examination of the Boy Who Lived.* Dallas, Tex.: Benbella Books, 2007.

Neal, Connie. *The Gospel According to Harry Potter: The Spiritual Journey of the World's Greatest Seeker.* Louisville, Ky.: Westminster John Knox Press, 2008.

———. *What's a Christian to Do with Harry Potter?* Colorado Springs, Colo.: WaterBrook Press, 2001.

———. *Wizards, Wardrobes, and Wookiees: Navigating Good and Evil in Harry Potter, Narnia, and Star Wars.* Nottingham, England: IVP Books, 2007.

Neilson, Stefan, Clara B. Allen, and Joe Hutton. *Character Education: The Legacy of the Harry Potter Novels: A Critical Review and Guide to Character Education for Parents and Educators.* Seattle, Wash.: Financial and Personal Success, 2001.

Neumann, Iver B., and Daniel H. Nexon. *Harry Potter and International Relations.* Lanham, Md.: Rowman and Littlefield, 2006.

Pyne, Erin. *A Fandom of Magical Proportions: An Unauthorized History of the Harry Potter Phenomenon.* Ann Arbor, Mich.: Nimble Books, 2007.

Randall, Eric. The *Pottersaurus: 1,500 Words Harry Potter Readers Need to Know.* Houston, Tex.: Pinewood Press, 2007.

Riphouse, Acascias. *The Harry Potter Companion.* College Station, Tex.: Virtualbookworm, 2004.

Schafer, Elizabeth D. *Exploring Harry Potter.* Osprey, Fla.: Beacham, 2000.

Schoen, Ben, Emerson Spartz, Andy Gordon, Gretchen Stull, and Jamie Lawrence. *Mugglenet. Com's What Will Happen in Harry Potter 7: Who Lives, Who Dies, Who Falls in Love and How Will the Adventure Finally End?* Berkeley, Calif.: Ulysses Press, 2006.

Stouffer, Tere. *The Idiot's Guide to the World of Harry Potter.* New York: Penguin, 2007.

Swinsinski, Anthony M. *Harry Potter! The Best Websites.* Port Orchard, Wash.: Lightning Rod, 2005.

Thomas, Scott. *The Making of the Potterverse: A Month-by-Month Look at Harry's First Ten Years.* Toronto, Canada: ECW Press, 2007.

Trevarthen, Geo. *The Seeker's Guide to Harry Potter.* Hampshire, England: O Books, 2008.

Vander Ark, Steven. *The Lexicon: An Unauthorized Guide to Harry Potter Fiction and Related Materials.* Muskegon, Mich.: RDR Books, 2009.

Van Young, Sayre. *The Unofficial Harry Potter Vocabulary Builder: Learn the 3,000 Hardest Words from All Seven Books and Enjoy the Series More.* Berkeley, Calif.: Ulysses Press, 2008.

Villaluz, Nancy Solon. *Does Harry Potter Tickle Sleeping Dragons?* Seattle, Wash.: Ramance Press, 2008.

Waters, Galadriel. *The Plot Thickens . . . Harry Potter Investigated by Fans for Fans.* Niles, Ill.: Wizarding World Press, 2004.

Waters, Galadriel, and Astre Mithrandir. *Ultimate Unofficial Guide to the Mysteries of Harry Potter: Analysis of Books 1–4.* Niles, Ill.: Wizarding World Press, 2002.

Waters, Galadriel, Astre Mithrandir, and E. L. Fossa. *Ultimate Unofficial Guide to the Mysteries of Harry Potter: Analysis of Book 5.* Niles, Ill.: Wizarding World Press, 2005.

———, Astre Mithrandir, and E. L. Fossa. *Ultimate Unofficial Guide to the Mysteries of Harry Potter: Analysis of Book 6.* Niles, Ill.: Wizarding World Press, 2007.

Zimmerman, W. Frederick. *Unauthorized Harry Potter and the Deathly Hallows News: Harry Potter Deathly Hallows and Half-Blood Prince Analysis.* Ann Arbor, Mich.: Nimble Books, 2005.

MINOR WORKS

Fantastic Beasts and Where to Find Them
(2001)

Rowling wrote this volume to appear as a textbook one might purchase in Diagon Alley. It is a textbook that, as one of the first pages proves, belongs to Harry Potter himself. *Fantastic Beasts* was produced as a companion to her other textbook, *Quidditch through the Ages*. These volumes were written for the charity Comic Relief, of which Rowling has always been fond and supportive.

Much like *Quidditch through the Ages*, this text is full of personal and humorous annotations from characters, including Harry, Hermione, and Ron; the foreword is written by Dumbledore, who acknowledges the significance that *Fantastic Beasts* is finally being made available to the Muggle community.

Newton "Newt" Artemis Fido Scamander is the fictional author of the text. According to the details Rowling provides, Scamander was known in the wizarding community before the publication of this book because of his creation of the Werewolf Register and a Ban of Experimental Breeding. Scamander received the Order of Merlin, Second Class, for his work in the field concerning magical beasts: magizoology.

In the introduction Scamander describes conducting his research by traveling the world and visiting all types of terrain, from bogs to mountains to caves. Scamander explains that the first edition of *Fantastic Beasts* was commissioned in 1918 and that now the text appears in its 52nd edition. The introduction also includes the topics "What Is a Beast?" "A Brief History of Muggle Awareness of Fantastic Beasts," "Magical Beasts in Hiding," and "Why Magizoology Matters."

In the section "Magical Beasts in Hiding" Scamander discusses how fantastic beasts have been protected from Muggles and how Muggles have also been protected from magical beasts. Beasts are sometimes placed in "safe habitats" protected by Muggle-Repelling Charms. Some of these habitats are also under constant watch by wizards because of the dangerous creatures kept there, such as dragons in their colonies. There are also strict laws about illegal breeding and selling of fantastic beasts; these provisions have reduced the number of beasts Muggles may accidentally encounter. Disillusionment Charms are also required by wizards who take their beasts, such as hippogriffs, out in public, to prevent Muggles from seeing them. Memory Charms are another way of responding to Muggles who see a fantastic beast. Obliviators from the Ministry of Magic modify the Muggle's memory so the sight of the beast is forgotten. In very difficult incidents that involve Muggles and beasts the Office of Misinformation is required to become involved; in such cases, members of the Ministry of Magic speak with the Muggle prime minister to develop a plausible explanation for the encounter with the beast or beasts.

Before delving into the encyclopedia of fantastic creatures, Scamander also explains the Ministry of Magic (M.O.M.) classifications for the beasts. The ratings applied to every magical creature denote how dangerous a creature is; the ratings range between one and five X's. The ranking of X's is explained as follows: X means a creature is boring; XX signifies that the creature is harmless and may be domesticated; XXX means that the creature can be handled by a competent wizard; if a creature receives a rating of XXXX, it is dangerous, it requires specialist knowledge, and only a skilled wizard may handle it. If a creature receives a rating of XXXXX, the creature is a known wizard killer and is impossible to train or domesticate.

The final and largest section of the book is called "An A–Z of Fantastic Beasts." An entry for a given creature is structured in a specific manner: Scamander supplies the scientific name of the beast along with other names the beast might be known by (sometimes accompanied by a picture), the M.O.M. rating, and then a description of its habits and history of its existence. The descriptions are very thorough and, in some cases, even include footnotes. For instance, the entry on centaurs has a footnote further explaining their M.O.M. rating of XXXX: "The centaur is given an XXXX classification not because it is unduly aggressive, but because it should be treated with great respect. The same applies to merpeople and unicorns"(6).

The catalog of beasts includes, but is not limited to, Acromantulas, basilisks, centaurs, demiguises, dragons, fairies, Flobberworms, gnomes, hippogriffs, leprechauns, manticores, Mooncalves, Nifflers, phoenixes, sphinxes, trolls, and winged horses.

Quidditch through the Ages (2001)

Meant to be an authentic book from the Hogwarts library and one of two volumes Rowling published in 2001, *Quidditch through the Ages* is a slim companion volume to *Fantastic Beasts and Where to Find Them;* both were written by Rowling as part of a fund-raising effort for Comic Relief. The proceeds from the two volumes were donated to charity projects funded by Harry's Books. On the back cover of the book Rowling explains in "About Comic Relief: A Note from J. K. Rowling" that funding supports "the education of children, the fight against child slavery, and the reuniting of parents and children separated by war." From these textbooks readers are also able to determine the ratio between Muggle and wizarding money as the back cover indicates that $3.99 is equivalent to "14 sickles and three knuts." In *Quidditch through the Ages* Rowling adopts the persona of Albus Dumbledore in the foreword, describing the book as a "popular title in the Hogwarts school library," and the persona of the magical historian Kennilworthy Whisp for the rest of the book, which is, as its title suggests, a history of the magical sport of Quidditch.

Most of the book provides a historical perspective on the game and its evolution. The first two chapters describe the history of brooms as a form of magical transportation and the history of broom games, various Quidditch predecessors. Whisp reviews Swedish broom races, as well as Irish, German, and Scottish games such as "shuntbumps." Chapter 3, "The Game from Quidditch Marsh," uses 11th-century diary excerpts from Gerdee Keddle to relate an eyewitness account of an early form of Quidditch. Also in this chapter is a letter from a century later using forms of contemporary Quidditch terms, suggesting the game had adapted to something like its contemporary structure, minus the Golden Snitch.

Chapter 4 accounts for the introduction of the Golden Snitch to the game; it was based on an adaptation from an early use of a small, agile bird called the "Golden Snidget." Since the bird used in early forms of the game was usually killed at the end and was feared to have become extinct, thus ruining the sport, more humane approaches prevailed, and a bewitched metal ball serving a similar purpose soon came into use in the mid-14th century. Whisp also notes in chapter 5 the evolution and increasingly stronger emphasis placed on "anti-Muggle security" as the game became more formalized.

"Changes in Quidditch since the Fourteenth Century," chapter 6, accounts for the more minor but important game changes that have refined the sport in the last six centuries. Whisp describes the pitch, balls, players, rules, and referees and some of the changes over time, including the replacement of baskets with hoops and the different roles of the keepers, beaters, and chasers. This chapter also includes a chart of common "fouls" in the game, of which there are more than 700.

Whisp examines the current state of Quidditch in chapters 7 through 10: "Teams of Britain and Ireland," "The Spread of Quidditch Worldwide," "The Development of the Racing Broom," and "Quidditch Today." Whisp notes the establishment of the British and Irish leagues in 1674 and gives brief histories of the 13 member teams including their distinctive maneuvers and notable accomplishments. Chapter 8 discusses notable teams around the globe—Asia, North Africa, Australia and New Zealand, South America, and Europe and how Quidditch has fared in each area. Chapter 9 outlines the various broom-making companies and a brief history of their contributions to the racing broom market, while the final chapter defines Quidditch moves such as the "Wronski Feint" and their origins. Readers can appreciate the minor details Rowling includes in this textbook since, for example, Muggle security measures, types of brooms, and Quidditch moves such as the "Wronski Feint" are mentioned in the series but not always explained comprehensively.

Readers interested in this wizarding sport will find details not available to them in the Harry Potter novels; further, comments and drawings from Hogwarts "student readers" add an element of humor to the work. For instance, the book includes a log of who has checked out the book, and unsurprisingly the names of Harry, Ron, and even Hermione appear. Readers are also privy to Harry and Ron's scribbled comments and exchanges over great Quidditch players and matches, further emphasizing their enthusiasm for the sport.

The Tales of Beedle the Bard
(2008)

First mentioned in the final book of the Harry Potter series, *Deathly Hallows, The Tales of Beedle the Bard* is bequeathed to Hermione in Dumbledore's will. The book proves invaluable to Harry, Ron, and Hermione during their quest to find Voldemort's Horcruxes and finally defeat the evil wizard.

After finishing the series, Rowling announced that she had written yet another book (related directly to Harry and his experiences). Rowling handwrote and illustrated seven copies of *Tales of Beedle the Bard,* which contained five stories: "The Wizard and the Hopping Pot," "The Fountain of Fair Fortune," "The Warlock's Hairy Heart," "Babbitty Rabbitty and Her Cackling Stump," and "The Tale of the Three Brothers." The last story helped Harry unlock the mystery of the Deathly Hallows in the final novel.

Rowling gave six of the seven handwritten copies to "those most closely connected to the *Harry Potter* books" and auctioned off the seventh copy at Sotheby's in London on December 13, 2007, to raise money for CHILDREN'S VOICE CHARITY, of which she is one of the founders. The winning bidders, art dealers of Hazlitt, Gooden, and Fox, paid £1.95 million for the work. They purchased the book on behalf of Amazon.com, which at first only posted some images of the work online out of respect of Rowling's rights. They kept the work private (except for taking it on tour to schools throughout Britain to the delight of many children) until 2008, when

Rowling authorized the publication of several versions of *The Tales of Beedle the Bard.* One version was released at bookstores around the world just as the other Harry Potter novels had been. The other version, a special collector's edition, is a replica of the seven handmade copies Rowling distributed to those key in making the Harry Potter series a success (with leather binding and a jeweled cover) and sold for a much steeper price (with the proceeds going to the CHILDREN'S HIGH LEVEL GROUP).

"The Wizard and the Hopping Pot" is the story of a wizard who has a magical pot that will brew any potion to aid someone in need. The wizard is generous and helps all those who ask. When the wizard dies, he leaves the pot to his son, with a shoe inside it. The son becomes angry that all his father left him was a pot with a shoe inside it. When people go to him for help, he ignores them all, and strange things happen to the pot: It grows a foot and later takes on the traits of a donkey. When he learns to be generous and use the pot to make potions that will assist his neighbors, the pot becomes calm. The wizard puts the shoe on the pot's foot, and they walk off together.

"The Fountain of Fair Fortune" tells the story of three witches on their way to a magic fountain, which, supposedly, will solve a problem for each of them. On their way the witches find solutions to their own problems. They travel to the fountain and realize their troubles have been addressed but remain ignorant of the fact that they solved their problems themselves, and the fountain had nothing to do with their success.

The third story, "The Warlock's Hairy Heart," tells the tale of a wizard who uses dark magic so that he never falls in love. When he is older and hears people gossiping about him, he decides to find a bride of whom everyone will be jealous. When a witch agrees to go to his house for dinner, she says she would love him if she knew he had a heart. The wizard takes her to the dungeon and shows the witch his heart, beating in a case. He puts the heart back inside himself and the witch hugs him. Later the wizard and witch are found dead in his dungeon.

"Babbitty Rabbitty and Her Cackling Stump" chronicles the story of a king who wants to be the only one able to do magic: He rounds up everyone who knows how to do magic in order to learn to do magic himself. The person who says he might teach the king magic is a fraud and turns to Babbitty, a woman who performs magic and who lives in a nearby cottage. The fraud says she must secretly help the king perform magic so that the king may save face in front of his people and so that the fraud's inability to do magic will not be discovered. If Babbitty does not comply, the fraud will reveal her to the authorities. When something goes awry during the performance, Babbitty runs off into the forest. Other adventures ensue in which the fraud is exposed and the king learns to regret his behavior, and at the end a rabbit jumps out of a tree stump, holding a wand between its teeth (it is assumed to be Babbitty).

The final story in *Tales of Beedle the Bard* is "The Tale of the Three Brothers," which also appears in *Harry Potter and the Deathly Hallows*. The story is about the adventure shared by three brothers who outsmart death. Death appears and grants them each a wish, and only the youngest brother asks for something that will impede death from finding him. The other brothers die while the youngest lives a full, long, and happy life, only succumbing to death when he chooses to do so.

Nonfiction Work

Since rocketing to fame as a fiction writer in the late 1990s, J. K. Rowling has published only a few nonfiction pieces in a variety of sources, including introductory essays to collections, a review, and a commencement speech.

One of the earliest pieces Rowling published in a medium other than a fictional novel was "A Good Scare," printed in *Time* and later published in other periodicals. It addressed the question posed to her by an interviewer, "what she thinks children should know about good and evil, magic and mayhem. Why did her series take a dark turn in this year's *Harry Potter and the Goblet of Fire?*" In the informal remarks published, Rowling discusses the moral obligations of a writer who chooses to "write about evil" to do so in a way that is vivid and accurate.

She describes reading the books to her daughter and the discussions that can emerge from her literary exploration of the seductive power of evil. Rowling also reinforces her opposition to censorship and asserts, "I don't think there's any subject matter that can't be explored in literature."

Reinforcing Rowling's admiration for the British writer JESSICA MITFORD, she published a review in the *Daily Telegraph* (London) in November 2006 of the newly released collection of Mitford's letters, *Decca: The Letters of Jessica Mitford*, edited by Peter Y. Sussman. Rowling begins the review, entitled "The First It Girl," with an admission of her own admiration for Mitford, one that she has spoken of in interviews many times before. The review highlights what the new book provides for readers beyond Mitford's own two autobiographies, and Rowling identifies specific examples of the way the collection "sing[s] with the qualities that first made her so attractive to me" and praises Sussman's "masterly job of editing" the letters, acknowledging that one footnote was able to "illuminat[e] at least one relationship that had eluded me through 27 years of reading about the Mitfords." Her only critique is the ordering of the letters in such a way that readers learn details of Mitford's husband's death prior to the love letters that captured their romance.

Several collections of essays and stories feature prefatory remarks by Rowling, including *Moving Britain Forward*, by Gordon Brown; *Magic*, edited by Gil McNeil and Sarah Brown; and *Harry: A History*, by Melissa Anelli. Consistent with the charity work Rowling has made her cause—through the organization currently known as GINGERBREAD but previously known as the National Council for One Parent Families—Rowling published a brief nonfiction piece in *Moving Britain Forward: Selected Speeches 1997–2006*, a collection of the speeches of Prime Minister Gordon Brown. Prefacing the section "Ending Child Poverty," which details Brown's political philosophy regarding the issue, Rowling describes her first meeting with Brown and offers reflections on her personal experience as a lone parent. She contrasts Brown's policies with those of the administration of John Major, who "stereotyped us as feckless teenagers who were 'married to the state' and whose children had been conceived as a means to secure a council flat'" (223). She praises Brown's refreshing attitude toward combating poverty as a "problem to be solved, not a well-merited punishment for failure to conform to some government-sanctioned ideal of family life" (223). Rowling passionately argues that poverty "is a bad place to live on your own, but the worst place on earth if you have a child with you" (224). Noting that poverty stifles creativity and talent and is the cause of numerous social problems, Rowling's short preface praises Brown's forward-thinking attitude through inclusion of a quotation from Brown, "We must never forget that poverty—above all the children of poverty—disfigures not just the lives of the poor, but all our society" (224).

Rowling wrote the foreword to *Magic*, a collection of stories "by some of Britain's most talented and acclaimed writers. It guarantees to immerse you in wondrous tales of all descriptions" (Brown 7). Rowling agreed to serve as ambassador for the Magic Million Appeal for the National Council for One Parent Families and in that role penned the foreword to *Magic*; Rowling explains that the "proceeds from the sale of this book will go towards the charity's Magic Million Appeal, whose funds help maintain the broad range of services offered to lone parents who want nothing more than to pull themselves out of the poverty trap while bringing up happy, well-adjusted children" (5). Rowling reflects on her experiences as a lone parent living in poverty and how she was "swamped with anger at the portrayal of single mothers by certain politicians and newspapers as feckless teenagers in search of the Holy Grail, the council flat, when 97 per cent of us [single mothers] have long since left our teens" (4). Rowling applauds those who purchase *Magic*, informing them that in purchasing the book, they "[offer] hope to families who are too often scapegoated rather than supported—families who could do with a lot less Dursleyish stigmatism, and a little more magic in their lives" (6).

Rowling rarely seems to approve of or participate in work by fans in the Harry Potter community. Her writing the foreword to *Harry, A History*, proves an exception. Rowling calls this book "a history of a

community" (xii), a community about which she knew very little until first searching "Harry Potter" on the Internet in 2002 (x). After repeatedly being asked why the Harry Potter series was so successful, Rowling realized that if she "tried to find this formula everyone was talking about [to make a successful book series], [she] would become self-conscious, start 'doing' J. K. Rowling rather than being her" (x). She adds that she avoided learning about Harry Potter fan activity for "self-protective" reasons (x).

When Rowling finally did peruse the Internet and began learning about the online Harry Potter community, she said that she was particularly impressed by the "professional" appearance of several of the Web sites, the Leaky Cauldron among them (for which Melissa Anelli, the book's author, serves as Web master) (xi). Rowling praises Anelli's thoughtful and thorough chronicling of the rise of Harry, particularly in the online world, and feels thankful for *Harry: A History*: "At long last I understand what was going on while I was holed up writing, trying to filter my exposure to Potter hysteria" (xi).

Another work of nonfiction that was widely publicized is Rowling's 2008 commencement address at Harvard's graduation. In "The Fringe Benefits of Failure, and the Importance of Imagination," delivered on June 5, 2008, at Harvard University, Rowling detailed the important decisions she made as a young college student, particularly her decision to major in modern languages and her relationship with her parents. Throughout the address Rowling draws upon her personal failings and successes as the source for life advice to the graduating seniors. In explaining her own life's low points as an unemployed single mother returned to England after a failed marriage, Rowling hopes to emphasize to the graduating class the value of failure in one's life, advising "[I] began to direct all my energy into finishing the only work that mattered to me. Had I really succeeded at anything else, I might never have found the determination to succeed in the one arena I believed I truly belonged." Conceding that poverty is neither "ennobling" nor to be "romanticised" and that failure is painful, she concludes this section of her address by admonishing, "You will never truly know yourself, or the strength of your relationships, until both have been tested by adversity."

The second key idea of Rowling's commencement speech is the importance of imagination, which she separates from her work as a fiction writer and discusses in a broader sense: "Imagination is not only the uniquely human capacity to envision that which is not, and therefore the fount of all invention and innovation." Rowling connects this theme with her work as a research assistant at AMNESTY INTERNATIONAL, describing some of the horrific stories about repression, violence, and brutality of which she learned during her time there. Rowling concludes that, while she learned much about human evil during that time, she also learned a great deal about human goodness and asserts that "humans can learn and understand, without having experienced. They can think themselves into other people's minds, imagine themselves into other people's places." This capacity for empathy underscores both her passion for human rights and her belief in the power of human imagination to transform social reality. In the address's conclusion she exhorts the Harvard graduating class to exercise their power of imagination and empathy to use their "status and influence to raise [their] voice on behalf of those who have no voice."

As National Public Radio reported, the speech was generally well received, though some graduating seniors felt as though Rowling's status as a children's writer (albeit the best-selling one in history) did not compare with some of the heavyweight commence-

ment speakers of years past ranging from Nobel Prize winners to heads of state. Other listeners from faculty to administrators to young children and teens (who had skipped school to hear the speech) were pleased and moved by Rowling's words.

WORKS CITED

Brown, Sarah. "Introduction." In *Magic,* edited by Sarah Brown and Gil McNeil, 7–10. London: Bloomsbury, 2002.

Rowling, J. K. "The First It Girl: J. K. Rowling Reviews *Decca: The Letters of Jessica Mitford ed. by Peter Y. Sussman.*" *Daily Telegraph.* 26 November 2006. Available online. URL: http://www.telegraph.co.uk/culture/books/3656769/The-first-It-Girl.html. Accessed September 1, 2009.

———. Foreword to *Harry: A History,* by Melissa Anelli, ix–xii. New York: Pocket, 2008.

———. Foreword to *Magic,* edited by Gil McNeil and Sarah Brown, 1–6. London: Bloomsbury, 2002.

———. "The Fringe Benefits of Failure, and the Importance of Imagination." *Harvard Magazine,* 5 June 2008. Available online. URL: http://harvardmagazine.com/commencement/the-fringe-benefits-failure-the-importance-imagination. Accessed August 25, 2009.

———. "A Good Scare." *Time Canada.* 30 October 2000. MasterFILE Premier. Available online by subscription. Accessed November 5, 2009.

———. "Introduction to Ending Child Poverty." In *Moving Britain Forward: Selected Speeches 1997–2006,* by Gordon Brown, edited by Wilf Stevenson. London: Bloomsbury, 2006.

PART III

Related People, Places, and Topics

Aeschylus was a Greek playwright and one of the earliest tragedians. Rowling uses an epigraph from Aeschylus's play *The Libation Bearers* in the prefatory material to *Harry Potter and the Deathly Hallows,* in order to hint at the "sins of the fathers" themes developed around the Malfoys and the Gaunts.

Aeschylus (525 B.C.E.–456 B.C.E.)   Ancient Greek playwright often cited as the founder of the tragedy. Few of his works survive to modern times; three of them—his trilogy *The Oresteia*—contain themes that resound in Rowling's series. *The Oresteia* concerns the House of Atreus, and the second play of the trilogy, *The Libation Bearers,* chronicles how Agamemnon's children seek revenge for his murder. The sins of the father, as it is commonly said, are visited upon the heads of his children. Such is the case in *The Libation Bearers,* as well as novels

in Rowling's own series. Significantly in the prefatory material of *Deathly Hallows,* Rowling includes a quotation from *The Libation Bearers.* The most obvious example of the tragic cycle Aeschylus describes in his play presents itself in the stories of the Malfoys and the Gaunts. Once Lucius Malfoy is imprisoned in Azkaban at the end of *Order of the Phoenix,* Draco is forced to assume a role in which he not only upholds his family honor but is punished for his father's inability to fulfill Voldemort's expectations that he orchestrate the death of Harry Potter (in *Chamber of Secrets*). Another example concerns Marvolo and Morfin Gaunt. Marvolo's pureblood fanaticism (and his outrageous behavior in supporting this belief) molds the behavior of his son Morfin, who also dies without questioning or dismissing the beliefs instilled in him by his father. Similarly Marvolo's elitist beliefs shape the destiny of his daughter, Merope, who is so tormented by her unrequited love for Tom Riddle, the Muggle neighbor, that she goes to great magical lengths to secure his love. His abandonment of her during her pregnancy ultimately shapes Tom Riddle, Jr./ Voldemort's entire life experience.

Alice's Adventures in Wonderland   See CARROLL, LEWIS

Amnesty International   Agency where Rowling found employment as a young woman. Rowling was a research assistant and bilingual translator for Amnesty International, working in PARIS, FRANCE, during part of her employment. The leading human rights organization in the world, Amnesty International describes itself as "a worldwide movement of people who campaign for internationally recognized human rights for all." The organization engages in education, research, reporting, lobbying, and demonstrations as part of its work. Rowling notes it was her "longest job," and her passion for human rights is demonstrated by both the causes to which she devotes herself, which are also important themes in the Harry Potter series. In 2008 she joined with a group of other celebrity children's authors to publish a letter in the London *Times* condemning political apathy toward the conflict in Darfur, Sudan, which has killed hundreds of thousands of Africans and left millions displaced. Rowling's social activism on behalf of children is also demonstrated by her charity, the CHILDREN'S HIGH LEVEL GROUP, which focuses on children's human rights. The author's commitment to human rights is also addressed in the Harry Potter series, primarily through Hermione Granger's tireless campaign on behalf of house-elves beginning in *Goblet of Fire* and dramatized through the character of Dobby, the house-elf introduced in *Chamber of Secrets*.

BIBLIOGRAPHY

"Rowling Adds Name to Call for Ceasefire in Darfur." *Australian*, 14 April 2008.

Arendt, Hannah (1906–1975) German-born political thinker and academic whose first major publication in the United States, *The Origins of Totalitarianism*, stirred controversy over her theories about the relationships among imperialism, anti-Semitism, and totalitarianism. On behalf of the *New Yorker* Arendt covered the trial of Adolf Eichmann, a top bureaucrat in the Nazi regime during the Holocaust; from this work emerged her book *Eichmann in Jerusalem: A Report on the Banality of Evil*. Arendt's philosophy is sometimes compared with Rowling's portrayal of the two sorts of "evil" in her series—the malicious, unredeeming hatred of Death Eaters and Voldemort and the institutional and bureaucratic pettiness of figures such as Dolores Umbridge, Cornelius Fudge, and Barty Crouch.

Austen, Jane (1775–1817) Considered by some critics to be the best woman writer in the English language, Jane Austen is also one of Rowling's favorite writers. Westman notes that Rowling claims to read Austen's novels in rotation each year. Like Rowling, Austen began writing when she was very young (Austen was only 12). Austen had an uncanny knack for capturing the dynamics of romantic relationships; this is one of the reasons she is so popular and commercially successful today. Similarly readers delight in Rowling's depiction of romantic entanglements— specifically the blossoming romances between Ron and Hermione and Ginny and Harry.

Rowling imitates Austen in yet another way. Austen, known for her subversive humor and portrayal of Regency-era England, expertly targeted members of society deserving of satire, such as the impossibly boring clergyman Mr. Collins. Likewise many of Rowling's critics wonder whether the former English prime minister MARGARET THATCHER serves as Rowling's satirical target in the character of Dolores Umbridge.

awards, Harry Potter books Rowling's Harry Potter series has been championed by critics and readers alike and has received scores of awards. *Sorcerer's Stone* won the following awards: *Parenting* Book of the Year Award 1998, the *School Library Journal* Best Book of 1998, New York Public Library Best Book of the Year 1998, the FCBG (Federation of Children's Book Groups) Children's Book Award

Writing at the turn of the 19th century, British novelist Jane Austen, like Rowling, delighted in subversive humor, subtle social critiques, and the pitfalls of romance.

for 1997, the Birmingham Cable Children's Book Award for 1997, Whitaker's Platinum Book Award in 2001, the Sheffield Children's Book Award for 1998, the Young Telegraph Paperback of the Year for 1998, the 1997 Gold Medal Smarties Prize, the 1997 National Book Award, and one of *Publishers Weekly* Best Book of 1998 awards. The book was also chosen as an ALA (American Library Association) Notable Book.

Chamber of Secrets won a plethora of awards, including the following: the Whitaker's Platinum Book Award in 2001, the Smarties Book Prize for 1998, the Bookseller's Association/Bookseller Author of the Year Award in 1998, the Scottish Arts Council Children's Book Award in 1999, the North East Scotland Book Award of 1998, the FCBG Children's Book of the Year Award in 1998, and the British Book Awards 1998 Children's Book of the Year Award.

The third novel in the series, *Prisoner of Azkaban,* also won several prestigious awards, including the Smarties Book Prize for 1999, the Whitbread Children's Book of the Year for 1999, the Whitaker's Platinum Book of the Year in 2001, an FCBG Children's Book of the Year Award for 1999, and the British Book Awards Author of the Year for 1999.

Goblet of Fire's awards include Whitaker's Platinum Book Award of 2001, the Scottish Arts Book Council Award in 2001, and the Hugo Award. *Half-Blood Prince* won the British Book Award's Book of the Year in 2006, and *Deathly Hallows* won *Newsweek*'s Best Book of the Year Award in 2007.

BIBLIOGRAPHY

Galaxy British Book Awards. "Book People Outstanding Achievement Award." Publishing News. Available online. URL: http://www.publishingnews.co.uk/bba/pnbb_shortlist_lifetimea.asp#1. Accessed November 22, 2009.

awards, Rowling Rowling herself has won a number of awards for her charitable work and her contributions to children's and adult literacy. In 2003 Rowling was awarded the Prince of Austria's Concord Prize, with a cash prize of 50,000 euros ($58,500). The award "recognizes scientific, technical, cultural, social, and humanistic work performed by individuals, groups or institutions worldwide" ("Rowling donates"). The novelist donated her prize to the International Reading Association's Developing Countries fund. In 2008 Rowling received the Book People Outstanding Achievement Award, which "recognises an enduringly popular author whose books have made an outstanding contribution to contemporary literature" (Galaxy). The award was presented to Rowling by the British prime minister Gordon Brown.

In 2009 Rowling was awarded the Edinburgh Award for her outstanding contributions to the city, both in her writing and her philanthropy. In accepting the award, Rowling commented "Edinburgh is very much home for me and is the place where Harry evolved over seven books and many, many hours of writing in its cafes. . . . So much has happened to me both professionally and personally since I moved here nearly 15 years ago, that to receive this recognition is particularly meaningful and special" ("*Harry Potter* Author").

Perhaps Rowling's biggest honor to date has been receiving the French Legion of Honor, awarded for outstanding civil or military conduct. The award was bestowed by the French president Nicolas Sarkozy and is the second Legion of Honor awarded within Rowling's family, as her great-grandfather received it in 1924 for battlefield courage. Rowling thanked the French people for the honor, apologizing for her poor accent and for conferring on her villain, Voldemort, a French name, though, as she explained, "I needed a name that evokes both power and exoticism" (Keaten).

Rowling has also received several honorary degrees, including a doctor *honoris causa* degree from Edinburgh University in 2004 and an honorary doctorate of laws degree from Aberdeen University in Scotland in 2006.

BIBLIOGRAPHY

"*Harry Potter* Author J. K. Rowling Honoured with Edinburgh Award." *Canadian Press,* 19 September 2008. Newspaper Source Plus. Available online by subscription. Accessed November 22, 2009.

Baum, L. Frank (1856–1919) Popular American novelist, playwright, and journalist whose most notable work is the Wizard of Oz series, made into a well-regarded film in 1939. The first Oz novel, *The Wonderful Wizard of Oz,* was met with great enthusiasm: The 10,000 copy first printing sold out in two weeks. Baum's series about the adventures of the Kansas farm girl Dorothy Gale in the make-believe (or is it?) world of Oz has drawn numerous comparisons to Rowling's Harry Potter series because of their shared audience and genre—fantasy novels for children—as well as some of their narrative conventions.

Geraldine Brennan introduced her discussion of the two series in the *Times Educational Supplement* by observing that both books were written "on the brink of a new century" and that each series is the tale of a "courageous but 'real' child who finds a gateway into the looking-glass world of magic, takes on the forces of evil and achieves a victory just decisive enough to leave the options open for a lucrative series." Both Harry and Dorothy move between their "home" worlds and their secondary, fantastic worlds. One tackles a "wicked witch" and the other an evil wizard, and both sets of novels have "crossover" between these two worlds, such as the character of Mrs. Figg, who Harry is surprised to discover is not just the decrepit baby-sitter he is left with by the Dursleys but also a Squib (a person of magical lineage who does not have magical powers). Her testimony at his trial in *Order of the Phoenix* over his use of underage magic is pivotal in securing his readmission to Hogwarts. Similarly in the film adaptation of Baum's first novel, friends and family from Kansas are "re-created" in Oz as the Scarecrow, the Wizard of Oz, the Tin Man, and the Cowardly Lion who assist Dorothy in her journey.

Both Rowling's and Baum's fantasy novels are unique entries in the children's fantasy tradition because of their employment of elements of the familiar and real world in their secondary, fantasy world. Much of the appeal of speculative fiction is the transporting of readers into entirely different worlds than those where they live. Rowling and Baum cleverly incorporate some of the familiar aspects of the real world in their fantasy worlds. As Greene and Martin note, Baum uses "cornfields . . . tin, circus balloons."

Other parallels have been drawn between the two series's thematic concerns and literary aspects, specifically their ability to be read as allegory, or an extended metaphor for some real-world concern. Baum's series has been interpreted by multiple critics as a political allegory detailing the turn-of-the-20th-century presidential campaign of William Jennings Bryan; the novel has also been read as an allegory for the political battle among agricultural interests, industrial workers, and politicians over the proposal to abandon the gold standard and back currency with both gold and silver. Each of the major characters of the Wizard of Oz series is associated, in this interpretation, with an interested party in this highly contentious 1896 public struggle. Parts of the Harry Potter series are similarly read allegorically, such as the interpretation of Dolores Umbridge's takeover of Hogwarts as critiquing the U.S. imposition of the No Child Left Behind Act on its schools or the possible modeling of Umbridge as a literary creation on MARGARET THATCHER and her conservative social policies of the 1980s.

Finally, as has Harry's, Dorothy's story has been examined in the framework of JOSEPH CAMPBELL's "monomyth," as Dorothy is an inadvertent heroine who is transported to a new realm in which she faces a series of difficult tasks including traveling to the Emerald City, gaining an audience with the Wizard, and traversing dangerous obstacles to procure the Wicked Witch of the West's broomstick. She ultimately returns to Kansas with newfound insight and appreciation for the family and community she had initially rejected.

BIBLIOGRAPHY

Brennan, Geraldine. "Harry Potter Follows the Yellow Brick Road." *Times Educational Supplement,* 19 November 1999.

Greene, David L., and Dick Martin. *The Oz Scrapbook.* New York: Random House, 1977.

BFG, The See DAHL, ROALD.

bildungsroman The term *bildungsroman* refers to a type of novel that originated in 18th- and 19th-century Germany. Sometimes called an "apprenticeship" novel, the bildungsroman focuses on the moral, social, and personal development of a central character, typically from adolescence to adulthood, particularly in response to the external environment with which the character interacts. The Harry Potter novels have sometimes been characterized as modern-day bildungsroman because they focus on the development of Harry as a character who learns to adapt to his new surroundings and embarks on a voyage of self-discovery.

The word *bildungsroman* was coined in the 1820s by the critic Karl Morgenstern. The term *Bildung* in German means "education," from the Latin word for "form," and this genre of novel has been called a "novel of formation" (Kontje 4). Though this genre is most often associated with German writers such as Goethe and his paradigmatic novel *Wilhelm Meister's Apprenticeship*, Marianne Hirsch has argued that the bildungsroman is "a European, rather than a purely German genre" (17). This argument could be illustrated by some of the most well-known novels considered to be examples of bildungsroman, including such British works as *Jane Eyre* by Charlotte Brontë and *Great Expectations* by CHARLES DICKENS and *Sentimental Education* by the French writer Gustave Flaubert. For some critics the story of Harry Potter is another entry in the bildungsroman genre. This case rests on the match between the features of the genre and the features of the Harry Potter series.

Contemporary Literary Criticism explains that a typical example of the bildungsroman centers on a "sensitive and gifted young man who encounters numerous problems and makes several false starts before he accomplishes his goals" (1). Hirsch's classic essay on the genre, "The Novel of Formation as Genre: Between Great Expectations and Lost Illusions," outlines seven qualities that define the genre, many of which Rowling's septalogy fits.

In Hirsch's model the bildungsroman focuses on one central character and his or her "growth and development within the context of a defined social order" (18), and it "aims at the formation of a *total personality*, physical, emotional, intellectual, and moral" (18). Harry's story begins with his introduction into an entirely new social order, the

wizarding world, and unfolds as he attempts to navigate this new environment and become part of it—even a leader within it. As he matures physically, he also grows intellectually through his academic study at Hogwarts, but his growth is not limited to that. Harry's moral compass evolves as he experiences new and challenging situations, whether navigating the demands of the Triwizard Tournament in *Goblet of Fire* or attacking Draco Malfoy with an untested and unknown spell in *Half-Blood Prince*. Harry learns from each of these situations and forms his moral compass with each new lesson.

For Hirsch the bildungsroman is also concerned with both the biographical and social elements of its protagonist: "Society is the novel's *antagonist* and is viewed as a school of life, a locus for experience" (18). Though Harry finds both friends and enemies within his new environment, the wizarding world, the challenges he encounters arise from within that world. Challenges Harry meets in the wizarding world besides his many confrontations with Voldemort/Tom Riddle in all his many incarnations include the iron rule of Dolores Umbridge, unraveling the complex and cryptic personality and history of his mentor Albus Dumbledore, and struggling to fight against an unjust class system and attitudes of elitism within wizardkind. Wizarding institutions such as the Ministry of Magic, and its many offices, impede Harry's progress, but from this obstruction personal growth results.

Further Hirsch argues that the bildungsroman is "a version of the quest story" (18). Harry's quest is both personal and epic: He seeks to develop a greater understanding of his identity by learning information about his parents and their lives, by understanding the history of the conflicts between the Death Eaters and the Order of the Phoenix and his role in them, and by engaging in a process of self-discovery that accompanies education. Additionally Harry's adventures become a quest of the more traditional sort as the climactic novel in the series centers on Harry's quest, along with his friends, to find the remaining Horcruxes that contain the parts of Voldemort's soul. The trio also seeks the tools that will allow them to destroy those pieces and the best way to defeat the evil forces threatening the social order.

Some critical debate centers on the Harry Potter books' privileging of plot over character development, which calls into question how effectively the books fit with Hirsch's fourth claim, that "it is the development of the selfhood that is the primary concern of the novel of formation, the events that determine the life of the individual, rather than all the events of that life" (18). Certainly it can be argued that the narrative trajectory of the books is profoundly focused on the way that the events in the plot shape Harry and his emerging identity, even though many readers cite the exciting plotline as responsible for the popularity of the books. For example, *Prisoner of Azkaban* relies heavily on a "surprise" ending and dramatic revelations such as Hermione's use of the Time-turner and Sirius's innocence, but throughout the novel Harry also develops a new confidence in his abilities as a wizard and an increased understanding of his relationship with the adults and peers in his life.

Less obvious but arguably present in Rowling's books is Hirsch's fifth assertion, that "the narrative point of view and voice, whether it be the first or the third person, is characterized by *irony* toward the inexperienced protagonist, rather than nostalgia for youth. There is always a distance between the perspective of the narrator and that of the protagonist" (18). Narrated in the third person, Harry and his readers experience the same initiation into the wizarding world, as they are both simultaneously introduced to the new environment. Similarly the distance between what Harry knows and what the narrator knows—and consequently the readers know—matches Hirsh's frame; often readers know better than Harry what his choices *should* be (such as Harry's extensive struggle in *Order of the Phoenix* to learn Occlumency and close his mind to Voldemort's intrusions) and experience a sense of frustration when Harry follows the wrong path.

Hirsh also comments on the function of the secondary characters who shape the protagonist's journey, including educators, companions, and lovers, and in this aspect Harry's story fits the mold of the bildungsroman. Educators, says Hirsh, "serve as mediators and interpreters between the two confronting forces of self and society" (18). Unquestionably the crux of Harry's story is not only his time at Hogwarts School of Witchcraft and Wizardry but also the development of his relationships with his teachers, especially Headmaster Albus Dumbledore. Dumbledore's perspicacious guidance sees Harry through his troubles with his evolving sense of self, his role in the battle with Voldemort and the Death Eaters, and his losses. Other strong educational influences in Harry's journey include Remus Lupin, who teaches him the Patronus spell that is essential to Harry's fights with the Dementors in all the novels including and after *Prisoner of Azkaban*; Minerva McGonagall serves as Harry's protector and guide throughout the series; and unbeknownst to Harry even his hostile relationship with Severus Snape eventually teaches him about loyalty, love, and service.

Also important to the protagonist of the bildungsroman are companions. Companions, according to Hirsh, "serve as reflectors on the protagonist, standing for alternative goals and achievements" (18). Harry's best friends, Hermione Granger and Ron Weasley, both serve as complements and sometimes foils to Harry's own aspirations and background. Hermione's academic successes and moral rigidity contrast with Harry's own somewhat lax approach to his schooling and his often impulsive decision making. At the same time Hermione learns from Harry's feats of derring-do that it is occasionally appropriate to break rules in the service of higher goals. Harry's other boon companion, Ron Weasley, serves a similarly important function. As a "native" of the world to which Harry is a latecomer, Ron is Harry's guide. At the same time, even though Ron seems, to Harry, to have the kind of life Harry dreams of—a loving set of parents, a sense of "belonging," a passel of siblings—Ron suffers his own set of troubles, which highlights the universal human condition. Further, through his friendship with Ron, Harry is able to work through some of the difficulties of human intimacy. For example, Harry and Ron's estrangement in *Goblet of Fire* emerges from the darker human emotions of mistrust and jealousy, and Ron's petulant abandonment of Hermione and Harry in *Deathly Hallows* helps Harry learn about forgiveness.

Finally, Hirsh notes that for the protagonist of the bildungsroman, lovers "provide the opportunity for the education of sentiment" (18). This is largely true in the Harry Potter books after *Goblet of Fire,* at which point Harry and his friends begin to experience the adolescent pangs of romantic interest. For Harry this first manifests itself with Cho Chang and then with Ginny Weasley. These two love interests fulfill their roles as educators of emotion just as Harry's teachers cultivate Harry's intellectual and moral development. In navigating his first relationship with Cho, Harry begins to understand the complex dynamics of romantic intimacy. This first relationship lays the groundwork for the more mature and long-lasting relationship that Harry develops with Ginny Weasley.

Finally, Hirsch observes that "the novel of formation is conceived as a *didactic* novel, one which educates the reader by portraying the education of the protagonist" (18). Rowling claims in interviews that though she is often compared with her fellow children's writer ROALD DAHL, her books, which avoid moralizing, are more clearly "moral" than those of Dahl, whose use of the absurd contrasts with Rowling's use of fantasy elements to contextualize the real-world concerns of her characters. Readers identify with Harry and the moral dilemmas, social challenges, and personal conflicts he experiences and learn from the challenges he navigates—successfully and unsuccessfully.

Though the Harry Potter series is not a perfect fit for the characteristics of the bildungsroman, it fits the definition of the model such that critical analysis of the books often characterizes the story line as a bildungsroman.

BIBLIOGRAPHY

Hirsch, Marianne. "The Novel of Formation as Genre: Between Great Expectations and Lost Illusions." *Genre* 12, no. 3 (Fall 1979): 293–311. In "The Bildungsroman in Nineteenth-Century Literature." *Nineteenth-Century Literature Criticism,* vol. 152, edited by Russel Whitaker, 1–129. Detroit, Mich.: Thomson Gale, 2005.

Kontje, Todd. "*Bildung* and the German Novel (1774–1848)." In *The German Bildungsroman: History of a National Genre.* Columbia, S.C.: Camden House, 1993. In "The Bildungsroman in Nineteenth-Century Literature." *Nineteenth-Century Literature Criticism,* vol. 152, edited by Russel Whitaker, 1–129. Detroit, Mich: Thomson Gale, 2005.

Bloomsbury Successful publishing firm based in London, England. Bloomsbury was the first to accept *Philosopher's Stone* for publication, after 12 local publishing firms rejected Rowling's manuscript.

book banning and censorship As the stories of Harry Potter became increasingly popular in Britain, in the United States, and across the globe (including their use in the public school curriculum), the numbers of legal challenges and attempts to keep the books out of schools and libraries also increased. These objections usually were led by parents, primarily on the basis of religion, though concerns over themes in the books that promoted delinquency and disobedience also arose. As early as 1999, the series topped the American Library Association's list of most-banned books from both public and private school libraries (Goldberg, "Censorship . . . Excommunicated" 17).

Some groups objected to what they viewed as an endorsement of either Satanism or witchcraft, as Barbara Comber and Helen Nixon described in 2001. Peter Denton outlined more specifically the biblical textual basis for objections to the series, including evangelical literalists who identify biblical passages that comment specifically on the sacred text's prohibition on "demonic" magical powers. Groups like the Concerned Women of America and their subgroup, the Culture and Family Institute, believe the book promotes "occult themes," and the Eagle Forum, an American "profamily," conservative group, believes the book promotes "the religion of witchcraft, or Wicca" (DeMitchell and Carney 159–160). Legal challenges have centered on whether the books promote a particular religious point of view, specifically "witchcraft" or Wiccanism. The legal case *Counts v. Cedarville School District* (2003), filed in

Arkansas, emerged from a decision by the board of education to restrict students' library access to the Harry Potter books and was challenged by a student at the school. Rejecting the two major claims—that the books promote disobedience and disruptive behavior and that they promote witchcraft/Wiccanism—the court ruled in the favor of the plaintiffs, finding that the restricted access infringed on the student's First Amendment rights (DeMitchell and Carney).

As a result of these objections, either the Harry Potter books were removed from public school and private school libraries (as well as county public libraries) or access was severely restricted. For example, in 2000 Holy Family Catholic School in Rockford, Illinois, removed the books from the school library because, as the principal stated, they presented astrology and witchcraft positively, an emphasis that is "contrary to the teachings of the Catholic church" (Goldberg, "Censorship . . . Excommunicated" 17). Schools in Michigan, Oregon, South Carolina, Colorado, Arkansas, Georgia, California, New York, and many other U.S. states faced similar legal challenges to library access to the books by parents, typically born-again Christians, who "felt the series threatened the fundamental morality of students" (Goldberg, "Censorship . . . Keeping" 21). Another parent and objector, Laura Mallory, in a Georgia case, claimed the series "teaches children and adults that witchcraft is OK for children" ("Censorship Roundup" 23). A related issue concerned public school teachers who "self-censored," that is, chose not to present the book in the classroom as a way of avoiding parent challenges.

Organizations as diverse as the American Booksellers Foundation for Free Expression, the National Coalition against Censorship, the Children's Book Council, and Americans United for Separation of Church and State have supported plaintiffs in lawsuits filed against book banning, and organizations such as the American Library Association and the Association of American Booksellers have sponsored Banned Books Week honoring as "heroes" teachers and parents who have resisted the banning of the Potter series in formal and informal ways; Mary Dana and Nancy Zennie were two such honorees for their founding of "Muggles for Harry Potter" in order to challenge restrictions on the series in the Zeeland, Michigan, case.

More extreme displays of anti-Potter activism are illustrated by book burnings, book shreddings, and book bannings that have been documented primarily but not exclusively in the United States, over the decade following the series's publication there. In 2000 and 2001 Pastor Jack Brock made headlines after orchestrating a book burning centered on the Potter series in Alamogordo, New Mexico, calling the series a "masterpiece of satanic deception" (Goldberg, "Pastor's" 19). The Reverend Douglas Taylor in Lewiston, Maine, shredded a copy of the book after being refused a permit for burning by city officials.

Potter apologists have responded to these critiques in scholarly, critical, and activist ways. Emily Griesinger's "Harry Potter and the 'Deeper Magic'" places the series in a Christian context and argues that the books are analogous to J. R. R. TOLKIEN's concept of the secondary world as a "longing for ideal worlds". She rejects the idea that supernaturalism is incompatible with Christian doctrine and texts. The widespread popularity of the series suggests that as more legal challenges are made and precedents set, the place of the series in the public school curriculum will be solidified.

BIBLIOGRAPHY

"Banned Books Week Organizers Laud Harry Potter Defenders." *American Libraries* 31, no. 10 (November 2000): 8.

"Censorship in the Cyber Age." *Reading Today* 18, no. 4 (February/March 2001): 22.

"Censorship Roundup." *School Library Journal* 52, no. 6 (June 2006): 23.

Comber, Barbara, and Helen Nixon. "The Harry Potter Phenomenon—Part 2." *Journal of Adolescent and Adult Literacy* 44, no. 8 (2001): 746–754.

DeMitchell, Todd, and Carney, John. "Harry Potter and the public school library." *Phi Delta Kappan* 87, no. 2 (2005), 159–165.

Denton, Peter. "What Could Be Wrong with Harry Potter?" *Journal of Youth Services in Libraries* 15, no. 3 (2002): 28–32.

Goldberg, Beverly. "Censorship Watch: Harry Potter Excommunicated." *American Libraries* 31, no. 9 (2000): 17.

———. "Censorship Watch: Keeping Harry Handy." *American Libraries* 31, no. 4 (April 2000): 21.

———. "Pastor's Potter Book Fire Inflames N. Mex. Town." *American Libraries* 33, no. 2 (2002): 19.

Griesinger, Emily. "Harry Potter and the 'Deeper Magic': Narrating Hope in Children's Literature." *Christianity and Literature* 51, no. 3 (2002): 455–480.

Ishizuka, Kathy. "Harry Potter Book Burning Draws Fire." *School Library Journal* 48, no. 2 (2002): 27.

———. "Pastor Shreds 'Harry Potter' Books." *School Library Journal* 49, no. 1 (2003): 22.

book dedications   Rowling's first novel in the Harry Potter series, *Sorcerer's Stone,* includes the following dedication: "For Jessica, who loves stories, for Ann, who loved them too; and for Di, who heard this one first." Jessica is Rowling's daughter (named after JESSICA MITFORD, one of Rowling's favorite writers). Ann is Rowling's mother, who passed away years before Rowling's Harry Potter stories were finally realized. Di, Rowling's sister, indeed would have heard the story of Harry Potter before, since the sisters have always been close.

The dedication for *Chamber of Secrets* reads, "For Seán P. F. Harris, getaway driver and foul-weather friend." Rumored to be the inspiration for the character of Ron Weasley, Harris is one of Rowling's closest friends. As a teenager Rowling loved escaping from her parents' home, and often Harris's car provided the means for that escape. His car, turquoise and white, serves as the model for the Ford Anglia the Weasleys fly (and similarly use to rescue Harry from his imprisonment at the Dursleys' in Little Whinging).

Rowling dedicates *Prisoner of Azkaban* to two of her closest female friends: "To Jill Prewett and Aine Kiely, the godmothers of swing." Rowling was roommates with Prewett and Kiely when she lived and taught in Portugal. She calls her friends "the godmothers of swing" because "Swing is the name of a disco that the three frequented in Oporto, looking for fun and male companionship after their classes ended for the night" (Kirk 55).

The dedication Rowling includes in the fourth novel of the series, *Goblet of Fire,* has an air of mystery to it: "To Peter Rowling, in memory of Mr. Ridley and to Susan Sladden, who helped Harry out of his cupboard." Peter Rowling is Rowling's father. Much less information exists about the true identities of Mr. Ridley and Susan Sladden. The Harry Potter Lexicon Web site has an image from the copy of *Goblet of Fire* Rowling gave to her father, and under the dedication she writes the following about Mr. Ridley: "If I had said Ronald (Weasley) Ridley, they would have tracked the poor bloke down . . . but that's why Ron's called Ron, of course!" ("Mr. Ridley"). Presumably Ridley was a friend of the Rowlings'. Susan Sladden's real identity is also unconfirmed, but in an interview with the *Washington Post* Rowling does make reference to a woman named Susan. Rowling explains that she met a woman named Susan at the church where her daughter, Jessica, was christened. During this time Rowling was a single mother. This same Susan would watch over Jessica so Rowling could have some time to herself. Susan hoped Rowling was out "kick[ing] up her heels" (Weeks), but instead Rowling relished using her time alone to write. Hence Rowling's thank you to Susan, "who helped Harry out of his cupboard"; without that time alone Rowling might never have been able to finish the first Harry Potter novel.

The dedication for *Order of the Phoenix* is for more members of Rowling's family: "To Neil, Jessica, and David, who make my world magical." Neil is Rowling's husband (Dr. Neil Murray), and Jessica and David are Rowling's children. Rowling also dedicates *Half-Blood Prince* to a family member—her newest family member—her daughter Mackenzie: "To Mackenzie, my beautiful daughter, I dedicate her ink-and-paper twin." Rowling calls *Half-Blood Prince* Mackenzie's "ink-and-paper-twin" because she was pregnant with Mackenzie while writing the novel (some fans were unreasonably disappointed to learn of Rowling's pregnancy out of fear that the publication of the sixth novel would be stalled because of it). Mackenzie was born on January 23, 2005; the novel was released on July 16, 2005.

The final novel in the series, *Deathly Hallows*, includes this dedication: "The dedication of the book is split seven ways: to Neil, to Jessica, to David, to Kenzie, to Di, to Anne, and to you, if you have stuck with Harry until the very end." Rowling honors her husband, daughters, son, sister, and mother; she also acknowledges the fans who have been dedicated to her work, and to Harry. Interestingly the text of the dedication is in the shape of a lightning bolt—a clever way for Rowling to refer to the star of her series and the scar that marked him almost his entire life. Another clever move is that her dedication is "split seven ways," a phrase that makes an important connection to the plot of the series and Voldemort's creation of seven Horcruxes, all of which Harry and his friends destroy victoriously.

BIBLIOGRAPHY

Kirk, Connie Ann. *J. K. Rowling: A Biography*. Westport, Conn.: Greenwood Press, 2003. Available online. URL: http://galenet.galegroup.com/servlet/LitCrit/cicctr/FJ3583450002. Accessed June 17, 2009.

"Mr. Ridley." The Harry Potter Lexicon. 14 August 2007. Available online. URL: http://www.hp-lexicon.org/Muggle/encyc/Muggle-r.html. Accessed October 3, 2009.

Weeks, Linton. "Charmed, I'm Sure." *Washington Post*. 20 October 1999. Available online. URL: http://www.accio-quote.org/articles/1999/1099-post-weeks.htm. Accessed October 3, 2009.

Bristol, England   City where Rowling spent most of her young life. She has been called "Bristol's Most Famous Daughter" by the British Broadcasting Corporation (BBC). Rowling lived in several towns considered part of the "Greater Bristol Area," including YATE, SOUTH GLOUCESTERSHIRE, ENGLAND (where she was born); WINTERBOURNE, SOUTH GLOUCESTERSHIRE, ENGLAND (where she and her family lived); and South Gloucestershire (where she attended St. Michael's school). She and her family moved from the area by the time she was 10 years old to TUTSHILL, ENGLAND, in Chepstow.

British boarding schools   Type of schools on which Rowling bases Hogwarts School of Witchcraft and Wizardry. Boarding schools are known for several important characteristics including the following: Students are "boarded" at the school, meaning that besides taking classes, they also take their meals at the school and sleep at the school (in dormitories or houses); students are divided into houses, and typically there is at least one head of house or dormitory; there is some type of disciplinary system in which older students—known as either prefects or monitors—help maintain order; and students spend the majority of the year at the school, going home usually only for short holidays throughout the year (or for perhaps a longer time during the summer months). Hogwarts is a boarding school because it has many of the characteristics mentioned: Students are divided into houses (each one with a head of house, such as McGonagall, Flitwick, Sprout, Snape, and Slughorn), students serve as prefects, and students spend the majority of the year at Hogwarts, sometimes remaining on campus for holidays including Christmas. These are only some of the major characteristics shared by British boarding schools.

The well-known British boarding school historian Vivian Ogilvie, in her landmark text *The English Public School*, also notes some important qualities inherent to British public schools (the equivalent of private schools in the United States). Hogwarts qualifies as a British public school (private school, in America) since students are hand-picked to attend the school: Someone not invited to attend (such as Petunia Dursley) will probably be denied permission to attend the school (again, exactly like Petunia Dursley). In *The English Public School* Ogilvie explains that a school can call itself "English" because the curriculum includes Latin and Greek; a school can call itself "public" because the institution itself is "private"; and the institution can call itself a "school" because it participates heavily in the "cult of athletics" (1). Hogwarts fits Ogilvie's definition. While readers do not witness students' taking classes simply devoted to classical languages, the spells they learn incorporate these languages, especially Latin. As discussed earlier,

Hogwarts qualifies as a "public" school because the admission to the school is carefully governed—making the access to the institution itself "private." Finally, Hogwarts can call itself a "school" because, as Ogilvie suggests, it participates in the "cult of athletics": When a Quidditch match looms in the near future, nearly every student (and professor) becomes distracted by the forthcoming match. Even McGonagall, usually reserved and academically focused, takes her Quidditch quite seriously. Hogwarts, then, fits the general picture for a British boarding school, and in turn, Rowling provides her readers with a brief snapshot of the British academic world.

BIBLIOGRAPHY

Ogilvie, Vivian. *The English Public School.* New York: Macmillan, 1957.

Campbell, Joseph (1904–1987) Authority on myth and folklore, whose use of the psychologist Carl Jung's notion of the "archetype" in his best-known work, *The Hero with a Thousand Faces,* became a touchstone for literary analysis in the last half of the 20th century. Campbell argues that the shared stories told by people across the world have a biological basis. His "monomyth" traces the commonly told heroic tale, which follows, in Campbell's estimation, a common pattern: A reluctant hero hears a call to adventure that he hesitantly accepts; the hero is given a resource or special gift by an older mentor for use in his or her journey; during his journey to a dangerous place, the hero faces literal or metaphorical demons; and in triumphing over them, he undergoes suffering. He or she takes the new insight and experience home to benefit the community.

Campbell's concept of the monomyth has often been applied to the Harry Potter series. Even a brief analysis reveals how closely Harry's story follows Campbell's structure. Though Harry is initially ecstatic to be freed from his oppressive Muggle adoptive family, he is less than ecstatic to find himself the "Boy Who Lived," the inadvertent "child of destiny" whose vanquishing of Voldemort has left him marked both literally and figuratively as the evil wizard's adversary. Throughout the series Harry finds himself repeatedly drawn into battles with evil, and he uses as a resource a number of gifts given him by his older and wise mentor, Dumbledore, including the Invisibility Cloak, Fawkes the phoenix, and the sword of Gryffindor.

BIBLIOGRAPHY

Campbell, Joseph. *Joseph Campbell: The Hero's Journey.* Edited by Phil Cousineau. Novato, Calif.: New World Library, 2003.

Carnegie Hall, New York, New York Well-known venue at which Rowling read from *Deathly Hallows* on Friday, October 19, 2007, for 1,000 contest winners and their guests. After the reading winners were allowed to ask questions, some of which led Rowling to reveal some highly important details about characters in the series. Fans were delighted to know that Neville Longbottom married the Hufflepuff Hannah Abbott, who became the landlady of the Leaky Cauldron pub. She explained that Lupin, after graduating from Hogwarts, could not find employment because he was a werewolf; in turn the Potters helped support him with their own money.

Probably the most shocking revelation of the night occurred when Rowling answered the question "Did Dumbledore, who believed in the prevailing power of love, ever fall in love?" Rowling then divulged that Dumbledore was gay and had actually been deeply in love with Grindelwald. He was attracted to Grindelwald's mind and was partly blinded by his love to the awful things Grindelwald believed in or was capable of doing. Upon her announcing Dumbledore was gay, a standing ovation, which lasted for minutes, ensued. Rowling told the crowd that had she known Dumbledore's sexual orientation would have pleased them so much, she would have told them years earlier.

Carroll, Lewis (1832–1898) English author and mathematician. Born Charles Lutwidge Dodgson on January 27, 1832, Dodgson later adopted the pen name *Lewis Carroll* and is best known for his works *Alice's Adventures in Wonderland, Through the Look-*

ing Glass, and What Alice Found There, and the poem
"Jabberwocky." In Carroll's most famous novels for
children Alice, a young girl, finds herself in "Wonderland," a world that seems built entirely on nonsense. Throughout the work Alice finds herself struggling with her size; different substances she ingests
cause her either to shrink drastically or to grow
taller than the trees. This constant shifting in size is
thought to represent Alice's development as a young
adult, and her changing size mirrors the struggles she
endures while navigating her way between the child
and adult worlds. The *Alice* stories were written to
please a friend's daughter, and while commonly considered works geared toward a youth readership, they
also appeal to adults as well because of their wordplay and logic problems. In *The Narrator's Voice: The
Dilemma of Children's Fiction*, Barbara Wall suggests
that the concept of "dual audience" (whether a narrator addresses only children, only adults, or children and adults simultaneously) began with Carroll's
Alice's Adventures in Wonderland.

Rowling's work seems influenced heavily by Carroll's. As Wonderland does for Alice, the wizarding
world presents Harry with a fantastic place wherein
he meets people and creatures who offer him guidance (though the advice he receives is, typically,
more helpful and logical than the direction Alice
is given by such characters as the Cheshire Cat or
the Mad Hatter). Both children are transported to
magical worlds in which they must learn to adapt and
survive. Harry, like Alice, finds himself weathering
trials as he shifts from a child to an adult.

Another important theme Rowling borrows from
Carroll's work is that of logic—logical reasoning
and logical fallacies. Alice finds herself in a world
where little makes sense; as a renowned mathematician Carroll enjoyed word problems and toying with
logic. For example, Alice encounters a number of
riddles in her journey through Wonderland such as
the bottles that she must drink and cakes she must
eat in order to move through various doorways or
out of houses. While Rowling seldom twists logic as
Carroll does, logic does appear in her works, notably
the infamous logic problem Hermione solves during
Harry, Ron, and Hermione's hunt for the Sorcerer's
Stone. In *Through the Looking Glass, and What Alice*

Lewis Carroll's work, *Alice's Adventures in Wonderland*,
shares many features with the Harry Potter stories,
including a "dual audience" of both adult and young
readers, the protagonist's transportation to a magical
world, and the main character's negotiation of the
transition from child to adult.

Found There the story opens with Alice's examining a mirror, wondering what lies on the other side.
This mirror motif presents itself in Rowling's work
as well: Harry becomes obsessed with the Mirror of
Erised and what he sees reflected there. Similarly in
Order of the Phoenix Sirius falls through a veil during a battle in the Department of Mysteries in the
Ministry of Magic. After he falls through the veiled
arch, Harry wonders what awaits on the other side.

As Carroll does, Rowling employs the concept
of dual audience in her works. An example of dual
audience at work in Carroll's *Alice's Adventures in
Wonderland* is the scene with the Caucus Race.
Alice and many of the creatures, soaking wet, need
to dry themselves. A Dodo suggests a Caucus Race,
during which the characters run in circles, racing,
and in the end everyone wins and receives a prize.
Child readers will find this a piece of delightful

The protagonist of *Alice's Adventures in Wonderland* shares similar challenges to the ones faced by Harry and his friends in *Harry Potter and the Sorcerer's Stone,* including bizarre chess games and logic puzzles.

nonsense, while adult readers can appreciate Carroll's satire on political practice.

A fine example of dual audience at work occurs in *Prisoner of Azkaban,* at the beginning of the novel. When Vernon Dursley sees Sirius Black's face on the Muggle news, he comments, "When will people learn . . . that hanging's the only way to deal with [criminals]?" After reading this, young readers understand that Dursley hates criminals and that he would rather they be killed, perhaps because they are dangerous. On the other hand, adult readers can appreciate Rowling's deeper message: Vernon Dursley supports the death penalty, and since the Dursleys are characters readers should dislike because of their rudeness, ignorance, and barbaric treatment of Harry, Rowling herself suggests that she does not support capital punishment.

BIBLIOGRAPHY

Wall, Barbara. *The Narrator's Voice: The Dilemma of Children's Fiction.* New York: St. Martin's, 1991.

Celtic mythology Influential mythology concerning wandlore in the Harry Potter series. The Celts valued the earth and nature highly; many trees and woods were considered sacred and symbolize various characteristics. In Rowling's series the wood of the wand almost always represents something significant about the wand owner.

Harry's wand, made out of holly, represents the "the death and rebirth symbolism of winter in both Pagan and Christian lore" (Collins). Harry's wand wood, then, is incredibly symbolic of his character since Harry does indeed die and find himself reborn during his final confrontation with Voldemort. Harry's mother, Lily, had a wand made of willow. As Collins explains, the willow is a sacred tree that people gathered around "to gain eloquence, inspiration, skills and prophecies." The characteristics of the willow align well with Lily's characteristics: She was a woman who was pleasant to everyone, she was a highly skilled witch, and of course, she served as inspiration for many—especially Harry, who consistently sees his mother in his greatest times of need (as when he feels lonely and sees her in the Mirror of Erised or when he battles Voldemort in both *Goblet of Fire* and *Deathly Hallows*). Another example of the use of Celtic mythology in the Harry Potter series concerns Draco's wand, which is made of hawthorn. According to Collins, "wands made of [hawthorn] are of great power." While Draco seems to function as more of a servant to Voldemort than a young man with the power to make all of his own choices, his wand represents, perhaps, his social standing: He is a member of the elite, and the wood his wand is made of confirms this.

BIBLIOGRAPHY

Collins, Ed. "Sacred Celtic Trees and Woods." 1999. Available online. URL: http://www.wicca.com/celtic/celtic/sactrees.htm. Accessed October 3, 2009.

Huey, Peggy. "A Basilisk, a Phoenix, and a Philosopher's Stone: Harry Potter's Myths and Legends." In *Scholarly Studies in Harry Potter: Applying Academic Methods to a Popular Text*, edited by Cynthia Whitney Hallett, 65–83. Studies in British Literature, vol. 99. Lewiston, N.Y.: Edwin Mellen Press, 2005.

Charlotte's Web   See WHITE, E. B.

Children's High Level Group   Organization cofounded by Rowling. In partnership with Baroness Nicholson of WINTERBOURNE, SOUTH GLOUCESTERSHIRE, ENGLAND, MEP (Member of the European Parliament), the organization began in 2005. Its mission is to "[work] at a political and practical level to ensure that UN minimum standards for the care of children are implemented across the whole of Europe and beyond."

Rowling was inspired to found the organization after reading an article about the treatment of mentally disabled children in the Czech Republic. The article described how the disabled children were forced to use cage beds; these beds, surrounded by wire mesh, prevented them from having any contact with other humans. They were kept in these cages most of the day. As Rowling relays on her Web site, she was especially moved, and disgusted, by the photo of a young boy trapped in one such cage. Rowling wrote letters to the MEP and Czech Republic government officials. Baroness Nicholson responded and asked Rowling to join her in her work with the Children's High Level Group; Nicholson was already doing a great deal of work to help the children of Romania, the benefits of which were many.

The Children's High Level Group (CHLG) has several initiatives already at work in Romania; the CHLG board hopes to put these initiatives into action in other countries as well. Their Community Action program educates institutionalized children about how to combat social prejudices and feel part of the community. The CHLG sponsors the Green Line, a phone line that children in need of support can call. CHLG also has helped improve care for infants and reduce the infant mortality rate in Romania through the creation and support of the Community Nurses program; these nurses are trained to educate troubled young Romanian mothers, in particular.

Children's Voice Charity   Campaign run by the CHILDREN'S HIGH LEVEL GROUP. The campaign focuses on protecting and improving the rights of primarily European children. The main missions of the Children's Voice Charity are to find adoptive or foster homes for children living in institutions and ensuring that those institutions maintain good living standards for the children waiting for homes. The proceeds from Rowling's auctioning off a copy of her work *The Tales of the Beetle Bard* went to the Children's Voice Charity. The amount was an astonishing £1,950,000.

Chipping Sodbury, South Gloucestershire, England   Town, located near BRISTOL, ENGLAND, that Rowling hails as her place of birth, even though YATE, SOUTH GLOUCESTERSHIRE, ENGLAND, is the town listed on her birth certificate. Chipping Sodbury has experienced growth because of its neighboring town of Yate, which has also seen rapid expansion since the year 2000.

Christopher Little Literary Agency   When Rowling completed her manuscript of *Philosopher's Stone*, she sent two copies of the manuscript to Christopher Little "because she like[d] his name" ("J. K. Rowling").

While Rowling was working as a French teacher in 1995, Little agreed to be her agent. Numerous publishers rejected the manuscript before it was accepted by BLOOMSBURY, a small independent British publisher. Little secured a favorable contract with the publisher, reserving Rowling's rights, giving Bloomsbury exclusive rights only in the United Kingdom, leaving Rowling free to negotiate highly lucrative contracts with foreign publishers and studios. At the time of publication of this work the agency continues to represent Rowling.

BIBLIOGRAPHY

"Christopher Little Literary Agency." Available online. URL: http://www.christopherlittle.net/. Accessed December 11, 2008

Church of Scotland   Religious institution of which Rowling is a member. Although raised an Anglican, Rowling now adheres to the Church of Scotland's practices. The church developed a program, Church without Walls, in an effort to assist people who find their relationships with Christ stifled because of an institution's structure or philosophy; the program helps spread Christ's teaching to people of all ages, ethnicities, and backgrounds. The church also participates heavily in fund-raising for human immunodeficiency virus/acquired immunodeficiency syndrome (HIV/AIDS) research. Interestingly, though many readers have decried the "Satanic" theme of magic and witchcraft in the Harry Potter series, other critics have identified strong Judeo-Christian themes in the books, as they are set in England and reflect the dominant religious affiliation of its white, Anglo-Saxon population; further, many readers consider Harry a Christ figure.

Clapham Junction, South London, England   Area located in London where Rowling rented an apartment. The location is of special importance to Rowling as it is where she began writing the Harry Potter series. Rowling explains that while she was riding the train from MANCHESTER, ENGLAND, to London, the idea of Harry and his adventures suddenly came to her. When she arrived at her apartment at Clapham Junction after the ride, she began writing immediately.

Cockcroft, Jason (unknown)   Illustrator for the British editions of *Order of the Phoenix, Half-Blood Prince,* and *Deathly Hallows.* He studied at the Falmouth School of Art. Cockcroft says his initial reaction to the news that he had been chosen to illustrate *Harry Potter and the Order of the Phoenix* was "excitement" but "then the fear kicked in" (Parr 50). Cockcroft says that he did not read any of the books for which he completed the illustrations, and instead, he "was given a very detailed brief—a description of a particular scene, with details on the appearance and expressions of characters present, the colours of the setting and clothes, and a general taste and texture of the atmosphere" (Parr 50). Cockcroft typically first

sketches his pieces in pencil, then uses acrylic paints. He considers being chosen to illustrate the final three novels in the Harry Potter series an immense honor.

BIBLIOGRAPHY

Parr, Lynn. "Designs on Harry Potter." Artists and Illustrators 2008. Available online. URL: http://www.lynnparr.co.uk/articles/jason%20cockroft.pdf. Accessed September 19, 2009.

Comic Relief   Social organization that benefited from the proceeds from the publication of Rowling's books *Fantastic Beasts and Where to Find Them* and *Quidditch through the Ages.* The organization's mission is to help establish "a just world free from poverty." Through the organization's relationship with the British Broadcasting Corporation, it promotes "positive change through entertainment." By encouraging charitable giving, the organization supports projects both in the United Kingdom and in Africa and other international locations. Rowling's charitable activities supported Comic Relief before the founding of her CHILDREN'S HIGH LEVEL GROUP with Baroness Emma Nicholson of WINTERBOURNE, SOUTH GLOUCESTERSHIRE, ENGLAND.

BIBLIOGRAPHY

"Who We Are." Comic Relief. Available online. URL: http://www.comicrelief.com/who_we_are. Accessed December 29, 2009.

Cooper, Susan (1935–)   English author of the Dark Is Rising series. The series consists of five novels published between 1965 and 1977: *Over Sea, Under Stone; The Dark Is Rising; Greenwitch; The Grey King;* and *Silver on the Tree.* The series is often read as a precursor to the Harry Potter series, not just because Cooper has authored books featuring terms Rowling adopted, such as *the boggart,* but because as a versatile British female author of fantasy novels for children, she is frequently compared to Rowling. Further Cooper, like Rowling, has been characterized as a writer in the fantasy tradition of C. S. LEWIS, J. R. R. TOLKIEN, and URSULA K. LEGUIN (whose Earthsea trilogy featuring a wizarding school draws many comparisons with Rowling). Cooper's Dark Is Rising books, as do Rowling's, employ an ordinary boy protagonist who suddenly finds himself given a special mission and role; her books also draw upon myth and folklore in creating characters, settings, and the "secondary world" her protagonist occupies.

Dahl, Roald (1916–1990) Renowned Welsh-born author, raised in England. He is best known for his fantasy works for children *Charlie and the Chocolate Factory, James and the Giant Peach,* and *Matilda.* Each of these novels features a youthful protagonist who possesses a special quality that leads to greatness. Reviews comparing Rowling's novels with Dahl's work are ubiquitous.

Dahl spent his youth in a number of private British boarding schools and in his fictional work incorporates numerous figures of oppressive and sometimes cruel adults, as does Rowling (for example, the Dursleys, many of the Death Eaters, as well as some Hogwarts teachers, including Snape). Before the 1960s Dahl was primarily a writer of short fiction for adults. Marriage and fatherhood (of five children) inspired him to pen fiction for children. His first major work of literature for children, *James and the Giant Peach* (1961), tells the story of a boy who travels in a giant peach with a motley cast of characters. *Charlie and the Chocolate Factory* traces young and penniless Charlie Bucket and his journey through the amazing candy factory of the highly secretive Willy Wonka. The title character of the eponymous novel *Matilda* is a put-upon youth whose parents do little to support her intellectual or personal growth and whose only confidante is her teacher, Miss Honey. As with many of Dahl's stories cruel or amoral adult characters are given a just punishment while the young protagonists are always vindicated.

One of Dahl's most celebrated novels, *The BFG,* chronicles the adventures of a girl named Sophie and the giant who kidnaps her. Luckily for Sophie, the BFG (Big Friendly Giant) abducts her, and the two become friends while fighting the other giants, all of whom are known for their repulsiveness and habit of eating children. The way in which Dahl manipulates the stereotype about giants, known for their meanness and brutality, appears in Rowling's work as well. Rowling reveals Hagrid's giant heritage in *Goblet of Fire,* and in turn readers learn that most giants in the wizarding world are unlike Hagrid, whose kindness and dedication to the order make him an exception from the rest of his species. As in the relationship Dahl's BFG has with Sophie, Hagrid remains kind to children and works tirelessly to protect them, especially Harry, Ron and Hermione. As British writers of fantasy novels for young readers, Dahl and Rowling are naturally compared. Though Rowling's use of magical and supernatural elements is an explicit part of the parallel world she creates in the Harry Potter series, Dahl similarly incorporates the strange and exotic into the everyday, such as the miniature Oompa Loompahs who work in Wonka's factory, Sophie's adventure with the BFG, Matilda's telekinetic powers, and James's giant traveling peach.

Rowling has in interviews acknowledged admiration for Dahl's work as well as recognized the ways that the two authors are similar, though she emphasizes that those similarities are "superficial," asserting that Dahl's characters are more cartoon-like than those found in the Potter series and that her books have a significant moral dimension that Dahl's books do not address.

Dale, Jim (1935–) Grammy Award–winning voice artist of the American versions of the Harry Potter audio books. Dale received recognition for his work with Rowling's series from the *Guinness Book of World Records* for providing the voices for 134 characters in the *Order of the Phoenix* audio book, which he later surpassed. He provides the voices for 146 characters in the audio version of *Deathly Hallows.*

Dante Alighieri (1265–1321) Italian author, best known for his literary masterpiece, the *Divine Comedy.* The first of three canticas in Dante's *Divine Comedy,* the *Inferno* is the best known. The

The structure of the Ministry of Magic and the Department of Mysteries are analogous to the nine circles of hell in *Inferno* in *The Divine Comedy,* by Dante Alighieri, pictured above.

Inferno chronicles Dante's journey through the nine circles of hell. The crimes of those trapped in hell worsen as Dante travels from the first circle to the ninth, which houses such traitors as Brutus and Cassius (who plotted to murder Julius Caesar) and Judas Iscariot (who betrayed Christ). Critics who have likened the circles of hell to the structure of the Ministry of Magic draw the parallel because some of the most mysterious and dangerous events occur deep underground, as in the Department of Mysteries. It is in this portion of the ministry where Harry and his friends must battle the ultimate traitors—Voldemort's Death Eaters—to possess the prophecy.

Dickens, Charles (1812–1870) English novelist. Widely considered to be the greatest (and most popular) novelist of the Victorian era, Dickens is well known for his novels, including *A Christmas Carol,* *Great Expectations, Bleak House, A Tale of Two Cities,* and *David Copperfield.* Rowling's character names and place-names are often referred to by critics and reviewers as "Dickensian," as they are plays on words, use onomatopoeia, or are unconventional.

Names of Dickens characters such as *Pip, Ebenezer Scrooge, Pecksniff, Chuzzlewit, Polly Toodle, Skimpole, Podsnap,* and even *Copperfield* mix words from common parlance with unique or underused words to create an effect that is sometimes comic, sometimes tragic, and sometimes merely literary. Others, such as *Pumblechook, Skiffins,* or *Wopsle* are silly-sounding inventions by Dickens. The author is also regarded for his innovative use of "type" names, or names that suggest some key feature of the character, for example, *Smallwood* in *Bleak House*

British author Charles Dickens, circa 1860. Rowling shares with Dickens a love of unique language and character names using onomatopoeia or plays on words.

or surnames such as *Sleary*, *Bounderby*, and *Sparsit* in *Hard Times*. The critic Harry Stone even claims that "names were always magical for Dickens," commenting on the author's habit of collecting names in notebooks and never settling for anything less than the perfect name.

Similarly readers often compare Rowling with Dickens because of her love of unconventional words and names that echo a distinctive aspect of a character or suggest commonly used words such as the archvillain Dolores Umbridge's surname, which resonates with the word *umbrage*, meaning "offense" or "resentment." Rowling draws upon a variety of other languages such as French in creating the names of her characters—for example, Voldemort—and shares with Dickens a similar love of the language in her creation of amusing surnames like *Shunpike* and familiar words like *Filch*.

BIBLIOGRAPHY

Harder, Kelsie. "Dickens and His List of Names." *American Name Society* 30, no. 1 (1982): 33–41.
Stoler, John. "Dickens' Use of Names in *Hard Times*." *Literary Onomastics Studies* 12 (1985): 153–164.
Stone, Harry. "What's in a Name: Fantasy and Calculation in Dickens." *Dickens Studies Annual* 14 (1985): 191–204.

Dodgson, Charles   See CARROLL, LEWIS.

Doyle, Roddy (1958–)   Irish playwright and novelist. Doyle is best known for his debut novel *The Commitments* (1988), later made into a feature film. His trilogy about the Rabbitte family has garnered critical praise for its wit, authenticity, and humor. Rowling has frequently cited Doyle as one of her major literary influences, calling him a genius and his dialogue "irreproachable." J. K. Rowling's official Web site (http://www.jkrowling.com/en/index.cfm) features a virtual bookshelf with links to her favorite causes and interests; many of her favorite authors are among the books on the shelf, including two by Doyle.

Duchess of Malfi, The   Drama by the English playwright John Webster. The play was first performed in the early 1610s and first published in

1623. As a famous playwright and contemporary of WILLIAM SHAKESPEARE, Webster would definitely have been part of Rowling's studies in literature. One of the main characters in the play, Ferdinand, supposedly suffers from lycanthropy (transforming into a werewolf). Ferdinand's lycanthropy remains one of the most famous examples of a werewolf in literature. Rowling's Remus Lupin—who is patient, kind, and usually very self-controlled—diverges significantly from lycanthropes such as Ferdinand, who are angry and violent.

Edinburgh Castle   Famous castle located in Edinburgh, Scotland. On July 16, 2005 (the release date for *Half-Blood Prince*), Rowling gave a reading from the book for a group of 70 children whose dreams included becoming professional reporters. After the reading each child was given an autographed copy of the sixth Harry Potter installment. The children were given the opportunity to read the novel in a specially designed room in the castle that mimicked Hogwarts and later attended a press conference at which they questioned Rowling about her latest work.

Edinburgh International Book Festival   One of the most famous book festivals in the world, held every August in Edinburgh, Scotland. The festival began in 1983 (occurring biennially but then annually since 1997 because of its popularity). Rowling gave a reading on August 15, 2004, from the newly released *Order of the Phoenix*. After the reading she answered questions posed by the audience and had a book signing.

Emerson, Ralph Waldo (1803–1882)   American author and philosopher. Emerson is most frequently associated with the mid-19th century American literary and philosophical movement transcendentalism; he is one of the most well-known essayists and philosophers of American letters. Rowling cites Emerson in her acknowledgment of finding her books on the list of the most banned books, posting his quotation "Every burned book enlightens the world" to punctuate her gratitude at being included among such writers as John Steinbeck, J. D. Salinger, and Mark Twain.

English folklore Rowling, famous for her creatures based often on those found in Greek mythology, also incorporates creatures famous in English folklore. Creatures such as boggarts, dragons, the grim, grindylows, hinkypunks, pixies, and red caps appear regularly in English folklore. Allan Kronzek and Elizabeth Kronzek's *The Sorcerer's Companion: A Guide to the Magical World of Harry Potter* is invaluably useful in tracing the appearances of creatures important in English myths for hundreds of years. According to the Kronzeks, "The Boggart is well known in Northern English folklore as a shape-shifting spirit that, while normally invisible, can materialize as a human, an animal, a skeleton, or even a demon" (24); they add that most boggarts simply like to cause mischief, but some can be quite dangerous. Rowling's revises the traditional role of the boggart then, by combining the characteristics of being mischievous and causing harm: All characters are glad when a boggart is locked up, but when seen, the creature transforms into the thing the viewer fears most. The Kronzeks argue that boggarts are quite stubborn; they do not simply go away. Similarly, through the use of the boggart Rowling suggests that what one fears most (which one sees when confronting a boggart) must be confronted, for the fear will not disappear otherwise.

Dragons have always been popular in the English literary tradition. The first epic in English, *Beowulf* (written between the years 700 and 1000), includes a major battle with a dragon. This dragon hoards treasure (common dragon behavior) and is roused when a human steals part of that treasure. A similar story appears in J. R. R. Tolkien's *The Hobbit*, approximately one millennium later. Dragons make frequent appearances in the Arthurian romances of the Middle Ages, and Edmund Spenser's Red Crosse knight has a famous encounter with a dragon in the first book of *The Faerie Queene*. These are only a few examples of dragons in the English literary tradition; nearly all of these dragons are known for their vicious tempers and fondness for violence. In the Harry Potter series Rowling's dragons fulfill the same role: They are dangerous creatures, to be feared. When the champions in the Triwizard

Tournament learn they will face dragons in the first task, they all experience high anxiety and worry how they will successfully survive their encounters with the vicious beasts. Rowling's own mythology asserts that dragons are some of the most dangerous magical creatures, as made clear in *Fantastic Beasts and Where to Find Them*. Rowling encourages readers to consider why dragons may behave so angrily; in *Deathly Hallows* Harry, Ron, and Hermione see a dragon who has been viciously abused by goblins while it guards the deepest vaults in the bank. Clearly the beast has been tortured; the dragon helps Harry, Ron, and Hermione escape. Rowling suggests that perhaps if treated more respectfully, dragons would be a little more friendly to humans.

Rowling also borrows the creature of the grim from preexisting English folklore. The Kronzeks explain that in British folklore grims are considered omens of death and usually only appear near churches or in graveyards: "According to English tradition, the church grim bears the heavy responsibility of protecting a graveyard" (97); grims "are usually invisible, but during stormy weather they can be seen roaming about the churchyard" (98). Rowling preserves the association that the grim functions as an omen of death (in Trelawney and most of her class's reaction to seeing the grim at the bottom of his teacup). Even though the grim is actually Sirius, Harry believes he sees the grim during the fateful and disastrous Quidditch match against Hufflepuff in *Prisoner of Azkaban*; while they play, an enormous storm rages. That is a time when, according to English folklore, one may see the grim. Besides these minor examples, readers may initially believe that Rowling revises some of the traditional myths about grims (as she did with the boggart) since they usually appear by churchyards. However, no grim actually exists in the story—the black dog readers encounter is merely Sirius. Rowling refers to an important creature in English folklore and represents it as it appears in most other folktales.

Other creatures Rowling incorporates from English folklore include grindylows and hinkypunks. Grindylows, according to the Kronzeks, fall into the category of "nursery bogies," which they define as follows: "Never really taken seriously by adults, nursery bogies have been invented to scare children away from dangerous or forbidden activities" (98–99). Since grindylows are water demons, their function may be to scare children to prevent them from standing close to water (specifically lakes) without supervision. Hinkypunks are small creatures who take delight in confusing (and usually injuring or even killing) people: With lost travelers as their targets, hinkypunks light lanterns that beckon them toward the small beasts. The hinkypunk then leads the lost soul to a place like a bog or a cliff, causing the traveler either to sink or to fall. According to the Kronzeks, "English folklore abounds with tales of travelers who wander" in wrong directions (108); perhaps these stories are so common because "so much of the English countryside is covered by marshes, bogs, and moors, which are treacherous to negotiate, particularly at night. Rather than blame the landscape itself, centuries of tradition have pointed the finger at supernatural beings" (108).

The Cornish pixies that swarm Gilderoy Lockhart's classroom in *Chamber of Secrets* also derive from English folklore. Cornish pixies "are known to help out people in need, but those who fail to do their share or forget to reward their wee helpers . . . are advised not to leave their prized possessions within reach" (Kronzek and Kronzek 190). Perhaps Lockhart should not have locked up the pixies he shared with his class; the usually friendly and helpful sprites probably gave Lockhart his comeuppance for their imprisonment. The Kronzeks also note that pixies are "quite distinctive in appearance," explaining that besides their "fiery red hair," pixies can easily be "identified by their pointed ears, turned up noses, and distinctive squint. . . . Pixies almost always dress in green and often wear a pointed cap" (190). Rowling significantly revises the appearance of the pixies in her work but still draws upon English folklore tradition by having these creatures appear in one of her novels.

The red caps Rowling mentions in the Harry Potter series also stem from English folklore. Red caps are goblins that make their homes in "the ruins of castles where bloody battles have occurred" (Kronzek and Kronzek 197). A red cap's appearance is very distinctive: "With long gray hair, fiery red eyes, and protruding teeth, the red cap might be mistaken for a very ugly old man, were it not for his distinctive red hat, which gains its color by being soaked in blood" (Kronzek and Kronzek 197). Red caps also brandish a rudimentary kind of spear that they stab people with: They do not hesitate to cause such injuries (and even murders) because "the blood of a fresh victim is just what's needed to brighten the color of [the] crimson cap" (Kronzek and Kronzek 197). Rowling's characters do not encounter red caps often, but one can clearly understand why Lupin, as professor of Defense Against the Dark Arts, saw fit to educate his students about these vicious little creatures.

Rowling's canon is distinguished by her ability to draw on and incorporate myths from various literary traditions. Instead of simply incorporating mythical creatures as they are traditionally known in English folklore, though, Rowling tends to revise either the creature's function or its appearance so the creature is still recognizable to readers familiar with English folklore but reflects Rowling's artistry and creativity. In turn she both participates in and experiments with the English folkloric traditions.

BIBLIOGRAPHY
Kronzek, Allan Zola, and Elizabeth Kronzek. *The Sorcerer's Companion: A Guide to the Magical World of Harry Potter*. New York: Broadway Books, 2001.

fan fiction Also known as fanfiction and fanfic, fan fiction is the practice of fans of a given piece of literature writing their own fiction based on the original work. Writers of fan fiction assume that their readers are already knowledgeable about the original work that serves as the fan writer's inspiration. Fan fiction writers use their fiction most typically as a means of furthering their own agendas about characters and situations from the original work. Fan fiction writers make use of many genres, ranging from songs to character sketches to lengthy stories with chapters. Fan fiction is not usually published formally in book form but commonly appears on various Internet sites (most notably, FanFiction.net). Because of their inclusion of graphic scenes (either sexual, violent, or both in nature), many fan fiction sites require writers to apply a rating, similar to that used by the Motion Picture Association (G, PG, PG-13, R, NC-17), to denote audience appropriateness.

Historically popular base material for fan fiction has included George Lucas's *Star Wars* and Gene Roddenberry's *Star Trek*. Fan fiction existed long before these series became popular, however; amateur writers have written their own continuations of classic stories for centuries. Presently, Rowling's canon supplies fans with a wealth of characters, places, and situations on which to expand in their own writing. In fact Rowling's work serves as the inspiration for many new writers to experiment with fan fiction. Rowling has been very supportive of her fans and their desire to write while using her creations as a base. She has described herself as flattered that so many writers use her work as a stimulus for their own fiction.

A subcategory of fan fiction, popular among some who write with Rowling's canon as their base, is slash fiction. The term *slash fiction* implies the existence of a romantic or sexual relationship, named for the slash (/) between the two character names indicating a romantic involvement (such as Draco/Pansy Parkinson), which is a direct comparison to the use of the ampersand (&), denoting a piece of fiction centered on two characters who are not romantically or sexually involved (such as Ron&Harry). Most recently, however, slash fiction has begun to refer specifically to fan fiction written about two male characters involved in a romantic or sexual relationship; similarly, some writers use the term *femslash* to denote fan fiction about two female characters involved in a romantic or sexual relationship.

The following is a brief summary of some of the most notable trends in fan fiction about the Harry Potter series. The most supported "ships" (short for *relationships*) include Ginny and Harry, Ron and Hermione, Harry and Hermione, Neville Longbottom and Luna Lovegood, Harry and Draco, Snape and Hermione, Hagrid and Madam Maxime, and Lupin and Sirius. Some of these relationships were dispelled by Rowling herself, including those of Neville and Luna and Harry and Hermione. Some supporters of the Harry/Hermione "ship" were infu-

riated when Rowling herself made comments that she had included quite obvious hints that Hermione and Ron would become a couple. A portion of the slash fiction involving Harry and Draco includes violent sexual encounters, often with Draco as the dominant male. Snape and Hermione "shippers" (a term referring to those who support a given relationship between characters) typically feel the two are an appropriate match for each other because Hermione's intelligence appeals to the professor; many of these shippers also think that Hermione, with her caring and nurturing ways, could offer comfort and love to the bitter older man, sometimes transforming him into a romantic interest and, in some cases, even the father of Hermione's child. Lupin/Sirius shippers support their union because the two men share a common bond as outcasts; their shared status allows them to offer comfort to each other, both emotionally and physically. A popular topic for general fan fiction on the Harry Potter series centers on the years before Voldemort murdered the Potters and tried to kill Harry. Many stories fill in the gaps from what readers know of James, Lily, and their friends while at Hogwarts. After the publication of the final book in the series, fan fiction about Snape, Lily, and James became quite popular; writers seized on the opportunity to depict Snape as they imagined him coping with the loss of Lily, first to James and then to Voldemort.

Even with the publication of *Deathly Hallows*, fan fiction still flourishes. Some fan fiction writers were frustrated by the epilogue for the seventh book, in which Rowling revealed who had married whom, who had children, and what jobs people went on to take, feeling their options for their fan fiction had been limited. Regardless, Rowling's works have inspired countless writers to experiment with and refine their own writing techniques and methods.

fantasy fiction   The Harry Potter books are generally considered examples of the literary genre of fantasy fiction, a much-theorized and broadly defined category. Influential theorists of the genre include Tzvetan Todorov, Colin Manlove, J. R. R. TOLKIEN, and Bruno Bettelheim, though many more critics have contributed arguments defining

the contours of fantasy literature. Manlove, Todorov, and other critics such as Ann Swinfen have acknowledged the debt that modern and contemporary fantasy fiction owes to older literary forms such as traditional fairy tales, myths, legends, folktales, and the early romance. In the 19th century literary works in the romantic and gothic traditions can be considered precursors to contemporary fantasy fiction. Regardless of the definition or the historical lineage, the Harry Potter books fall squarely within this genre.

No single definition of what constitutes the literary genre of fantasy seems fully to satisfy the critics and scholars who theorize about its boundaries. Many critics return to the notion of what Todorov describes as a literary creation that is occupied with or makes use of the "marvellous"; Todorov himself wrote in *The Fantastic: A Structural Approach to a Literary Genre* (1970) that, in a work of fantasy, "in a world which is indeed our world, the one we know, a world without devils, sylphides, or vampires, there occurs an event which cannot be explained by the laws of this same familiar world" (25). Readers and characters experiencing this "real" world must then find an explanation for the event that has violated the law, and thus the "fantastic occupies the duration of this uncertainty" (25). In the Todorovian sense J. K. Rowling's novels do not strictly fulfill the definition of fantasy of Todorov's model, because in Rowling's books explanations for the magical events are revealed to readers and characters simultaneously, whereas Todorov's theory proposes that fantasy novels do not clearly explain how and why events have unfolded. In Rowling's books most questions are resolved quickly—the rules of the magical world, for example—and even more enduring narrative questions such as the method that Voldemort uses to return from his incapacitated state and how the psychic link between Harry and him was formed are eventually explained to readers.

Greg Bechtel more clearly explains that for Todorov, "fantasy exists only so long as the narrative remains ambiguous as to the 'true' explanation of the portrayed events" (143). Further, one of the limitations of Todorov's structuralist approach to fantasy is that it seems primarily perhaps only concerned with works of fantasy in which events that defy explanation by natural law intrude on a real world familiar to readers and not to account for the "secondary world" model endorsed earlier in the 20th century by Tolkien in his 1939 lecture "On Fairy-Stories" (appearing in print form in 1947 and subsequently in 1966): the "fictional presentation of an internally consistent imaginative world" (Bechtel). Clyde Northrup's 2004 essay in *Modern Fiction Studies* outlines "The Qualities of a Tolkienian Fairy-Story," fleshing out Tolkien's most original contribution to fantasy theory, the notion of the "secondary world," or a created universe with its own internally consistent and logical natural laws, which is, as Swinfen notes, "the furthest removed from everyday experience". Rowling's novels seem partially to fulfill Tolkien's paradigm in that, as many reviewers and critics have observed, Rowling creates a rich, innovative, and fully imagined world that exists in parallel to the "real world" of 1990s London, England. It is not entirely considered a secondary world because of the interaction between the Muggle world and the wizarding community that occurs (often with either hilarious or tragic results) throughout the series. For other types of fantasy the critical explanations of Tolkien provide clarification and have had significant influence on subsequent theories of the fantastic. Naturally Tolkien's own series of novels in the Lord of the Rings series are examples of novels whose characters occupy the created world of Middle Earth and its adjacent realms. Lloyd Alexander's *Chronicle of Prydain* is another example of such a subgenre, as is URSULA K. LEGUIN'S Earthsea series.

Swinfen's definition is perhaps the broadest: "the sub-creative art, with its quality of strangeness and wonder, and the kind of novels which such art produces. The essential ingredient of all fantasy is the 'marvellous,' which will be regarded as anything outside the normal space-time continuum of the everyday world" (5); thus, her definition encompasses a wider range of fiction (animal fantasy, parallel worlds, secondary worlds, etc.) Works such as Richard Adams's *Watership Down*, *The Chronicles of Narnia* by C. S. LEWIS, and *The Wizard of Oz* by L. FRANK BAUM all involve elements of what has been called "animal fantasy," which, as Swinfen has claimed, "tends to be set in the primary world and also borrows more heavily from its antecedent literature" (17–18). They are all further usefully categorized as examples of what Swinfen calls "worlds in parallel," along with books like *The Phantom Tollbooth* by Norton Juster, Madeleine L'Engle's *A Wrinkle in Time,* the 1884 satire *Flatland* by Edwin Abbott, and *Charlotte Sometimes,* by Penelope Farmer. The Harry Potter stories belong to this category, as the wizarding world exists alongside the Muggle world, where a "precarious balance must be maintained between the two distinct worlds, and where the awareness of one world is constantly coloured by awareness of the other" (44). This could also be said of Phillip Pullman's His Dark Materials novels, which part way through the trilogy introduce the characters who seemingly occupy a secondary and tertiary world to the "real world" of contemporary Earth.

One of the persistent critical debates about fantasy literature since the initial theorizing has been the historical association of—indeed, accusation of—fantasy literature with juvenile readers, often prompting criticism that takes apologetics as its central project. Swinfen's study, for example, is entitled *In Defense of Fantasy.* Swinfen claims that many of the high fantasies traditionally regarded as aimed at young readers actually "operate on an adult level of meaning" (3), and Tolkien similarly claims that good fantasy literature (what he calls fairy stories) is "worthy to be written for and read by adults" (Kurtz 575). Both writers seem to be responding to early claims made by critics like Bettelheim who suggested that the moral lessons conferred by fantasy literature primarily benefit child readers (Kurtz 574). Residing on the line between "genre" fiction and "formula" fiction, fantasy literature, especially "high fantasy," often uses such recurring tropes as elves, fairies, swords and sorcery, magic, wizards, magic, quests, or Arthurian and/or medieval settings. Some literary critics associate high fantasy, then, with lack of originality because of its reliance on stock characters, settings, plotlines, or protagonists.

As such the Harry Potter books have been subject to similar accusations, with critical division over whether Rowling's books originally and uniquely draw upon multiple literary traditions and incorporate elements of myth, folklore, linguistics, and other motifs in new and inventive ways, or whether they are simply derivative and two-dimensional in their use of those motifs. Similarly, though the books were originally conceived of as targeting a youth audience, their readership grew over the 10-year span of the books' publication, with a noticeable shift after *Sorcerer's Stone* and *Chamber of Secrets* to darker, more complex themes (even simply heftier volumes produced), beginning with *Prisoner of Azkaban* and beyond.

Interestingly Rowling said in an interview with *Newsweek* that she did not "really like fantasy," or that perhaps more accurately, she had not read much of it. She admitted, "It didn't occur to me for quite a while that I was writing fantasy" (Jones).

Readers interested in a thorough but compact overview of the development of the canon of criticism on fantasy literature as a genre will want to read "Understanding and Appreciating Fantasy Literature," a bibliographic essay by Patti Kurtz, published in *Choice,* the American Library Association periodical for collection development and scholarly research.

BIBLIOGRAPHY

Bechtel, Greg. "There and Back Again: Progress in the Discourse of Todorovian, Tolkienian and Mystic Fantasy Theory." *ESC* 30, no. 4 (2004): 139–166

Jones, Malcolm. "The Woman Who Invented Harry." *Newsweek,* 17 July 2000. MasterFILE Premier. Available online by subscription. Accessed August 25, 2009.

Kurtz, Patti. "Understanding and Appreciating Fantasy Literature." *Choice* 34, no. 3 (December 2007): 571–580.

Manlove, Colin. *The Impulse of Fantasy Literature.* Kent, Ohio: Kent State University Press, 1983.

Northrup, Clyde. "The Qualities of a Tolkienian Fairy-Story." *MFS: Modern Fiction Studies* 50, no. 4 (2004): 814–837.

Swinfen, Ann. *In Defense of Fantasy: A Study of the Genre in English and American Literature since 1945.* London: Routledge, 1984.

Todorov, Tzvetan. *The Fantastic: A Structural Approach to a Literary Genre.* Translated by Richard Howard. Ithaca, N.Y.: Cornell University Press, 1970.

Flying Dutchman Ship famous in European maritime legend. The *Flying Dutchman* is a spectral ship that is fated to sail for eternity. It is usually viewed as a bad omen signaling disaster. Some critics have seen the Durmstrang ship that takes students to the Triwizard Tournament in *Harry Potter and the Goblet of Fire* as an allusion to the *Flying Dutchman* of myth and folklore.

Fry, Stephen (1957–) British entertainer who provides the voice for the British version of the Harry Potter series audio books. Fry also provides voice-overs for some video games based on Rowling's series.

Gallico, Paul (1897–1976) American novelist best known for his books *The Snow Goose, The Poseidon Adventure,* and the Mrs. Harris series. His book *Manxmouse* is cited in several interviews with Rowling as a childhood favorite of hers. She calls the book in an interview with Barnes and Noble "funny, magical . . . imaginative." It is the story of the adventures of a ceramic mouse who comes to life.

Gingerbread Organization offering assistance to single-parent families. Formerly known as the National Council for One Parent Families, the organization merged with Gingerbread and now is known simply as the latter. Gingerbread's motto reads, "Single parents, equal families." Rowling supports the Gingerbread organization in the role of president, a capacity she has served in since 2007. Rowling was an ambassador for the organization for seven years before accepting her role as president. Having been a single parent herself, Rowling can identify with and feels particularly invested in the Gingerbread organization.

The organization believes that "through working together, we can make change happen and build a fair society for all families" ("J. K. Rowling Official Site"). Gingerbread has a toll-free hotline that single parents can call for advice on issues ranging from child-care to employment to tax and welfare benefits. Knowing the distress single parents face and experience regularly, the site advises visitors, "Don't delay, call today." The site offers a wealth of links to helpful advice including "What to Do When a Relationship Ends," "Managing Your Household Bills," and "Claiming Income Support and Child Tax Credit." These resources and the organization's mission to educate the public about single parents and their struggles make Rowling proud to be Gingerbread president. She has said, "I am truly honored to be made President of [Gingerbread . . .]. It is gratifying to be a part of a charity which works so hard to support single parents at ground level, while giving them a voice in the national arena" ("J. K. Rowling Becomes President").

BIBLIOGRAPHY

"J. K. Rowling Becomes President of One Parent Families." Gingerbread. 16 November 2004. Available online. URL: http://www.gingerbread.org.uk/portal/page/portal/Website/About%20the%20charity/What%20we%20do/JK%20Rowling/JK%20Rowling%20-%20President. Accessed September 20, 2009.

J. K. Rowling Official Site. Available online. URL: http://www.jkrowling.com/textonly/en/links_parent.cfm. Accessed September 20, 2009.

Goudge, Elizabeth (1900–1984) Prolific author of books for children and adults. She is best known for her award-winning works *Green Dolphin Country* (published in the United States as *Green Dolphin Street*) and a children's novel that J. K. Rowling has repeatedly cited as one of her childhood favorites; Rowling received a copy of the 1946 novel *The Little White Horse* from her mother when Rowling was eight years old. The story of a 13-year old orphan named Maria Merryweather who journeys to mysterious Moonacre manor, *The Little White Horse* shares some narrative similarities to the Harry Potter series: Both protagonists are orphans, and both characters discover a previously unrecognized part of their identity as part of the novel's plot. Magic beasts and other elements of high fantasy are also common to the Potter series and Goudge's novel.

GrandPré, Mary (1954–) Illustrator for American editions of the Harry Potter series. GrandPré most enjoys illustrating children's books because "she can focus on a big project for a long time, using brighter colors to create larger, simpler pieces. And it allows her to indulge in her love of magic, fantasy, and whimsy" ("Meet Artist"). GrandPré's talents also shined in the film *Antz*, for which she served as part of the illustration team. GrandPré created her illustrations for Harry Potter without talking to Rowling about her ideas. The illustrator says that it was best for her not to talk to Rowling during her artistic process "Because it allows each person to do their job cleanly and clearly, I think, because they don't want too many creative visions blending and getting muddy. J. K. has her own ideas of what things look like as she writes. Then I think, as an illustrator, I kind of have to have my own idea as I read the book" ("Meet the Illustrator"). GrandPré adds that "the best part about working on Harry Potter is being invited to be connected to this really wonderful ongoing story. . . . She's just a joy to illustrate for because her writing is so rich. I'd say that's the best part of working on Harry Potter—that you have so much wonderful stuff to work with."

BIBLIOGRAPHY

"Meet Artist Mary GrandPré." Scholastic. Available online. URL: http://www.scholastic.com/harrypotter/books/illustrator/. Accessed September 2, 2009.

Greek and Roman mythology One of the most frequently praised aspects of Rowling's series is her use of a multilayered and rich mythological, folkloric, and literary tradition to create Harry's wizarding world. Rowling draws upon a number of figures and creatures from Greek mythology in creating the magical atmosphere of her books.

The Greek myth of Hercules and his 12 labors or challenges bears some relation to Harry's own struggle against the many tasks throughout the series. Hercules was half-god and half-mortal and completed the 12 labors in order to help humanity. Harry's own defeat of a number of challenges—from the traps he must navigate in *Sorcerer's Stone* to the battle with the basilisk in *Chamber of Secrets* to the navigation of the maze in *Goblet of Fire*—is undergirded by his responsibility for saving wizardkind from the evil machinations of Lord Voldemort. This hero story is also mirrored in Greek myths about Apollo.

Other mythological connections have been made between the lore and mythology of the ancient Greeks and the narrative conventions of Harry Potter. For example, like Mount Olympus, the home of the Greek gods, Hogwarts serves as a foundation for the great thinkers and sorcerers of the wizarding world. Dumbledore can be interpreted as an all-powerful but kindlier version of the king of the gods, Zeus, while Voldemort is the dark godlike force of Mars or Hades. Gilderoy Lockhart demonstrates characteristics of Narcissus, the young man who fell in love with his own reflection, and Janus, the two-faced god, is alluded to in the character of Quirrell.

Some character names are drawn from Greek myth including that of Sibyll Trelawney, who claims heritage from Cassandra, the daughter of King Priam and Queen Hecuba who was granted the gift of prophecy by Apollo; because of his unrequited love for her, he balanced the gift with the curse that no one would ever believe her predictions. This is a particularly rich backdrop for the character of Trelawney because of the frequency with which she is dismissed or considered fraudulent by other characters. Trelawney's first name echoes the mythical Sibyl, a "fortune teller who asked for eternal life but forgot to ask for eternal youth" (Schafer 138).

Originally found in Greek and then Roman literature and art, Cerberus is the three-headed dog that guards the gates of the underworld (Hades), whose purpose is to prevent the dead from crossing the river Styx back into the world of the living. Rowling draws upon the figure of Cerberus in the character "Fluffy," the three-headed dog guarding the Sorcerer's Stone in the first novel. Fluffy's responsiveness to musical entrancement is unique to Rowling; when Hercules is required as one of his 12 labors to capture the dog alive, he simply overpowers rather than enchants him.

In ancient Greek mythology centaurs are creatures that are half-man, half horse; they appear on Attic vase paintings and are often seen as occupying a marginal space between humanity and the animal world because of their hybrid status. Rowling draws upon this historical association as the centaurs in Harry Potter's world are both defined by a complicated moral structure (for example, a doctrine of noninterference with nature, the ethical consequences of spilling innocent blood) and a kind of violent brutality epitomized by their exiling of Firenze when he decides to assist humans and their attack on Dolores Umbridge at the end of *Order of the Phoenix.*

Although the phoenix originated in the mythology of continental India and Egypt, its route to widespread recognition in Western culture has been through Greek mythology. The phoenix, a mythical firebird, traditionally lived 500 years and at the end of its life cycle was regenerated from flames. It is associated with immortality and resurrection both because of its ability to regenerate from fire and the healing power of its tears. Rowling draws heavily on the phoenix mythology in the figure of Fawkes, who is friend and familiar to Headmaster Albus Dumbledore and who goes to Harry's aid more than once throughout the series. In *Chamber of Secrets* it is Fawkes whose healing tears enable Harry to continue in his fight against teenage Tom Riddle's apparition and defeat the basilisk; readers learn that the phoenix feather that is the core of Harry's wand—and Voldemort's—is from Fawkes's tail. In *Goblet of Fire* the bird's song helps gird Harry for the fight against Voldemort and gives him the strength to recount the tale to Dumbledore at the novel's end.

Less directly referenced but perhaps implied is the ancient Greek story of the minotaur, the half-ox, half-man creature that was relegated to the labyrinth built by Daedalus. The famous labyrinth is suggested by the third task of the Triwizard Tournament when the four champions must navigate treacherous traps and dangerous creatures to locate the tournament trophy. The unicorn, as well, has its origins in ancient mythology, found in Mesopotamian, Chinese, and Indian as well as Greek myths. Legend holds that by drinking from the unicorn's horn, the drinker could prevent various ailments. The unicorn becomes central to *Sorcerer's Stone* when the disembodied Voldemort who is occupying Professor Quirrell's body kills and drinks the blood of the unicorn in the Forbidden Forest.

The figure of the basilisk, popularly reused in modern fantasy film, literary works, and gaming, originates in Roman mythology. Rowling draws upon the traditional associations and mythical descriptions of the basilisk as a legendary serpent whose glance is fatal. The basilisk that is discovered to be controlled by Voldemort in *Chamber of Secrets* and that haunts the water pipes of Hogwarts fits the accounting of the basilisk by Roman naturalist Pliny the Elder, who described it in *Naturalis Historia* (Natural History) as "not above twelve fingers-breadth long: a white spot like a starre it carrieth on the head, and setteth it out like a coronet or diademe: if he but hisse once, no other serpents dare come neere." Pliny further explains, "He killeth all trees and shrubs not only that he toucheth, but that he doth breath upon also: as for grasse and hearbs, those hee sindgeth and burneth up, yea and breaketh stones in sunder: so venimous and deadly is he," revealing Rowling's preservation of the ancient associations of the basilisk as a poisonous and dangerous snake.

BIBLIOGRAPHY

Huey, Peggy. "A Basilisk, a Phoenix, and a Philosopher's Stone: Harry Potter's Myths and Legends." In *Scholarly Studies in Harry Potter: Applying Academic Methods to a Popular Text,* edited by Cynthia Whitney Hallett, 65–83. Studies in British Literature, vol. 99. Lewiston, N.Y.: Edwin Mellen Press, 2005.

Pliny the Elder. *Naturalis Historia.* Translated by Philemon Holland. 1601. Available online. URL: http://penelope.uchicago.edu/holland/pliny8.html. Accessed October 6, 2009.

Schafer, Elizabeth. *Beacham's Sourcebooks for Teaching Young Adult Fiction: Exploring Harry Potter.* Osprey, Fla.: Beacham Publishing, 2000.

Greenfield, Giles (unknown)   Illustrator for *Harry Potter and the Goblet of Fire*, published by BLOOMS-BURY. He is known for his illustrations in books for children, including the *World of Mother Goose*.

Grimm, Jacob (1785–1863) **and Wilhelm** (1786–1859)   Commonly known as the Brothers Grimm; writers of the well-known collection of fairy tales *Grimm's Fairy Tales*. The brothers Jacob and Wilhelm collected and recorded in writing fairy tales, loved by generations, in the early 1800s. Their tales include grisly murder and graphic details and do not always end happily. The brothers wrote the collection to preserve some of the Germanic heritage; they did not work explicitly to write a book that would function as entertainment. The tales have appeared in many editions, some of which have had the unpleasant details edited out. Their collection of stories remains influential and important to Rowling's work, which also shares stories about scary creatures in forests or omens of death. As the Grimms do with their admiration for their Germanic lineage, Rowling also pays homage to and preserves her British heritage in her works.

Harry Potter and the Doomspell Tournament   Working title of the fourth novel in the series, *Goblet of Fire*. As late as spring 2000, only a few months before the book's publication, the novel was being listed under its working title. In an interview with the American popular culture magazine *Entertainment Weekly*, Rowling confessed that she could not make up her mind but settled on *Goblet of Fire* instead of *Doomspell Tournament* or *Triwizard Tournament* because it had a "cup of destiny" feel.

Harry Potter and the Pillar of Storgé   *Harry Potter and the Pillar of Storgé* was a rumored title for Rowling's sixth book, *Half-Blood Prince*. Upon hearing the rumor, Rowling immediately denounced it as a hoax, commenting that she would not use *storgé* in a title, and that whoever started the rumor should "get a grip."

Hons and Rebels   Autobiography of JESSICA MITFORD, whom Rowling cites as one of her greatest influences. *Hons and Rebels* details Mitford's growing up as an aristocrat in England during the 1920s. She discusses her exploits with her sisters Nancy, Diana, Unity, and Deborah, all of whom are known for their own exploits or eccentricities, including becoming the duchess of Devonshire (Jessica) and falling madly in love with Adolf Hitler (Unity). Mitford explains how her faith in communism contributed to her status as outsider in her own family. Mitford also chronicles how she divorced herself from her family by marrying her second cousin, Esmond Romilly, causing an enormous scandal. *Hons and Rebels* showcases Mitford's political activism, the trait that, above any other, Rowling admires most about Mitford.

HP Education Fanon, Inc.   Nonprofit corporation based in Texas, that organizes a series of well-attended Harry Potter Symposia, beginning with Nimbus 2003 at Walt Disney World in Orlando, Florida, and following with the Witching Hour in Salem, Massachusetts, in 2005; Lumos 2006, in Las Vegas, Nevada; Prophecy in Ontario, Canada, in 2007; Portus in Dallas, Texas, in 2008; Azkatraz in San Francisco, California, in 2009; and in 2010, Infinitus, in Orlando, Florida, home of the World of Harry Potter Theme Park.

BIBLIOGRAPHY

"Infinitus 2010." HP Education Fanon. Available online. URL: http://www.infinitus2010.org/. Accessed December 6, 2008.

Kafka, Franz (1883–1924)   Jewish, Czech-born novelist who is widely considered to have best captured the dizzying pace and zeitgeist of modern life; in Kafka's narratives characters are alienated, disoriented, and confused, and they struggle to make sense of the often surreal and bizarre circumstances in which they find themselves. His most famous works include *The Metamorphosis*, *The Trial*, *The Hunger Artist*, and *The Penal Colony*. Some critics have drawn comparisons between Rowling's portrayal of the Ministry of Magic and Department of Mysteries in *Order of the Phoenix* and Kafka's use of the faceless, deadened bureaucracy that emerged from industrialization. In addition, the main character in *The Trial*, Josef K., finds himself being tried for an unnamed crime; similarly, a number of Rowling's characters in the latter half of the series find themselves detained or tried for noncrimes or crimes they have not committed.

Kensington, West London, England   Location of one of Rowling's homes, an extremely wealthy neighborhood. Her house in Kensington has six bedrooms and is in Earls Terrace, where the average price of a home is roughly £4.3 million.

Killiechassie House   One of Rowling's homes, located in PERTH AND KINROSS, SCOTLAND. The house ranks as one of the 100 finest homes in the country. Rowling married her husband, Neil Murray, in the house's library. She purchased the home in 2001.

Knight of the Legion of Honor   Known in France as the Légion d'honneur, the award was established by Napoleon in 1802. France's most distinguished award, it is typically reserved for those of French origin, but Rowling was granted the prestigious honor as an exception. President Nicolas Sarkozy awarded Rowling this title on February 3, 2009. Rowling (who speaks fluent French) was greatly honored and upon receiving the Knight of the Legion of Honor, apologized to the French crowd witnessing the ceremony for giving her villain Voldemort a name that, when translated from French, literally means "to fly/flee from death." She assured the crowd, who laughed with her as she explained, that she in no way meant her choice to be an insult to the French people. President Sarkozy commended Rowling for her overwhelmingly positive influence on children's reading habits.

Knowles, John   (1926–2001)   American writer best known for *A Separate Peace* (1959), a BILDUNGSROMAN chronicling the lives of the male students at an American private school during the final years of World War II. Besides the obvious connection between Knowles and Rowling as writers fond of the bildungsroman genre, both writers explore the effects of war on adolescents in a school setting. Knowles captures the lighthearted spirit of the young men at the Devon School, who seem protected from the outside world and the terror of war. Hogwarts functions as a type of haven as well, where, until *Half-Blood Prince*, students also find refuge from the war raging between Voldemort, and his followers and the rest of the wizarding community.

Tragedy eventually strikes the Devon School as well, and Gene (the main character of *A Separate Peace*) loses his best friend, Finny, who dies after a terrible accident. The novel is about Gene's reflections on his past and the experience of losing his best friend. Similarly throughout the Harry Potter series Harry thinks often of those whom he has lost in the war against Voldemort. Both Gene and Harry realize that while some of their most painful memories involve the schools they attended as boys, the experiences they had at those same schools helped them become men.

Leaky Cauldron, The   Web site about the Harry Potter universe, which Rowling has publicly praised as her favorite fan-based Web site. Found at http://www.the-leaky-cauldron.org/, the site promotes itself as "The most trusted name in Potter." Because of its careful organization and respect for Rowling and her art, the site has won awards including *Entertainment Weekly*'s "Best of the Web" and "Essential Fan Site" list, and Rowling's own prestigious award, "J. K. Rowling's Fan Site Award."

The Web site serves a diverse community of fans, appealing to visitors because of the many purposes the site serves. It diligently posts reliable information about happenings in the Harry Potter world, ranging from updates on the series's films to events Rowling sponsors. The site not only informs Potter fans but allows them to express their own creativity; subscribers can submit artwork or FAN FICTION to be posted, and the site boasts a large number of craft projects ranging from recipes to interior design to woodwork.

The site also supports several chatrooms and offers a newsletter to keep fans informed of new developments. Fans can be entertained with the wealth of activities on the site, including games and extensive quizzes. The Leaky Cauldron also sponsors a range of contests for its viewers and hosts "The Cauldron Shop," an online store at which fans can buy everything related to Harry Potter.

Possibly what makes this site so important is its educational value. Though it offers many enjoyable activities and games associated with the Harry Potter world, the site also works to teach fans about the series and encourages them to think critically about larger issues in the novels. The site's "HP 101" provides basic information about the series and was created to help educate those unfamiliar with Rowling's work.

Lee, Harper (1926–) Novelist of the American South who won the Pulitzer Prize for her best-known (and only) novel, *To Kill a Mockingbird*, considered one of the greatest novels of the 20th century. The story of a black man on trial for raping a white woman, it is narrated through the eyes of a six-year-old girl, Jean "Scout" Finch, whose attorney father is defending the accused. As a coming-of-age novel, the book has inspired parallels to the Harry Potter series because of the two protagonists' journey to maturity as they grapple with moral and human questions about prejudice and tolerance, knowledge and ignorance, racism, and social stigma.

Le Guin, Ursula (1929–) American-born science fiction and fantasy writer, Le Guin is the winner of numerous awards and one of the best-known female science fiction and fantasy writers. Le Guin has often used her fiction as a platform for tackling controversial social issues informed by her progressive feminism; works in which she addresses such issues include *Left Hand of Darkness* and *The Lathe of Heaven*, for example. Her early novels were published primarily in the 1950s after she had some difficulty finding a publisher interested in her innovative and unconventional style.

In the late 1960s she was asked by the editor of Parnassus Press to write a young adult novel, in response to which she produced the first in her popular Earthsea series, *The Wizard of Earthsea*, the story of the adventures of a young wizard named Ged. It is this set of works that Rowling finds her own novels most frequently compared with, and both Rowling and Le Guin's complex and multilayered fantasy worlds have been compared with J. R. R. TOLKIEN'S Lord of the Rings and C. S. LEWIS'S Narnia series. Five novels and a story collection make up the Earthsea oeuvre. As does Rowling, Le Guin takes on substantive themes in her young adult novels, such as virtue, courage, love, coming of age, and cosmological balance.

Though Rowling's works share many commonalities with Le Guin's, Le Guin seems to have little respect for the Harry Potter author. When Le Guin was asked to share her thoughts about the Harry Potter series, she said: "I have no great opinion of it. When so many adult critics were carrying on about the 'incredible originality' of the first Harry Potter book, I read it to find out what the fuss was about, and remained somewhat puzzled; it seemed a lively kid's fantasy crossed with a 'school novel,' good fare for its age group, but stylistically ordinary, imaginatively derivative, and ethically rather mean-spirited" ("Chronicles of Earthsea").

BIBLIOGRAPHY

"Chronicles of Earthsea." *Guardian*. 9 February 2004. Available online. URL: http://www.guardian.co.uk/ books/2004/feb/09/sciencefictionfantasyandhorror. ursulakleguin. Accessed October 3, 2009.

Lewis, C. S. (Clive Staples Lewis) (1898–1963) Ireland-born writer with training in philosophy and literary studies. Lewis is best known as the author of the Chronicles of Narnia, the seven-volume fantasy series for children imbued with Lewis's Christian vision and sometimes read as an allegory for Christ's death and resurrection (particularly the first volume, *The Lion, the Witch and the Wardrobe*). Rowling's books are frequently compared with the Narnia series because of their similar creations of "secondary worlds" in the fantasy tradition.

Lewis was a prolific writer in multiple genres— fiction, letters, philosophical treatises, religious allegories, poetry, and literary criticism. Lewis became widely known during his lifetime as a leading Christian thinker and defender of the faith, frequently giving public talks to diverse audiences. Lewis's books more clearly and substantively engage a religious worldview than Rowling's do, even though some critics read Harry Potter's world as operating out of the Judeo-Christian tradition even if they do not explicitly endorse or embrace a religious message as Lewis's do.

However, evidence that suggests that Lewis is a direct influence on Rowling as an author is mixed. According to a *Time* magazine interview with Lev Grossman, "Rowling hasn't even read all of C. S. Lewis' Narnia novels, which her books get compared to a lot. There's something about Lewis' sentimentality about children that gets on her nerves". Grossman quotes Rowling: "'There comes a point where Susan, who was the older girl, is lost to Narnia because she becomes interested in lipstick. She's become irreligious basically because she found sex,' Rowling says. 'I have a big problem with that'." Alan Jacobs, by contrast, claims in his essay in *First Things* that Rowling "has expressed her love for the Narnia books—one of the reasons there will be, God willing, seven Harry Potter books is that there are seven volumes in the Narnia series" (36).

Certainly it is verifiable that Rowling read Lewis's Narnia series as a young girl and if direct influence is not documented, indirect comparisons are frequently made not simply because of their shared use of an "alternate world" but also because of their orphan protagonists, even if Rowling's series is sometimes found wanting in "moral seriousness" in comparison with Lewis's works. Joy Farmer notes that both series use magic as a way of talking about "spiritual reality" (55). Other shared themes include mortal loss and grief, human and supernatural evil, the clash of good and evil, and religious allegory. Free will, sin, forgiveness, and temptation are among the religious questions also explored by both Lewis and Rowling, according to Farmer.

BIBLIOGRAPHY

Farmer, Joy. "The Magician's Niece: The Kinship between J. K. Rowling and C.S. Lewis." *Mythlore* 88 (Spring 2001): 53–64.

Grossman, Lev. "J. K. Rowling Hogwarts and All." *Time* (25 July 2005), 60–65. Available online. URL: http://www.time.com/time/magazine/article/0,9171,1083935-1,00.html. Accessed November 30, 2009.

Lightmaker   Private company responsible for the design, implementation, and maintenance of Rowling's personal Web site. The company is best known for its talent in making accessible, creative, and unique Adobe Flash designs. The company also designed the personal Web site of Emma Watson, who plays Hermione Granger in all the Harry Potter films.

Little White Horse, The   See GOUDGE, ELIZABETH.

Madwoman in the Attic, The   Collection of feminist literary criticism that discusses the representation of female literary characters in works by Victorian authors including JANE AUSTEN, George Eliot, and the Brontë sisters, among others. Written by the literary scholars Sandra Gilbert and Susan Gubar, the collection is considered the landmark work of second-wave feminism. The title refers to *Jane Eyre*'s Bertha Mason, Rochester's first wife, whom he keeps barricaded in the attic. The work is relevant to Rowling's series for two reasons in particular: First, as a British female writer, Rowling participates in the tradition of the writers whom Gilbert and Gubar explore. Second, perhaps in homage to Charlotte Brontë's Bertha Mason, Rowling places Trelawney—her version of the "mad woman"—in what equates to Hogwarts' attic—the top of the North Tower. As Gilbert and Gubar do, Rowling challenges her readers to consider how her female characters, such as Trelawney, are confined to certain spaces, both literally and metaphorically.

BIBLIOGRAPHY

Gilbert, Sandra, and Susan Gubar. *The Madwoman in the Attic: The Woman Writer and the Nineteenth-Century Literary Imagination.* New Haven, Conn., and London: Yale University Press, 2000.

Manchester, England Rowling lived here in the early 1990s. Rowling has described many times how after spending the weekend looking at apartments, she was stranded on a delayed train going from Manchester to London. She was suddenly struck with the idea for the Harry Potter series.

McCann, Madeleine (2003–) Madeleine McCann, a three-year-old British girl on vacation with her parents in Portugal, disappeared from the resort where she was staying with her siblings and parents in May 2007. Rowling supported the investigation by authorizing posters of the missing girl to be hung at bookstores where the seventh Potter novel was being sold in July 2007 and donated nearly a half million dollars to the reward fund. As of press time the investigation into McCann's disappearance had been shelved, after all leads have been exhausted.

BIBLIOGRAPHY

"Madeleine Case Timeline." BBC: British Broadcasting Corporation. Available online. URL: http://news.bbc.co.uk/2/hi/uk_news/7376805.stm. Accessed July 21, 2008.

Merchiston, Edinburgh Location of the apartment in which Rowling wrote the first novel in the Harry Potter series, *Sorcerer's Stone*. She faced some of her greatest hardships while living there alone with her first daughter, Jessica. The apartment remains very dear to Rowling since, as she says, it was there that she "turned her life around completely," adding that she feels she "really became [herself] there" (Houston).

BIBLIOGRAPHY

Houston, Stephen. "Rowling in Tears on Return to Harry's Lowly Birthplace." *Times* (London) (December 23, 2007). Available online. URL: http://www.timesonline.co.uk/tol/news/uk/article3087368.ece. Accessed September 2, 2009.

Mitford, Jessica (1917–1996) English author of social critique and autobiography. Mitford is best known for her scathing exposés, particularly the 1963 book *The American Way of Death* skewering the U.S. funeral industry. A collection of Mitford's investigative journalism, *Poison Penmanship: The Gentle Art of Muckraking*, was published in 1979. Rowling named her first child, her daughter Jessica, after Mitford. Rowling's admiration for the English author can be seen in the Harry Potter series's own turn toward social critique in the last four novels.

MuggleNet Web site devoted to Rowling, the Harry Potter series, and all things related to Harry Potter. The site, located at http://www.Mugglenet.com, was founded in 1999. Fans flock to MuggleNet for its many user-friendly features such as chatrooms, discussion forums, and Mugglecast, a podcast in which hosts discuss scores of topics including the illustrators of the books, debates about characters, and reactions to news about the series. The staff updates the site daily by posting news items or offering Harry Potter–related surveys and quizzes. Fans can browse thousands of pictures, visit the MuggleShop, or even submit their own art or fiction based on the series.

Multiple Sclerosis Society of Scotland Society for which Rowling remains a major donor. The effects of multiple sclerosis are many, stemming from nerve cell damage. As Rowling informs readers on her Web site, Scotland has the highest rate of multiple sclerosis, as one in 500 people suffers from the condition. Rowling's mother died of multiple sclerosis; this is a charity about which she is extremely passionate and generous. Thanks to a large donation from Rowling, complemented by donations from others, the Multiple Sclerosis Society of Scotland created a new research center. In a press release Rowling commented, "It means a great deal to me to be able to provide support for this much needed research centre. It is an extremely exciting step forward in the on-going battle to try to unlock the mysteries of MS and which will hopefully, one day, lead to a cure."

mythology See CELTIC MYTHOLOGY; ENGLISH FOLKLORE; GREEK AND ROMAN MYTHOLOGY.

Nazis Members of the Nazi Party who supported the National Socialism movement in Germany under Adolf Hitler; Hitler's dictatorship lasted from 1933 to 1945. Many readers believe that Hitler serves as a model for Voldemort and that Hitler's most dedicated and strict followers—the Schutzstaffel (which translates literally to "protection guard"), known also simply as the SS—provide models for Rowling's Death Eaters.

Before his reign as a fanatical tyrant responsible for committing the world's largest genocide, Hitler was admired by many Germans because of his commitment to socialism and later, after he was elected chancellor in 1933, his ability to rebuild the country's infrastructure. Similarly Voldemort was well liked as a boy at Hogwarts; teachers were proud of his accomplishments, and he was quite successful. Like Hitler, Tom Riddle, Jr., would become a man far different from what those who knew him earlier in life could have ever predicted. Hitler did not always have the ability to instill fear in others; once he had amassed a great deal of power, however, people were forced to bend to his will or suffer the consequences. This situation also parallels Voldemort's. During the time that Voldemort worked to transform into one of the most feared wizards of all time, he did not pose much of a threat. Once he amassed power, however, he could force almost anyone (regardless of whether the person supported him) to act as he commanded, either through fear or through force (with the use of the Imperius or Cruciatus Curse, for example).

Voldemort's Death Eaters also clearly resemble Nazis; more specifically, one might liken them to Hitler's SS, the select group of Nazis who performed some of the most heinous war crimes in world history. Bellatrix Lestrange, Voldemort's most devout and dangerous follower, bears many similarities to Heinrich Himmler, who was one of the most powerful and feared Nazis under Hitler's reign. Himmler, often considered one of the most notorious mass murderers of all time, justified his crimes with his fanatical faith in the Nazi ideology that the "master race" was constituted only of Aryans: Caucasians, typically with fair hair, fair skin, and blue or green eyes. Interestingly enough the Malfoys—who strongly support Voldemort (Lucius himself is a Death Eater)—fit the description of "perfect Aryans." As did Himmler, Bellatrix spouts her pureblood fanaticism and uses those beliefs as her justification to mock, torture, and murder those who do not share her blood status.

The information that readers learn about Gellert Grindelwald and Albus Dumbledore in *Deathly Hallows* also raises some striking similarities between these men and Hitler and his regime. Grindelwald and Dumbledore, for a time, agreed that "for the greater good" Muggles must be shown "their place" and learn to live dominated by wizardkind (a belief reflected powerfully in the Ministry of Magic fountain once the ministry falls to Voldemort's rule: the fountain bears the slogan "Magic Is Might" and shows humans underneath a wizard and witch). Though Dumbledore's fascination with Grindelwald's genocidal tendencies fades quickly, Grindelwald's thirst for power and domination strongly aligns him with Hitler. Significantly Dumbledore defeats Grindelwald in the year 1945, the same year that World War II ended. Grindelwald, as did Hitler, falls and the Allies (and the order) are victorious.

Nesbit, E. (Edith Nesbit) (1858–1924)   One of the most renowned children's authors in late 19th- and early 20th-century England. Her most famous works center on the Bastable family; other notable works include *The Wouldbegoods*, *The Treasure Seekers*, and *The Railway Children*. Nesbit is best known for the magical worlds she created for her child readers; she was an important participant in a literary tradition in which Rowling would also take part. Her works, as do Rowling's, allow readers to escape from mundane, dreary everyday life to fantastic places. Rowling has also documented her admiration for Nesbit and her fondness for Nesbit's books when she was a young reader.

Critics have commented on Nesbit's employment of the "dual audience" concept, meaning that she addressed more than one audience simultaneously in her work: both children and adults. The same holds true for Rowling: While her first few novels were geared specifically for children, the last five books (in particular) were written to appeal to children and adults. Both writers could speak to their young readers, while commenting on more serious cultural issues that adults could consider more carefully.

A useful example of dual audience in Nesbit's work centers on a character—the Pretenderette—whom some of her child characters encounter. The children in Nesbit's work realize that the Pretenderette is a woman not to be trusted; consequently, the character reflects Nesbit's own antagonistic reaction (one similar to that of some of her adult contemporaries) to the woman's suffrage movement. Similarly, when Vernon Dursley comments that the only way to handle criminals like Sirius Black (whom he hears about on the Muggle news) is to hang them, Rowling speaks to a dual audience. Child readers understand that Black is a dangerous criminal; they may not, however, appreciate the subtle comment Rowling makes about the death penalty in this instance, and that characters like the narrow-minded, selfish, greedy Dursleys are the type of people who support the death penalty.

Once and Future King, The See WHITE, T. H.

One Parent Families See GINGERBREAD.

Oresteia, The See AESCHYLUS.

orphans in literature Literary tradition most prominent in 19th-century Britain. Rowling participates in this tradition with the Harry Potter series, whose protagonist is an orphan. The tradition reflects the contemporaneous societal concerns about poverty and homeless children. Some of the most notable 19th-century British literary orphans include Jane in Charlotte Brontë's *Jane Eyre*, Heathcliff in Emily Brontë's *Wuthering Heights*, Becky in William Makepeace Thackeray's *Vanity Fair*, and characters in CHARLES DICKENS's works, including *Oliver Twist*, *Bleak House*, and *Great Expectations*.

As orphans these characters commonly feel alone in the world and become the embodiment of lone-

liness. Even when they find (as they usually do) someone who functions as their mentor or guide, the orphans ultimately must rely on themselves to survive. Though he finds a group of faithful friends (Hermione and Ron among others) and several mentors (Dumbledore and Lupin among them), Harry consistently feels he is an outcast and must confront issues of loneliness (instigated by the loss of many whom he has come to love including his parents, Sirius Black, and Dumbledore). However, like many orphans, he is not overcome by this sense of loneliness and provides readers with a sense of hope: He is a child who is determined to succeed and does.

Paris, France City where Rowling studied abroad. Rowling spent the third year of her undergraduate career at the University of Exeter in Paris: While there, she learned more about the French language (which she sought a degree in) while teaching English as a foreign language. Her biographer Connie Ann Kirk writes of Rowling's stay in Paris that Rowling "was able to sample more cultures than just French because she shared an apartment with an Italian, a Russian, and a Spaniard" (45).

BIBLIOGRAPHY

Kirk, Connie Ann. *J. K. Rowling: A Biography.* Westport, Conn.: Greenwood Press, 2003. *Literature Criticism Online.* Available online. URL: http://galenet.galegroup.com/servlet/LitCrit/cicctr/FJ3583450002. Accessed June 17, 2009.

Perth and Kinross, Scotland Location of one of Rowling's homes, KILLIECHASSIE HOUSE. The town boasts beautiful landscapes, including many walking trails and world-famous lochs. Rowling purchased her home in Perth and Kinross in 2001 and lives there with her husband and children.

Porto (Oporto), Portugal Location where Rowling taught for the English Encounter Schools. According to Rowling's biographer Connie Ann Kirk, when Rowling first interviewed for the job (which she had seen advertised in the *Guardian*), Rowling "had a rather gothic appearance . . . that

Crowds gather at a California bookstore for the much-anticipated release of *Harry Potter and the Deathly Hallows. (Photo by Zack Sheppard/Used under a Creative Commons license)*

did not make her a prime candidate for a teacher at this school" (54). Rowling met two of her greatest friends in Porto: Aine Kiely and Jill Prewett. She formed a lasting and close friendship with these women (to whom she dedicated *Prisoner of Azkaban*). In Porto Rowling taught night classes for students ranging between eight and 62 years old (Sexton 47, Kirk 55). Rowling's favorite students were the teenagers because of their passion; their interests fueled her own and eventually led to her becoming the head of the department responsible for teaching the teenage students (Kirk 55). Since she taught at night, Rowling spent most of her days writing the first Harry Potter novel. Two of Rowling's major life events also occurred in Porto: Rowling met and married her first husband Jorge Arantes and gave birth to her daughter Jessica.

BIBLIOGRAPHY

Kirk, Connie Ann. *J. K. Rowling: A Biography.* Westport, Conn.: Greenwood Press, 2003.
Sexton, Colleen. *J. K. Rowling.* Minneapolis, Minn.: Lerner, 2006.

Pottermania   Term used to explain the general and sometimes fanatical interest in the Harry Potter series. *Pottermania* serves as an umbrella term under which a wide variety of activities fall. Among the best examples of Pottermania are the release parties for the Harry Potter books, which became popular beginning with *Goblet of Fire.* Bookstores around the world stayed open or reopened at midnight the days the books went on sale. In many instances bookstores were too small to hold the number of customers waiting eagerly for the latest installment in the Harry Potter series.

Many bookstores began hosting parties the evening before the release at which fans could play Harry Potter–related games, compete in trivia tournaments, have their faces painted, have their fortunes told via a crystal ball or their tea leaves read, taste foods and drinks mentioned in the books, participate in costume contests, or even have their pictures taken with character look-alikes. To combat the problem of who would get his or her copy first, many bookstores resorted to issuing bracelets with numbers on a first-come, first-served basis. In some cases police were called in to prevent fans from lining up more than a day in advance. But whether it was London, England, or Maple Grove, Minnesota, fans waited diligently in line, sometimes for as long as 20 hours, in order to be among the first to purchase their copy of the latest Harry Potter book in their town.

Other activities associated with Pottermania are the design and maintenance of hundreds of Web sites devoted to the Harry Potter universe. Some of the sites are devoted to only one character and were created out of affection and love; others are more serious in nature, post updates regularly, and attempt to educate visitors. Among some of the most reliable, accessible, well-organized, and creative sites are The LEAKY CAULDRON, the Harry Potter Lexicon, and MUGGLENET. These sites provide a forum in which fans (whether new or highly dedicated) can join to discuss their passions, compete in trivia challenges, or learn how to knit like Molly Weasley and Hermione Granger. Some Web sites also provide podcasts, covering topics ranging from discussions on the film adaptations to debates on characters in Rowling's canon.

FAN FICTION is another important activity associated with Pottermania. Fans who write stories based on Rowling's characters and world compose fan fiction. The genres used by those who write fan fiction include both prose and poetry. Closely associated with the practice of writing fan fiction is the activity of writing songs based on the series; the music of these artists and performers is known as WIZARD ROCK, otherwise known as "wrock." Popular bands of this genre include Harry and the Potters, Draco and the Malfoys, and even the Whomping Willows. These bands are not mainstream, but they have a group of dedicated fans who sometimes follow a band's tour across a state or even across the country. These bands receive especially warm receptions at conventions centering on the Harry Potter series.

These conventions, sometimes local but often international, provide another venue for fans to gather. Some of the conventions and conferences are held merely to celebrate Rowling's art and meet fellow fans; others, however, are more serious and academic. These gatherings have become increasingly popular since the publication of *Goblet of Fire*. Two such conventions are the Witching Hour, held in 2005 in Salem, Massachusetts, and Enlightening 2007, held in Philadelphia, Pennsylvania. The Witching Hour proves a good example of an international conference on Harry Potter. The conference saw nearly 1,000 fans gather to watch the film adaptations of the books, write fan fiction or produce fan art, play Muggle Quidditch, or dress up as their favorite character from the series. There was also an academic programming track, which encouraged participation from Harry Potter scholars around the world. Lectures on how to incorporate Rowling's series into a physics course or debates on whether Snape was good or evil initiated thoughtful conversations.

Enlightening 2007 was a conference of a different nature. Hosted by the nonprofit organization Bonding over Books, the conference was designed for families; the primary mission of the conference was to encourage families to read together. As such this conference modeled itself closely on Hogwarts, and while children between five and 18 years of age attended classes, their parents and guardians attended discussions that encouraged them to appreciate the complexities of the novels and supplied them with strategies for reading and discussing them with their children. Summer academic camps, such as the Muggle and Wizarding Academy, have also been created to cater to student interest in the series; at camps like this, students work on interdisciplinary projects with fellow campers while studying traditional subjects such as mathematics, science, English, and art and the way they are presented and work in Rowling's universe.

Another activity (although not as popular because of the cost) for "Pottermaniacs" or "Pott-heads," as they are sometimes called, is traveling to Great Britain to tour the locations where the Harry Potter movies were filmed. And as a result of popular demand, a Harry Potter–themed amusement park is now open in Orlando, Florida.

Pottermania, light hearted as it may seem, has provoked a great deal of criticism. Tammy Turner-Vorbeck in her essay "Pottermania: Good, Clean Fun or Cultural Hegemony?" considers the ramifications of the Harry Potter phenomenon, paying special attention to the creation of child consumers through the mass production of items associated with the series. Turner-Vorbeck is not the only critic to question the effects of Pottermania. Stephen Brown has written about the marketing of the series and the accompanying consumerism and examined the ways Rowling herself uses images and ideas from commodity capitalism within the books—including advertising, product branding, and salesmanship.

Others feel troubled and even angry about the mania over the series, but for reasons concerning moral and ethical issues. Countless critics have attacked the series as "evil," and some (like Richard Abanes in *Harry Potter and the Bible*) suggest that Rowling uses her work as a recruitment tool to gather followers of Satan. Critics who oppose using or allowing the series in schools (or publishing it in general) tend to have concerns about whether Harry and his friends can be viewed as role models for child readers, the violence in the books, the way in which death and its repercussions are presented, the sexist and stereotypical portrayals of certain characters (women most specifically), the lack of diverse characters, the inclusion of a gay character—Dumbledore—(even though this information is never explicitly revealed in any of the novels), and the students' use of magic (the practice of which is problematic to members of several faiths, but most commonly Christian). The mania surrounding the Harry Potter series has made it an obvious target for attack; while many of the claims about the series deserve respect, consideration, and analysis, some

are made by critics who have not read the books (or have read them haphazardly), and in turn, the series is awarded even more attention, and Pottermania only escalates when devoted fans respond.

BIBLIOGRAPHY

Brown, Stephen. "Harry Potter and the Marketing Mystery: A Review and Critical Assessment of the Harry Potter Books." *Journal of Marketing* 66, no. 1 (2002): 126–130.
Turner-Vorbeck, Tammy: "Pottermania: Good, Clean Fun or Cultural Hegemony?" In *Critical Perspectives on Harry Potter*, 2d ed. [Revised and expanded version of *Harry Potter's World* (2002)], edited by Elizabeth E. Heilman, 13–24. New York: Routledge, 2008.

Potters, the   Neighbors of Rowling when she was a girl. Rowling explains she was fonder of their last name than her own. Mrs. Potter, Rowling notes, claims her son and Rowling used to pretend they were wizards. Her son has claimed to be the inspiration for Harry. Rowling has denied both of these claims.

Rank, Otto (1884–1939)   Noted Austrian psychoanalyst and close friend and colleague of Sigmund Freud. Rank's work has been used to analyze Harry Potter as a literary hero. His *Der Mythus von der Geburt des Helden (The Myth of the Birth of the Hero)* is most relevant to Rowling's series. Rank divides his work into three main sections: exploring how the myth of the hero is universal, discussing specific instances of the hero in works from a range of cultures and periods, and analyzing the patterns revealed in these heroes. Rank created a list of "hero traits," including (but not limited to) the following: The hero's parents are noble or of high stature; his birth is preceded by difficulty; a prophecy or oracle warns against his birth; he is found in some receptacle, such as a basket; he is raised by lowlings; he seeks revenge for his lost father; he is marked by some type of scar (as was Odysseus); and, finally, the hero achieves rank and honors. According to these traits Harry Potter can be classified as a hero.

RDR Books Independent publishing firm named as one of the top 100 Independent Book Publishers. The firm supported STEVE VANDER ARK's publication of the work and research conducted for his Web site the Harry Potter Lexicon. Rowling firmly protested the publication of this work. RDR's lawyers asserted that the publication of the *Lexicon* is in no way a threat to Rowling, whose own books are published and sold on an astronomical scale. RDR Books's struggle with publishing Vander Ark's *Lexicon* is supported by the Right to Write Fund, an organization sponsored by the Center for Ethics in Action. The firm eventually published the work in 2009.

Rowling, Kathleen (?–1974) Rowling's paternal grandmother. Rowling did not have an official middle name, and because she admired and loved her grandmother deeply, she chose to pay homage to her by taking her first name, *Kathleen,* and making it her own middle name, thereby creating the now-famous *J. K. Rowling.*

Runcie, James (1959–) Author and filmmaker. He made the film *J. K. Rowling . . . A Year in the Life,* which follows Rowling as she completes the last Harry Potter book, *Deathly Hallows.* The film includes rare private footage of Rowling writing the end of the seventh book, as well as the book's delivery to her agent. The film also chronicles parts of Rowling's life before she began the series and what she plans to do now that she has finished it.

St. Michael's Church of England Primary School School Rowling attended as a child. It is located in the village of WINTERBOURNE, SOUTH GLOUCESTERSHIRE, ENGLAND. The school began as a few rooms located above the George and Dragon Pub but expanded to the size of a typical school, moving to the street of Linden Close in 1970. It is rumored that Rowling's headmaster at St. Michael's, Alfred Dunn, was her inspiration for the headmaster of Hogwarts School of Witchcraft and Wizardry, Albus Dumbledore.

Scholastic Rowling's American publisher. Scholastic publishing was founded in 1920 and has been a strong force in children's educational and literary texts. Scholastic paid $105,000 for the rights to publish the American edition of *Sorcerer's Stone* and has published all seven of Rowling's Harry Potter novels.

Shakespeare, William (1564–1616) Widely acknowledged as the greatest writer in the English language, William Shakespeare is known for his plays, sonnets, and lyrical poems. Rowling references some of Shakespeare's works by assigning names to some of her characters that also appear in Shakespeare's canon. The most obvious reference is the name *Hermione;* Shakespeare's Queen Hermione appears in *The Winter's Tale* and pretends to be turned to stone, much as Rowling's Hermione is petrified in *Chamber of Secrets.* Another notable reference is the wizarding band the Weird Sisters, who perform at the Yule Ball in *Goblet of Fire;* the name refers to the three witches in *Macbeth.* The director Alfonso Cuarón capitalizes on this connection between Rowling and Shakespeare in *Prisoner of Azkaban.* The choir sings a tune with the words "Double, double, toil and trouble, fire burn and cauldron bubble; double, double, toil and trouble, something wicked this way comes," quoting *Macbeth* act 4, scene 1. Cuarón's choice to utilize this particular line from *Macbeth* is fitting since Shakespeare's play and *Prisoner of Azkaban* focus on the theme of the hunger for power. Even though Voldemort does not play a major role in the third installment in the Harry Potter series, his lust for power is closer to being attained because of Peter Pettigrew, who plays a large part in the novel and who, more significantly, assists Voldemort in returning to human form in *Goblet of Fire.*

slash fiction See FAN FICTION.

Squidward Screen name used by Rowling in chatrooms discussing theories about the Harry Potter series. Rowling did not reveal her true self but used the moniker to talk directly with fans. She offered theories on what would occur in remaining books, but chatroom participants dismissed her, to her amusement.

Taylor, Thomas (1973–) Illustrator for BLOOMSBURY's *Philosopher's Stone*. Taylor attended the Norwich School of Art and Design and continued to study illustration at Cambridge University. His artwork for the first Harry Potter novel was his first commissioned piece. Described as the artist who determined what Harry would look like, Taylor received somewhere between 200 and 300 pounds sterling for his illustration (Thorpe). According to Catherine Porter, an expert on books for children, "Taylor's preliminary pencil and watercolor drawing for the front cover of the first book, *Philosopher's Stone*, were sold at Sotheby's last year for an astonishing £85,750. . . . Porter suspects this drawing will prove the quintessential piece of Potter memorabilia, as it represents the first visual image of the bespectacled trainee wizard" (Thorpe).

BIBLIOGRAPHY

Thorpe, Vanessa. "Harry Potter Beats Austen in Sale Rooms." *Observer*. 20 January 2002. Available online. URL: http://www.guardian.co.uk/uk/2002/jan/20/books.booksnews. Accessed September 25, 2009.

Thatcher, Margaret (1925–) Former prime minister of the United Kingdom from 1979 to 1990 and a possible model for Rowling's despicable Dolores Umbridge. She is the only woman to have held this office. She was a member of the Conservative Party. Thatcher's early years as prime minister suffered from devastating unemployment rates and high inflation. The problems in educational institutions from the mid-1970s to the late 1980s were unparalleled in the preceding century of British history. Thatcher cut education budgets, and students suffered. She rescinded the practice of giving free milk to students at lunchtime, spawning the chant "Thatcher, Thatcher, milk snatcher" by many youngsters; she also implemented admission charges at museums where access had previously been free.

Some critics link Rowling's character of Dolores Umbridge with Thatcher. Both were women in important positions, and both neglect student needs in pursuit of their (or their party's) own needs. This linking, however, may be too harsh. Near the end of Thatcher's term as prime minister, members of her

Margaret Thatcher in 1975. Thatcher served as prime minister of the United Kingdom from 1979 to 1990. Some critics speculate she served as the inspiration for Rowling's character of Dolores Umbridge. *(Photo by Marion S. Trikosko)*

supporting staff, such as Kenneth Baker, passed several educational reform acts that improved the state of education in Britain.

One of Thatcher's most well-known observations is "There is no such thing as society," which she made during remarks that too many people were blaming the government and "society" for situations with which they were unhappy. Thatcher explained that "society" does not exist; rather, individuals exist and must take responsibility for their own decisions. This neoconservative philosophy about personal responsibility may have sparked Rowling's critique in *Order of the Phoenix*.

Through the Looking Glass, and What Alice Found There See CARROLL, LEWIS.

Tolkien, J. R. R. (1892–1973) Best known as the author of the Lord of the Rings trilogy and *The Hobbit*, J. R. R. Tolkien is one of the most recognized names in FANTASY FICTION. He is widely regarded as influential as both a novelist and a critic, and J. K. Rowling's wizarding world is often compared with Tolkien's Middle Earth because of both writers' abilities to craft a fully imagined, three-dimensional secondary world.

Tolkien was born as John Ronald Reuel Tolkien in 1892 to a bank manager, Arthur Reuel Tolkien, and Mabel Tolkien. He was educated at the University of Leeds and served in the British Infantry Regiment the Lancashire Fusiliers during World War I. In addition to his career as a writer, Tolkien occupied a number of academic posts throughout his life, including as a professor of Anglo-Saxon literature and language at Oxford University, a professor of English language and literature, and numerous fellowships at British universities. He was as well known among his academic colleagues as a leading philologist as he was among devotees of fantasy fiction for his Lord of the Rings series.

Rowling's books have been compared with Tolkien's not simply in their ability to create a vividly imagined alternate universe but also in each writer's interest in myth, folklore, language, linguistics, and philology. William Compson's biography of Rowling notes that the author read the Lord of the Rings trilogy (originally published in 1954–55) for the first time as a university student at Exeter, though she claimed in some sources that she initially read the trilogy as a teenager (Kirk 45). Most frequently compared are the series' creations of an alternative world—the wizarding society that Harry enters and the lands of Middle Earth that Tolkien's hardy band of adventurers travels in the trilogy. The books differ in that Rowling's secondary world is really a parallel world and the characters in her books travel between the wizarding and Muggle cultures. Further, Muggle London is portrayed as the same "real world" London, England, Earth, that readers occupy, whereas Tolkien's characters live entirely in Middle Earth.

Rowling and Tolkien also incorporate similar themes in their novels; both series center largely on an epic battle between good and evil. The three novels in Tolkien's series, *The Fellowship of the Ring, The Two Towers,* and *The Return of the King,* are examples of high fantasy, drawing upon such stan- dard elements as swords, sorcery, and multiple races of fantasy creatures (both traditional and invented, including elves, dwarfs, hobbits, giants, orcs, as well as humans). The crux of the books' plotline is control over a powerful ring, referred to as the "One Ring," that confers multiple magical powers (such as, but not limited to, invisibility) upon its wearer. As one of several sets of rings forged by the evil wizard Sauron with the help of elvin blacksmiths, the One Ring is malevolent and gives the wearer control over the wearers of other rings. The books trace the protagonist, Frodo Baggins, as he and his friends journey to Mount Doom to destroy the ring. Though Tolkien himself has rejected readings of the Lord of the Rings as an allegory for World War II, readers have been attracted to such interpretations, comparing figures of modern history such as Adolf Hitler with the power-hungry wizard Sauron.

Rowling's books similarly tackle a battle of good and evil between the dark wizard Voldemort (and his minions, the Death Eaters) and Harry Potter, under the leadership of his mentor Albus Dumbledore. As Frodo does, Harry becomes drawn, somewhat unwillingly, into the epic battle, but, in the end both reluctantly step into their roles as hero and defeat their own demons and external threats. Like Tolkien, Rowling incorporates a set of powerful objects in the story line, finally explained in *Deathly Hallows*; the three Hallows—the Resurrection Stone, the Invisibility Cloak, and the Elder Wand—are coveted items that grant their possessor many powers, just as the One Ring of Middle Earth has the power to corrupt its owner.

Finally, the two writers are linked by their shared fascination with language (Rowling earned a bachelor's degree in French, and Tolkien, worked as a philologist). The Tolkien biographer T. A. Shippey observes that Tolkien's character names were drawn from Nordic and English myth and literature and Anglo-Saxon vocabulary: For example, Tolkien transformed the Anglo-Saxon word *ent* into a race of giant trees in his trilogy and contracted two Norse words for "staff" and "elf" to create the name of his great wizard, *Gandalf.* Rowling's own fascination with and passion for language(s) have been well documented. She draws upon French and Latin to create character names such as *Draco Malfoy* (cognates for the Latin for dragon and the French for bad faith, respectively) and Voldemort's name, as well, is French in origin, translating literally to "fly from death" (from the French verb *voler*, the preposition *de*, and the noun *morte*), an etymology that reinforces the character's obsession with immortality.

BIBLIOGRAPHY

Abanes, Richard: *Harry Potter and the Bible: The Menace Behind the Magick.* Camp Hill, Pa.: Horizon Books, 2001.
Compson, William. *The Library of Author Biographies: J. K. Rowling.* New York: Rosen Publishing Group, 2003.
Kirk, Connie. *J. K. Rowling: A Biography.* Westport, Conn.: Greenwood Press, 2003.
Shippey, T. A. *J. R. R. Tolkien: Author of the Century.* Boston: Houghton-Mifflin, 2001.
———. *The Road to Middle-Earth.* London: Allen & Unwain, 1983.

Tutshill, England   Town where Rowling lived as a child. The area, located in the countryside and near the Forest of Dean, afforded Rowling and her sister plenty of opportunities for adventure. Tutshill lies on the border between England and Wales.

University of Exeter   University that Rowling attended, from which she earned degrees in French and classics. Rowling admits that she wanted to study literature but was pressured by her parents to pursue an educational path that would lead to more job opportunities, hence her enrollment as a French major (since with such a degree she could obtain a variety of jobs, including that of an interpreter or translator). While working toward her degree in French, she spent a year abroad in PARIS, FRANCE. The University of Exeter awarded her an honorary doctorate in 2000.

The university's motto is "Lucem sequimur," meaning "We follow the light." The university has roughly 15,000 students, including both undergraduates and postgraduates. The University of Exeter is known for its rigorous academic programs in subjects ranging from mathematics to teacher training to religious studies. Exeter was named University of the Year in 2007.

Vander Ark, Steve (?–)   Creator and editor in chief of the Harry Potter Lexicon Web site. Vander Ark founded the Lexicon in 2000 and has maintained and updated the site since. He planned to take the information pooled over the years and transform it into a type of encyclopedia on the Harry Potter universe; when Rowling heard about his plans, she accused him of plagiarism, alleging that he was trying to make a profit based on her own artistic creations. Rowling also explained that she felt that the book should not be published because it is mainly a regurgitation of facts she has already shared with her readers, rather than a work including new insights, analysis, or observations. A trial, covered in detail and the catalyst for a media frenzy, ensued between Rowling's team and RDR BOOKS, the publishing firm supporting the publication of Vander Ark's book. Vander Ark states the following on the Lexicon Web site: "The Lexicon holds J. K. Rowling and her fans in the highest regard. Her respect is of the utmost importance to us, as is the trust of our readers. We will do everything in our power to earn and keep that respect." Vander Ark was crushed by Rowling's accusations, especially since she had always held the Lexicon and Vander Ark in such high regard; he broke down in tears on the stand, assuring the judge and jury that he still admired Rowling.

During the trial Rowling stated that "even though she loved fan sites, she hoped to write 'the definitive Harry Potter encyclopedia, which will include all the material that never made it into the novels' and donate the proceeds to charity" (Kearney). Rowling vigorously argued other reasons why Vander Ark's work should not be allowed to be published: "I cannot, therefore, approve of 'companion books' or 'encyclopedias' that seek to pre-empt my definitive Potter reference book for their authors' own personal gain. . . . The losers in such a situation would be the charities that I hope, eventually, to benefit" (Kearney). The presiding judge, Robert Pattison, agreed that Vander Ark's book (as it existed at the time of the trial) did infringe on Rowling's rights. But with revisions (such as making the book much shorter), Vander Ark's book was eventually published in 2009 under the title *The Lexicon: An Unauthorized Guide to Harry Potter Fiction.*

BIBLIOGRAPHY

Kearney, Christine. "Rowling, Warner Brothers Sue over Harry Potter Book." 31 October 2007. Available online. URL: http://www.reuters.com/article/peopleNews/idUSN3133972420071031. Accessed October 4, 2009.

Volant Charitable Trust   Trust established by Rowling, named in honor of her mother, Ann Rowling (née Volant). According to the Volant Charitable Trust Web site (http://www.volanttrust.com/), Rowling established the trust to fund two major causes. The first major cause is research on multiple sclerosis (Rowling's mother died of MS in 1990); the second is "charities and projects, whether national or community-based, at home or abroad, that alleviate social deprivation, with a particular emphasis on women's and children's issues" (Volant).

BIBLIOGRAPHY

"Volant Charitable Trust." Available online. URL: http://www.volanttrust.com/. Accessed November 21, 2009.

Warner Brothers   Now part of the AOL Time/Warner conglomerate, Warner Brothers Studios obtained the film rights to the Harry Potter series in 1998, about the same time that Rowling negotiated publication rights in the United States with SCHOLASTIC, a leading U.S. publisher of children's books. Details of neither deal have been disclosed, though Rowling generally receives a sizable percentage of the profits from the distribution of the films and merchandising associated with the productions and the series. The company works separately from Rowling, maintaining the Harry Potter "brand" as part of its marketing, film enterprise, and merchandising operations. As Jarrod Waetjen and Timothy Gibson have described, AOL Time Warner assigned merchandising of the Potter series to Warner Brothers Consumer Products, involving licensing and merchandising strategies and a "strict style guide" that is "entitled the Consumer Products Program of Witchcraft and Wizardry" (18).

Harry Potter fans have had conflicts with Warner Brothers because of the tight hold the company maintains over the series as a brand and commodity. For example, in December 2000 the company aggressively defended its ownership of the Harry Potter chapter title "The Boy Who Lived" when a fan established a Web site of the same name. In response to activism by fans defending their rights to create such Web sites, Warner Brothers has created a Harry Potter Webmaster Community where Web masters can register their nonprofit sites.

BIBLIOGRAPHY

Waetjen, Jarrod, and Timothy A. Gibson. "Harry Potter and the Commodity Fetishism: Activating Corporate Readings in the Journey from Text to Commercial Intertext." *Communication and Critical/Cultural Studies* 4, no. 1 (2007): 3–26.

White, E. B.   (1899–1985) American writer best known for his literature for children including *Charlotte's Web, Stuart Little,* and *The Trumpet of the Swan.* Rowling's novels—and *Sorcerer's Stone,* in particular—share many similarities with White's most famous novel, *Charlotte's Web* (first published in 1952). White's celebrated novel follows the story of a pig named Wilbur and his spider friend Charlotte. Born the runt of the litter, Wilbur is eventually sold to a farmer who plans to raise him for food. Wilbur makes fast friends with Charlotte. She consoles him and decides that if Wilbur became famous, the farmer probably would not kill him. Charlotte starts weaving messages into her web about Wilbur, writing things like "Radiant" and "Some pig!" Wilbur does become famous and avoids being killed. Charlotte dies, and Wilbur sees that some eggs she laid before her death hatch so that Charlotte can live on through her children.

The first important similarity between *Charlotte's Web* and *Sorcerer's Stone* concerns the plot and characters of the novels. Harry and Wilbur share many characteristics. They have a similar status: Wilbur is the runt, and the Dursleys treat Harry poorly and act, at times, as if he does not exist. Wilbur and Harry find support from mentor figures in Charlotte for Wilbur and Dumbledore for Harry. Perhaps the most significant parallel between Wilbur and Harry is that both characters experience a change in status and fulfill their destinies while honoring their mentors. Wilbur transforms from a runt into a show-stopping pig; Harry, ignored most of his young life, becomes the most famous man in the wizarding world. Wilbur saves Charlotte's eggs so that her children may live full lives of their own. Harry destroys Voldemort, finishing the battle Dumbledore began so long ago, and in the process transforms into a savior for wizards and Muggles alike.

The record-breaking sales of *Charlotte's Web* and *Sorcerer's Stone* are the other factor that makes these works so similar. *Publishers Weekly*'s survey "Best-Selling Children's Books" conducted in December 2001 confirms *Charlotte's Web* as the best-selling children's paperback of all time (Roback and Britton), but despite nearly 50 years worth of sales to its advantage, White's beloved classic will probably one day be ousted by Rowling's first novel.

BIBLIOGRAPHY

Roback, Diane, and Jason Britton, eds. "All-Time Bestselling Children's Books." *Publishers Weekly*, 17 December 2001.

White, T. H. (1906–1964)   British author best known for his tetralogy The Once and Future King, a fantasy retelling the King Arthur legends to a 20th-century audience. Inspired by Thomas Malory's original 15th-century *Le Morte d'Arthur*, White set to writing the first in the series of four books, *The Sword in the Stone*, published in 1938. Subsequent books in the series appeared in 1939 and 1940, and a four-book collection was published in 1958. Numerous comparisons have been drawn between Harry Potter and the teenage protagonist of White's novels, King Arthur, known familiarly in the first book as "Wart." Evelyn Perry has noted that both the Harry Potter series and White's series feature adolescent male protagonists who have

an inherent power and greatness that are unrecognized during their youth; both protagonists, because of the poor treatment they receive as children, develop a sense of humility and a passion for justice that follow them even into adulthood once they have risen above their low status. Each has a "noble mage"—Dumbledore and Merlyn—who has orchestrated the young boy's living situation as part of a larger plan for his life. In both boys' cases, their experience of isolation and abuse as youths is key to developing their moral compass as adults—with empathy, compassion, fairness, and equality central qualities of their worldviews as literary heroes. Both boys also learn a great deal at the feet of their mentor and surrogate father, the magicians Merlyn and Albus Dumbledore.

BIBLIOGRAPHY

Perry, Evelyn M. "Metaphor and MetaFantasy: Questing for Literary Inheritance in J. K. Rowling's *Harry Potter and the Sorcerer's Stone*." In *Scholarly Studies in Harry Potter: Applying Academic Methods to a Popular Text*, edited by Cynthia Whitney Hallett and Debbie Mynott, 241–275. Lewiston, N.Y.: Edwin Mellen Press, 2005.

Wildsmith, Michael (unknown)   Photographer whose pictures are on the covers of the adult versions of the Harry Potter series, published by the Canadian-based Raincoast Books.

Winterbourne, South Gloucestershire, England
Village in South Gloucestershire, England. Rowling lived here until she was nine years old and attended St. Michael's Church of England Primary School. This is also the village in which Rowling befriended her neighbors, The Potters, whose last name appealed to her; Rowling herself admits that Harry's surname is based on her Winterbourne neighbors'.

Wizard of Oz, The   See Baum, Frank.

wizard rock   Genre of music inspired by Rowling's Harry Potter series. Also referred to as "wrock," short for the combination of the words *wizard* and *rock*. The most notable wizard rock bands include Harry and the Potters, Draco and the Malfoys, the Remus Lupins, the Whomping Willows, and the Moaning Myrtles. Similar to writers of FAN FICTION, the songwriters compose material based on the universe Rowling has created. Some of the artists write about events that have already transpired (as in Harry and the Potters' hit "We've Got to Save Ginny Weasley from the Basilisk"), while other artists, such as the Remus Lupins, remind readers to "make love, not horcruxes." Most of the members of wizard rock bands dress as characters of Rowling's series, usually like the character for which their bands are named. The documentary *The Wizard Rockumentary: A Movie about Rocking and Rowling* explores the wizard rock phenomenon in detail.

BIBLIOGRAPHY

The Wizard Rockumentary: A Movie about Rocking and Rowling. Dirs. Megan Schuyler and Mallory Battista. Gryffinclaw Productions, 2008.

Wizarding World of Harry Potter   In spring 2010 Universal Studios in Orlando, Florida, opened the theme park ride and attraction "Harry Potter and the Forbidden Journey," named by Rowling. The Forbidden Journey makes up just one part of the larger Wizarding World of Harry Potter, an addition to the Universal Studios Islands of Adventure theme park. The Miami attraction replicates Harry Potter's world as authentically as possible; guests enter through Hogsmeade, a replica of Hogwarts School of Witchcraft and Wizardry, and into shops such as Honeydukes, Ollivander's, Zonko's, Owl Post, Dervish and Banges, and Three Broomsticks. Rides are named Dragon Challenge and Flight of the Hippogriff, both high-intensity roller coasters. Stuart Craig and Alan Gilmore (production designer and art director, respectively, for the films) were hired to re-create the visual richness of the films in the theme park experience.

BIBLIOGRAPHY

"The Wizarding World of Harry Potter." Universal Studios. Available online. URL: http://www.universalorlando.com/harrypotter/. Accessed December 6, 2008.

Wright, Cliff (1963–)   Illustrator for cover artwork for the BLOOMSBURY versions of *Harry Potter and the Chamber of Secrets* and *Harry Potter and the Prisoner of Azkaban*. A graduate of the Brighton College of Art, he is best known for his illustrations of animals. He was selected to illustrate the famous children's work *Wind in the Willows* (written by Kenneth Grahame, a story famous for its animal cast). While Bloomsbury seemed pleased with THOMAS TAYLOR'S illustrations for *Philosopher's Stone*, Vanessa Thorpe reports that "Bloomsbury dropped Taylor after the first book in favor of a more experienced artist, Cliff Wright." Wright was asked to provide the illustration for the cover of *Goblet of Fire* also, but because of a falling out with Bloomsbury, he angrily declined, since "the publishers had lost his original artwork for the third novel" (Thorpe).

BIBLIOGRAPHY

Thorpe, Vanessa. "Harry Potter Beats Austen in Sale Rooms." *Guardian* (UK). Available Online: http://www.guardian.co.uk/uk/2002/jan/20/books.booksnews. Accessed January 20, 2002.

Wyedean School   School Rowling attended in Sedbury, Gloucestershire, England. The school is coeducational and serves roughly 1,100 pupils. Rowling was head girl at Wyedean; there she also met one of her closest friends, Sean Harris, who is rumored to be the inspiration for the character of Ronald Weasley. Several critics and biographers argue that Rowling did not enjoy her years at Wyedean. The school dedicated a library to her, but Rowling has not returned to the school, even though she has visited other schools in its vicinity. One of her former teachers, the science master John Nettleship, is rumored to be the basis for Severus Snape.

Yate, South Gloucestershire, England   Town located near BRISTOL, ENGLAND, that is officially listed as Rowling's place of birth on her birth certificate. Rowling, however, usually says that she was born in CHIPPING SODBURY, SOUTH GLOUCESTERSHIRE, ENGLAND, a nearby town.

PART IV

Appendices

Bibliography of J. K. Rowling's Works

Fiction

Harry Potter and the Philosopher's Stone. London: Bloomsbury, 1997.

Harry Potter and the Sorcerer's Stone. New York: Scholastic, 1998.

Harry Potter and the Chamber of Secrets. London: Bloomsbury, 1998.

Harry Potter and the Chamber of Secrets. New York: Scholastic, 1998.

Harry Potter and the Prisoner of Azkaban. London: Bloomsbury, 1999.

Harry Potter and the Prisoner of Azkaban. New York: Scholastic, 1999.

Harry Potter and the Goblet of Fire. London: Bloomsbury, 2000.

Harry Potter and the Goblet of Fire. New York: Scholastic, 2000.

Harry Potter and the Order of the Phoenix. London: Bloomsbury, 2003.

Harry Potter and the Order of the Phoenix. New York: Scholastic, 2003.

Harry Potter and the Half-Blood Prince. London: Bloomsbury, 2005.

Harry Potter and the Half-Blood Prince. New York: Scholastic, 2005.

Harry Potter and the Deathly Hallows. London: Bloomsbury, 2007.

Harry Potter and the Deathly Hallows. New York: Scholastic, 2007.

Quidditch through the Ages. New York: Scholastic, 2001.

Fantastic Beasts and Where to Find Them. New York: Scholastic, 2001.

The Tales of Beedle the Bard. New York: Scholastic, 2008.

Nonfiction

"The First It Girl: J. K. Rowling Reviews *Decca: The Letters of Jessica Mitford ed. by Peter Y. Sussman.*" *Daily Telegraph,* 26 November 2006. Available online. URL: http://www.telegraph.co.uk/culture/books/3656769/The-first-It-Girl.html. Accessed November 5, 2009.

Foreword to *Harry: A History,* by Melissa Anelli. New York: Pocket, 2008, ix–xii.

Foreword to *Magic,* edited by Gil McNeil and Sarah Brown. London: Bloomsbury, 2002, 1–6.

"The Fringe Benefits of Failure, and the Importance of Imagination." *Harvard Magazine,* 5 June 2008. Available online. URL: http://harvardmagazine.com/commencement/the-fringe-benefits-failure-the-importance-imagination. Accessed November 5, 2009.

"A Good Scare." *Time Canada.* 30 October 2000. MasterFILE Premier. Available online by subscription. Accessed November 5, 2009.

"Introduction to Ending Child Poverty." In *Moving Britain Forward: Selected Speeches 1997–2006,* by Gordon Brown, edited by Wilf Stevenson. London: Bloomsbury, 2006.

BIBLIOGRAPHY OF SECONDARY SOURCES

Abanes, Richard. *Harry Potter and the Bible: The Menace behind the Magick.* Camp Hill, Pa.: Horizon Books, 2001.

Anatol, Giselle Liza, ed. *Reading Harry Potter: Critical Essays.* Contributions to the Study of Popular Culture 78. Westport, Conn., and London: Praeger, 2003.

Baggett, David, and Shawn Klein. *Harry Potter and Philosophy: If Aristotle Ran Hogwarts.* Chicago: Open Court Press, 2004.

Beahm, George. *Muggles and Magic: J. K. Rowling and the Harry Potter Phenomenon.* Charlottesville, Va.: Hampton Roads, 2004.

Benson, Kristina. *Harry Potter A–Z: The Unofficial Harry Potter Encyclopedia.* N.P.: Equity Press, 2007.

Blake, Andrew. *The Irresistible Rise of Harry Potter.* London: Verso, 2002.

Boyle, Fionna. *A Muggle's Guide to the Wizarding World: Exploring the Harry Potter Universe.* Toronto, Canada: ECW Press, 2004.

Bridger, Francis: *A Charmed Life: The Spirituality of Potterworld.* London: Longman & Todd, 2001.

Burkart, Gina. *A Parent's Guide to Harry Potter.* Downers Grove, Ill.: InterVarsity Press, 2005.

Compson, William: *J. K. Rowling.* New York: Rosen Publishing Group, 2003.

Dickerson, Matthew T., and David O'Hara, eds. *From Homer to Harry Potter: A Handbook on Myth and Fantasy.* Grand Rapids, Mich.: Brazos Press, 2006.

Duriez, Colin. *Field Guide to Harry Potter.* Downers Grove, Ill.: IVP Books, 2007.

Eccleshare, Julia. *Beatrix Potter to Harry Potter: Portraits of Children's Writers.* London: National Portrait Gallery, 2002.

———. *Guide to the Harry Potter Novels.* London: Continuum, 2002.

Ellis, Bill. *Lucifer Ascending: The Occult in Folklore and Popular Culture.* Lexington: University Press of Kentucky, 2003.

Fraser, Lindsey. *Conversations with J. K. Rowling.* New York: Scholastic, 2001.

Gaines, Ann *J. K. Rowling.* Hockessin, Del.: Mitchell Lane, 2005.

Gillatt, Gary. *The Magical World of Harry Potter: The Unauthorised Guide to the Adventures of Harry Potter.* Richmond, Va.: Reynolds & Hearn, 2001.

Granger, John. *The Hidden Key to Harry Potter: Understanding the Meaning, Genius and Popularity of Joanne Rowling's Harry Potter Novels.* Hadlock, Wash.: Zossima Press, 2003.

———. *Looking for God in Harry Potter.* Carol Stream, Ill.: Tyndale House, 2004.

———. *Unlocking Harry Potter: Five Keys for the Serious Reader.* Hadlock, Wash.: Zossima Press, 2007.

Granger, John, ed. *Who Killed Albus Dumbledore? What Really Happened in* Harry Potter and the Half-Blood Prince? *Six Expert Harry Potter Detectives Examine the Evidence.* Hadlock, Wash.: Zossima Press, 2006.

Gross, Edward: *The Making of the Potterverse: A Month-by-Month Look at Harry's First 10 Years.* Toronto, Canada: ECW Press, 2007.

Hallett, Cynthia Whitney, ed. *Scholarly Studies in Harry Potter: Applying Academic Methods to a Popular Text.* Lewiston, N.Y.: Edwin Mellen Press, 2005.

Harmin, Karen Leigh: *J. K. Rowling: Author of Harry Potter.* Aldershot, England, and Berkeley Heights, N.J.: Enslow, 2006.

Harry Potter Special Issue. Topic: The Washington and Jefferson College Review 54 (2004).

Heilman, Elizabeth E., ed. *Harry Potter's World: Multidisciplinary Critical Perspectives*. New York: RoutledgeFalmer, 2002.

Highfield, Roger. *The Science of Harry Potter: How Magic Really Works*. New York: Viking, 2002.

Hill, Mary. *J. K. Rowling*. Danbury, Conn.: Scholastic Library, 2003.

Houghton, John. *A Closer Look at Harry Potter: Bending and Shaping the Minds of Our Children*. Eastbourne, England: Kingsway, 2001.

Kern, Edmund M. *The Wisdom of Harry Potter: What Our Favorite Hero Teaches Us about Moral Choices*. Amherst, N.Y.: Prometheus Books, 2003.

Killinger, John. *God, the Devil, and Harry Potter: A Christian Minister's Defense of the Beloved Novels*. New York: Thomas Dunne Books, 2002.

Kirk, Connie Ann. *From Shakespeare to Harry Potter: An Introduction to Literature for All Ages*. Philadelphia: Xlibris, 2004.

———. *J. K. Rowling: A Biography*. Westport, Conn.: Greenwood Press, 2003.

———. *The J. K. Rowling Encyclopedia*. Westport, Conn.: Greenwood Press, 2006.

Kronzek, Allan Zola, and Elizabeth, Kronzek, *The Sorcerer's Companion: A Guide to the Magical World of Harry Potter*. New York: Broadway Books, 2001.

———. *The Sorcerer's Companion: A Guide to the Magical World of Harry Potter*. 2d extended ed. New York: Broadway Books, 2004.

Lackey, Mercedes, and Leah Wilson, eds. *Mapping the World of Harry Potter: Science Fiction and Fantasy Writers Explore the Best Selling Fantasy Series of All Time*. Dallas, Tex: Benbella Books, 2006.

Langford, David. *The End of Harry Potter? An Unauthorised Guide to the Mysteries That Remain*. London: Gollancz, 2006.

Lovett, Charles C. *J. K. Rowling: Her Life and Works*. New York: SparkNotes, 2003.

Mammen, Lori. *Harry Potter and the Sorcerer's Stone by J. K. Rowling: Teacher Guide*. San Antonio, Tex.: Novel Units, 2000.

Manlove, Colin. *From Alice to Harry Potter: Children's Fantasy in England*. Christchurch, New Zealand: Cybereditions, 2003.

Markell, Kathryn A., and Marc A. Markell. *The Children Who Lived: Using Harry Potter and Other Fictional Characters to Help Grieving Children and Adolescents*. New York: Routledge, 2008.

McCarthy, Shaun. *All about J. K. Rowling*. Austin, Tex.: Heinemann Library, 2003.

Meister, Cari. *J. K. Rowling*. Edina, Minn.: Abdo, 2001.

Mulholland, Neil, ed. *The Psychology of Harry Potter: An Unauthorized Examination of the Boy Who Lived*. Dallas, Tex.: Benbella Books, 2007.

Nel, Philip. *J. K. Rowling's Harry Potter Novels: A Reader's Guide*. New York and London: Continuum International Publishing Group, 2001.

Nexon, Daniel H., and Neumann, Iver B., eds. *Harry Potter and International Relations*. Lanham, Md.: Rowman & Littlefield, 2006.

Perry, Phyllis Jean. *Teaching the Fantasy Novel: From The Hobbit to Harry Potter and the Goblet of Fire*. Portsmouth, N.H.: Teacher Idea Press, 2003.

Pezzi, Bryan. *J. K. Rowling*. New York: Weigl, 2005.

Price, Joan. *J. K. Rowling*. Milwaukee, Wis.: World Almanac Library, 2005.

Randall, Eric D. *The Pottersaurus: 1,500 Words Harry Potter Readers Need to Know*. Albany, N.Y.: Plain English Legal Publications, 2007.

Schafer, Elizabeth D. *Exploring Harry Potter: The Unapproved Beacham's Sourcebook*. Beacham's Sourcebooks for Teaching Young Adult Fiction. Osprey, Fla.: Beacham Publishing Group, 2000.

Sexton, Colleen. *J. K. Rowling: Biography*. Minneapolis, Minn.: Lerner/Twenty-First Century Books 2006.

Shapiro, Marc: *J. K. Rowling: The Wizard behind Harry Potter*. 2d rev. ed. New York: St. Martin's Press, 2004.

Shields, Charles J. *Mythmaker: The Story of J. K. Rowling*. Philadelphia: Chelsea House, 2002.

Steffens, Bradley: *J. K. Rowling*. San Diego, Calif.: Lucent Books, 2002.

Vander Ark, Steve. *Harry Potter Lexicon*. Muskegon, Mich.: RDR Books, 2007.

Ward, Stasia. *Meet J. K. Rowling*. New York: PowerKids Press, 2001.

Whited, Lana A., ed. *The Ivory Tower and Harry Potter: Perspectives on a Literary Phenomenon*. Columbia: University of Missouri Press, 2002.

Wiener, Gary, and Penny J. Parks, eds. *Readings on J. K. Rowling*. San Diego, Calif.: Greenhaven Press, 2004.

J. K. ROWLING CHRONOLOGY

1965
Rowling born on July 31.

1967
Rowling's sister, Diane, born on June 28.

1969
The Rowling family moves to Winterbourne.

1970
Rowling starts primary school.

1974
The Rowlings move to Tutshill.
Rowling's grandmother Kathleen dies; after her, Rowling takes the middle initial K.

1976
Rowling begins school at Wyedean.

1980
Rowling's mother, Anne, is diagnosed with multiple sclerosis.

1983
Rowling enters Exeter University.

1986
Rowling spends a year studying abroad in Paris, France.

1987
Rowling graduates from Exeter. She moves to London and begins working for Amnesty International.

1990
Rowling has the idea for the Harry Potter series and begins writing.
Ten years since her diagnosis, Rowling's mother, Anne, dies.

1991
Rowling moves to Oporto, Portugal, to teach English.

1992
Rowling meets Jorge Arantes, a journalist.
Rowling and Arantes marry in October.

1993
Rowling gives birth to her daughter, Jessica, on July 27.
Rowling moves to Edinburgh, Scotland, with Jessica after leaving Arantes.

1994
Rowling continues working on the manuscript for *Philosopher's (Sorcerer's) Stone*.

1995
Rowling sends samples of *Philosopher's (Sorcerer's) Stone* to various literary agents; Christopher Little decides to represent Rowling.
Rowling divorces Arantes.

1996
Rowling begins teaching at Leith Academy.
Bloomsbury, a British publishing house, makes an offer to Christopher Little to publish Rowling's first Harry Potter novel.

1997

The first Harry Potter book is published in Britain in June by Bloomsbury under the title of *Harry Potter and the Philosopher's Stone*.

Scholastic buys the rights to publish the first Harry Potter book in America, but under the title *Harry Potter and the Sorcerer's Stone*.

1998

Chamber of Secrets published in Britain in July.

Scholastic Books publishes *Sorcerer's Stone* in September.

Rowling receives the British Book Awards' Author of the Year Award. She also receives the Bookseller's Association Author of the Year Award.

Rowling sells the rights to make films based on the first four Harry Potter novels to Warner Brothers.

1999

Chamber of Secrets published in the United States on June 2.

Prisoner of Azkaban published (on July 8 in Britain, and on September 8 in the United States).

Rowling receives her second Bookseller's Association Author of the Year Award.

Rowling begins her long-standing support for the Multiple Sclerosis Society of Scotland.

2000

Goblet of Fire published on July 8; it is the first Harry Potter novel to be released on the same day in Britain, Australia, Canada, and the United States.

Rowling establishes the Volant Charitable Trust.

2001

Two Hogwarts textbooks written by Rowling—*Quidditch through the Ages* and *Fantastic Beasts and Where to Find Them*—are published in March; a large portion of the proceeds benefit the charity Comic Relief.

Warner Brothers releases *Sorcerer's Stone* on film in November.

Rowling marries her second husband, Dr. Neil Murray, on December 26.

Rowling receives the Order of the British Empire Award.

2002

Warner Brothers releases the film version of *Chamber of Secrets* in November.

2003

Order of the Phoenix published on June 21.

Rowling and Murray's son, David, is born on March 24.

Rowling receives the Prince of Asturias Award for Concord.

2004

Film version of *Prisoner of Azkaban* is released by Warner Brothers in June.

Rowling receives the W. H. Smith Fiction Award.

2005

Rowling and Murray's daughter, Mackenzie, is born on January 23.

Half-Blood Prince published on July 16.

Warner Brothers releases the film *Goblet of Fire* in November.

Rowling founds the Children's High Level group with Emma Nicholson.

2007

The film version of *Order of the Phoenix* is released in July.

Ten days after the American release of the film of *Order of the Phoenix*, the final Harry Potter novel—*Deathly Hallows*—is published on July 21.

Time magazine staff considers Rowling for their annual honor of "Person of the Year"; Rowling is chosen as runner-up.

Rowling receives a Blue Peter Gold Badge.

Rowling awarded the position of president for Gingerbread (formerly known as One Parent Families).

2008

Rowling publishes *The Tales of Beedle the Bard*.

Rowling serves as the guest commencement speaker at Harvard.

Rowling receives the Edinburgh Award and the James Joyce Award. She also receives the British Book Awards' Lifetime Achievement Award and the Outstanding Achievement Award from the South Bank Show Awards.

2009
Warner Brothers releases the film version of *Half-Blood Prince* in July.

Rowling receives France's Legion of Honor Award.

2010
Deathly Hallows, part 1, released in the UK and US on November 19, 2010.

2011
Release date of July 15 for part 2 of the film *Deathly Hallows*.

CAST INFORMATION ON HARRY POTTER FILMS

Harry Potter and the Sorcerer's Stone

Harry Potter and the Sorcerer's Stone (also known as *Harry Potter and the Philosopher's Stone*) was released in the United States on November 16, 2001, with the following cast:

Albus Dumbledore	Richard Harris
Argus Filch	David Bradley
Dean Thomas	Alfie Enoch
Draco Malfoy	Tom Felton
Dudley Dursley	Harry Melling
Filius Flitwick/Gringotts Teller	Warwick Davis
Fred Weasley	James Phelps
George Weasley	Oliver Phelps
Ginny Weasley	Bonnie Wright
Gregory Goyle	Josh Herdman
Griphook the Goblin	Verne Troyer
Harry Potter	Daniel Radcliffe
Hermione Granger	Emma Watson
Lee Jordan	Luke Youngblood
Madam Hooch	Zoë Wanamaker
Minerva McGonagall	Dame Maggie Smith
Molly Weasley	Julie Walters
Mr. Ollivander	John Hurt
Nearly Headless Nick	John Cleese
Neville Longbottom	Matthew Lewis
Oliver Wood	Sean Biggerstaff
Percy Weasley	Chris Rankin
Petunia Dursley	Fiona Shaw
Quirinus Quirrell	Ian Hart
Ron Weasley	Rupert Grint
Rubeus Hagrid	Robbie Coltrane
Seamus Finnigan	Devon Murray
Severus Snape	Alan Rickman
the Sorting Hat	Voice of Leslie Phillips
Vernon Dursley	Richard Griffiths
Vincent Crabbe	Jamie Waylett
Voldemort	Richard Bremmer

Directed by Christopher Columbus
Produced by David Heyman
Music by John Williams
Screenplay by Steve Kloves
Cinematography by John Seale

Harry Potter and the Chamber of Secrets

Harry Potter and the Chamber of Secrets debuted on November 15, 2002, with the following cast:

Albus Dumbledore	Richard Harris
Aragog	Voice of Julian Glover
Argus Filch	David Bradley
Arthur Weasley	Mark Williams
Colin Creevey	Hugh Mitchell
Cornelius Fudge	Robert Hardy
Dean Thomas	Alfie Enoch
Dobby the House-Elf	Voice of Toby Jones
Draco Malfoy	Tom Felton
Dudley Dursley	Harry Melling
Ernie MacMillan	Louis Doyle
Filius Flitwick	Warwick Davis
Fred Weasley	James Phelps
George Weasley	Oliver Phelps
Gilderoy Lockhart	Kenneth Branagh
Ginny Weasley	Bonnie Wright
Gregory Goyle	Josh Herdman
Harry Potter	Daniel Radcliffe
Hermione Granger	Emma Watson
Justin Finch-Fletchley	Edward Randell
Lee Jordan	Luke Youngblood

Lucius Malfoy	Jason Isaacs	Lucius Malfoy	Jason Isaacs
Minerva McGonagall	Dame Maggie Smith	Madame Rosmerta	Julie Christie
Moaning Myrtle	Shirley Henderson	Minerva McGonagall	Dame Maggie Smith
Molly Weasley	Julie Walters	Molly Weasley	Julie Walters
Nearly Headless Nick	John Cleese	Nearly Headless Nick	John Cleese
Neville Longbottom	Matthew Lewis	Neville Longbottom	Matthew Lewis
Oliver Wood	Sean Biggerstaff	Oliver Wood	Sean Biggerstaff
Percy Weasley	Chris Rankin	Percy Weasley	Chris Rankin
Petunia Dursley	Fiona Shaw	Peter Pettigrew	Timothy Spall
Pomona Sprout	Miriam Margolyes	Petunia Dursley	Fiona Shaw
Ron Weasley	Rupert Grint	Remus Lupin	David Thewlis
Rubeus Hagrid	Robbie Coltrane	Ron Weasley	Rupert Grint
Seamus Finnigan	Devon Murray	Rubeus Hagrid	Robbie Coltrane
Severus Snape	Alan Rickman	Seamus Finnigan	Devon Murray
the Sorting Hat	Voice of Leslie Phillips	Severus Snape	Alan Rickman
		Shrunken Head	Lenny Henry
Tom Marvolo Riddle	Christian Coulson	Sirius Black	Gary Oldman
Vernon Dursley	Richard Griffiths	the Sorting Hat	Voice of Leslie Phillips
Vincent Crabbe	Jamie Waylett		
Young Rubeus Hagrid	Martin Bayfield	Stan Shunpike	Lee Ingleby
		Sybil Trelawney	Emma Thompson
		Tom the Innkeeper	Jim Tavaré
		Vernon Dursley	Richard Griffiths
		Vincent Crabbe	Jamie Waylett
		Wizard	Warwick Davis

Directed by Christopher Columbus
Produced by David Heyman
Music by John Williams
Screenplay by Steve Kloves
Cinematography by Roger Pratt

Directed by Alfonso Cuarón
Produced by David Heyman and Mark Radcliffe
Music by John Williams
Screenplay by Steve Kloves
Cinematography by Michael Seresin

Harry Potter and the Prisoner of Azkaban

Harry Potter and the Prisoner of Azkaban debuted on June 4, 2004, with the following cast:

Albus Dumbledore	Michael Gambon
Argus Filch	David Bradley
Arthur Weasley	Mark Williams
Cornelius Fudge	Robert Hardy
Dean Thomas	Alfie Enoch
Draco Malfoy	Tom Felton
Dudley Dursley	Harry Melling
Ernie MacMillan	Louis Doyle
Ernie Prang	Jimmy Gardner
Fred Weasley	James Phelps
George Weasley	Oliver Phelps
Ginny Weasley	Bonnie Wright
Gregory Goyle	Josh Herdman
Harry Potter	Daniel Radcliffe
Hermione Granger	Emma Watson
James Potter	Adrian Rawlins
Lee Jordan	Luke Youngblood
Lily Potter	Geraldine Somerville

Harry Potter and the Goblet of Fire

Harry Potter and the Goblet of Fire debuted on November 18, 2005, with the following cast:

Alastor "Mad-Eye" Moody	Brendan Gleeson
Albus Dumbledore	Michael Gambon
Amos Diggory	Jeff Rawle
Argus Filch	David Bradley
Arthur Weasley	Mark Williams
Barty Crouch	Roger Lloyd-Pack
Barty Crouch, Jr.	David Tennant
Cedric Diggory	Robert Pattison
Cho Chang	Katie Leung
Cornelius Fudge	Robert Hardy
Dean Thomas	Alfie Enoch
Draco Malfoy	Tom Felton
Dudley Dursley	Harry Melling

Ernie MacMillan	Louis Doyle	Arabella Figg	Kathryn Hunter
Fleur Delacour	Clémence Poésy	Argus Filch	David Bradley
Frank Bryce	Eric Sykes	Arthur Weasley	Mark Williams
Fred Weasley	James Phelps	Bellatrix Lestrange	Helena Bonham
Gabrielle Delacour	Angelica Mandy		Carter
George Weasley	Oliver Phelps	Cedric Diggory	Robert Pattison
Ginny Weasley	Bonnie Wright	Cho Chang	Katie Leung
Gregory Goyle	Josh Herdman	Cornelius Fudge	Robert Hardy
Harry Potter	Daniel Radcliffe	Dean Thomas	Alfie Enoch
Hermione Granger	Emma Watson	Dolores Umbridge	Imelda Staunton
Igor Karkaroff	Predrag Bjelac	Draco Malfoy	Tom Felton
James Potter	Adrian Rawlins	Dudley Dursley	Harry Melling
Lee Jordan	Luke Youngblood	Elphias Doge	Peter Cartwright
Lily Potter	Geraldine Somerville	Emmeline Vance	Bridgette Millar
Lucius Malfoy	Jason Isaacs	Ernie MacMillan	Louis Doyle
Madame Olympe Maxime	Frances de la Tour	Frank Longbottom	James Payton
Minerva McGonagall	Dame Maggie Smith	Fred Weasley	James Phelps
Moaning Myrtle	Shirley Henderson	George Weasley	Oliver Phelps
Molly Weasley	Julie Walters	Ginny Weasley	Bonnie Wright
Neville Longbottom	Matthew Lewis	Grawp	Tony Maudsley
Nigel	William Melling	Gregory Goyle	Josh Herdman
Padma Patil	Afshan Azad	Harry Potter	Daniel Radcliffe
Parvati Patil	Shefali Chowdhury	Hermione Granger	Emma Watson
Peter Pettigrew	Timothy Spall	James Potter	Adrian Rawlins
Petunia Dursley	Fiona Shaw	Kingsley Shacklebolt	George Harris
Rita Skeeter	Miranda Richardson	Kreacher	Timothy Bateson
Ron Weasley	Rupert Grint	Lee Jordan	Luke Youngblood
Rubeus Hagrid	Robbie Coltrane	Lily Potter	Geraldine Somerville
Seamus Finnigan	Devon Murray	Lucius Malfoy	Jason Isaacs
Severus Snape	Alan Rickman	Luna Lovegood	Evanna Lynch
Sirius Black	Gary Oldman	Minerva McGonagall	Dame Maggie Smith
Vernon Dursley	Richard Griffiths	Molly Weasley	Julie Walters
Viktor Krum	Stanislav Ianevski	Neville Longbottom	Matthew Lewis
Vincent Crabbe	Jamie Waylett	Nigel	William Melling
Voldemort	Ralph Fiennes	Nymphadora Tonks	Natalia Tena
		Padma Patil	Afshan Azad
Directed by Mike Newell		Parvati Patil	Shefali Chowdhury
Produced by David Heyman		Percy Weasley	Chris Rankin
Music by Patrick Doyle		Petunia Dursley	Fiona Shaw
Screenplay by Steve Kloves		Remus Lupin	David Thewlis
Cinematography by Roger Pratt		Ron Weasley	Rupert Grint
		Rubeus Hagrid	Robbie Coltrane
		Seamus Finnigan	Devon Murray
		Severus Snape	Alan Rickman
		Sirius Black	Gary Oldman

Harry Potter and the Order of the Phoenix

Harry Potter and the Order of the Phoenix debuted on July 11, 2007, with the following cast:

		Vernon Dursley	Richard Griffiths
		Vincent Crabbe	Jamie Waylett
		Voldemort	Ralph Fiennes
Alastor "Mad-Eye" Moody	Brendan Gleeson	Young James Potter	Robbie Jarvis
Albus Dumbledore	Michael Gambon	Young Peter Pettigrew	Charles Hughes
		Young Remus Lupin	James Utechin

Young Severus Snape	Alec Hopkins
Young Sirius Black	James Walters

Directed by David Yates
Produced by David Heyman and David Barron
Music by Nicholas Hooper
Screenplay by Michael Goldenberg
Cinematography by Slawomir Idziak

Harry Potter and the Half-Blood Prince

Harry Potter and the Half-Blood Prince debuted on July 15, 2009, with the following cast:

Albus Dumbledore	Michael Gambon
Argus Filch	David Bradley
Arthur Weasley	Mark Williams
Bellatrix Lestrange	Helena Bonham Carter
Blaise Zabini	Louis Cordice
Cormac McLaggen	Freddie Stroma
Dean Thomas	Alfie Enoch
Draco Malfoy	Tom Felton
Fenrir Greyback	Dave Legeno
Filius Flitwick	Warwick Davis
Fred Weasley	James Phelps
George Weasley	Oliver Phelps
Ginny Weasley	Bonnie Wright
Gregory Goyle	Josh Herdman
Harry Potter	Daniel Radcliffe
Hermione Granger	Emma Watson
Horace Slughorn	Jim Broadbent
Katie Bell	Georgina Leonidas
Lavender Brown	Jessie Cave
Lily Potter	Geraldine Somerville
Luna Lovegood	Evanna Lynch
Madam Pomfrey	Gemma Jones
Marcus Belby	Robert Knox
Minerva McGonagall	Dame Maggie Smith
Molly Weasley	Julie Walters
Mrs. Cole	Amelda Brown
Narcissa Malfoy	Helen McCrory
Neville Longbottom	Matthew Lewis
Nigel	William Melling
Nymphadora Tonks	Natalia Tena
Pansy Parkinson	Scarlett Byrne
Remus Lupin	David Thewlis
Romilda Vane	Anna Shaffer
Ron Weasley	Rupert Grint
Rubeus Hagird	Robbie Coltrane

Seamus Finnigan	Devon Murray
Severus Snape	Alan Rickman
Tom Marvolo Riddle, age 11	Hero Fiennes-Tiffin
Tom Marvolo Riddle, age 16	Frank Dillane
Vincent Crabbe	Jamie Waylett
Wormtail	Timothy Spall

Directed by David Yates
Produced by David Heyman and David Barron
Music by Nicholas Hooper
Screenplay by Steve Kloves
Cinematography by Bruno Delbonnel

Harry Potter and the Deathly Hallows

At press time the film versions of *Deathly Hallows*—parts 1 and 2—had not yet been released. Their projected release dates are as follows: November 19, 2010 (part 1), and July 15, 2011 (part 2).

Deathly Hallows: Part I

As of press time, the confirmed cast includes:

Aberforth Dumbledore	Ciarán Hinds
Albert Runcorn	David O'Hara
Albus Dumbledore, age 17	Toby Regbo
Arthur Weasley	Mark Williams
Aunt Muriel	Matyelok Gibbs
Bathilda Bagshot	Hazel Douglas
Bellatrix Lestrange	Helena Bonham Carter
Bill Weasley	Domhnall Gleeson
Charlie Weasley	Alex Crockford
Dobby	Voice of Toby Jones
Dolores Umbridge	Imelda Staunton
Draco Malfoy	Tom Felton
Dudley Dursley	Harry Melling
Elphias Doge	David Ryall
Fenrir Greyback	Dave Legeno
Fleur Delacour	Clémence Poésy
Fred Weasley	James Phelps
Gellert Grindelwald	Jamie Campbell Bower
George Weasley	Oliver Phelps
Ginny Weasley	Bonnie Wright
Gregorovitch	Rade Serbedzija
Griphook	Warwick Davis
Harry Potter	Daniel Radcliffe
Hermione Granger	Emma Watson
Kreacher	Voice of Simon McBurney

Lucius Malfoy	Jason Isaacs
Luna Lovegood	Evanna Lynch
Mad-Eye Moody	Brendan Gleeson
Mafalda Hopkirk	Sophie Thompson
Minerva McGonagall	Dame Maggie Smith
Molly Weasley	Julie Walters
Mr. Ollivander	John Hurt
Mundungus Fletcher	Andy Linden
Narcissa Malfoy	Helen McCrory
Neville Longbottom	Matthew Lewis
Nymphadora Tonks	Natalia Tena
Percy Weasley	Chris Rankin
Peter Pettigrew	Timothy Spall
Petunia Dursley	Fiona Shaw
Remus Lupin	David Thewlis
Rita Skeeter	Miranda Richardson
Ron Weasley	Rupert Grint
Rubeus Hagrid	Robbie Coltrane
Rufus Scrimgeour	Bill Nighy
Severus Snape	Alan Rickman
Vernon Dursley	Richard Griffiths
Viktor Krum	Stanislav Ianevski
Voldemort	Ralph Fiennes
Xenophilius Lovegood	Rhys Ifans

Directed by David Yates
Produced by David Heyman and David Barron
Screenplay by Steve Kloves

Deathly Hallows: Part II

As of press time the confirmed cast includes:

Aberforth Dumbledore	Ciarán Hinds
Albus Dumbledore, age 17	Toby Regbo
Arthur Weasley	Mark Williams
Bellatrix Lestrange	Helena Bonham Carter

Bill Weasley	Domhnall Gleeson
Dobby	Voice of Toby Jones
Draco Malfoy	Tom Felton
Fenrir Greyback	Dave Legeno
Firenze	Voice of Ray Fearon
Fleur Delacour	Clémence Poésy
Gellert Grindelwald	Jamie Campbell Bower
Ginny Weasley	Bonnie Wright
Gregorovitch	Rade Serbedzija
Harry Potter	Daniel Radcliffe
Hermione Granger	Emma Watson
Horace Slughorn	Jim Broadbent
James Potter	Adrian Rawlins
Lavender Brown	Jessie Cave
Lily Potter	Geraldine Sommerville
Lucius Malfoy	Jason Isaacs
Luna Lovegood	Evanna Lynch
Minerva McGonagall	Dame Maggie Smith
Molly Weasley	Julie Walters
Mr. Ollivander	John Hurt
Mundungus Fletcher	Andy Linden
Narcissa Malfoy	Helen McCrory
Nymphadora Tonks	Natalia Tena
Percy Weasley	Chris Rankin
Pius Thicknesse	Guy Henry
Pomona Sprout	Miriam Margoyles
Remus Lupin	David Thewlis
Ron Weasley	Rupert Grint
Rubeus Hagrid	Robbie Coltrane
Rufus Scrimgeour	Bill Nighy
Seamus Finnigan	Devon Murray
Severus Snape	Alan Rickman
Voldemort	Ralph Fiennes

Directed by David Yates
Produced by David Heyman and David Barron
Screenplay by Steve Kloves

Index

11/12

last 6/17
8/22

WHA102412